IN SEARCH OF PEACE

MR BYRNES' TRAVELS ~ from Yalta to the Paris Peace Conference

1 Big Three Meeting, Yalta
Jan. 22, '45 — Feb. 12, '45

2 Big Three Meeting, Potsdam
July 6, '45 — Aug. 7, '45

3 Foreign Ministers Council, London
Sept. 4, '45 — Oct. 8, '45

4 Big Three Foreign Ministers, Moscow
Dec. 12, '45 — Dec. 29, '45

5 U.N. General Assembly, London
Jan. 7, '46 — Jan. 25, '46

6 Big Four Foreign Ministers, Paris
Apr. 23, '46 — May 18, '46

7 Big Four Foreign Ministers, Paris
June 13, '46 — July 14, '46

8 21-Nation Peace Conference, Paris
July 27, '46 — Oct. 17, '46

Total approximate mileage – 77,000
Dates cover from time of departure to return to Washington

K. VOUTE

SPEAKING FRANKLY

JAMES F. BYRNES

SPEAKING FRANKLY

By James F. Byrnes

Harper & Brothers Publishers

New York and London

10–7

To the Memory of
My Mother
Elizabeth E. Byrnes

Contents

Illustrations

See other side for transcription of these notes.

Mr. Stettinius reads from a report:

"I have a brief statement as to Dumbarton Oaks. 'It is agreed that five governments which have permanent seats on the council should consult each other prior to the United Nations Conference as to the establishment of trusteeships.' "

Mr. Churchill: "I absolutely disagree. I will not have one scrap of British territory flung into that area. After we have done our best to fight in this war and have done no crime to anyone I will have no suggestion that the British Empire is to be put into the dock and examined by everybody to see whether it is up to their standard. No one will induce me as long as I am Prime Minister to let any representative of Great Britain go to a conference where we will be placed in the dock and asked to justify our right to live in a world we have tried to save."

The President: "I want Mr. Stettinius to finish the sentence he was reading because it does not refer to the matter you have been speaking about."

Mr. Churchill: "If we are out I have nothing to say. As long as every bit of land over which the British Flag flies is to be brought into the dock, I shall object so long as I live."

Mr. Stettinius: "The only thing contemplated as to territorial trusteeship is to provide in the Charter of the world organization the right to create a trusteeship if it desires to do so. Later on, we have had in mind that the Japanese mandated islands be taken away from the Japanese. We have had nothing in mind with reference to the British Empire."

Mr. Churchill: "So far as the British Empire is concerned, we ask nothing. We seek no territorial aggrandizement. If it is a question solely of dealing with enemy territory acquired during the war, it might be proper to put them into some form of trusteeship under the United Nations."

Foreword

> If we could first know *where* we are, and *whither* we are tending, we could better judge *what* to do and *how* to do it.
>
> ABRAHAM LINCOLN

THERE were a number of friends who beguiled me into writing this story. Their arguments were that while the events were fresh in my memory and I was still able to read my shorthand notes, I would, by speaking frankly, render a public service.

For some time I had been urging a people's peace and expressing the opinion that the people could not intelligently influence the peace unless they were told the facts about our negotiations. With this background, you can appreciate how easily I was flattered into believing that I might help the people who are interested in making peace to know where we are, so that they might better judge what to do and how to do it.

In the four months that have passed, as I have worked long hours on this manuscript, I have forgiven those friends but have not forgotten them. Also I have realized that writing is a profession and that it is not my profession. Instead of attempting to qualify as a professional and to acquire a literary style, I have tried to tell, in an informal and conversational way, of our efforts to make the peace settlements.

After completing the manuscript I was surprised and displeased to note the frequency of the capital "I." Now it is too late to do anything about it. In extenuation, I hope it will be recalled that this is a story of events and discussions in which the writer was a participant and it was difficult to avoid the frequent use of the "I."

This does not purport to be a story of our foreign relations since the cessation of hostilities. It is confined to our peace-making efforts and to events incident to those efforts. For example, there is no reference to our relations with our South American neighbors. This is because, in telling the story of the peace settlements, there is little reason to discuss our relations either with the South American Governments or the Canadian Government.

In writing this story I have had occasion to mention many persons who were associated with me in the various conferences. There were many others without whose assistance we could not have presented our cause, and whose names are not mentioned. Their services I warmly remember and deeply appreciate.

Many times during the preparation of this manuscript I also have had reason to thank those hard-working and nearly always anonymous members of the secretariat of the various conferences. Their carefully compiled records were invaluable in drawing together the many threads which form the pattern of our peace negotiations. I had many notes of my own, but only at Yalta, where I was serving as an adviser and not taking part in the debates, was I able to make a complete stenographic record.

Throughout the book there are many direct quotations. These are taken either from my notes, from the records of the secretariat or, in some cases, from memoranda made immediately after conversations. Nevertheless, they are subject to human error. This is particularly true in quotations of statements made by Soviet and French representatives. It should be remembered that, in those cases, the quotations are the words of the translator rather than those of the speaker. Wherever I had any reason for doubt, however, I have not used quotations but have tried instead to reflect the spirit as well as the letter of the statements, the events, and the atmosphere in which they occurred.

I have tried, in short, to give you a seat at the conference table. Some critics may say it is too early for these facts to be made known. My answer is that if it were possible to give the people of this world an actual, rather than a figurative, seat at the peace conference table, the fears and worries that now grip our hearts would fade away.

JAMES F. BYRNES

SPARTANBURG, S. C.
JULY 1, 1947

BOOK I

INTRODUCTION TO WORLD LEADERSHIP

Chapter I

Awakening to Danger— and Responsibility

A HUNDRED THOUSAND voices awakened me to danger. Acres of Germans in even furrows stretched before me and from them rose a chorus of praise for military might and its apostle, Adolf Hitler. It was no nightmare. It was Nuremberg, Germany, in September, 1937. Like most Americans, I had watched the rise of this man Hitler with a somewhat detached concern, but here was a scene that could not be regarded with detachment.

Domestic as well as international affairs had brought Mrs. Byrnes and me to Europe. I was a delegate to the Inter-Parliamentary Union meeting in Paris, and as chairman of the Senate Committee on Unemployment and Relief I wished to see how Europe was handling its unemployment problem. We had not planned to visit Nuremberg, but in Munich, an official of the German Foreign Office whom we had met on board ship, persuaded us we could not properly evaluate Germany's program for economic recovery without witnessing the Annual Congress of the Nazi Party.

What was spread before us, however, was a program not for economic recovery but for armed aggression. Twelve thousand troops marched past our stand, accompanied by the rumble of scores of tanks and motorized weapons, while 450 planes swept across the skies above the stadium. As the demonstration reached its climax, Hitler rode across the field in an open automobile standing erect and with right arm uplifted in the Nazi salute. An exultant cry arose from the multitude. But I was frightened—frightened by the specter of war.

While we were in Berlin the government announced the first civilian air raid drill. We heard women complaining because they had to buy blackout curtains. Two years before the war started, the German people already were doing what our people barely succeeded in doing two years after it started.

My concern mounted as we traveled through Germany. In Hamburg and Bremerhaven we witnessed the enthusiastic welcome given the troops returning from Nuremberg. The people were proud of their new and rapidly growing army. In rural districts and in the cities there was talk of war. The older folks were fearful; the younger people were enthusiastic. But nearly all supported the restoration of an armed might they fervently believed to be a natural German right and a German necessity.

These impressions were in sharp contrast with what we had seen in France. There, the contest between capital and labor was bringing that country to an economic impasse. Stores and factories were closed from Saturday noon until Tuesday morning. Demands were made in some industries for even fewer working hours. But in Germany, only an overnight train trip away, factories were working longer and longer hours. The slogan JOY THROUGH WORK appeared everywhere. The Germans were as busy increasing production as the French were busy decreasing it.

We went to London. Because of what we had seen in Germany, I asked the British officials we met what their government was doing in the way of military preparedness. The alarm had sounded for them, but only a few were responding. These few had succeeded in launching a preparedness program a few months earlier. Consequently, when we visited the Birmingham area, I did find some plants producing military equipment twenty-four hours a day.

Even Britain's limited program had aroused strong opposition from the pacifists. The weekend we returned to London there was a huge peace parade. I went to see it and to listen to the comments of the other onlookers. The slogans were the same as those at home: WE DIDN'T RAISE OUR BOYS TO BE CANNON FODDER, PEACE ON EARTH, and the like. The marchers were good people—the same kind of people we had in every state in our Union—who wanted to proclaim their desire for peace and their hatred for war. As those earnest, uneven ranks passed down the street, I saw again the thousands of tough disciplined troops, goosestepping by Hitler at Nuremberg. And this parade for peace seemed all in vain.

Surmise deepened into certainty when I combined the German display of military power with what I had learned on a trip to the Pacific two years earlier. A large Congressional party, headed by Vice President Garner, had gone to Manila to witness the inauguration of Manuel Quezon as the first President of the Philippine Commonwealth. There, Americans in all walks of life had expressed to us their concern over the increasing indications of Japan's aggressive intentions. Therefore, when we stopped in Japan I made a special effort to inquire into Japanese naval appropriations and naval construction. A study of the Japanese budget for 1936 readily revealed that at least half of the total was devoted to the army and navy. Members of our Embassy staff were convinced that the published budget disclosed only part of the naval appropriations. The published figures were alarming enough in themselves and when we returned to this country I urged the President to seek means for acquiring still more accurate estimates of Japan's naval strength.

Equally disturbing was the structure of Japan's political and economic life. I had begun by inquiring into the Japanese textile industry primarily because of its competitive relationship to the chief industry of South Carolina. I ended with a realization that industry, banking, shipping, in fact the whole economic and political life of Japan, were centrally controlled. The power of Japan rested with a small group of men who could set the entire nation on any course they desired.

It was clear that neither in Japan nor in Germany was there an opportunity to appeal to the judgment of the millions. It was the decisions of leaders and not the desires of people that prevailed.

On October 1, 1937, we returned from Europe and as soon as I could, I reported to President Roosevelt what we had seen and heard and my conclusion that we must immediately give serious thought to the nation's defense.

The President told me I only confirmed what he had concluded from the reports of our official representatives abroad. He was greatly disturbed about the developments in Europe. Even more, he was disturbed about the difficulties of awakening our people to a realization of the true situation.

I told him that the sentiment of the people, as reflected in the Congress, would make it difficult for us to secure increased appropriations for Army and Navy. He was determined, however, to do his best to make people see the necessity for increased appropriations, and I promised to help him.

It was on October 5, 1937, that the President made his famous Chicago Quarantine Speech. It was a strong speech. For many reasons it had to be. There was our traditional desire to be free of Europe's troubles and the belief, born of desire, that aggressive nationalism could be confined to the European continent. There also was the disillusionment from our venture into European politics after World War I which still lingered on. As a people we hated war and we prized our isolation.

There were other immediate factors.

Our support of our Army and Navy in peacetime was always a reluctant one. Reluctance in many cases turned to outright opposition in the years of the depression when there was great strength in the argument that the revenue we raised should be spent for relief and not for military preparedness. It was argued that the people of the world had enough of war in World War I. In addition, the Senate Munitions Committee had given encouragement to the pacifists; had helped foster the simple theory that war was a creature of the munitions makers' thirst for profits. Producers of military supplies were labeled "Merchants of Death." International bankers were charged with creating the markets for the products of those merchants.

Every time I brought a naval appropriations bill to the floor of the Senate, I had to face those pacifist slogans and arguments. They commanded large public support. To hear them, crowds with a high proportion of women and of students invariably would fill the Senate galleries. Senator Lynn J. Frazier usually spoke in criticism of the Navy, but the pacifists' outstanding spokesman was Senator Gerald P. Nye of North Dakota. His sincerity I never questioned; but I often wondered if he had ever considered why, out of all that large congressional group to visit Japan in 1935, he was the one member the Japanese Naval Command had wired prior to our landing seeking to honor him with a banquet. Nye declined the "honor." Later when we were leaving Japan on our return trip he showed me a book recording the story of the development of the Japanese Navy which had been sent to him at the ship by an admiral of the Japanese Navy. I am sure he was embarrassed. He should have been.

Since the early days of his administration, President Roosevelt had faced opposition as he sought to strengthen our defense establishment. He had allotted funds for public works to naval construction projects and he had obtained authority to increase the Army's enlisted strength from 115,000 to 165,000 men.

The President was disappointed by the failure of the people to respond to his Chicago speech. He waited until the turn of the year and then began in earnest the drive to arouse the Congress and the public.

"It is an ominous fact," he told the Congress in a special message on January 29, 1938, "that at least one-fourth of the world's population is involved in merciless, devastating conflict in spite of the fact that most people in most countries, including those where conflict rages, wish to live at peace."

He then called for a 20 per cent increase in the naval building program, construction of two battleships and two cruisers, experimental construction of small vessels and the pitifully small sum of twenty million dollars for Army materiel. Our regular Army then ranked eighteenth among the standing armies of the world.

But public sentiment was such that the campaign to increase our military and naval appropriations was an uphill fight. Attention was concentrated on the alphabet—WPA, PWA, AAA, CCC, NRA, and all the others. And the alphabet took all the revenues. It was hard to reduce them and impossible to abolish them. The nearest approach to immortality on earth is a government bureau.

The annexation of Austria in March 1938, the Munich agreement, and the consequent dismemberment of Czechoslovakia in September were shocks to the American people. But appropriations for the Army and Navy were still hard to get through Congress. To stimulate public interest, the President started the new year, 1939, with another special message to Congress on defense problems. This time he asked for an appropriation of half a billion dollars, primarily for the Army and Navy air arms.

On May 27, Secretary Hull submitted letters to the House and Senate asking for repeal of the act that placed an embargo on the shipment of arms to a nation at war. He explained that the law should be left flexible and that repeal would help us to stay out of war if it should, unfortunately, start in Europe. Shortly thereafter, during a conversation at the White House, President Roosevelt told me he greatly feared Hitler would start a war during the summer. When, on July 11, the Senate Foreign Relations Committee voted 12 to 11 to postpone consideration of the bill repealing the Arms Embargo, it was a keen disappointment both to the President and to Secretary Hull. Three days later, the President sent a message to Congress expressing his regret and appended a strong statement from Mr. Hull appealing for action without delay. It emphasized that without repeal our influence to preserve peace would be weakened. The appeal was in vain.

The Congress adjourned, but Hitler did not. He and his Foreign Minister, Joachim von Ribbentrop, were busily negotiating with the Soviet Union the nonaggression pact that was concluded on August 28. Two days later the Nazi armies invaded Poland and the word "blitzkrieg" came into our vocabulary.

In accordance with existing law, President Roosevelt proclaimed our neutrality and invoked the Arms Embargo. At the same time he called a special session of Congress to convene September 21 to consider repeal of the embargo. And on November 4, Congress voted the repeal we had been seeking since May.

At the outset the President realized the necessity for bipartisan action in the emergency confronting him. In order to make such an appeal, he held a meeting in his office on the day preceding the opening of Congress, attended by representatives of the two political parties, including Vice President Garner, Secretary Hull, Alfred M. Landon, Colonel Frank Knox, Speaker Bankhead, Senate Leaders Barkley and McNary, and Senators Pittman, Byrnes, Minton and Austin, and Representatives Bloom, Rayburn, Martin and Mapes.

It was a serious meeting of serious men.

In response to his appeal for the co-operation of the two great parties, frank statements were made by those present. Landon thought the Congress should be kept in session. He thought the judgment of the Congress and the executive safer than the judgment of a single individual, meaning, of course, the President. Of the Republican representatives, no one made a more impressive statement than Frank Knox, the vice presidential candidate in the preceding election. A few days later the President remarked upon the splendid statement of Mr. Knox, who had said the war would spread, and that we neither were able to stay out of it nor prepared to get into it. He declared we should forget all about political parties, close ranks, and prepare to defend our country.

When the President made up his mind to appoint two Republicans to his Cabinet, I was not surprised that he selected Knox as Secretary of the Navy, and I was delighted at his choice of the talented and courageous Henry L. Stimson as Secretary of War.

The President asked me to ascertain from Senator Lucas of Illinois whether he would approve the confirmation of Knox. Lucas promptly advised me he approved the appointment and a few hours later said he also had talked with Mayor Kelly of Chicago. He quoted Kelly as saying that, although Knox's newspaper had consistently opposed him, political considerations must be entirely disregarded in the emergency we were facing. He then added he would be glad to see Knox appointed. This statement from Mayor Kelly, the head of a large Democratic political organization, was an encouraging demonstration that political considerations had become of secondary importance.

When the senatorial members of the group who had met with the President returned to the Capitol, Senator McNary, the Republican leader of the Senate, stated he wanted to advise me and I might advise the President that, while he had said little at the conference, the President could count on his wholehearted co-operation. McNary was one of the ablest Republicans in or out of Congress and in the days that followed, he lived up to his promise to co-operate. Time after time when some proposal connected with the preparedness program was pending, which by the enforcement of Senate rules could have been delayed, he would consent to immediate consideration and give his influential support to the legislation. He and Senator Austin, who was then the minority whip, quietly helped to speed the passage of many measures for our defense.

Notwithstanding the success of the Nazis in Poland, a large portion of the American public still was not aware of the danger confronting us. In the absence of action on the western front people began referring to the "phony war." The feeling was as widespread as the phrase, and was reflected in Congress. Early in the spring we had completed hearings on the Naval Appropriation Bill, providing for construction of additional battleships and cruisers. Conversation with my Senate colleagues forced me to conclude that passage of the bill without destructive amendments was very doubtful, so I deliberately delayed consideration of it in the Senate. Some of the appropriations were made immediately available. The Navy wanted them. But I wanted to be sure of getting the bill through without amendments reducing appropriations for new construction. From statements made by our Intelligence officers and from the opinions of our military leaders, I was convinced that with the coming of spring the Nazis would attack on the western front. They did. And when they did I brought up the Naval Bill in the Senate. It passed in three hours, as reported by the Appropriations Committee.

Our difficulties were not confined to materiel. The Army had in its higher ranks many officers who were good men, but who, in the opinion of General Marshall, were too old and not good enough for the terrific task ahead of us.

In August 1940, General Marshall appeared before the Senate Appropriations Committee to testify on a defense appropriation bill. During a recess, he told me that his greatest difficulty was his inability to promote younger officers of unusual ability. Possession of such authority, he said, was essential to the proper reorganization of the Army. He told me he had requested Chairman May, of the House Military Affairs Committee, to introduce the necessary legislation some months before but had been unable to get action on it.

His needs were so impressive that I requested him to have one of his technicians draft an amendment that would accomplish the purpose he desired and stated I would try to help him. Under the rules of the Senate, the amendment could not be added to an appropriation bill in committee but when the bill was reported to the floor, I offered an amendment, adopted without objection, providing that "In time of war or national emergency determined by the President, any officer of the Regular Army may be appointed to higher temporary grade without vacating his permanent appointment."

When we met in conference with the members of the House Appropriations Committee, I explained the urgency of the proposal and they accepted it. On September 9 it became law and under its provisions the War Department began the task of promoting over the heads of officers of high rank the younger officers who thereafter led our armies to victory. Before the end of the year, 4,088 of these promotions were made. Among the officers advanced were men like General Eisenhower, General George C. Kenney, General Carl A. Spaatz, General Mark Clark and the late General George S. Patton. Eisenhower was promoted over 366 senior officers.

It was the disaster at Dunkirk that at last aroused our people, but they reacted in a curiously divided way. Our hatred of war was at odds with our growing recognition that the conflagration was creeping ever closer to our shores. The compromise that emerged from this conflict of heart and mind was a willingness to build up our own defenses but a determination to avoid involvement.

The division of sentiment among the people was reflected in the political conventions.

The Republicans, meeting in Philadelphia on June 24, included in their platform a declaration: "The Republican Party is firmly opposed to involving the nation in foreign war."

The political leaders of the Democratic Party, appreciating what a strong appeal this declaration would make to the voting mothers, were exceedingly anxious that the Democratic convention should offset the Republican declaration.

The President had asked me to represent him on the floor of the convention. He was particularly anxious that I interest myself in the foreign relations declaration of the platform. When the Platform Committee met, it was apparent that we were in for a fight. Senator Burton K. Wheeler, an astute and able legislator, wanted a declaration against participation in the war. His views were shared by Senators David I. Walsh and Pat McCarran, as well as other members of the committee. Several proposals were offered. I asked Senator Wagner, the chairman of the committee, to postpone consideration of the foreign relations section until I could talk with the three Senators to see if we could agree upon a satisfactory declaration. Wagner appointed Mayor Kelly to confer with us also.

The three Senators were insisting upon a statement: "We will not participate in foreign wars and we will not send our armies, navies or air forces to fight on foreign lands outside the Americas." They advised me of threats from many delegates to bolt the convention if they didn't get a direct pledge of this kind. I finally told them that if they would agree to the words "except in case of attack" I would submit it to the President and the Secretary of State. They agreed. This, actually, was my third talk with the President on the subject and this time he had Secretary Hull with him. Hull was slow to agree. I pointed out that if we were attacked anywhere in the world we would fight and send forces abroad. After all, we would not send armies abroad to fight without declaring war, and it was the function of Congress to declare war. The President and Secretary Hull agreed.

The declaration was adopted unanimously by the committee and the convention. I did not like the "plank." I feared it would cause Hitler to conclude, as the Kaiser did in 1917, that we would not fight and that he would be encouraged to act on that assumption. But the views expressed by members of the Platform Committee made it clear it was the best we could hope for. The alternative would be a bitter fight in the convention that would disclose a serious split in the President's party and impair his prestige abroad. It was a good illustration of competition between the two political parties for the approval of a bloc of voters.

With France gone, and the grim bombardment of Britain in full swing, the President moved ahead on his own initiative. He sold to Britain rifles and other weapons from our World War I stockpile to help replace those left behind on the French beaches. The deal for exchanging fifty overage destroyers in return for bases was negotiated. There was a great protest that the President had no authority to dispose of these destroyers. When I talked to him about it, he called attention to a supporting legal opinion from Attorney General Jackson. However, from the President's attitude, I suspected he was more concerned whether public sentiment would support his action. He had determined to take that chance even with the election only a few months away.

It was about this time that Congress began its debate over the first peacetime military draft in our history. It was significant that this controversial legislation was being pushed by the administration a short time before a presidential election. The fact that Representative James W. Wadsworth, a loyal Republican, had joined with Senator Edmund R. Burke, a Democrat, in sponsoring the bill made the measure a bipartisan one. It passed just before the election, and it is doubtful if it affected many votes.

The acceptance of Selective Service by the people served to show that the public had responded to the developments in Europe.

From then on the people were often ahead of the President and the Congress. They saw the world-wide scope of the conflict. They realized the urgent necessity of aiding our friends and obtaining time in which to prepare.

Shortly before Christmas, 1940, President Roosevelt disclosed at a press conference his plan "to eliminate the dollar sign" from our aid to those fighting against Hitler. The idea was elaborated still further by the President when he appeared before the new Congress on January 8, 1941, to deliver his message on The State of the Union. Meanwhile, work had begun on drafting legislation to put the plan into action. A draft prepared by Oscar S. Cox, then an assistant to the general counsel of the Treasury, was used as a basis for soliciting advice and suggestions from many people.

On January 10, the bill was introduced simultaneously in the Senate and House by Senator Alben W. Barkley and Representative John W. McCormack, the majority leaders. In the House the symbolic number,

H. R. 1776, was attached to what finally became, on March 11, the Lend-Lease Act. '

When the new Congress was organized there were two vacancies on the Senate Foreign Relations Committee, which was to handle the lend-lease legislation. Senator Carter Glass and I received the assignments. My principal activity from then on was to help secure passage of this legislation. Mr. Cox and Assistant Secretary of War John J. McCloy were assigned to furnish whatever information was desired by committees or by individual Senators and Congressmen. We had to admit to opponents that little of what we would lend and lease for use in the prosecution of the war would ever come back. Our justification had to be that it would enable other men to fight the enemy while we trained and equipped our own armed forces. The bill was brought to the floor of the Senate on February 17 after a favorable vote of 15 to 8 in committee. The ranking members of the Foreign Relations Committee conducted the debate on the floor and ably presented our cause which won by a vote of 60 to 31.

After passage of the legislation, the fight was transferred to the Appropriations Committee, of which, under the chairmanship of Senator Glass, I was also a member. An initial appropriation of seven billion dollars to implement the lend-lease program was approved.

In June 1941, Justice McReynolds, of Tennessee, announced his retirement from the Supreme Court, and I was appointed to fill the vacancy.

During the months that followed, I did not participate in any way in the preparations for national defense and had only such information as I got from the press and from visits with the President.

The invasion of Russia on June 22 left only one other major power free from war, but the sinking of the *Robin Moor* and the attacks on the *Greer* and the *Kearney* made it clear we would not escape much longer. Congress responded by further amending the Neutrality Act and voting more funds for defense. The President and Secretary Hull also were deeply concerned over the trend of events at the eastern end of the Axis. Japan's move into French Indo-China exposed aggressive intentions which could not be obscured by the "peace missions" of Ambassador Kurusu to the United States. The President finally was prompted to send an appeal for peace directly to the Emperor on Saturday, December 6. He received his response when the Japanese, without warning, attacked Pearl Harbor the following day.

The Tuesday after Pearl Harbor Sunday, the Supreme Court met to hear arguments in a case between the Bethlehem Shipbuilding Company and the United States of America. I must confess I found it very difficult to concentrate on the arguments that morning. The issue involved arose out of the company's construction of ships for the government during World War I. At any other time it would have seemed important, but right then it appeared of little consequence in the light of the news bulletins still pouring in from Pearl Harbor and our growing realization of their consequences.

Early Wednesday morning, I went to see the President. He was still in his bed, which was covered with dispatches and memos. Some of his papers were on the floor. He had been awake for hours studying the information and planning the future. I had hardly walked into the room before he began giving me the details of the disaster. Only then did I fully realize the extent of the damage to our ships. The President was alternately sad, determined, and hurt. He could not understand how such a thing could happen to the Navy of which he was so proud.

As we talked, he rang for his valet, arose, and began to shave. So our conversation was just moved to the bathroom. He had finished lathering when I changed the subject by saying:

"Mr. President, you know, before your fight on the Supreme Court was over I had concluded you were wrong, and my service on the Court has only confirmed that view."

His razor stopped in mid-stroke. It was a sore point with him. He turned to me with a look both of inquiry and annoyance, but I went right on.

"You urged that Justices be retired at seventy. From my experience, I've decided they shouldn't be appointed until they reach seventy."

His good humor was restored. He laughed as I told him about the case of the day before.

"I've been in the middle of crises ever since I entered public life," I told him, "but yesterday with the nation confronted with the greatest crisis in its history, the best I could do was to spend hours listening to arguments about the payment for ships that were built twenty-three years ago. I was thinking so much about those ships sunk at Pearl Harbor that it was difficult to concentrate on arguments about ships that were built at Bethlehem in 1918."

It was said half in jest. As we moved back into the bedroom the President made it clear he was taking me seriously. He pointed out that our entry into the war would require the passage of considerable legislation, the assumption of additional executive powers and the reorganization of much administrative machinery. Prompt action was required, he said, and because of my long experience in the Congress he wanted to call on me for help. The President thereupon ordered all war legislation cleared by Attorney General Francis Biddle, and asked him to consult with me.

This created a problem. The issues referred to me required consultation with leaders of the House and Senate as well as officials of the executive departments, and it was often difficult to explain how a Supreme Court Justice was connected with the heterogeneous questions that came my way. But we were at war—and we were frightened.

On December 15, I was studying the Overman Act of World War I, which had authorized President Wilson to reorganize government agencies for more effective prosecution of the war. It suddenly occurred to me that here was the solution to my problem. Reorganization was necessary now, and it would be easy for the President to announce that, since I had been chairman of the Senate Committee on Government Reorganization, he had asked me to make a survey and advise what changes were necessary. I recalled that back in 1913, during my second term in the House, President Taft had appointed Associate Justice Charles Evans Hughes to serve as chairman of a commission created by Congress to investigate second-class mail rates. So there was a precedent created by a Justice for whom I had the greatest admiration.

Acting on this impulse, I sent a brief memo to the President outlining both my problem and the suggested answer.

"I want to avoid the words 'liaison' and 'coordinator,'" I wrote him. "They would destroy even a good man."

But my message had hardly reached the White House when I began to fear that a public announcement might restrict my ability to help. The President agreed that I could work for him more effectively if I did so quietly and unobtrusively. So the announcement was never made.

Requests for emergency legislation came streaming in from virtually every agency of the government. The need for several of the requests was not readily discernible. Individual action on each of them would require consideration by at least a dozen congressional committees. Days and weeks of precious time would be lost.

In a conference with the Attorney General, and Oscar Cox, who had become his assistant, it was decided that these matters could best be handled in an all-inclusive bill. In that way, only one committee on each side of Capitol Hill would be concerned, and the popular proposals would carry along the more controversial issues. For example, Postmaster General Frank Walker had a proposal to extend free postage to all members of the armed forces. It was certain to win almost unanimous support—so it became Title X of the over-all bill.

Meanwhile, Speaker Sam Rayburn and Majority Leader Alben W. Barkley approved the idea of an omnibus bill. They selected the respective committees and conferred with the chairmen. As a result, the Second War Powers Act was sponsored by the chairmen of the Judiciary Committees of the House and Senate. It was approved by the Senate in eight days and was through the House by the end of February.

Organization of war production was another urgent problem. Labor had pledged its co-operation and William Knudsen was doing an excellent job in enlisting the support of the industrialists. But we simply were not organized for production on the scale necessary to supply our Allies and our own armed forces too. The divisions of power and the resultant conflicts were such that production actually was being delayed. There seemed to be more agencies than decisions. And there were as many suggestions on what should be done to remedy the situation as there were agencies. The press and public demanded a change.

Harry Hopkins was then chairman of the Munitions Assignment Board. He was living in the White House and was consulted by the President on many subjects. During a telephone conversation with Hopkins on January 2, Harry asked me to send him any ideas I might have on the production problem. That afternoon I sent him a two-page memorandum saying first that the proposal for a Ministry of Supplies, made popular by the current visit of Prime Minister Churchill and his Supply Minister, Lord Beaverbrook, would require transfer of the procurement organizations of the Army and Navy and thus would cause confusion, conflicts, and loss of time the nation could not afford.

Instead of still another board, my memo to Hopkins urged that the President appoint one man charged with the duty of supervising and expediting procurement. That man could have any type of board he wanted, but when a controversy arose, he should decide it. The memo to Hopkins continued:

"You say, 'All right—find the man.' If you demand perfection, you will never select a man. There are some things we do know. If you bring in an executive who has had experience only in a particular industry, he will have to be educated in the methods of government as well as to the needs of the various services. If you will recall how much you knew about the machinery of government when you first came to Washington, you will appreciate how little the average executive knows about the methods that must be pursued by the heads of the various agencies in the Production Organization. If you now have in the government service a man who has served his apprenticeship, who has some appreciation of the problems of the procurement divisions of the Army, Navy and other Services, and who has the ability to make other men work, appoint him, instead of bringing in another new man."

"We no longer need for political or prestige purposes a man with a big name," I wrote. "All you need now is a man who can do the job. If any one of the 'Stars' becomes temperamental and wants to resign— let him go. He will find it uncomfortable at home. . . . Pick the best man you now have on the team and let the heathen rage."

Monday, January 12, "Pa" Watson called to say the President wanted to see me. A few minutes later Hopkins telephoned to ask that I stop by his room before seeing the President. He was in bed, sick, but able to attend to business. He said he had discussed the problem briefly with the President but as the President had been reluctant to go into it he had not pressed him.

Hopkins said he had not shown the President my memorandum but had simply discussed the subject generally. I asked for the memorandum and presented it to the President.

"I've been considering the appointment of a commission," he said after he had read it, "but the more I think it over the closer I come to the conclusion you've expressed here."

I urged prompt action.

"If I had to make a selection this morning, I would pick Donald Nelson," he went on. "He was here last night for a dinner we had for Lord Beaverbrook. I hadn't known him too well, but last night I heard him discussing the sugar situation and a number of production problems, and I was impressed by the soundness of his views."

"I have not come to recommend any man but only to urge action," I told him. And warned, "The man will last only as long as it is recognized that he has your complete confidence."

With that, I had to leave as it was almost time for the Court to convene. The incident remains in my mind as this was the only time I ever arrived late either for a sitting or for a conference of the Court.

That afternoon General Watson asked me to come see the President the next morning. When I arrived Director of the Budget Harold Smith was there, and told me the President had asked him to draft an executive order embodying the ideas of the memorandum. Harry Hopkins joined us and we prepared a press release announcing the establishment of the War Production Board and Nelson's appointment as Chairman. Harry was anxious to have the President act at once.

"Every hour of delay gives more people an opportunity to know what the President is planning," Harry said. "The first thing we know somebody who has different ideas will be in here trying to change his mind. And," he added, "the news will leak to the press."

The President, however, insisted, quite correctly, that he must first advise Vice President Wallace, whose job as Chairman of the Economic Defense Board was being abolished by the order. He said he would see Wallace early that afternoon. I returned to the White House late in the day to see a final draft of the executive order. I learned there had been a delay. Wendell Willkie had called on Mr. Roosevelt. He enjoyed talking with Mr. Willkie, and became so engrossed in the conversation that he was behind his schedule of engagements. Consequently, it was not until almost six o'clock that he told the Vice President of his decision. The announcement was made shortly thereafter.

In the summer, while the Court was in recess, I was tired and wanted to go home for two weeks. But the President for some time had been worried about the wage and price situation and he requested me to confer, before I left, with Judge Samuel I. Rosenman, who afterwards became his personal counsel. Judge Rosenman had been designated to reconcile the various views on the best method of stabilizing our economy. The judge had worked out general outlines of a plan for an Office of Economic Stabilization, which reasonably satisfied the heads of agencies concerned. After making a few suggestions, I left at last for South Carolina.

Not many days had passed when a wonderful afternoon nap was interrupted by Mrs. Byrnes calling:

"Jim, the White House wants you on the telephone."

It was the President. It was essential, he said, to create without delay an agency with sufficient power to enforce ceilings upon prices and wages. He asked what I thought the Congress would think of his establishing by executive order the Office of Economic Stabilization and giving it such powers. He feared that, if the proposal were placed before Congress, it would take months to obtain its passage.

"Mr. President, I think you have got to submit this matter to Congress if you want it to succeed," I replied. "This regulation of wages and prices is so controversial, it touches so many people so directly, that enforcement will be difficult without congressional authorization. It's going to be tough enough with it."

A few minutes later Secretary Ickes telephoned. He had heard about the proposal the President was considering and the old "curmudgeon" wanted me to urge the President to submit it to the Congress. When I said the President indicated he would do so, Harold was genuinely pleased.

The legislation was introduced and the bill became law on October 2, 1942. That day, the President sent me a message requesting me to come see him the next morning.

It was another of our many bedside talks, but it is especially memorable to me because it marked the end of my service in the legislative and judicial branches of the government and my first entry into the executive department.

There was hardly time for a "good morning" before the President said he wanted me to get a leave of absence from the Court and accept the appointment as Director of Economic Stabilization.

I deeply appreciated his suggestion but told him no one had the power to give a leave of absence to a Justice of the Supreme Court, that the

Justice alone was responsible for the discharge of his duties. I stated that the job of regulating wages and prices would involve so many decisions with political implications that it would not be right for me to remain on the Court.

"But you will remember," I continued, "that the first time I saw you after Pearl Harbor, right in this room, I offered to assist in any way that I could. If you think this appointment is important to the prosecution of the war, I will, without hesitation, resign from the Court and accept it."

"Jimmy, most of my time is devoted to the consideration of problems intimately and directly connected with the conduct of the war. It just isn't possible for me to devote sufficient time to the domestic problems. All these new agencies we have had to create mean an increasing number of jurisdictional conflicts which come to me for decision. I want you to settle those conflicts for me; I'll issue an executive order giving you power to settle them, and I'll let it be known that your decision is my decision."

Then, with a quick flicker of a smile, he added:

"The Director of Economic Stabilization is an important job, but it will be less important than the other duties I want you to perform for me by direct delegation. Will you do it?"

I told the President I would, and within the hour sent him my resignation from the Supreme Court.

It wasn't easy to leave the Court. No man trained in the law could lightly do so. I liked the work and liked my associates. But as a young member of the House during World War I, I had been deeply impressed with the vital part the home front plays in the winning of a war. And I had seen what a tragic role the home front had assumed in losing the peace. This appointment, I felt, would give me an opportunity to help Franklin Roosevelt achieve for this country the dream of Woodrow Wilson.

How I felt is accurately reflected in my first speech as Director of Economic Stabilization. It was delivered to the New York *Herald Tribune* Forum on November 16, 1942, and dealt largely with the danger of inflation. It ended with these words:

"If anything like inflation happened, our people would not be ready to take the part which we are pledged to take to organize the world for peace. There could be no greater tragedy. After a while, by drastic national action and radical social planning we would recover, but there would have passed the time when our leadership must be asserted if peace and order are to be established in a prostrate world. This, the strongest and most powerful nation in the world, must keep its own house in order. We must be in a position, when the war is over, to turn our energies, our productive resources to the arts of peace. We must show the way to a world of expanding freedom. We must show the way to a lasting peace."

The fight to hold wages and prices was a bitter struggle. It was a struggle against the desires of producers to obtain increased prices and of workers to win increased wages. Senators, Representatives, labor leaders, businessmen, farmers, and spokesmen for groups of all kinds would present their special case. Whenever they could, they would go to the President to present their complaint.

The President was good at taking them on. After listening sympathetically, he would say, "You know, Justice Byrnes is temperamental on this subject. I do not want to talk with him about it but you should go over and see him." They would take his advice. I saw many people. In fact, it was a job in which I made many acquaintances and no friends!

The effort to hold the line on wages and prices should have started with the beginning of the war. Because we entered the fight late, it was always an uphill battle. I became tired of saying, "I'm sorry but it can't be done." The line was bent in many places but it held much better than I ever expected it would.

From October 15, 1942, when the office really began operating, until April 1943, the cost of living index increased 4.3 per cent. Then we drafted and the President issued what was known as the Hold-the-Line Order. It gave even greater power to hold prices and wages. It brought to my office in the White House all the leaders of organized labor and organized agriculture.

Shortly thereafter, I concluded that the job of mobilizing our resources for the prosecution of the war had become so big that I could not devote adequate time both to it and to the problems of economic stabilization. After talking with the President, he suggested I draft the order establishing the Office of War Mobilization.

At my suggestion he asked Judge Vinson to become Director of the Office of Economic Stabilization. Vinson didn't hesitate one minute. He resigned from the Circuit Court of Appeals and ably and courageously administered the Hold-the-Line Order. From April 1943, until his resignation in April 1945, the cost of living index rose only 3.2 per cent. In the twenty-two months following his resignation and the abandonment of the Hold-the-Line Order the increase was 20.2 per cent.

Day after day the problems faced by the Office of War Mobilization demonstrated the direct and often critical relationship between the economic power of this country and the fate of the world. The number of kilowatts we generated and consumed determined directly how many airplanes would be over European and Asiatic targets. The rate at which we produced and transported petroleum acted almost as a speedometer on the movement of our armed forces. The amount of steel that

went into ships or war plants had to be weighed against the probable
need for pontoons to bridge the Rhine or the Irrawaddy. Every statistic
on our farm production was scanned anxiously because it determined
not only the number of soldiers we could support abroad but also the
balance between life and death for thousands of our Allies.

Dramatic evidence of this awful fact was placed on my desk on
November 22, 1943. The President had radioed a message from Teheran.
He urgently requested data on how much our output of landing craft
could be expanded and how rapidly deliveries could be made. Every
agency was immediately summoned because I knew the request involved a decision by the three heads of government at Teheran on the
opening of a second front.

On November 24, I wired the President that by the end of May,
1944—six months hence—we could deliver to our own seaports the
following: 570 LSTs, 665 LCILs, 950 LCTs, 8,469 LCMs, 12,496
LCVPs and 99 LCCs. But to do it, we would have to give them priority
over all other munitions including supplies promised for the Russian
front. And it would require, in addition, slowing down our output of
army trucks, naval shipping and high octane gasoline. Actually we did
better than was promised.

Information on this critical item helped the principals at Teheran plan
for the invasion of the European mainland in the summer of 1944. It
was America's ability to produce that made possible our landing in
Europe on schedule. Stalin acknowledged it once in a toast by saying:
"Without American production the United Nations could never have
won the war."

Even so, our productive capacity ran a race with time. How close we
risked disaster I saw on a visit to the European front in October 1944.
Near Cherbourg was one of the launching sites for the Nazis' V-bombs.
It was placed in what had been an old rock quarry and was well camou-
flaged. When the Germans were driven out they had not quite completed
the construction of a concrete roof that would have been thoroughly
bombproof. Had our invasion been delayed many months beyond June
6, it is entirely possible that from such sites as these, bombs would have
rained on England so effectively that we might never have succeeded
in gathering and launching our invasion force.

It was the daily collision with these facts that prompted me to say to
the National Press Club at a lunch on September 27, 1944:

"This generation of Americans can nobly gain or meanly lose the
hope of the world. If America can use her productive powers for peace
as she uses them for war, we shall nobly gain that hope. If America cannot use her productive powers for peace, America and the whole world
will lose. . . . It is not a theory to be held but a condition to be met."

Chapter 2

Yalta—High Tide of Big Three Unity

DURING Christmas week of 1944, I was in the President's study talking to him about the shipping problem. As he looked up from the memorandum I had given him, he said:

"Jimmy, I want you to go with me on this trip to the Crimea."

It was a complete surprise. He had talked with me about the forthcoming meeting with Stalin and Churchill a number of times, but there had been no hint that I should be a member of the party.

"You know what went on at the other meetings," he added, "and as Director of Mobilization you have acquired a knowledge of our domestic situation that will be of great service in settling the economic questions that are certain to come up."

"When you are out of town," I told him, "the machinery doesn't stop. Problems like the one we are now discussing constantly arise. I think I should remain here and work on those problems."

He insisted, however, that I should go. I agreed, but was not happy about it.

We did not discuss it again until the day scheduled for our departure. That afternoon the OWMR staff met to discuss the problems that were expected to arise during my absence. The discussion convinced me more than ever that I should not go. I left the meeting and went over to see the President. He was having his hair cut by John Mays, the colored man who has greeted guests at the front door of the White House on all formal occasions for thirty-six years. Mays came to the White House from South Carolina during the administration of President Taft, and ever since has acted as barber and enjoyed the confidence of the residents of the White House. He is not only courteous and dignified, he is wise and discreet.

As Mays continued clipping, I again urged that I should remain in Washington. I outlined the problems we anticipated during the month he would be away. He had been so absorbed in foreign affairs he did not appreciate the number of questions and decisions then devolving on the Director of War Mobilization and Reconversion. In fact, I had tried, in so far as possible, to keep domestic issues from intruding upon his consideration of foreign problems. The President persisted in his view that I should go, and I finally agreed. That night we left for Norfolk, where, in the early morning darkness of January 23, we boarded the heavy cruiser USS *Quincy*, which was to take us as far as Malta.

When we left Washington the President was suffering from a severe cold. On board ship it grew worse and he stayed in his cabin most of the time. He would come to lunch and dinner and after dinner attend a moving picture. But only once or twice was he able to sit on deck, until we reached the Mediterranean.

We were at sea on the President's birthday, January 30, and his daughter, Mrs. John Boettiger, made the birthday dinner a gala occasion. Gifts purchased from the ship's commissary were presented to the President. His devoted Filipino chef insisted on providing a birthday cake. But others had the same idea. The commissioned officers presented one; so did the enlisted men and the warrant officers. When four cakes arrived, one of our group, who remembered that the President had just been inaugurated to serve a fourth term, went out and procured a fifth cake. A large candle was stuck into it which the President was challenged to blow out.

Although he responded to the gaiety of the occasion, I was disturbed by his appearance. I feared his illness was not due entirely to a cold and expressed this concern to Mrs. Boettiger. She thought my opinion arose from observing him during the moving pictures, when she usually sat on one side of the President and I on the other. She explained that, while looking at the pictures, the President would have his mouth open because of his sinus trouble and that this made him look badly, but he was not really ill. Dr. McIntyre also expressed the belief that the President's appearance was due to the combination of sinus infection and cold. Since he had so often "bounced back" after an illness, I dismissed my fears.

By the time we reached Malta he had improved greatly. As the *Quincy* approached its anchorage we saw Prime Minister Churchill, in navy uniform, waving a greeting to the President from the deck of the H. M. S. *Sirius* across the channel. Shortly thereafter he and his daughter, Section Officer Sarah Oliver, came aboard for lunch. There were ten of us at lunch and discussion of the approaching conference was only general. The President did, however, confide to Churchill his plans to visit King Ibn Saud on his return trip to discuss the Palestine question. He wanted to bring about peace between the Arabs and the Jews. Churchill wished him good luck but didn't seem very hopeful that the President would meet with success. He didn't.

That night the President traveled for the first time in the Sacred Cow. Months earlier I had tried to induce him to use this airplane, built for his use and provided with an elevator which could be lowered from the plane to the ground, for his trips to Hyde Park and Warm Springs. He told me he disliked to fly; he disliked the monotony of looking at the clouds. His other objection was more surprising. He thought an unnecessary expense had been incurred in fitting a plane solely for his personal use. He said he had not been consulted about it and he did not approve it. This from a man who often had been accused of being the greatest spender ever to hold the office of President!

So far as I could see, the President had made little preparation for the Yalta Conference. His inauguration had taken place the Saturday before we left and for ten days preceding that he had been overwhelmed with engagements. On the cruiser, the President, Admiral Leahy and I, on four or five occasions, usually after dinner, discussed some of the questions to be considered, particularly the proposal for the United Nations. But not until the day before we landed at Malta did I learn that we had on board a very complete file of studies and recommendations prepared by the State Department. I asked the President if the Department had given him any material and he advised me it was all in the custody of Lieutenant William M. Rigdon. Later, when I saw some of these splendid studies I greatly regretted they had not been considered on board ship. I am sure the failure to study them while en route was due to the President's illness. And I am sure that only President Roosevelt, with his intimate knowledge of the problems, could have handled the situation so well with so little preparation.

Secretary of State Edward R. Stettinius, who had gone ahead by air, joined us at Malta. We were met also by Mr. Hopkins who had been visiting in London, Paris and Rome. Harry was sick. He took off for Yalta in the first available airplane and during the conference was confined to his bed most of the time. His great courage caused him to attend every session of the conference, but immediately after adjournment he would retire to his room. Members of our delegation frequently held meetings there because Dr. McIntyre insisted he remain in bed.

There were some uneasy minds in our party as we took off from Malta. Our pilots were unfamiliar with the airfield at Saki where, we understood, there had been a considerable snowfall. We had conflicting reports on the hazards of the drive from Saki across the mountains to Yalta. There also was some fear of typhus, as we were told the Germans had left the place infested with vermin.

These worries were based on an underestimation of the prodigious effort the Russians exerted to demonstrate their hospitality. The landing strip at Saki was swept clear of every snowflake. The road from the field to Yalta, eighty miles away, was guarded by an unbroken line of Soviet troops, many of them girls—girls with guns. Livadia Palace, which was our headquarters and the scene of the meetings, was immaculate. We were told the Germans had completely ransacked it, leaving behind only two paintings out of all the furnishings in the huge building which had been a summer home for the Czars. Although some of the conveniences we fortunate Americans are accustomed to were missing, the Russians, with only three weeks advance notice, had done an amazing job in completely renovating the place.

As we were shown to our rooms we were told what they had been used for when the Czars were in residence. We soon learned Fleet Admiral Ernest J. King had been assigned to the Czarina's boudoir. He was reminded of it throughout the conference.

The Yalta Conference opened on Sunday, February 4, 1945, on a rising tide of Allied victories. The German counteroffensive in the west had been stopped in the bloody snow of the Ardennes Forest, and we were preparing to launch our drive across the Rhine. The Russians had begun the drive on Germany's eastern frontier that was to end in Berlin three months later. The situation was such that at one time President Roosevelt and Marshal Stalin engaged in light banter as to whether they should wager that the Red Army would get to Berlin before the American Army recaptured Manila.

Our chief objective for the conference was to secure agreement on the Dumbarton Oaks proposals for the creation of an international peace organization. But the rapid advance of our armies required also that urgent consideration be given to European political and military problems. It was natural, then, that the President, with the agreement of the other members, opened the conference with the suggestion to discuss "what we shall do with Germany."

Stalin immediately made it clear that he wanted to discuss the terms of the German surrender, the future form of the German state or states, reparations, and the allocation of a zone of occupation to France.

In the fall of 1944 the Soviet Union and the Provisional Government of France had entered into a treaty of friendship. It was immediately obvious at Yalta, however, that the treaty and the friendly words exchanged over it by the diplomats had not changed in any degree Marshal Stalin's opinion on the contribution of France to the war. He thought France should play little part in the control of Germany, and stated that Yugoslavia and Poland were more entitled to consideration than France.

When Roosevelt and Churchill proposed that France be allotted a zone of occupation, Stalin agreed. But it was clear he agreed only because the French zone was to be taken out of the territory allotted to the

United States and the United Kingdom. And he especially opposed giving France a representative on the Allied Control Council for Germany. He undoubtedly concurred in the opinion expressed to the President by Mr. Molotov that this should be done "only as a kindness to France and not because she is entitled to it."

"I am in favor of France being given a zone," Stalin declared, "but I cannot forget that in this war France opened the gates to the enemy." He maintained it would create difficulties to give France a zone of occupation and a representative on the Allied Control Council and refuse the same treatment to others who had fought more than France. He said France would soon demand that de Gaulle attend the Big Three's Conferences.

Churchill argued strongly in favor of France's being represented on the Council. He said the British public would not understand if questions affecting France and the French zone were settled without her participation in the discussion. It did not follow, as Stalin had suggested, that France would demand de Gaulle's participation in the conferences of the Big Three, he added. And, in his best humor, Mr. Churchill said the conference was "a very exclusive club, the entrance fee being at least five million soldiers or the equivalent."

Stalin, however, feared there would be such a demand. He said General de Gaulle was "very unrealistic," and reiterated that even though "France had not done much fighting in the war, yet de Gaulle has demanded equal rights with the Soviets, the British and the Americans, who have done the fighting."

President Roosevelt did not take issue with Stalin on de Gaulle. The President had great admiration for France and its people but he did not admire de Gaulle. On several occasions he referred to a conversation at Casablanca in which de Gaulle compared himself with Joan of Arc as the spiritual leader of France, and with Clemenceau as the political leader.

President Roosevelt's first opinion was not to insist upon giving France representation on the Allied Council if she were allotted a zone. As the argument proceeded, however, the President said he wished to consider further that phase of the question and asked that action be delayed. The following day Mr. Hopkins, Averell Harriman, our Ambassador to the Soviet Union, and I urged upon the President the view that France should be represented on the Council, that they could not accept a zone without such representation, and that any other action would greatly humiliate them. The President finally reached the same conclusion, and he later succeeded in inducing Stalin to agree with him.

The major problem in connection with the surrender of Germany arose from an informal suggestion, broached at Teheran, that the future security of Europe required Germany to be cut up into a number of individual states.

The discussion was brief but there seemed to be general agreement among all three that Germany should be divided into an unspecified number of states. Marshal Stalin was of the opinion that the Germans in surrendering should be told about this plan. Mr. Churchill suggested that the questions involved were so complex that further study should be made. The President then suggested that the Foreign Ministers study the matter and submit recommendations within the next thirty days.

At the later meeting in London, in which Ambassador John C. Winant represented the United States, no agreement was reached. When Mr. Hopkins saw Marshal Stalin late in May it was apparent that the Soviet leader had changed his views and had reached the conclusion that we and the British were opposed to dismemberment. He said it was evident there was no agreement at Yalta; and that at the London meeting the British had interpreted the Crimean discussions to represent not a positive plan but something to hold over Germany's head in case of bad behavior. He suggested that the matter be discussed at the forthcoming meeting of the Big Three at Potsdam. By the time that meeting occurred, however, the thinking of all three governments had veered away from dismemberment and the issue did not arise.

During all the consideration of the German question at Yalta, reparations were the chief interest of the Soviet delegation.

At the conference table Marshal Stalin sat between Mr. Molotov and I. M. Maisky, Deputy Commissar for Foreign Affairs. Maisky had served as the Russian Ambassador in London for eleven years, and at Yalta often acted as interpreter as well as adviser to Stalin. It was he who presented the Soviet proposal on German reparations.

"Our plan foresees that reparations in kind should be demanded from Germany in two ways," Mr. Maisky explained. "First, withdrawals from the national wealth of Germany. That means factories, land, machinery, machine tools, rolling stock of railways, investments in foreign enterprises, and so on. Second, yearly payments in kind after the war in the course of ten years."

He proposed that 80 per cent of all German industry should be withdrawn, specifying the iron and steel, engineering, metal and chemical industries. He added that aviation plants, facilities for the production of synthetic oil and all other military enterprises and factories should be withdrawn entirely.

"By withdrawal I mean to confiscate and carry away physically and use as reparations payments," he emphasized.

Retention of 20 per cent of Germany's heavy industry would be adequate to sustain the country's economic life, he said. All reparations should be terminated within ten years and the removal of factories and other wealth should be completed in two years. German enterprises important as war potentials should be internationalized with representatives of the three powers sitting on the boards of these enterprises for as many years as the three countries should desire.

Reparations funds should be paid only to those countries that had sustained direct material losses such as damage to factories, land and homes and the losses of personal property by citizens, Mr. Maisky maintained. Because such losses were so huge he proposed that a system of priorities be established among the countries to receive reparations based on their contribution to the winning of the war and the value of their direct material losses.

He then stated that reparations should be fixed at twenty billions of dollars and that the share of the Soviet Union in the reparations fund should not be less than ten billion dollars.

Mr. Churchill responded first to Mr. Maisky's statement. He recalled the experience of the United Kingdom after World War I.

"The process was a very disappointing one," he said. "With great difficulty about 1,000 million pounds was extracted from Germany, and that would never have been extracted if the United States, at the same time, had not loaned Germany a larger sum."

"Removal of plants and factories to a certain extent is a proper step," he declared, "but I am quite sure you will never be able to get out of ruined Germany for Russia alone anything like 215 million pounds a year." He pictured Britain's losses and heavy debts and referred to the severe losses of other countries which must be considered in allotting reparations.

"Secondly," Mr. Churchill continued, "there arises in my mind the specter of an absolutely starving Germany.

"If our treatment of Germany's internal economy is such as to leave eighty million people virtually starving, are we to sit still and say, 'It serves you right,' or will we be required to keep them alive? If so, who is going to pay for that? . . . If you have a horse and you want him to pull the wagon you have to provide him with a certain amount of corn—or at least hay."

"But the horse must not kick you," Mr. Maisky objected.

Mr. Churchill switched to a nonkicking illustration by saying:

"If you have a motorcar you must give it a certain amount of petrol to make it go. I am in favor of having a reparations inquiry committee set up to explore this subject with the object of getting the most we can in a sensible way."

In presenting the position of the United States, President Roosevelt pointed out that after the last war we loaned to Germany billions of dollars, and emphasized "We cannot let that happen again."

"We are in the position of not wanting any of Germany's manpower," the President said. "We do not want any of her machinery, tools, or her factories. There will be some German assets in the United States that might be credited against what Germany owes the United States, but it will amount to very little." After the meeting I advised the President that the best estimate placed the value of German assets in this country at 150 million dollars and that the value certainly would not exceed 200 million. He later used these figures to point out what an exceedingly small amount we would receive in contrast to other nations.

The American people want the Germans to live, the President told the conference, but do not want them to have a higher standard of living than other states, such as the Soviet Republic. He stressed that the United States would emerge from the war in poor financial condition and that we would have no money to send into Germany for food, clothing or housing.

"All I can say is that we will do the best we can in an extremely bad situation," the President said, and concluded by adding we would support the creation of a reparations commission as proposed by the Soviet Union.

Marshal Stalin then entered the discussion. "The root of the trouble the last time," he asserted, "was that reparations were demanded in money. Then, the question arose of transferring the German mark into foreign currencies. That was the rock upon which reparations broke down."

Marshal Stalin urged that the three powers that carried the burden of the war should have priority in reparations. He said it must be admitted that "France did not have any sacrifice to compare to the three powers I have in mind." And then to clinch the argument, he said, "France at this time has in the war eight divisions while the Lublin government has ten divisions." There is no doubt that his opinion as to the claims of a government was influenced by the number of its divisions. He is credited with having said at Yalta, when reference was made to the views of the Pope, "How many divisions does he have?" The Marshal did not make that statement at Yalta. But it was the yardstick he frequently used.

Stalin concluded his statement with a proposal that a decision be made as to whether reparations should be based upon the contributions made in the prosecution of the war or upon the losses sustained, or whether both should be considered. During the discussion, the President made a statement which still remains a source of misunderstanding between ourselves and the Russians. He said the Reparations Commission "should take, in its initial studies as a basis for discussion, the suggestion of the Soviet government, that the total sum of reparations should be twenty billions and that fifty per cent of it should go to the Soviet Union."

This language was later incorporated in the Conference Protocol, the document prepared by a committee appointed to set forth in writing the agreements reached during a conference. The protocol, which on the last day of the conference was submitted to the heads of government for final approval, also contained the statement that the Reparations Commission could consider "the use of labor" as a possible source of reparations. There was no discussion of this proposal at the conference table except a passing reference by the President in which he said the United States "cannot take manpower as the Soviet Republics can." Later I learned the language was added by Mr. Maisky, the Soviet representative, and subsequently agreed to by the other delegations. At any rate, I did not know of it at the time I left Yalta. Had I known it, I would have urged the President to oppose the inclusion in the protocol of any provision for the use of large groups of human beings as enforced or slave laborers. The program later drafted by the Reparations Commission contained no provision for "the use of labor." But I regret to say that Germans and Japanese still are being held in Allied hands for use as laborers.

In the days that followed Yalta, as our armies fought their way into Germany from the east and the west, and as our combined air power and artillery pounded the cities of Germany into rubble, it became fully apparent there was no adequate answer to Prime Minister Churchill's contention that Germany would be unable to reimburse the Allies for all the losses inflicted on the people in the various Allied countries.

Closely related to the reparations issue was the problem of fixing Poland's boundaries. President Roosevelt said, at the outset of the discussion, that the United States felt that Poland's eastern boundary should generally follow the so-called Curzon Line. He still held, he said, the view he had expressed at Teheran that it would be desirable to adjust the southern end of the line so that the city of Lwow and at least a portion of the oil fields should be inside Polish territory.

Prime Minister Churchill pointed out he had supported the Curzon Line in Parliament including the Soviet Union's retention of Lwow. The claim of the Soviet Union to this area, he said, "is one not founded on force but upon right." But if the Soviet Union made a "magnanimous gesture to a much weaker power" such as that suggested by the President, Mr. Churchill said, Britain "would admire and acclaim the Soviet position."

Marshal Stalin replied with an impassioned statement.

"The Curzon Line is the line of Curzon and Clemenceau and of those Americans who took part in 1918 and 1919 in the conference which then took place," Stalin declared. "The Russians were not invited and did not take part. . . . Lenin was not in agreement with the Curzon Line. . . . Now some people want that we should be less Russian than Curzon was and Clemenceau was. You would drive us into shame. What will be said by the White Russians and the Ukrainians? They will say that Stalin and Molotov are far less reliable defenders of Russia than are Curzon and Clemenceau. I could not take such a position and return to Moscow with an open face."

At this point, Stalin stood at the conference table as he spoke. It was the only time during the entire conference that he exhibited his strong feelings in such a manner.

"I prefer the war should continue a little longer although it costs us blood and to give Poland compensation in the west at the expense of the Germans," he continued. "I will maintain and I will ask all friends to support me in this. . . . I am in favor of extending the Polish western frontier to the Neisse River."

Mr. Churchill doubted the wisdom of extending the western boundary of Poland to the Neisse River. He agreed that Poland's western boundary should be moved into what had been German territory but asserted "it would be a pity to stuff the Polish goose so full of German food that he will die of indigestion." He estimated that the taking of territory in East Prussia as far west as the Oder would necessitate the moving of six million Germans.

Stalin protested that the number would be much smaller because "where our troops come in, the Germans run away."

Churchill reminded him that consideration must be given "to where those Germans are that run away," and asked, "will there be room for them in what is left of Germany?"

Privately, Churchill expressed to me the opinion that placing the line at the Neisse River would mean the transferring of nearly nine million Germans. Such a number, he asserted, could never be absorbed in what would remain of Germany.

The discussion was long and earnest but Stalin finally accepted the Curzon Line in principle and the following somewhat equivocal statement on Poland's frontiers was approved for inclusion in the protocol:

"The three heads of government consider that the eastern frontier of Poland should follow the Curzon Line with digressions from it in some regions of five to eight kilometres in favour of Poland. They recognize that Poland must receive substantial accessions of territory in the North and West. They feel that the opinion of the new Polish Provisional Government of National Unity should be sought in due course on the extent of these accessions and that the final delimitation of the western frontier of Poland should thereafter await the peace conference."

Not only Poland's boundaries but Poland itself was one of the most serious issues of the entire conference. More time was spent on this subject than on any other. Because of the intensity of the argument, Mr. Roosevelt would assume a role more of arbiter than of advocate although he, as well as Prime Minister Churchill, urged the establishment of a new Polish government in Warsaw.

The Soviet Union, on the other hand, wanted to continue the Lublin government. Stalin was willing to add a few persons but he wanted to make certain that those who were added did not affect the Soviet Union's control of the government.

The President said he favored a Polish government which would resolve all the political differences by "creating a government of national unity, a government which would represent all the political parties." Such a government, he maintained, should be provisional, and should regard as its primary duty the establishment of a permanent regime. He said the United States wished to have Poland on friendly terms with the Soviet Union and he felt if the conferees should solve the Polish question, they could make it easier to establish peace in the world.

"Britain," the Prime Minister said, "declared war on Germany in order that Poland should be free and sovereign. Everyone knows what a terrible risk we took and how nearly it cost us our life in the world, not only as an Empire but as a Nation. Our interest in Poland is one of honor. Having drawn the sword in behalf of Poland against Hitler's brutal attack, we could never be content with any solution that did not leave Poland a free and independent sovereign state."

He repeated the sentiment expressed by the President saying that Poland should not be "free to entertain hostile designs against the peace and safety of the Soviets."

Mr. Churchill eloquently painted the danger which arose from the continuing existence of two Polish governments. He urged that provision be made for a free election and that, in the meantime, effective guarantees could be made to secure the lines of communication of the Soviet army.

Stalin displayed great earnestness in replying.

"For the Russian people, the question of Poland is not only a question of honor but also a question of security. Throughout history, Poland has been the corridor through which the enemy has passed into Russia. Twice in the last thirty years our enemies, the Germans, have passed through this corridor. It is in Russia's interest that Poland should be strong and powerful, in a position to shut the door of this corridor by

her own force. . . . It is necessary that Poland should be free, independent in power. Therefore, it is not only a question of honor but of
life and death for the Soviet state."

In every subsequent discussion the Soviet Government has used this
argument to justify what it has done in Poland. Their idea of a friendly
government is a government completely dominated by them. The Lublin
government fitted this description and Stalin did not want to take any
chances with representatives of other political parties. Later I discussed
the subject with Mr. Molotov. I could not impress him with my views
that Soviet security would be better assured by having in Poland a
people who were friendly, rather than a government that was friendly
only because it was dictated to by the Soviet Union. Unsuccessfully, I
argued that governments would come and go, but that if the Soviet
Government's conduct in Poland won the friendship of the people, the
friendship of the government would be assured.

After the first discussion of Poland, President Roosevelt wrote a
letter to Stalin suggesting that delegates from the Warsaw and London
governments, and representatives of the several political factions in
Poland not represented in those governments, meet to consider the
formation of a new Polish Government. The letter became the basis of
further discussions.

The conferees debated the President's proposal for several days.
Finally they agreed on a declaration providing, among other things:
"The provisional government which is now functioning in Poland should
therefore be reorganized on a broader democratic basis with the inclusion
of democratic leaders from Poland itself and from Poles abroad. This
new government should then be called the Polish Provisional Government of National Unity."

A commission, composed of Mr. Molotov, Mr. Harriman and Sir
Archibald Clark Kerr, was appointed to consult, first, in Moscow with
members of the Lublin government, with democratic leaders from within Poland, and others from abroad, with a view to reorganizing the
government along the lines indicated.

The declaration pledged the Provisional Government to the holding
of free and unfettered elections as soon as possible on the basis of universal suffrage and secret ballot.

As the conferees neared what we thought was agreement on this
troublesome issue, President Roosevelt asked:

"How long will it take you to hold free elections?"

"Within a month's time," Mr. Molotov replied.

The election which, by our standard, was not "free," actually was
held twenty-three months later on Jaunary 19, 1947.

The day we arrived at Yalta I learned for the first time of a draft declaration of policy on the liberated areas that had been prepared by the State Department. The President did not like the declaration as drafted, but it greatly impressed me and I undertook to see if it could be revised to meet his objections. After conferences with Secretary Stettinius and other State Department officials a draft was prepared which received the President's approval.

When Secretary Stettinius presented the paper, several amendments were suggested by Foreign Secretary Eden and Foreign Minister Molotov. These were accepted and the paper was placed before the Big Three.

The declaration referred to "a principle of the Atlantic Charter—the right of all peoples to choose the form of government under which they will live—the restoration of sovereign rights and self-government to those peoples who have been forcibly deprived of them by the aggressor nations."

It then asserted:

"To foster the conditions in which the liberated peoples may exercise these rights, the three governments will jointly assist the people in any European liberated state or former Axis satellite state in Europe where in their judgment conditions require (a) to establish conditions of internal peace; (b) to carry out emergency measures for the relief of distressed peoples; (c) to form interim governmental authorities broadly representative of all democratic elements in the population and pledged to the earliest possible establishment through free elections of governments responsive to the will of the people; and (d) to facilitate where necessary the holding of elections."

Agreement was quickly reached among the Big Three. At least, we thought there had been a meeting of minds, but, ever since, there has been continual disagreement between the Soviets and ourselves as to its proper interpretation.

The discussion of the proposal was brief. Stalin opened it by saying, "On the whole, I approve of the declaration."

The President called attention to the paragraph containing the agreement to "facilitate if necessary the holding of elections," and Stalin quickly replied: "I accept that."

"Poland will be the first example of operating under this declaration," the President said. . . . "I want the election in Poland to be beyond question, like Caesar's wife. I did not know Caesar's wife, but she was believed to have been pure."

Stalin smilingly replied:

"It was said so about Caesar's wife, but, in fact, she had certain sins."

I only hope the lady had fewer sins than, in our view, this declaration has had violations. It seems to me there is no question as to the intention of the parties to the agreement. We thought it was a step forward. But it proved to be a very faltering step.

When the draftsmen assisting the Foreign Ministers agreed to include in the declaration a statement that certain things would be done by the three governments "where in their judgment conditions require," the Soviets were able to say—as they so often did—whenever they disliked to act, that in their judgment conditions did not require action.

The American public greeted the publication of this declaration with enthusiasm. Editorial writers commented on it favorably. From the close of the Yalta Conference to the present day it has been a source of conflict between the Soviet Union and ourselves. But it is the basis on which we have shown the world that Russian actions in eastern Europe have been in violation of Russia's pledged word. In that respect it has been useful.

In October 1943, Secretary of State Cordell Hull had taken with him to Moscow the first proposal that finally developed into the Dumbarton Oaks plan for a United Nations organization. He and the President believed it would be far easier to obtain agreement on a plan for a peace organization while the war was still in progress. How right they were!

At the conclusion of the Dumbarton Oaks Conference, in the autumn of 1944, the only major point remaining at issue was the formula for voting in the Security Council. The Soviet delegation had insisted that all decisions in the Security Council must be by a unanimous vote on the part of the major powers. We agreed that no decision committing our military forces to action should be taken without our consent but did not believe the right of veto should extend to all matters.

We finally had devised a compromise formula which we hoped the Soviets could be persuaded to accept, and the President sent it direct to Marshal Stalin on December 5. At the same time, the State Department prepared and delivered to the Soviet and British embassies in Washington lengthy statements in explanation and support of the President's proposal.

We sought to meet the Soviet insistence that the votes of the five permanent members of the Security Council must be unanimous on all questions by suggesting that Paragraph 3 in the section of the plan dealing with voting procedure in the Security Council should state that unanimity would be required for all categories of decisions except one: in those decisions involving promotion of peaceful settlement of disputes, a permanent member of the council would not cast a vote if it were party to the dispute in question. Such cases, we believed, would be quasi-judicial in character and no nation should be placed above the law in an organization based on the principle of equality under the law. Where the decisions might require the use of force, we felt justified in placing the permanent members in a special position, since they would have to bear the principal responsibility for such action.

It was on the second day of the conference that Secretary Stettinius formally presented our proposal, and the President then asked for its immediate consideration. In supporting the plan, the President referred to the agreement reached at Teheran in which the three heads of government declared: "We recognize fully that supreme responsibility resting upon us and all the United Nations to make a peace that will command the good will of the overwhelming mass of the peoples of the world and banish the scourge and terror of war for many generations."

Conflicting reports of the exchange that followed were presented in the Security Council of the United Nations in the spring of 1947 by the Soviet and the British representatives during a discussion of the veto power and its relationship to the control of atomic energy. Because of this, and because the veto power has remained one of the most controversial issues of the United Nations structure, it may be of interest to present here the major portion of my shorthand record of the views expressed on the veto issue at Yalta.

Since the United States, as the author of the proposal, had clearly stated its position, the exchange was almost entirely between Prime Minister Churchill and Marshal Stalin. It follows:

Prime Minister: "The peace of the world depends upon the lasting friendship of the three great powers, but His Majesty's Government feel we should be putting ourselves in a false position if we put ourselves in the position of trying to rule the world when our desire is to serve the world and preserve it from a renewal of the frightful horrors which have fallen upon the mass of its inhabitants. We should make a broad submission to the opinion of the world within the limits stated. We should have the right to state our case against any case stated by the Chinese, for instance, in the case of Hongkong. There is no question that we could not be required to give back Hongkong to the Chinese if we did not feel that was the right thing to do. On the other hand, I feel it would be wrong if China did not have an opportunity to state its case fully. In the same way, if Egypt raises a question against the British affecting the Suez Canal, as has been suggested, I would submit to all the procedure outlined in this statement. I would do this without fear because British rights would be preserved under paragraph 3 when our veto would kill action if we chose to use it.

"I presume, Mr. President, if Argentina raises a question against the United States, that the United States will submit to all the procedure of the last five paragraphs and would not vote on the issue. However, the United States could raise its fundamental objections in respect to all the measures to be taken under paragraph 3. . . .

"His Majesty's Government see no danger from their point of

view in associating themselves with the proposals of the United States. We see great advantage in the three great powers not assuming the position of rulers of all of the rest of the world without even allowing them to state their case. It would not be right for us with the great power we possess to take that position, denying them the right to state their case, and to have measures taken to adjust difficulties short of the powers set out in paragraph 3, on which powers we rely if we are not convinced by our friends and colleagues on the Security Council."

The Marshal: "I would like to have this document to study because it is difficult on hearing it read to come to any conclusion. I think that the Dumbarton Oaks decisions have, as an objective, not only to secure to every nation the right to express its opinion, but if any nation should raise a question about some important matter, it raises the question in order to get a decision in the matter. I am sure none of those present would dispute the right of every member of the Assembly to express his opinion.

"Mr. Churchill thinks that China, if it raised the question of Hongkong, would be content only with expressing opinion here. He may be mistaken. China will demand a decision in the matter and so would Egypt. Egypt will not have much pleasure in expressing an opinion that the Suez Canal should be returned to Egypt, but would demand a decision on the matter. Therefore, the matter is much more serious than merely expressing an opinion. Also, I would like to ask Mr. Churchill to name the power which may intend to dominate the world. I am sure Great Britain does not want to dominate the world. So one is removed from suspicion. I am sure the United States does not wish to do so, so another is excluded from the powers having intentions to dominate the world."

Mr. Churchill: "May I answer?"

The Marshal: "In a minute. When will the great powers accept the provisions that would absolve them from the charge that they intend to dominate the world? I will study the document. At this time it is not very clear to me. I think it is a more serious question than the right of a power to express its intentions or the desire of some power to dominate the world."

Prime Minister: "I know that under the leaders of the three powers as represented here we may feel safe. But these leaders may not live forever. In ten years' time we may disappear. A new generation will come which did not experience the horrors of war and may probably forget what we have gone through. We would like to secure the peace for at least fifty years. We have now to build up such a status, such a plan, that we can put as many obstacles as possible to the coming generation quarreling among themselves."

The Marshal: "I think that the task is to secure our unity in the future, and, for this purpose, we must agree upon such a covenant as would best serve that purpose. The danger in the future is the possibility of conflicts among ourselves. If there be unity, then the danger from Germany will not be great. Now we have to think how we can create a situation where the three powers here represented, and China—"

Prime Minister: "—and France."

The Marshal: "Yes, and we will keep a united front. I must apologize to the conference. I have been very busy with other matters and had no chance to study this question in detail. As far as I understand what was said in the American proposal, all conflicts are being divided into two categories—conflicts which demand sanctions of a military nature; the other category includes conflicts which could be regulated by peaceful means without military sanctions. Then I understand that, in the consideration of conflicts of both kinds, it is contemplated there should be first a free discussion of the conflict. I understand, also, that in considering the disputes of the first category, which demand military sanctions, that a permanent member being a party to the dispute has a right to vote. But in conflicts of the second category, which could be regulated by peaceful means, and do not require sanctions, the party in dispute is not allowed to vote.

"We are accused of attaching too great importance to the procedure 'how to vote.' We are guilty. We attach great importance to the question of voting. All questions are decided by votes and we are interested in the decisions and not in the discussions. Suppose China is a permanent member and demands Hongkong be returned to her. I can assure Mr. Churchill that China will not be alone. They will have some friends in the Assembly. That would be true of Egypt in the case mentioned."

Prime Minister: "I could say 'no.' I would have a right to say that the powers of the World Security Organization could not be used against us if we remained unconvinced."

The Marshal: "There is another danger. My colleagues in Moscow cannot forget the case which occurred in 1939 during the Russian-Finnish War, when Britain and France used the League of Nations against us and eventually expelled us and isolated us."

The President: "It is entirely satisfactory for the Marshal to have sufficient time to study the proposal."

I was deeply disturbed by the clear evidence that Stalin had not considered or even read our proposal on voting in the Security Council even though it had been sent to him by diplomatic air pouch on December 5. This was February 6, and it occurred to me that if in those sixty-three days he had not familiarized himself with the subject, he could not be greatly interested in the United Nations organization. It was all the more impressive since this certainly was the only proposal on the agenda with which he was not entirely familiar. My concern remained even though at the next day's meeting Mr. Molotov announced the Soviet Union's acceptance of our proposal, which was later adopted in substantially the same form at San Francisco.

The discussion on the United Nations then turned to what governments should become members. There followed this colloquy:

The Marshal: "I have a list of the states that declared war on Germany. It means that they become future members of the Assembly. Among those states are ten which have no diplomatic relations with the Soviet union. [Most of these ten were South American republics.] We are to meet with them to build up international security. How is it possible to build up international security with states that have no diplomatic relations with us at all? Perhaps the conference would discuss this matter."

The President: "I think most of them would like to establish diplomatic relations with the Soviet Union. They just have not got around to it yet. At the same time it should be recognized that most of the states that have not recognized the Soviet Union have been sitting with the Soviet representatives at Bretton Woods and other places in conferences that have been held."

The Marshal: "That is right. But it is difficult to build up international security with states that do not want to have anything to do with the Soviet Union."

The President: "I think the easiest way to establish complete diplomatic relations with them is to invite them. This whole question involves a matter of history which should be explained.

"Four years ago the Acting Secretary of State, Mr. Welles, told the South American republics it was not necessary to declare war on Germany but that it was necessary to cut off diplomatic relations. So there are five or six republics which think they should be invited because they took the advice of the United States at that time. This matter was brought to my attention one month ago. As a result, I sent a letter to the Presidents of these six republics, explaining that if they want to attend the Conference of United Nations they should declare war. I think one, Ecuador, has done so, but has not yet had a chance to sign the Declaration of the United Nations. Paraguay will do so in a week or ten days. Peru and Uruguay will soon declare war. The result is that it would be a little embarrassing if, after they declared war, they should then be excluded from coming to the meeting. Quite frankly, it was a mistake of Mr. Welles in not advising them to declare war instead of merely breaking off diplomatic relations.

"In the meantime all these nations have helped us in the conduct of the war. A large part of the raw materials for the manufacture of munitions has come from them. The result is, I am in a difficult position.

"In addition to those nations that have signed, there are a small number called associated nations which have worked with us. They broke diplomatic relations but did not declare war."

The Marshal: "What about Argentina?"

The President: "The Argentines are not in it at all."

The Marshal: "But the Argentines broke relations with Germany."

The President: "But have not been accepted as an associated nation."

The Marshal: "I am not for the Argentines. I do not like them; but I do desire there should be no logical contradiction. If we invite the nations that declared war and also the associated nations that have broken relations, there is then a category of nations like Argentina. This means Turkey and some other countries would come. I think the nations which declared war would feel not quite at ease with those nations that have not declared war, but were saving all the time, trying to speculate on who would win and who generally were not straight in their behavior."

The President: "My idea would be to invite only those associated nations that have helped us on the condition that they declare war."

The Marshal: "When should they act?"

The President: "Right away. Put a time limit on them."

The Marshal: "Say, the first of March."

The President: "All right, the first of March."

Mr. Churchill also approved this solution, citing Turkey as an example of a state that had remained neutral heretofore and had been encouraged to do so. Although somewhat reluctant, Marshal Stalin likewise agreed.

Immediately after announcing the Soviet Union's acceptance of the President's proposal on voting procedure in the Security Council, Mr. Molotov expressed the hope that Byelorussia, the Ukraine and Lithuania would be admitted to the United Nations. In any event, he said, he hoped the first two would be admitted. Marshal Stalin made a forceful plea in support of the suggestion.

Prime Minister Churchill supported the Soviet request, stating: "My heart goes out to White Russia, bleeding from her wounds while beating down the tyrants."

Not wishing to agree, and yet not wanting to oppose Churchill and Stalin directly while the issue of the international organization was in the balance, the President made this statement: "The British Empire has great populations in its dominions, like Australia, Canada and South Africa. The Soviet Government has great masses of population like the three dominions mentioned. The United States has no colonies but has a large population. Brazil is smaller than the Soviet Union but larger in area than the United States. There are many countries with small population, like Honduras and Liberia. We must study the question of whether any country should be given more than one vote. I do not want to break down the principle of one vote to each nation. Therefore, we can decide on the general plan of a meeting to organize the association and then before the meeting, through the Foreign Secretaries, or at that meeting, we can decide these questions and I will be glad to take them up."

There was no dissent. Because I was strongly opposed to granting the Soviet request, I thought the President had done a good job and that we might hear no more of the proposal. But at the conference table the next afternoon the President began reading a report of the meeting of the Foreign Ministers which had just been handed him and said:

"Paragraph 2 is that it will be for the conference to determine the list of the original members of the organization. At that stage the delegates of the United Kingdom and the United States will support the proposal to admit to original membership two Soviet Socialist republics."

The report was agreed to.

I learned later that at the Foreign Ministers meeting, Mr. Eden, who wanted to be certain of the admission of all members of the British Commonwealth including India, which was not an independent state, agreed with Mr. Molotov on the votes for Byelorussia and the Ukraine. Mr. Stettinius then also agreed to the arrangement. As the meeting opened, the Secretary advised the President of the action which the President later announced, and the heads of government approved.

I was surprised at the agreement which, in my opinion, was very unwise. After the meeting I urged my view upon the President. I reminded him that before we left Washington he had told a group of Senators that if Stalin proposed granting membership to Byelorussia and the Ukraine, he would insist upon membership for each of our forty-eight states. The truth is, the Soviet republics are no more independent than the states of our Union.

I recalled to him how effectively the opponents of the League of Nations had argued that the British, because of their dominions, would have five votes in the Assembly while we would have but one. Our people had come to realize that the dominions were independent states and frequently held views different from the United Kingdom, but that was not true of the Soviet republics. I feared the opponents of the United Nations might use the allotment of three votes to the Soviet Union as effectively as the foes of the League had used the argument against the British votes twenty-six years earlier. I urged the President at least to ask that the United States be granted a number of votes equal to those of the Soviet Union. The President feared it was too late but said he would consider it.

I convinced Hopkins that, at the very least, we should secure such an agreement from Stalin and Churchill whether or not we afterward exercised the right. He then joined me in urging the President to withdraw his agreement regarding the two Soviet republics unless Russia agreed the United States also should have three votes. The President finally told us he would present it to Marshal Stalin. On the last day I spent at Yalta, February 10, the President wrote him a letter which stated:

> I am somewhat concerned lest it be pointed out that the United States will have only one vote in the Assembly. It may be necessary for me, therefore, if I am to insure wholehearted acceptance by the Congress and people of the United States of our participation in the World Organization, to ask for additional votes in the Assembly in order to give parity to the United States.
>
> I would like to know, before I face this problem, that you perceive no objection and would support a proposal along this line if it is necessary for me to make it at the forthcoming conference.

The following day Marshal Stalin advised the President that he entirely agreed with him that "since the number of votes for the Soviet Union is increased to three in connection with the inclusion of the Soviet Ukraine and Soviet White Russia among the members of the Assembly, the number of votes for the USA should also be increased.

"The number of votes for the USA might be increased to three as in the case of the Soviet Union and its two basic republics," he said. "If it is necessary I am prepared officially to support this proposal."

President Roosevelt also asked Churchill for his views, and Churchill stated he would support the President in any proposal he made to achieve American equality with other nations.

When I arrived in Washington there was waiting for me in the White House Map Room the following cable:

For Justice Byrnes from Mr. Hopkins
THE PRESIDENT HAS RECEIVED COMPLETELY SATISFACTORY REPLIES FROM THE PRIME MINISTER AND MARSHAL STALIN ON ADDITIONAL VOTES TO ACHIEVE PARITY FOR THE UNITED STATES, IF NECESSARY. IN VIEW OF THE FACT THAT NOTHING ON THIS WHOLE SUBJECT APPEARS IN THE COMMUNIQUÉ, THE PRESIDENT IS EXTREMELY ANXIOUS NO ASPECT OF THIS QUESTION BE DISCUSSED EVEN PRIVATELY.

I assumed he had some very good reason for not wishing this matter to be discussed, and I complied with the request.

The President and his advisers concluded not to ask at San Francisco for compliance with the agreement that we have as many votes as were given to Russia. He did not again discuss the subject with me, and I did not know he had changed his mind. I admit that the public opposition to Russia's three votes as against our one was not so great as I had expected. But nevertheless I think we should have insisted at San Francisco on the agreement made at Yalta. I felt then and feel now that the smaller states would have opposed the request of the Soviets and the United States. This course would have been just and it would have resulted in both governments having only one vote. That would have been the best solution.

In granting three votes to the Soviet Union, we established a precedent. The Soviets do not overlook precedents favorable to themselves. At the Peace Conference in Paris, for example, Byelorussia and the Ukraine were members. They will demand membership in every other conference. This means the Soviet Union has three arguments as well as three votes. They never fail to make the three arguments or cast the three votes.

The Paris Peace Conference agreed upon two kinds of recommendations, one requiring only a majority vote, the other requiring a two-thirds vote. The Soviet representatives announced that in the Council of Foreign Ministers they would not consider any recommendation adopted by less than a two-thirds vote.

There were twenty-one members of the peace conference. Therefore, eight votes in opposition to a recommendation would prevent its receiving the two-thirds endorsement. When the Soviets opposed a proposal, it was much easier for them to secure these eight votes because they had three votes to start with. Had the Soviets possessed only one vote, or had the United States been given three votes, as was agreed at Yalta, many of the recommendations which received thirteen votes, one short of two-thirds, would have been adopted.

Another agreement was made at Yalta which was to confront me later. This was the "Top Secret" Protocol in which it was agreed that in return for Soviet participation in the war against Japan, the Kurile Islands would be "handed over" to the Soviet Union. It also provided that "the former rights of Russia violated by the treacherous attack of Japan in 1904 shall be restored," and listed these as the return of the southern half of Sakhalin Island, internationalization of the Port of Dairen, the lease of Port Arthur as a Russian naval base, and joint Russo-Chinese operation of the Chinese Eastern and South Manchurian railroads. The United States was to use its influence to have China agree to that part affecting China's territory.

I did not know of this agreement, but the reason is understandable. At that time I was not Secretary of State. Mr. Stettinius was Secretary.

Because of problems that had arisen in Washington, the President wanted me to return with Admiral King, who was leaving at noon on February 10. We expected the conference would end that evening and that the President would leave the following day. But that afternoon Stalin requested the President to remain one more day. He said they could not conclude their work and he wished to discuss some matter he deemed important. The President complied. The agreement as to the Kurile Islands was reached in private conversations among the Big Three instead of at the conference table, and the protocols, including this one, were signed on February 11. Had I been in Yalta that day it is probable I would have learned of it.

When the President returned, he did not mention it to me and the protocol was kept locked in his safe at the White House. In the early summer I learned that President Roosevelt had undertaken to induce China to make the concessions affecting Port Arthur, Dairen, and the railroad, but it was not until some time after I became Secretary of State that a news story from Moscow caused me to inquire and learn of the full agreement. I presented the matter to President Truman and he requested Admiral Leahy to transfer to the State Department those documents at the White House containing agreements with foreign governments. I wanted to know how many IOUs were outstanding.

In considering the wisdom of these Pacific agreements entered into by President Roosevelt, one should be fair enough to consider the circumstances under which the promises were made. It was six weeks after the serious German counterattack on the western front. Although progress was being made in both the east and the west, neither the President nor anyone else at that time knew how long the Germans could hold out and how many casualties we would suffer before they surrendered. The President had with him at Yalta the Joint Chiefs of Staff. They knew the situation.

The evidence is clear that the agreement was, in great part, a military decision. The military leaders already had their plans for the invasion of Japan under way. They undoubtedly gave the President their estimate of what such an invasion would cost us in human lives with Russia in the war and what the cost would be if Russia were out of the war. They naturally wanted Russia in the war to engage the Japanese armies in the north. But once Stalin knew our plans for invasion were under way, he knew also that we would want his armies and he could demand more for them. Mr. Stalin is not bashful about making demands.

Nor should President Roosevelt be criticized for keeping the agreement secret. The Soviet Union was party to a treaty with Japan and we could not announce Russia's intention to go to war with her. Furthermore, Russia's military strength was then concentrated on the German campaign. Any hint of the agreement would have been an invitation to the Japanese troops on Russia's borders to launch an invasion. It was in the interest of all of us to allow the Soviets ninety days after Germany's surrender to transfer troops from the European front. It is, therefore, quite understandable that both Marshal Stalin and President Roosevelt wished to maintain strict secrecy.

Toward the end of the conference, Marshal Stalin entertained at dinner. At the time, the press quoted one of the Americans present as saying forty-five toasts were proposed. I am willing to believe it, but the simple statement certainly is misleading. Unexplained, it would indicate the diners were thoroughly intoxicated. The fact is that with each toast, the diners took only a sip of wine and many made the gesture without the sip. The dinner lasted four hours. Forty-five sips of wine in four hours, during which time enough food was consumed to last twenty-four hours, did not intoxicate any one of that group. As for me, I do not drink wine.

About the time we reached the soup course, I noticed Mr. Vyshinski, who was sitting near me, pouring water into his vodka glass. Since vodka is the color of water, I decided if he could do it, I could. In the confusion incident to everyone's standing up when a toast was proposed, I would pour water into my vodka glass. It was not very stimulating, but I do know what took place at the dinner. Because of some of the reports in the United States about Soviet officials getting intoxicated, it is only fair to say that all those with whom I have come in contact have been most temperate. Never have I seen a Soviet representative at a social affair who showed the slightest evidence of intoxication.

The Marshal was generous in the toast he proposed to Churchill and particularly generous in his remarks proposing the health of the President, whom he described as the "chief forger of the instruments which had led to the mobilization of the world against Hitler."

The Prime Minister toasted Marshal Stalin as the "mighty leader of a mighty nation whose people had driven the tyrants from her soil." The President spoke with pride of the unity that characterized the relations among the three countries, and expressed the hope it would continue.

One statement of Stalin's that interested me was: "It is not so difficult to keep unity in time of war since there is a joint aim to defeat the common enemy, which is clear to everyone. The difficult task will come after the war when diverse interests tend to divide the Allies. It is our duty to see that our relations in peacetime are as strong as they have been in war."

I can testify to the accuracy of his prophecy, and I share his views as to our duty.

When toasts had been proposed to all the military chieftains and the heroes of the war on land, sea, and in the air, I proposed a toast "to the people of our respective countries—the workers on farms and in factories—who did not wear the uniform but whose contribution made possible our victories." The Marshal left his place and came to clink his glass with mine in approval of the sentiment. The truth is, he is a very likeable person.

The report of the Yalta Conference was released simultaneously from London, Moscow and Washington on Monday afternoon, February 12. All the Allied nations responded favorably and American public opinion was especially enthusiastic. The Philadelphia *Record* called the conference the "greatest United Nations victory of the war." The New York *Herald Tribune* declared that "the overriding fact" is that the conference "has produced another great proof of Allied unity, strength and power of decision." And *Time Magazine* asserted: "all doubts about the Big Three's ability to co-operate in peace as well as in war seem now to have been swept away."

That was how I felt about it. There is no doubt that the tide of Anglo-Soviet-American friendship had reached a new high. But President Roosevelt had barely returned to American soil when the tide began to ebb.

Chapter 3

The Tide Begins to Turn

BACK home, in February 1945, there was a huge amount of work to plunge into. The shortage of manpower was critical and the proposed National Service Act, generally called the "work-or-fight" bill, was the center of controversy both on Capitol Hill and among the agencies concerned. Our entire production program was under review in anticipation of the end of the war in Europe. Plans for post V-E Day lend-lease, surplus property disposal and emergency relief were being made; and the policies for reconverting our industrial establishment from war to peacetime operations were being shaped.

During my absence these plans had been greatly advanced through the tireless efforts of the people in my office, including General Lucius D. Clay, whom I had induced the War Department to assign to my office a few months earlier. Assisting him was Fred Searls, a New York industrialist—a quiet, unassuming man, with extraordinary knowledge of industrial processes. Throughout the war, he ably filled a number of responsible positions, refusing salary and reimbursement for expenses and avoiding publicity. He served his country well.

The previous June, when the bill to expand the Office of War Mobilization into the Office of War Mobilization and Reconversion was under consideration in Congress, I had stated to the committee I was not asking for power for myself in the postwar era, because I would not remain in the government to administer the reconversion program. We then thought little would be done in the way of reconversion until the European war ended. However, immediately following our return from Yalta, we decided that the emphasis should immediately shift from mobilization to reconversion.

It was, therefore, necessary for me to give some thought to the manner and timing of my departure from government service. It seemed only fair that the man who would have to assume responsibility for administering the reconversion program should take charge as soon as possible, and should not be placed in the position of having to administer policies he had no part in drafting.

Nevertheless, the question of timing troubled me. We knew V-E Day could not be far distant, but there was a danger that what was evident in Washington might not be so clear to the GI, who still had to fight his way across the Rhine. I did not want to take any action, however desirable for domestic reasons, that would carry to the fighting fronts the remotest suggestion that there was a slackening of effort, enthusiasm or support by those in responsible positions at home.

By mid-March we had established a foothold on the east bank of the Rhine and had received word from Field Marshal Alexander that high German officers had proposed a meeting in Switzerland to arrange for the surrender of the German Army in Italy. Consequently, when we started moving across the Rhine in force on March 23, I concluded it was wrong to postpone action any further, and the following day I presented to the President a letter of resignation, asking that it become effective April 2. I fixed that date because the law required the filing of a quarterly report with the President and Congress on April 1, and necessarily I had to submit that report.

When the President tried to persuade me to remain, I reminded him of his promise the previous fall that with the end of the war in Europe I could leave. I told him that I had left the Court only to undertake a wartime task; that I did not want to become the head of an agency or bureau in time of peace. I convinced him that the man who was going to direct the reconversion program should be given an opportunity to share in drafting that program, and it was essential therefore that the change be made.

We discussed many things, including the plans for the occupation of Germany. He understood the War Department was planning to send Assistant Secretary of War, John J. McCloy, to Germany to head our organization. I informed him McCloy had decided to remain with Secretary Stimson and that my deputy, General Clay, had been selected by the War Department for the assignment. To my surprise, he did not know General Clay. I told him I had obtained his assignment to my office, because, after dealing with officials of all the departments, I had found no man more capable than Clay and no army officer who had as clear an understnding of the point of view of the civilian. The President remarked that I was unusually enthusiastic about Clay and asked that I bring him in for a talk. The President was leaving that day for Hyde Park but would be spending a day in Washington the following week en route to Warm Springs. We agreed the three of us would get together that day. Shortly after the President arrived in Hyde Park he telephoned me to ask that I reconsider my resignation, and then, when I did not change my mind, he asked that I suggest a successor. I recommended Judge Fred M. Vinson, who had succeeded me as head of the Office of

Economic Stabilization. The President indicated agreement and said we could discuss it when he returned.

The President was unusually nervous the day of his return. During our talk he told General Clay he was glad he was going to Germany and he wanted the general, who was an engineer, to know of his idea of establishing a TVA in Central Europe to develop greater electrical power and relieve Europe's chronic coal shortage. Clay stood at attention. The President did not give him a chance to say a word, and as soon as the President had finished Steve Early came into the room. I knew the President was behind his schedule and asked Clay to wait outside for me. I remained for a few minutes to ask about Vinson and the President told me he would appoint Vinson, and asked me to talk to him because he had a number of engagements to fill before leaving that afternoon for Warm Springs. He would telephone Fred later in the day.

When I left the President's office and rejoined Clay, I said jokingly: "General, you talk too much."

"Mr. Justice," Clay replied, "even if the President had given me a chance, I doubt that I could have talked to him because I was shocked at his appearance."

Clay had not seen the President for some time. For forty-one crowded, exciting months, I had been at work in the White House and, because I saw him frequently, I did not realize, as Clay did, the change in his appearance. Although, when we parted, I had felt that an eventful chapter in our relationship was ended, I certainly did not appreciate that for him the end of life's journey was only a few days away. While waiting for Judge Vinson's appointment to be confirmed, I talked to the President on our direct line to Warm Springs several times and he professed to be feeling much better. I concluded that he was staging a "comeback" as he had done on many previous occasions.

On April 8, I returned to Spartanburg, where the friendly people who are my neighbors gave me a warm welcome. Four days later, with millions of people all over the world, I was stunned by the radio announcement that President Roosevelt was dead.

The Secretary of the Navy, James V. Forrestal, telephoned that he was sending his plane to Spartanburg to bring me to Washington because he thought I might be of some service during the next few days and he knew I would want to attend the President's funeral.

Early the next morning I called to see President Truman. He was overwhelmed by the responsibilities suddenly thrust upon him but was rapidly familiarizing himself with the status of pending problems. That afternoon I returned to the White House and he requested me to ride with him the next morning to meet the train bringing the body of President Roosevelt, and to accompany him on the sad journey to Hyde Park.

On the train returning to Washington the President and I discussed many matters. As I had been out of the White House only a few days, I was able to acquaint him with the status of many serious problems in our foreign and domestic relations. In the course of this conversation the President said he would like me to attend the forthcoming United Nations Conference in San Francisco as his representative.

"Mr. President, I appreciate your suggestion very much, but I don't think you ought to send me," I replied. "The delegation already is appointed. It is a representative group and includes some very able people. Experience has shown that a personal representative of the President under such circumstances usually causes great dissatisfaction in a delegation. Almost invariably relationships become more personal than representative." President Truman agreed.

The following day he told me he wished to appoint me Secretary of State. I did not want in time of peace to be head of an agency considering reconversion problems but I did want to take part in the making of the peace. I said I would accept the appointment, and we agreed that neither the change nor the announcement should be made until the end of the San Francisco Conference which was just about to meet.

Probably no new President ever faced a swifter pageant of great events than did Mr. Truman in his first weeks in office. The collapse and surrender of Germany and the San Francisco Conference held the center of the stage before a world audience that was stirred by victory and filled with high hopes for the future.

But those of us who were familiar with Soviet activities following the Yalta Conference found our high hopes mingled with great concern.

Before President Roosevelt's death, in fact, even before his return from Yalta, difficulties had arisen with the Soviet Union regarding the action to be taken on the agreements reached. The two major points of difficulty were Poland and Rumania.

In the Declaration on Liberated Europe the three governments had exchanged pledges to "concert during the temporary period of instability in liberated Europe the policies of their three governments in assisting the peoples liberated from the domination of Nazi Germany and the peoples of the former Axis satellite states of Europe to solve by democratic means their pressing political and economic problems." It stated further that the three governments "will jointly assist" the peoples of this area "to form interim governmental authorities broadly representative of all democratic elements in the population and pledged to the earliest possible establishment, through free elections of governments responsive to the will of the people." And finally, it added that "when, in the opinion of the three governments, conditions in any European liberated state or any former Axis satellite state in Europe make such action necessary, to discharge the joint responsibilities set forth in this declaration."

Nevertheless, on February 24, only two weeks after the conference, when the American and British members of the Allied Control Council for Rumania requested a meeting of the council, their request was refused by the Soviet chairman. On that same day, Ambassador Harriman was instructed to indicate to the Soviet Government our desire to see an orderly development of the Rumanian situation under the Allied Control Council or else consultation among the three countries on a higher level.

Three days later we got our answer. Mr. Molotov's deputy, Andrei Vyshinski, went to Bucharest and presented a demand for the dismissal of the Radescu government and the formation of a new Rumanian government. At the same time, Mr. Molotov informed our Ambassador that the Radescu government was unable to maintain order and fulfill the armistice terms and that the Allied Control Council would take the necessary measures and keep the Allies informed.

Mr. Harriman was instructed immediately to inform the Soviet Government that we could not accept a provisional government in Rumania made up of representatives from one political party. His instructions also stated that measures should be taken to support the present government in maintaining order; that freedom of press should be granted in accordance with the armistice agreement; that all political groups should be disarmed; and that full three-member consultations should take place in the Allied Control Council on major political matters.

Mr. Molotov told Mr. Harriman that three power consultations were going on with Vyshinski in Bucharest.

On March 5, our Ambassador presented a letter to Mr. Molotov stating that the question of the Radescu government was a matter for direct consultation and agreement by all three governments. He advised Molotov that the Soviet member of the Allied Control Council had not kept the United States representative informed and that the Soviet military authorities had weakened the ability of the Radescu government to maintain order. He followed this with another note the next day rejecting the idea that the intermittent contacts with Vyshinski constituted the tripartite consultations agreed upon at Yalta.

While these exchanges were taking place between our Ambassador and Foreign Minister Molotov in Moscow, here is what was happening in Rumania:

On February 27, Mr. Vyshinski had arrived in Bucharest and requested an audience with the King that evening. He was received by the King and Foreign Minister Constantine Visoianu. Mr. Vyshinski stated that General Radescu was incapable of maintaining order; that the Soviet government was unwilling to interfere in Rumania's internal affairs but had the responsibility of seeing that order was maintained behind the front and, therefore, asked that the Radescu government be dismissed immediately and replaced by a government based on "the truly democratic forces of the country." He was told that consideration would be given his request.

Burton Y. Berry, our political representative in Bucharest, was unable to obtain an interview with Vyshinski. He then informed Vyshinski in writing of the American point of view—that no decisive action should be taken prior to consultation.

According to the information sent us by Mr. Berry, Mr. Vyshinski the next day demanded an audience with the King and asked for his decision on the suggestion of the previous evening. The King replied he had communicated this information to General Radescu and had started consulting party leaders for the purpose of choosing another Prime Minister. Vyshinski declared this answer was unsatisfactory. Then, the report stated, Vyshinski looked at his watch and told the King he had just two hours and five minutes to make it known to the public that General Radescu had been dismissed. By eight o'clock, he added in emphasis, the King must tell the public the name of his successor.

The Rumanian Foreign Minister reminded Mr. Vyshinski that the King was a constitutional monarch and had to proceed in a constitutional manner; that he could only consult party leaders and follow their advice in selecting some individual to form a government. Vyshinski retorted that Radescu was protecting Fascists and by retiring ten officers the previous day under a royal decree had performed an unfriendly act toward the Soviet Union. That decree, he said, must be annulled immediately. The King acceded to this request and Mr. Vyshinski left. In leaving he slammed the door so hard that the plaster around the door frame was cracked badly. It has never been fixed; it remains to testify to the strength of his feeling and of his arm.

The King announced that he had asked Prince Stirbey to form a government. Prince Stirbey tried to comply but could not induce the Communists to join in forming a government. Shortly afterward Mr. Vyshinski sent word to the King that the Communist leader, Petru Groza, was the choice of the Soviet government. Nevertheless, the King continued to consult party leaders and on the evening of March 1, Vyshinski again saw the King to inform him personally that the Soviet Union wanted Groza appointed. The King then decided to charge Groza with the formation of a government.

Because the first Cabinet suggested by Groza was not representative of the people, the King refused to accept it. Vyshinski then sent word that cancellation of the Groza appointments would be considered by the Soviet Government as a hostile act. Mr. Vyshinski was quoted as saying that unless the King accepted the Groza government by the afternoon of the following day, he would not be responsible for the continuance of Rumania as an independent state.

At the same time Groza announced that the Soviets had promised great improvement in relations between the Soviet Government and Rumania, mentioning the return to Rumania of control over its transportation system, the cession of Transylvania from Hungary and a relaxing in the terms of the armistice. The result was that the King summoned the leaders of the historic parties Monday night and appealed to them to disregard political considerations and support his action in accepting the Groza government.

The leaders of the historic parties could not agree and the King was urged by some to abdicate. However, he concluded he could best serve the people by not deserting the country. On Tuesday night, March 6, the Groza government was sworn in and immediately afterward Marshal Malinovsky arrived in Bucharest where he and Vyshinski had an audience with the King. They told the King that they could not concentrate upon front line activities if they had unrest behind the lines. The Rumanian government had failed in the past to maintain order, they said, and it would not be permitted again.

On March 7, the day after the Groza government was installed, Mr. Molotov informed our Ambassador in Moscow that the questions raised in his letter of March 5 had lost point since the crisis in Rumania had been overcome by the formation of a new government.

The following September, while in London, Mr. Molotov urged that we recognize the Rumanian government. I told him we had not recognized the Groza government because of the character of the government which had been installed by virtue of a two-and-a-half hour ultimatum given to the King by Vyshinski. Mr. Molotov then admitted that Mr. Vyshinski had "helped in the formation of the government," but said the Soviet Government had acted because "there was very serious danger of disorder and civil war."

These developments, of course, had been reported in full to President Roosevelt. As a result, instructions had been sent to Mr. Harriman to propose to Mr. Molotov the establishment of a joint committee in Bucharest to safeguard the application of the principles announced in the Declaration on Liberated Europe. Mr. Molotov's rejection of this proposal was blunt. In a note dated March 17 he stated that no action was required; that our proposal would emasculate the Allied Control

Council, and asserted it was untrue that our representative on the council had never been consulted.

All of this occurred while the Allied armies were closing in on Berlin and President Roosevelt was anxious to avoid giving aid and comfort to the enemy by a public display of disunity. The President told me he had grave misgivings about the future. However, he decided that, for the time being, our protest should be filed through our Ambassador and that he would resort to direct communication to Stalin only after other efforts were exhausted.

In the fall of 1944, Churchill and his Foreign Minister, Anthony Eden, had visited Moscow and, while there was no formal agreement, we knew they had reached the informal understanding that, if the British found it necessary to take military action to quell internal disorders in Greece, the Soviets would not interfere. In return, the British would recognize the right of the Soviets to take the lead in maintaining order in Rumania.

The British heartily disapproved of Soviet actions in Rumania but they did not want to take the initiative in protesting to Stalin. The President felt that the Rumanian situation did not offer the best test case of our relations with the Soviets. Great Britain and the United States had no armed forces in Rumania. It was under the exclusive control of the Red Army. The President knew that the Soviets had to maintain a line of communication from the homeland through Rumania to their armies in Germany. He knew the Soviets would claim the action taken was necessary to protect their armies and he knew we could not obtain from Rumanians, who were under the domination of the Red Army, information to contradict the Soviet claim of interference with the army. He felt that Soviet action in Poland was more clearly in violation of the Yalta agreement.

The Yalta decision on Poland contained the following sentence:

"Mr. Molotov, Mr. Harriman and Sir A. Clark Kerr are authorized as a commission to consult in the first instance in Moscow with members of the present Provisional Government and with other Polish Democratic leaders from within Poland and from abroad, with a view to the reorganization of the present government along the above lines."

On March 2, the day after President Roosevelt delivered his optimistic and widely acclaimed report on the conference to a joint session of Congress, a disturbing message was received from Ambassador Harriman. He reported that Molotov was insisting that only Poles who had been recommended by the Provisional, or Lublin, Government should be invited to consult with the commission. Molotov's list of those who should be invited to come to Moscow from London included only one name that appeared also on the list we had submitted. He stoutly refused to invite Mikolajczyk, the liberal leader of the Polish Peasant Party, who was with the exiled Polish Government in London and who had been warmly recommended to Marshal Stalin by Mr. Roosevelt.

The Soviet Foreign Minister was firm in his view that the Lublin government should be the "kernel" of the Provisional Government of National Unity. Our representative, together with the British member of the commission, refused to accept this interpretation of the Yalta agreement. They pointed out that the language of the Yalta Protocol and the discussion preceding it showed it was to be a "new" government, not an expanded Lublin government. The impasse which thus developed finally caused the President and Prime Minister Churchill to communicate directly with Marshal Stalin.

Toward the end of March, the Prime Minister had expressed to President Roosevelt the belief that the agreements at Yalta were breaking down and there would be serious consequences unless something were done to change the situation. On March 27, President Roosevelt replied that he too had been "watching with anxiety and concern the development of the Soviet attitude" since Yalta. He added he was "acutely aware of the dangers inherent in the present course of events, not only for the immediate issue involved but also for the San Francisco Conference and future world co-operation." He included in his message a draft of a telegram he proposed to send to Marshal Stalin.

President Roosevelt dispatched his message to Stalin on April 1, and the Prime Minister also sent a communication supporting the President's position.

The President opened his message by stating he could not conceal "the concern with which I view the development of events" since Yalta. He expressed his regret at "the lack of progress made in the carrying out, which the world expects, of the political decisions which we reached at Yalta, particularly those relating to the Polish question," and added that he could not understand the "apparent indifferent attitude" of the Soviet Union. The President said he felt the situation arose from the Soviet interpretation of the Yalta agreement as meaning that the new Provisional Government should be little more than a continuation of the present Warsaw government. The President emphasized that he could not reconcile that position either with the agreement or with the discussions preceding the agreement. He said he must make it plain to the Marshal that "any such solution which would result in a thinly disguised continuation of the present government would be entirely unacceptable, and would cause our people to regard the Yalta agreement as a failure." If the right of the commission to select the Poles to be invited to Moscow for consultation were either limited or shared with the Warsaw government, he went on, the foundation of the Yalta agreement would be destroyed. President Roosevelt said that he would not bar or veto any candidate proposed by Molotov for the consultation, and that our Ambassador should be accorded the same confidence. He told Stalin that there should be a maximum of political tranquility in Poland and that we should use our influence to see that dissident groups ceased measures and countermeasures against each other. He also urged that, in view of our responsibilities, representatives of the American and British members of the commission be permitted to visit Poland, reminding Stalin that Molotov himself had suggested this at an early meeting and subsequently withdrew the suggestion.

The President pointed out "how important it is, for the successful development of our program of international collaboration," to settle the Polish question. Otherwise, he warned, "all the difficulties and dangers to Allied unity" they had considered at Yalta "will face us in an even more acute form."

As for Rumania, the President said he could not understand why the developments there did not fall within the terms of the Yalta Declaration of Liberated Areas, and he asked Stalin "personally to examine the exchange of notes between our governments on this subject."

In concluding this message, the President took note of an exchange of messages about the desirability of having Mr. Molotov attend the San Francisco Conference. The President, on March 24, had sent a message urging that Molotov attend in which he had said "I am afraid Mr. Molotov's absence will be construed all over the world as a lack of comparable interest on the part of the Soviet Government in the great objectives of this conference."

After expressing regret that Molotov could not attend, Stalin added in the last paragraph of his reply:

"As regards various interpretations, you understand, this cannot determine the decisions which are to be made."

The President, after warning that the attitude of the Soviet Government on the Polish and Rumanian questions was having an adverse effect on public opinion, took note of Stalin's dismissal of possible public reaction to Molotov's absence, and concluded his message with this wise and true statement:

"I am sure you are aware that genuine popular support in the United States is required to carry out any government policy, foreign or domestic. The American people make up their own mind and no governmental action can change it. I mention this fact because the last sentence of your message about Mr. Molotov's attendance at San Francisco made me wonder whether you give full weight to this factor."

On April 7, Stalin replied, admitting that the Polish question had reached a dead end and charging this was because the Ambassadors of the United States and Great Britain had departed from the Yalta agreement. They had taken the position, he said, that the existing Provisional Government should be completely liquidated and an entirely new government formed. Mr. Harriman, he contended, had stated in the commission that it was possible no member of the Provisional Government would be included in the Polish Government of National Unity—a statement Harriman denied having made.

Stalin maintained the Big Three had agreed at Yalta to invite five persons from Poland and three from London, but that the British and American Ambassadors now urged that each member be given the right to invite an unlimited number of people from Poland and London. The Marshal said that only Polish leaders should be invited who would recognize the decisions of Yalta, including the decision about the Curzon Line, and who were "really striving to establish friendly relations between Poland and the Soviet Union." Knowing, as we did, Stalin's usual interpretation of the phrase "friendly relations" we were sure this could only mean a leader who would strive to establish a government willing to accept orders from the Soviet Union.

In his reply to Mr. Churchill, Stalin also indicated that he might withdraw his opposition to inviting Mikolajczyk provided Mikolajczyk would make a public statement recognizing the decisions of the Yalta meeting and declaring that he favored the establishment of friendly relations between Poland and the Soviet Union. Stalin refused to agree that American and British observers be allowed in Poland, taking the position that the Poles would consider this an insult to their national dignity.

The President and Churchill decided they would send a joint message in reply to Stalin. While the State Department and the Foreign Office were preparing the joint reply, President Roosevelt died.

In those closing days of his life he also was annoyed and particularly disturbed by still another incident; one which was on his mind when he wrote his last message to Mr. Churchill, just before his death.

On March 11, the Allied Commander-in-Chief in Italy, Field Marshal Alexander, learned through the Office of Strategic Services that General Kesselring and several German Staff officers were willing to meet in Switzerland to discuss the surrender of the German Army in Italy. The Combined Chiefs of Staff approved Alexander's plan to send his Deputy Chief of Staff to Bern but instructed him to wait until the Soviet Government was informed. When Ambassador Harriman gave this information to Mr. Molotov, the latter declared that the Soviet Government wished to take part in any such discussions and would send three Red Army officers. Thereupon, the Combined Chiefs of Staff informed the Soviet Government that nothing would be done at Bern except to arrange for a meeting at Allied headquarters in Caserta, Italy, where the Soviet representatives would be welcome. The directive also instructed that it be made clear to the Soviet Government that, should the Germans offer to surrender, Alexander as supreme commander on that front, would conduct the negotiations and make the necessary decisions.

The Soviet Government replied that inasmuch as their officers could not participate in the discussions they would not be sent to Caserta. The message "insisted" that the negotiations be stopped.

A few days later Stalin sent a message to President Roosevelt stating that if the same situation had been presented on the Russian front he would not have objected to the participation of British and American representatives in the discussions. He recognized, he said, the great importance of the negotiation that had taken place because it affected the military situation on the eastern front.

President Roosevelt replied that no negotiations had taken place and assured Stalin that he would be kept fully informed. The next message from the Soviet leader was the one that deeply offended Mr. Roosevelt.

Stalin referred to the statement that no negotiations had taken place and asserted that it was evident the President had not been advised by his own military leaders. Stalin said the information given him by his Red Army advisers showed that negotiations had been completed and that, as a result of them, Kesselring was going to open up the German front to permit the American Army to advance. In return for this military assistance, Stalin said, the United States and Britain had agreed to secure easier peace terms for Germany. In accordance with this agreement, Stalin charged, the Germans already had moved three divisions from the Italian front to the Russian front, and the American Army had been permitted to advance in Germany.

Despite his personal reaction to this message, President Roosevelt managed to write a dignified reply. The movement of the three German divisions from the Italian to the Russian fronts, the President pointed out, had begun several weeks before the information regarding the desire of the Germans to negotiate had even reached Field Marshal Alexander and therefore the negotiations could not have been responsible in any way for the troop transfer. Stalin would have to believe him to be honest and truthful, the President declared. General Eisenhower would not have entered into any negotiations without informing him. No negotiations such as Stalin described had taken place, and from the receipt of the first message from the Germans, instructions had been issued to keep the Soviet authorities fully informed.

In the last paragraph of his message, the President gave vent to some of his feelings.

He deeply resented, he said, the "vile misrepresentations" of Stalin's informers which reflected upon the President of the United States and his trusted subordinates, and indicated a belief that Stalin's informants wished to destroy the friendly relations between the two countries. He thought it would be a tragedy if, just as victory for the Allies seemed assured, such misrepresentations should disturb the unity that had existed and that was necessary for complete victory.

To this message Stalin replied that he did not question the President's honesty or truthfulness but repeated his belief that he had received accurate information from his Red Army advisers. He had reason to regard them as accurate, he said, because only a short time earlier General Marshall and the general of the British Army had been kind enough to send word to the Russian commanding general that the Germans were concentrating at a certain point in preparation for attack upon the Russian lines. The Russian officers, however, knew that the information was wrong and that the German drive was to take place at another point. The Red Army had concentrated its forces at the place it thought best and had stopped the German drive. He recognized, he said, that the Germans may have misled the American and British officers deliberately, but the incident served to show the accuracy of his Red Army officers. He wished, nevertheless, to thank the Americans for this effort to be helpful. On the whole, Stalin's message was more conciliatory than the previous ones and President Roosevelt, on April 11, sent Stalin a message saying he was glad the unfortunate incident was now over.

Meanwhile, the negotiations with the Germans had been postponed for other reasons and in the interim the Combined Chiefs of Staff made a proposal that was accepted by the Soviet military leaders. It provided that each of the three powers should observe all surrender negotiations, but that a surrender on any one front would not be delayed because of the absence of any one of the powers.

Nevertheless, Stalin's charges and his apparent willingness to believe we had secretly concluded a separate peace, coupled with the exceedingly objectionable language of at least one of his messages had greatly offended Mr. Roosevelt. And when President Truman assumed office and read these messages he fully sympathized with the view and attitude of President Roosevelt.

On the same day that President Roosevelt received his last message from Stalin, he received one from Prime Minister Churchill. It stated that he had to make a statement in the House of Commons within a few days, dealing primarily with Poland but necessarily requiring a discussion of Russian relations. He was exceedingly anxious not to say anything that would affect adversely the military situation at that critical hour and he asked President Roosevelt for advice.

Although the President by that time was greatly disappointed by the Soviet attitude, he was philosophical about it. He had reached the conclusion—which I was to reach months later—that there is no easy formula to guide one in getting along with the Soviets. Thus, on April 12, an hour before he died, President Roosevelt, replying to the Prime Minister's request for advice about his speech to Commons, sent this message:

I would minimize the general Soviet problem as much as possible because these problems, in one form or another, seem to arise every day and most of them straighten out as in the case of the Bern meeting.

We must be firm, however, and our course thus far is correct.

The message was sent from Warm Springs and bears all the earmarks of having been written by the President himself. The advice is as good today as it was on the day it was written.

It is idle to speculate on what the course of history would have been had President Roosevelt lived, but these messages dispose of the legend that our relations with the Soviet Union began to deteriorate only after his death.

The President's deliberate efforts to cultivate the good will of Marshal Stalin have led some observers to underestimate the strength of his affection and admiration for Mr. Churchill. It was a feeling that was genuine and that was cordially reciprocated. It was the kind of friendship that permitted frankness in their conversations with each other and about each other.

Whenever Mr. Churchill was a guest at the White House, the President would complain to those of us who had to carry on business with him that Mr. Churchill had kept him up late. But even as he complained about his guest, it was clear that the President had greatly enjoyed the conversation of the previous evening. Once at Yalta, when we were preparing for dinner at the end of a long session, the President grumbled that the lengthy session was "Winston's fault because he had made too many speeches."

"Yes, he did," I replied, "but they were good speeches."

The President chuckled and replied:

"Winston doesn't make any other kind."

It is true, if my observations at Yalta provide a typical example, that the President used all his charm and his genius for promoting human relationships to make the Big Three meetings harmonious. The value of these qualities in those early days cannot be overestimated. But the Soviet leaders did overestimate the ultimate extent of the President's generosity and his willingness to compromise on principles.

Two other elements figured in the deteriorating situation. During the war the issues that faced the Big Three and the decisions they made together were primarily military. As we approached the end of hostilities, political questions began coming to the fore and these, of course, became issues between victors. President Roosevelt had sensed this. In fact, in his speech on The State of the Union made on January 6, 1945, he warned that "the nearer we come to vanquishing our enemies the more we inevitably become conscious of differences among the victors." That was why he was so insistent that the United Nations should be established while the war was still in progress.

The second element is a corollary of the first. This is the fact that the end of the war and the lifting of censorship brought to public attention differences that had been known to few except a restricted group of officials.

Just after the President's death, there was, in fact, a momentary rise in our hopes that the barometer of our relations would cease falling. This was caused by an interview with Marshal Stalin in which Ambassador Harriman requested that Mr. Molotov be sent to the San Francisco Conference.

"President Roosevelt has died but his cause must live on," Marshal Stalin told our Ambassador. "We shall support President Truman with all our forces and with all our will."

He then asked the Ambassador to inform President Truman of his statement and say that he would send Molotov to San Francisco to let the world know his attitude.

Meanwhile, the State Department had prepared the joint message on Poland in answer to Stalin's communication of April 7. This message, which President Roosevelt had directed the State Department to prepare, was sent by President Truman and Mr. Churchill on April 18. It began by seeking to correct the "completely erroneous impression you have apparently received in regard to the position of the British and United States governments" and by denying that our Ambassadors had asked for the right to invite to Moscow for consultation an unlimited number of Poles. They called attention to the statement in President Roosevelt's message of April 1 that "in order to facilitate the agreement, the commission first of all might select a small but representative group of Polish leaders who could suggest other names for consideration by the commission." "The real issue between us," said Truman and Churchill, "is whether or not the Warsaw government has the right to veto individual candidates for consultation." No such interpretation could be found in the Yalta agreement, they said, and they expressed the belief that the Soviet Union was reverting to the position it had assumed originally at Yalta but which had been modified in order that agreement could be reached.

By the time Mr. Molotov reached Washington, President Truman had studied the agreements at Yalta and had read much of the correspondence between President Roosevelt and Marshal Stalin, particularly those messages dealing with Rumania, Poland and the Bern incident. He was so disturbed by the swift collapse of what we thought had been agreements and the consequent dissipation of the cordial spirit of Yalta that he called a meeting of the Secretaries of State, War and Navy, the Chief of Staff and Admiral Leahy to discuss our relations with the Soviets. Later when Mr. Molotov called at the White House, President Truman spoke very frankly about some of our problems, and the Polish situation in particular. From what I learned upon my return to Washington, it was not a very harmonious meeting and ended rather abruptly.

At San Francisco, efforts at collaboration were marred by disagreement on almost every issue. It started the first day with the question of the chairmanship. With the announcement that sixteen Polish resistance leaders, who were discussing problems of reorganizing the government with the Russians, had been arrested, President Truman decided some action had to be taken to halt the increasing deterioration in our relations. He therefore suggested to Marshal Stalin that Harry Hopkins go to Moscow, on what was to be his last mission.

Hopkins had served his government well on many occasions, but the record of this mission does him special credit. Ambassador Averell Harriman, who had come home to confer with the President on the Polish problem, returned with Hopkins to take part in the talks. And, of course, Chip Bohlen went along to interpret for them and to advise them. The report of their conversations with Marshal Stalin, which they sent to the President, is an illuminating chapter in the story of our relationships with the Soviet Union. It was of great interest to me as I was educating myself for the work ahead.

The conversations were marked by the frank exchange of views and the interesting revelation of Soviet thinking.

Stalin expressed concern over what seemed to be a cooling of American friendship once it became clear Germany was defeated and Russia's help was no longer needed. He gave examples he felt supported this impression.

He cited the action of the United States in agreeing to the admission of Argentina to the United Nations in violation of President Roosevelt's statement at Yalta and declared he was forced to question the value of agreements between the major powers if their decisions could be upset by votes of such countries as Honduras.

He said our stand that France should be made a member of the Reparations Commission was an insult and an attempt to humiliate the Soviet Union, since France had concluded a separate peace with the Germans and opened her frontier to them.

The Yalta agreement, he insisted, contemplated that the Lublin government would form the basis of the new Polish government and that no other procedure was reasonable. "Even though the Russians are a simple people," Stalin added, "the West often made the mistake of regarding them as fools."

He was particularly irritated by the manner in which lend-lease shipments had been suspended at the end of the European war. The fact that ships with supplies bound for Russia even had been unloaded indicated to him that the cancellation order was an effort to put pressure on the Soviet Union. This, he declared, was a fundamental mistake and the United States should understand much could be gained from the Russians only if they were approached on a friendly basis.

In the case of the German Navy and merchant fleet, he had sent a message to the President and the Prime Minister suggesting that one-third be turned over to the Soviets. Not only had he received no reply, he said, but he had acquired instead an impression that the request was to be rejected.

These complaints were surprising to us at home. They revealed an extreme sensitivity and an amazing degree of almost instinctive suspicion.

Mr. Hopkins forcefully and tactfully presented the position of the United States. As for the German ships, it was our intention that they should be divided equally among the three and we thought that the matter could be settled at the forthcoming meeting of the Big Three. He explained that the cancellation of lend-lease was necessary under the law because lend-lease was authorized only for the purpose of prosecuting the war. With the German war ended and with the Soviet Union not yet a participant in the Japanese war, further shipment could not be justified. The order to unload the ships was the mistake of an official who had nothing to do with policy, and the order had been withdrawn quickly. He reminded the Marshal of how liberally the United States had construed the law in sending foodstuffs and other nonmilitary items to their aid.

Stalin readily acknowledged the accuracy of Hopkins' statement. If proper warning had been given there would have been no feeling about the matter, he said, pointing out that advance notice was important to them because their economy is based on plans. The way in which the shipments had been halted made it impossible for him to express, as he had intended, the great appreciation of the Soviets for the lend-lease aid given to them.

Hopkins told the Marshal that what disturbed him most was the revelation that Stalin believed the United States would use lend-lease as a pressure weapon. The United States, he asserted, is a strong nation and does not need to indulge in such methods. With this, Stalin said he was fully satisfied with our explanation.

Ambassador Harriman explained the Argentine question. The difficulty was due to the fact that, after Secretary Stettinius had obtained the agreement of the South American republics for the admission to membership of the Ukraine and Byelorussia, Mr. Molotov had also raised the question of inviting the existing Polish Government to the conference. There certainly had been no agreement at Yalta to invite the Polish Government, and this action by Mr. Molotov caused the South American republics to insist that the Argentine be admitted. We not only had fulfilled our commitment to support the admission of the two Soviet republics, but we had gone further and had obtained support for the motion from the South American republics. Mr. Stettinius had therefore felt that, since our neighbors had supported him in his efforts in behalf of the Ukraine and Byelorussia, he should accede to their wishes and support the admission of Argentina.

Stalin said simply that what had been done could not be changed and it all belonged to the past.

With these questions out of the way the discussion proceeded to the principal cause of Hopkins' trip—the situation in Poland.

Throughout the conversations Hopkins kept emphasizing that, in the eyes of the American people, the Polish question had become a symbol of our ability to work out mutual problems with the Soviet Union and that an impasse on this issue would threaten our whole relationship with our Soviet Allies. Our people were deeply disturbed, Hopkins said, because the Soviet Union was acting independently on a problem that should be worked out jointly. He stressed that we had no interest in Poland other than a desire to see a truly independent government established which would protect what we regarded as basic freedoms and which would be friendly to the Soviet Union.

Marshal Stalin repeated the statements he had made at Yalta on the vital interest of the Soviet Government in Poland. He felt that before the war the policy of European governments had been to keep Poland hostile toward Russia, and that this could not be permitted again; Poland must be friendly and must be strong. He admitted unilateral action had been taken but asked Mr. Hopkins to consider that the Soviet Army was in Poland, that an army's lines of communication must be protected and its authority maintained.

During this discussion, Stalin made a very interesting reference to his conception of the United States in world affairs. Whether the United States wished it or not, he said, we were a world power and would have to accept world-wide responsibilities. Without our intervention in the last two wars, Germany could not have been defeated.

In fact, he added, the history of the last thirty years shows that the United States has more reason to be a world power than any other state, and he therefore recognized our right to participate in the Polish question.

There was considerable discussion as to which Poles should be invited from outside and inside Poland to meet in Moscow and consider establishing a provisional government which would carry out the Yalta pledges on the holding of elections.

During these talks Stalin revealed a willingness to believe that we would secretly sponsor the names of men hostile to the Soviet Union or associated with hostile groups. In the strongest terms Hopkins assured him we had no such intent and would drop from consideration any person who appeared to fall in either category.

Stalin agreed to invite Mikolajczyk and an agreement was reached on the personnel of the Polish Committee. As a result, a new government was subsequently formed which pledged itself to hold free elections. On the basis of the new government's pledges, Poland was admitted to the United Nations and the first official telegram I signed as Secretary of State dealt with diplomatic recognition of the Provisional Polish Government.

While Hopkins and Harriman were conferring with Stalin, in the San Francisco Conference a controversy over voting procedure in the United Nations organization had arisen. The Soviet delegation insisted that a dispute could not even be discussed by the Security Council without the unanimous vote of the five permanent members, unless the situation clearly was one that could be settled by peaceful means. In effect, the Soviet position meant that even the council's agenda could be subject to a veto. To many at the conference it seemed that the deadlock was complete.

On one occasion during this period, our former Ambassador to Russia, Joseph E. Davies, and I were talking to President Truman. Davies was telling the President of some matters connected with his mission to London. The President mentioned his concern over the impasse at the San Francisco Conference. I suggested he take advantage of Hopkins' presence in Moscow to present directly to Marshal Stalin our view that the veto should not apply to procedural questions. The President sent a message to Hopkins who presented it to Stalin.

As soon as our point of view had been presented, Mr. Molotov intervened to defend the Soviet position. The conversation between Marshal Stalin and his Foreign Minister, as interpreted by Bohlen, made it clear that the Marshal had not understood the issue involved. He told Molotov he thought it was an insignificant matter and that the American position should be accepted. In expressing his agreement, he cautioned against what he termed a tendency on the part of small nations to create and exploit differences among the great powers in order to gain the backing of one or more of them for their own ends. "A nation need not be innocent just because it is small," he said.

This incident was especially interesting for two things: First, it revealed that the Russian leader was not informed on what was the crucial issue of the San Francisco Conference on International Organization; and, second, it demonstrated that when matters are brought to Stalin's attention it frequently is possible to get a quick decision even when it requires reversing openly the decision of his Foreign Minister.

The agreements reached in the Hopkins conversations constituted an advance over the deadlock of the preceding ninety days, but it was clear they constituted no advance over Yalta. It meant that in June we would establish in Poland the Provisional Government that we had agreed in February should be established promptly. It did not mean we had solved the Polish problem.

Not only Poland and Rumania but other developments worried us. On April 18, the Soviets invited the other Allies to send representatives to Vienna, but then took the position that they could not proceed until an agreement was reached by the European Advisory Commission regarding zones in the city of Vienna and the provisional control machinery. The British, supported by the United States, maintained that it was impossible to agree about zones until our representatives reached Vienna and learned what conditions were there. Finally, on May 19, Stalin agreed that our representatives could visit Vienna for that purpose and with the understanding that the zones would be determined by the European Advisory Commission. When our representatives reached Vienna they were not allowed to see anything outside the city limits and after a short stay were ordered to leave by June 10 or 11.

We continued to worry about the differences revealed by the San Francisco Conference, the difficulties being encountered in the Reparations Commission meeting in Moscow, the conflicting points of view already arising in the Allied Control Council in Berlin, Marshal Tito's bellicose behavior in the Trieste area, and growing tension in Iran, Greece and Turkey.

The successful conclusion of the San Francisco Conference was a big factor on the credit side of the ledger as we analyzed the situation in preparation for the forthcoming meeting of the Big Three. It had been agreed, during Hopkins' visit in Moscow, that this would be held in Berlin on July 15.

On Tuesday, July 3, my lifelong friend, Chief Justice Richard S. Whaley of the United States Court of Claims, administered the oath making me Secretary of State. To the friends who had gathered for the ceremony on the rose-covered east portico of the White House, I made this statement:

"The making of enduring peace will depend on something more than skilled diplomacy, something more than paper treaties, something more even than the best charter the wisest statesman can draft. Important as is diplomacy, important as are the peace settlements and the basic charter of world peace, these cannot succeed unless backed by the will of the peoples of different lands not only to have peace but to live together as good neighbors. . . .

"Today there can be no doubt that the peoples of this war-ravaged earth want to live in a free and peaceful world. The supreme task of statesmanship the world over is to help them to understand that they can have peace and freedom only if they tolerate and respect the rights of others to opinions, feelings and way of life which they do not and cannot share."

Three nights later I boarded the President's special train for the journey to Newport News, where the USS *Augusta* was waiting to take us to Europe, to Potsdam—the first step down the long road toward peace.

Chapter 4

Potsdam—The Success That Failed

WE WORKED hard on board the *Augusta*. Memoranda had been prepared in the State Department to cover every subject which conceivably could arise at the conference. Every morning throughout the trip, Ben Cohen, H. Freeman (Doc) Matthews, and Charles E. (Chip) Bohlen would meet with me in my cabin to consider these papers. A new Secretary of State could not have asked for a finer trio of advisers.

Ben, in his quiet, shy way, has had a hand in important issues ever since the early days of the Roosevelt administration. He was with me through all my work at the White House. In addition to having a genuine affection for him, I regard his mind as one of the best I have ever encountered. There is no more selfless and devoted public servant than Ben Cohen. Doc, the chief of the State Department's European Division, is a veteran foreign service officer, who combines with his vast and intricate knowledge of foreign affairs keen political sense and sound judgment. He is representative of the finest men in our career service and I relied upon him heavily. Chip is another in this category. After spending some years in the Soviet Union, he has served through a crucial period as the State Department's expert on Russian affairs. Chip, I believe, is the only man who has attended all the Big Three meetings with President Roosevelt and President Truman. He has seen these meetings from the unique position of both interpreter and adviser. He was invaluable to me.

The four of us spent many hours in long and earnest discussion of the State Department memoranda. On many issues, President Truman's Chief of Staff, Fleet Admiral William D. Leahy, would join us. In these meetings we would agree on recommendations to present to President Truman. At least once a day during the entire trip the President and I would go over them. When the President approved a proposal, it was then prepared for presentation to the conference. Consequently, by the time we landed at Antwerp on July 15, 1945, we had our objectives thoroughly in mind and had the background papers in support of them fully prepared.

We wanted to reach agreement on four major issues: *first,* the machinery and the procedures for the earliest possible drafting and completion of peace treaties; *second,* the political and economic principles which would govern the occupation of Germany; *third,* plans for carrying out the Yalta Declaration on Liberated Europe, with the hope of ending the constant friction which had prevailed over Russian policy in eastern Europe since the Crimea Conference; and, *fourth,* a new approach to the reparations issue in view of the inability of the Reparations Commission to reach agreement.

There were other goals, also. Among them was our desire to speed Italy's entry into the United Nations in recognition of the part her people played in the last year of the war in Europe and her declaration of war against Japan. Then, we had a plan for insuring free navigation of all of Europe's inland waterways.

When we arrived at the "Little White House" in Babelsberg, the Berlin suburb that had been the center of the German film colony, we learned that Marshal Stalin would be delayed a day. This gave us a chance to do a little sightseeing; the President, Admiral Leahy and I drove into Berlin. We were greatly impressed by the streams of people walking along the road. They were mostly grandparents and children. As a rule they carried their possessions on their backs. We did not know where they were going and it is doubtful that they did, but when we reached Berlin we were convinced they were headed in the wrong direction. Despite all we had read of the destruction there, the extent of the devastation shocked us. It brought home the suffering that total war now visits upon old folks, women, and children, besides the men in uniform.

Shortly after his arrival, on July 17, Stalin came to call on the President. We had to remember to call him Generalissimo rather than Marshal Stalin, for he had been accorded the new title in recognition of the Red Army's great successes. It was the first time the President and Stalin had met. After a very pleasant conversation, the President quite informally asked Stalin, Molotov, and Pavlov, the capable Soviet interpreter, to stay and have lunch with him. They accepted. The conversation was general in nature and cordial in spirit. The President was favorably impressed by Stalin, as I had been at Yalta. In speaking of our visit to Berlin, I asked the Generalissimo his views of how Hitler had died. To my surprise, he said he believed that Hitler was alive and that it was possible he was then either in Spain or Argentina. Some ten days later I asked him if he had changed his views and he said he had not.

At lunch the Generalissimo was as entertaining as he usually is on such occasions. He complimented the President on the wine that was served. While the President was thanking him, Stalin asked the Filipino waiter to unwrap the towel from the bottle, because he wanted to see the label. I was glad he did; it was a California wine.

Shortly after lunch, we left for the first of our many three-mile drives to Potsdam and to Cecilienhof Palace where the meetings were held. As always, when they are hosts, the Russians had made painstaking preparations. Cecilienhof Palace had been the country estate of the former Crown Prince Wilhelm, and provided ample accommodations for the conference. It is a two-story brown-stone mansion beautifully situated on Gribnitz Lake. Its four wings form a square with a courtyard in the center, which the Red Army had brilliantly carpeted with a twenty-four-foot wide Red star of geraniums. Each head of government was provided with a suite of rooms for his personal use and each delegation had a conference room and offices for its staff.

The conference room itself was impressively large and pleasantly bright. At one end a huge window reached up the full two-story height of the room, letting in light and giving the conferees a sweeping view of beautifully landscaped gardens.

The group that sat down at the large oaken table at 5:10 P.M. on July 17 included, besides the President and me, former ambassador Joseph E. Davies, Admiral Leahy and Chip Bohlen from the United States delegation; Prime Minister Churchill, Foreign Minister Anthony Eden, Mr. Attlee, Sir Alexander Cadogan, and an interpreter from the United Kingdom delegation; and from the Soviet Union, Generalissimo Stalin, Foreign Minister Molotov, Mr. Vyshinski, Mr. Andrei A. Gromyko, who was then the Soviet Ambassador in the United States, the Soviet Ambassador to Great Britain, F. T. Gousev, and Mr. Pavlov.

It was fortunate that the room was large because each of these delegations had grouped behind them other members of their delegations. This group would change as various issues before the conference called for the aid of different technical advisers. As I recall it, our delegation that opening day included Ambassador Averell Harriman, Under Secretary William L. Clayton, Reparations Commissioner Edwin W. Pauley, Counselor Ben Cohen, Assistant Secretary of State James C. Dunn and Doc Matthews.

At Stalin's suggestion, President Truman was made chairman and he immediately presented for consideration some of the proposals we had prepared aboard the *Augusta*. It was evident that the other heads of government appreciated the President's efforts in having proposals ready for discussion.

The first of these papers was the proposal to establish the Council of Foreign Ministers. It had been agreed at Yalta that there should be regular consultation of the Foreign Ministers to deal with the difficulties we knew would arise after the war. But it had not been intended that those meetings should be concerned with peace treaties. At Yalta, peace had still seemed so remote that the question of how it should be brought about was not, to my knowledge, ever discussed. The machinery for making the peace was, therefore, one of the first things we began to work on in planning for the Berlin Conference.

As a Member of Congress I had followed closely the peace conference proceedings at the end of World War I and I was convinced that this time we had to follow a different procedure. If we waited until the end of the war with Japan and then held one peace conference, attended by all the states at war, with no preliminary draft to use as a basis for the treaties, there would be endless bickering. The logrolling, the interplay of conflicting interests, plus the sheer number of issues and people, would result, I was sure, in such confusion that the conference would last a year if, indeed, it could ever end successfully. Even the Versailles Conference had finally found it necessary to assign to a few of the great powers the duty of treaty-drafting. Those states not represented on the drafting committee had little opportunity to know what was in a treaty and why. Consequently, when agreement was reached among the great powers, the smaller Allied nations had little more opportunity to examine or amend the treaties than did the defeated Germans.

We had to devise a system that would facilitate agreement among the major powers and at the same time provide the smaller states with ample opportunity to express their views.

Fortunately, the procedure initiated by Secretary Hull and carried out by Secretary Stettinius in the establishment of the United Nations organization provided good precedent. The accomplishments at San Francisco demonstrated the wisdom of the earlier conversations at Dumbarton Oaks and at Yalta where the big powers had reached agreement on the more important points at issue.

Ben Cohen and I prepared the plan for the creation of the Council of Foreign Ministers. When I presented it to President Truman for his consideration, we suspected what later we found to be true: the Soviet Union did not wish to act promptly on a German treaty. We knew that because of the many serious problems presented, and because there was no German government, some delay was inevitable. But we thought a start should be made promptly and that our experience with the Italian and Balkan treaties would make it easier for us to agree on Germany's problems.

I visualized for him the council's operation, in these terms: The council would consider first the treaties with Italy and the Balkan enemy states because these were the least controversial. The Foreign Ministers would agree on certain general principles and appoint deputies to draft treaties based on these principles. The Foreign Ministers, shortly thereafter, would take up the German treaty, agree on fundamental problems such as frontiers, and local governments, and then appoint different deputies to begin drafting a German settlement. The peace treaties based on these general agreements would then be presented to all the United Nations for their consideration and amendment in the same way the Dumbarton Oaks proposals were reviewed at the San Francisco Conference. A similar course ultimately would be followed for Japan.

After consideration the President approved the plan. This was shortly before I became Secretary of State. The President submitted our memorandum to the State Department for comment. The Department officials had been thinking along similar lines and recommended the procedure.

It was a good theory. But it was faulty in one assumption. I had assumed that at the end of hostilities an era of peace would be so deeply desired by those nations that had fought the war in unity that the inevitable differences of opinion could be resolved without serious difficulty.

It is true that following Yalta we had been somewhat disillusioned. Such things as the Bern incident and the Soviet violation of the agreements on Poland and Rumania warned us that in the days to come we would encounter serious differences and would have to overcome deepseated suspicion. However, fresh in our minds were the words of President Roosevelt's last message to Prime Minister Churchill, based upon his experience with the Russians, that such difficulties would straighten out.

Today it is easy for one to say that President Roosevelt's advice and our assumption were not warranted. It is a trite but true statement that "hindsight is better than foresight." But, if one can recall the attitude of the people of the United States toward the Soviets in the days immediately following the German surrender, he will agree that, as a result of our sufferings and sacrifices in a common cause, the Soviet Union then had in the United States a deposit of good will, as great, if not greater than that of any other country. It is little short of a tragedy that Russia should have withdrawn that deposit with the recklessness and the lack of appreciation shown during the last two and a half years. Our assumption that we could co-operate, and our patience in trying to co-operate, justify the firmness we now must show.

Our optimism certainly was not lessened by the speed with which the proposal to establish the Council of Foreign Ministers was approved at the conference table. Both Churchill and Stalin asked questions on our inclusion of China on the council; the Russian delegation continued to oppose the admission of France to the ranks of the great powers. When Churchill suggested that the Foreign Ministers consider whether the council should be composed of four or five members, Stalin quickly added, "or three members."

The Foreign Ministers met the following morning, and we agreed that China's part should be limited to Far East problems and those of world-wide importance. Mr. Molotov reiterated the view that France should participate in the drafting of only the Italian and the German treaties. We finally agreed that each treaty should be drafted by the states which signed the armistice with that particular enemy, and, that in the case of Italy, France would be regarded as a signatory of the armistice.

We submitted our recommendations to the chiefs of state that afternoon. Churchill inquired about a phrase stating that the council should draft treaties "with a view to their submission to the United Nations." I explained that this was required by the Declaration of the United Nations, which all of us had signed. Stalin then made a statement which carried a significance that we did not appreciate until later months. The inclusion of such a phrase in the document, he said, made no difference as "the three powers would represent the interests of all."

With this brief exchange, the proposal of the American delegation for the creation of a Council of Foreign Ministers charged with the responsibility of preparing peace treaties became the first approved act of the Berlin Conference.

The high state of our hopes is indicated by my notes of a luncheon conversation with Mr. Molotov on July 24. We discussed plans for the first meeting of the council to be held in London in September. I expressed the belief that we should organize the council and agree upon directives to guide our deputies and their staffs in the preparation of treaty drafts. I then added that the Ministers should be able to finish their work in about ten days, and that the effective performance by the deputies of their work would keep our subsequent meetings as short. Mr. Molotov appeared to be very pleased with this view. We discussed the appointment of deputies, the relationship of the council to the United Nations and the desirability of beginning work on the Italian treaty upon our return home. On all these points we appeared to be in complete accord.

We went to the meeting of the heads of government encouraged by our apparent agreement. The debate that followed perhaps should have stifled my optimism, but it didn't. It dealt with another of the proposals that President Truman had presented at the opening meeting of the conference—the implementation of the Yalta Declaration on Liberated Europe.

Our paper stated flatly that the obligations assumed in the Yalta Declaration had not been carried out. A continuation of this situation, it went on, would be regarded throughout the world as evidence of lack of unity and would undermine confidence in the sincerity of the jointly proclaimed aims. We proposed joint action in reorganizing the governments of Bulgaria and Rumania to permit participation of all democratic groups as a prelude to establishing diplomatic relations and concluding peace treaties. We also suggested that our three states should help the interim governments in holding "free and unfettered elections."

The discussions that churned around this paper and the issues it raised are worthy of note. They form the background for many weary hours of negotiating.

Stalin's initial response to our paper was simply that the Soviet Union had a proposal of its own to present on the subject. Molotov presented it at the meeting of the Foreign Ministers the next morning. It was devoted largely to a severe attack on Greece. Eden angrily termed the attack a "travesty of fact," pointing out that international observers, including representatives of the Soviet Union, had been invited to observe the Greek elections. Unfortunately, the same could not be said of Rumania or Bulgaria, he added. And he concluded by saying that the British Government "took the gravest exception" to the charges in the Soviet paper, and the matter could only be reported to the Prime Minister.

Mr. Molotov replied that the charges were directed only against the Greek Government. He asserted that the British had more representatives in Rumania and Bulgaria than the Soviet Union, and, citing British and and American press reports as evidence, he charged that there were greater excesses in Greece than in either Rumania or Bulgaria.

My contribution to this exchange was to repeat a statement which I was to make many times. It is one which, I fear, Mr. Molotov never fully understood or believed. "The United States," I told him, "sincerely desires Russia to have friendly countries on her borders, but we believe they should seek the friendship of the people rather than of any particular government. We, therefore, want the governments to be representative of the people. If elections are held while there are restrictions not only on newspaper and radio correspondents but upon our own governmental representatives as well, the American people will distrust any government established as a result of such an election. We do not wish to become involved in the elections of any country, but, because of the postwar situation, we would join with others in observing elections in Italy, Greece, Hungary, Rumania and Bulgaria."

This discussion contains arguments heard scores of times during ensuing months. Whenever the Soviets were faced with an issue that annoyed them or placed them on the defensive it was standard operating procedure for them to gather up a sheaf of British and American press reports from Greece and launch a counterattack. Mr. Molotov always seemed ready to enjoy the blessings of other nations' free press.

A few days later our paper came up for discussion again, providing an interesting demonstration of the Soviet bargaining technique.

"The Soviet Union," Molotov said, "can not agree to the supervision of elections. I can understand, though, that other Allies want better facilities for their representatives in these countries. Now that the war is at an end, there is every reason to give greater freedom both to these representatives and to the press. They will have every opportunity to be informed fully regarding the elections."

Having stated an opposition and a promise, he then lodged a complaint that the Soviet representative on the Allied Control Council in Italy was not receiving proper attention. He followed these parries and thrusts with an offer to discuss our proposal regarding elections *if* we would agree to accord diplomatic recognition to Rumania and Bulgaria.

Eden explained that formal recognition was constitutionally impossible for Britain until peace was concluded. I told him that our recognition of a country had to be based on our own estimate of it rather than on its value as a bargaining point. But Mr. Molotov is a difficult man to discourage and the effort to effect a trade of diplomatic recognition in return for the ends we desired went on and on.

Most of the Soviet bargaining effort was centered on Italy. We had asked for modification of Italy's armistice terms in recognition of her help in the war against Germany and of her declaration of war against Japan. We had proposed that the drafting of an Italian peace treaty be the first order of business for the Council of Foreign Ministers.

Both Generalissimo Stalin and Mr. Molotov were determined that no favor should be granted to Italy that was not also granted to Hungary, Rumania and Bulgaria. One essential difference was pointed out to them constantly: all foreign representatives were free to travel about in Italy and report their observations. During one of these exchanges, Mr. Churchill was stating that the British mission in Bucharest had been "penned up with a closeness approaching internment," when Stalin broke in to ask him how he could make such unverified statements.

Mr. Churchill reddened slightly; he said that the Generalissimo would be astonished at the catalogue of difficulties encountered by the British mission. "An iron fence has come down around them."

"All fairy tales," Stalin exclaimed, and maintained that British representatives in Rumania were accorded the same courtesies received by Soviet officials in Italy.

Not until the end of the conference, when we linked this question to that of reparations, did we secure Soviet acceptance of Section 10 of the protocol. This stated, first, the desirability of concluding peace treaties and resuming normal relations with all five countries. It then stated that the three powers "have included the preparation of a peace treaty with Italy as the first among the immediate important tasks to be undertaken by the new Council of Foreign Ministers." It then referred to the other four countries, in a way that permitted concurrent preparation of peace treaties with them if this were found feasible. We met the problem of recognition with the statement that "the three governments agree to examine each separately in the near future, in the light of conditions then prevailing, the establishment of diplomatic relations with Finland, Rumania, Bulgaria and Hungary to the extent possible prior to the conclusion of peace treaties with those countries."

The problem of the press was met by this statement: "The three governments have no doubt that in view of the changed conditions resulting from the termination of the war in Europe, representatives of the Allied press will enjoy full freedom to report to the world upon developments in Rumania, Bulgaria, Hungary and Finland."

I must admit we did have some doubt, but this was the strongest commitment for freedom of the press that we were able to achieve after many hours of discussion devoted to the issue.

In the meantime, the Soviet Union had placed on the table a second series of charges against Greece in obvious retaliation for a British paper directed against Yugoslavia. When agreement was finally reached on the foregoing section of the protocol, Mr. Bevin pointed out that the agenda carried two papers against Greece and one against Yugoslavia. He proposed that all three be dropped. Stalin quickly replied "Yes, welcome." It was a good demonstration of the seriousness with which some of the charges and countercharges were made.

Another irritant running throughout the conference was the question of American- and British-owned industrial equipment in Rumania that had been seized by the Russians. As an example of the Soviet conception of property rights, it was a forewarning of the difficulties we were to encounter on reparations. Before the war American and British firms had substantial holdings in Rumanian oil enterprises involving the ownership of highly valuable equipment. The Germans, of course, confiscated this equipment when they overran Rumania; our people assumed that when Rumania was liberated this equipment naturally would be returned to them. We were amazed to find, however, that the Red Army had carried off much of the equipment as war booty and insisted on the right to a large quantity of what remained. We could not admit that the Russians had a right to take, as war booty, property owned by their Allies. Stalin, Molotov and Vyshinski all stoutly maintained that this equipment did not belong to our nationals but was German property which they had a right to confiscate. Some of it had been bought in Germany before the war by American and British interests. But the Soviets insisted that since the property was German in origin it did not belong to us.

Mr. Vyshinski presented much of the Russian case. He is an able and aggressive lawyer. When he sits across the table looking at you with his cold, gray, piercing eyes and arguing his case with relentless precision, it is easy to understand his selection as Chief Prosecutor in the Soviet Union's great "purge" trials.

The question of ownership became fairly technical in such problems as equipment replacement and identification. Only after long argument were we able to appoint Soviet-American and Anglo-Soviet committees of experts to investigate the legitimacy of our claims.

On the opening day of the conference, Stalin announced his desire to discuss the question of trusteeship, stating that the Soviet Union "would like some territory of the defeated states." His delegation accordingly submitted a paper proposing that the Soviet Union be named trustee of one of the Italian colonies. The Atlantic Charter was a forgotten pledge. He wanted territory—indicating his conception of a trusteeship.

When the item was reached on the agenda, Mr. Churchill was reluctant even to discuss it. The President immediately made clear our belief that it was a matter for the peace conference and the United Nations but that no bars should be raised against discussion. Thereupon, Mr. Churchill delivered an impassioned statement.

"Britain," he said, "expects no gain out of this war. We have suffered terrible losses. Our losses have not been so heavy in human life as those of our gallant Soviet Ally. We have come out of the war, however, a great debtor in the world. There is no possibility of our regaining naval equality with the United States. We built only one capital ship during the war and lost ten or twelve. But in spite of the heavy losses we have suffered, we have made no territorial claims—no Königsberg, no Baltic states, nothing. We therefore approach the question of the colonies with complete rectitude.

"The British, of course, have great interests in the Mediterranean," Mr. Churchill added, "and any marked change in the status quo will need long and careful consideration," and he asked the Generalissimo to state what it was the Soviet Union desired.

"We would like to learn if this meeting will consider whether Italy is to lose her colonies," Stalin replied. "In that event, we can decide to what states they should be transferred for trusteeship."

"I had not considered the possibility of the Soviet Union desiring to acquire a large tract of the African shore," Mr. Churchill declared. "If this is the case, it will have to be considered in relation to many other problems." The question, he said, properly belonged to the peace conference and the ultimate administration of the colonies was a matter for the United Nations.

The President finally intervened. He suggested that the question be referred to the Foreign Ministers for further discussion, and there was a noticeable relaxation of tension around the big table as this suggestion was accepted.

When the Foreign Ministers met to consider it, Mr. Molotov immediately proposed that a definite determination be made of the future status of these colonies. I reminded him of President Truman's declaration that such a decision could be made only in connection with the peace treaties. When I pointed out that work would begin on them within one month, he agreed to wait.

The Soviet desire to reach into the Mediterranean was more modestly but nonetheless importantly expressed in connection with the control of the Dardanelles. Mr. Churchill first raised the issue. He had discussed it previously with the Generalissimo and now he expressed once again his willingness to join in a revised agreement that would insure free passage through the Straits for both the naval and the merchant ships of the Soviet Union in peace or in war. He felt it important, however, that Turkey should not be alarmed unduly, and pointed to the concern aroused by Russia's requests for the provinces of Kars and Ardahan, and for a naval base in the Straits.

"This," Mr. Churchill said, "has led Turkey to fear for the integrity of her empire and her power to defend Constantinople."

Both Stalin and Molotov explained that the request for the provinces had resulted from Turkey's proposal to the Soviet Union of a treaty of alliance. They contended that, aside from the fact that these provinces had been part of Russia under the Czar, the Soviet Union was justified, when entering into a treaty of alliance, to fix the boundaries it would thereafter be obliged to defend. The Montreux Convention, Stalin described as "inimical" to the Soviet Union since it gave Russia the same rights granted the Japanese Emperor. Turkey, he maintained, was too weak to give any effective guarantees of free passage and it was, therefore, only right that the Soviet Union should be enabled to defend the Straits.

"The American government will agree to a revision of the Montreux Convention," the President said. "We believe, however, that the Straits should be a free waterway open to the whole world and guaranteed by all of us."

That presented the issue. The Soviets wanted the free navigation of the Straits guaranteed by the Soviets, or by the Soviets and Turkey.

This meant their armed forces would be on Turkey's soil. We wanted the free navigation of the Straits guaranteed by the United Nations.

The thinking of the Soviet leaders in connection with the Dardanelles is unrealistic. For a hundred years Russia has coveted this section of its neighbor's territory. A hundred years ago the fortifications they now seek would have been of great military value. Today, without complete air superiority, their fortifications in the Straits would be of little value.

At this point, President Truman declared he was convinced that a great step toward ending Europe's recurring wars could be taken if the barriers to free passage of goods and vessels could be eliminated. He then presented the proposal we had prepared providing for free and unrestricted navigation of inland waterways.

This proposal, Stalin said, he was not prepared to discuss, since it had not been on the agenda. Despite several subsequent efforts by the President and by me, the best we could obtain was an agreement to refer the proposal to the Council of Foreign Ministers for later consideration. When it came to drafting the communique of the conference, Stalin objected to any mention even of this action, giving no reason other than that it was unnecessary and that the communique was already too long.

On July 25, the conference recessed, because the votes cast in the British election several weeks earlier were to be counted the following day. Mr. Churchill had brought the leader of the Opposition, Mr. Clement R. Attlee, to the conference, so that there would be continuity of representation regardless of the outcome of the election.

The day before the two Britons left for home to hear the results, I asked Mr. Churchill what he thought of his chances of remaining in office. He said he had no idea of the result but that the people who professed to know about elections had been betting that the Conservative Party would maintain a sizeable majority of the seats in the House of Commons. He felt very confident of victory. Mr. Attlee, on the other hand, impressed me as believing that his party would make a fine showing but would be defeated.

It made an interesting point that in the midst of our wrangling over how elections should be conducted in the liberated areas, these two leaders, weeks after the votes had been cast in England and by the armed forces overseas, were entirely unaware of the landslide that had taken place to sweep the Labor Party into power. The result was a surprise to all of us who had discussed the matter with them.

When the new Prime Minister returned to Potsdam, he brought Ernest Bevin to succeed Anthony Eden as Foreign Minister. As personalities, Attlee and Bevin differ from Churchill and Eden about as much as it is possible for people to differ. Mr. Attlee, in appearance and certainly in manner, gives one the impression of being a university professor. In speaking, he makes no pretense of oratory but presents his ideas clearly and carefully. He is exceedingly modest; there is nothing of the actor in him, and it is difficult to picture this earnest, serious man having great appeal for masses of people.

Soon after their arrival, Mr. Attlee and Mr. Bevin called on the President and the four of us discussed the work of the conference. The President mentioned the Soviet demand for East Prussia and indicated on a map the changes in the boundary lines of Germany, Poland and the Soviet Union that thus would be effected. Mr. Bevin immediately and forcefully presented his strong opposition to those boundaries. His manner was so aggressive that both the President and I wondered how we would get along with this new Foreign Minister. Some time later I told Mr. Bevin of the impression he had made on us at our first meeting, adding that we soon came to admire his bluntness and directness. He rather enjoyed my statement. And indeed it did not take me long to learn to respect highly his fine mind, his forthrightness, his candor, and his scrupulous regard for a promise. I have not only a high regard for his ability but a genuine affection for him as a man.

Britain's stand on the issues before the conference was not altered in the slightest, so far as we could discern, by the replacement of Mr. Churchill and Mr. Eden by Mr. Attlee and Mr. Bevin. This continuity of Britain's foreign policy impressed me. Later, in London, an incident occurred which demonstrated that I was not the only one so impressed. During the session of the United Nations General Assembly, Mr. Bevin made an important speech on British foreign policy. An Englishwoman, who had followed foreign affairs closely and who, naturally, had contrasted Ernest Bevin's bulk of at least 250 pounds with Anthony Eden's tall slender frame, sat in the gallery with an American friend listening to Mr. Bevin's speech. During the course of it, she turned to her companion and remarked, "Anthony Eden is making a good speech, but he seems to have gotten a little stout."

With the arrival of the new British leaders, the conference resumed and we started work in earnest on the most difficult issue before us— Germany.

We had arrived in Potsdam to face what amounted to a *fait accompli,* so far as the Polish-German frontier was concerned. Prior to Yalta, the three powers had agreed to divide Germany into four zones of occupation, and they had made a positive declaration in Section VI of the Yalta Protocol that the final delimitation of the western frontier of Poland should await the peace conference. Although the protocol would seem to permit no misunderstanding, we learned before leaving the United States for Germany that, without any consultation either with the United Kingdom or with the United States, the Soviets had transferred all the German territory east of the Neisse River to Poland for administration.

Both President Truman and Prime Minister Churchill promptly asked for an explanation of this unilateral action in establishing, for all practical purposes, another zone. Such a course, the President maintained, not only was contrary to agreement but would make the settlement of problems such as reparations far more difficult.

The Soviet defense was that the Germans had fled before the Russian armies, and, since it was necessary to have some government in the area, they had permitted Poland to take over its administration. Generalissimo Stalin agreed that no one of the powers had the right to create a new zone, but said that the Soviet government had to be assured of stable conditions in the rear of the Red Army. He then admitted that Poland was actually removing from this area substantial amounts of coal, which we contended certainly should be considered part of reparations payments.

The President asked how the reparations issue could ever be settled "if part of the German territory is gone before we reach agreement on what reparations should be."

Stalin remarked that everything the President said was irrelevant since "no frontiers had been ceded at the Crimea Conference except for the provisions that Poland would receive territory."

"The western frontier question is open," Stalin said, "and the Soviet Union is not bound."

The President repeated: "You are not?"

"No," Stalin replied.

We were concerned also by the huge displacement of population resulting from this action of the Soviets. Although Stalin claimed "no single German remained in the area to be given to Poland," an area that had a prewar German population of nearly nine million, our information indicated that there were at least two million Germans left there. Later, representatives of the Polish government admitted the presence of approximately a million and a half Germans, but contended that many of them would leave voluntarily if the area were assigned to Poland.

President Beirut of Poland argued his country's claim to eastern Germany at a meeting of the Foreign Ministers on July 24. He pointed out that, if all the area they asked were given them, Poland would still be smaller in total area than before the war because, in accordance with the Crimea decision, 180,000 square kilometers of territory in the east would be transferred to Russia. He asserted, however, that the eastern German area would give Poland a sounder economy and a more homogeneous population.

Mr. Churchill had pointed out that this Soviet-supported plan would take nearly one-fourth of the arable land within Germany's 1937 frontiers. Not only would the German food supply be cut, he stressed, but more than a million Germans would be forced into the western zones, "bringing their mouths with them."

Time after time, in discussing the claims of Poland and the question of recognizing the existence of Polish administration of the area during the occupation, the President repeated that there could be no transfer of territory until there was a peace conference. In addition, we specifically refrained from promising to support at the German Peace Conference any particular line as the western frontier of Poland.

Our deliberate avoidance of a promise on the Polish border is emphasized by the promise we did make in the protocol about the transfer of the city of Königsberg to the Soviet Union, when we said: "the President of the United States and the British Prime Minister have declared that they will support the proposal of this conference at the forthcoming peace settlement."

To remove even an excuse for Poland or the Soviet Union to claim that the line had been established or that there was any promise to support a particular line, the Berlin Protocol declared: "The three heads of government reaffirm their opinion that the final delimitation of the western frontier of Poland should await the peace settlement."

In the light of this history, it is difficult to credit with good faith any person who asserts that Poland's western boundary was fixed by the conferees, or that there was a promise that it would be established at some particular place.

We had recognized from the outset, however, that we would have to accept for the time being the Polish administration of this part of the Soviet zone. It was an accomplished fact and we could not force the Russians to resume the responsibilities they had voluntarily resigned. However, no agreement even on the temporary administration was reached until we came to grips with the issue of reparations.

Ever since Yalta the great variance between the Soviet Union and ourselves on the subject of reparations had been apparent. We agreed that reparations should be obtained through payments "in kind" rather than in currency. But the meetings of the Commission on Reparations between the Yalta and Potsdam meetings had demonstrated that our agreement extended no further.

There was, first of all, the figure of twenty billion dollars, with one-half, or ten billion dollars, to go to the Soviet Union. Mr. Maisky had advanced this figure at Yalta and President Roosevelt had accepted it as a "basis for discussion" in the Reparations Commission. When the commission met at Moscow repeated efforts by our representative, Mr.

Edwin Pauley, failed to elicit from Mr. Maisky any data to support this figure. At Potsdam, both Generalissimo Stalin and Mr. Molotov kept pressing for the establishment of a definite figure. We finally succeeded in eliminating from the agreed declaration any mention of a total amount either in terms of dollars or tonnages of equipment.

The major impasse at the Moscow Reparations Commission meetings arose from our insistence that there could be no reparations from current output until Germany exported enough goods to pay for essential imports. Here, too, we were guided by our experience in World War I when American loans paid for German purchases of raw materials, which were then converted into goods for delivery to other countries as reparations payments. We were determined that we would not again pay for Germany's reparations and, therefore, maintained that necessary imports and advances must constitute a first charge against any German production available for export.

Our desire to treat the reparations issue as one part of the over-all economic planning struck a snag of reality. We had expected that no property other than war booty would be removed from Germany by any of the armies of occupation without a strict accounting so that its value could be charged against whatever reparations program was later agreed upon. But, even before the conference opened, we had received reports that the Soviet army was removing property and equipment that could in no sense be classified as war booty. Some of these reports were such that we were reluctant to believe them. But there was little room for doubt after our arrival in Germany where we not only received eye-witness accounts but ourselves encountered corroborating evidence.

The house assigned to the President and his party had been the home of a motion picture executive who, we were told, had been taken to Russia. His wife was acting as charwoman in one of the homes assigned to other members of the American delegation. "The Little White House" had been completely stripped of its furnishings, but had been refurnished for the conference with furniture taken from still other homes.

Assistant Secretary Clayton and Mr. Pauley were shown a point on the line between the American and Russian zones where the Soviets, before the dividing line was finally fixed, had taken machinery from a plant which eventually was left in our zone and moved it into their area not more than two-hundred yards from the line. There it was left in an open field. The International Telephone and Telegraph Company's plant in Berlin, they found, had been stripped of nearly all its machinery. They visited other plants where rayon, ice and optical instruments had been made, and observed similar conditions.

Mr. Pauley had discussed the matter at length with Mr. Maisky, who admitted that the occupying power could not rightfully remove property without accounting to the other powers unless that property could be classified as war booty. Mr. Maisky tried to devise a definition of war booty that would include furniture, bath fixtures, silverware, coal, and other nonmilitary supplies. He found it an impossible task.

Finally, at a meeting of the Foreign Ministers on July 23, I asked Mr. Molotov whether it was true that the Soviet authorities had taken large quantities of equipment and materials, including even household goods, out of their zone.

"Yes, this is the case," Mr. Molotov replied. If it was worrying me, he went on, he would agree to deduct from their reparations plan a suitable figure to cover removals already made and he suggested 300 million dollars as a proper amount. When I objected, he quickly responded with an offer to reduce their reparations claims from ten to nine billion to cover removals already made "and thus dispose of the question."

But at Paris, at New York and at Moscow in the spring of 1947, Molotov was again demanding ten billion dollars.

Further complicating the problem of property removals was Poland's action in eastern Germany, where, Stalin admitted, the Poles were taking coal from the Silesian mines. This area, Mr. Molotov maintained, "must of necessity be considered differently."

We considered these practical problems in our delegation at considerable length. We knew that, if reparations were to be drawn from all Germany we would have to demand an accounting from the Soviets. We were sure they could not even approximate an accurate valuation of what had been taken, and we realized that the effort to establish and maintain such an accounting would be a source of constant friction, accusations and ill-will.

Mr. Clayton, Mr. Pauley and I concluded that the only way out of the situation was to persuade each country to satisfy its reparations claims out of its own zone. I discussed this idea with former Ambassador Joseph E. Davies and he, too, thought it was the solution. Then, with the approval of the President, I arranged for a private interview with Mr. Molotov on July 23.

The United States, I said, was "deeply concerned" at the development of the reparations issue. We had always favored the adoption of a policy by which the three powers would treat the entire German economic question as a whole, but we did not see how the Soviet Union's position on war booty, removals, and so on, could be reconciled with an over-all reparations plan. We were very much afraid, I stressed, that "the attempt to resolve these conditions in practice would lead to endless quarrels and disagreements between the three countries at a time when unity between them is essential." Therefore, under the circumstances, we believed it wise to consider the possibility of each country's taking reparations from its own zone.

Approximately 40 per cent of the value of "industrial equipment deemed unnecessary for a peace economy" was located in the Soviet zone. We proposed that 10 per cent of such industrial equipment in the western zones be given to the Soviets. If the Soviets desired certain additional equipment or materials from the British or American zones, these could be exchanged for food or coal needed for the German population in the west.

Mr. Molotov promised to give this proposal to Generalissimo Stalin for his consideration.

The day before Mr. Attlee and Mr. Bevin were to arrive, Mr. Molotov returned to the subject with the complaint that we were seeking to reverse a decision made at Yalta by not accepting the twenty-billion dollar total reparations proposal. I tried many ways to help him understand that acceptance by Roosevelt "as a basis for discussion" was not a commitment.

"If you ask me for a million dollars and I tell you I will discuss it," I told him, "it does not mean I will write a check for it." That didn't get the point over. So I pointed out that we not only had accepted the proposal as a basis for discussion but that Mr. Pauley had been in Moscow for thirty-five days and discussed it; then he had come to Berlin and we had continued to discuss it, and for the many reasons I had previously explained to him we had decided, after this discussion, that the figure was not practical.

As soon as Mr. Attlee and Mr. Bevin returned I visited them and, after several hours discussion, obtained their agreement in principle to our proposal. The next day the President and I arranged to see Generalissimo Stalin and Mr. Molotov, but the Generalissimo was ill with a cold. Molotov came.

We declared our agreement to an equal division of the German fleet and merchant marine among the three powers, for which the Russians had been pressing very vigorously since the beginning of the conference. We urged him to accept our plan for reparations. Mr. Molotov thereupon announced that the Soviet Union was prepared to accept our proposal "in principle" but wished to settle certain "details." The major "detail" was the amount of equipment that would be turned over to the Soviet Union from the Ruhr and he suggested two billion dollars' worth as an appropriate amount!

We explained that the placing of a dollar value on the equipment was impossible and we could only agree to offer a certain percentage of the equipment to be declared available for reparations. Mr. Molotov was most insistent about having a total dollar value set because otherwise "a percentage figure would be meaningless."

During this conversation he asserted that the Economic Committee had not done so well. I knew this was a criticism of his representative,

Mr. Maisky, for his inability to justify in some way the removals from the Soviet zone. But I did not realize how serious a matter it is for a Soviet representative to fail to have the right answers. Since that criticism, Mr. Maisky, who had served as Ambassador at London for ten years and spoke English fluently, has not been seen at a conference.

On July 31, I told Mr. Molotov there were three outstanding issues: reparations, Poland's administration of a part of the Soviet zone, and our paper entitled "Admission to the United Nations" dealing with Italy and the Balkan states. I submitted a proposal containing the only concessions we were willing to make and requested that Mr. Molotov present the three proposals to Generalissimo Stalin so that they might be discussed at the afternoon session. I told him we would agree to all three or none and that the President and I would leave for the United States the next day.

When the conference opened that afternoon the President immediately suggested that the three proposals be discussed and called on me to present them. I did so, emphasizing that it was all one proposition.

Generalissimo Stalin expressed disapproval of "the tactics of Mr. Byrnes," in asking for consideration of the three proposals at one time. I replied that we had been considering them one at a time for three weeks; that we were now making concessions in one solely for the purpose of reaching a compromise on the three in order to bring the conference to an end. Therefore, we insisted on this procedure. The Generalissimo renewed his protest and then began to bargain. First, he suggested a fantastic increase in reparations. Then, he proposed that the amount of capital equipment to be removed from the western zone in return for products such as food, coal, timber, and so on, be increased from 12 per cent to 15 per cent. I said if he would withdraw his other demands and agree to the other two proposals in dispute, we would agree to the 15 per cent. He agreed and the conference ended shortly thereafter.

Molotov dropped, for the time being at least, his proposal for the joint administration of the Ruhr, a major objective of the Soviet Union in western Europe. Agreement quickly followed on such matters as the economic principles to govern the occupation of Germany, including the compact to treat the country as an economic unit; the orderly transfer of German population; and the revision of the Allied Control Council procedure in Rumania, Bulgaria and Hungary to meet, in part, some of the requests made in our paper on implementing the Yalta Declaration on Liberated Europe.

We agreed to urge our representatives to act promptly on the procedure for the trial of major war criminals. It would take some of the joy out of war if the men who started one, instead of a halo around the head, got a rope around the neck.

Note that nowhere in the Potsdam Protocol is there any provision for the payment of reparations from current production. All prior discussions were superseded by the formal reparations agreement at Potsdam. The Soviet Union's renewal one year later of its demand for ten billions of dollars of reparations from current production and its continued use of German labor is inexcusable.

There is even less justification for requiring Germany to pay reparations out of current production when it is considered that the prewar value of taxable property in the Silesian area alone, which is only a part of the region now administered by Poland, was 11,300,000,000 dollars. Poland invariably argues that it is entitled to this area because of the 180,000 square kilometers of its territory east of the Curzon Line transferred to Russia by the Yalta decision. In addition there is East Prussia, which we have pledged to the Soviet Union and which had taxable property valued at two and a half billion dollars. The resources of these areas certainly should be considered as part of the reparations settlement.

Even if the figures were less generous, I think we should realize that, modern war being what it is, it is shortsighted and futile for any country to seek approximate compensation for losses it has sustained.

Because Generalissimo Stalin made so clear in the discussion of reparations at Potsdam that he "disliked the tactics of Mr. Byrnes," I thought he was seriously offended. It was therefore a surprise and a good indication of Russian appreciation of firmness in negotiating that just before the final gavel was to fall on the Potsdam Conference he asked the President for permission to say a few words about "Mr. Byrnes who has worked harder perhaps than any of us."

"He has brought us together in reaching so many important decisions," Stalin added.

The President expressed the hope that the next time the Big Three met it would be in Washington.

"God willing," Stalin replied.

The conference ended in good spirits. But the American delegation that headed for home probably was less sanguine than the one that had departed from Yalta. Events had shown that agreements reached in conference must be hammered out on the hard anvil of experience. We thought, however, that we had established a basis for maintaining our war-born unity. Our efforts in relation to eastern Europe had been less successful than we had hoped. We had failed to exempt Italy from reparations. We thought we had succeeded in the case of Austria. We felt we had made genuine progress in the agreements about Germany, although there was ample ground for our fears that it would be a long time before we could get the Soviets to start work on a German settlement. Nevertheless, we believed our agreement on reparations enabled us to avoid denouncing their unilateral action in removing people and property from their zone.

Certainly, no one of us suspected that the first treaties of peace would be concluded only after sixteen more months of almost continuous negotiation. We considered the conference a success. We firmly believed that the agreements reached would provide a basis for the early restoration of stability to Europe.

The agreements did make the conference a success but the violation of those agreements has turned success into failure.

WORKING ON BOARD USS AUGUSTA ON THE WAY TO POTSDAM

Charles E. Bohlen, H. F. Matthews, James F. Byrnes and Benjamin V. Cohen

BOOK II

THE TREATIES—FIVE STEPS TOWARD PEACE

Chapter 5

Setback at London

ON MAY 9, 1947, I appeared before the Senate Foreign Relations Committee which was considering the peace treaties with Italy, Bulgaria, Rumania and Hungary. The committee was under considerable pressure, primarily from Italian-American groups, to delay action. The arguments for delay were really intended to accomplish the defeat of the treaties. After describing how the United States had held the initiative throughout sixteen months of difficult negotiations, I urged the committee to consider the consequences if the treaty were to be delayed and we were to give up our leadership. I then asked the Senators to remember the words of President Roosevelt in his last State of the Union message on January 6, 1945.

> Perfectionism, no less than isolationism or imperialism or power politics, may obstruct the paths to international peace. Let us not forget that the retreat to isolationism a quarter of a century ago was started not by a direct attack against international co-operation but against the alleged imperfections of the peace.
>
> In our disillusionment after the last war we preferred international anarchy to international co-operation with nations which did not see and think exactly as we did. We gave up the hope of gradually achieving a better peace because we had not the courage to fulfill our responsibilities in an admittedly imperfect world.
>
> We must not let that happen again, or we shall follow the same tragic road again—the road to a third world war.

We should remember these words as we seek to conclude treaties of peace with Austria, Germany and Japan, and as we watch the evolution of international relations within the framework of the United Nations.

Happily, the committee and the Senate acted in the spirit of these words and President Roosevelt's wisdom. The committee unanimously endorsed the treaties, and the Senate, on June 5, 1947, approved the Italian treaty by a vote of 79 to 10, and ratified the others by a voice vote.

Good government lies in seeking the highest common denominator.

This is as true in international councils as it is in the county court house. The story of our effort to obtain this common denominator in the four European treaties is told here not only for its intrinsic interest and importance but as one means of evaluating the solution to the many problems that lie ahead.

I had been Secretary of State two months when we boarded the *Queen Elizabeth* on September 5, 1945, for London and the first meeting of the Council of Foreign Ministers. Those twenty-eight days spent in the United States after the return from Germany were full of action. There had been the second atomic bomb; Russian entry into the Japanese war; Japan's surrender; arrangements for the occupation of Japan; the visits of the French President, General de Gaulle, and his Foreign Minister, Georges Bidault; postwar lend-lease settlement problems; intensified efforts to bring China's divided factions together; departmental appointments, including the nominations of Dean Acheson as Undersecretary, Ben Cohen as counselor, and Donald Russell, Spruille Braden and William Benton as Assistant Secretaries; and, finally, the very important preparation for the London Conference.

On the boat we started to work in earnest on the proposals and alternative proposals that had been prepared by the State Department experts. John Foster Dulles, a leading Republican spokesman on foreign affairs, had accepted my invitation to join the delegation, and together we met with the State Department advisory staff twice a day to plan the position of the United States on all the issues before the Council.

One of the things that gave us particular concern in these talks was the unmistakable evidence of Russian expansion. I had secured the Yalta agreement on the Kuriles, Sakhalin, Dairen and Port Arthur from the Map Room, in the White House. At Potsdam we had encountered the Soviet demands that Poland be given a large portion of eastern Germany to compensate for the Polish territory east of the Curzon Line taken over by the Soviets; her demands for Königsberg; for a share in the administration of the Ruhr; and for control of the Dardanelles. Her determination to dominate the Balkan states had become apparent, and at Potsdam she had made a bid for control of one of Italy's North African colonies, preferably Tripolitania.

This last request was especially disturbing because events had convinced me that the Soviets' interest in this territory was primarily military. Throughout the war they had shown a tendency to enter into multilateral arrangements when they were economic in character and demonstrably of direct benefit to them, but to prefer unilateral action where military and security considerations were involved.

We finally decided that our policy should be to promote the independence of these colonies, which covered over a million square miles of territory and had more than three million inhabitants. While preparing for independence they should be administered under a trusteeship set up within the United Nations Charter. The problem was: Who should be the trustee? Some of the State Department officials had recommended that Italy continue as trustee for the United Nations. At first that seemed the easiest solution but there were strong reasons against it.

Italy's record of administering the colonies was one of inefficiency and oppression. Consequently, in the African campaign the native inhabitants were sympathetic to the Allied cause and had given great assistance to the British. The British had promised the Senussi tribes, in recognition of their help, that Italy would never again be placed in control of their territory and their people. Investigation disclosed that every year Italy had been in control of the colonies she had incurred financial loss, notwithstanding the fact that her civilian employees were paid pitifully small salaries. As long as the United States was appropriating relief funds for Italy, it did not seem wise to allow Italy to assume such a financial burden.

It was difficult to foresee what kind of government would prevail in Italy. The colonies had proved of no value to her except as a place for military training and, under the treaty we were considering, she would have no need for great areas for training troops. But above and beyond these considerations was our belief that a trusteeship should be established solely to assist the inhabitants of the colonies to develop the capacity for self-government so that the people might be granted independence. With these thoughts in mind, I asked one of my aides to prepare a draft of a proposal for a collective trusteeship under the United Nations.

I was glad we had come to London to begin work on drafting treaties of peace. The devastation of war that surrounded us seemed to me to be a desirable reminder of the grave responsibility that was ours. From my observations on short walks or quick drives around the city I concluded that fifteen years at least would be required to repair the damage. But I am always more impressed with people than with buildings and I was deeply moved by the patience and the courage of the British people. About all the end of the war had brought them was a reduction in casualty lists, but they accepted all the rationing and regulations in a spirit that was in sharp contrast to the clamor at home over the few remaining shortages and controls.

The council convened on September 11, and we immediately encountered serious differences of opinion over its organization and its agenda. There was even, to my surprise, a request from Molotov to discuss the control of Japan. Two days passed before we were able to get started on the Italian treaty.

It was agreed that a British draft would be used as the basis for our work. Issues which were to become old friends immediately appeared. They were the Italo-Yugoslav border, the Dodecanese Islands, and the Italian colonies. Mr. Molotov would not discuss the border problem unless the Yugoslavs were present; he would not discuss the Dodecanese until we discussed the Italian colonies. So I suggested that we invite the Yugoslavs and the Italians to come and present their case, and proceeded to present the proposal on the Italian colonies, which we had completed immediately after our arrival.

Our proposal provided that an administrator be appointed by the United Nations Security Council of which the Soviet Union was a permanent member. This administrator would be an international civil servant appointed from any one of the member nations. He would have an Advisory Council composed of one representative each from Britain, France, the Soviet Union, and the United States, plus Italy, and a representative of the people of the territory. Should the administrator fail to discharge his responsibilities in a manner satisfactory to any one of the states on this Advisory Council, any one of them could bring the matter to the attention of the Trusteeship Council. Our plan also called for the termination of the trusteeship at the end of ten years.

"This plan would give assurance that the Italian colonies will not be developed for the military advantage of anyone," I stated. "It would be left to the Security Council to determine, if necessary, the points in these colonies at which strategic bases might be established. This plan would give heart to the peoples of the world, since it shows that the states on this council intend to carry out their promises and permit these peoples to select at the earliest possible moment the government under which they would live."

Mr. Bidault preferred to make Italy the trustee power, particularly since the Trusteeship Council had not yet been established and there was no indication of how a collective trusteeship would work. Dr. Wang Shih Chieh immediately expressed the Chinese delegation's full approval of our proposal. Mr. Bevin said this was a new proposal and he would have to study it. He referred to Britain's wartime promise to the Senussi tribes. He was not ready to commit himself. He wished to know if other proposals would be considered because he wanted the dominions to have the opportunity to give their views to the deputies. It was then Mr. Molotov's turn.

The Soviet delegation, he said, proposed that the principle of trusteeship be applied to some of the Italian colonies with individual countries being made trustee for each of the colonies. He doubted our ability to agree on an administrator. He would not conceal, he added, the desire of the Soviet Government to claim an individual trusteeship, and proceeded to base his claim on the damages inflicted by the ten divisions and three brigades of Italian Blackshirts that had invaded the Soviet Union. Pointing to the "wide experience" of the Soviet Government in "establishing friendly relations between different nationalities," he proposed this experience be applied to Tripolitania and assured the council that ten years would be adequate to prepare the territory for independent existence.

In a private conversation, Mr. Molotov proposed to me that each of the three powers: the United States, United Kingdom and Soviet Union, should administer one of the colonies. I told him we could not agree to that.

Our delegation, I told him, had concluded it would be far more difficult to agree on administration by individual governments than on an individual administrator who could not be charged with exploiting the colony for commercial or military advantage. These areas must constitute a trust and must not be regarded as spoils of war or compensation for damage done in the war. Dividing these three colonies among three states without restrictions on military developments would not serve peace but would sow the seeds of trouble.

The following afternoon Mr. Bevin presented the British position. With characteristic bluntness he said that Britain could not agree to the Soviet claim to an individual trusteeship over Tripolitania. Since the claim was based on the damage caused by Italian troops in Russia, he was forced to point out that Britain and the dominions were fighting Italy long before Italy and Russia were at war. Britain, he went on, recognized the interest of the Soviet Union in eastern Europe and had therefore supported Russia's claims, and he expressed his surprise that Russia did not recognize a similar interest on the part of his country in the Mediterranean. Bevin then declared his support for our proposal, subject to modifications. He did not want to be tied to the American draft as it applied to Somaliland and Eritrea. But as for Libya and Tripolitania, he agreed "because it was a great, new and untried experiment and because Britain wished to avoid conflict in this area between the great powers." With regard to Eritrea and Somaliland, he suggested that the deputies consider the right of Ethiopia to an outlet on the sea and seek territorial adjustments among those countries that would "give these peoples a better chance to live."

This latter suggestion, of course, was acceptable to us. Mr. Bidault's opinion was still reserved. France, he said, could not accept our proposal, "even in principle" until the details were more definite and he pointed out that Libya was bordered by an important part of the French Union. Obviously, he feared the effect that the promise of independence for Tripolitania would have in French territory.

Mr. Molotov was precise and specific. He wanted to discuss Tripolitania. The Soviet Union had a sea outlet in the north, he asserted, and in view of its vast territory should have one also in the south, "especially so since we now have the right to use Dairen and Port Arthur in the Far East."

"The Soviet Union should take the place that is due it," he said, "and therefore should have bases in the Mediterranean for its merchant fleet. We do not propose to introduce the Soviet system into this territory apart from the democratic order that is desired by the people." And then, he added, "This will not be done along the lines that have been used in Greece."

In a private conversation with Mr. Molotov it became apparent that another difficult misunderstanding in language had arisen between ourselves and the Russians. At the San Francisco Conference when the question of establishing a trusteeship system within the United Nations was being considered, the Soviet delegation had asked Mr. Stettinius what the American attitude would be toward the assumption by the Soviet Union of a trusteeship. Mr. Stettinius replied in general terms, expressing the opinion that the Soviet Union was "eligible" to receive a territory for administration under trusteeship. Mr. Molotov took this to mean we would support a Soviet request for a trusteeship. He told me he was surprised that we were opposing his request for Tripolitania. He admitted the letter contained no specific commitment as to the Italian colonies, but asserted that these colonies provided the only opportunity that the Soviet Union would have to acquire a trusteeship, and therefore a commitment was certainly implied.

He repeated this so often I finally said:

"In the United States any citizen is eligible to become President, but that does not mean every citizen is going to be President. If you keep repeating that there is a commitment to support any request you make, for a trusteeship, you will soon come to believe it yourself."

I saw I had not convinced him, so I tried again.

"If I tell a man I think he is eligible to own a house, I do not mean that if he asks for the Soviet Embassy, I must support his demand for the house."

That did not help. He still professes to believe that because of Secretary Stettinius' statement it is our duty to find a satisfactory territory that the Soviet Union can administer as trustee.

Those were the opening arguments. With variations and embellishments they were repeated throughout the next sixteen months until it became clear the issue could not be settled at present. Consequently, unless there is a prior agreement, the military government will continue for one year after the Italian treaty comes into force. If the four states do not reach agreement within that year, the disposition of the colonies will be decided by the General Assembly of the United Nations, where unanimous agreement is not required.

Nor could we reach any agreement on the Dodecanese Islands. Four members of the council believed they should go to Greece but Mr. Molotov insisted that a decision on these islands could be made only in connection with a decision on the Italian colonies.

As to the Italo-Yugoslav border, the initial statements of position disclosed that all members of the council were generally agreed that Trieste should be made a free port. The chief problem was Mr. Molotov's lone stand that the city be placed under Yugoslav sovereignty despite the fact that its population was overwhelmingly Italian. The position of the council members was not changed in any marked degree by the arguments presented on September 18 by the representatives of Yugoslavia, Italy, South Africa, Australia and New Zealand. But immediately after this hearing I proposed that experts be sent to the territory with directions to determine a line that would, primarily, follow ethnic divisions but which would also take economic factors into consideration. Molotov accepted this suggestion but afterward regretted the action because the line his expert recommended could not be justified under the directive.

Another issue on which Mr. Molotov faced four-to-one opposition was that of reparations. The Soviet proposal called for payment by Italy of reparations totaling 600 million dollars of which 100 million would go to Russia. The other members of the council held that after Italy repaid advances for relief there would be little left for reparations payments.

Although I had come to the conference thinking the Foreign Ministers might reach agreement on general principles to guide the deputies in detailed work on the treaties within ten days or two weeks, it was apparent by the end of the first week that this was a vain hope. We had spent hours talking about procedure. France wanted to discuss the control of Germany. Molotov wanted to discuss German reparations. He also raised the question of the Control Council in Japan. We had made little progress on the Italian peace treaty and the Soviet delegation was insisting that Britain and the United States extend diplomatic recognition to their puppet governments in eastern Europe.

It was the latter demand that appeared to me to be the main stumbling block of the conference. On Sunday morning I determined I must make Mr. Molotov understand why we refused to recognize governments installed and maintained by the Soviet Union. The Soviet official was spending the day in the country but arrangements were made for us to meet at the Russian Embassy at 5:30.

I opened the conversation by saying "It is essential for the future of the world that our nations continue to co-operate and that we should endeavor to adjust our differences in such a way as to preserve our unity of purpose." I then emphasized that "the United States is not interested in seeing anything but governments friendly to the Soviet Union in adjacent countries."

"I must tell you I have doubts as to this, and it would not be honest to hide it," Mr. Molotov replied. He went on to say that the doubts rose from the attitude of the United States in the case of Rumania. The former Radescu government, he said, "was hostile to the Soviet Union and yet received British and American support but when the Groza government, which was friendly, had been established, both the United States and Britain had withdrawn support."

"The Yalta Declaration on the Liberated Countries had been warmly received by the American people," I told him. "You will remember, I am sure, that the Groza government was installed during President Roosevelt's administration. We know it was installed as a result of a two-and-a-half hour ultimatum to the King by Mr. Vyshinski. Since that time, the exclusion of our press representatives, the treatment accorded our official representatives and other actions has confirmed our doubts as to the character of this government.

"Our objective," I said, "is a government both friendly to the Soviet Union and representative of all the democratic elements of the country." I pointed out that the misunderstandings that had arisen after Yalta over Poland had been worked out and I suggested we try to agree on the composition of a Rumanian government as we had in the case of Poland.

Mr. Molotov refused to accept the Polish case as a precedent. In Rumania, he said, such a course would lead to civil war. Only after an election was held, he maintained, would it be possible to consider reorganizing the government.

I pointed out that the government then would not be a provisional one but an elected one and that if we joined in establishing a representative provisional government, the results of an election held by such a government would be accepted by our people.

"Are all parties represented in the British and American governments?" Mr. Molotov inquired.

"No," I replied, "but in the case of Rumania we are speaking of a temporary government and not one based on elections. Because of the manner in which the Groza government has been established and because of its subsequent actions, any elections held under its auspices would be suspect in the eyes of the American people."

Mr. Molotov then attacked Greece and asked why we should maintain a different attitude toward one country than toward the other.

"It is a question of facts," I told him. "In Greece correspondents had been allowed to go in, move about freely, and report without censorship what they had seen. As a result, the American people were informed about Greece and felt the situation was not the same as that described by you. In Rumania, correspondents have not been allowed any such facilities and the actions of the Groza government have led us to believe it is not representative of the people."

"Apparently," Mr. Molotov remarked, "in Greece the correspondents are happy but the people are not; whereas in Rumania the people are happy but the correspondents are not. The Soviet Government attaches more importance to the feeling of the people."

Although our representatives believed an overwhelming majority of the people in Rumania opposed the Groza regime, I chose not to argue this with him but rather to seek some formula for resolving our differences. But he kept insisting that our refusal to recognize Groza could only mean we desired to see established a government hostile to the Soviet Union. After repeatedly insisting this was not true and failing in every effort to reach an understanding, I finally gave up and went home.

It was a gloomy Sunday evening for the American delegation. We talked over this interview and the problems it raised for a long time. It seemed that the Soviet Union was determined to dominate Europe. We could see no solution to our problems but we knew we must continue to search for one.

The events of the following day gave us no encouragement. In all the treaties, we had proposed a strict limitation on armed forces and the establishment of inspection commissions to insure that the limitation was observed. The Rumanian treaty was under consideration, and Mr. Molotov immediately announced his opposition to our proposal.

Mr. Bevin pointed out that the last two wars had started in small states, Serbia and Poland, and we must hereafter see that small states neither start war nor become the first victims of war.

"If we encourage these small states to maintain peace rather than armies, and to develop their economies," he said, "it will also keep the big states out of trouble."

Mr. Molotov said it had never occurred to him that "if one disarmed a state it could lead a quieter life." And, in the same note of sarcasm, he asked:

"Do you really have so many people in your countries that you can send them out as inspectors, and consuls and so on?"

Mr. Bevin, who felt very strongly about the activities of the Red Army in Rumania, inquired how that country had acquired all the people it had there now.

I interrupted to say that I regarded the issue as a serious one.

"The world is war weary," I stated. "In every country soldiers want to return home. In the countries where they are in occupation, they should return home as soon as possible. The peoples of the world look to this council for action that will establish permanent peace. It would be the greatest favor we could do these countries, all of which are poor, if we relieve them of the burden of armaments. We have given assurances through the United Nations to prevent aggression against any country. Why, then, do any of these countries need large armies?"

But we made no progress and so proceeded to equally fruitless discussions of other treaty clauses.

Wednesday evening Mr. Molotov came to my office and we went over the same ground in almost the same terms. He persisted in believing that there was some hidden motive in our stand based on hostility toward the Soviet Union. Nothing I could say would dissuade him and I understand he later said he wished he could find out what it was I wanted so we could negotiate.

I was impressed by the repeated statements made by Stalin, Molotov, and others that the Soviet Union sought security. Ever since Yalta, when Marshal Stalin recounted how Poland twice within twenty-five years had been used as a corridor for invading Russia, this fear had kept cropping up in Russian policy. It was present in Molotov's demand that governments wholly subservient to Russia should be maintained in Rumania, Bulgaria and Hungary. Therefore, I thought that if we could give them assurance on this score perhaps the obstacle blocking the conference could be removed. In any event, we would eliminate that argument. So, the following morning, I arranged for another private talk with the Soviet Foreign Minister.

I recounted my conversation with Generalissimo Stalin at Yalta and said that I had been impressed by his observation that twice within twenty-five years Russia had been invaded through the Polish Corridor and by his fear of a revival of German military power.

"As you know," I went on, "the United States, historically, is reluctant to enter into political treaties, but I want to ask you if the Soviet Government would consider desirable a twenty-five-year treaty between the four principal powers for the demilitarization of Germany. If the Soviet Government thinks this a good idea, I am prepared to recommend it to the President and both of us could recommend it to the Congress. The details we will have to work out, but I would like your views as to whether such a treaty would be a real contribution toward removing the fear of a recrudescence of German aggression—a fear that plays a large part in the policies of various European states.

"If you think well of the idea," I concluded, "we can then talk to the French and the British."

He said he could not give the definite views of his government but personally he thought it was "a very interesting idea." He would report it to Moscow and we could discuss it again in a few days. With that, he returned to the question of Rumania and told me that unless we withdrew our paper he would have to reply to it because it was, in effect, a challenge directed against the Soviet Union.

I told him he had every right to make a statement but that he could rest assured I would reply to him.

There were two meetings the next day and both of them were tense as the arguments that Mr. Molotov and I had been having privately were at last brought out into the open.

"In Rumania," Mr. Molotov asserted, "there is the Groza government which enjoys the support of the overwhelming majority of the population, and no one can deny this. . . . I ask; is not the reason that the American Government opposes this government the fact that it is friendly to the Soviet Union?"

He declared that our feeling that the Rumanian Government is undemocratic "does not correspond with the facts," and then added:

"The Rumanian Government is liked by the Rumanian population but not by the American Government. What should be done? Should we overthrow it because it is not liked by the United States Government, and set up a government that would be unfriendly to the Soviet Union? In such an undertaking the Soviet delegation will not be able to assist the American delegation."

I pointed out to Mr. Molotov that at Yalta the heads of government had agreed to favor interim governments that would be broadly representative and committed to the holding of early elections.

"At Potsdam," I continued, "the President had stated not once but a dozen times that the United States could not recognize the present governments of Rumania and Bulgaria. There was difference of opinion between the President and Generalissimo Stalin, but Generalissimo Stalin never once questioned the motives of the United States." I pointed out the steps we had taken to extend recognition to Poland, Finland and Hungary, and asserted these actions proved conclusively that "the statements made by Mr. Molotov regarding the motives of the United States Government are both unfair and untrue."

This exchange was typical of the debate throughout the morning. That afternoon, Mr. Bevin declared his support of the United States' position. Mr. Molotov, of course, rose to the challenge, but I could see that further discussion would only contribute bitterness and therefore declined to make any additional statements about Rumania. Mr. Molotov then concluded the discussion by charging that the other members of the council were "conducting an offensive" against him on the issue of Rumania.

It was the next day, September 22, that broke the back of the London Conference.

Just before 10 A.M. Mr. Molotov's secretary called to say that the Russian delegation could not be present for the scheduled meeting at 11, but asked if I would meet Mr. Molotov at 11 :30. I arrived promptly and discovered he wanted to discuss Japan. The instructions he had received from Moscow undoubtedly had been sent before the receipt of his message regarding my suggestion for a nonaggression treaty, he explained. His government had informed him that it was timely to conclude a treaty directed againt a revival of Japanese aggression, particularly in view of the manner in which terms of surrender were being carried out in Japan. He urged the establishment of a Control Council for Japan.

This was not the first time Molotov had raised the question of the control of Japan and it was not the last. I thought it was just an element in his campaign of counterattack. Nevertheless, we were placed in an embarrassing situation.

The British also had previously proposed the establishment of a Control Council for Japan. Australia was pressing hard for a greater share in the determination of occupation policies. Japan was not on the agenda for the London meeting. I wanted first to get the views of our occupation forces, and therefore was not prepared to discuss it. I said that the heads of government at Potsdam had instructed us to devote ourselves to the immediate task of drafting the five European treaties. I assured Mr. Molotov I would take up the Japanese question as soon as I returned home and would communicate with him.

While our conversation was in progress, Mr. Bevin walked in. It was obvious that Molotov had asked him to come in at noon and that he had arrived too early. Mr. Molotov made it clear that he wanted to continue the discussion with me, and Bevin withdrew. When, at noon, he rejoined us, Mr. Molotov immediately said that he wished to propose a reorganization of the Council of Foreign Ministers on the ground that the work was being retarded through an initial mistake which had in effect violated the decisions of the Berlin Conference. This mistake, he said, had been made on the opening day, September 11, when it had been decided that France and China could participate in the discussion of the peace treaties for Finland, Rumania, Bulgaria and Hungary. He took the position that France and China should absent themselves completely except when the council was discussing treaties for countries with which they had signed armistice terms as provided in the Berlin declaration. This would exclude China from all the European treaties and France from all except the German and the Italian treaties.

Mr. Bevin and I both asserted that our clear understanding of the

Berlin decision was that while France and China could not vote upon any proposal under the circumstances cited, they could certainly take part in the discussions, and that to ask them to withdraw now would be an unnecessary humiliation.

As soon as I could get away I put in a telephone call to the President. He was at the Jefferson Islands Club, so I outlined the situation to Admiral Leahy and asked him to communicate with the President as soon as possible and make sure the President's understanding of the Potsdam decision was the same as mine. Then I drafted a message to Generalissimo Stalin which I suggested the President send. It urged Stalin to agree that China and France could continue participating in discussions on all treaties but could vote only on treaties for those countries with which they had signed armistice terms. The message, which the President sent, asserted that Mr. Molotov's stand would create a bad impression throughout the world.

"It would be charged," it said, "that the three big powers are denying the other members of the council even an opportunity to present their views." It argued that this was "too small a matter to disrupt the council and delay progress toward peace and better understanding."

When Mr. Molotov presented his proposal at the late afternoon meeting of the council it was, of course, a shock to the other members. Our most earnest persuasion had no effect whatever on Mr. Molotov. Late that evening, I arranged to see Mr. Bidault who, I knew, was furious. I was afraid he would walk out of the council and deliver a public blast, which I was anxious to avoid while there was any chance of receiving a favorable reply from Generalissimo Stalin. Despite his justifiable anger, Mr. Bidault promised to co-operate, and he did.

Stalin's reply confirmed the position taken by Mr. Molotov against the participation of France and China. The conference had come to an impasse.

I made several efforts to compromise our differences. On September 28, at a meeting with Mr. Molotov and Mr. Bevin, I submitted a compromise which I hoped would work. In the first step, it gave in to Mr. Molotov's insistence that the first draft of the treaties should be prepared only by those countries which had signed surrender terms. This meant only Britain and the Soviet Union in the case of Finland; Britain, the Soviet Union and the United States for the Rumanian, Hungarian, and Bulgarian treaties, with France joining the group only for the Italian treaty. But, because of our interest in participation by the small states, we proposed a second step on which, I served notice, we would be most insistent.

It provided that, after the treaties had been drafted, all of them would be submitted to a peace conference that would include "the five members of the Security Council, together with all European members of the United Nations and all non-European members of the United Nations which supplied substantial military contingents against European members of the Axis."

This was so worded because Molotov took the position that the Soviet Union would not attend if Argentina were invited.

Mr. Molotov wanted three separate peace conferences. He said the Soviets could not be prepared to discuss the Italian treaty during 1945. When Mr. Bevin asked him why, he replied it would be easier for him to get ready if the United States agreed to an Allied Control Council for Japan! This was in addition to his earlier demand for recognition of the three Balkan governments as a prerequisite for an Italian peace treaty. It illustrated his technique. Because we wished to proceed with the peace treaty he would delay the treaty, hoping thereby to force us to agree to various proposals in which he was interested.

The following day, I made one more effort. I submitted an additional paragraph to our peace conference proposal. It provided that "after full and free discussion by the invited states the final approval of the terms of the treaties of peace will be made by those of the invited states which were at war with the enemy states in question."

This, I hoped, might satisfy Mr. Molotov's desire to restrict the number of states sharing in the final decisions. My hope was in vain.

We had come to the crossroads. We saw there would be no agreement unless we yielded to the Soviet demands. We were determined to yield no further. Yet we were reluctant to let the first test of the peace-making machinery result in complete breakdown.

The people were anxious for peace. The public at home did not have the clear view of Soviet ambitions that the President and I got at Potsdam, and which was revealed even more clearly here at London. We had refrained, after Potsdam, from publicly expressing our concern because of our desire to maintain friendly relations with our Russian Allies. The first meeting of the council would be a complete failure and I realized that the failure would be attributed to me.

Mr. Molotov had concluded that I was unfriendly to Russia, and he declared that our policy had changed since President Roosevelt's death. His attitude was understandable. At the first meeting in Teheran, his need was for a second front and for further lend-lease aid. Both of these requests were agreed to by President Roosevelt. At Yalta the President had agreed to the transfer to Russia of the territory east of the Curzon Line and to offset this had agreed that there should be some extension of the western boundary of Poland. He had agreed to the transfer of the Kuriles and the remainder of Sakhalin, and to the transfer by China of Port Arthur and of certain rights in Dairen. At Potsdam, we had agreed to support at the peace conference the claim of the Soviets for Königsberg and the valuable territory of East Prussia. We had recognized for the time being their *fait accompli* in eastern Germany, and had made a reparations settlement they then regarded as acceptable.

Now, at London, Mr. Molotov saw no chance of taking home any packages. He could not understand why we would not accept his interpretation that "friendship" between our governments required that we let the Soviets establish complete suzerainty over the Balkan states. As far as I was concerned, Christmas was over—it was now January 1, and we had many bills to pay. Instead of issuing more I.O.Us, I wanted to collect some we held. One of these I felt was the Yalta pledge on the treatment of the liberated states.

To make the sacrifice Mr. Molotov demanded, I was convinced, would constitute a defeat for the Allies and the principles we had espoused. Only by refusing to bow to Soviet domination could we establish sound relations for the future. Our attitude was a shock to them. At that time, immediately after the end of hostilities, the Soviet Union enjoyed the admiration and the good will of most of our people. The Soviet leaders knew of our people's strong desire for peace and they thought we would not dare let the conference fail.

Our stand at London required them to make a re-evaluation; it made them realize they could not force us to accept their position. It was, in a very real sense, a test of strength. Most of all, it was a test of whether we really believed in what we said about one world and our desire to build collective security, or whether we were willing to accept the Soviet preference for the simpler task of dividing the world into two spheres of influence.

Our fight to have France and China remain in the council was generally applauded, and our fight for the peace conference and for the right of the smaller states to participate in the peace won for us the good opinion of those states. And it forced the Soviets to begin to reorient their policy. Their shift toward collective action within the United Nations is slow and grudging; it is still in process, but it will continue only so long as and only to the extent that the Soviets are forced by world opinion to co-operate.

Before closing the conference we tried to reach agreement on the customary protocol enumerating the questions on which agreement had been reached. But Mr. Molotov refused to sign any agreement which was based on the decision of the council on September 11 making France and China participants in the discussion. In one of the several heated discussions on the protocol, Mr. Bevin referred to Mr. Molotov's denunciation of his own previous action as "the nearest thing to the Hitler theory I have ever heard."

The effect was electric. Mr. Molotov rose from the table and started angrily toward the door. He slowed down a little as he approached it and gave the blunt Briton a chance to call him back and withdraw the statement—which he did.

Five more meetings failed to bring any further progress. Actually, we had realized for several days that no agreement was possible, but Dr. Wang Shih Chieh had urged us to continue our efforts a little longer. The final day of the conference Dr. Wang was presiding. It soon became apparent to all of us that a Russian filibuster was under way. The only plausible reason for it was the fact that the next day I was scheduled to be chairman and Mr. Molotov seemed to feel it would be desirable to have the council break down while an American was presiding. During a recess I expressed this opinion to Dr. Wang. He said that since the sessions had been extended at his request, he was willing to assume the responsibility of presiding at the breakdown.

The session extended fruitlessly into the late evening hours and, finally, Dr. Wang picked up his gavel and declared:

"I happen to be the man who has prolonged the session until today. As I hear no request for another meeting, I declare the council adjourned. My earnest hope is that a future meeting of the council will be arranged by the governments concerned."

It was courageous action by Dr. Wang. It is typical of the statesmanship exhibited by Chinese diplomats wherever I have observed their work. China's difficulties certainly cannot be attributed to the caliber of its foreign representatives. From my experience, I know of no nation which has been more ably represented in international conferences than China.

As I look back on this London meeting now, about the only pleasant experience of the entire meeting that I can recall occurred during a state dinner given by Prime Minister Attlee. Despite the splendor of the setting and the friendly efforts of our host, the tense mood of our meetings pervaded the dinner. The speeches were short and restrained and were finished long before it was time for the dinner to end. During an especially long lull in the proceedings, Mr. Bevin began quietly to sing. "Ernest," I said, "you can't sing and neither can I, but I have a military aide here who can sing."

"If you have such a man, why don't you produce him?" he immediately responded.

"You won't like him," I joked, "because all he knows is Irish songs. It's too bad, though, that this is St. James Palace, because he is the best singer of Irish songs you ever heard."

"Go ahead," Bevin urged, so I told Colonel Hugh A. Kelly, an architect and old friend from Jersey City who was the security officer of the American delegation, that Mr. Bevin wished him to sing an Irish song.

He must have been taken aback, but he rose to the occasion splendidly. Soon, he was standing in the middle of the room and was directing the whole group of nearly a hundred, including the Prime Minister and Mr. Molotov, in a hearty "community sing." Mr. Molotov asked for a repeat performance of "Johnny Doughboy Found a Rose in Ireland."

Everyone had a wonderful time. The final and most conclusive evidence of this fact came as we were leaving. The dinner had been served by a butler who was as stiff, correct, and impassive as we always imagine British butlers to be. Colonel Kelly was getting into his coat when the butler suddenly bowed and said:

"Begging your pardon, sir, I wish to say that precedent was set here tonight. But all of us had a ripping good time."

With the break-up of the council I headed for the United States knowing I had to face criticism. The public's disappointment was quite understandable. Immediately upon my return, I delivered a report to the people by radio in which I presented as complete a picture as possible without stimulating a wave of disillusionment that would adversely affect our future relations with the Soviets. The public response was gratifying. I decided then that hereafter the people would have to be more fully informed if we were to maintain a firm position in international affairs with full public support.

I resolved, too, that the deadlock had to be broken; peace was too important to be lost by default.

The chief cause of our difficulties appeared to be our failure to agree on the recognition of Rumania and Bulgaria; so that problem was tackled. I wanted to make certain that our views on conditions in these countries were not based on erroneous or prejudiced information and therefore arranged for Mark Ethridge, editor of the Louisville *Courier-Journal*, an outstanding liberal, to visit the Balkans. I instructed State Department officials not to give him the information sent in by our representatives in these two countries, as I wanted him to approach his investigation with an open mind.

Simultaneously, we sought to demonstrate to the Soviets that, where efforts were made to comply with the spirit of the Yalta agreement, we would not withhold diplomatic recognition. Therefore, on October 20, we joined with the other three powers in recognizing the Provisional Government of Austria. And on November 2 we recognized the Provisional Government of Hungary.

In accordance with our Potsdam agreement, we initiated discussions on a revision of the Montreux Convention. On November 7, we sent a proposal on the control of the Dardanelles to the signatories, which stated our willingness to join in a multilateral guarantee of free access to the Straits and our opposition to a settlement confined to the Black Sea powers.

In addition, I accepted an invitation to speak before the New York *Herald Tribune* Forum on October 31, in which my message was directed largely toward the Kremlin. I emphasized our recognition of the importance to the Soviet Union of having friendly states as neighbors. I declared "America will never join any groups in those countries in hostile intrigues against the Soviet Union," but went on to say: "The policy of the good neighbor, unlike the institution of marriage, is not an exclusive arrangement. The best neighbors do not deny their neighbors the right to be friends with others."

The speech stressed the importance of the United Nations in promoting security, and then asserted: "We cannot have the kind of co-operation necessary for peace in a world divided into spheres of exclusive influence and special privilege." And I closed the speech with words I hoped the Kremlin would ponder: "There must be one world for all of us or there will be no world for any of us."

Meanwhile, I had asked Ambassador Harriman to request an interview with Generalissimo Stalin who was then on vacation in the Crimea. I wanted him to present to Stalin directly an amended proposal for a peace conference, setting forth the list of states to be invited, and to discuss the situation in Rumania and Bulgaria in the light of the steps we had taken to show our desire for co-operation.

The result was a revelation. When the Ambassador started to present our views on these European questions, Stalin interrupted to say that what he wanted to hear about was our view on the control of Japan. Mr. Harriman was as surprised as he was unprepared, and my surprise was even greater.

At London when Mr. Molotov had raised the question of Japan at the same time that he was killing days discussing procedural questions, we had concluded it was simply part of his war of nerves. Ambassador Harriman, who was present at London, agreed with me that the Balkan issue was the crucial one. Now, we suddenly realized we had been wrong. The remarkable performance that had led to the breakdown of the London Conference had been stimulated by the Russians' belief that they were not being consulted adequately by our officials in Japan. There was confirmation of the Russian attitude in the fact that the Soviet military representative in Tokyo, General Kuzma N. Derevyanko, had returned to Moscow.

Shortly after we had received this surprising information from Ambassador Harriman, Prime Minister Attlee and Prime Minister King came to Washington to confer with the President on procedure for controlling atomic energy. The agreement that emerged from this meeting injected still another important element into the already complex problem of international relations.

A few days later it was Thanksgiving Day and I was alone in my office, taking advantage of the holiday quiet to think over several problems. Suddenly I recalled that at Yalta it had been agreed that the three Foreign Ministers should meet every three months. So many things had taken place thereafter that there had been no need to schedule a specific meeting. A meeting of the three Foreign Ministers might get the peace-making machinery in motion again. I thought it was worth a try, so next morning a cable was sent to Mr. Molotov referring to the Yalta agreement that the three Secretaries should meet regularly and pointing out that they had met informally at San Francisco, Potsdam, and London, but not in Moscow. I suggested, therefore, that a meeting be held in the Russian capital. I felt sure that, Russian hospitality being what it is, the Soviet Government would extend the invitation and I believed that if we met in Moscow, where I would have a chance to talk to Stalin, we might remove the barriers to the peace treaties.

Of course, a proposal for a meeting under such circumstances was in violation of accepted diplomatic procedure. Many of the diplomats and columnists reminded me of that procedure and declared that no such conference should be held without first having diplomatic exchanges to assure agreement on the questions at issue. But in view of what had taken place, I knew there was no chance of reaching agreement by correspondence or through Ambassadors. The peace of the world was too important for us to be unwilling to take a chance on securing an agreement after full discussion. Furthermore, the first General Assembly of the United Nations would meet in January, and this would be our only chance personally to urge Stalin and Molotov to join with us in sponsoring our proposed resolution on atomic energy control.

So, against the advice of the diplomats and the columnists, I went to Moscow.

Chapter 6

Moscow Ends an Impasse

EVEN the journey to Moscow was tense. We were told that we could not fly over the Soviet Union without Russian navigators, and they met us on a snow-covered runway at Berlin on December 14. There was no usable airport between Berlin and Moscow, so our plane had to carry enough gas to make a return trip if an emergency developed. When we were supposed to be about sixty miles from Moscow, the navigators told Mr. Bohlen that they had lost their way. They were trying to identify farm homes projecting from the snow-covered earth. It would have been difficult under any circumstances, but it was virtually impossible in the heavy snow storm. They had us flying so low that I was afraid we would collide with the first sizable hill that came along.

"There are no mountains here," Bohlen told me.

"I could accept your assurance," I told him, "if only you could tell me where 'here' is."

The navigators and pilot asked for permission to "shop around" for ten additional minutes. The pilot said there was just enough gas to permit that and still have a margin for the return to Berlin. I agreed, but told them that Napoleon and Hitler had tried to reach Moscow and had failed and that I, too, would have no objection to an immediate retreat.

When the ten minutes were almost gone, the navigators sighted a familiar building. They knew then where we were, and in a few more minutes we were back on the route to Moscow. Even then we landed at the wrong airport, but no airport has ever looked so good to me.

Russian hospitality, however, was equal to the challenge of the weather. The officials of the Foreign Office had foreseen the possibility of our landing at a different airport and had divided the group of official greeters, so, although Mr. Molotov was not on hand, we were received with appropriate ceremonies.

On our drive to Spasso House, the home of the American Ambassador, the snow storm prevented me from seeing much of the city. I was disappointed, because, as one feels about all places that are difficult to get to, I was curious about Moscow. But I consoled myself with the thought that I would get to see it later. As usual, I was an optimist. I doubt if anyone else has spent even a fraction of the time I did in Moscow and has seen so little of the city. Besides Spasso House, where we worked and managed to get a few hours of sleep each night; Spridinovka House, where the council held its sessions; and the Kremlin, where we had our meetings with Stalin, the only other thing I saw in Moscow was the Opera House where the Foreign Ministers were entertained by the Soviet Government.

The meeting opened at 5:00 P.M., December 16, and at my suggestion Mr. Molotov was made chairman. In recognition of Generalissimo Stalin's concern over the situation in the Far East, I had suggested including on the agenda proposals for the creation of a Far Eastern Commission to function in Washington and of an Allied Council to be located in Tokyo; a paper on the creation of a unified administration for Korea as a prelude to the establishment of an independent Korean government; and a review of American policy in China, including the disarming of Japanese troops in North China. We agreed also that there would be informal discussions on the Soviet occupation of Manchuria, the withdrawal of British troops from Indonesia and from Greece, and the withdrawal of Soviet troops from Iran. The remainder of the agenda included in accordance with my original suggestions, proposals for a United Nations Commission to consider the control of atomic energy, the reconvening of the Council of Foreign Ministers and the resumption of the work of their deputies, and, conditions permitting, the recognition of the present governments of Rumania and Bulgaria. At Mr. Molotov's request, the first item on our list, atomic energy, was placed at the end of the agenda. It was just his way of informing me that he regarded the subject as one of little importance.

Our proposal on peace conference procedure was based on our last position at London in which we had acceded to the Russian stand on the preparation of first drafts but had insisted that these drafts be submitted to a peace conference. The only change was in the final paragraph. It now provided that, after the peace conference had considered the draft treaties and made recommendations, the final drafts would be prepared by the states that had signed the armistice terms; in other words, Britain, the Soviet Union, the United States and France for the Italian treaty, with France dropping out for the Rumanian, Bulgarian, and Hungarian treaties, and both France and the United States dropping out for the Finnish treaty.

This final paragraph was in accordance with a proposal Stalin had advanced in his vacation meeting with Ambassador Harriman. We had accepted it reluctantly but we knew it was the only way we could get the Soviets to agree to call a peace conference.

The following day Mr. Molotov presented his counterproposal which failed to advance the situation beyond the London stand of the Soviet delegation. It provided that at the peace conference each treaty could be considered only by those countries which actually had waged war against that particular enemy. As a practical matter, this meant that there really would be a separate conference for each treaty. For the Bulgarian and Hungarian treaties only five countries would be qualified, under Mr. Molotov's definition, even to take part in peace conference discussions. They would be the Big Three, Yugoslavia and Greece for the Bulgarian treaty, with Czechoslovakia replacing Greece for the Hungarian treaty. Discussions on the Rumanian treaty would be limited to the Big Three, and only the Soviet Union and Britain would consider the Finnish treaty. In the case of Italy, the participants would be the Big Three, France, Greece, Canada, Yugoslavia, Australia, New Zealand, South Africa, Brazil and Ethiopia—a maximum of twelve states.

This was clearly so unacceptable that I simply proposed that we pass to the next item on the agenda, and waited until the next day when a private conversation was arranged between Mr. Molotov, Mr. Vyshinski, Ambassador Harriman and myself. Then I frankly expressed my disappointment at the Soviet proposal, especially since our paper had been prepared with regard for the views expressed by Generalissimo Stalin in his conversation with Mr. Harriman. Mr. Molotov protested that his proposal corresponded exactly with the Generalissimo's statements. Mr. Harriman then outlined his understanding of the conversation, pointing out that on the first day of his talks with Stalin, the Generalissimo had presented views in accord with the current Soviet proposal. On the second day, however, Stalin had agreed that there should be one conference, at which states included on a list we had presented would have an opportunity to present their views—provided the appropriate members of the Council of Foreign Ministers retained the right to "determine the final peace terms."

Mr. Molotov was willing to concede the right of the United States to express its opinions in connection with the Finnish treaty, but no further progress was made.

When we met on December 18, I immediately presented a list of states eligible for invitation to a peace conference under the terms of our proposal. This list included "all members of the United Nations which actively waged war with substantial military forces against the European members of the Axis." There were twenty-one.

"The war was one war," I stressed. "As partners in a common venture each of the Allies served where it could serve best. China performed a great service by holding the Japanese and giving the United States an opportunity to furnish more aid to those engaged in Europe. Norwegian shipping helped to supply our air force in its bombing operations. These states should have the opportunity to come to a peace conference and present their views. This would do no harm and would give the world confidence in the fairness of the Big Three."

Mr. Bevin supported me, declaring it would be unjust if Norway, for example, which had lost one-third of its seamen in the war, should be excluded from taking part in the peace. A long meeting brought no results, so we decided to try one of our "informal" meetings at which attendance is restricted. Mr. Molotov referred to my list and said India would have to be dropped—"it is not an independent state; it has no Foreign Office of its own," and, if India were to come, the three Baltic Soviet republics—Latvia, Lithuania and Estonia—would have to be invited. Mr. Bevin, of course, could not agree to exclude India, which had sent large contingents of troops to the European theater.

That night, Ambassador Harriman, Mr. Bohlen and I went to the Kremlin for the first of our meetings with Generalissimo Stalin. I wanted to present my views to Stalin before Molotov took positions from which he would find it difficult to withdraw. I wanted to see the man who had the power to decide.

The Kremlin, of course, has a reputation as a place of mystery and, being an appreciative reader of good mysteries, I looked forward to my first journey into its inner chambers. Before we reached Stalin's office we were ushered through three successive chambers, each with several identical doors. I had just begun to ponder on how carefully Stalin was guarded when it suddenly occurred to me that any foreigner might get a similar impression on a visit to the White House. When one goes to see President Truman, there is a large outer hallway to pass through. Then one is escorted into the waiting room presided over by Bill Simmons, the tactful White House doorkeeper. After that, one goes through the office of the President's secretary, Matthew J. Connelly, and finally reaches the President's oval office. The principal apparent difference was that in the Kremlin everyone was in uniform.

Stalin's greeting was businesslike, but cordial. After presenting a personal letter from the President, I assured him of our belief that there were no conflicts between us we could not solve.

"Our only desire," I said, "is to live in peace, increase the comfort of the American people, and help our friends abroad restore the damages of war through economic assistance."

Stalin replied that he fully shared this desire, and we agreed that in view of our different customs and traditions it was understandable that we should sometimes interpret the same question differently. He volunteered the belief that so far we had succeeded quite well in settling our differences.

I then sketched the discussions with Mr. Molotov on our proposed list of states, which I noticed he had before him. I pointed out that if India and the three Baltic states were admitted to the peace conference "this would mean that Britain would be there with five dominions and the Soviet Union would be there with five republics.

"It would be difficult for me to explain such a decision in the United States," I told him. "I would have to add to the list five states, including my own state of South Carolina!"

Molotov interjected that even if India were dropped, Britain would still have four dominions represented.

"The Soviet Union and the United States are strong enough to stand alone, and I am sure Mr. Molotov can adequately protect the interests of the three Soviet republics at the conference," I replied. "We have made important concessions in this matter of the peace treaties, and it is not too much to ask that our list for the conference be approved."

Stalin said he could see no concession on our part since the list was identical with the one Mr. Harriman had shown him in October. I explained that the concessions related to the preparation and final approval of the treaties rather than to the list. He contended that the Armistice in each case had been signed by those who had shed blood in the war against that country, and that they should be the ones to sign the peace. Belgium and Holland, for example, had not fought against Rumania and Italy. He then recounted the contributions of the Baltic republics and offered to accept our list with the addition of these states. He was sure, he said, that we would soon have to recognize these republics, but he realized it would be embarrassing for the United States if the United Kingdom and the Soviet Union had six votes while the United States had but one. This situation, he said, must be met. One way was to give the United States six votes. He recalled that he had agreed with President Roosevelt at Yalta that the United States could have two additional votes in the General Assembly of the United Nations if we wished.

I concluded he would not want to reverse Molotov's decision that night but might do so later, so I urged him to give the matter further thought in the hope that we could find a solution. He agreed to do so.

The next afternoon, Mr. Molotov excused himself from the conference table. When he returned, he came to me and said that the Generalissimo had just telephoned to inform me that he would accept our list of states.

The conference then quickly agreed that a peace conference should be held in Paris not later than May 1. But this agreement was followed by a long wrangle over who should sign the peace treaties when they were concluded, and whether China and France should be invited to concur in this Moscow agreement or should merely be informed of it. We finally compromised by both informing *and* inviting concurrence!

The day before Christmas, we received China's favorable reply. There was no word from the French. I was anxious that, as a Christmas gift, the world should know that a peace conference would be held. Unsuccessfully I tried to reach Mr. Bidault by telephone. I learned he was very busy—getting married to his charming wife. Finally, I suggested we simply announce our own agreement and state that France and China had been invited to concur. I had suggested Paris as the site of the conference but we deleted mention of it pending a French reply.

And so, on Christmas morning, 1945, people throughout the world learned that five months of negotiation had at last brought agreement on the holding of a conference to help restore "peace on earth."

The solution we reached was not ideal, but it did assure the small states an opportunity to be heard. While the larger states were not to be bound by the recommendations of the peace conference we were in a position, by exercising the unanimity rule, to refuse a final treaty which arbitrarily rejected the recommendations of the peace conference. Experience proved the value of the peace conference, and the record shows that practically all of its recommendations adopted by a two-thirds vote were written into the treaties.

With this agreement reached, we turned again to the question of Rumania and Bulgaria. On the third day of the conference I had called on Mr. Molotov and presented to him a copy of the report Mark Ethridge had submitted on Rumania and Bulgaria. We had intended to publish it, I told him, but instead we had held it for discussion, in the hope that Mr. Ethridge's findings furnished a basis for an understanding.

Even before looking at it, Mr. Molotov deprecated the report, saying that Ethridge, of course, knew I was opposed to recognizing these governments and therefore must have been influenced in his judgment.

I pointed out to him the instructions I had given Mr. Ethridge, which were repeated at the opening of the report, and which made it clear he was a completely free observer. After an independent, unprejudiced investigation Mr. Ethridge found not only that these governments failed to meet the Yalta Declaration, I told him, but that they were authoritarian, dominated by one party, and forcibly excluded from representation large democratic segments of the population. I asked him particularly to note that in Rumania Mr. Ethridge had found former pro-Fascist collaborators and even pro-Nazi Iron Guardists occupying key government posts.

Mr. Molotov had made quite a point of the fact that elections had been held in Bulgaria, and I asked him to note Mr. Ethridge's comment that these elections signified nothing and that Ethridge had, in fact, been told a month in advance how they would come out. As for Rumania, Mr. Ethridge merely confirmed what both of us knew about Mr. Vyshinski's activities and the repressions which had followed the installation of the Groza government.

I asked him to give special consideration to Mr. Ethridge's recommendations that the Soviet Union join with us in an agreement similar to those reached on other former enemy countries in eastern Europe.

After giving Molotov two days to consider the Ethridge report, I submitted papers to the Foreign Ministers suggesting action to be taken toward each of these countries. These papers proposed, with variations necessitated by differing conditions, that the three powers join in suggesting a reorganization of the present governments to include all leading democratic elements. Mr. Molotov strongly objected. He contended that nothing could be done in Bulgaria as elections had taken place which the Soviet government considered free and unfettered. Any interference after these elections, he maintained, would be greatly resented by the Bulgarian people. He dismissed the opposition to the government with the observation that opposition parties always are dissatisfied. As for Rumania, he contended that King Michael's request for three-power assistance in establishing a government would never have been made except at the instigation of the American and British representatives there. This, I assured him, was untrue, but he chose not to believe me. The Ethridge report he also dismissed, saying it merely reiterated my views and could have been written without the trip ever having been made.

Once again it appeared that the only hope was to take up the matter directly with the Generalissimo, and I went to see him the following night. The engagement was set for 10 P.M. This is just about the time I usually go to bed, but is about the time the Generalissimo starts to work.

We first discussed the question of withdrawing all foreign troops from Iran, and then I expressed a desire to talk about the Balkans "as I have been having a difficult time with Mr. Molotov on this subject."

Stalin smiled broadly and said that this was unexpected news.

"It is terribly important to settle this matter and to proceed with the peace treaties so that we can be in a position to render them economic assistance," I asserted. Then I quickly outlined the situation. I concluded by saying that if we could reach no agreement I would be compelled to publish the Ethridge report.

Stalin replied that if I felt it necessary to publish the Ethridge report he would ask Mr. Ehrenberg, who also was an impartial man and had visited these countries, to publish his views.

This would be most unfortunate, I told him, as the two reports would tend to separate rather than unite our two countries on this question. I expressed my confidence that with his help and understanding we could find representatives of the democratic parties who were also friendly toward the Soviet Union.

Given a mutual desire to settle the problem, means could be found to do so, he said, and then referred to accusations in our press that the Red army had exerted pressure on the Bulgarian elections. This, he declared, was untrue and he pointed to Hungary, where, despite the presence of Soviet troops, the election had not resulted in a Communist victory. The alleged action, he stressed, was unworthy of the Soviet Union which asked only that near-by states should not be hostile. This did not mean that only Communist parties could be regarded as friendly, he said, but he asked me to remember that during the war Hungarian troops had reached the Don River and Rumanian troops had reached the Volga.

Since elections had been held in Bulgaria it was impossible to ask for a reorganization there, but he finally agreed it would be possible to advise them to include in the government two truly representative members of two important political parties not then represented. He stressed that there could be no pressure—merely advice. He assented to my suggestion that the advice should come from the Soviet Union. I made it clear that we would reserve the right to decide whether necessary conditions had been created to warrant recognition. In the case of Rumania, he conceded it would be less difficult to make changes. After considerable discussion it was agreed to send a commission, composed of the American and British Ambassadors in Moscow and Mr. Vyshinski, to Bucharest to work out with the government the addition of representatives of other parties, and to insure the restoration and maintenance of civil liberties. Stalin asked me to convey his acceptance of this proposal, which I originally had made in London, to Mr. Bevin. I agreed to inform the British Foreign Minister and added jokingly that even though we were supposed to have a bloc with Britain I had not informed Bevin about my proposal to Mr. Molotov for this meeting in Moscow as soon as I should have.

The Generalissimo smiled and, in the same spirit, replied that this obviously was only a cloak to hide the reality of the bloc.

The next day I presented to the meeting the proposals regarding Rumania and Bulgaria which we believed Stalin had agreed to. However, we immediately entered into an all-day argument with Messrs. Molotov and Vyshinski over the wording of them. The argument was still under way when we adjourned for the Christmas Eve dinner given us by the Generalissimo.

At dinner I was seated on Stalin's right and Bevin was on his left. I told him that our newspapers had represented him as being ill and that I was happy to see him looking so well. He said his recent vacation had been his first one in many years and that he realized, after the strain of the war, that he was not so young as he once was. He had attended to many important matters while away, he continued, but he had rested also and now felt better than he had in years. He was determined, he said, to take a vacation every year.

In all sincerity I proposed a toast to him, expressing the hope that he would continue to take vacations for many years to come and continue to enjoy good health. I added: "whom war hath joined together, let not peace put asunder." I thought it was good, but from the Russian's lack of appreciation, I concluded they were all bachelors or, in any event, were not familiar with our marriage ceremony. I felt sure they did not dissent from the sentiment.

My talks with the Generalissimo that night, like those during the two earlier interviews, were marked by their encouraging combination of frankness and cordiality. One of the issues on which I placed particular emphasis was the situation in Iran.

At our first meeting on December 19, I told him we were concerned about the events in Iran because of the pledge President Roosevelt had entered into with him and Prime Minister Churchill at Teheran in 1943. In that pledge, the three leaders recognized "the assistance which Iran has given in the prosecution of the war against the common enemy, particularly by facilitating transportation of supplies from overseas to the Soviet Union." The declaration promised that "any economic problem confronting Iran at the close of hostilities should receive full consideration" along with those of other members of the United Nations. It expressly declared that they were "at one with the Government of Iran in their desire for the maintenance of the independence, sovereignty and territorial integrity of Iran."

Developments within Iran prior to the Moscow meeting indicated that the pledge was in danger of being broken. The Iranian Government had protested that when it dispatched 1,500 troops toward the province of Azerbaijan to quell what the Iranians said was an insurrection encouraged by foreign sources, the force had been stopped en route and ordered by the Red army to turn back. The Iranian Government thereupon asked for the withdrawal of all foreign troops. We promptly issued an order to the remaining American troops to evacuate and I sent a message to the Soviet Union and the United Kingdom urging that they take similar action.

The Iranian protest was still pending and I told the Generalissimo that, unless we fulfilled the Teheran Declaration, Iran very likely would place its complaint before the forthcoming meeting of the United Nations in London. As a signatory of the declaration, the United States would feel obliged to support Iran's right to be heard. We felt it would be difficult to explain how the Soviet Army of 30,000 would have been endangered, as they had asserted, by the presence of 1,500 Iranian soldiers.

Stalin outlined what he termed "the pertinent facts" in the matter. The Baku oil fields in the south of Russia lay close to the border and this created a special problem. These fields had to be safeguarded against any possible hostile action by Iran against the Soviet Union, and no confidence could be placed in the Iranian Government. Saboteurs might be sent to the Baku oil fields to set them on fire, he continued. Since the Soviet Union had a right, by treaty, to maintain troops in Iran until March 15, it did not want to withdraw before that date. At that time, he said, it would be necessary to examine the situation and see whether or not it was possible to evacuate the soldiers. The decision would depend upon the conduct of the Iranian Government. He pointed out that a 1921 treaty with Iran gave the Soviet Union the right to send troops into northern Iran if there was a possible danger from an outside source.

I told him I was greatly surprised to learn that he considered the Iranian Government hostile in view of his declaration at Teheran, and in view of the report made to me by General Connolly, the commanding general of our forces in Iran, that the Government had co-operated well with both the Red Army and the American forces in moving supplies through to the Soviet Union. While he had a right to maintain his troops in Iran until March, I pointed out that he was not required to do so. The United States, incidentally, had always regarded March 2 as the deadline date rather than March 15, as cited by Stalin.

Stalin told me that the Soviet Union had no designs, territorial or otherwise, against Iran and would withdraw its troops as soon as they felt secure about the Baku oil fields.

The more I thought about Generalissimo Stalin's excuse for retaining troops in Iran, the less confidence I had in the Soviet position. It was absurd to claim, as he had, that the Red Army of 30,000 well-trained and fully equipped troops must stop the poorly trained and inadequately equipped Iranian force of 1,500 from marching toward Azerbaijan on the public highway because it feared a disturbance would be created. His statement that he feared saboteurs from little Iran would come over into the Soviet Union and set fire to the Baku oil fields seemed an equally poor excuse for maintaining a large army inside the borders of Iran. And his admission that the question of withdrawal would be examined on the evacuation date showed that our worries about his fulfilling the Teheran Declaration were justified. Consequently, I determined to make another effort to get him to understand our position regarding that obligation.

Iran was the first thing I took up with him at our second meeting. I told him I was "seriously disturbed" at the prospect that the issue would be raised at the first meeting of the United Nations. It was exceedingly important, I added, that the great nations keep their pledges to the smaller powers. If Iran raised the issue at London it would be unfortunate, I warned him, because, under the facts as we knew them and in view of our solemn pledge, we would be forced to support the position of Iran. The United States would greatly regret having to oppose the Soviet Union in the very first meeting of the United Nations and I hoped, therefore, that we could take action at Moscow that would forestall this possibility.

We discussed Mr. Bevin's proposal that a Three-Power Commission be appointed to go to Iran and seek a solution to the numerous aspects of the problem. He was noncommittal regarding the Bevin proposal, and I said once again that we hoped no action would be taken in Iran that would cause a difference between us. To this, the Generalissimo replied: "We will do nothing that will make you blush."

On Christmas Day, the council resumed the argument on the Balkan and Iranian problems. We finally reached substantial agreement on Rumania but were at a complete impasse on Bulgaria. Molotov and Vyshinski argued for a draft stating that the Cabinet could include only people loyal to the existing government. Mr. Bevin and I pointed out that this wording could exclude all prodemocratic elements except those that had sworn allegiance to the government we were seeking to broaden; in practice, it could be used to nullify our agreement. Mr. Bevin pointed out that he had been fighting Mr. Churchill for thirty years and that, under such a ruling, he could not now be in the British Government.

The afternoon of December 25, I had a private conversation with Mr. Molotov. Among other things, he said he thought that "the British proposal on Iran in general is acceptable." He asked for my views. I told him I would accept it because I was particularly anxious to avoid having the Iranian question raised in the General Assembly. When the conference met that night, Molotov offered several amendments to Mr. Bevin's proposal. Bevin accepted all except one which left in doubt the date for the withdrawal of troops. He claimed that that date had been fixed by treaty and that the proposed amendment, therefore, was unnecessary.

In view of our private conversation I thought Molotov would finally agree to Bevin's language. However, when we met the afternoon of December 26, it was clear that the Soviet High Command had changed its attitude. Molotov announced that the Iranian case was not properly on the agenda and "cannot be considered." Bevin complained that he had accepted practically every amendment the Soviets had proposed. He said he had understood, as a result of a conversation he had had with Stalin, that the Soviet Union would agree to his proposal.

"It is sufficient that views have been exchanged," Molotov replied. "No decisions have been reached. The question was not on the agenda and there is no need to mention it in the communiqué."

"What is my next step?" Bevin asked.

"You know that well," Molotov answered.

Bevin, with some feeling, said he thought he understood the situation and greatly regretted it.

The heated arguments on Bulgaria and Iran were jeopardizing our agreements on other issues, so I suggested that we resume, in London, consideration of the pending problems. Members of the staff were asked to prepare the protocol to be signed by the three Foreign Ministers. This was completed about 2:30 in the morning and in a formal meeting the protocols in two languages were presented for signature. That meant there were nine copies that each of us had to sign. Mr. Bevin signed first and the papers were passed to me. After signing, I arose to say good-by to a member of the British delegation seated near me.

Suddenly Mr. Molotov sent one of his aides to me and asked that I return to the table. He said that his staff had, "by mistake," included the Soviet document on Bulgaria in the Russian text of the protocol. He asked if, after all, it could not be accepted. We promptly said it could not. He then suggested that we might combine the first half of my proposal with the second half of his draft. I told him we could not do things by "halves"; that since he had come halfway, he should accept the American proposal. To my amazement, he did.

Mr. Bevin then facetiously asked him to look in his pocket to see if he could not find another "mistake" that would satisfactorily end our discussions on Iran. In good humor, Mr. Molotov said he regretted that he could not. The protocol was then amended for signature.

It was 3:30 A.M. December 27. I was dead tired; all of us were. Mr. Molotov and Mr. Vyshinski probably were less exhausted than the rest of us because they customarily begin their working day at noon and often extend it past midnight. They were more accustomed to a steady succession of late hours than an American who long ago had learned that his constituents expected him to be at his office at nine in the morning. Our airplane was scheduled to take off at 7:30. I packed, had a short nap, talked to the American newspaper and radio correspondents, and got to the airport on time. It seemed terribly early, but Messrs. Molotov and Vyshinski were there to see us off.

The man who, three nights later, sat before a radio microphone in Washington to report to the American people was far happier than the one who had sat before the same microphone upon his return from London only fifteen weeks earlier. The proposal for a peace conference, rejected at London, had been accepted at Moscow, with the participating states selected in accordance with the American list. After ten months' experience in trying to secure Soviet compliance with the Yalta agreement on the Balkans, we fully appreciated the difference between promise and performance. But Ambassador Harriman, Chip Bohlen and others, who had been living with this problem, felt we had made progress in securing a much more specific agreement than that made at Yalta.

On the question of Japanese policy, which had been an important factor in Soviet obstinacy at London, we had won full approval of the plans President Truman and I had prepared prior to my departure for Moscow. We had secured agreement on the presence of our troops in China and had stimulated a restatement by Stalin of his support of the National Government of China. Coming at a time when General Marshall was beginning his effort to bring about a unified and democratic China, this seemed an important gain.

And on the subject of atomic energy, which I had expected to make difficulties, the Soviet Union had agreed to join in sponsoring, with no material change, the resolution previously approved by the United Kingdom and Canada for the creation of a United Nations Atomic Energy Commission.

The only important question on the conference agenda not resolved was the proposed appointment of a commission to try to solve our common problems in Iran. I was therefore surprised and disappointed to find a portion of the press criticizing our agreements as "appeasement." Some of the criticism I recognized as personal in character. Some of it came from people who obviously had been misled in their thinking—largely as a result of Soviet censorship of the news from Moscow on the conference. But much of the criticism, unfortunately, came from people so unreasonably anti-Soviet in their views that they would regard any agreement with Russia on any subject as appeasement.

No one who had shared my experience at Potsdam, London and Moscow doubted that there were still many trying days ahead. But we did face the new year of 1946 with greater hope as a result of the Moscow Conference. Perhaps the rest of the world did too. I hoped so.

Chapter 7

London Again and Paris Twice

FIVE days after returning from Moscow I had to fly back to London for the first session of the General Assembly of the United Nations. My primary concern was the adoption of the resolution to establish a United Nations Commission on the control of atomic energy, and I announced before leaving Washington that I would return as soon as the Assembly acted on this issue.

But life in London was not to be so simple. The problems of Moscow followed us there. Ambassador Harriman came to London to report that the committee composed of Mr. Vyshinski, Sir Archibald Clark Kerr and himself had made no progress in Bucharest toward a reorganization of the Groza government. The efforts to broaden the Bulgarian Government were equally unproductive. And the problem of Iran was becoming more acute.

Iran's representative in London called on me and asked whether he should file his country's complaint against the continued presence of Soviet troops in Iran and interference in Iranian affairs with the Security Council. He said Mr. Bevin had declined to advise him and he therefore hoped that I would. I told him that I, too, hesitated to offer advice, that the Security Council was just being organized, that it had not even adopted rules of procedure, that only the most urgent matters should be placed before the Security Council while it was being organized. However, I told him I would gladly listen to the facts of his case, give the matter consideration, and advise him the following day. Without waiting, he filed his complaint. The Soviet delegation conceived the idea that Mr. Bevin had inspired the Iranian representative to do this. From the latter's statements to me, I am sure the Russians were mistaken. Nevertheless, because of their suspicion, the Soviet delegation two days later filed a complaint against the presence of British troops in Greece; the Ukrainian delegation filed a similar charge against the British troops in Indonesia. The debates that ensued were acrimonious and created a situation conducive to anything but agreement.

This was the atmosphere that prevailed when the deputies of the Foreign Ministers gathered at Lancaster House, a few blocks away from the United Nations meetings, on January 18, 1946, to begin the actual drafting of the peace treaties.

With the unanimous adoption by the General Assembly of the atomic energy resolution on January 24, I left for home. But already there were indications the deputies would encounter the same barriers that had blocked the Ministers' agreement at the September meeting. At our suggestion, the Italian treaty was taken up first, not only because the Potsdam agreement had named Italy as first, but also because the question of France's right to take part in discussions on the others remained unsettled.

March arrived and the deputies were still as far apart as ever on the three main issues: reparations, the colonies, and the Italian-Yugoslav border. On the latter issue, there had been at least some action. A commission of experts was appointed to visit the area with instructions to determine a frontier that would (a) leave a minimum number of Italians and Yugoslavs under alien rule and (b) take into account local geographic and economic factors. Our able deputy, James C. Dunn, appointed Philip E. Mosely to represent us on this commission; the commission arrived in Trieste on March 9.

The deputies then turned to a study of draft treaties for the three Balkan states, submitted by the Soviet delegation. At this point, the French deputy tactfully withdrew. The Soviet drafts were very brief documents; in fact, little more than an extension of the armistice terms. Nevertheless, some progress was made toward securing agreement to the amendments offered by the British and the United States.

At Moscow we had agreed there would be a peace conference "after the completion of the drafts" and "before May 1." As the weeks went by, the deputies reached agreement on so few clauses it was clear that drastic action would have to be taken if we were to keep our promises to the world. I sent a message to the other members proposing that the council meet in an effort to speed up the work of the deputies and suggested that this meeting be held in Paris. We had agreed that Paris should be the site of the peace conference and I was eager to have the council meet there also. I was reasonably sure that in Paris, where the Communists were very active in French politics, Mr. Molotov would be much less obdurate in opposing French participation in discussions on all treaties. The earliest date we could agree on was April 25.

At the first session, Mr. Bidault proposed rules of procedure that provided for the participation of all four delegations in the discussions of all five treaties. Although he had opposed such an arrangement for months as a matter of vital principle, Mr. Molotov quickly agreed. This, however, marked about the limit of his concessions.

The agenda was the subject of our first disagreement. Mr. Bidault was eager to discuss questions involving Germany and I had submitted the United States' draft treaty for the disarmament and demilitarization of Germany for a period of twenty-five years. In addition, we proposed that special deputies begin work on a peace treaty for Austria. Mr. Molotov was willing to discuss Germany, but he dismissed our treaty proposal as wholly inadequate and flatly refused even to put the question of Austria on the agenda.

I saw that if we were going to make any progress Mr. Molotov and I must try to get together. So I invited him, Mr. Vyshinski and Mr. Pavlov, the interpreter, to dine with Mr. Cohen, Mr. Bohlen and me.

Although our dinner was to be a quiet private affair, the constant effort made to protect Mr. Molotov, as well as Generalissimo Stalin, was not relaxed. The afternoon of the dinner, Soviet security officers came to the United States delegation office in the Hotel Meurice and asked to be shown the suite where we were to dine. My secretary, Miss Cassie Connor, gladly showed them through the apartment which Mrs. Byrnes and I occupied. As no criticisms were made, we assumed they were entirely satisfied with the arrangements.

That evening when the guests arrived, the security officer who accompanies Mr. Molotov wherever he goes was with them. Even though we had an American MP at each end of the hall, Mr. Molotov's guard took his station in the hall where he had a view of all doors to the five-room suite, which included my offices.

Mrs. Byrnes and Miss Connor left the apartment to go down to the hotel dining room for dinner. The guard evidently paid little attention to those leaving the apartment because, when they returned and Mrs. Byrnes tried to enter the bedroom, he raised his hands and shook his head. His gestures, in any language, meant that she could not enter. In words which would have been understood in South Carolina or Washington she insisted that this was her room, and that she had left it only a short while before. But the gentleman was firm—she could not enter. The ladies finally retreated to the office to plan a campaign to capture the bedroom. They enlisted the help of the Army by calling upon one of the MPs stationed in the hall. He spoke no more Russian than they did, but the uniform apparently convinced the Soviet guard that the ladies could be trusted in the apartment. His orders no doubt had been that no one could enter the suite. With the help of the MP, another crisis in Russo-American relations was avoided.

Probably Mr. Molotov is neither aware of nor responsible for the somewhat unusual methods of the guards assigned to him. These security officers are perhaps directed by an organization similar to our Secret Service. I suspect Mr. Molotov sometimes shared my own desire to escape the constant surveillance to which all of us were subjected—by our host government if not by our own.

In London, Scotland Yard assigned Captain Black, a most efficient officer, to watch me and he never let me get out of the hotel without him. In Paris, an English-speaking plain-clothes officer, René Houvenaghel, was always on the job. I got away from him only once—and that was after a particularly depressing meeting during the peace conference. Mrs. Byrnes, who shared my depression, suggested that we take a walk. I was not only depressed, I was tired of being watched. And, over Mrs. Byrnes' objections, we slipped out a side door of our hotel to escape detection. I thought we had escaped our security officer and that idea alone tended to raise my spirits. After we had walked half an hour I happened to look back—there was Houvenaghel. An employee of the hotel had reported our leaving and he had followed us. With both "the law" and my wife against me, I did the only thing a man could do under the circumstances: I confessed my guilt and promised not to offend again.

Many times when the security officer was with me I felt in much greater danger than I was that night. Every day we were driven to the meetings; our car traveled behind two motorcycle policemen, who raced through Paris traffic at fifty miles an hour, each of them blowing a tiny whistle. Paris streets are crowded with bicyclists and every one of them dislikes traffic policemen and has utter contempt for a whistle. I tried to get the escorts to go slower. But they persisted in dashing madly through red lights. To protect ourselves we had to keep up with them, even though our tenseness increased with every jump in the speedometer.

I have digressed from the dinner with Mr. Molotov, but it was just about as relaxed as one of those rides through Parisian traffic. Before we reached the dining room, Mr. Molotov began to complain bitterly about the attitude of the United States in the Iranian case, which had been argued in the Security Council at New York since our last meeting. He charged that our actions were not those of a friend and that his government was the victim of an "anti-Soviet campaign" in which the Iranian case and the Security Council were being used to advance an offensive. I first reminded him of the efforts made at Moscow, both with him and with Generalissimo Stalin, to deal with the Iranian situation. These talks had had the specific intent of preventing the Iranian case from being brought before the United Nations. At that time I had clearly stated it would be necessary for us to oppose the Soviet Government if the case did become a Security Council issue. Mr. Cohen and I outlined in detail the actual course of events in the Security Council, and stressed that, once Soviet troops had remained in Iran beyond the treaty date, it was no longer possible to arrange matters privately; the issue then had to be met in the light of public opinion.

Because the dinner opened on this note of discord, it is not surprising that our later discussions of the treaties, and the United States' proposals about Germany and Austria, met with little success. The next morning I went over the situation with Vandenberg and Connally—we agreed there was little prospect for early agreement on the issues before the council.

The council, however, quickly agreed on the limitation of the Italian Navy, the disposition of surplus naval units, three minor rectifications of the French-Italian border, and on a committee to study a fourth French-proposed change in the Tenda-Briga area. Then we came to the question of the colonies. Mr. Molotov advanced a new proposal: two-power trusteeships with the Soviet Union and Italy together administering Tripolitania. This ran into strong British opposition and Mr. Bevin made a counterproposal that all of Libya, including Tripolitania and Cyrenaica, should be given immediate independence. The French joined the Russians in opposing this suggestion. Finally, Mr. Molotov said he would accept the French proposal for Italian trusteeship. We continued our stand for a collective trusteeship but later said we would accept the French proposal if the others were in agreement and if there were a definite promise to give the colonies their independence in ten years. The French could not agree to this, and the British would not approve the French proposal. So I announced that we would stand by our collective trusteeship plan.

The discussions on the transfer of the Dodecanese to Greece continued to produce no results as Mr. Molotov insisted settlement of this question had to await the disposition of the colonies.

Our longest and most difficult hours were spent on the question of the Italian-Yugoslav border. The four-man commission that had gone to the province of Venezia Giulia spent four weeks there, and then had submitted four individual recommendations. The Soviet representative's recommendations corresponded closely to the claims of the Yugoslavs. The boundary lines proposed by the American, British and French representatives were identical in the north but they separated going southward. The French line, which represented roughly a compromise between our line and the Soviet line, did not take certain geographic and economic considerations into account, but it did appear to balance the two minority groups most equitably. The available population statistics were quite unreliable but our best estimates showed the French line leaving 130,000 Italians in Yugoslavia and 115,000 Yugoslavs in Italy. Only the Soviet member of the commission recommended that Trieste, with a population that was 80 per cent Italian, should be taken from Italy.

On May 3, Vice Premier Kardelj of Yugoslavia and Premier de Gasperi of Italy presented the arguments of their governments. They were largely the same ones we had heard in London. Nor was the situation advanced after more than five hours of debate by the Ministers the following day. Mr. Molotov gave full support to the Yugoslav claims. He charged that Italy would use Trieste as a military base, a springboard for the extension of Italian influence into adjacent territory populated by Croats and Slovenes. We must not punish our ally Yugoslavia, he declared, by severing Trieste, which he termed the head, from the body of the province, even though the city was predominantly Italian. I pointed out that a line giving Yugoslavia over 300,000 inhabitants and several thousand square miles of territory it had never had before could hardly be called punishment. I offered to go still further and accept as a compromise the French line which would give the valuable Arsa coal mines to Yugoslavia. I also suggested the holding of a plebiscite in the disputed area. Neither of these proposals was acceptable to Mr. Molotov and, as neither Mr. Bevin, Mr. Bidault nor I were willing to make further concessions, there was nothing to do but turn to consideration of the other treaties.

In a final effort to bargain, Mr. Molotov invited Mr. Cohen, Mr. Bohlen and me to dinner in his suite at the Soviet Embassy. He suggested that, if we would agree to cede to Yugoslavia all Venezia Giulia, including Trieste, it would be possible for him to take a different attitude about the colonies and about reparations. But he indicated that his concession on the latter point would be at the expense of Greek and Yugoslavian claims. The Soviet Union, he stated flatly, could not renounce its claim for 100 million dollars, which it thought an excessively modest sum. When we stated our inability to make such an agreement, he and Mr. Vyshinski launched into a whole series of propaganda charges that the United States was engaged in a policy of "imperialist expansion." They cited the presence of American forces in Iceland and in China, and charged us with seeking bases in Turkey, Egypt and Iran. I was tempted to answer in the same spirit, but instead pointed out how ridiculous it was to describe 720 air-base mechanics and service troops in Iceland as an "imperialist" threat to the Soviet Union, and reminded him that we had discussed the Chinese situation in detail at Moscow and had issued a joint statement on the subject. As for the Middle East, we had no plans or desires for any bases.

"Our basic policy is to obtain the removal of troops from countries other than Germany and Japan at the earliest possible moment," I told him in our discussion after dinner. "For this reason we have urged the conclusion of a treaty with Austria so that our troops there may be withdrawn. But it is the Soviet Government, which has forces there many times larger than those of any other Allied nation, that refuses this suggestion. No one in the world fears the United States or its intentions. I am sorry to say this cannot be said of the Soviet Union."

Mr. Molotov, in support of the charges of Anglo-American imperialism, even went back to 1919 and the American expedition to Siberia during the postwar revolution. The next morning he talked to Mr. Bevin the same way, commenting that while Bevin claimed nineteenth century imperialism was dead it had to be pointed out that twentieth century imperialism was very much alive, as evidenced by British troops and bases in Greece, Egypt, Iraq, Indonesia, and elsewhere. Bevin's denial of these charges did not discourage Molotov from waging a similar propaganda campaign later in the Security Council and General Assembly of the United Nations.

It was on this note that we began work on the other treaties. It was not surprising, therefore, that Mr. Molotov regarded the American proposals to guarantee equality of opportunity in economic affairs and free navigation on the Danube simply as additional efforts at imperialist expansion and capitalist domination.

When I told Senators Connally and Vandenberg about our dinner conversation with Molotov, they shared my pessimism. In this atmosphere there was virtually no hope of securing agreement on any controversial issues. Therefore, on May 8, I proposed we acknowledge the first anniversary of V-E Day by calling the long-promised peace conference. I suggested June 15 as the date in order to give the deputies time to prepare and circulate a report on the agreed clauses and to present the views of the four delegations on the still unsettled clauses.

Both Mr. Bevin and Mr. Bidault indicated their agreement. Mr. Molotov maintained, that, in accord with the Moscow agreement, it would be impossible to hold the peace conference until there was unanimous agreement on all "basic issues." In effect, this gave the Soviet delegation a veto as long as there was disagreement on any issue it considered "basic." But my suggestion apparently had some effect because the deputies' report the next day showed that they had been able, overnight, to reach agreement on nineteen additional points. For the next week we continued our effort to call the peace conference, but throughout the hours at the conference table, at informal meetings and at private talks, Mr. Molotov remained adamant. He was evidently determined to delay the withdrawal of his occupation armies.

In an endeavor to make some progress we proposed the appointment of special deputies to begin work on the German treaty, but that too was rejected. The only accomplishment of the entire week was a revision of the Italian armistice which abolished the Allied Commission and removed most military controls.

On May 16, we wearily agreed to take a recess and meet in Paris again on June 15. "Building the foundations of a people's peace in a war-shattered world is a long, hard process," I confessed to the American public in my radio report on May 20. "A people's peace cannot be won by flashing diplomatic triumphs. It requires patience and firmness, tolerance and understanding. We must not try to impose our will on others, but we must make sure that others do not get the impression they can impose their will on us."

Having failed to make June 15 the date for the peace conference, I had tried July 1 and July 15, with no more success. But, I told the radio audience, "when a world short of goods and short of food is crying for the return of conditions of peace, we cannot indefinitely delay the making of peace and the withdrawal of troops from occupied areas," and I served notice that if a peace conference were not held during the summer the United States would bring the matter to the attention of the United Nations. Although it was never intended that the United Nations organization should become involved in the peace settlement, Article 14 of the Charter does authorize the General Assembly to "recommend measures for the peaceful adjustment of any situation, regardless of origin, which it deems likely to impair the general welfare or friendly relations among nations." We were fast approaching, I felt, such a "situation."

"We must take the offensive for peace as we took the offensive for war," I added, and expressed my faith that "there is no iron curtain that the aggregate sentiments of mankind cannot penetrate."

Mr. Molotov's reaction to this speech was quick and violent. He released a statement to the Soviet press repeating his charges that Anglo-American capital was instigating new aggressive wars and was aiming at world domination. My reference to an offensive for peace, he said, was in reality an "offensive against the Soviet Union in disregard of the interests of peace."

Nevertheless, when the deputies resumed their work during the recess the Soviet representative was at last willing to negotiate in concrete terms on the economic sections of the five treaties. Consequently, there were an appreciable number of additional agreed clauses ready for us when we returned to Paris.

Premier Nagy of Hungary visited Washington during this "recess." While here he publicly announced that he favored international control of the Danube—a surprising demonstration of independence on the part of a satellite state. He wanted to secure the return of Hungarian gold removed by the Germans and captured by our forces. We ordered the commanding officers of our zone to return the gold to Hungary and any other property which was clearly Hungarian-owned.

On June 14, we left again for Paris. This was my eleventh trip across the ocean in less than a year. For the trip, the President had placed his plane, the Sacred Cow, at our disposal. In the party, as usual, were Senator and Mrs. Connally, Senator and Mrs. Vandenberg, Ben Cohen, Chip Bohlen, Mrs. Byrnes, and my secretary, Miss Cassie Connor, who had acquired in this quest for peace treaties a mileage record almost as extensive as mine.

The American delegation returned to ornate Luxemburg Palace for the second Paris session determined to do all in our power to see that invitations for a peace conference were issued. We expected all kinds of delay but felt that when Mr. Molotov realized he could not get any more concessions, he would agree. The meeting opened with the almost customary preliminary skirmishes. The American delegation had circulated a draft treaty for Austria which we asked to have placed on the agenda. Mr. Molotov was unwilling to discuss our draft but did accept Mr. Bidault's suggestion that an "examination of the Austrian question" be included on the agenda. He then countered with a request that the "political situation in Italy" be examined, using the demonstrations which had accompanied the Italian referendum of June 2 on the abolition of the monarchy as an opportunity to criticize Anglo-American occupation policies. We surprised him, I think, by readily assenting to hold this discussion. But for the next eleven days progress was agonizingly slow. Then, on June 27, the log jam suddenly showed signs of breaking up.

The break came most unexpectedly at the end of a long meeting that had started with a fruitless discussion of our proposal to include in the treaties a mere statement of principle that the Danube should be a free waterway. With almost monotonous insistence, Mr. Molotov had maintained that the Danube must be controlled by the riparian states. We had spent the entire afternoon on such items as the limitation of the Bulgarian Navy, the rectification of the French-Italian border in the Tenda-Briga area, and miscellaneous clauses of the Rumanian treaty. Our agreement on some of the economic clauses of this treaty prompted me to say in humor as much as in hope:

"We should make it a good afternoon and settle the question of the Dodecanese."

To my amazement, Mr. Molotov replied that "the Soviet delegation has no objection to that proposal."

"Did Mr. Molotov say that he agreed the islands should go to Greece?" Mr. Bevin, who had tried repeatedly to settle the issue, asked in disbelief.

The Soviet representative promptly said that he had, and immediately asked that we proceed to the next question.

"Let me have a minute or two to recover," I exclaimed.

Mr. Molotov calmly suggested some other "good agreements" might be made. I proposed we discuss the question of the Italian colonies. He said that the matter could be settled on the basis of the American proposal to postpone a decision for a year after which, if agreement was not reached, the General Assembly of the United Nations would be asked for a decision. After drafting work by the deputies, this was subsequently approved.

But the twin issues of reparations and Trieste remained unsolved. In a discussion on June 18 the United States had renewed its suggestion that the Soviet Union be allowed 100 million dollars in reparations to be met from four sources: wartime industrial equipment not readily convertible to civilian use, Italian assets in the Balkan states, the Italian merchant ships, *Saturnia* and *Vulcania,* and naval vessels and other war booty captured by the American and British navies.

Molotov claimed that war booty could not be considered a source of reparations. Strictly speaking, he was correct. War booty belongs to the governments that capture it. But Molotov asserted the Soviet Union was entitled to a share of the Italian naval vessels because, at the Potsdam Conference, the United States and Britain had agreed to let Russia share in the allocation of German naval vessels which we had taken as war booty. We told Mr. Molotov that since naval vessels were war booty, the Soviet Union was not entitled to any of them; that the German vessels had been allotted to the Red Navy purely as a gift. There had been no promise that we would forever continue to make such gifts of our war booty. They did not divide their war booty.

The other three sources of reparations he accepted, but claimed our valuation of these assets was far too high. He placed the total at approximately 30 million dollars. The balance, he said, should be made up from current production. We left the question open by suggesting an inspection of the merchant ships and a study of means to determine the valuation of the other sources.

Three days later, Mr. Bidault took up the Trieste issue by suggesting, very cautiously, a temporary international regime for the city. The other three members of the Council received the suggestion with comparable caution. That evening, Messrs. Molotov, Vyshinski and Pavlov came to my rooms at the Hotel Meurice for a private conversation with Mr. Cohen, Mr. Bohlen and me. Mr. Molotov made what apparently was a final effort to obtain Trieste for Yugoslavia. We maintained we could never agree to Yugoslav sovereignty over this Italian city and suggested that both sides give some consideration to Mr. Bidault's proposal.

The next day I proposed that we issue invitations for a peace conference on July 15 and that we utilize the intervening period to seek settlement of the remaining issues. Those that remained unsolved on the fifteenth we would simply report to the assembled twenty-one nations.

Although Mr. Molotov maintained the suggestion was premature, both Mr. Bevin and Mr. Bidault joined in strong urging the immediate issuance of the invitations. We finally decided to begin, on Monday the twenty-fourth, a review of progress on all the treaties and, the following Friday, to consider again the American demand for the peace conference.

Monday morning, Mr. Molotov asked me to meet him again in my room that afternoon for another talk on Trieste. There, he proposed that Trieste and its adjacent area be declared an autonomous state under the sovereignty of Yugoslavia and controlled by an international statute to be drafted by the four powers. We pointed out that this was quite different from Mr. Bidault's idea which provided for United Nations administration and a governor appointed by the United Nations, but we promised to consider it. The next afternoon we repaid his visit.

"We have analyzed your suggestion and feel it would create an impossible situation," I said. "With Yugoslav sovereignty and a Yugoslav governor there would be little for the representatives of the four powers to do and there would be no connection whatever with the United Nations. The United States cannot accept Yugoslav sovereignty over the Trieste area. I recognize that the Soviet Union cannot accept Italian sovereignty. We are willing, therefore, to consider any proposal that offers a way out—either United Nations' administration as proposed by Mr. Bidault or leaving the issue to the peace conference for decision. I prefer the latter, for then the responsibility will rest upon the twenty-one nations."

Mr. Molotov then asked whether the problem of reparations could be disposed of "in a positive fashion" if the Trieste issue were settled. I stated I did not think this would create insuperable difficulties.

"The United States does not wish to finance reparations for others," I added. "But, a plan might be agreed upon whereby the Soviet Union could supply Italy with certain raw materials out of which Italy could manufacture goods the Soviet Union desires as reparations."

He then asked if the United States would sign all the peace treaties, including the one with Bulgaria, if agreement could be reached. I told him I saw no difficulties on that score but would meet that question when it arose. I then asked him if he could persuade the Bulgarian Government to carry out the Moscow decision. The only reply he would give was that his government had tried, but the opposition parties in Bulgaria had refused and the failure thus rested on them. With this "position sounding" we parted.

The following afternoon, Mr. Bidault suggested a restricted night meeting at which each Foreign Minister would be accompanied by only two advisers.

As on all such occasions, Senators Connally and Vandenberg accompanied me. Mr. Molotov at first reiterated the proposal he had made at our private conversation and then took one more step toward the French proposal. Instead of a Yugoslav governor, he proposed two governors, one Italian and one Yugoslav, to administer in concert. This idea naturally aroused no enthusiasm and finally Mr. Bevin remarked that the procedure of the conference seemed to be not to decide anything. Mr. Molotov's wry rejoinder was that the Briton should not underestimate his own services in producing that result.

Having concluded on this note, it is little wonder that the agreement the next day on the Dodecanese and on the Italian colonies took us by surprise. Even then, there was still much to be done and the yielding process was slow and grudging. To keep the log jam moving, I asked that the calling of the peace conference be placed on the agenda of our next meeting. Mr. Molotov objected but I served notice that I, at least, would discuss it. The next day everyone but the Soviet representative agreed that the conference should be called on July 20. And he maintained the decision must be postponed for a few days to consider a new proposal on Trieste that Mr. Bidault had presented.

The Trieste issue then entered a crucial phase. We didn't like the free territory idea but, since this was the only way out of the dilemma, we were determined that the regime would be set up so that it had a chance to work. Mr. Molotov first proposed a territorial outline that was impossible: It cut the port off from its shipyards, it severed the city from its water supply, and placed its power transformers in Yugoslavia. He wanted four-power rather than United Nations supervision. We refused to budge from our position that responsibility should lie with the Security Council rather than with a rival four-power commission.

We felt that the success of the free territory would be a matter of vital interest to all the United Nations and not merely the four powers. The four powers had not shown ability to work harmoniously elsewhere and there was no reason to expect a different situation in supervising the free territory. By placing responsibility in the Security Council, eleven states would share the obligation. There was no excuse for a rival organization. We also felt that the United Nations would have greater prestige than a four-power organization created for this sole purpose. We believed that if the integrity and independence of the free territory were threatened by aggression, it would be the duty of the Security Council to furnish military protection and it would be unwise for a four-power commission to have a military force for the same purpose.

On July 3, we renewed our campaign for the peace conference. This time, Mr. Molotov said he could not agree until the question of reparations was settled, but he was finally pressed into suggesting September 1 as a possible date. The other three Foreign Ministers objected to such delay but at least we had his commitment in principle. We ended our session at 8:30 with the feeling that July 4 would be a decisive day.

The morning of the Fourth was a glorious morning. Senator Connally Senator Vandenberg, Ambassador Caffery and I took part in ceremonies arranged by the American Legion near the monument to George Washington, and then we marched to the statue of Rochambeau where we also placed flowers in memory of the Frenchman's contributions to our freedom.

We met that day at 5:00 P.M. As soon as the deputies had made their customary report, Mr. Bidault suggested the meeting be adjourned for half an hour to permit the four Ministers to meet in his office for a private discussion of the question of setting a date for the peace conference. In his office he explained he had proposed this meeting in the hope that we could settle the question of the peace conference and reparations simultaneously.

I immediately declared we had repeatedly stated our willingness to re-examine the questions of reparations and would do so once the date of the peace conference was set. The United States objects, I said, to being told what it must do on other questions in order to secure agreement on the holding of the conference. Mr. Molotov denied that such tactics were being employed. Mr. Bidault then renewed his efforts at compromise and, in response, Mr. Molotov asked about reparations from current production. At this point I interrupted to say that, while we appreciated Mr. Bidault's efforts, we could not discuss reparations until a date was set for the peace conference. The American people would not like the appearance of a threat, I asserted, and would interpret any agreement under such circumstances as a deal in order to obtain a peace conference.

Mr. Bevin was even more pointed in his remarks. He said he could not face Parliament if he went out of this room with the implication that he had bought the peace conference from the Soviet Union for 100 million dollars.

Mr. Molotov appraised the situation and made his decision. There was no intention of buying anything, he said. He merely asked that the legitimate claims of the Soviet Union be considered. He therefore agreed that the council should take up in regular session first, the date of the peace conference, and then reparations, with the expectation that both questions would be settled that day. With that, we returned to the council room and in five minutes reached agreement on July 29 as the date for convening the peace conference and instructed the deputies to draft the invitation.

The United States delegation then submitted a reparations proposal—which immediately became the center of six tiring hours of debate. At one o'clock, the morning of July 5, we wearily agreed that the Soviet Union should receive 100 million dollars in reparations. This figure is to be made up from industrial equipment not necessary for Italy's peace economy, Italian assets in the Balkan states, and the balance from current production for which the Soviet Union would furnish the necessary raw materials. Mr. Molotov was willing to let the other claims for reparations be fixed at the peace conference.

We expected that the invitations would be issued the next day, but we grossly underestimated the resourceful stubbornness of Mr. Molotov. He objected to the invitations being issued in the name of the Council of Foreign Ministers because that would make China one of the sponsoring powers and, more importantly, he insisted that we must first agree on rules of procedure for the conference. Four more days of bitter controversy ensued. Mr. Molotov proposed rules of procedure which would have left the peace conference virtually powerless to do anything but approve the work of the four Ministers. Mr. Bevin, of course, could not agree to rules that would give the British dominions little opportunity to present their views effectively. Again and again, I told Mr. Molotov the United States would not agree to the imposition of rules on an assembly of sovereign nations, and maintained that the conference had a right to determine its own procedure.

At Mr. Bidault's suggestion, we finally resorted to another private conference. The Soviet representative accepted the proposal that draft rules of procedure accompanying the invitations should merely be "suggestions" from the Council. Included in these rules was the provision that recommendations would be made by a majority vote of two-thirds. Mr. Molotov had sought persistently to negotiate the rules point by point, but I had refused. I had made it clear the United States would not be bound by these rules, and I could not permit "suggestions" to achieve through point-by-point negotiation the same status as agreed treaty clauses. At the end of the discussion I repeated a statement I had made many times:

"I wish it clearly understood," I said, "that when the conference convenes the United States will feel entirely free to accept or reject on its merits any amendment or new proposal which might be offered."

This statement, which is but one of many like it that I made during this discussion, is important because Mr. Molotov's later effort to ignore it provided one of the bitterest controversies of the peace conference.

Agreement at last was reached and the invitations to the peace conference finally went out the next day, July 9.

The story of this agreement would be incomplete without acknowledging that it was brought about by the mediation of Mr. Bidault. He is, in fact, quite a remarkable man. Before the war he was a professor. During the war he became a leader of the underground forces, and was taken as a prisoner of war. When he was released and returned to France, he entered politics. For a man who had no experience in that field, he showed unusual aptitude. Under his leadership, the party known as the Mouvement Republicain Populaire (MRP) elected the largest number of delegates to the Chamber of Deputies, and as a result, he was called upon to form a government. Later he became the provisional President of France as well as Foreign Minister. He had a coalition government composed of Communists, Socialists and members of his own party. When a man can be successful directing such a government in France even for nine or ten months he is certain to be helpful in presiding over the deliberations of the Council of Foreign Ministers. With his constructive mind and engaging personality he brought about agreement on several very controversial questions.

When Mr. Bevin dropped the chairman's gavel late in the evening of July 12 with the declaration, "Gentlemen, we will meet at the peace conference," I was tired and sorely tempted to follow the suggestion of the President and the members of my staff to take a vacation in Switzerland prior to the conference.

But much could be done in two weeks at home. The foreign service legislation and other such matters were pending; there were Far East and South American problems to be dealt with. Therefore, on Monday night, July 15, I found myself once again before the radio microphones in Washington delivering another report to the American people.

"The draft of treaties agreed upon are not the best human wit could devise," I admitted. "But they are the best which human wit could get the four principal Allies to agree upon. They represent as satisfactory an approach to the return of peace as we could hope for in this imperfect and war-weary world."

After outlining the major provisions of the drafts and the agreements reached I spoke of the "great struggle and tremendous difficulties the four governments had in harmonizing their views" and then added:

"I am ready to believe it is difficult for them to understand us, just as it is difficult for us to understand them. But I sometimes think our Soviet friends fear we would think them weak and soft if they agreed without a struggle on anything we wanted, even though they wanted it too. Constant struggle, however, is not always helpful in a world longing for peace."

Chapter 8

The Paris Peace Conference and Its New York Finale

WE PREPARED for the peace conference believing that the voice of the United States could be raised on behalf of both political parties and a large majority of the American people. This spirit was reflected by the response of the people of Washington to a friendly suggestion from the Washington *Post* that the American delegation be given a hearty send-off. The huge crowd that lined the road to the National Airport and crowded the field to cheer us on our way was a source of genuine encouragement during the eleven weeks of the conference. This moving demonstration of our people's desire for peace made the twelve months of work and over sixty thousand miles of travel to obtain the conference and its promise of peace more than worth while.

The French Government and people did everything they could to provide an appropriate setting for peace making. The French excel as hosts but even their best efforts failed to dispel the harsh feelings that held over from the closing days of the Council of Foreign Ministers meetings.

Social activities constitute a physical endurance test and I had to decline all invitations except those extended by the heads of government and the Foreign Ministers. I must admit, however, that there is virtue in the social life at such gatherings as the peace conference. As long as men meet socially and continue to discuss their problems there is a chance to solve them. This idea exists in many ways, among many people. It is recognized even by our Supreme Court where each Justice, upon entering the conference room from which the group marches into the Court, shakes hands with every other Justice present. It seemed to me, when I first became a member of the Court, that this was absurd because I had often just concluded talking with one or more of the Justices. I learned, however, that many years ago a Chief Justice established the custom on the theory that no matter how heated the arguments of the Justices might have been the previous day, they would be able to reconcile their differences if they started the day with a handshake and on speaking terms. I did not forget this lesson from the Court in my dealings with the representatives of other countries. It was especially valuable during the tense days of the Paris Conference.

We approached the conference from a point of view entirely different from that of the Soviet Government, and that fact produced conflict from the very start. We believed the discussions should be full and free; that the countries which had helped to win the war should have the widest latitude in suggesting amendments and proposals for the peace, and that their recommendations should carry great weight. We believed that a lasting peace had to be a people's peace.

The Soviet attitude, however, seemed to be that the conference should simply and speedily confirm the agreements made in the Council of Foreign Ministers and that establishment of the conditions of peace was primarily, if not exclusively, the concern of the great powers.

In accordance with our belief, I announced in my opening speech that the United States would support the agreements made in the council, but, as I had stated in the council, I would vote on each proposal of procedure regardless of the suggestions submitted by the council. Should the conference, on any question of substance not agreed to by the council, make a recommendation by a two-thirds majority, I would exert every effort to secure adoption of that recommendation by the council regardless of how the United States voted in the peace conference. Mr. Molotov immediately charged that our position, which was also taken by the United Kingdom, was a violation of an agreement made in council on rules of procedure for the conference. The first time I overlooked his accusation, but when it was renewed with the evident purpose of giving offense, I read from the record of the council six different statements I had made reserving for the United States the right to vote for any amendment on procedure. I stated I had made the reservation so often only because I knew the tactics of Mr. Molotov.

"In the light of this record," I declared, "only Mr. Molotov would say that I had agreed to support the suggested rules of procedure."

I pointed out that, when he had lectured the United States and the United Kingdom for "inconsistency" in supporting an amendment to the rules of voting procedure, he had closed his statement by offering an amendment himself to the same section of the rules.

"Now, only Mr. Molotov would do that," I added.

The debate on procedure was as long as it was bitter. For nearly three weeks Mr. Molotov and Mr. Vyshinski used all their talent as parliamentarians to restrict participation by the small and medium powers. This was contrary to the interest and desires of these powers. In addition, the tactics of the Soviet delegation in questioning the motives of those who differed from them and in charging the formation of blocs when there was no justification for the charge were so offensive that some delegates who had come to the conference thinking the Foreign Ministers of the western states were unfair to the Soviet Union changed their minds. From that time on these delegates were very critical of the Soviets and generally were found voting against them. The Soviet delegation declared that when the treaties were returned to the Council of Foreign Ministers they would disregard, as lacking in authority, any recommendation passed by a simple majority. But on many of the votes the Soviet proposals were defeated by more than a two-thirds majority.

Mr. Molotov assumed that we and the British had organized a bloc against him. The fact is I never attended a meeting that would even suggest such an effort. Later in the conference he even charged that we instigated amendments offered by the smaller powers. Many of these amendments supported objectives that had been included in our original proposals for the treaties. But we had been obliged to drop them because of the Soviet veto in the council. Because Molotov exercised a tight control over the votes and the actions of his supporters, he assumed that we did the same. It was inconceivable to him that Belgium, the Netherlands, South Africa, Australia or New Zealand, for example, could have ideas of their own, and that we would hesitate to try to influence their views. So he charged us with the formation of "blocs" aimed at destroying the work of the council.

"Whence comes this talk of blocs?" I was finally impelled to ask. "By what right do those who vote ballot after ballot with the Soviet Union call those of us, who do not always agree with the Soviet Union, a bloc? When the New Zealand proposal to have all recommendations made by a simple majority vote was defeated in the commission by a bare 11 to 9 votes, no one complained that the proposal had been rejected by a Soviet bloc; but when the Soviet proposal on voting procedure is defeated by the overwhelming vote of 15 to 6 here in this conference, the charge is made that the defeat was brought about by an Anglo-Saxon bloc. What loose and wicked talk this is!"

When the fight on procedure neared its end, I cabled Senator Connally and Senator Vandenberg, urging them to join the delegation. I needed them to defend the United States against the criticism now being directed against us by the satellites as well as the Soviet Union. As in the past, they immediately responded to my request. And they did a most effective job.

Senator Connally became the American representative on the commission handling the political sections of the Italian treaty, assisted by Assistant Secretary of State James C. Dunn and an outstanding foreign service officer, Sam Reber. Senator Vandenberg represented us on the commission in charge of economic questions in all the treaties, with the aid of Willard Thorp, now an Assistant Secretary of State. The other American commission assignments were as follows: The Commission on the Rumanian treaty, Mr. Averell Harriman, then our Ambassador in London; the Bulgarian Commission, our Ambassador in Paris, Mr. Jefferson Caffery; the Commission on Hungary, our Ambassador in Moscow, General Bedell Smith. On the Military Commission which dealt also with naval questions, we had Vice Admiral Richard L. Connally, Brigadier General Jesse D. Balmer, and Captain Roland K. Pryce.

At nine o'clock each morning these gentlemen would meet with me and various State Department experts. Each representative on the commission would make a report so that every member of the delegation knew the status of the discussions in all the commissions and, when desirable, could obtain the judgment of the delegation on a controversial issue. It was a harmonious and smooth-working team. No Secretary of State ever received more loyal or more capable support.

At one of the first plenary sessions, Prime Minister de Gasperi of the new democratic Italy, appeared in order to present his country's cause. He and his delegation were treated as representatives of an enemy state. No delegate greeted him except Mr. Bidault, who was presiding and who, in a formal way, presented him. The Italian Prime Minister presented his case tactfully but with dignity and courage. As he left the rostrum to return to the seat assigned to him on the last tier, he walked down the center aisle of the silent chamber, past many men who knew him. No one spoke to him. It impressed me as unnecessarily cruel. Like others, I had met him in London. So, when he approached the United States delegation I stood and shook hands with him. I then sent him a message inviting him to my apartment that afternoon. I wanted to encourage this man who had suffered personally at the hands of Mussolini and now was suffering at the hands of the Allied nations.

Before leaving Washington for Paris I had secured authority to help the new government of Italy in a matter of great importance to them. We had paid for supplies furnished our armies in France but the House Appropriations Committee had objected to our Army paying for supplies purchased in Italy on the ground that Italy was an enemy state. Because of their action, payments were held up by the Treasury. I presented this matter to Representatives Clarence Cannon and John Taber, chairman and ranking Republican, respectively, of the House Appropriations Committee. These two gentlemen frequently are criticized by free-spending officials. From my long experience I know they strive only to protect the money of the taxpayers and I have always found them sympathetic to a deserving cause. When I told them the supplies were furnished after Italy was fighting on the side of the Allies, they promptly stated they would withdraw their objection.

Knowing that Prime Minister de Gasperi was humiliated by his reception at the peace conference, I took the occasion that afternoon to inform him of the United States Government's decision. But I warned him our decision would not be announced until agreement was reached on the Italian treaty. Otherwise, I explained, the claimants for reparations from Italy might increase their claims.

There were times when we thought the conference would never end. On every subject where there was the slightest controversy, the Soviet Union would present its views and then several of the satellite states would make supporting speeches. Since each speech was made in three languages, progress was difficult. Not until representatives of other states, without any formal meeting or understanding but by general accord, began refraining from making speeches, and calling for votes instead, did the work start moving forward.

Nevertheless, it seemed to me that the course of the Soviet delegation and its satellites was not wholly discouraging. It seemed incredible to me that Mr. Molotov and Mr. Vyshinski would devote so much time to the consideration of the proposals before the commissions and in the plenary sessions and thereafter refuse to give consideration to the recommendations of the conference.

In the course of these debates, there were few accusations which were not directed against the United States and the United Kingdom. We were charged with seeking alliances with "Fascists," with attempts to "enslave" Italy through "foreign trusts and cartels," with using our capital to "subjugate" weaker nations, and numerous other crimes as heinous as they were ridiculous.

We sought, in so far as possible, to avoid indulging in debate of this kind, but there were occasions when answers had to be made. One of these was the speech made by Mr. Molotov after the ex-enemy states presented their views on the treaty drafts. It was an intemperate speech in which he supported the attacks of the former enemy states against our ally, Greece, and contrasted Italy unfavorably with the Russian-dominated Balkan governments. It also constituted a direct attack on American and British peace policies.

"Peace in this interdependent world," I told the conference in reply, "cannot be furthered by ignoring the repeated abuse and misrepresentation which have been leveled against America from this floor." I strongly objected to "the Soviet Government's giving the impression to the conference that other ex-enemy states are more democratic than Italy because they have harmonized their viewpoints with the Soviet Union. . . . The United States believes in the sovereign equality of nations. We are opposed to making the small nations satellites of the larger states."

I referred to Mr. Molotov's charge that certain large powers had enriched themselves during the war and asked if he could possibly mean the United States, which has spent over 400 billion dollars in fighting the war, and had sent over 11 billion dollars of lend-lease aid to the Soviet Union. I pointed out that we sought no territory nor reparations in contrast to the large territories and hundreds of millions of dollars allotted to the Soviet Union by the treaty drafts.

"The United States must also repudiate the suggestion of the Soviet delegation that the economic clauses proposed by the United States and based upon the principle of equality . . . are part of an effort to exploit the ex-enemy countries for the selfish advantage of the United States."

On one occasion when Mr. Vyshinski was repeating the charge that the United States was trying to dominate the world with "hand-outs," I noticed he was heartily applauded at the end of his remarks by two of the Czechoslovakian delegates seated two rows in front of our delegation. I had just been told that the Czechoslovakians had been allotted a credit of 50 million dollars for the purchase of surplus property. The credit had been given because of representations that the government needed financial help for the reconstruction of the country. I inquired and learned that the Czechoslovakian government had entered into a contract to transfer to Rumania 10 million dollars of this "emergency" credit. The transfer was to carry an interest rate of 6 per cent plus an administration fee of 7 per cent, giving the Czechs a very nice profit, since they were to pay only 2⅜ per cent interest on the money borrowed from us.

I immediately cabled instructions to the State Department to stop the extension of credit to Czechoslovakia. A few days later the very able and attractive Foreign Minister of that country, Mr. Jan Masaryk, came to see me, bringing with him Clementis, a member of his delegation, who was a Communist representative in the government. Mr. Masaryk asked what was disturbing the friendly relations between our two countries. I told him our friendly relations need not be disturbed but that there would be an end to relief appropriations or credits to a government whose officials could applaud a denunciation of the United States as a government seeking to dominate the world by "hand-outs." I assured him we wished to be friendly with Czechoslovakia and we did not want to offend them further by giving them hand-outs, particularly in view of the violent arguments against us in the Czech press. I also told him how shocked I was by the Rumanian transaction and said the credit was extended to Czechoslovakia because we relied upon their representations that they needed it. If Rumania needed assistance from us, I said, they should ask for it; Czechoslovakia could not act as a broker for us.

Mr. Masaryk advised me—and I knew he was sincere—that he had known nothing of the transaction with Rumania and he regretted such action. He said he would inquire into the facts. The other gentleman knew the facts, but explained that the bargain was not completed. With that, I told him it had not been completed because I knew about it and stopped it.

Later, I received information which mitigated slightly the action of the Czech government. A representative of our Treasury Department, visiting in Czechoslovakia, was approached by a Czech official. The Czech asked the Treasury representative about the Rumanian transaction. The American replied he had nothing to do with such matters but then added that the proposition might be submitted to our government for consideration. Czech officials later cited this statement in justification of the agreement with Rumania, saying that they assumed the United States would not advance the credit if we were opposed to the Rumanian transaction.

During this same period a crisis in our relations with Yugoslavia— a country about the size of New York and Pennsylvania, containing 16 million people—occurred. There, Marshal Tito, who had fought in the Russian revolution and was a thoroughly trained Communist leader, had worked his way into control. We had had difficulties with him a year earlier when it had appeared that Yugoslav troops would seek to take Venezia Giulia by force. The Yugoslavs had finally withdrawn to the Morgan line but skirmishes continued intermittently all along the line. The other source of friction had been airplane travel. The Army's Air Transport Service operating between Rome and Vienna passed through Udine in northern Italy to Klagenfurt in Austria. It was impossible for our planes to travel the sixty-five miles between these two points in a straight line because the northwest tip of Yugoslavia jutted out between them and, because of Yugoslav protests, our planes had been ordered to stay away from that territory. The order was often difficult to obey as the territory is rugged and many navigational hazards exist. Pilots must fly through a pass where mountains are 9,000 feet high and surrounding peaks reach as high as 18,000 feet. In bad weather it was easy to get lost and in any weather it was a temptation to clip the corner. No friendly country would have complained, but the Yugoslavs charged us with 176 violations of her frontiers. Our Army denied the charges.

On August 9, an army transport, carrying seven Americans, a Turk, and a Swiss, lost its way, strayed over Yugoslav territory, was attacked by two Yugoslav fighter planes, and forced to make a hazardous landing in a wheat field. The Turkish Army officer was wounded. The other eight were immediately interned in a Belgrade hotel. On August 19, another transport en route to Rome radioed Udine that it was over Klagenfurt. It was never heard from again, but Klagenfurt reported it had been attacked and sent down in flames by Yugoslav fighters. The bodies of the five Americans were found five days later.

The State Department asked for information and Marshal Tito made a belligerent speech in which he charged us with sending "whole squadrons" of military planes over Yugoslavia. I sent for the Vice Premier of Yugoslavia, Edward Kardelj, who headed his country's delegation to the peace conference. I told him the news I had received and asked for an explanation. He said he had none other than the general information that our planes had flown over his country on several occasions although they had been told not to do so.

"Yugoslavia claims to be a friendly government and your planes can fly over our territory at any time," I told him. "But even if you were not friendly and one of your planes, flying over Canada, got lost and happened to fly over the United States and was grounded, the officials of the United States would feel it their duty to do everything in their power for the safety and comfort of the Yugoslav crew and its passengers. Any official who failed to do so would be reprimanded by our government. The idea of a United States Army plane, under such circumstances, firing upon a plane of Yugoslavia, killing its crew and passengers, is something the American government would never be guilty of and is something for which the American people will not forgive Yugoslavia."

I demanded that he communicate with his government to obtain an explanation. At the same time I communicated with Under Secretary of State Dean Acheson and he sent an official demand through diplomatic channels. Upon receiving a very unsatisfactory reply, I issued instructions to notify the Yugoslavs that unless we received a satisfactory reply to our demands within forty-eight hours we would call upon the United Nations Security Council to take appropriate action.

The atmosphere at the conference was tense as the news of the American ultimatum spread among the delegations. Before long, I noticed a member of Mr. Molotov's group leave his delegation and go over to the Yugoslav table and whisper to Mr. Kardelj. Both Mr. Molotov and Mr. Kardelj then walked out of the conference chamber through different doors. A member of our delegation saw them in earnest conversation in the anteroom and noticed that Mr. Molotov was doing most of the talking. It may not have been a conference about our message, but, in any event, we received a satisfactory reply before the forty-eight hours were over.

During this period the pilot and co-pilot of the first airplane were flown to Paris to see me. The pilot told me that, while they were being kept prisoners in a hotel in Belgrade, they were prevented from communicating with the American Ambassador or any other American. He learned that one of his passengers was an UNRRA official and suggested he try to communicate with UNRRA officials in Belgrade. The UNRRA man did so, but his request was denied. Within an hour after this request was rejected, they looked out the window and saw an American-made locomotive over at the railroad depot with the letters UNRRA printed on it. They knew that 70 per cent of the cost of that locomotive had been furnished by the American taxpayers and the thought contributed little to the comfort of their internment.

The incident was ended, but it was not obliterated from the minds of the American people. And this, together with the experience with Czechoslovakia, led me to believe that when UNRRA expired, any new appropriations by Congress for foreign relief should be allocated by the United States and should go to those countries who would not denounce us for granting them the relief they asked for. I felt that if our representatives could get sufficient information to pass judgment on loans made by the Export-Import Bank we should be able to acquire the data needed to pass judgment on requests for relief.

Meanwhile, the tiring work of the conference went on, with sessions lasting into the early hours of the morning. I was chairman during much of the debate on the economic clauses, and I congratulated myself on succeeding in moving the adjournment hour from 2:30 A.M. to 1:00 A.M. The economic clauses of the five treaties were almost identical and, when a roll call was taken on the economic section of the Italian treaty, I hoped that roll calls would not be demanded on the same provisions in all the other treaties. But the Soviet delegation had other ideas.

Notwithstanding the fact that the commissions for each of the enemy states were made up of all the countries that had been at war with that particular state, and that in the commissions roll calls had been taken on all important issues, most of the arguments were repeated in plenary session and then roll calls were demanded again. The results rarely varied, but Mr. Molotov never gave up trying. Even when a resolution of a subcommittee had received a two-thirds majority vote in the plenary session, he would demand a roll call on the minority motion as well. The result was two roll calls on a resolution each time it came up for consideration in each of the five treaties. Tactics such as these by Mr. Molotov and his satellite associates served to create the western bloc that he charged us with seeking to build. Had we wanted to create a bloc he did the job far too effectively for us to have interfered.

Many nights I returned to the hotel from the conference depressed as well as exhausted. A few weeks before, when I left Washington, a reporter at the airport asked how I felt as I returned to the conference, and I replied that, in the words of the old Negro spiritual, I was "standing in the need of prayer." One night, when the prospects for peace were indeed gloomy, Mrs. Byrnes handed me a package of mail forwarded from Washington. Most of the letters were from persons who had heard or read my statement at the airport, and they told me they were praying for the success of the conference and for my efforts. None of them were from chronic letter writers. They were from good people who yearned for peace and believed in the efficacy of prayer. They will never know the comfort their messages gave me.

Toward the end of the conference, Mr. Molotov made a quick trip to Moscow. I assumed he desired to confer with his associates there and I was pleased. The attitude toward the United States adopted by him and by Mr. Vyshinski had been so unfriendly throughout the conference that I felt that any change resulting from his Moscow discussions would be a change for the better. It could hardly be for the worse.

When consideration of the treaties was completed, the Yugoslav delegation declined to attend the last meeting of the conference. The chairman of that delegation sent a letter to the President of the conference stating that because of dissatisfaction with the recommendations on Trieste, Yugoslavia would not attend the meeting and would not sign the treaty. Because of their continued threats not to sign the treaty unless the conference acceded to their views on Trieste, our delegation had offered, and the conference had approved by a majority vote, a proposal that no state refusing to sign the treaty could receive the benefits provided in it. Later, at the Council of Foreign Ministers' meeting in New York, I urged this proposal and when Mr. Molotov agreed to the provision I no longer doubted that Yugoslavia would sign the treaty.

The conference began with twenty-six unagreed articles before it in addition to all the articles agreed upon in the council, and in all, some three hundred amendments were considered. But the real issues of the conference focused on Trieste, the total of reparations obligations, and the control of the Danube.

The council had been unable to agree on the terms of a statute to govern the free territory of Trieste and had appointed a special commission to work out a report. As might be expected, this committee presented to the conference four different draft proposals. We had prepared our draft with an eye on the unhappy experience of the League of Nations with the free city of Danzig. Because the High Commissioner appointed by the League had been powerless to protect the integrity of that city after a well organized Nazi minority had captured control of the local legislature, we were determined that the Governor of Trieste should be invested with strong powers. This created the anomaly of the western democracies advocating appointment by the Security Council of a governor having almost dictatorial powers, while the eastern dictatorship sought to place control in a popularly elected legislature. We were determined, however, to do our utmost to protect the area from infiltration and similar tactics that would pave the way for a coup aimed at delivering Trieste to Yugoslavia, as Danzig had been delivered to Germany.

In addition to giving the Governor the role of a figurehead, the Soviet draft would have joined Trieste to Yugoslavia, and provided for joint administration of Trieste's railways, and the right of free settlement and employment in each other's territory. The conference finally approved, by a vote of 15 to 6, a French compromise on the statute much closer to the American and British drafts than to the Soviet proposal.

The reparations debate was equally difficult, but the conference finally approved for the Finnish, Rumanian and Hungarian treaties the figure of 300 million dollars which had been fixed in the Soviet armistice terms in 1945. We urged the council to take cognizance of the economic chaos prevailing in Hungary by advocating a reduction in reparations payments of one-third, but without success. Bulgaria's reparations payments to Greece and Yugoslavia were set at 125 million dollars, although the figure was opposed by the Slav bloc as being too high.

The biggest reparations fight, of course, centered on Italy. The smaller Allied states submitted claims totaling billions. Since we had agreed in the council to support 100 million dollars for the Soviet Union, these claimants could not be wholly denied, but we did try to give them some sense of proportion by showing that we could, if we wished, present reparations claims totaling 20 billions. The British submitted a similar claim for 11 billion, which they also had no intention of pressing. The conference finally recommended 100 million dollars each to the Soviet Union, Yugoslavia and Greece, and 25 million to Ethiopia. Albania's claim was denied. We sought to lighten Italy's burden by liberalizing the other economic clauses in the treaty for such items as compensation for Allied property, assets in Allied countries, and costs of occupation.

Harsh words were piled high on the American and British proposals aimed at guaranteeing equality of economic opportunity in the Balkan states and for unrestricted use of the Danube. The Soviet representatives professed to believe our purpose was to challenge their control of eastern Europe. We took the position that we wanted to put into action, in the treaties, the principles that had been agreed upon at Yalta. But we were charged with plans to accomplish capitalist "enslavement" of the Balkan people. During much of this debate, the United States was ably represented by Senator Vandenberg and Mr. Willard Thorp, assisted by Mr. Jacques Reinstein. They managed to obtain provisions in the treaties requiring that the ex-enemy states must grant to each of the United Nations, on a reciprocal basis, nondiscriminatory treatment in matters of trade and equal status with their own nationals in conducting business within the country. Also, guarantees were included for equal economic opportunity and for equal rights in negotiating civil aviation agreements for a period of eighteen months, by which time the ex-enemy states, it was assumed, would come within the jurisdiction of the United Nations agreements in these fields.

Senator Vandenberg led our fight for freedom of commerce and navigation on the Danube. He and Mr. Bevin pointed out that there had been international control of the Danube since 1856, but Mr. Molotov dismissed these agreements as "imperialistic treaties" and maintained that the Danube rights concerned the riparian states alone. In an eloquent speech on September 30, Senator Vandenberg urged adoption of a joint Anglo-American resolution affirming the free commerce and navigation principle; it called for convening, within six months after the treaties come into force, a conference to establish a new international traffic regime on the Danube; the Big Four and the riparian states would participate. The resolution, slightly modified, was adopted by the conference and was included in the final draft of the treaty.

While these three issues were the principal centers of controversy at the conference there were, of course, many other difficult questions such as the territorial and minorities disputes which had proved so troublesome after World War I. These included Hungary's loss of Transylvania to Rumania, the latter's transfer of northern Bukovina to Russia, and Russia's acquisition from Finland of Petsamo and naval base rights at Porkkala. There were also such claims as that of Greece for northern Epirus in southern Albania, which was countered by a Soviet-supported claim by Bulgaria for the Greek province of western Thrace.

In the midst of all these claims and counterclaims, Italy and Austria provided the conference with a timely demonstration of statesmanship by working out an enlightened agreement insuring basic human rights for the German-speaking peoples in South Tyrol, which remained with Italy. We tried to use this as an example of reasonable bilateral negotiations to help solve such problems as Czechoslovakia's desire to transfer back to Hungary its Magyar minority, but met with indifferent success.

In all, the peace conference passed on to the Council of Foreign Ministers fifty-three recommendations voted by at least a two-thirds majority and forty-one others adopted by a simple majority. This list made it quite clear, when the conference finally adjourned on October 15, that the Council of Foreign Ministers was faced with more weeks of tedious effort before the treaties would be completed.

Although the conference had not accomplished all we had hoped for, we did feel that our months of effort to obtain it were well and wisely spent. Our contention that wisdom was not a monopoly of the Big Four and that the smaller powers could make important contributions to the treaties had been thoroughly vindicated. The value of their recommendations is proved by the number subsequently included in the treaties.

The council opened its meeting in New York on November 4, 1946, and for once, there was no debate on procedure. We immediately began consideration of the peace-conference recommendations for the Italian treaty. Otherwise, there was little change. In fact, if the setting had not been the tower of the Waldorf-Astoria Hotel, I might have thought I was back in London a year earlier.

The setting, however, was a matter of concern to us for, this time, we were the host government and were responsible for making all the arrangements. Finding suitable accommodations in New York was a major problem. The shortage of hotel space had been made even more acute by the arrival of several thousand delegates for the session of the United Nations General Assembly, which had opened on October 23. The problem was not solved until the president of the Waldorf-Astoria, the late Mr. Lucius Boomer, volunteered to give up his thirty-seventh floor suite for use as the council chamber and for committee meetings, and arranged to clear large areas on the sixth and seventh floors where we established seventy-three offices.

After months of unrelenting negotiation, I thought I appreciated the difficulties involved in preparing peace treaties. But the duties of acting as host gave me still greater understanding. For example, we had to recruit switchboard operators who not only were skilled and thoroughly reliable but who could also speak the languages of the council group. A special switchboard was installed so that each delegation flashed a different colored light on the board whenever a member of its staff picked up the telephone. Thus it was possible for an operator speaking the language of that delegation to take the call. Providing reasonable security for the leading delegates and their papers required a detail of 150 military policemen and an untold number of FBI agents and New York City policemen.

Never before had I realized the magnitude of some of the mechanical aspects of treaty making. In the five weeks of the New York session, 855,000 pages of documents were mimeographed. The minutes of each meeting, the record of each motion made and agreement reached had to be checked and rechecked in each language and with each delegation. This painstaking work of supervising documents was ably handled by L. E. Thompson and Edward Page of the State Department's Eastern European Division, who worked with me also on policy questions affecting that area.

The work of preparing documents, in fact, went on for two months after the delegates went home. Language experts had to check the texts of the treaties in the three official languages and prepare a text in the language of each ex-enemy country. This meant four language versions for each of the five treaties. Approximately 143,000 maps had to be cut, folded and inserted into the treaty texts. The entire job, which required the production of twenty versions totaling, in all, 44,000 volumes, was under the direction of Dr. Warren Kelchner, the chief of the State Department's Division of International Conferences.

While these were new situations, the ones at the conference table were old. Mr. Molotov and Mr. Vyshinski entirely disregarded the recommendations of the conference and argued just as they had been arguing for the past thirteen months. The representatives of Yugoslavia came before the council and presented their case for control of the city of Trieste in substantially the same words they had used at London in September and October, 1945, and which they had persistently voiced at Paris.

I confess it was tiresome. It must have been particularly so for Senators Vandenberg and Connally who, as usual, sat at my side while I, as Secretary, did all the talking. It did not help that each time I made a statement it would be repeated in Russian by Mr. Bohlen and then in French by another interpreter. The best statement cannot be interesting in three languages. Usually, during these translation periods, the Senators, Ben Cohen, and other members of our delegation would hand me notes suggesting how to meet a new proposal or answer an argument that had been made. But, at times, there was nothing to do but wait for the translator to finish. During those periods the Senators would draw doodles. They were quite artistic; I think an artist would say they belonged to the "futuristic" school. Ben Cohen would sketch the persons sitting at the table, and some of his sketches actually were recognizable.

By then, the Senators had become quite expert in diagnosing Mr. Molotov's tactics and motives. They are realists to begin with, and their long experience in the Senate has enabled them to judge whether a man is trying to improve the language of his proposal or whether he is simply killing time. Ben Cohen possesses a different type of mind. Because a thing is right, he cannot understand why Mr. Molotov does not agree to it. For instance, he felt very strongly about the Austrian situation and the hardships the Austrians were enduring as a result of continued occupation. Several times when I had exhausted efforts to induce Mr. Molotov to proceed with the Austrian treaty, Ben would write a note suggesting a new approach and urging me to make one more effort. It was utterly impossible, Ben would feel, for Mr. Molotov to object to this new approach—but he would.

Vandenberg and Connally would admire my patience as much as they would deplore my lack of judgment.

The council in New York took up a great number of the peace conference recommendations before an agreement was reached on one. And that agreement was due to the action of Mr. Bevin. The article dealt with early deliveries of goods for reparations. The British delegation had fought very hard against it at Paris but it was adopted by a vote of 14 to 7. When we came to it, Mr. Bevin said:

"The clause acquired authority through a two-thirds vote in the conference. I withdraw the objection."

"Then, may we consider that this recommendation is accepted by the Council of Ministers?" Mr. Couve de Murville, who had taken Mr. Bidault's place in the Council, asked.

"I ought to say I was very strong on this in Paris," Mr. Bevin replied. "I do not propose to stand in the way in spite of that. I confess it will impose great difficulties on Italy, but I withdraw the objection."

"Mr. Chairman," I put in, "I think it might be noted that this is the first recommendation of the conference to be adopted."

"Britain still leads in some things," Mr. Bevin added.

At this point, Mr. Molotov made his first comment on the clause. With an attempt at humor, he turned to Bevin and said:

"We wish her as much success in the future."

We proceeded to go through all the recommendations of the conference, and with each article the Soviet representative made more emphatic his refusal to follow Mr. Bevin's example in acknowledging the majority will of the peace conference.

Personal relations between us, however, had greatly improved. From the day of his arrival in this country, Mr. Molotov refrained at the council meetings from directing criticism at the United States. During the peace conference there had been no private dinner conversations such as Mr. Molotov and I had had during council sessions. In New York, with the improved relationships, we reverted again to pleasant social exchanges. During the fourth week of the meeting, Mr. Molotov came to see me at my apartment in the Waldorf Hotel and asked what could be done to make better progress in our deliberations.

"I must tell you frankly," I replied, "that since you have rejected practically all of the recommendations of the peace conference adopted by at least a two-thirds vote, I see no hope for agreement. Beginning with London, over a year ago, I have done everything in my power to secure agreement on the treaties. It is with the greatest reluctance, therefore, that I have come to the conclusion we will not be able to agree upon the treaties. Having become reconciled to this, I think we should agree to disagree without having any of the bitter exchanges that marked some of the debates at Paris."

Mr. Molotov was surprised. He was not prepared for such a statement from the United States delegation which had worked so unceasingly for the treaties through so many months. He replied he was not so pessimistic; he thought we could reach agreement.

"For months I have refused to be pessimistic," I told him. "But I have at last realized that we do not share the same desire for treaties of peace. If we do not have the same objective, there is no purpose in further debate. I am particularly anxious that we should not announce our inability to agree in such a way as to frighten the peace-loving people of the world. Time is a great healer and a year from now other individuals may find it possible to agree."

Although Mr. Molotov was reluctant to believe my statement was serious, I closed our conversation on a strong note of resignation to the impossibility of securing treaties.

The day after my visit with Mr. Molotov, the Yugoslav representative, Mr. Simic, who then was also the Yugoslav Ambassador to the United States, requested an interview with me.

He opened the conversation by urging a modification in the boundary line between Yugoslavia and the free territory of Trieste. In return, he said, Yugoslavia was willing to make concessions on Italy's reparations payments. It was obvious to me that Mr. Molotov was merely employing this method to test our position. If I showed willingness to negotiate with Mr. Simic, it would be a good indication to Mr. Molotov that I had not meant what I had said to him about ending our efforts to reach agreement.

"Mr. Ambassador, there is not the slightest use in our discussing your proposal," I told him. "We have reached the conclusion that under the present circumstances it is not possible to obtain treaties that will genuinely contribute toward peace. I have told Mr. Molotov that I think we should end our work and avoid the recriminations that have marked many of our past discussions. Therefore, it is futile even to discuss your suggestion."

Mr. Simic said he thought it would be most regrettable to toss aside the efforts of months. I agreed, but said that I saw no alternative. He tried to reopen the subject, but each time I would simply state that we had exhausted our efforts. The demands made by Mr. Molotov for the conclusion of treaties, I said, made continuation of the status quo the more attractive alternative. I told him that the Italian Government would be satisfied if we announced disagreement and that I did not see how Yugoslavia would be hurt.

In a conversation the following day Mr. Molotov inquired if I held to the view I had expressed during our private conversation. I told him I did. He said again that he thought I was too pessimistic.

"If you really entertain that view," I replied, "I would be glad if you would express some justification for your hope."

Mr. Molotov indicated he was ready to agree to some of the recommendations of the peace conference. I told him that if he took that attitude, I might revise my opinion on the outcome of the treaties.

When the council met for its next formal session, Mr. Molotov announced his agreement to some of the peace conference recommendations and proposed slight modifications for others. He realized that I meant what I had said and that he could secure no further concessions.

When Mr. Molotov decides the time has come to agree, he does it in a big way. He proposed amendments to some of the recommendations which were merely changes in words rather than substance. We were quite willing to co-operate in this face-saving and within a few days we had reached agreement on all the controversial issues. His abrupt change in attitude is accurately reflected by the fact that when the council session opened he objected to virtually all the conference recommendations; but the treaties, as finally approved, contained forty-seven of the fifty-three recommendations adopted by at least a two-thirds majority, and twenty-four of the forty-one which failed to receive a two-thirds vote but were adopted by a simple majority.

These agreements were all the more notable since they had been reached in the midst of a debate on armaments control at the General Asssembly of the United Nations a few miles away at Flushing Meadows, and during continued friction on the familiar issues of Greece and Iran. But on all of these questions, reasonable measures of progress were made.

With the close of the Assembly on December 16, five days after the adjournment of the council session, we were able to return to Washington believing that at last we had passed one important milestone on the long road to peace.

The treaties, as I stated in my radio report at the end of the Paris Conference, were "not written as we would write them if we had a free hand," but I was convinced they were as good as we could hope to get by general agreement for a long time to come. They did represent an important step in the restoration of stability. As long as the armistice terms remained in effect, all five of these countries were subject to uncertainty and interference in every phase of their national life. No planning for the future, particularly in respect to economic development, was possible under these conditions.

The treaties also paved the way for the withdrawal of Allied forces from Italy, Bulgaria and Finland and the reduction of garrisons in Rumania and Hungary. The Trieste issue was settled in such a way as to give reasonable hope that serious conflict may be avoided in the future. Italy has been disarmed so that aggressive action cannot be supported, and Yugoslavia, despite its militant nationalism, will hesitate, I believe, to challenge the authority of the Security Council in this area. While the reparations penalties against Italy were heavier than we believed wise, at least we succeeded in arranging for alleviating the methods of payment.

Perhaps most important of all, the treaties will make possible the entry of the ex-enemy states into the United Nations and their participation in the benefits and responsibilities of such specialized agencies as the International Bank, the Monetary Fund, the Food and Agriculture Organization, and the International Trade Organization. Thus, these countries will be able to join the other United Nations in cooperative action to stabilize and improve their living conditions and their economic, social and cultural relations with the rest of the world.

CONFERENCE TABLE AT POTSDAM

Reading left to right around the table from President Truman: Bohlen, Davies, Cadogan, Eden, Churchill, Birse (interpreter), Attlee, Clark Kerr (now Lord Inverchapel) in striped suit behind Attlee, Vyshinski, Molotov, Stalin (other Russians unidentified), Admiral Leahy, Byrnes.

BOOK III
UNFINISHED TREATIES

Chapter 9

Central Europe—the Crucial Test

IN GERMANY and Austria we face the crucial test of our ability to create the conditions of peace in Europe and, in fact, the world. Geographically, this area is the heart of the European continent. Economically, it has provided much of Europe's lifeblood through its mines, its industries, its agriculture and its transportation system. And politically, it is the tinderbox which has ignited two world-wide conflicts within twenty-five years and which holds the fuel that—without skill, effort, patience and statesmanship—will start still another.

Sincere and well-intentioned people have held the view that the German problem should have been settled first. Virtually everything that has happened since the end of the war has confirmed in my mind the wisdom of concluding the lesser treaties first. The record of those negotiations amply demonstrates the ingenuity of the Soviet delegation at bargaining and log rolling in the pursuit of their objectives; it illustrates their willingness to block agreement on a noncontroversial, universally accepted proposal in order to obtain concessions on some wholly unrelated issue they consider important. Such tactics would have had free play if all the complex problems of the German and Austrian settlements had been added to those of the five lesser treaties. The restoration of peace in any area would have been delayed for years to come.

We have opened the way for withdrawal of occupation armies from a large segment of Europe. When the armies are gone, 80 million people in these five countries will have a reasonable chance to select the kind of government under which they wish to live and to work out their destiny. We have stripped away countless opportunities for confusion, procrastination, and pressure. We are now able to face more directly and clearly the crucial problem of Germany and Austria.

We should recognize that the Soviet Union, alone of all the major powers, was not eager to obtain an early peace settlement. Particularly in the case of Germany, the Soviet Union was content with any policy that contributed to delay. This permitted them to continue occupying the productive zone assigned to them, to continue drawing off its resources, to continue indoctrinating the population in the Soviet way of life, and suppressing those who maintained other beliefs. Delay also permitted them to keep armed forces in Poland for the ostensible purpose of protecting lines of communication to Germany.

Soviet armies, unlike ours, live in large part off the land. They are subject to little, if any, pressure from a public or parliament that is eager to remove from the tax rolls the burden of maintaining armies of occupation. Even the men of the Red Army, unlike ours, are often content to remain where life, in all the rubble of defeat, still is richer than most of them have ever known.

The same considerations have helped to delay a settlement with Austria, where the continued maintenance of armies of occupation not only serves immediate Soviet purposes there but also permits the retention of troops in Rumania and Hungary to protect lines of communication. In the past we have learned that the Russian phrase, "protection of lines of communication," has a very broad meaning when translated into action in the internal affairs of these countries.

The case of Austria is one of the most unhappy illustrations of our difficulty in making an agreement mean the same thing to the Russians that it means to us.

In October 1943, at Moscow, Cordell Hull—one of the greatest Secretaries of State this country has known, a man I am proud to call a friend, and a counselor I had the privilege of consulting during my service in the Cabinet—scored an outstanding success of his diplomatic career. Among the agreements he helped achieve was a Big Three declaration that Austria should be restored as an independent and democratic state.

The Red Army broke into Austria early in April 1945, and soon thereafter captured Vienna. Almost immediately, it was announced that a provisional government had been formed, a government we declined to recognize primarily because it was chiefly Viennese rather than national in its composition.

A congress of political leaders from all sections of Austria was held late in September as a result of which the power of the Communist Minister of Interior was sharply restricted. The control of election machinery, the police and public security were taken from the Interior Ministry and placed under a five-man commission on which the three major parties were represented.

On October 20, 1945, we recognized Austria's Provisional Government, and, on November 23, under the supervision of the Allied military authorities, it held a "free and unfettered" election. The elected government—headed by the veteran Socialist, Karl Renner, as President, and Leopold Figl as Chancellor—was recognized by the four occupying powers on January 7, 1946.

The fate of Austria, however, continues to lie in the hands of the Allied Council. Until a treaty is concluded defining Austria's position as an independent state, the council will remain the supreme authority. As in the case of Germany, Austria (which is only slightly larger than South Carolina) and its capital city, Vienna, are each divided into four separate compartments; and, as in Germany, the Soviet zone is not only the largest but it contains important industries and the best agricultural land.

The elections of 1945 reflected a general return to the political line-ups that prevailed prior to the Nazi Anschluss with the Socialist and the People's parties predominant, representing roughly a division between the urban and the rural areas. The Communist Party received less than 5 per cent of the total vote. Since these elections, Soviet policy toward Austria has altered noticeably. It is not unfair to describe this policy now as one that seems to punish the Austrians for their association with the Germans during the Nazi occupation, and one that tries to make Austria an economic if not a political dependent of the Soviet Union.

But when we were at Potsdam, the elections had not taken place. Decisions on Austria were made with relative ease. In fact, it was the Soviet delegation that suggested that the authority of the Renner provisional government be extended into all the zones. With the British, we finally agreed to examine the question once our troops had entered their zones.

The question of Austria first entered the Potsdam discussions when Prime Minister Churchill complained that although the country had fallen to the Allies in April, it was then July 20 and British forces had not yet been permitted to move into their zone of occupation. The situation, he declared, was "not satisfactory"—a typical bit of British understatement.

Stalin pointed out that agreement on zones had just been reached, owing largely, he said, to the delay of the French. He chided Churchill for being indignant and said the situation had been made difficult because Field Marshal Alexander had acted "less skillfully" than the British and American commanders in Germany. Alexander, he said, "behaves as if Russian troops were under his control."

The affair was straightened out quickly. Two days later Stalin announced that Soviet troops had begun withdrawing to their own zone. Later in the conference he acceded to Churchill's request for assistance in feeding the Viennese in the non-Russian zones since the city's food supplies normally came from the eastern, Russian-occupied area.

With this issue amicably settled, we turned to the question of reparations. Mr. Molotov proposed that Austrian reparations should be fixed at 250 million dollars, payable in goods over a six-year period. He designated the Big Three and Yugoslavia as the recipients. The British and the United States not only renounced any desire for reparations from Austria but maintained that, in accordance with the Moscow Declaration of 1943, we should treat Austria as a liberated area and not as an enemy country, and should exact no reparations from her.

The United States, Mr. Molotov replied, had not been occupied by Austrian troops, whereas the Austrians had wrought great devastation in the Soviet Union; they could not, therefore, go unpunished.

We appreciated, I told him, the sacrifices of the Soviet people in human lives for which there could be no material compensation. Mr. Molotov said he was talking about property and not about lives. I reminded him of our huge war expenditures and asserted that, in computing losses, there was little difference between losing a building and paying for the cost of such a building. He then asked if we would agree to the taking of plants and materials as reparations from Austria and Italy.

I replied that we could not agree to the theory that Austria, a liberated country, should pay reparations but we would agree that plants that could only be used for war purposes might be taken from Italy as reparations.

He dismissed this qualification by saying materials used for war purposes were "war booty" and could be taken anyway. I also pointed out that Austria, even then, required relief from UNRRA; that it would be wrong for a country to pay out reparations to the Allies while receiving relief from those Allies.

At the next-to-the-last meeting of the Big Three on August 1, when the conference protocol was being examined, the new British Prime Minister, Mr. Attlee, said he understood Generalissimo Stalin had agreed previously that Austria would not be called on for reparations. He was not quite clear on it, he said, and asked if this were a "firm" decision.

"It is," Stalin replied. "The agreement should be stated in the protocol."

We soon found, however, that Mr. Molotov was determined to get at least the equivalent of reparations in a somewhat different fashion. The loophole is in the section of the protocol dealing with reparations from Germany—it makes available for reparations "German assets" in the Soviet zone of occupation in Austria. During seven years of occupation, the Nazis, often through transfers made under duress or by use of outright force, had acquired large interests in the entire Austrian economy including the oil fields, the banks, Danube shipping, and so on. The Soviet Government claimed that this made such properties "German assets" and, therefore, available to Russia. No one of the other three occupying powers could have anticipated this interpretation of the Potsdam agreement, and no one could accept it. It certainly is in conflict with the declaration issued by the Allies in London in January, 1943, which declared that transfers of property obtained by force or duress would not be recognized. Removal of the assets claimed by the Soviets would wreck Austria's economy; leaving them in Austria under Soviet ownership and control would mean the end of Austria as a sovereign state.

The Austrian government sought to curb Russian seizure of all these assets by nationalizing them, but the Soviet authorities ignored the law on the ground that it violated the Potsdam agreement. Up to this writing, all efforts to solve this issue through diplomatic channels—in the Allied Council and in the Council of Foreign Ministers—have been unsuccessful. The experience of our representative on the Control Council, General Mark Clark, and my own experience in the Council of Foreign Ministers force me to the conclusion that the Soviet Union has no intention of concluding a treaty with Austria as long as it can be avoided; that it desires a prolonged occupation during which time every effort will be made to gain control of the economic and political structure of the country and firmly tie it into the Eastern bloc.

At Moscow, in December 1945, I tried to discuss the problem of German assets in Austria and proposed lightening Austria's economic burden by reducing the occupation forces. On the first point, all I could get was Mr. Molotov's promise to give the subject consideration. On the second, my proposal first stimulated a charge that the Austrians were seeking to "insinuate" Fascists into the government. Then a paper was presented charging the British, particularly, with rebuilding the Austrian Army and also Nazi and anti-Communist White Russian units with the ostensible purpose of directing them against the Soviet Union.

Mr. Bevin replied with a blunt memorandum declaring that the allegations, "which are entirely without foundation, are categorically rejected." They displayed, he said, a distrust that is "deeply resented." He asserted that Soviet representatives in Austria must be "listening to fictitious tales maliciously recounted to them by persons seeking to create suspicion and ill feeling between the Allies." He pointed out that a four-power commission was now investigating these charges in all the zones and proposed that this procedure be followed in all such cases both in Austria and in Germany.

That was as far as we progressed at Moscow in our talks about Austria.

In February 1946, the United States informed the other members of the Council of Foreign Ministers that we wanted to discuss the treaty with Austria at the next meeting in Paris. On April 25, the first day of the session, I tried to have the question included on our agenda. Mr. Molotov immediately objected, saying his delegation had not had an opportunity to study the paper we had submitted.

"There is no parallel between Austria and the other countries and the treaty with Austria calls for special consideration," Mr. Molotov said. "The Soviet delegation is not ready to give it consideration at this time. Of course, we will study with full attention the proposal of Mr. Byrnes and will advise when we are ready to discuss it."

I tried again, during a private conversation with Mr. Molotov and Mr. Vyshinski, on April 28, and was told the Austrian Government had not shown itself capable of cleaning out the Nazis, and occupation forces would have to remain for at least another year. I proposed that the deputies begin a study of an Austrian treaty and was told it was a matter that had to be considered by the Ministers.

Toward the end of the meeting, when we were considering the agenda for our session to begin June 15, I proposed that the Austrian treaty be included and that the deputies prepare a treaty draft for all of us to consider. Mr. Molotov contended that such action was "inadvisable" since the deputies would have their hands full with the five treaties under consideration. Mr. Bevin then suggested that the four powers exchange drafts of treaties in the interim and plan to discuss them in June. Mr. Molotov refused to make any commitment except to "take steps to intensify and expedite the preparation for discussion of the question of a treaty with Austria"; whereupon Mr. Bevin served notice that the British delegation would press, "in whatever way was open to it," for the consideration of an Austrian treaty in June.

Mr. Molotov reiterated that the council was completely occupied with the treaties already under consideration and added:

"May God help us to complete the work on the treaties which are now before us."

Since it was clear that Mr. Molotov was lending little assistance, I could only reply that I hoped, indeed, that God would do so.

That was the extent of our progress on Austria at the first Paris council session.

During the recess, the United States sent the other members of the council a draft treaty with Austria so that there would be a basis for discussion when the council reconvened. This time, Mr. Molotov did not directly oppose the inclusion of the subject on the agenda, he merely asked that a decision be postponed. The council then accepted Mr. Bidault's suggestion that we place at the end of the agenda the subject, "Examination of the Austrian Question." On June 26, the British submitted a second draft, but no action was taken until the final day of the session, July 12. Then I asked that the deputies be instructed to study these two drafts and any others the French and Soviet delegations might submit, with a view to arriving at an agreed proposal. It was "inconceivable," I said, that we should conclude treaties with ex-enemy states before even considering a treaty with Austria, which all the council members regarded as a liberated country whose sovereign freedom they were pledged to restore.

Mr. Molotov thereupon presented a four-point resolution which, first, called attention to the recent agreement in the Allied Council increasing the authority of the Austrian Government. Second, it asserted that there were 437,000 displaced persons in the western zones of occupation, many of whom were pro-Nazi Yugoslav Chetniks and Ustashis, Hungarian Salashists, Russian and Ukrainian White Guards, and members of General Anders' Polish Army, whom he described as "Fascists." Mr. Molotov proposed that the council find that these displaced persons "constitute a grave danger to the neighboring democratic states," and agree to their "imperative and urgent" evacuation. Third, the resolution stated that the "successful accomplishment" of this evacuation was a necessary prerequisite to restoring Austria's full independence. And, last, Molotov's resolution would permit the deputies to begin preparing an Austrian treaty only after the other five treaties were completed.

We immediately agreed that the problem of displaced persons was urgent, and pointed out that the United Nations was then considering it. Both Mr. Bevin and I objected to making the solution of this question a prerequisite for beginning work on a treaty. Nor could we endorse the allegations in the resolution without first determining the facts. Mr. Bevin then referred to the problem of defining German assets in Austria and asked that a four-power commission be appointed to find a solution. Mr. Molotov refused to discuss it, saying it was not on the agenda. I pointed out that the matter of displaced persons had not been on the agenda either, but we had discussed it.

With that, the Austrian discussions stopped. We made no further progress in Paris.

In New York we tried again. This time Mr. Molotov responded with a proposal that both Germany and Austria be considered at a meeting of the council to be held at Moscow in March. Mr. Bevin and Mr. Couve de Murville, who was acting in the absence of Mr. Bidault, joined me in urging that deputies be appointed to begin preliminary work at once. Two days later, on December 11, Mr. Molotov agreed to the appointment of deputies for both the Austrian and the German treaties and it was decided they should begin work in London on January 14. Then, again, I raised the question of German assets in Austria; Mr. Molotov said he was not prepared to discuss it. I agreed not to press the issue as long as it was understood that the deputies would consider it.

Having sought from February to December to initiate work on a treaty for Austria, I realized that the end of the task was far ahead of us, and that a German treaty belonged to the still more distant future. The United States delegation decided that the next best thing was to try again to reduce the Allied occupation forces throughout Europe. Such action, we contended, would lift a heavy burden from the victors as well as the vanquished. We proposed that the four powers agree to reduce their forces to 10,000 in each of the four zones in Austria by April 1, and in Germany to the following numbers by that date: 200,000 in the Soviet zone, 140,000 each in the American and British zones, and 70,000 in the French zone. This reduction, we asserted, would permit a corresponding cut in the number of troops along lines of communication. We proposed a limit of 20,000 in Poland and 5,000 each in Hungary and Rumania.

Mr. Molotov said that this was a new question and that he was not prepared to consider it. Mr. Bevin asked if Mr. Molotov would be prepared to discuss it if it were raised at the meeting in Moscow and the latter indicated his assent. But, at Moscow, when Secretary Marshall again presented the proposal, Mr. Molotov would not agree.

During the Moscow meeting, the efforts of Secretary of State Marshall to conclude a treaty with Austria met with little success. The Austrian Treaty Commission, then created, has made virtually no progress. We will find at the council meeting, scheduled to take place in November, that the issue was merely postponed six more months. There is no certainty that we will reach agreement on a treaty even at that meeting. Our past experience certainly does not encourage optimism.

We must remember that we are not dealing with an enemy state. The treaty involved has the relatively simple objectives of re-establishing Austria's independence and fixing its frontiers. But we will be fortunate indeed if April, 1948—the third anniversary of its liberation from the Nazis—finds Austria restored to the freedom and independence that were pledged it by the Big Three in 1943.

In the case of Germany, our initial agreements were as satisfactory as the subsequent developments have been discouraging. At Potsdam, we gave primary consideration to the German problem. Even while we pressed successfully for the agreement to conclude the lesser treaties first, we took the initiative in securing approval for a set of political and economic principles to govern the occupation of Germany. These principles could have opened the way to an early and equitable peace settlement.

Politically, these principles not only provided for removal and punishment of all Nazis, but they set up the framework within which German political life could be reconstructed on a democratic basis. They directed the reorganization of the judicial and educational systems in accordance with democratic ideals, and they promoted the cause of free local governments and free trade unions. While insisting upon decentralization of the German political structure, they provided for central German administrative agencies in the fields of finance, transportation, communications, foreign trade and industry.

In the economic sphere, these principles called for prohibiting all armaments production, restricting the peacetime needs of industries convertible to war uses and eliminating centralized economic controls such as cartels. The three powers agreed that Germany should be treated as a single economic unit in which primary emphasis would be placed on the development of agriculture and peaceful domestic industries. There were to be common Allied policies on industrial production, mining, transportation and communication, agriculture, wages and prices, foreign trade, currency and banking.

Reparations, we originally had hoped, would be included in this list as well. But the wholesale removal of property by the Red Army prior to Potsdam forced us to conclude that an over-all accounting was an impractical hope and we turned to the plan of handling reparations on a zonal basis. Even then, it was provided that production available for export should be used to pay for necessary imports first and then for reparations; a provision which clearly called for over-all economic planning and administration.

Another aspect of the reparations agreement made at Potsdam has not received the attention it deserves. The recommendation made at Yalta that the "use of German labor" should be considered by the Reparations Commission as a possible source of reparations was dropped by the Big Three at Potsdam and the protocol signed there contained no provision for, or reference to, the use of labor as reparations. Yet it is a deplorable fact that thousands of Germans and Japanese are still being held as enforced laborers in violation of solemn international pledges.

In the closing days of the war against Germany we took so many prisoners it was difficult to care for them behind the lines, and guarding them required so many troops that General Eisenhower decided to transfer many of them to the custody of the liberated nations. But these prisoners surrendered to the United States Army and we therefore retained responsibility. The prisoners held in the United States we endeavored to return promptly. We encountered some resistance from their employers who found the labor profitable, but both Secretary of War Patterson and I were insistent. Notwithstanding the problems in getting necessary transportation, the last of the German and Italian prisoners in this country were returned home in the fall of 1946.

The Geneva Prisoners of War Convention, in letter and spirit, contemplates the repatriation of prisoners as soon as possible after the end of actual fighting. The Soviet Union was not a signatory of that convention but Great Britain and France were.

Because of the obligations I felt the convention placed on the Allied powers, I thought they, too, should exert every effort to expedite the return of prisoners. But, I could not well complain of others until we had returned our prisoners. On September 12, 1946, the British announced a program that would return the last of their prisoners to their homes in October, 1948. This seemed to me to be very slow, but at least it was a planned schedule. That same month, I suggested informally to the French a program for returning these prisoners for which we were responsible.

At that time, France still held approximately 600,000 of the prisoners transferred by General Eisenhower, of which 40,000 were working in coal mines, 280,000 were working on farms and the balance were in miscellaneous occupations.

The French asked me to withhold any formal action for a short time, which I did. But on December 2, 1946, I asked all three governments holding prisoners for us—France, Belgium and Luxemburg—to agree to complete repatriation by October 1, 1947. My message pointed out that eighteen months had elapsed since the end of hostilities and that, since the idea of forced labor was repugnant to the American people, we believed those prisoners not charged with war crimes should be returned. The French answered that while they realized the prisoners must be returned, they were so short of labor that they needed a longer period to complete the repatriation.

In mid-1947 we had in our zone in Germany approximately 573,000 displaced persons. We support them and will not force them to return to the countries of their origin as long as there is reason to believe they would be punished for political reasons.

I had suggested to French officials that they offer work to these people, but when their representatives went to Germany they expressed a preference for German workers. I believe it was the French Communists who objected to bringing in the anti-Communist Poles, Balts and Slavs. But the more quickly the German prisoners in France are returned to Germany, the more quickly will France want to find employment for the displaced persons now in camps in Germany and Austria.

On March 13, 1947, our government announced that an agreement had been reached with the French under which approximately 450,000 prisoners, including those captured by French forces as well as our own, would be released at the rate of 20,000 per month. This means that the last of the German prisoners will not be returned home until about four years after the end of the war. The agreement further provided that the prisoners, upon release, would be given a choice of repatriation or of remaining in France as voluntary workers. We should be certain that contracts are offered to the prisoners for whom we are responsible, under circumstances that protect their freedom of choice.

We know little about the prisoners of war in the Soviet Union, German or Japanese. Generalissimo Stalin told Mr. Hopkins in June, 1945, that they had about two million prisoners of whom 1,700,000 were Germans. He said they were being used in the Ukraine, White Russia and in the Moscow area on reconstruction projects, in the coal mines and in the timber industry. The Germans, he observed, had been so underfed that they were poor workers; he preferred the Hungarians, who were better fed. In March, 1947, the Soviet Government claimed to have returned over one million Germans and to have 890,000 left.

An over-all agreement on the repatriation of German prisoners finally was obtained at the last meeting of the Council of Foreign Ministers in Moscow. The agreement, reached on April 23, provides that all German prisoners shall be returned by December 31, 1948, and thus will have virtually the same effect as the French-American understanding. I still believe that we should have insisted that France return the prisoners for whom we are responsible by October 1, 1947. In any event, I hope that this issue, which should have never become a part of the reparations question, will be settled by the dates now agreed upon. Forced labor camps are a symbol of Hitler's regime that we should eliminate as rapidly as possible.

This story provides one more example of the many instances where what we thought was an understanding turned out to be no agreement at all. That is why I have stated that the Potsdam agreements on Germany failed. Because they failed it has become popular to criticize them. But the fault does not lie with the agreements. The refusal of the Soviet Union to join wholeheartedly in the collaborative effort necessary to fulfill them was and is the very heart of the German problem. This fact, however, did not become evident to us until some months after Potsdam because the French, without intending to, assumed much of the burden that the Soviet Union was quite willing to share.

France was not represented at Potsdam and therefore did not feel bound by the agreements made there; in fact, it objected strongly to some of them. These objections were placed before President Truman and me by General de Gaulle and Mr. Bidault during their visit to Washington a few weeks after our return from Germany.

Their worries centered on the plan to establish central German administrative agencies and on the disposition of the Rhineland, the Ruhr and the Saar. General de Gaulle feared that these acts were the prelude to the reconstruction of a centralized German state. To re-establish

German unity now, he contended, would be even more dangerous than in the past, because Germany might come under the influence of a strong and powerful Slav bloc rising in the east. The very fact that Germany was now weak, he said, "makes that country all the more susceptible of becoming the political instrument of other powers." The extension of Poland into eastern Germany, both of the French leaders argued, shifted Germany's center of gravity toward the west and therefore endangered the security of France. They asked for the separation of the Rhineland from Germany for administration by France, for the annexation of the Saar, and the transfer of the Ruhr to an international regime.

President Truman and I tried to convince them that the establishment of a central administration for such things as transportation and currency was not creating a highly centralized German government. The security of France, we asserted, could be promoted far more effectively by the United Nations than by slicing away sections of German territory. Only through joint action of all nations, we argued, could the maximum of security be realized.

We were unsuccessful in our efforts, and Mr. Bidault renewed his arguments at the first meeting of the Council of Foreign Ministers in London. France, he said, would continue to oppose creation of a central German authority in the absence of a decision on Germany's western frontier. The French feared that extension of German administration into the Ruhr and the Rhineland would prevent them from acquiring in the peace settlement the control they desired. In proposing an international regime for the Ruhr they were tactfully vague because they did not wish to precipitate the issue of Russian participation in the regime. Nevertheless, this provided Mr. Molotov with an opportunity to renew his proposal for four-power control of the Ruhr. It was suggested that the issues be studied by the deputies but the three of us finally agreed to Mr. Molotov's proposal that the matter should be pursued for the time being "through diplomatic channels."

All the political parties in France insisted that the government take the position stated by Mr. Bidault, but that position has blocked revival of healthy economic activity; it has also given the Soviets an excuse for delay for which they do not have to assume responsibility. I understand why the French are fearful, but I believe they should take a fresh look at the situation. They should withdraw their opposition to central administrative agencies essential to economic unity. There is even less reason for their position since Mr. Bevin and I, long ago, gave assurances in writing that in the peace settlement we would support the cession of the Saar to France. The continuation of their stand will not affect the Soviet position. Russia will maintain its opposition to the cession of the Saar until the final hours and then seek to secure, in exchange for agreement, French support on some other question.

As might be expected, little progress was made after London "through diplomatic channels"; and so, before going to Paris in April, I determined to insist that we start work on the German settlement. The American delegation, therefore, proposed the appointment of special deputies who would undertake two distinct tasks: prepare a report on immediate occupation problems and begin work on a German treaty. The division of Germany into four water-tight compartments, preventing the exchange of people, commodities, and even ideas, I pointed out, was forcing the United States to spend 200 million dollars a year to furnish food which ordinarily would come from the Russian zone. Production of goods for export would have to be increased in order to pay for the food we were bringing in; in such a situation we could not continue dismantling industrial plants to send to Russia for reparations.

The second duty assigned to the deputies, we urged, need not wait until a German government was established. We should agree among ourselves, we maintained, on the nature of the peace settlement and the kind of German government that should be created. Then, both the occupying powers and the German people would know how to proceed.

Our proposal was generally acceptable to France and Britain but Mr. Molotov refused to consent to the appointment of deputies. Even more disappointing was his rejection of our additional proposal for a twenty-five year treaty among the Big Four to block a resurgence of German militarism.

I had first discussed this proposal with Mr. Molotov informally at London in September and had been encouraged by his interest. But when we heard no more from him about it, I put it on the list of items to be discussed with Generalissimo Stalin during the Moscow meeting.

I waited until the Christmas Eve dinner which the Russian leader hospitably tendered us. After a toast-laden dinner marked by its cordiality, we moved into the drawing room for coffee. While it was being served, the Generalissimo and I sat down for a quiet chat; only his interpreter, Mr. Pavlov, was with us. I told him I had been disappointed not to hear from Molotov about the treaty we had discussed in London. He said his Foreign Minister had mentioned it to him, but it was evident from the questions he asked me that no serious consideration had been given to the proposal.

"Such a treaty will give all European states assurance that the United States would not return to a policy of isolation," I told him. "I have often recalled how you expressed at Yalta your fear of another invasion by Germany. You then asserted that the continued co-operation of the four Allies in keeping Germany demilitarized would relieve your fears and perhaps influence your actions in the Balkan states."

Stalin replied that it was the best proposal he had yet heard.

"The United States has always been reluctant to enter into such treaties," I added, "but our experience in trying to stay out of Europe's wars has been so disastrous I am confident our people would support a treaty under which the major powers would join forces to keep Germany disarmed. The Senate will have to ratify such a treaty but I think they will do so and I am willing to make the effort."

"If you decide to fight for such a treaty," Stalin said, "you can rely on my support."

With this conversation in mind, I started preparing a German treaty draft as soon as we returned to the United States. To minimize the possibility of misunderstanding, I followed as closely as possible the language agreed upon in the Allied declaration of June 5, 1945, on demilitarization during the occupation period. I also included a provision in which I have had a deep interest: That, following the conclusion of a peace treaty with Germany, the four major powers should maintain an inspection force. On this force would be men with engineering knowledge and similar specialized skills, to prevent the establishment of or conversion of industries capable of producing weapons of war. Should these technically skilled inspectors report a treaty violation, the four powers would call upon the German Government to order the manufacturer to stop these dangerous activities. A refusal would permit the four powers to take whatever steps they thought necessary to force compliance.

Such a compact would eliminate the need to maintain large armed forces in Germany. A disarmed Germany would never fail to comply with an order from the Allied headquarters if the government knew a violation would bring the air forces of one or more of the four powers over their land within a few hours.

Action under the treaty I proposed could be taken upon a majority vote. Of course, with four powers, it would take three to constitute a majority. The obvious purpose of this was to prevent any one state from blocking prompt action. This elimination of the veto power may be one reason for Soviet opposition, but if so, it is one reason Mr. Molotov has never mentioned. Under Article 107 of the United Nations Charter, punitive action is permitted against a former enemy state by the governments responsible for such action.

President Truman heartily approved of the proposal. He was so sure it would be accepted he began referring to it as the Byrnes treaty. I also discussed it with Senator Connally and Senator Vandenberg. The latter, in fact, had forcefully presented a similar idea in his notable speech to the Senate in January, 1945. In addition, I presented the plan to a group of Senators who had been appointed by the chairman of the Foreign Relations Committee to confer with me on matters such as this. These Senators, of course, had to reserve their decision until the treaty was before them in final form but they endorsed the plan in principle.

After receiving this general concurrence, in early February I sent copies of the proposed treaty to the Soviet Union, the United Kingdom and France with the request that they regard it as a basis for discussion and feel free to suggest amendments or alternate drafts. Mr. Bevin and Mr. Bidault quickly said that they endorsed the treaty, subject to some amendments they would offer. Just before leaving Washington for Paris, I received a message from Mr. Molotov stating simply that he had certain objections.

At dinner with Mr. Molotov on April 28, I asked him to let me know what those objections were. To my surprise, he stated that the treaty appeared to postpone the question of German disarmament until after the occupation. An agreement already existed, he said, that Germany should be disarmed immediately and he proposed that a commission be appointed to verify how it was being carried out. When this investigation was completed, he added, the question of future controls could be embodied in a separate treaty.

He already knew, but I nevertheless outlined for him, the whole background leading up to our drafting of this treaty, beginning with the conversation at Yalta in which Stalin had expressed fear of a revival of German militarism.

"This treaty," I said, "will serve as added insurance against your fears of a renewed attack by Germany and it will remove any element of doubt about the United States bearing its full share of the burden of safeguarding the peace. I must tell you frankly that there are many people in the United States who are unable to understand the exact aim of the Soviet Union—whether it is a search for security or merely expansion. A treaty such as this, and a similar treaty for Japan, will effectively take care of the question of security."

The Soviet Union, he replied, is "in favor of a twenty-five year demilitarization treaty both for Germany and Japan," but he emphasized the importance of carrying out the previous agreement for the immediate disarmament of Germany. We had a long discussion in which we were joined by Mr. Vyshinski and Mr. Cohen. Ben and I did our best to persuade Molotov and Vyshinski that our treaty did not postpone the disarmament of Germany but on the contrary was based on the assumption that disarmament would be completed at once and that the treaty would insure the maintenance of Germany's demilitarization.

The next day I raised the subject in the council and Mr. Molotov repeated substantially the same arguments. He said he would consider our proposal carefully but thought that the "burning question" before the council was the proper completion of the present agreement. I read to him the opening words of our draft which referred to the previous agreement between our governments "to effect the total demilitarization and disarmament" and went on to say that nothing in the proposed treaty "shall delay or prevent the completion of that process."

To meet Mr. Molotov's argument regarding lack of action on the existing demilitarization agreement, I communicated with General Clay in Berlin. A few days later he proposed to the Allied Control Council the apopintment of a commission to visit the four zones and report on the progress of demilitarization. When I reported this action to the council, Mr. Molotov said his government would support it. However, it did not alter his views on the treaty.

When the treaty was again considered, Mr. Molotov adopted a tactic the Russians often employ—he assumed the offensive. The period of the treaty, he said, was not long enough; it should run for at least forty years. I immediately agreed to make it that. It was, he went on, "completely inadequate" and "cannot be a reliable guarantee of security in Europe and the world," as its provisions for disarmament and demilitarization were not sufficiently comprehensive. I reminded him that when I had submitted the treaty I had told him that the language of the disarmament and demilitarization sections had been taken from an agreement issued June 5, 1945, on behalf of our governments by Generals Zhukov, Montgomery, deLattre de Tassigny, and Eisenhower, and that I knew of no better qualified men to draft a demilitarization program. However, if it was not sufficiently comprehensive, I suggested that we amend it.

Mr. Molotov then returned to his previous statement that such a treaty was useless in the absence of any immediate action to disarm Germany. I pointed out that General Clay in the Allied Control Council in Berlin had proposed the appointment of a commission to investigate the status of disarmament in all four zones; that Mr. Molotov had said his government would support it but that every member had agreed except the Soviet representative, who insisted the inquiry should not extend to the demilitarization of industrial plants. If he really wanted an investigation, I said, he could instruct his representative in Berlin to agree and the inquiry would be started promptly.

He then complained that the treaty "evades and disregards" such problems as democratizing Germany. I explained that economic and political objectives for the future would be set forth hereafter in any treaty agreed upon at a peace conference. I said, further, that this particular treaty which provided the method and the necessary force to require compliance should not be confused with a political-economic treaty.

The discussion made it clear that he had no idea of discussing the treaty in a serious manner but was simply looking for excuses for delay. And my patience was exhausted when he continued: "The treaty ignores the necessity of delivering to the Soviet Union reparations totaling at least 10 billion dollars, which President Roosevelt had agreed to at Yalta." Reparations payments, he continued, "naturally" must include commodities out of current production as well as equipment, and he then referred to the "unlawful statement" by General Clay that no more reparations deliveries would be made.

"When the United States is willing to make a drastic departure from its policies of the past and offers this treaty in order to help insure security for Europe," I replied, "we resent having that offer met with irrelevant arguments on reparations and minor difficulties of the occupation.

"You have misquoted President Roosevelt," I added. "My shorthand notes as well as the protocol itself show that the President stated simply that the Soviet proposal should be referred to the Reparations Commission as a basis for discussion." At Potsdam, President Truman and Generalissimo Stalin agreed to a reparations program which recognized the impossibility of obtaining this sum and which deliberately and intentionally stated no amount in dollars.

"Other agreements were made at Potsdam," I continued, "including a provision that reparations payments should leave enough resources to permit the Germans to live without external assistance. Still another agreement provides that exports should first be used to pay for necessary imports. Notwithstanding this, the United States is having to support the people in its zone at a cost of 200 million dollars a year. It was also agreed that Germany should be treated as an economic unit but this is not being done. Therefore, when you complain about General Clay's action, you should remember his action is taken only to obtain justice for the United States under the Potsdam agreement."

By the time Mr. Molotov and I had finished our exchange it was 8:30 P.M. Our tempers as well as our appetites were on edge so I quickly accepted Mr. Bevin's suggestion that the discussion be continued the following day.

The next morning, Mr. Bevin and Mr. Bidault made strong statements in general support of our position. The British people regard the resurgence of Germany as the greatest menace to peace, Mr. Bevin said, and, although he might have some amendments to offer later, his government warmly approved the treaty for the long-term disarmament and demilitarization of Germany. There are three approaches to maintenance of peace in Europe, he continued: first, a balance of power between states of equal strength; second, domination by one power or by two blocs of powers; and third, united control by the four powers with the co-operation of their Allies. It is this last approach, he stressed, that the British Government believes is the most likely to produce stability.

Mr. Bidault, in his statement, declared it was necessary that measures be undertaken to destroy the "militaristic Prussian character" of Germany, and the American treaty should constitute "the crown of the edifice." It would not be an obstacle to reparation, denazification, or any of the other essential tasks of the occupation, he insisted, but would make more concrete the solidarity of the Allies against the danger of a resurgent Germany and would guarantee the security of Europe with the "indispensable" support of the United States.

Both these statements were impressive but they were unsuccessful in swaying the stand taken by Mr. Molotov. When Secretary of State Marshall again proposed consideration of the twenty-five or forty-year treaty at Moscow in April, 1947, the Soviet Foreign Minister offered new reasons for opposing it. Some of the reasons and the amendments he offered were so irrelevant and absurd they indicated a deliberate intent to make certain they could not be accepted.

I have been forced to the conclusion that following Stalin's promise, on December 24, 1945, to support the treaty, the Soviet High Command or Politburo concluded they did not want the United States involved in the maintenance of European security for the next twenty-five or forty years. The pressure of American power would restrict the freedom of action which the Soviet Union, as the predominant military power in Europe, might otherwise enjoy. The same assurance that made the treaty attractive to Mr. Bidault caused Mr. Molotov to disagree. I feel satisfied it is Mr. Molotov who is responsible for the Soviet position. From the very first, his indifference was in contrast to Stalin's enthusiasm.

It does not follow that Mr. Molotov will continue to oppose the treaty. He should be convinced by now that, treaty or no treaty, we intend to maintain our interest in Europe. But when he decides to support it, he will probably announce: "The Soviet Union offers a paper for consideration," and he will produce a draft of a treaty containing some reasonable amendments. He will offer it as a great concession to us and probably ask that we in turn agree to give him the two things he wants: 10 billion in reparations and a part in the control of the Ruhr.

When we made no progress at Paris in the discussions on our treaty, the council, on July 10, turned once again to the American proposal for the appointment of deputies to work both on immediate German problems and a draft treaty.

Mr. Bidault opened what proved to be a highly significant three-day discussion. He outlined the French position that, until the boundaries of Germany were set, no determination of policy could be made. He renewed the French plea for the Saar, international control of the Ruhr, and separation of the Rhineland from Germany. His second objective was assurance of larger coal deliveries from Germany. This request was directed primarily at the British as he was highly doubtful that he would ever get much coal from the Polish-operated mines in Silesia. But he agreed that deputies should be appointed to begin work on these and other problems.

Mr. Bevin also agreed to the appointment of deputies and asserted that Britain would support France's claim to the Saar. He placed particular emphasis on the necessity of securing a decision for immediate implementation of the Potsdam compact to treat Germany as an economic unit. Support of their zone, he said, was costing the British taxpayer 320 million dollars annually and it could not continue. The reason, he went on, was that surplus food from other zones, primarily the Soviet zone, was being removed from Germany.

Mr. Molotov said "no"; deputies could not be appointed until the Ministers had settled other issues. One, of course, was the Soviet demand for 10 billion dollars in reparations, and the other was control of the Ruhr. He coupled with this latter proposal the charge that disarmament and demilitarization were not being carried out in the western zones.

This was a familiar issue by now. The previous November, the Russians had charged that the British were maintaining remnants of the Nazi armies in their zone. The British had proposed an investigation by the Allied Control Council in all the zones with the understanding that a precedent would thereby be established for handling similar allegations. The matter was then dropped by the Soviet representative. Later the British submitted to the Control Council in Berlin reports that war matériel was still being manufactured in the Soviet zone and proposed an investigation of the industrial demilitarization of the country. When we had proposed an investigation early in May, Mr. Molotov had said he would support it, but his representative in Berlin blocked any action. Now, when the charges were renewed, I proposed again that the Allied Control Council set up a commission to investigate progress both in the dismantling of war plants and the destruction of arms and armed forces. Mr. Molotov contended in reply that such an investigation would be meaningless until we had decided on an over-all plan for Germany's economic disarmament.

Mr. Bidault then entered the argument. He had the impression, he said, that the members of the council "were on a merry-go-round," in which case he was "going to ride his own horse and say something more about coal."

I urged that we could get off the "merry-go-round" by appointing deputies who would narrow the points at issue and thus permit a more fruitful discussion at another session of the council. Mr. Molotov asked why I would not agree to holding a special session of the council in November.

"I have no objection to such a meeting," I replied, "but why put off until November what we can do today? What I fear is that when November comes and we propose to take up this question, the Soviet representative will suggest referring it to the deputies and another five months will pass before they get to work. I would like to get to work now."

We know now that this fear was fully justified. Mr. Molotov withheld agreement on the appointment of deputies for Germany until December 11 at the Council of Foreign Ministers meeting in New York. With Ambassador Robert D. Murphy representing the United States, the deputies met in London in January to hear the views of the smaller Allied nations who had fought against Germany and to consider the procedure for drafting a German peace treaty. We know what little progress was made at the meeting in Moscow during March and April 1947. The world now is looking toward the next meeting of the council scheduled for November, two and one-half years after the surrender of Germany, hoping for the first signs of genuine progress toward a settlement.

Chapter 10

A Course of Action

THE EARLY conclusion of peace treaties with Germany and Austria is essential to the restoration of Europe's political and economic health. The barriers of military zones, the burdens of military occupation, and the uncertainty of the future, all of which paralyze Europe's "heart land," cripple our friends and Allies as much as they bring indiscriminate punishment to Germany and Austria.

As this is written, it is almost two years since we gathered around the big table at Cecilienhof Palace in Potsdam, preparing what we believed would be an adequate blueprint for a lasting structure of peace. The blueprint has failed to fulfill our hopes. It is necessary, therefore, to evaluate the situation and plan a new course of action.

The most significant statement of Soviet policy toward Germany was made by Mr. Molotov in the Council of Foreign Ministers at Paris on July 10, 1946. The importance he attached to the speech is shown by the fact that it was released to the press in advance—an act as unusual for Soviet diplomats as it is routine for us. This first and still authoritative expression of Soviet atttude toward Germany is worthy of special note in any effort to plan for the future.

Mr. Molotov opened his speech with a strong appeal to the Germans— criticism of all suggestions that Germany should be transformed into a primarily agrarian state.

"It would be incorrect," he said, "to adopt the course of Germany's annihilation as a state or that of its agrarianization, including the annihilation of its main industrial centers." He reiterated the point in various ways. "Our purpose is not to destroy Germany," he went on, "but to transform Germany into a democratic and peace-loving state which, besides its agriculture, will have its own industry and foreign trade. . . . The policy of Germany's annihilation as a state or that of her agrarianization and annihilation of her principal industrial centers will result in making Germany a center where dangerous sentiments of revenge will be nourished and will play into the hands of German reactionaries and will deprive Europe of tranquility and peace."

Then he turned to the Ruhr, where he managed to create a two-headed horse.

Talk about the separation of the Ruhr from Germany originates "in the same policy of destruction and agrarianization of Germany, for it is easy to understand that, without the Ruhr, Germany cannot exist as an independent and viable state." But, he added, "the Ruhr should be placed under an interallied control of four countries with the object of preventing the revival of war industries in Germany." Thus he tried both to leave it and to take it away.

The future form of the German state was his next concern and he criticized the "fashionable" talk of splitting Germany into autonomous states and similar proposals, such as federalizing Germany. Allied authorities in the western zones, he said, "have encouraged the idea of a federal structure for Germany," without regard for the desires of the German people, while the Soviet Union holds "it is incorrect to impose upon the German people some one or other solution of this question." No action of this kind should be taken, no territory should be separated from Germany, except as a result of a plebiscite. He did not, of course, make any reference to the Soviet Union's support of Poland's claim for Silesia and all the territory east of the Oder and Neisse rivers.

"We should not put obstacles in the way of the increase in the output of steel, coal and manufactured products of a peaceful nature in Germany," he stated. He then mentioned the recent action of the Allied Control Council in fixing the levels at which German industries would be allowed to operate in the future, and added: "It should now be admitted that peaceful industries in Germany must be given an opportunity to develop on a wider scale. . . ." He avoided admitting that, when the levels of industry were fixed by the Control Council, the Soviet representative had voted for the lowest figure and it was only by the most urgent insistence of the American and British representatives that a higher figure was set.

He dealt finally with the question of a German peace treaty.

"Before talking about a peace treaty with Germany it is necessary to solve the question of setting up an all-German government. . . . But even when a German government has been set up *it will take a number of years* to check up on what this new German Government represents and whether it is trustworthy. . . . A future German Government must be such a democratic government as will be able to extirpate the remnants of Fascism in Germany and which will at the same time be able to fulfill Germany's obligations toward the Allies. Amongst other things and above all it will be bound to carry out reparation deliveries to the Allies. Only when we become satisfied that the new German Government is able to cope with these tasks and is really honestly fulfilling them in practice will it be possible to speak seriously of concluding a peace treaty with Germany."

Here, in this last statement, was confirmation of our fears that unless forced by world opinion to do so, the Soviet Union would not agree to a treaty of peace with Germany for years to come. They would utilize their veto power on the Allied Control Council and in the Council of Foreign Ministers to secure adoption of their conception of a "democratic" government; to secure a part in the control of German industry, the industries of the Ruhr in particular, and to enforce the payment of 10 billion dollars of reparations.

It was an effective speech. It was timed to win the favor of the German people who were about to vote in various municipal elections. Their dislike of the quietly enunciated claim for reparations was more than offset by his announced opposition to dismemberment and to cession of territory without approval by plebiscite. But the part of the statement that was particularly heartening to the Germans was that which denounced all proposals to annihilate German industry and to "agrarianize" the country. I realized at once the strength of this appeal. It was clearly calculated to play on the widespread German fear of the so-called "Morgenthau Plan," which had been widely discussed in the American press.

In October 1944, while the war was still in progress, I was in Paris. At the Guest House, where I lived, there was a sergeant who spoke German. Each night he would interpret for me the Berlin broadcasts; these invariably included an appeal to the people of Germany not to consider the proposals of the Allies to surrender. Surrender, they warned, meant enforcement of the "Morgenthau Plan" which would destroy all industry and turn Germany into an agricultural state. The plan was greatly exaggerated to inspire the Germans to fight and die rather than surrender. Molotov's speech was aimed at the German people who had listened to those broadcasts day after day, and had been educated to expect only the harshest treatment from the United States. He capitalized on the confusion in the minds of the German people about American policy.

I had to admit the effectiveness of the effort because there *had* been confusion in our own country on the policy of the United States toward Germany. The truth is, there had even been much confusion in the Cabinet on the subject.

My mind went back to an occasion at the White House, in the latter part of August 1944, when President Roosevelt had discussed the kind of peace he proposed for Germany. He said that some well-meaning but misguided officials of the State Department were planning what he regarded as a "soft" peace for Germany. That, he said, was not his plan.

The German people should be taught their responsibility for the war and for a long time should have only soup for breakfast, soup for lunch, and soup for dinner. It did not sound like President Roosevelt. He was angry.

About that time he appointed a Cabinet committee to consider the peace for Germany, consisting of the Secretary of State, Mr. Hull, the Secretary of the Treasury, Mr. Morgenthau, and the Secretary of War, Mr. Stimson.

There was a wide difference of opinion among the members of this Cabinet committee. On September 9, 1944, they held a meeting in the President's office which was also attended by Mr. Hopkins.

Secretary Stimson took the position that they were all trying to devise protection against a recurrence of attempts by Germany to dominate the world. They differed, he said, as to the method. He contended that Mr. Morgenthau's remedy would substantially obliterate the industry of Germany. He quoted Mr. Morgenthau's plan for the Ruhr and surrounding industrial areas as providing that:

"This area should not only be stripped of all presently existing industries but so weakened and controlled that it cannot in the foreseeable future become an industrial area—all industrial plants and equipment not destroyed by military action shall either be completely dismantled and removed from the area or completely destroyed, all equipment shall be removed from the mines and the mines shall be thoroughly wrecked."

These resources, Secretary Stimson argued, constitute a natural and necessary asset for the productivity of Europe. He urged that such assets should be conserved and made available for the benefit of the European continent. His thought was that the internationalization of the Ruhr or the trusteeship of its products would constitute a treatment of the problem in accord with the needs and interests of the world.

Secretary Stimson objected also to the proposal in Mr. Morgenthau's plan that so-called archcriminals should be put to death by the military without provision for any trial and upon mere identification after apprehension. Mr. Stimson contended that the procedure should embody at least the rudimentary aspects of the Bill of Rights. If these criminals were punished in a dignified manner consistent with the advance of civilization, he asserted, it would have a greater effect upon posterity.

About the same time, the President and Secretary Hull asked me to consider becoming the American High Commissioner for Germany. I had previously told the President of my desire to leave the Office of War Mobilization and Reconversion at the end of hostilities but this new proposal did not appeal to me. Nevertheless, I promised to consider it and to study the plan that had been outlined for the occupation. Mr. James Riddleberger, who has ably directed the administration of German affairs in the Department of State through the postwar period, brought me the plan for occupation and offered to answer any questions. It impressed me as intended to enforce a punitive peace somewhat along the lines suggested to the President by the Secretary of the Treasury. I shared the President's opposition to what he regarded as a "soft peace" but I thought the plan was unnecessarily harsh and not wise for the future of Europe.

One provision struck me particularly. Its phraseology was tantamount to saying that the principal war criminals should be tried and hanged. I asked if any consideration had been given to the possibility that some of those charged might be acquitted or that a mistrial might occur. Mr. Riddleberger agreed that the language was questionable. In justice to the State Department, he added, I should be informed that much of the plan, including that section, had been prepared by representatives of the Treasury Department. Shortly thereafter, I informed the President and Secretary Hull that I could not accept the appointment, since I did not think I was qualified for the task.

The difference in the Cabinet committee did not come to a head until President Roosevelt and Prime Minister Churchill met in Quebec in September 1944. Secretary Hull did not attend because, he told me, the President had said that only military matters would be discussed. There evidently was a change of plan because Secretary Morgenthau did attend. Nor did Secretary Stimson go, but after the meeting was under way he sent the President his views on the postwar program for Germany.

It developed that the Quebec Conference was very important. Agreements were reached, for example, on the zones to be occupied by the British and American forces in Germany. We accepted the southern zone after Mr. Churchill agreed that Bremerhaven in the British zone, should be made part of the American zone to insure us the use of a major port for the transportation of men and supplies.

Another important decision, on September 14, dealt with the continuation of a very generous lend-lease program to Britain during the war with Japan.

Differences arose about this agreement. In a memorandum handed the Secretary of State by the Secretary of the Treasury, on September 20, it was stated that "the President thought a committee should be set up and suggested that Mr. Morgenthau should head it, representing him, and that Mr. Stettinius who had taken such a large part in lend-lease should also be a member." However, the memorandum from the White House contained simply the record of the conversation in Quebec and did not include this paragraph. Mr. Leo T. Crowley, then in charge of Foreign Economic Administration, presumably was to administer lend-lease. Mr. Crowley and the President discussed carrying out lend-lease for the British. He said that the President had instructed him to continue administering lend-lease and to consider British requests as he considered all other requests and without regard to the Quebec agreement.

The question of how the lend-lease program for the British should be carried out did not become an acute controversy between the departments because of President Roosevelt's death and because of the short time that elapsed between the surrender in Europe and the Japanese surrender.

Mr. Churchill and Mr. Roosevelt, however, on September 15, had approved with their initials a memorandum on postwar Germany, which was subsequently called the "Morgenthau Plan." The President followed the views held by the Secretary of the Treasury instead of those held by the Secretaries of State and of War. The portion of the agreement which immediately attracted the attention of officials in Washington was the reference to the "metallurgical, chemical and electric industries in Germany." The memorandum stated that experience had shown that these industries could be converted from peace to war and that the governments which had suffered at the hands of the Germans should be entitled to remove the machinery they needed to repair their losses.

"The industries referred to in the Ruhr and in the Saar would, therefore, necessarily be put out of action and closed down," the memorandum stated. "It was felt that these two districts should be placed under somebody under the world organization which would supervise the dismantling of these industries and make sure they were not restored by subterfuge.

"This program for eliminating the war-making industries in the Ruhr and in the Saar is looking forward to converting Germany into a country primarily agricultural and pastoral in its character;

"The Prime Minister and the President were in agreement upon this programme."

Secretary Hull did not approve of this program. On September 25, he advised the President to effect a firm agreement with the governments of Great Britain and the Soviet Union on policy to be adopted regarding Germany, stating that we had followed a principle of placing matters of this kind on an agreed tripartite basis. As of that date, he added, the State Department had no indication that the British Government would be in favor of completely eradicating German industrial productive capacity in the Ruhr and Saar. He said he did not know the views of the Soviet Government.

It is difficult to understand how Mr. Churchill approved the memorandum of the "Morgenthau Plan." Certainly, later at Yalta, he deplored a peace that smacked of vengeance. And at Potsdam, he argued that heavy industries should not be reduced to a point that would necessitate financial assistance from other governments to maintain Germany's economy. After Potsdam, when the four powers agreed upon a level of industry for Germany, the British government advocated a higher level of production than any of the four powers.

It is equally difficult to understand President Roosevelt's attitude in view of what occurred immediately thereafter.

In reply to the Secretary of State, the President sent him a memorandum, dated September 29. However, it did not reach the State Department until October 2.

In it the President stated that he did not think any good purpose would be served at that stage by having the State Department, or any other department, sound out British and Russian views on the subject of German industry.

"The real nub of the situation," the President asserted, "is to keep Britain from going into complete bankruptcy at the end of the war." The President said that somebody had been giving statements to the newspapers "which are not fundamentally true." And, he added, "No one wants to make Germany a wholly agricultural nation again and yet somebody down the line has handed this out to the press. I wish we could catch and chastise him."

The President stated further that he could not go along with the idea of seeing the British Empire collapse financially while Germany at the same time was building up a potential rearmament to make another war possible in twenty years. While mere inspection of plants would not prevent this, the President concluded, "no one wants complete eradication of German industrial productive capacity in the Ruhr and Saar."

On the same day that the President's memorandum was written, September 29, Secretary Hull was submitting to the President a paper obviously drafted before the receipt of the President's message. Mr. Hull said:

"The Cabinet committee has not been able to agree upon a statement of American policy for the postwar treatment of Germany. The memorandum submitted by the Secretary of the Treasury is decidedly at variance with the views developed in the State Department. In the meantime I have received your memorandum of September 15 with the statement of views respecting the Ruhr, Saar, etc. and the conversion of Germany into an agricultural and pastoral country, which was formulated at Quebec. This memorandum seems to reflect largely the opinions of the Secretary of the Treasury in the treatment to be accorded Germany. I feel I should, therefore, submit to you a line of thought that has been developing in the State Department on this matter."

This, Secretary Hull followed with a statement of policy. In the economic section he stated that, among others, our objectives were to make Germany incapable of waging war and to eliminate German economic domination of Europe permanently. To achieve these two objectives, the Secretary said, it would be necessary (*a*) to destroy all war plants that could not be converted to peaceful purposes, and to prevent their reconstruction; and (*b*) to force conversion of all other war plants to the manufacture of peacetime goods.

Secretary Stimson seemed to share, in a general way, the views of Secretary Hull. In a conversation with the President he expressed his attitude. The President told Secretary Stimson that they were not far apart in their ideas, and that he had no intention of turning Germany into an agrarian state. The Secretary, however, called the President's attention to the language of the Quebec agreement stating that the program "is looking forward to converting Germany into a country primarily agricultural and pastoral in its character." Mr. Stimson had genuine affection for the President and great admiration for the part he had played throughout the war. He expressed the hope that the President would not approve a peace of vengeance. The President agreed with Mr. Stimson and told the Secretary of War he did not know how he had initialed that particular language in the Quebec agreement. It must have been done, he said, without much thought.

That the Quebec agreement on postwar Germany became a cause of considerable anxiety to the President is evident from the fact that the day before he wrote his long memorandum of September 29 to Secretary Hull, the President sent a memorandum to Mr. Crowley reading as follows:

"You have been making studies from the economic standpoint of what should be done after the surrender of Germany to control its power and its capacity to make war in the future. This work must be accelerated and, under the guidance of the Department of State, you should be furnished assistance in the work and when requested to do so, in personnel, by making available specialists to work with the military authorities, the Foreign Service, and such other American agencies, to see to it that Germany does not become a menace again to succeeding generations."

The President told Crowley he would make public the fact that he had requested him to make the study. Mr. Crowley's report was furnished to the State Department and considered in drafting the plan finally agreed upon.

The interdepartmental discussion on a German program continued until March 25, when a paper prepared by the State Department, after consultation with the Secretary of the Treasury and the Secretary of War, was signed by representatives of the three departments, and then was approved by President Roosevelt. This memorandum was used by Assistant Secretary of State Clayton when he represented us on the Economic Committee at Potsdam. It said nothing about making Germany an agricultural and pastoral state. Nor did Mr. Churchill, who had initialed the Quebec program, mention it to President Truman or to me. The fact is, it was not mentioned to us by anyone at Potsdam. There, our proposal formed the basis of the program of economic and political principles for Germany and was approved by the heads of government.

Mr. Molotov, of course, had learned from our press about the confusion in our government as a result of the agreement between President Roosevelt and Prime Minister Churchill at Quebec. Knowing how the German people feared any plan that would turn a nation of skilled industrial workers into a nation of farm workers, Mr. Molotov successfully played on those fears. The Soviet-controlled press in the Soviet zone misrepresented our views almost daily. Communist leaders in Berlin spread rumors that the United States was disgusted with the European situation and within a short while would withdraw its armed forces.

On July 11, the day following Mr. Molotov's significant declaration of Soviet policy toward Germany, I made a general statement of the American position. I made it brief because I wanted to keep attention focused on the immediate objectives of appointing deputies and putting them to work. I intended to withhold a detailed statement of our German policy until the Council of Foreign Ministers was prepared to act on the German question. Later I changed my mind. Since the Soviet delegation had forced a postponement of action on Germany until November, and since the Soviet campaign of misrepresentation in Germany continued, I decided to make a full statement of our German policy immediately. I did not think it proper to make such a declaration in Paris while the peace conference was in session; therefore, I decided to go to Germany and talk to the occupation forces, military and civilian, in the American zone. General Clay encouraged me to do this. He informed me that a policy statement in Germany would be very helpful to his organization and he quickly initiated arrangements for a meeting at Stuttgart.

At his request, we went first to Berlin where we took a train in order that, en route to Stuttgart, we might see the country and the destruction wrought by the war. We traveled in the train that the Nazi government had built for Hitler's personal use. It certainly was more luxuriously equipped than the train used for the President of the United States. Hitler's suite consisted of two rooms and a large lavender-tiled bathroom. Mrs. Byrnes and I felt a little strange in these rooms formerly occupied by Hitler and Eva Braun.

We welcomed the diversion of seeing the many American GIs who were in evidence all along the route. At one station there was a troop train on the opposite side of the platform and one of our boys was out on the steps of the train making a speech to some fifty or sixty Germans. I am sure they did not understand a word the youngster was saying, but that didn't discourage him. Suddenly he stopped in the middle of a sentence and flattered me by crying out, "Look who's here! Hi, Jimmy."

We arrived in Stuttgart shortly before noon on September 6. At the bomb-scarred station the minister-presidents of the districts of Württemberg, Bavaria and the Duchy of Hesse, in the American zone, were waiting to see us. I was anxious to meet them because they represented our first experiment in re-establishing local self-government and democratic processes in Germany. They reported the progress they were making and expressed a belief that the Germans in the British zone would like to have similar efforts at local self-government initiated but had not yet made much progress. Senator Connally and Senator Vandenberg asked them some questions. We spent half an hour with them and then proceeded to the Württemberg Staatstheater, the only large gathering place still standing in Stuttgart.

Generals McNarney and Clay had made every effort to provide an impressive setting for a declaration of American policy, but I am sure their plans did not include one item that was on the program. As I walked on the stage with General McNarney, Ambassador Murphy and the two Senators, the band was playing "Stormy Weather." I was tempted to ask the general if he had instructed the band to play symbolic music. General Clay, who seeks to avoid the spotlight, was seated in the audience.

I opened the speech by declaring that the American people have learned that we live in one world, that "peace and well-being are indivisible and that our peace and well-being cannot be purchased at the price of the peace and well-being of any other country.

"I hope the German people will never again make the mistake of believing that because the American people are peace loving, they will sit back hoping for peace if any nation uses force or the threat of force to acquire dominion over other people and other governments. . . . We intend to continue our interest in the affairs of Europe and of the world. We have helped to organize the United Nations. We believe it will stop aggressor nations from starting wars. Because we believe it, we intend to support the United Nations organization with all the power and resources we possess."

I then turned to the question of the kind of peace the United States believed should be enforced in Germany. We had long since, I said, stopped talking of a hard or a soft peace because what we wanted was a lasting peace. "We will oppose harsh and vengeful measures which obstruct an effective peace. We will oppose soft measures which invite the breaking of the peace."

We must first of all free Germany from militarism and give the German people an opportunity to "apply their great energies and abilities to the works of peace" and "in time, to take an honorable place among the members of the United Nations."

"It is not in the interest of the German people or in the interest of world peace that Germany should become a pawn or a partner in a military struggle for power between the East and the West."

With this general statement, I then turned to specific actions that were required. Germany should do her part to repair the devastation that had been inflicted on her neighbors twice in a generation. The United States wanted to see the Potsdam agreements on demilitarization and reparations fully carried out so that Germany's war potential would be reduced by the elimination of her war industries and by the reduction and removal of heavy industrial plants not required for her peacetime economy. This should not be carried so far as to deprive Germany of the levels of industry necessary to maintain average European living standards without assistance from other countries.

"In fixing the levels of industry no allowance was made for reparations from current production," I stated. "Reparations from current production would be wholly inconsistent with the levels of industry now established under the Potsdam agreement," and I then added that the United States would not agree to greater reparations payments than those agreed on at Potsdam.

The Potsdam agreements had not been carried out, I explained, because the Allied Control Council had been unable to agree on the treatment of Germany as an economic unit. It was impossible to achieve the standards set by the Allied Council in the absence of economic unity. It was the American view, I added, that central German administrative agencies should be established to develop a common financial policy; and a nation-wide organization of transportation, industry and foreign trade.

"Germany must be given a chance to export goods in order to import enough to make her economy self-sustaining," the speech continued. "Germany is a part of Europe, and European recovery, particularly in Belgium, the Netherlands and other adjoining states will be slow indeed if Germany with her great resources of iron and coal is turned into a poor house."

With this statement of economic principles, I turned to the political sphere. The purposes of the occupation did not contemplate "a prolonged alien dictatorship" of German economy or political life, but rather the building of a political democracy "from the ground up." We believed the German people should be given primary responsibility for running their local affairs. We should administer them so that the political structure would be decentralized and local responsibility developed. We do not believe, I stressed, "that large armies of alien soldiers or alien bureaucrats, however well motivated and disciplined, are in the long run the most reliable guardians of another country's democracy." We wanted the Allied governments to lay down the general rules "under which German democracy can govern itself" so that Allied occupation forces could be limited "to a number sufficient to see those rules are obeyed." That was why, I explained, we had proposed a treaty that would make certain a force would be available for a twenty-five or forty year period to insure that Germany did not rearm. I then made a statement that the army newspaper, *Stars and Stripes,* described as being "just what the doctor ordered."

"Security forces will probably have to remain in Germany for a long period. I want no misunderstanding. We will not shirk our duty. We are not withdrawing. We are staying here and will furnish our proportionate share of the security forces."

Meanwhile, we favored the early establishment of a provisional government, which "should not be hand picked by other governments" but which should be composed of "democratically responsible" chief officials of the several states or provinces established in each of the four zones. Under the authority of the Control Council, this government should see that the central administrative agencies functioned properly and it should prepare a draft of a federal constitution.

"The time has also come to define the boundaries of the new Germany," I continued. Austria already was recognized as a free and independent country. At Potsdam, the heads of government had agreed to support the Soviet desire for the transfer to Russia of the city of Königsberg. As for Silesia and other eastern areas, I pointed out that their transfer to Poland for administrative purposes had been made by the Soviet Union before the Potsdam meeting. But, I emphasized, the Protocol of the Potsdam Conference makes clear "the heads of government did not agree to support at the peace settlement the cession of any particular area." We did agree at Yalta that territory east of the Curzon Line should be transferred from Poland to Russia, and we did believe that there should be a compensating revision of Poland's northern and western frontiers. The extent of the area to be ceded, however, "must be determined when the final settlement is agreed upon."

We could not deny the right of France to the Saar, I said, but so far as the Ruhr and Rhineland were concerned, "the United States will not support any encroachment on territory which is indisputably German or any division which is not genuinely desired by the people concerned." We were determined that the resources of these regions must never again be used for destructive purposes. We, therefore, will "favor such controls over the whole of Germany, including the Ruhr and Rhineland, as may be necessary for security purposes" but "will not favor any controls that would subject the Ruhr and Rhineland to the political domination or manipulation of outside powers."

I closed the speech by declaring that the German people must realize it was German arms that had sought "to dominate and degrade the world." The United States consequently could not "relieve Germany from the hardships inflicted upon her by the war her leaders had started," but we would seek to give the German people "an opportunity to work their way out of these hardships so long as they respect human freedom and cling to the paths of peace."

As I finished, the army band struck up our national anthem and the entire audience, including the German leaders, rose to their feet. The place, the occasion and particularly the audience of civilian and military occupation authorities made it an especially moving moment. As the last notes died away, Senator Vandenberg, who had been away from the United States many weeks, turned to me and said, "The 'Star Spangled Banner' never before gave me such a thrill."

This declaration of American policy was given wide publicity in the American and British zones, and to a slightly lesser degree in the French zone. A German translation was superimposed over my voice in a radio transmission carried by radio stations in all except the Soviet zone. In the Soviet zone, the Soviet-licensed newspapers, with one exception, ran the story on the second page, and the longest reference to it was 140 lines.

After a short delay, the Communist-controlled press throughout Europe launched a campaign of severe criticism. In Poland, the declaration on the Polish-German frontier especially was attacked. It was claimed that the United States was violating an agreement reached at Potsdam. But the facts clearly showed otherwise. It will be remembered that, when we complained about the unilateral action of the Soviets in assigning a portion of their zone to Poland, Stalin told the President "the western frontier question is open, and the Soviet Union is not bound," and the final protocol stated: "The three heads of government reaffirmed their opinion that the final delimitation of the western frontier of Poland should await the peace settlement." Stalin's statement to the President was true when he made it, but, on August 16, just fifteen days after the signatures were affixed to the Potsdam Protocol, the Soviet Union concluded a treaty with Poland which recognized the Oder-Neisse line as the western boundary of Poland.

The Stuttgart speech made it impossible for the Soviets to continue talking one way to the Poles and another way to the Germans. Forced to choose, they announced they would support Poland's claim to the territory. German leaders then asserted that this stand was in conflict with promises made to them and much of the support of the Communist cause in Germany began melting away. I am confident that, as a result of our statement of policy, the sphere of influence the Soviets had hoped to extend into Berlin was moved back into Polish-controlled territory.

Upon our return to Paris, representatives of several European governments expressed to me their approval of the American program for Germany. Mr. Bevin was among those who offered congratulations. He said the program was substantially that which the British were prepared to offer. Mr. Molotov never mentioned the subject, but from what some of his staff were quoted as saying, my speech received no applause at the Soviet Embassy.

From Switzerland, Winston Churchill sent a message of congratulations and, as he was stopping in Paris en route to London about a week later, asked if we could meet. I immediately informed the British Ambassador that I would be happy to come to the Embassy to see Mr. Churchill. The Ambassador was anxious to keep Mr. Churchill's presence in Paris a secret. Mr. Churchill, who had just received a great ovation in Geneva and in Brussels, was not hiding from anyone and seemed irked by the steps taken to insure secrecy. I shared his irritation. To this day I do not know the reason for the secrecy, but I co-operated with the Ambassador, and, to my surprise, he succeeded in keeping the visit a secret. I scarcely suspected I could get away from the Hotel Meurice, go to the British Embassy, and spend two hours with Mr. Churchill, without being detected by the watchful eyes and ears of the exceedingly alert American correspondents. The only explanation was that it was Saturday afternoon and our correspondents had adopted the French habit of declaring a holiday for that afternoon. It was even more difficult for me to understand how Ambassador Duff Cooper with only grudging co-operation from Mr. Churchill could get the former Prime Minister in and out of Paris without the press knowing it.

Mr. Churchill simply wanted to state his approval of the American stand at Stuttgart and to discuss current problems. He did not criticize any official of His Majesty's Government, but I gathered that, as leader of the opposition, he was not informed about what was happening in Britain's foreign relations and he was not happy about it. We talked of many things. Toward the end of our conversation, Field Marshal Smuts called, and we continued our discussion of world problems. Then I left these two great men. May they never grow old.

To some of the political leaders of France, the Stuttgart speech was disappointing because of our stand against separation of the Ruhr and the Rhineland, and our insistence on central administrative agencies. They were, however, gratified at our pledge to support French claims to the Saar at the peace conference, and by the positive declaration that we intended to keep in Germany our proportion of occupation forces.

Because of the reaction of some French leaders, I accepted the opportunity offered by the American Club in Paris to emphasize further our determination to help maintain European stability and peace, in a speech I delivered on October 3.

"The people of the United States did their best to stay out of European wars on the theory that they should mind their own business and that they had no business in Europe," I stated. "It did not work. The people of the United States have discovered that when a European war starts, our own peace and security inevitably become involved before the finish. They have concluded that if they must help finish every European war, it would be better for them to do their part to prevent the starting of an European war."

I then urged upon the French the value of our proposed forty-year treaty. The United States, I stressed, not only wanted to see Germany disarmed and demilitarized before the peace settlement but also wanted to make sure that Germany would remain disarmed and demilitarized for forty years *after* the peace settlement.

"So long as such a treaty is in force," I said, "the Ruhr could never become the arsenal of Germany or the arsenal of Europe. That is a primary objective of the proposed treaty.

"The United States is firmly opposed to the revival of Germany's military power. It is firmly opposed to a struggle for the control of Germany which would again give Germany the power to divide and conquer. It does not want to see Germany become a pawn or a partner in a struggle for power between the East and the West."

I also explained we were seeking to develop a sense of local responsibility in Germany so that the people would look to the states rather than to the central government.

"We want to see the federal government of Germany created by the states, and not the states created by the central government."

The speech helped to reassure the people of France that the United States wanted to see a Germany created that would respect the freedom of her own inhabitants and would not threaten the security of her neighbors, particularly the security of France.

The Stuttgart speech, Secretary Marshall announced at Moscow in the spring of 1947, continues to represent American policy toward Germany.

The policy of the Soviet Union also remains as it was revealed by Mr. Molotov at Paris in July 1946. The last day of that session of the council, and two days after Mr. Molotov's pronouncement on Soviet policy toward Germany, Mr. Cohen, Mr. Bohlen and I were the dinner guests of the Soviet Foreign Minister. At the end of the dinner I told him that, since he had known beforehand he would not agree to starting work on the German and Austrian treaties, I deeply regretted that he had not come to me and frankly told me so. We would thus have prevented much heated debate which did not accomplish anything but was calculated to do harm. In a perfectly disarming way, he agreed that I was right and said it would have been better if the debate had not taken place.

"Why, then," I asked, "don't you tell me what is really in your heart and mind on the subject of Germany?"

The Soviet Union, Molotov replied, wanted what it had asked for at Yalta—10 billions of dollars in reparations, and also participation with the United States, the United Kingdom and France *in a four-power control of the industries of the Ruhr.*

Since that time there has been much speculation on the ambitions of the Soviet Union in Germany. Soviet representatives probably will make many other claims for themselves and the satellites, but I am sure the statement made by Molotov that night represents the real desires of the Soviet High Command.

Of the two demands, the Russians have greater interest in participating in the control of the Ruhr industries. The coal and iron of that area cause the Soviets to regard it as the arsenal of Europe. They want to share in all decisions on the allocation of Ruhr products. Our experience in the Allied Control Council demonstrates how impractical this proposal is. For over two years the Control Council has been trying to come to some agreement on relations between the zones. The members of the Control Council have had just as much difficulty in reaching agreements as have the Foreign Ministers. We can find another example in Korea, where we are supposed to have a joint administration with the Russians. Only in June were we able to resume discussions that were discontinued a year ago because of our inability to agree. If it is impossible to reach agreements on any front, except after months of discussion, it would not be practical for the four powers to control the various industries of the Ruhr. They would be able to agree upon few questions connected with any industry. Four-power control would be an effective way of destroying the industries of the Ruhr, which, properly supervised, are vital to an economically healthy Europe.

During discussions on the Ruhr, France indicated that it favored control by the Allied governments of western Europe. France did not mention participation by the Soviet Union. The idea of the Soviets agreeing to any international supervision of the Ruhr which does not include them is so unrealistic it has not been seriously discussed by other governments.

The industries of the Ruhr should be considered in the peace treaty along with the rest of Germany's industries. When a treaty is agreed upon, the control of German industries should be turned back to the owners. Our interest and our duty is to see that these industries are not thereafter converted to the manufacture of weapons of war. That can be done by the kind of joint inspection contemplated in the forty-year treaty I have proposed. I think this is one of several reasons why the Soviets oppose the treaty. They know there are many people who have advocated international control of the Ruhr industries. If the forty-year treaty should be agreed to, most of these people would be satisfied, and it would lessen the Soviet's chances of getting hold of the Ruhr industries.

Wisdom and justice will prevent the United States from ever acceding to the Soviet demands either on the Ruhr or on reparations. Mr. Molotov, however, has said these are essential prerequisites to any peace settlement. Since we believe an early peace settlement is of vital importance to the restoration of stability throughout Europe, we are forced to consider what we must do.

The first step already has been taken. At Paris, on July 11, 1946, I announced the action which we had determined to take only as a last resort—the merger of the zones of occupation, with or without the Soviet Union.

I began by expressing the hope that the council would agree "at this meeting" to the establishment of the central German administrative agencies necessary to secure economic unity in Germany. To satisfy Mr. Bidault's fears, I stated that we would agree to the continuation of French administration of the Saar until Germany's western boundaries were determined. But if, I added, the council could not agree to these central agencies, the United States "as a last resort makes another suggestion." I declared that no zone of Germany was fully self-sustaining and the treatment of any two zones as an economic unit would improve conditions in both zones. I pointed out that officials in our zone had recently discussed common agricultural policies with British officials for the exchange of some products.

"Pending agreement among the four powers to implement the Potsdam agreement requiring the administration of Germany as an economic unit," I announced, "the United States will join with any other occupying government or governments in Germany for the treatment of our respective zones as an economic unit.

"The continuation of the present situation will result in inflation and economic paralysis. It will result in increased costs to the occupying powers and unnecessary suffering to the German people. The United States is unwilling to share the responsibility for the continuance of such conditions. We feel it our duty to exhaust every effort to secure the co-operation of the occupying powers in administering Germany as an economic unit."

The following morning, Mr. Bevin announced that His Majesty's Government would agree in principle to the American merger proposal. General Clay, in Berlin, then began negotiations with Lieutenant General Sir Brian Robertson representing the United Kingdom; these continued until the meeting of the Council of Foreign Ministers in New York.

During the negotiations in Berlin and Washington, agreement was reached on all questions except one—the share of the annual deficit which should be borne by each government. The deficit in the American zone for 1947 was estimated at 200 million dollars and that for the British zone was placed at 400 million. Both the American and British representatives believed the deficit would be progressively reduced and that the merged zone could be made self-sustaining in three years. In these terms, the issue was placed before Mr. Bevin and me.

Officials of the British Treasury contended, Mr. Bevin told me, that Britain did not have the necessary dollars to meet the deficit for the next three years and he therefore urged the United States to carry 60 per cent of the burden. I replied that, in view of the much larger deficit in the British zone, we were assuming an additional 100 million dollars anyway when we agreed to an even division and that we, therefore, could not approve the 60 per cent suggestion. Our representatives in Germany might be mistaken in their self-confidence, I added, but they firmly believed that, if they had charge of the British zone with its industries and coal mines, they would wipe out most, if not all, of the deficit. I then proposed quite seriously that we would pay 60 per cent of the total deficit if Britain would exchange zones with us.

With a smile, Mr. Bevin replied, "You know His Majesty's Government would not agree to that." I admitted that I had doubted that Britain would want to trade their heavily industrialized zone and its rich natural resources for our largely scenic and agricultural zone. I pointed out, however, that my suggestion would provide him with a good answer to make to the British Treasury officials, who were pressing him. He then agreed to an even division of the cost. I thought it unwise for Britain to be put in the position of a poor relative or a junior partner by contributing less than 50 per cent. They are a proud people. It would be apt to cause irritations. It seemed much better to aid Britain in some other way.

The difficulties of the British in meeting the estimated deficit in their zone should not be minimized. When they were negotiating for the loan we made them in the spring of 1946, they had not counted on having to use dollars to provide food for Germans. This was a large, unforeseen drain on their dollar balances. This fact, quite correctly, I believe, influenced my judgment on another point: the date on which we would begin to pool exports from the merged zones. I supported the British contention and the resulting decision will save them 30 million dollars.

I had hoped the French would join us in the merger. That was one of the reasons I announced our decision in regard to the Saar. The French wanted the Soviets to agree to the Saar proposal also, but Mr. Molotov reiterated his opposition. This was disappointing because I knew the French coalition government would be hesitant to join us in a move that certainly would offend the large French Communist Party. The French Communists were greatly embarrassed by Mr. Molotov's refusal to assist a universally supported French objective, and would have welcomed another issue to divert attention from the Russian stand on the Saar. Subsequently, in September 1946, I advised the French Government in writing that, in the peace settlement, we would support the claim of France to this region. The United Kingdom extended a similar assurance. But the Government of France did not join us.

It is my hope that the French, before long, will accept our invitation, which is a continuing one, and merge their zone and its 6 million people with the British and American zones, where there is hope of making 46 million people self-supporting within three years. The offer remains open to the Soviet Union as well, so that all four powers may carry out the Potsdam pledge to treat Germany as an economic whole.

Allied co-operation, however, is not a part of the Soviet program and Soviet officialdom has greeted the merger with loud protests. Probably no other single event since the end of the war has been so bitterly and continually attacked by Moscow. It is a signal to the Soviet officials that the veto they have exercised so effectively since Potsdam is no longer inviolate. It is evidence that we refuse to follow indefinitely a course that conforms only to Mr. Molotov's conception of what is best. It is a demonstration that the western powers are willing to act in support of their interests and what they believe to be the interests of the vast majority of European peoples, and also of the Soviet Union.

Our next action must be the conclusion of treaties with both Germany and Austria. The key to the problem is Germany.

By July 1946, the best agreement I had been able to obtain on the preparation of a peace treaty with Germany was a promise to consider the question in New York in December. In New York, the best we could do was to agree to take up the German and Austrian questions at a meeting in Moscow in March of 1947. After six weeks of negotiation in Moscow, the German question was virtually where it had been the previous July. The Ministers adjourned to meet again, in November 1947, to resume the discussion. Unless the Soviet Union changes its position by November, there will be no agreement except to adjourn to another date in 1948. Secretary Marshall, Mr. Bevin and Mr. Bidault did everything in their power at Moscow to reach agreement on questions of importance. They were unsuccessful because of Soviet opposition.

We must bear in mind Mr. Molotov's statement at Paris on July 11, 1946, that "even when a German government is formed, *several years* must elapse before it would be wise to sign a treaty with them." We must also recall his further statement that there is no necessity for us to hurry; that "we should spend the next year thinking about what should be done with Germany."

Nor should we forget what happened during the consideration of the treaty with Italy and the Balkan states. At Moscow, in December 1945, we agreed after long argument that a peace conference would be held at Paris not later than May 1, 1946. At Paris, after long discussion, Mr. Molotov took the position that, notwithstanding this agreement, invitations to a peace conference could not be issued until the Council of Foreign Ministers unanimously agreed upon all provisions of the treaties the Soviet Union regarded as fundamental. We argued that we should issue the invitations, agree as far as possible, and then submit to the conference those questions still unsettled when the conference convened. In this way, the Soviet representative has the power to deny the Allied nations not members of the Council of Foreign Ministers even the opportunity to consider a treaty with an enemy state until every question that the Soviet Union considers important has been settled to its satisfaction.

World opinion may force the council at its forthcoming session in November 1947, at London, to give serious consideration to the German question blocked by the Soviet Union at the last meeting in Moscow. But we must realize that even then the Soviets will exercise the same veto weapon to obtain concessions from the United Kingdom, France and the United States before they will agree to issue invitations for a peace conference.

We have had one experience of this kind. It is enough to last for a long, long time. The Indian was right when he said: "Fool me once, shame on you; fool me twice, shame on me."

Because I first proposed to President Truman that the Council of Foreign Ministers be established as the machinery to prepare drafts of all the peace treaties, one will realize how reluctant I am to conclude that it can no longer serve the purpose for which it was established. In proposing it, I assumed that all the members of the council would be anxious to secure peace. We accepted the idea that there should be unanimous agreement among the members of the Council. We never conceived that such a worthy principle would be employed by one member of the Council to enforce his views on all the others. We did not conceive it because we assumed that we were all animated by a common purpose, the early restoration of peace. Now I am not sure that is true. And, if the leaders of the Soviet Union continue in every possible way to delay the restoration of peace, and continue to keep their troops in Germany, in Austria, and in the adjoining states through which they maintain lines of communication to Germany and Austria, other means of making peace will have to be found.

There are more controversial problems involved in the German settlement than in all the Italian and Balkan treaties. Consequently, it would be easy for any member of the council to delay the work and to give plausible reasons for the delay.

Even if we cleared these hurdles and made such concessions that invitations to a peace conference could be issued, we still would not be heading down a clear track. The Paris Peace Conference was in session from July 29 to October 15, 1946, and we may safely assume that a peace conference for Germany will continue much longer. Then, if our previous course is followed, the recommendations of the peace conference will be submitted to the Council for a final decision on which of the recommendations are to be included in the treaty.

Viewed in this light, the procedure we have followed, under the most favorable circumstances we can presently imagine, places prospects for a peace settlement in Europe in the far distant future. In the interest of peace and security, of the economic and political well-being of millions of people in Allied as well as ex-enemy states, we cannot permit such prolonged delay.

Secretary of State Marshall, during the meeting of the council in Moscow, announced that if agreement could not be reached soon on a treaty for Austria, the United States would consider submitting the problem to the General Assembly of the United Nations, for recommendations under Article 14 of the Charter. I understood his attitude and sympathized with him. Confronted with a similar situation during discussions on the Italian and Balkan treaties, I made a similar statement in my radio report to the American people after the first Paris session of the Council of Foreign Ministers.

Upon further consideration, however, I concluded that this course could not be helpful. The Charter of the United Nations does not give the General Assembly power to take action. It has power only to recommend. Formerly, I had hoped that if the General Assembly made recommendations, the power of world opinion, as reflected in those recommendations, would induce the Soviet Union to accept them. Now I am inclined to believe this would not occur.

The Soviet Union would argue to the world that the recommendations were made by an Assembly which includes among its members many states that were not even at war with Germany. The Soviet spokesmen would point out that determination of important and controversial questions, such as control of the Ruhr, would be decided by the votes of South American states, Arab states, and other smaller states which made no substantial military contributions to the defeat of the German armies. To make the General Assembly of the United Nations the center of such a controversy would be to place upon it a burden it was not intended to bear. Rebuff would seriously impair its prestige and undermine it in the confidence of the people of the world.

We should adopt another course of action. The United States should ask those powers that constitute the Council of Foreign Ministers, including, of course, the Soviet Union, to agree to the holding of a peace conference early in 1948.

At Moscow, Secretary Marshall proposed that the next peace conference should include all the states at war. He suggested that a resolution, to be adopted, must receive not only two-thirds of all votes cast but also two-thirds of the votes of the states that made military contributions. This proposal is in accord with the objective we held from the outset—participation in the making of the peace by all the United Nations that helped to win the war. At the same time, the proposed voting procedure would prevent the states that made only economic contributions from having an undue amount of power in the conference.

If one member of the Council of Foreign Ministers rejects our proposal for an early peace conference, the other members should proceed to call it. They should do it in such a manner that the way would be left open for the dissenting member of the council to join and to become one of the sponsoring powers if it should later decide to do so. France, for example, chose not to be one of the sponsoring powers for the San Francisco Conference although it later became one of the permanent members of the Security Council. As in that case, the other powers should continue to urge the dissenting power, or powers, to join them in sponsoring and sharing in the peace conference.

Each of the sponsoring powers should be asked to prepare treaty drafts for the peace conference. Undoubtedly, they would try to agree on as many clauses as possible before the conference. It has been nearly two and a half years since the German surrender and during that time the German question has been discussed by the four powers time and time again. At Potsdam, three of the Big Four discussed and concluded agreements on political and economic principles and reparations. The French have formulated and expressed their views at length. If, after all this, the four powers don't know what their positions are, they never will.

In the Paris Conference we have ample precedent for handling these drafts and all other questions of procedure. As at Paris, the conference should appoint, from its membership, commissions to consider different phases of the treaty drafts submitted by the sponsoring powers. There would, for example, be a commission to consider political questions, one for economic questions, and another for military questions. If desired, subsidiary bodies could be set up to consider different phases of these issues. These commissions could then prepare drafts of those sections of the treaty within their jurisdiction. In this way, all the states that fought the war against Hitler would have a part in drafting the treaty. If we are going to hold a peace conference ultimately and have a treaty considered by commissions, as we did at Paris, why not hold it now?

We must make it plain that we are not trying to make a separate peace or to dictate the terms of the peace. We would not attempt to force the acceptance of any particular plan. We would submit our plan and urge the British, the French and the Soviet Union to submit plans as well. The members of the conference could then make their decision.

In view of our experience we must face the possibility that the Soviet Union may refuse to join its war partners in a peace conference. This would indeed be disheartening to the peace-loving people of the world and every sober-minded person must hope that this will not occur. The possibility need not, however, stop us from initiating the course I suggest.

By the time the conference takes place, the merged British-American zone probably will be operating successfully. I hope, in addition, that the 48 million people in this merged zone will by that time be joined by the 6 million people of the French zone, if not those of the Soviet zone. The treaty of peace can be signed by the government or governments in the zones that have been unified.

There are, in fact, several ways in which German ratification could be obtained. At Moscow, Secretary Marshall proposed that when a constitution is presented to the German people for approval in a plebiscite, they should also be asked to vote on a directive to whatever government is established to accept an Allied peace treaty. This is a good proposal. If it is not agreed to, we might then consider submitting the treaty itself to a plebiscite. The German people then would have to decide whether to accept the treaty or continue to live indefinitely under military government and military occupation.

It may be objected that the latter course creates the impression that the treaty must be acceptable to the German people. But I think such an impression would be offset by removing from the accepted German government the political handicap of having negotiated a treaty that many Germans will probably regard as oppressive. I do not believe, however, that they will consider it as oppressive as the continuation of the present situation.

Before acting without the Soviet Union, we should once again invite the Soviet Government to join us in the treaty.

That treaty, like the treaties with Italy and the Balkan states, should provide that a country that does not sign it shall not share in any of its benefits. If the Soviet Union declines to sign the treaty, it certainly should not receive any further reparations payments from the western zones and should receive none of the other benefits that would surely accrue to them as a result of the settlement.

One may say: But suppose the Soviet Union declines to sign the treaty, what then?

If Soviet troops are withdrawn from Germany, no action by other nations will be necessary. But if the Red Army is not withdrawn, we must, as a last resort, go to the Security Council of the United Nations. The problem then will no longer be one of drafting peace treaties—a function the United Nations was never intended to perform. We will then be facing a situation likely to endanger the peace—the kind of situation the United Nations *was* created to meet.

The Soviet Union has declared its adherence to the Atlantic Charter which states that none of the signatories seek territorial aggrandizement. The Soviet Union has solemnly pledged in the United Nations Charter to refrain "from the threat of force or use of force against the territorial integrity or political independence of any state, or in any other manner inconsistent with the Purposes of the United Nations."

Eastern Germany, like all other parts of Germany, is to be held by armies of occupation temporarily and only until a treaty of peace is agreed upon. For the Soviets to keep troops there after an overwhelming number of the Allied nations have reached a peace settlement would be evidence of their intention to hold indefinitely territory allotted to them only for the period of occupation. Such action would constitute a threat to the peace of the world and the United Nations should therefore require the Soviet Union to withdraw from Germany.

But, one may add, the Soviet Union will veto any action by the Security Council.

Because I do not believe it is wise to suggest a course of action unless one is willing to carry it through, it is proper to discuss the contingency that might arise. We should not start something we are not prepared to finish.

First of all, let me say I do not believe the Soviet Union will force us to take measures of last resort. The Soviet Government will not, I believe, remain away from the peace conference and thus isolate itself from the rest of the world. If it should, I do not believe the Red Army would try to hold permanently all of eastern Germany. However, if I misjudge them, and they do go to the point of holding eastern Germany and vetoing a Security Council directive to withdraw occupation forces, we must be prepared to assume the obligations that then clearly will be ours. If our action is to be effective, we must be clear in our own minds and must make it clear to all that we are willing to adopt these measures of last resort if, for the peace of the world, we are forced to do so.

By "we" I do not mean the United States alone. The United States wants no separate peace. We trod that path once before. We want to make the peace collectively—with all the Allies if possible. But if it is not possible to secure the co-operation of all states, we should seek to enlist the assistance of as many as are willing to join in the task.

In the Charter of the United Nations, all of us have pledged "to unite our strength to maintain international peace and security" and "to take effective collective measures for the prevention and removal of threats to the peace, and for the suppression of acts of aggression or other breaches of the peace." A veto by one member does not relieve the rest of us of these obligations. They are pledges we must be prepared to fulfill.

I hope, believe, and I pray that the leaders of the Soviet Union will never force us to this course of last resort. But they must learn what Hitler learned—that the world is not going to permit one nation to veto peace on earth.

Chapter 11

Toward Peace in Asia

WE MUST never forget that World War II began in the Pacific.

The first scene of the drama that ended on board the USS *Missouri* on September 1, 1945, took place in Manchuria in the same month in 1931. The scenes that followed were of varying interest to us in the United States—Italy's invasion of Ethiopia in 1935, civil war in Spain in 1936, Japan's attack on China in 1937, the fall of Austria and Czechoslovakia in 1938, and Hitler's invasion of Poland in 1939. But all of them led us inexorably to the tragic action at Pearl Harbor on December 7, 1941.

If we regard Europe as the tinderbox of possible world conflagration, we must look upon Asia as a great smoldering fire. There, civilization faces the task of bringing a huge mass of humanity, the majority of the people on this earth, from the Middle Ages into the era of atomic energy.

In China, unfortunately, the end of one war has brought the beginning of another. Our most earnest efforts there, for the present at least, have failed. But Japan has made heartening progress toward matching in the political, economic, and social fields its earlier swift absorption of the technical aspects of modern civilization.

The feudalistic control of Japan's economy by a few families has been proscribed; state religion and the worship of the Emperor as a deity have been abolished; the right of the people to organize and to elect their representatives freely has been established. These, and similar changes are a start toward a democratic society; they and the speed with which they have been effected is in contrast to the usually slow tempo of human affairs. Much of this progress is due to the wise administration of General Douglas MacArthur. Some of it comes, I believe, from our decision to continue the institution of the Emperor under our own conditions and to use it as an instrument for carrying out the instructions and policies of the Supreme Allied Commander.

Immediately upon becoming Secretary of State, I learned about the differences of opinion in the State Department as to whether, at the time of surrender, we should insist on the removal of the Emperor. Before we left for Potsdam, I was presented with memoranda setting forth the varying views. These went into a brief case bulging with the problems of war and peace in the Pacific.

President Truman and Generalissimo Stalin discussed Russia's entry into the war against Japan at their first meeting on July 17. The Generalissimo said he had not yet succeeded in reaching an agreement with the Chinese—a prerequisite to the Soviet declaration of war. He told the President that his negotiations with Premier T. V. Soong would be resumed again after the conference. Among the questions still unsettled was a regime for the port of Dairen. President Truman declared that the United States wanted to make sure Dairen was maintained as an open port. Stalin replied that, if the Soviet Union obtained control of the port, it would have that status. I pointed out that, under the agreement President Roosevelt had entered into at Yalta, China was to retain control of Dairen.

We received a report that Soong had told his government the Soviet Union was making claims extending beyond the Yalta agreement. Since the negotiations were taking place in accordance with a commitment made by President Roosevelt, I was interested. I was afraid Soong would find it difficult to resist Soviet pressure and would make additional concessions if he were in doubt about our attitude. Therefore, with the approval of the President, I sent a message to the Chinese Government saying we would not advise making any concessions that went beyond the terms of the Yalta agreement.

The Chinese and Russians subsequently reached agreement, but events have shown that our concern about Dairen was justified. Two years after Japan's defeat, Dairen still is not a free port. Before a ship can enter the port, it is necessary to obtain clearance from Moscow, not only for the vessel but also for its personnel.

At a later meeting Stalin told the President and me that the Japanese Ambassador in Moscow had asked whether the Soviet Union would agree to act as a mediator to bring about the settlement of the war. This request, Stalin said, did not indicate a willingness to surrender unconditionally as the Allies demanded; it was phrased so generally that Mr. Molotov simply told the Ambassador that he would discuss the matter with him later. Subsequently, Stalin said, the Japanese Ambassador presented another message. This stated that the Emperor wished to send Prince Konoye to Moscow with a message saying that Japan wanted to end the war but had decided to fight on with all its strength as long as unconditional surrender was demanded. Stalin added that a letter was then sent to the Ambassador stating that the character of the indicated message was general, contained no specific proposal, and therefore it was impossible to give a definite reply. President Truman expressed his approval of Stalin's action.

Meanwhile, Secretary Stimson informed us that he had received reports from New Mexico on the test of the atomic bomb on July 16. The reports made it clear that the bomb had met our highest hopes and that the shock of its use would very likely knock our already wavering enemy out of the war. Before the experiment we had agreed that, if it proved a success, we would not use it without issuing a final solemn warning to the Japanese.

Secretary of War Stimson, on July 2, had submitted to the President a wise memorandum setting forth a proposed message to Japan. Using this memorandum as a basis, the President prepared a draft of a declaration to be issued jointly by the United States, the United Kingdom and China. The President and I spent some time on it. Then Prime Minister Churchill made some suggestions which were adopted. The declaration to which Mr. Churchill agreed followed the general lines of Secretary Stimson's proposal except that it did not contain a reference to the future status of the Emperor. The proposed declaration then was sent to Chiang Kai-shek for his approval.

On Thursday, July 26, the conference recessed to enable Mr. Churchill and Mr. Attlee to go to London to receive the results of the British election. President Truman utilized the opportunity for a trip to the headquarters of the American zone of occupation at Frankfurt. I accompanied him. Wherever the President reviewed troops abroad, commanding officers managed to have the band play "The Missouri Waltz," and presented to the President the Missourians among the commissioned officers of the outfit. Like all Senators and ex-Senators, the President is "state conscious." He liked it, and by the end of the day he had almost concluded Missouri had won the war. He enjoyed making to me the facetious charge that South Carolina had not participated in the war. The President rode in an open car, first with Brigadier General Doyle O. Hickey and later with Major General A. G. Bolling, commanding the Third Armored and the 84th Infantry Divisions. After each stop he would tell these officers that I had not yet found any South Carolinians among the troops. Finally, Pfc. Warren E. Baker, who was driving the President's car, could stand it no longer. He swung around in the driver's seat and said:

"Mr. President, I would like to say that I am from South Carolina, and I live just around the corner from the Secretary of State."

The President laughed heartily and at the next stop told me the story. He liked the courage of the young private in telling the President of the United States in the presence of a Major General that he was mistaken. The boy did demonstrate pride in his state and also the spirit that helped to make what I believe was the greatest army in the world.

When we returned to the "Little White House" that evening there were two messages for the President. The first one was from Ambassador

Winant with the surprising news of Churchill's defeat and the second was from Generalissimo Chiang Kai-shek approving what is now known as the Potsdam Declaration.

The declaration was immediately released for publication and a copy was sent by special messenger to Mr. Molotov. It pointed out that the combined forces of the three Allies "are poised to strike the final blows upon Japan," and that the experience of Germany "stands forth in awful clarity as an example to the people of Japan." It warned that the might converging on Japan "is immeasurably greater" than that which laid waste Germany.

"The full application of our military power, backed by our resolve," the declaration continued, "will mean the inevitable and complete destruction of the Japanese armed forces and just as inevitably the utter destruction of the Japanese homeland."

The declaration then set forth in seven paragraphs the terms under which the government of Japan was called upon to proclaim its unconditional surrender. They were phrased so that the threat of utter destruction if Japan resisted was offset with hope of a just though stern peace if she surrendered. It is tragic that the Japanese chose to reject this offer.

Mr. Molotov telephoned later in the evening asking that the declaration be held up two or three days. When he was told it already had been released he seemed disturbed. The next day I explained it had not been submitted to him before release because we did not want to embarrass the Soviet Union by presenting it with a declaration affecting a country with which it was not yet at war. He did not say he desired to make any change but said simply that we should have consulted him.

Two days later, on July 29, Mr. Molotov called again. It had been agreed that the President and I would meet with him and Generalissimo Stalin, but Mr. Molotov informed us that Stalin was ill that day. He had instructed Mr. Molotov to discuss with us the immediate cause of the Soviet Union's entry into the war. The Soviet Government, Molotov said, considered that the best method would be for the United States, Great Britain, and the other Allies to address a formal request to the Soviet Government for its entry into the war. He added that the Soviet Government was assuming, of course, that the agreement with the Chinese Government would be signed before his country entered the war.

The request presented a problem to us. The Soviet Union had a non-aggression pact with the Japanese. The Soviet Government also had had a similar pact with Hitler, but it was the Nazis who had violated that one. We did not believe the United States Government should be placed in the position of asking another government to violate its agreement without good and sufficient reason. The Soviet Union had notified Japan a few months earlier of its intention to abrogate the treaty but it would still be in force for nearly a year. The President was disturbed.

As for myself, I must frankly admit that in view of what we knew of Soviet actions in eastern Germany and the violations of the Yalta agreements in Poland, Rumania and Bulgaria, I would have been satisfied had the Russians determined not to enter the war. Notwithstanding Japan's persistent refusal to surrender unconditionally, I believed the atomic bomb would be successful and would force the Japanese to accept surrender on our terms. I feared what would happen when the Red Army entered Manchuria. Before it left Manchuria, my fears were realized.

When the agreement on Russian participation in the war was reached at Yalta, the military situation had been entirely different. President Roosevelt and our military leaders wanted the Soviet Union in the war. No one of them could have anticipated the difficulties we encountered after Yalta. However, an agreement had been made and we had to stand by our obligation.

Ben Cohen and I spent hours trying to decide how the President could properly reply to the Soviet request. It was Ben who suggested that we call the Soviet Government's attention to its obligations under the Charter of the United Nations.

The President approved the idea. It was late at night. The staff had gone. With Ben's suggestion as a starter I went to a typewriter and drafted the letter which the President later approved.

It first mentioned the Moscow Declaration of October 30, 1943, signed by the Soviet Union, the United States, the United Kingdom and China. That declaration provided that "for the purpose of maintaining international peace and security pending the re-establishment of law and order and the inauguration of a system of general security, they will consult with one another and as occasion requires with other members of the United Nations with a view to joint action on behalf of the community of nations." The letter then pointed out that Article 106 of the proposed United Nations Charter provided that the four powers would continue to act on the basis of the Moscow Declaration until the Charter came into force. It then cited Article 103 of the Charter, providing that "in the event of a conflict between the obligations of the Members of the United Nations under the present Charter and their obligations under any other international agreement, their obligations under the present Charter shall prevail."

The President's letter then concluded:

"Though the Charter has not been formally ratified, at San Francisco, it was agreed to by the Representative of the Union of Soviet Socialist Republics and the Soviet Government will be one of the permanent members of the Security Council.

"It seems to me that under the terms of the Moscow Declaration and the provisions of the Charter, above referred to, it would be proper for the Soviet Union to indicate its willingness to consult and co-operate with other great powers now at war with Japan with a view to joint action on behalf of the community of nations to maintain peace and security."

The President later told me that Generalissimo Stalin expressed great appreciation of the communication. He should have. The Soviet Government's statement announcing its entry into the war did not include a reference to Section 103 of the Charter, but our finding it for Mr. Molotov will enable the Soviet historian to show that Russia's declaration of war on Japan was in accordance with what they like to claim is their scrupulous regard for international obligations.

We arrived back in Washington the afternoon of August 7. The day before, we had received word aboard ship that the first atomic bomb had been dropped on Hiroshima. The day after our return, Nagasaki received its atomic blast and the Soviet Union declared war on Japan, to be effective August 9. In the early morning hours of August 10, we received, through the Swiss Government, a message from the Japanese that they were ready to accept the terms of the Potsdam Declaration "with the understanding that the said Declaration does not comprise any demand which prejudices the prerogatives of His Majesty as a Sovereign Ruler."

The message had come in during the night, but the President and I were not called until early morning. I immediately rushed to the White House where the Secretaries of War and Navy soon gathered. Admiral Leahy urged that the Japanese offer be accepted promptly. I told the President I would like a little time to think about a reply to the message.

"I do not see why we should retreat from our demand for unconditional surrender," I said. "That demand was presented to Japan before the use of the bomb and before the Soviet Union was a belligerent. If any conditions are to be accepted, I want the United States and not Japan to state the conditions."

The President agreed with me, and asked me to draft a reply.

In my office I drafted a reply, which the President approved when I presented it to him an hour later. About noon Secretary Stimson telephoned to say he had seen the draft and highly approved of the message. It stated:

> From the moment of surrender, the authority of the Emperor and the Japanese Government to rule the state shall be subject to the Supreme Commander of the Allied powers who will take such steps as he deems proper to effectuate the surrender terms.
> The Emperor will be required to authorize and ensure the signature by the Government of Japan and the Japanese Imperial General Headquarters of the surrender terms necessary to carry out the

provisions of the Potsdam Declaration, and shall issue his commands to all the Japanese military, naval and air authorities and to all the forces under their control wherever located to cease active operations and to surrender their arms, and to issue such other orders as the Supreme Commander may require to give effect to the surrender terms. . . .

The ultimate form of government of Japan shall, in accordance with the Potsdam Declaration, be established by the freely expressed will of the people.

The message was sent on August 11, and we waited tensely for a response. I was confident the Japanese would accept, but the feeling of responsibility for thousands of lives was inescapable. I telephoned our Minister in Switzerland, Mr. Leland Harrison, and asked him to call me as soon as he received a Japanese reply and say whether or not the Japanese accepted unconditional surrender. I wanted to eliminate the hours a coded cable would consume.

A few minutes after 4 o'clock on August 14, I got the telephone call; it ended the longest wait I have ever experienced. As soon as Mr. Harrison had read me the contents of the Japanese note, I asked the War Department to set up a radio circuit with London, Moscow and Chungking and then rushed out to the Pentagon Building to carry on a teletype conversation with the Foreign Ministers in these three capitals. I informed each one of Harrison's message, said we regarded the Japanese reply as a complete acceptance of the Potsdam Declaration, and suggested a time for simultaneous release of the news. The teletype clicked off so many different replies I realized it would be impossible to reconcile them quickly.

On the other hand, I did not believe this happy news should be withheld from the people of the world because of an argument on the time of release. So I ended the discussion by stating that at 7:00 P.M., Eastern War Time, the hour that seemed most suitable, President Truman would announce the surrender, and invited the other governments to do likewise. By 5:30 I had reported the conversation to the President and received his approval for the arrangements. At 6:00, the Chargé d'Affaires of the Swiss Legation, Mr. Max Grassli, arrived at my office with the Japanese message read to me over the transatlantic telephone. An hour later President Truman announced the end of the world's most horrible conflict.

Some day the complete story will be written of the events in Japan preceding the surrender. From the interrogation of high-ranking officials and from the documents that came into the possession of our authorities, it is evident that five weeks before the surrender Japan had no idea of Stalin's intentions. In fact, the Japanese were no more certain of the Soviet Union's entry into the war than the Soviets had been of Hitler's intentions five weeks before he invaded Russia. Nor were they any more certain than we had been of Japanese intentions five weeks before Pearl Harbor.

Not until July 6, 1945, when China's Foreign Minister, T. V. Soong, was in Moscow, did the Japanese become suspicious of Soviet intentions. At that time, Foreign Minister Togo said, "Soong, we know to have been received well by the Russians and to have conferred with Stalin. . . . This may result in some sort of treaty." And he added with evident surprise, "It is *even* reported in some quarters that the Soviet Union would soon enter the war against Japan." This would indicate that, even then, the Japanese intelligence was not very efficient.

It is evident that at the time Ambassador Sato, the Japanese envoy in Moscow, presented Japan's mediation request to Mr. Molotov, the Emperor already had concluded that their cause was hopeless. His advisers, however, apparently believed they could avoid the Emperor's removal and also save some of their conquered territory.

Also clear, from his messages to the Japanese Foreign Office, is the fact that Ambassador Sato in Moscow was a realist and a courageous representative. He advised the Japanese Government that the message sent to him was so general in character the Soviets would not consider it; that they would not be convinced by pretty phrases having no reality and that, unless Japan was ready to surrender, there was no use wasting time sounding out the views of the Soviet Government.

Ambassador Sato told his Foreign Office that the Soviets had insisted upon the unconditional surrender of Germany and certainly would join the Americans and British in insisting upon the unconditional surrender of Japan. He said he knew his views were not in accord with the communications from His Majesty and even though "my offense is great," nevertheless "I want to preserve the lives of hundreds of thousands of people who are about to go to their death needlessly." And he stressed that "Japan has no choice but to accept unconditional surrender."

Had the Japanese Government listened to Sato and surrendered unconditionally, it would not have been necessary to drop the atomic bomb. But his advice was ignored as the militarists clamored for a negotiated peace. On July 21 the Japanese Government advised its representative in Moscow:

> We cannot consent to unconditional surrender under any circumstances. Even if the war drags on and more blood must be shed, so long as the enemy demands unconditional surrender, we will fight as one man against the enemy in accordance with the Emperor's command.

The Japanese Government communicated with the Soviets instead of Sweden or Switzerland in order to advise the Russians that they were prepared to meet fully their demands in the Far East. They hoped, by granting Soviet demands, to secure Soviet aid in negotiations. They also hoped, by such discussions, to find out definitely whether the Soviets were going to enter the war.

The Japanese Cabinet did not decide to surrender until the atomic bomb had been dropped on Hiroshima.

The records of the Japanese Foreign Office show that on August 10 the Soviet Ambassador to Tokyo presented Togo a message stating the Soviet's endorsement of the Potsdam Declaration and the existence of a state of war with Japan. In return, the Foreign Minister handed the Soviet Ambassador, for transmission to his government, a copy of the message sent that morning through Switzerland, announcing Japan's willingness to surrender upon condition that we made no demand prejudicing the prerogatives of His Majesty as a sovereign ruler. This was the message I answered on the eleventh which resulted in the surrender on the fourteenth.

The Japanese surrender had come earlier than we expected, but it did not find us unprepared. A co-ordinating committee, composed of representatives from the State, War and Navy departments had been at work for some time preparing general orders to govern the surrender and the occupation. One crisis, however, immediately confronted us: Who should have the honor of accepting the surrender of the Japanese?

The Great Powers had agreed that General MacArthur should act as their representative as well as ours in accepting the surrender. But officers of the Navy soon registered their keen disappointment at this arrangement. Secretary Forrestal presented their arguments: The war in the Pacific had been their show primarily; the bluejackets and Marines had advanced island by island from Pearl Harbor to Tokyo; they had destroyed the Japanese Navy. Therefore, MacArthur could sign for the Allies but Admiral Nimitz should sign for the United States. My service in the Senate as chairman of the Committee on Naval Appropriations may have influenced my view, but I responded sympathetically to Mr. Forrestal's arguments; I wanted the Navy in the picture. Arrangements had already been made, but I promised Forrestal I would try to think of a way by which Admiral Nimitz could take part in the signing along with General MacArthur.

When Secretary Forrestal is really interested in a cause, he doesn't sleep, and he doesn't let others sleep. That night the telephone awakened me. It was Secretary Forrestal, suggesting that the surrender ceremonies take place on board the battleship USS *Missouri*. I was sufficiently awake to recognize what the Army would call a "Navy trick." Had he said simply, "a battleship," it would have remained a debatable question, but when he named the Missouri, I knew the case was closed. The President, upon receiving the suggestion, of course, thought it an excellent idea. Thus was averted a great crisis in army-navy relations.

The people of the Soviet Union, however, may not know of Forrestal's victory. After the Christmas Eve dinner that Generalissimo Stalin gave during our meeting in Moscow in December 1945, a moving picture of the Soviet Army entering Manchuria was shown to us. It pictured Japan's preparation for war as being directed only against Russia; the tumultuous reception given the Red Army by the people of Manchuria and, finally, the signing of the terms of surrender. According to the film, the principal participants in the surrender ceremonies were representatives of Japan and the Soviet Union. The Supreme Commander, General MacArthur, was in the background. The scene was described as "signing the surrender terms" on "a battleship." There was no statement that the battleship was the *Missouri* or even that it was a United States' ship. The entire scene might well impress many Russians as the ending, on a Soviet battleship, of a private war between Russia and Japan. It showed me that the Soviets are keenly aware of the effectiveness of propaganda through moving pictures. I was not surprised to learn that the Soviet Government is now promoting the exhibition of Soviet films in European countries.

While we had borne the major burden in crushing the military power of Japan, we had always regarded the war as one war against the Axis, and we intended that the occupation of Japan should be an Allied responsibility. As early as August 22, we invited the Soviet Union, Great Britain and China to join us in setting up a ten-power advisory commission to carry out the aims of the Potsdam Declaration and the surrender terms. The Soviet Union and China promptly accepted, but Great Britain objected because the commission would have only advisory powers. Australia and New Zealand wanted more decisive roles. Consequently, the establishment of a commission was delayed.

As soon as the Council of Foreign Ministers met in London in September, I began talks with Mr. Bevin in an effort to settle our differences. But before we had progressed very far a new element was injected into the situation. Mr. Molotov came to see me, on instructions from Moscow. He wanted to complain of the way in which the surrender terms were being carried out. He complained particularly about the way the Japanese Army was being demobilized. It was dangerous, he said, merely to disarm the Japanese and send them home; they should be held as prisoners of war. We should do what the Red Army was doing with the Japanese it had taken in Manchuria—make them work.

I pointed out to him that the Potsdam Declaration, to which the Soviet Union had adhered, pledged that "Japanese military forces, after being completely disarmed, shall be permitted to return to their homes with the opportunity to lead peaceful and productive lives." I assured him that we would hold all those suspected of war crimes but said that we would not hold prisoners to work for us.

No one can say accurately how many Japanese prisoners have been taken to the Soviet Union. In mid-1947, the best guess was that approximately 500,000 were still there. Transportation difficulties delayed the return of many of our Japanese prisoners, but they *have* been returned. As long as we were holding either Japanese or Germans, we could not very well insist that our Allies comply with the Geneva Convention on Prisoners of War and the clearer promises of the Potsdam Declaration. I have described in an earlier chapter our efforts in returning the Germans. The positive statements concerning prisoners in the Potsdam Declaration make the use of Japanese as slave laborers even less excusable. The time has come when the United States should demand that its Allies comply with the Potsdam Declaration.

At London, however, when Mr. Molotov said that Japanese should be made prisoners, he even expressed the fear that our policy would lead to a revival of Japanese aggression. Assistant Secretary Dunn pointed out to him that our proposal to set up a Far Eastern Commission would give his government an opportunity to express its views on Japanese policy, including the disarmament of prisoners. I said that I thought we should have a demilitarization treaty for Japan similar to the German Treaty. I assured him that, when I returned home, I would discuss it with President Truman.

Despite our assurances, Mr. Molotov two days later opened the session of the council by reading a prepared statement in which he suggested the establishment of an Allied Control Council for Japan. The council would be composed of the United States, Great Britain, the Soviet Union and China, with the American representative acting as chairman. The council would have far-reaching powers, much greater than those Mr. Bevin had suggested. Through two long meetings, I argued against including on the agenda the subject of establishing a Control Council in Japan. The other members, on the whole, supported me, for they were eager to proceed with the European treaties, and at the time Mr. Molotov's request appeared to be just another phase of his campaign for delay.

On September 26, at my request, Mr. Bevin, Mr. Molotov and I met in an effort to solve our differences on the right of France and China to participate in all the discussions of the council. But Mr. Molotov immediately reverted to the Soviet proposal for the establishment of a Control Council in Japan. The policies being pursued by General MacArthur made him wonder, he said, whether it was "useful for the Soviet Government to continue having a representative in Tokyo." I repeated that I was not prepared at this session of the council, called to begin work on the

European treaties, to discuss the Japanese question. I again assured him that I would go into the matter thoroughly as soon as I returned home, and would communicate with him.

The Soviet delegation, he said, was unable to understand why it was impossible to discuss this question during the present meeting, and he wished to ask whether or not the one or two billion dollars of gold which the Americans had found in Japan, according to newspaper reports, had anything to do with this situation.

Had the Foreign Minister of Great Britain, France or China made such a statement, one would have known that it was deliberately intended to be insulting. But, from the way in which it was expressed and particularly in the light of Soviet actions elsewhere, I concluded Mr. Molotov did not intend it as an insult.

Mr. Molotov had admitted at Potsdam that the Red Army had indulged in large-scale removals of property and had suggested that one billion dollars be deducted from his reparations claims to cover them. Notwithstanding the embarrassment he seemed to feel about this at Potsdam, the Red Army repeated a few weeks later in Manchuria its performance in Germany. Soviet troops removed from the soil of their Chinese Allies everything they could carry away. It was therefore quite understandable that when Mr. Molotov read the story, later proved to be untrue, that our soldiers had found two billion dollars in gold, he should expect us to do just what the Red Army would do under similar circumstances—remove the gold and refuse to talk about Japanese affairs until the wealth was safely hidden in the United States.

In London, I tried once again, in a private conversation with Mr. Molotov, to persuade him that the establishment of the Far Eastern Advisory Commission was logically the first step in considering how the occupation of Japan was to be directed. But my efforts met with no success.

Meanwhile, I had been urging Mr. Bevin to agree to our proposal, submitted on August 22, for the creation of the Far Eastern Advisory Commission. I agreed informally that when the commission met, we would support a proposal that it should be authorized to meet in Tokyo as well as in Washington and that India should be made a member. The Cabinet then authorized Mr. Bevin to accept our proposal. With Britain's approval obtained, I hoped Molotov would withdraw his new proposal and revert to his earlier approval of our August 22 proposal. I immediately wrote him a letter stating that, since the four powers now were agreed, a meeting of the commission would be held on October 30, and I hoped a Soviet representative would be there. He replied that the situation had changed since the Soviet Union had agreed to our August 22 proposal and that his government now asked for the establishment of a Control Council. As I left for Washington, it still was uncertain whether a representative of the Soviet Union would be on hand for the commission's first meeting.

This situation was a part of the whole state of our relations with the Soviet Union which deeply disturbed me during October 1945. I felt that as long as we continued to communicate with each other concerning our problems, they might be reconciled. But during those weeks there was no communication.

I thought it wise to give the Soviets the benefit of every doubt, since we wanted to progress in the task of peace making. Therefore, we prepared a modification of our proposal for a peace conference on the European treaties—the issue we thought was mainly responsible for the deadlock of the London session of the council. I wanted this proposal to get to Stalin, who was then on vacation. A message to the head of a government must be signed by the President, so we drafted a letter and asked the President to have Ambassador Harriman deliver it for him personally. The President made the letter a most cordial one.

On October 25, Ambassador Harriman called on Stalin at Gagri. After he had read the President's letter, which had been translated into Russian, Stalin looked up and said, "The Japanese question is not touched upon."

When this message came in from Harriman, I immediately realized that we had miscalculated at London. We had thought it was the peace conference issue that was behind Molotov's obstructive tactics. Stalin's question made us realize that they were more angry about Japan.

Harriman was equally surprised, but fortunately he had been with us in London and was able to explain our August 22 proposal in detail to Stalin. He made it clear he was not authorized to negotiate regarding Japan. He added he knew I was most anxious to devise a method of informing and consulting with the Soviet Government and our other Allies on Japanese policy, provided that, if there was disagreement, the United States would not be interfered with in carrying out the occupation policy.

Although Harriman was able to steer the conversation back to the question of the peace conference, Japan remained uppermost in Stalin's mind. He opened the second day of his talks with our Ambassador by returning to the subject.

He was unwilling, he said, to send a representative to the forthcoming meeting of the Far Eastern Advisory Commission because, as Molotov had stated in London, the situation had changed since our invitation had been accepted. Stalin had, in fact, recalled his representative in Tokyo, Lieutenant General Derevyanko, because, he claimed, the general was neither informed nor consulted and, under such circumstances, could not accept responsibility for actions taken by General MacArthur in the name of the Allies.

The Soviet Union, Stalin declared, was being treated as a satellite state and not as an Ally, and this did not become the dignity of his nation. He complained that the Japanese press and radio had been allowed to vilify the Soviet Union; that changes in the government had been made without informing or consulting him; and that Japanese banks had been closed without any information being issued on the disposition of their assets.

Ambassador Harriman explained that General MacArthur was carrying out the surrender terms agreed to by the Soviet Government and that all assets were being held for eventual disposition by the Allies. He pointed out that, even before the surrender terms had been signed, we had proposed the establishment of the Advisory Commission to consider just such matters as the Generalissimo was mentioning, and he urged that a Soviet representative be sent to the forthcoming meeting in Washington where he could get the information his government wanted.

Stalin was not satisfied. He said his representative in Tokyo had been treated "like a piece of furniture" and he feared further differences would arise if he sent a representative to the Washington meeting. If the United States wished to come to an agreement with the Soviet Union, he insisted, it could only be done properly in negotiations between our two governments. He called attention to the fact that Russia had maintained thirty to forty divisions on the Manchurian border throughout the war, had engaged the Japanese with seventy divisions and had been ready, if their offer had been accepted, to assist in the occupation of Japan.

Because this statement undoubtedly will be heard frequently in the discussion of the Japanese peace treaty, it should be recorded that while Generalissimo Stalin's statement was correct, it is also true that Japan's thirty or forty divisions on the Manchurian border did not seriously affect the Japanese war effort. As a result of the successful operations of the United States Navy, the Japanese early in the war lacked the ships necessary to move men and supplies to the battlefields of the Pacific. With their forces immobilized, it was just as easy for the Japanese to maintain their divisions on the Manchurian border as elsewhere. Conceivably, the Japanese could have used these forces for land operations in China, but we know now that this would not have materially affected the final outcome of the war.

We had barely received Harriman's report on his conversations when the Far Eastern Advisory Commission gathered for its first meeting, and elected Major General Frank R. McCoy, the United States representative, as chairman. It then adjourned for a week to give the Soviet Union another chance to send a representative.

The fact is, the commission was unable to operate effectively from the very outset. Although the United Kingdom and Australia were willing to co-operate with us, they were not satisfied with a purely advisory role. I soon realized we must try to work out an arrangement which, while protecting General MacArthur from undue interference, would nevertheless meet the desire of our Allies for more extensive participation.

Many conferences and long debates took place before we finally agreed upon a draft proposal for a Far Eastern Commission and an Allied Council. This proposal was approved by the President, and I presented it at the first meeting of the three Foreign Ministers in Moscow on December 16. Discussion of our proposal extended through six meetings. The chief issues were Mr. Molotov's opposition to making India a member of the commission, his desire to insert the word "Control" in the name of the Allied Council, Mr. Bevin's request to include Australia on the council and, finally, the voting procedure in the commission.

For a while I feared that agreement would be delayed so long that it would be impossible to obtain China's concurrence before we adjourned. But on December 24, Mr. Molotov announced his willingness to admit India to the commission. It was agreed that the commission would act upon majority votes of the eleven members, including the votes of the United Kingdom, the Soviet Union, China and the United States. Mr. Bevin likewise accepted a suggestion that on the four-member Allied Council in Tokyo, the United Kingdom, Australia, New Zealand and India should have one representative in common.

The new Far Eastern Commission began functioning in Washington on February 26, 1946. It has authority to decide upon the principles which control the administration of Japan, and its decisions are put into directives issued to the Supreme Allied Commander by the United States Government. This means, of course, that no basic policy may be adopted without our concurrence, and, pending agreement in the commission, we are free to give interim directives on all urgent matters.

Only three questions were excepted from this authority. These three questions, on which the commission must decide by a majority vote which includes ours, are: (a) changes in the control system as set forth in the surrender terms, (b) fundamental changes in the Japanese constitutional structure, and (c) changes in the government as a whole as distinguished from shifts involving individual officials. It has not been our policy to dictate wholesale alterations in the government, and the authority of General MacArthur to make individual changes or fill vacancies has been unimpaired.

The council continues to advise and consult with the Supreme Commander in Tokyo. At the time the commission and the council were established, I stated that the authority of General MacArthur should not be obstructed by the inability of the commission to agree on policy or of the council to agree on advice for carrying out that policy. Nearly two years have passed and events have proved that the two bodies have not interfered with MacArthur's administration. He and his staff have continued to carry out their difficult task with an efficiency that has won the plaudits of the people in other Allied nations besides the United States.

There were other Japanese questions on Mr. Molotov's mind at Moscow. He asked first about plans for disposing of the Japanese Navy and, secondly, about the Japanese islands. Two months before the Moscow meeting, we had proposed that what was left of the Japanese Navy should be scuttled. Britain and China had agreed, but Mr. Molotov had replied that his government wanted one-fourth of all surface vessels from destroyers on through the lesser tonnages. He also had asked about the merchant fleet. Secretary Forrestal had said the naval vessels requested had little practical value and, with his approval, we had agreed rather than argue the point with Mr. Molotov. The merchant fleet, I told Mr. Molotov, was being used to repatriate Japanese, and we believed it should ultimately be considered in connection with the reparations settlement.

I don't know why Mr. Molotov felt it necessary to raise the issue again in the Council unless he wanted me to restate our position before the other Foreign Ministers. Apparently, he did not know that I had sent them the same message I had sent him. His other motive may have been to create an opportunity to submit a claim for a part of the Japanese fishing fleet. Mr. Bevin quickly pointed out that the fishing fleet was essential to maintain Japan's food supply. Even though the Japanese were defeated, he said, "It is necessary for them to go on living somehow."

Mr. Molotov then turned to the question of the Japanese mandated islands.

The United States, I replied, had not yet formulated its views and I knew of no agreements concerning Japanese islands in the Pacific except two: (a) the declaration at Cairo in November 1943 that Japan should be required to surrender territories acquired by conquest, and (b) the Yalta agreement regarding South Sakhalin and the Kurile Islands. The last of these I had learned about only some weeks after becoming Secretary. Mr. Bevin said the British Cabinet had not known of the Yalta agreement until some time after it was made, nevertheless they had no intention of going back on it.

After the Moscow meeting and through most of 1946 we studied actively the question of what should be done with the islands entrusted to Japanese care by the League of Nations. Shortly before the meeting of the Council of Foreign Ministers in New York in November, the President held a meeting of the Secretaries of State, War and Navy to determine our policy.

The State and War departments felt that, since Japan had received these islands under a mandate from the League of Nations, our rights were not superior to those delegated by the League and that therefore, if possible, the United Nations should declare them a strategic area to be administered by us under a United Nations trusteeship agreement. We pointed out that at San Francisco the United States delegation, by direction of President Roosevelt, had been a strong advocate of the trusteeship system. We argued that we could not properly adopt a policy that would show a lack of confidence in the system we had urged upon the United Nations. Japan had violated her mandate and therefore we could seek a decision from the United Nations on these mandated islands, while those islands that belonged to the Japanese, such as the Ryukyus, would have to await disposition by the peace conference.

The Secretary of the Navy was very reasonable. He did not want us to do anything that would show lack of confidence in the United Nations, but because he felt keenly the loss of life these islands had cost us, he wanted to make certain that the terms of the arrangement would permit the Navy to maintain adequate bases. He expressed fear that once negotiations were under way, subordinate officials of the State Department or some delegate to the United Nations might compromise and accept an arrangement that would jeopardize the proper maintenance of the bases. When I assured him that no changes in the United States proposal would be accepted without the approval of the President or the Secretary of State, he said he was satisfied with the trusteeship proposal. Shortly thereafter, our able representative to the United Nations, Mr. Warren R. Austin, placed our proposal before the Security Council.

The United Nations General Assembly was in session during the meeting of the Council of Foreign Ministers in New York, and some of the pending trusteeship proposals were up for approval, in the hope that the United Nations Trusteeship Council could be established.

The Charter provides that each trusteeship agreement must be acceptable to the "states directly concerned." I held that while the trusteeship agreement for strategic areas had to be approved by the Security Council, the United States, as the country in possession of the mandated islands, was the only state "directly concerned." Mr. Dulles, who was our representative on the Trusteeship Committee in the General Assembly, had taken the position that the definition of "states directly concerned" should not be determined until the Trusteeship Council was established but he had been strongly opposed by the Soviet representative, Ambassador Nikolai V. Novikov.

Mr. Molotov asked me to agree that the five permanent members of the Security Council should be regarded as "states directly concerned" in all cases. He suggested that the five powers exchange letters confirming this understanding. The Soviet Union probably would have no objection to the United States' proposal for a strategic trusteeship over the Japanese mandated islands, he said; nevertheless his government would like to have an agreement that all trusteeship proposals must have the approval of the five permanent members. If this were done, he added, two or three trusteeship agreements could be approved at that session of the General Assembly so that the Trusteeship Council could be organized.

Such a definition of "states directly concerned," I replied, was a matter of Charter interpretation within the United Nations itself, and should not be the subject of a bilateral arrangement between our two governments. I then added that I would bear his position in mind when considering the ultimate disposition of the Kurile Islands and the southern half of Sakhalin. This brought a very quick response. The Soviet Union, he said, did not contemplate a trusteeship arrangement for the Kuriles or Sakhalin; these matters had been settled at Yalta. I pointed out to him that Mr. Roosevelt had said repeatedly at Yalta that territory could be ceded only at the peace conference and he had agreed only to support the Soviet Union's claim at the conference. While it could be assumed that we would stand by Mr. Roosevelt's promise, I continued, we certainly would want to know, by the time of the peace conference, what the Soviet Union's attitude would be toward our proposal for placing the Japanese-mandated islands under our trusteeship. Mr. Molotov quickly grasped the implications of this remark. When the United States trusteeship agreement was voted upon later by the Security Council, I was delighted, but not surprised, to see that the Soviet representative voted in favor of our proposal.

The other Far Eastern territorial question that figured prominently in our discussions at Moscow was Korea.

The United States, United Kingdom and China had agreed at Cairo on December 1, 1943, that "in due course Korea shall become free and independent." At Yalta, President Roosevelt and Generalissimo Stalin had agreed informally that Korea should win its independence and that if a transition period were necessary, a trusteeship should be established. For forty years Korea had been exploited by Japan. The Japanese had permitted relatively few Koreans to secure an education and had made it difficult for them to obtain the important positions in trade and industry that would have given them administrative experience. As a result, there was some question whether the people were sufficiently trained to assume the responsibilities of government immediately. The desire to help the Koreans develop the skills and experience that would enable them to maintain their independence was the inspiration for President Roosevelt's acquiescence in the trusteeship idea.

When we went to Moscow we were troubled by the fact that Korea had, in fact, been split in two. At the time of the Japanese surrender, the military leaders agreed that all Japanese troops north of the 38th parallel would surrender to the Red Army and all troops south of that line would surrender to our Army. This arrangement was accepted by the Soviet

Union and was included in Order No. 1 issued to General MacArthur. But what was intended as a division for military convenience has become a closed boundary between the Soviet and American zones of occupation.

Our delegation therefore submitted a paper to the conference proposing the establishment of a Joint Soviet-American Commission to unify the administration of such matters as currency, trade and transportation, tele-communications, electric power distribution, coastal shipping, and so on. It also proposed that a four-power trusteeship be established which would "endure for no longer period than necessary to allow the Koreans to form an independent, representative and effective government."

A few days later, Mr. Molotov submitted a Soviet proposal for a Joint Commission on urgent problems of economic unification, the establishment of a provisional government and a four-power trusteeship to last for five years. In the interest of promoting agreement, we accepted the Soviet draft with a few amendments and it was included in the Moscow protocol.

But "trusteeship" to the Koreans meant only a continuation of outside control, which under the Japanese had brought them much suffering, and the postponement of their long-sought independence. The complaints against the Trusteeship proposal prompted me to issue a statement saying:

"The joint Soviet-American Commission, working with the Korean provisional democratic government, may find it possible to dispense with a trusteeship. It is our goal to hasten the day when Korea will become an independent member of the society of nations."

This hope, unfortunately, has not been sustained by subsequent events. The Soviet-American Commission met in January 1946 to carry out the mandate of the Moscow agreement. But what seemed to us unequivocal language, once again, apparently, was different in Russian. To us it seemed clear that the country should be considered as an economic and administrative whole. The Soviet commander, however, saw the problem as one of arranging exchanges between and the co-ordination of two entirely separate zones. Today, a year and a half later, they are still separate zones, and progress toward setting up a provisional government has been equally disappointing.

The Soviet representative has insisted that only those political parties which had not opposed the idea of trusteeship should be consulted in forming a government. But most Koreans, with the exception of the Communists, had opposed it. The United States maintained that, in accordance with the doctrine of free speech, an expression of opposition should not keep anyone from being consulted. We insisted on meeting with representatives of all political parties; as a result, the commission adjourned in a deadlock in May 1946. In the spring of 1947, at Moscow, Secretary Marshall succeeded in arranging for the Joint Commission to resume negotiations, but these have as yet produced no concrete results.

In the United States zone, Koreans rapidly are replacing Americans in administrative positions. An interim legislative assembly composed of forty-five elected members and forty-five appointed members met for the first time in December 1946. The purpose was not to encourage a movement for separate governments in Korea but to prepare the Koreans for responsibilities of self-government.

Whenever a provisional government is established, I fully expect the Soviet Union will propose that the Soviet-American Commission be withdrawn and that the proposed period of trusteeship be eliminated. This latter proposal, particularly, will be popular with the Koreans. But the Soviet Union may have another purpose in mind. In the Soviet Zone, the Red Army has trained an army of Koreans estimated to number from 100,000 to 400,000 men. The withdrawal of the Joint Commission and Soviet-American occupation forces would leave the Soviet-trained army the only effective military force in Korea. Undoubtedly, this army would attempt to take charge of whatever government then existed. Therefore, as a condition to withdrawal of the commission, we must require that this army be disbanded.

Korea does not need an armed force trained either by Russians or by Americans. What it needs is economic assistance. The fertilizer plants in the Soviet zone were converted by the Japanese to the manufacture of explosives. The Soviet commander has refused the American zone adequate shipments of fertilizer. Consequently, fertilizer will have to be imported in the immediate future if the depleted soil of the southern zone is to be productive.

Korea's industrial plants need rehabilitation. This requires coal, raw materials, and replacement parts. If the Joint Commission remains for two or possibly three years and American representatives can supervise financial assistance, the United States might furnish the help that is needed to set Korea's industrial machinery in motion.

The United States and the Soviet Union are committed to the establishment of a unified, independent and democratic Korea. Our government must continue its interest until that promise is fulfilled and Korea is able to take its place as a sovereign equal in the family of the United Nations. This is one of the important steps toward lasting peace in Asia.

Another essential step is to conclude an early peace treaty with Japan. Nearly two years of occupation experience have given us sound basis for judgment. Under the policies administered by General MacArthur great progress has been made. The time has come when we should agree upon the terms of the peace treaty so the people of Japan may know what the future holds for them and may begin the work of rehabilitation, guided by the blueprint provided by the Allied nations.

For reasons I have given in connection with Germany, I do not think the Council of Foreign Ministers should prepare the preliminary draft of the Japanese treaty. The Soviet Union, which entered the war a few hours before the first offer of surrender, should not insist upon peace machinery which gives them the power of veto. On the other hand, it is quite understandable that a government like Australia, whose armed forces fought the Japanese from Pearl Harbor to the day of surrender, feels that it should play a larger role in the Japanese peace settlement than it had in the drafting of the five European treaties.

We should immediately announce that we believe a peace conference should be held, and fix an early date. The eleven governments on the commission are those that made substantial military contributions in the war against Japan and are the ones that should prepare the preliminary draft of the peace treaty. Through their work on the commission, all eleven have been giving careful consideration to Japanese problems for nearly two years. They should be able, without difficulty, to prepare drafts of a treaty for consideration by the peace conference.

The peace conference should include all the states at war with Japan.

Decisions of the drafting powers and of the peace conference should be by a two-thirds vote, including two-thirds or seven out of eleven powers that made substantial military contributions. Every effort should be made to secure unanimity, but a two-thirds vote should be decisive and a treaty based on such decisions should be submitted to the governments for signature. The veto power, of course, cannot be entirely eliminated since there is no way in which an Allied nation that is a member of the peace conference can be forced to sign a treaty. But it cannot prevent others from signing it.

The governments unwilling to accept the decision of a two-thirds majority would remain in a technical state of war with Japan. I believe, however, that the treaty with Japan, like those with Italy and the Balkan states, should provide that any government refusing to sign it will not receive any of the benefits of its provisions.

In adopting the procedure recommended here we would, of course, be giving up our right to veto any provision with which we disagree. This would be a magnanimous gesture on the part of the country which was largely responsible for defeating the Japanese. It also would be an expression of confidence in our Allies and in our ability to reach, by a two-thirds vote, satisfactory agreements on the treatment of Japan.

In drafting the peace treaty there should be no serious controversy on territorial questions. The United States undoubtedly will stand by President Roosevelt's agreement on the Kuriles and Sakhalin. I see no objection to Japan's keeping the islands of the Ryukyu group north of Okinawa. From Okinawa south, it is my hope that the islands will be placed under a United Nations trusteeship. For sentimental reasons, the United States will want a trusteeship interest in Okinawa.

The question of reparations is certain to be most controversial. The Far Eastern Commission's discussions on this subject have been marked by the Soviet representative's insistence that the industrial equipment removed from Manchuria must be excluded from any reparations settlement. These removals, the Soviets insist, must be regarded as "war booty." One Soviet representative has placed an estimated value on these removals of 97 million dollars. Reparations Commissioner Pauley, on the basis of his investigation in June 1946, has placed direct damage at more than 858 million dollars and the total damage, including deterioration and cost of replacement, at over two billion dollars.

The Soviet position is indefensible. Of course, this industrial equipment must be included in the reparations settlement. It cannot be war booty. It does not include weapons of war. Its return to Manchuria is impractical, but the least that can be done to repair the damage is to charge it against the Soviet Union's share of reparations.

We have taken this position in the Far Eastern Commission. We have been supported in it by nine other nations. But the Soviet Union, through its use of the veto, has been able to block action in the commission.

At the time of the Peace Conference we should propose a forty-year treaty to insure the demilitarization of Japan, similar to the treaty we proposed for Germany. In this case, however, any violation of the treaty should be reported to the Ambassadors or Ministers of the states that drafted the treaty, who would constitute a Commission of Enforcement. As in the German treaty, decisions would be made by a majority vote.

Both in the peace treaty and the demilitarization treaty we must look forward to a long period of involvement in Japanese affairs. The great progress we have made in the last two years can be lost if we do not make sure that the changes become a permanent part of the Japanese way of life. The spiritual disarmament of a people is a much more difficult task than their physical disarmament. To instill the democratic concept of the individual in the Japanese requires a major social revolution. It can be accomplished permanently only if we make certain that a whole new generation of Japanese is educated in accordance with this democratic ideal. Unless this is done, the newly won rights of labor to organize, of farmers to own their land, of women to participate in public life, and of political parties to operate without fear, can be dissipated and destroyed. We must work intelligently with the new generation and we must make a just economic settlement so that that generation will have a promise of stability and an opportunity to create a better way of life than under the old order.

I have said relatively little about China. This is primarily because the record of our effort there is well known. Unhappily, that record shows little success. China still is a long way from peace. The future which could hold so much for that great country and its millions of people is still only a promise. It is one of the great tragedies of our times that a nation so rich in human and material resources is split by fratricidal conflict.

The one safe generalization that can be made about China is that it stands on the threshold of great change. We should encourage and assist that change whenever possible. China needs the physical and human engineering skills that we possess. The intelligent and persevering application of those skills can prevent China's change from becoming an upheaval that could well endanger the peace of the world. But the initiative for applying them must come from within China herself if they are to succeed.

Awareness of China's importance is by no means confined to the United States. My own experience as well as events have made clear the interest of the Soviet Union in this great area bordering its eastern frontiers. Outer Mongolia has become virtually a Soviet protectorate. At Yalta, Stalin successfully quoted as his price for entering the Japanese war, joint control of the two railway systems in Manchuria, a free port at Dairen, and a naval base at Port Arthur. And, when I went to Moscow in December 1945, Mr. Molotov's great interest in China was clearly revealed by his insistent efforts to discover what aims, hidden or otherwise, the United States might have toward China.

Fortunately, I arrived in Moscow well prepared for Mr. Molotov. Before Ambassador Hurley's resignation, the State Department had prepared a statement of policy on China, the first draft of which I showed the Ambassador a few days before he resigned. As soon as President Truman appointed General Marshall his personal representative in China, I asked the General to study the draft so that he could help prepare the final statement for presentation to the President.

The Sunday before I left for Moscow, Under Secretary Acheson, General Marshall and members of his staff met in my office. By the end of the morning's discussion, we had agreed upon the statement of policy that subsequently was approved by the President and released to the public on December 15. Thereafter the President made no change in that policy except upon the recommendation of General Marshall or with his approval.

At our very first meeting in Spiridonovka House, Mr. Molotov asked that the question of American troops in north China be discussed. I agreed and presented him with a prepared statement giving the exact number of troops in north China. I explained that they were there at the request of the Chinese Government to assist in disarming 325,000 Japanese. I assured the Soviet Government the troops would be withdrawn as soon as this mission was completed, and pointed out that General Marshall had gone to China as the President's personal representative to help effect a truce that would end China's internal strife and permit the disarming of the Japanese.

The next day I presented to the council President Truman's statement of American policy toward China. It reiterated that our troops were in north China to disarm the Japanese, a mission that was being delayed by the country's internal strife, and it stressed our belief that the antagonists should cease fighting and join in a national conference of all political parties to unify the country.

These statements did not satisfy Mr. Molotov and he raised the question again two days later. This time I explained in detail our obligations to the Allies to make certain that the Japanese in north China were disarmed, how this task had been assigned primarily to the Chinese Nationalist forces, how they were prevented from accomplishing it because the Communist armies stood between them and the Japanese troops, how we had delayed taking action to disarm these Japanese ourselves because it was a duty that had been assigned to the National government by the Supreme Commander, and since we all recognized that government, we thought they should be given a fair opportunity to discharge it. I assured him that if it became necessary we would go in and disarm the Japanese so that our troops could then return home.

Mr. Molotov said he felt Chiang Kai-shek's government exaggerated the strength of the Communist forces. He observed that Chinese never wished to do any fighting themselves but prefer that others do it for them. The continued existence of these Japanese forces, he asserted, was "intolerable" and dryly remarked that after eight years of war Chiang Kai-shek should have learned how to handle the Japanese, particularly after they had capitulated.

A few days later, Mr. Molotov resumed the offensive by suggesting that a date be fixed for the simultaneous withdrawal of American and Russian troops from China. Once again I explained that the disarmament of the Japanese was a different problem from the one the Red Army had faced in Manchuria. But a few minutes later he was asking the same question he had been asking since the first day of the session.

"Mr. Molotov, you must be asking these questions because you like the sound of my voice," I said. "I can only give you the answer I have given you every time you have asked the question. For your advance information, when you ask the same question tomorrow, you will get the same answer."

That evening I was to see Generalissimo Stalin. I was weary of going through my routine with Molotov so I added this question to the items to be discussed.

I told Stalin of my discussions with Molotov, who was present, and I reminded him how he had declared at Potsdam that Chiang Kai-shek's government was the only possible government in China and that the Chinese Communists were not real Communists at all. In response, he pointed out that the Soviet Union had a treaty recognizing Chiang. He had no objection to the presence of our troops there, he added, but he merely wished to be informed about it. If the Chinese people became convinced Chiang Kai-shek was depending on foreign troops, Stalin remarked, Chiang would lose his influence.

Taking some matches, I placed them on the table, indicating the relative location of the Japanese troops and the Communist troops along the railroad in North China and the troops of the National government. Stalin became deeply interested and inquired about the size of the Communist forces in the Tientsin area. I replied that Mao Tse Tung, the Communist leader, claimed to have 600,000 in that area. Stalin laughed at the statement. Pointing to the match representing National government forces in the North China area, which I said numbered about 40,000, he asked me what had become of the army of one and a half million that Chiang was supposed to have. I told him our Navy and Army had not seen them. Stalin laughed heartily and said all Chinese were boasters who exaggerated the forces of their opponents as well as their own. He paid a compliment to General Marshall, saying that, if anyone could settle the situation in China, he could.

As a result of this discussion with Stalin the council reached an agreement the following day on the statement that was included in the protocol. It reaffirmed that the three governments recognized the need of a unified and democratic China under the National Government, and stated that the Foreign Ministers of the United States and the Soviet Union were "in complete accord as to the desirability of withdrawal of Soviet and American forces from China at the earliest practicable moment consistent with the discharge of their obligations and responsibilities."

In September 1946, General Marshall reported to the President that it seemed useless to remain in China much longer. President Truman authorized him to return whenever he thought his mission should be concluded. In Paris, I told China's Foreign Minister of our decision. He immediately expressed fear that General Marshall's departure would suggest to the Chinese people that the United States had lost interest in China's affairs. I assured him of our friendly interest but emphasized that the general could not remain indefinitely when neither faction would accept his advice.

Every effort had been made to insure the success of General Marshall's mission. In addition to his own great prestige, he was accorded the prestige and authority of a personal representative of the President of the United

States. At Moscow, we had secured from the Soviet Union an official re-affirmation of their support of the National Government as the only legiti-mate government in China. And the President, in his statement of policy on December 18, 1945, had held out to the Chinese this attractive promise:

"When conditions in China improve we are prepared to consider aid in carrying out . . . projects, unrelated to civil strife, which would en-courage economic reconstruction and reform in China and which, in so doing, would promote a general revival of commercial relations between American and Chinese businessmen."

General Marshall continued his efforts until January 1947, but the war-ring groups were still no nearer settlement. We then had to decide whether Ambassador Leighton Stuart should continue the efforts to bring the two factions together. John Carter Vincent, chief of the Far East Division and an experienced foreign service officer, took the position that he should not; that, if General Marshall could not bring about unity, it would be unwise to ask any other official to force our views upon the factions. I agreed with Vincent.

Many of us have had the unhappy experience of intervening in the domestic quarrel of some couple, and we have learned that, when our ad-vice is not wanted by either, the best course is to withdraw. This is as true of nations as it is of married couples. In both cases our action is motivated by friendship. But if we are to stay friendly with the couple it is always necessary to wait until at least one of them is tired of fighting. In interna-tional as well as domestic affairs, there are times when the best thing to do is—to do nothing.

In our approach to the myriad troubles of Asia we should always re-member that we start with a tremendous reservoir of good will. The ful-fillment of our promise of independence to the Philippines and our acts of friendship toward the independent Kingdom of Siam stand as beacon lights to millions of Asiatics who are looking toward an expansion of their political and economic freedom. In all the change that inevitably lies ahead in Asia, we must make sure our actions do not drain this reservoir of good will. Our own safety and security, as well as the peace of the world, de-pend upon our success in being on the side of progress in Asia.

King George VI, Ernest Bevin, and James F. Byrnes following a dinner discussion of the atomic energy resolution and other matters then pending before the United Nations General Assembly. St. James Palace, January 1946.

BOOK IV

WORK AHEAD

Chapter 12

Building a People's Foreign Policy

THIS GENERATION of Americans has learned that the United States is a principal trustee of the world's peace and freedom. What the United States says and does affects the lives of people in the most remote areas of this earth. The words and deeds of a member of the Cabinet or of the Congress often reaches into more homes than those of many Kings and Presidents. Even Generalissimo Stalin, in his last talks with Harry Hopkins, acknowledged the world-wide interests and responsibilities of the United States and declared that our country has more reason to be a world power than any other.

Leadership and its inherent responsibilities we have accepted with reluctance—reluctance that two costly wars have not wholly overcome. But without our initiative, the United Nations probably would not have been created to promote and maintain international peace and security. Without our determined effort, it is doubtful whether ravages of war can be removed quickly enough to give the United Nations a chance to work.

The responsibilities that clearly are ours will be discharged in the years ahead only if we develop in international affairs a policy that truly reflects the will of our people. I am convinced that to build a people's foreign policy we must pursue three primary objectives.

First, we must have a foreign policy that is bipartisan in its origin and development; that is national rather than political in its conduct and its character; and that, consequently, is a continuing policy worthy of the confidence of other nations.

Second, we must have an institution that is responsive to the will of the people and able to translate our policies into effective action.

And, third, we must leave behind the era of secret diplomacy. We must make sure that our people have an opportunity to know the problems their diplomats confront so that they can judge properly the proposed solution. The right of the people to know is a basic element in the development of a people's foreign policy.

These objectives, I know from experience, are not easy to attain. But the story of what I encountered in my pursuit of them may be of some service in the work that lies ahead.

My conviction on the first objective stems from World War I. In November 1918, I was in Paris with Representatives Carter Glass and Richard S. Whaley of South Carolina. Out of all our talks with military and diplomatic representatives, I was particularly impressed by the comments of General Tasker H. Bliss, our military representative on the Supreme Council at Versailles. Among other things, he told us that, with the approach of peace, his associates lost much of their idealism; they talked less about ending all wars and more about reparations and territorial gains. He thought there was little chance of establishing international machinery to preserve peace unless President Wilson came to France and could make a successful appeal over the heads of politicians.

When I returned to Washington, I spoke to President Wilson about my conversation with General Bliss. He told me that in the latter days of the war he relied on Bliss more than on any other representative in Europe. However, he could not do as General Bliss suggested, he said, because he could not speak French and any appeal he might make would lose its force when translated into another language. When I visited him again a short time later, he then told me he had decided to go to Europe. To this day, I remember his words:

"I am going," he said, "in the hope that I may redeem the pledge I made to the mothers of the world that we were fighting a war to end wars."

He was not making a speech to me. He stated it simply as the reason for his decision.

In the early days of World War II, I told this story to President Roosevelt and expressed the opinion that Wilson lost his great fight for the League of Nations because he did not take with him at least one Republican Senator. President Roosevelt shared my opinion.

At Yalta, immediately after the Big Three agreed to support the Dumbarton Oaks proposal and before he left the conference table, President Roosevelt instructed Secretary Stettinius to name, as members of the delegation to the San Francisco Conference, Senator Connally and Senator Vandenberg. They worked in harmony with Secretary Stettinius at San Francisco and their wholehearted co-operation was largely responsible for the almost unanimous vote by which our adherence to the United Nations was approved by the Senate.

Before the first meeting of the Council of Foreign Ministers, I decided to invite a prominent Republican, well informed on international affairs, to accompany me. It did not occur to me then that a Senator could be away for as long a time as the treaty-drafting business was likely to consume. I consulted Senator Vandenberg. He suggested that I invite Mr. John Foster Dulles, who for years has been keenly interested in our foreign relations and is exceptionally well qualified. Mr. Dulles accepted the invitation, notwithstanding his business commitments, and was of great assistance. Later I recommended to President Truman that Mr. Dulles be a member of our delegation to the first meeting of the General Assembly of the United Nations. He accomplished much and continued his service at the meeting of the General Assembly in New York.

Our participation in the United Nations constantly and deliberately has been bipartisan. At both sessions of the General Assembly, our delegation included, in addition to Mr. Dulles, the top-ranking Democratic and Republican members of the Foreign Affairs Committees of both the Senate and the House, Senators Connally and Vandenberg and Representatives Bloom and Eaton. At the first session at London one of the delegates was my friend John G. Townsend, former Senator from Delaware, chairman of the Republican Senatorial Campaign Committee, and a man respected by all Senators.

When Edward R. Stettinius resigned as head of the permanent delegation to the United Nations, I recommended to the President that he appoint the Vermont Republican, Senator Warren R. Austin, as chief of our permanent mission to the United Nations. The President was delighted with the suggestion. He liked Austin, having been closely associated with him in the Senate. Throughout his Senate career Austin had shown an extensive knowledge of and a keen interest in foreign relations. He had made a great contribution to the success of the Chapultepec Conference and, in fact, since 1939, has co-operated wholeheartedly in the prosecution of the war and the preparations for the peace.

After we agreed at Moscow to resume work on the preparation of peace treaties at Paris, I asked Senators Connally and Vandenberg to go with me as advisers. They generously agreed and served through the meetings of the council and also during the peace conference. I discussed with them every phase of our foreign relations. In 1946 they spent 213 days away from Washington attending international conferences. No two legislators ever served their country more loyally or more efficiently than they did at those meetings.

Because Senator Vandenberg represented the political party opposed to the administration, and because he enjoyed the confidence of the overwhelming majority of his party, his support enabled us to speak of our foreign policy as the American policy.

At the conference of the Council of Foreign Ministers each delegation has five seats at the table. Seated with me were the two Senators, the deputy in charge of the work on the treaty under discussion, and the interpreter. Each Foreign Minister can bring to the conference room an additional eight or ten members of his staff. It makes quite an audience. Consequently the Ministers frequently hold private meetings in the hope that the absence of an audience may promote agreement. When these meetings are held each Foreign Minister is allowed to bring two associates in addition to the interpreter. To all such meetings, I asked the two Senators to accompany me. I preferred to have their counsel rather than the aid of the technicians of the State Department, as helpful as these gentlemen always were. Also, I wanted the Senators to know at first hand every stage of the treaty making.

The political party in power cannot ask the opposition party to share responsibility for the conduct of our foreign relations unless the leaders of the opposition are fully advised of our policies. This is true when the Congress and President are of the same party. It is particularly true when a majority of the Congress and the Chief Executive are not of the same political party. The executive branch of the government cannot announce a policy of importance requiring congressional action and then inform the leaders of the opposition. Even if the opposition leaders think the proposal unwise they must support it or create abroad the impression of dissension. A policy of by-passing the Congress would make impossible a bipartisan policy.

While Senator Vandenberg and Senator Connally were with me I sought their counsel not only on the treaties but on other matters connected with our foreign relations that were submitted to me by the Department each day. They were helpful and, though I know they were frequently and skillfully tempted, not once did either of them give to newspaper friends advance information of our plans.

The participation of Senators Connally and Vandenberg in the meetings of the Council of Foreign Ministers, the peace conference and the United Nations served to let the people of the world know that the foreign policy of the United States was a continuing policy and would not end with the defeat of a political party. It enabled me, during the ceremony at the Washington airport which marked our departure for the Peace Conference, to address this statement to the people of the world:

"The situation is entirely different from that which existed after World War I. Then we were badly divided. This time there is no division between the Executive and the Congress as to the making of peace. This time there is no division between the great political parties as to the making of peace. . . . We are all working together not as partisans of any political party or of any branch of the Government; we are working together as Americans. . . . We are deeply conscious that if we as a nation are to exert our influence on the affairs of the world, we must be united."

But during our stay in Paris, I was to experience one more demonstration that bipartisanship does not necessarily insure unity. Long before the Paris meeting, I had learned that the most conscientious effort to make a just peace would not receive united support at home. I have already reported the criticism I encountered when, at London, the Council of Foreign Ministers could not agree. I was prepared for that. But I was not prepared for some of the criticism I received when, at Moscow, we did agree.

The story of the Moscow meeting, I have told; the long negotiations, the final session which ended at 3:30 A. M., our take-off for the United States four hours later at 7:30 A. M., December 27. My statement that we were thoroughly exhausted when we landed at Washington at noon on the twenty-ninth will be fully understood. Nevertheless, I went directly to the State Department and to work.

Upon asking when I could see the President, an employee at the White House told me that the President was cruising down the Potomac and expected to remain on his boat for several days. I requested that a message be sent to him saying that I had returned and would like to report to him at his convenience and that I expected to make a radio speech the following evening about the work of the conference.

Shortly thereafter, I received an invitation to visit the President that afternoon on his boat, which was anchored near Quantico. I took a plane and reached Quantico about 4:30.

After I had reported to the President on what had happened at the conference, he expressed wholehearted approval of my action. He asked me to remain for dinner. There were present, as I recall, members of the President's staff who frequently accompanied him on such trips: Admiral Leahy, George Allen, General Vaughan, Clark Clifford, Charles Ross, Matthew Connelly, General Graham, and Judge Rosenman, who was working on a speech the President was to deliver the following week.

While we were at dinner, the President asked me to repeat what I had said to him about the conference, and I did so. From time to time the President interrupted to express his approval. There was no expression of disapproval or approval by any other except Admiral Leahy, who said that my report made him feel much better about the situation but that he did not approve of the agreement on Rumania and Bulgaria. I reminded him that both of us had been at Yalta and at Potsdam when President Roosevelt and President Truman had entered into agreements on the same subjects, seeking to establish provisional governments that would include representation of all political parties and that would provide for free elections and the four freedoms. These agreements, I added, had not been kept by either of the two states or by the Soviets. The Moscow agreement, I told him, was simply one more effort to achieve the objective of the Yalta and Potsdam agreements. At Moscow we had secured what previously the Soviets had opposed—the agreement to send Ambassador Harriman, Ambassador Clark Kerr, and Mr. Vyshinski to Rumania to seek ways to carry out the agreement. The effort might not be successful, I said, but the result could not be any worse than the previous situation. I asked what he would have done. I received no information.

Immediately after dinner I asked to be excused because I had to fly back to Washington; because of the rain and sleet then falling I feared a low ceiling at Washington. There was no further discussion of our foreign problems.

The President invited me to come back New Year's Eve and spend the night on the ship, and I promised to return.

When I went ashore I found that the sleet had covered the wings of my plane and it was impossible to use it. Therefore, I had to return to Washington by automobile. The marine officer who kindly offered to drive me to Washington found he had undertaken an exceedingly difficult task as the sleet kept all the windows and windshield of the car covered with ice. Consequently, it was late when I reached home. That automobile trip, following the long journey from Moscow, made December 29 a far from perfect day. But when I walked in the door at home, Mrs. Byrnes handed me a message that gave the day at least a perfect ending. It was from my thoughtful friend and counselor, Cordell Hull. It said:

> *My dear Jim:* My heartiest congratulations on the splendid progress made at the Moscow Conference. Understanding, confidence, friendliness, and the whole spirit of international co-operation have been greatly improved by the work of this conference.

The next night I made to the people my radio report on the conference. I explained the agreements reached and observed that they "should bring hope to the war-weary people of many lands." I also expressed the belief that "the meeting in Moscow did serve to bring about better understanding."

When I returned to the President's ship, the night of the thirty-first, he congratulated me on the report. He said the party on board had listened the previous night and considered it a convincing statement.

Within a few days, however, one or two newspaper columnists wrote that the President had wired me to come to his ship and had expressed strong disapproval of my agreements. They stated that there was ill feeling between the President and the Secretary of State. There was a general understanding among the newspaper correspondents that the information came from the White House and critics felt encouraged to attack me when it was rumored that the criticisms were shared by the President's official family.

The fact is the President did not on that occasion nor at any other time express to me disapproval of any position I took at the meetings of the Council of Foreign Ministers or any other meetings. Nor did he ever express to me disapproval of any statement I made on our foreign policy.

In the President's letter to Stalin written before the Moscow Conference, the President approved most of the proposals agreed to at Moscow.

My experience with the Moscow agreements demonstrated that in the pursuit of a truly national foreign policy one has to be prepared for criticism from both the right and the left. Had these agreements been as favorable to the Soviet Union as some critics have charged, the Soviets would not have violated them. And the fact that ever since then we have been protesting against these violations indicates that they were in the best interests of the liberated states.

However, the person or persons inspiring the stories of dissension between the President and myself continued their efforts. In at least one press conference the President denied such dissension, but the stories persisted. A man who holds public office learns to disregard misrepresentations, but I admit these untrue stories did not make life any easier for me in the strenuous days of early 1946.

My hope for united support of our foreign policies received a serious setback when, on September 12, 1946, while I was in Paris, Secretary of Commerce Henry A. Wallace made a speech at Madison Square Garden contending that the policy which had been approved by the President, and carried out by me, was too harsh to the Soviet Union and that a more conciliatory approach to them was necessary. I was not greatly surprised by the Secretary's action. Previously, he had made a statement to the New York *Times* referring to our negotiations with Iceland for the use of the airfield we had built there. His statement was effectively used by the Communists in Iceland and it had obstructed the efforts of the State Department to secure an agreement important to the defense of this hemisphere.

In Paris, the importance of Mr. Wallace's Madison Square Garden speech was magnified in the minds of the representatives of foreign governments by newspaper reports quoting President Truman as saying at a press conference that he approved the Wallace speech in its entirety. This report stimulated widespread discussion among the govermental representatives attending the peace conference; it inspired inquiries to our representatives in various capitals. Foreign Ministers wondered whether in my various public statements I had correctly presented American policy.

Senator Vandenberg issued a statement saying that he wanted to co-operate with the administration but he could co-operate with only one Secretary of State at a time.

Senator Connally declared that he supported the policy we had announced and had been following.

I concluded that I should not make a public statement; that the matter called for correction by the President.

Of course, the position of our delegation was a very unhappy one. So far as possible, I tried to avoid delegates to the conference or the other Foreign Ministers because I wanted to avoid answering questions about whether the policy of our government had changed. Our difficulties were increased rather than lessened when Mr. Wallace announced on the White House steps that he and the President had agreed that the Secretary of Commerce would make no more speeches until after the peace conference. To the delegates in Paris, this implied that the President had not objected to a later renewal of his attacks on our foreign policy.

While I had no direct communication with the White House, I learned of developments from the press and from several messages sent to me by Assistant Secretary of State Donald Russell. As a result, on September 18, I sent the President a message, reminding him that, on the advice of a physician, I had given him my resignation in April. By agreement, my resignation would take effect upon the completion of the treaties. My message further stated:

"If it is not possible for you, for any reason, to keep Mr. Wallace, as a member of your Cabinet, from speaking on foreign affairs, it would be a grave mistake from every point of view for me to continue in office, even temporarily. Therefore, if it is not completely clear in your own mind that Mr. Wallace should be asked to refrain from criticizing the foreign policy of the United States while he is a member of your Cabinet, I must ask you to accept my resignation immediately. At this critical time, whoever is Secretary of State must be known to have the undivided support of your administration and, so far as possible, of the Congress.

"I shall, of course, remain here until my successor arrives. In case you are not ready to make that appointment promptly, you can, of course, appoint someone other than the Secretary of State to head the United States delegation at the Peace Conference."

The following day I was informed that the President wished to talk with me over the telephone. We had difficulty getting a clear signal and finally I was told that a third party was on the channel and the telephone company's operator was unable to "clear the line" for our conversation. I then asked the President if we might arrange for a teletype conversation. He kindly consented. There is a teletype instrument in the White House, and one in our Embassy in Paris. I went to the message room of our Embassy and dictated to the operator this statement:

I realize that in reaching the agreement announced by Mr. Wallace you were trying to reconcile the difference in views held by us on the one hand and by Mr. Wallace on the other.

But Mr. Wallace's last statement leaves the representatives of our government abroad, as well as other governments, in more doubt than ever as to just what American foreign policy will be.

Mr. Wallace has reiterated that he stands by his New York speech which he does not deny was intended to be critical of our foreign policy. There is little difference in a member of the Cabinet issuing to the press statements that he stands by his criticism of your foreign policy and making such criticisms from a platform.

Mr. Wallace has promised to refrain from speaking until the present Paris Peace Conference concludes, but the form of his statement indicates that he will continue to press publicly his own ideas on foreign policy which differ from your ideas and that you recognize his right as a member of your Cabinet to do so.

When the administration itself is divided on its own foreign policy, it cannot hope to convince the world that the American people have a foreign policy.

The position of the delegation in this particular conference is not restored by Mr. Wallace's agreement not to speak during this conference when he remains a member of your official family and indicates in effect that he will renew his criticism of your present foreign policy as soon as the conference is over. We are promised only a moratorium from criticism of your policies by your own administration.

The world is today in doubt not only as to American foreign policy, but as to your foreign policy.

This particular peace conference is only a stage in the peace-making process. The conference makes only recommendations to the Council of Foreign Ministers which upon the adjournment of the conference will meet to draft the final treaties. Then while the Foreign Ministers are at the most critical stage of their negotiations, Mr. Wallace can resume his public criticisms of our policies and says he will do so.

Moreover, this conference deals only with some of the treaties, and the making of peace with Germany, Austria and Japan is still ahead of us. This conference is only a start and nothing done will have finality if there is not continuity in our foreign policy.

You and I are confronted with most serious problems entirely disassociated from the conference and demanding unity at home.

When the representatives of other governments know that as soon as the conference ends we will again have conflicting statements made by your Secretary of State and your Secretary of Commerce, your delegation here cannot contribute much to the making of the peace. As a matter of fact, since these attacks upon us by a member of the Cabinet, our efforts have been greatly handicapped.

When the conference ends and the Council of Foreign Ministers meets to make the final decision, each day I would be confronted with statements of Mr. Wallace in conflict with views expressed by me. I would then have to insist upon being relieved. It is far better for the administration to let us come home now, rather than for us to return October 23, by which date we hope the conference will adjourn.

If Wallace is influenced by any ill feeling toward me it is possible that if you accept my resignation he might be willing to support your foreign policies or at least refrain from attacking such policies.

To me the important thing is to try and restore confidence in our policies.

I sincerely hope that when you appoint someone you can announce that you are wholeheartedly and undividedly behind the foreign policy of the United States as it has been heretofore determined by you and as it is being carried out; that our foreign policy is an American foreign policy and not the policy of any party or faction; that no change in American foreign policy is desired or contemplated by you. If for any reason you wish to modify your policy in any way, I hope that whatever policy you determine upon you will announce it as the American policy to which we are going to adhere, and that while a private citizen can express his views in opposition, that no member of your cabinet can express views in conflict with your policies.

I have been urging on every Foreign Minister with whom I have talked that the American policy as fixed by you was a permanent bipartisan policy and they could rely upon it that it would not be shifting from time to time and it would not even shift if there were a change in parties because for the first time we had the co-operation of the Republicans. Any statement that in six weeks the policy will be re-examined and discussed with Mr. Wallace whose statements have caused such consternation will cause these Foreign Ministers to doubt the stability of our policy.

I respectfully submit that if Mr. Molotov believed that on October 23 there would be a re-examination of the question of permitting Wallace to again attack your policy he would derive great comfort. No other member of the Cabinet would claim the right or be allowed to criticize your policy. The fact that it is not decided now that a man who stays in the Cabinet must support your policy is bound to hurt us. The work of our delegation is at a standstill. Representatives of the other delegations keep our delegation busy asking whether the administration will permit Wallace to make another speech attacking us. These governments would never permit a member of the Cabinet to do such a thing and they cannot understand how we would permit it unless his views were shared or there was a serious division of sentiment among the people. I do not want to ask you to do anything that would force Mr. Wallace out of the Cabinet. However, I do not think that any man who professes any loyalty to you would so seriously impair your prestige and the prestige of the government with the nations of the world. This is particularly true, if you showed him telegrams such as we have received from Greece. You and I spent 15 months building a bipartisan policy. We did a fine job convincing the world that it was a permanent policy upon which the world could rely. Wallace destroyed it in a day.

It is not proper for me to quote the President's statements. But I think it is proper to say that, as a result of the conversation, I knew he did not intend to change his policies or leave any doubt about his views. He did not tell me what action he would take. However, the following day the

President settled the matter in a manner satisfactory, I hope, to the overwhelming majority of the people of the United States.

With the resignation of Secretary Wallace, confidence in the American policy was restored. Senators Connally and Vandenberg continued to serve in support of our foreign policy with unswerving loyalty. The Wallace incident took place during a national campaign which resulted in the shifting of the majority rule in Congress from the Democrats to the Republicans. Senator Connally met opposition in his primary election, but would not abandon his work in Paris where he was helping his country and come home to help himself. Senator Vandenberg, who also was a candidate for re-election, not only took no part in the campaign but was barely able to get back to Michigan to vote; he urged other Republicans to support the bipartisan foreign policy.

The results of our efforts to maintain a bipartisan foreign policy were clearly indicated by the overwhelming approval of the Senate in its vote on June 5, 1947, ratifying the five treaties thus far concluded. When I was informed of the vote, I could not help but recall again the unhappy months after World War I when President Wilson struggled with a disgruntled and determined Senate that finally defeated his efforts for peace. And I renewed my hope that never again would our policy makers repeat President Wilson's mistake; that hereafter the responsible leaders of both parties would be kept informed of our policies from the beginning of their formulation to their ultimate conclusion.

The second element in the development and maintenance of a people's foreign policy is the caliber of the institution responsible for our foreign affairs. It has often been popular to use the State Department as a whipping post for shortcomings in the conduct of our foreign affairs that actually are due to our own indifference.

The organization and operation of the State Department still needs continuing study. It grew from an organization that numbered nine hundred people before the war to one of some 3,000 people who were scattered in eighteen buildings throughout Washington. A few months after I assumed office, the personnel of the Department had been almost doubled by the transfer to it of all or part of such war agencies as the Office of Strategic Services, the Office of War Information, the Foreign Economic Administration, and the Surplus Property Administration. The transfer of these wartime agencies did not make me very happy. The job of acting as "undertaker" for war agencies necessarily is a bad one. The most capable people are impelled to leave a dying organization, to find permanent work with a live and growing organization. Morale sags and problems multiply.

But, more important, I do not believe that functions primarily adminis
trative in character should be assigned to the State Department.

The State Department must be a policy-making department. It cannot
be run like one which is charged with conducting a variety of operations.
The amount of time a Secretary of State must give to decisions on carrying out operating functions, necessarily is taken away from the important
questions of foreign policy.

Because I thought the State Department should be maintained as a
policy-making department, I opposed the efforts of the War Department
to transfer to the State Department control of our occupation organizations in Europe and in the Pacific. The State Department is not adapted
for such work. It cannot recruit an efficient organization because the appointees could, at best, be promised only temporary employment far removed from their homes. If the burden of carrying on shipping, maintenance of transportation, policing, inspection and all the myriad duties of
occupation forces were transferred to the State Department, its capacity
to define wisely important foreign policies would be seriously hampered.
We should retain the efficient organizations that have been developed by
Generals McNarney and Clay in Germany, General Clark in Austria, and
General MacArthur in Japan.

The proponents of the transfer argue that there is a division of authority between the War Department and the State Department, but I do not
believe the argument is sound. There is such a division in all matters
affecting foreign policy. The President determines our foreign policy.
He makes his decisions upon the recommendations of the Secretary of
State. The policy as determined must be executed by the War and Navy
departments whose personnel, by training and experience, are best qualified to conduct the necessary operations. Until there is a treaty of peace,
the job of occupation is as much the job of the Army as is the job of
making war. Of course, it is a disagreeable task, but the army of no other
power has quit the job and our army should not.

There must, of course, always be close co-ordination between the State,
War and Navy departments. A policy which, in today's world, is not defined with one eye on our power to back it up, is hardly a policy at all.
Since the early days of the war not only have the Secretaries of State,
War and Navy held frequent consultations but a Co-ordinating Committee made up of representatives from these three departments meets regularly to consider common problems.

In February 1946, I agreed to a proposal made by the Joint Chiefs of
Staff which eventually will greatly promote the efforts to achieve co-
ordination. This was the proposal to establish the National War College
as a combined training institution for high ranking officers of State, War
and Navy. It began its operations July 1, 1946. Foreign service officers

have been assigned to the college and the new institution is already doing a most effective work.

In October 1945, I proposed that the President issue an executive order establishing a Council of National Defense consisting of the Secretaries of State, War and Navy, so that our foreign and our defense policies could be fully co-ordinated. The draft order provided that the Chief of Staff of the Army and the Chief of Naval Operations serve as advisers to the Council on military matters. In addition to maintaining its own secretariat, the council also would have under it a unified intelligence service. The proposal was never approved, but many of its objectives were incorporated into the legislation to merge the Army and Navy into a Department of National Defense. As this legislation is put into practice, the problem of co-ordinating our foreign and our military policies must be given continuing study.

One who was Secretary of State a total of 562 days, 350 of which were spent at international conferences, cannot claim to have effected many fundamental changes in an institution like the State Department. In fact, during the early months of my tenure we made a conscious effort to help the Department recover from an acute attack of "reorganization jitters." But one innovation was introduced. It did not win any public attention but I regard it as one of the more significant undertakings in the conduct of our foreign affairs.

When I became Secretary, I attempted to obtain a broad statement of our policy. I thought there should be a basic operating guide for a realistic foreign policy. No such document had been drawn up. Many officials of the State Department could outline our policy for a particular area, but it was readily apparent that the statement was only their idea of what our policy was. There was no authoritative text, duly considered and approved, which set forth our national objectives the world over. I asked that the formulation of statements of policy be given a top priority in the work of the Department.

Country committees for every nation in the world were created. These committees sought to draw up a rounded program that tied our political, economic, intelligence and information activities into a commonly conceived program. After this group had prepared a draft statement it was sent to our Missions abroad for review and criticism. It was my opinion that too much policy was determined without consulting the man on the spot who was in daily contact with the situation in that country. Also, I thought, if he helped to shape the policy he would be better able to follow a consistent program. Certain of the larger Embassies received many or all of the statements for comment. When the suggestions from the field had been received and studied a final policy statement was prepared by the men who lived with these problems. As they were approved, these became our operating guides. To meet changing conditions, I directed that these policy statements be reviewed and revised every six months.

There is little sense in determining policy in the Department unless that policy is made known to our representatives throughout the world. In past years I have visited Embassies where the representatives of our State Department and the Navy and Army attachés each had different opinions about our government's policy toward that particular country. When our own people didn't know our policy, one could not expect a foreign government to know it. Copies of our policy statements were also sent to the Joint Chiefs of Staff.

When these "country" statements were completed, I asked that "area" committees be set up to review the policies set forth for each country in that area to make sure that our aims were consistent. At this point, we decided to bring in fresh minds to review the statements with critical detachment. The "area" committee for Latin America was the first one created. It was composed of Professors Samuel F. Bemis of Yale University, Dana G. Munro of Princeton University, and Dexter Perkins of the University of Rochester, all of them outstanding scholars of Latin-American diplomacy. I had not had an opportunity to extend this program further when my resignation became effective.

I was glad to be able to hand to Secretary Marshall statements of American foreign policy on every country in the world and covering every facet of our interests. He may differ with some of those policies, but at least he can determine definitely and in a few minutes what they are, and change them to accord with his views.

These statements carry an added advantage. They require the development of a consistent program of action. And they force the responsible officers to look ahead, to plan for the crises of tomorrow.

The best planned organization, however, depends for its strength on the caliber of its people.

Immediately after becoming Secretary I found that attending conferences abroad made it impossible for me to attend many staff meetings so I requested Under Secretary Acheson to preside at these meetings. Each morning he met with the office directors of the Department. While I was abroad Mr. Acheson kept me informed about any important problems considered by the group. When I was home, he would confer with me about them, usually late in the afternoon. It was seldom that either of us left the Department before seven o'clock. I could not have devoted myself so completely to the task of peace making in the conferences abroad had I not known the work of the Department was being efficiently carried on under the direction of a man with the unusual ability and energy of Under Secretary Acheson.

I want to pay tribute also to the generally high quality of the men who have made the diplomatic service their career. The vast majority of the career foreign service officers I have met are able, conscientious, hardworking men, capable of earning far more than the comparatively low salaries our government has paid them.

And I would like to destroy the legend of the diplomat as a stripedpants cookie pusher. Today's diplomat knows that the social graces are far less valuable to him than the ability to work intensively for long hours with little opportunity for rest or relaxation. Members of my staff at the various international gatherings more than once found themselves working around the clock. The fact is that during my year and a half as Secretary of State, out of all the men in the service of the Department who called on me, I can recall only two who arrived wearing striped trousers and spats—and those two were political appointees!

It should be clear, then, that I intend no disparagement when I say that our foreign service was, and to a large extent, still is inadequate for the tasks we must discharge in world affairs. I am particularly pleased that during my period as Secretary of State action was taken to help remedy this situation. The passage of the Kee-Connally bill "to improve, strengthen, and expand the Foreign Service," which was signed by the President on August 13, 1946, was the first legislation dealing with foreign service personnel in twenty-two years—a period which brought vast changes in the scope and responsibilities of our foreign service.

Work to obtain this legislation had been started under Secretary Hull and was continued by Secretary Stettinius. It was pending before Congress when the Council of Foreign Ministers adjourned its first session in Paris on May 16 and was one of the reasons why I resisted the temptation to take a vacation during the one-month recess and returned home instead. Long experience had taught me that in Congress, as in other places, things do not happen unless somebody makes them happen.

With Assistant Secretary Donald Russell, I went to the Congress and enlisted the aid of friends. Thanks again to the co-operation of both political parties, the bill was given special handling to insure a vote before adjournment and was adopted in both the House and the Senate by unanimous consent. It marked a long step forward toward the fulfillment of the second objective I have stated.

As a result of this act, salaries can be raised so that no longer will it be necessary to appoint men of wealth as our Ambassadors. At the same time that salaries were advanced all down the line, more rigid requirements on training and promotion were provided. The bill seeks to make our foreign service truly representative of our government and people by making it possible for the best qualified men and women in the country, in or out of the government, to have tours of duty with the foreign service in any of its ranks. Among the most important provisions, in my opinion,

was one that calls for more frequent and varied assignments in this country. Its purpose is to prevent these sentinels of the United States from
losing touch with American life. I recall Woodrow Wilson saying, "It is
easy to send an American to London or Paris, but it is hard to keep an
American there." A man who represents his country abroad, no less than
the man who represents his people in Congress, needs to return frequently
to the "grass roots."

In other ways, too, the State Department is becoming increasingly sensitive to public opinion. Each day a digest of representative newspaper editorials and opinions of radio commentators is placed on the desks
of Department officials and sent to our missions overseas. Letters and
petitions from individuals and organizations are analyzed for evidence of
opinion trends. The Public Liaison Division, for example, keeps in touch
with all types of voluntary organizations throughout the country, not only
to help them keep informed on foreign affairs but to get their criticism
and suggestions on pending issues. Behind these efforts is the firm realization that our foreign policy must be responsive to and have the firm support of the American people.

A basic prerequisite to a people's foreign policy is, of course, a well-
informed public. In the field of international relations the world is still
suffering a hangover from the era when international agreements were
secret and private arrangements between rulers. But the United States,
at least, is rapidly leaving the habits of that era far behind.

The war interrupted the trend away from secret diplomacy. Military
and political agreements then were often so interrelated, secrecy was required in the interests of the war effort. All the meetings between President Roosevelt, Prime Minister Churchill and Generalissimo Stalin were
held in secrecy with the press excluded. Although many newspapermen
may have learned indirectly of the conferences, the discussions and the
agreements, they refrained from publishing them in accordance with the
wartime voluntary press censorship.

But at Potsdam, even though the war in the Pacific was still continuing,
the press was restless under the agreement denying them information on
what was occurring at the conference. American newspapers and radio net-
works had many representatives stationed in Berlin to cover the conference. However, the suburb of Potsdam, which was the scene of the conference, was in the Russian zone, and they were not permitted to go
there. The press complained bitterly, but they received no detailed report
until the President returned and made his report to Congress. Because
of the agreements in connection with the Japanese war, some secrecy
was thoroughly justified. But since then I have often wished that more

information could, at that time, have been supplied our people on European problems.

When the Council of Foreign Ministers met in London, there was no military reason for secrecy. But the best arrangement we could secure was for a daily issuance of a communiqué containing the subjects discussed and any agreement reached. It did not, however, report the statements or positions of individual members. This seemed an advance over Potsdam, but it turned out to be no advance at all. Each Minister assigned a representative to a committee charged with the drafting of a communiqué. But the communiqué, like everything else, required unanimous agreement. The Council itself reached so few agreements that there was little for the committee to report except the debates, which were prohibited material. Under these circumstances, the correspondents did the only thing they could do—tried to get information from someone connected with the delegations who presumably had been instructed not to give it. Consequently, the reports of the meetings not only were inadequate but were often inaccurate.

Trouble began with the very first communiqué. The Soviet representative did not want to give out any statement. The others argued that a communiqué should be issued stating at the very least that the Council had agreed to take up the Italian treaty and would begin with the study of a text submitted by the British delegation. After a long argument, the Soviet representative finally agreed to the release of the following uninformative communiqué:

> The Council of Foreign Ministers held its second meeting at 4 P.M. and adjourned at 6:30 P.M. Owing to the number of documents which have to be translated and studied it was decided to meet next at 11 o'clock on Friday instead of tomorrow as planned.

A soothsayer rather than a reporter was required to get any news out of a statement like that. Similar statements followed. Our communiqués were shorter than the average weather report and soon an effort was made to make them less accurate than one.

The Council had discussed a complaint from the Soviet Union that France was failing to repatriate Soviet citizens. France in turn complained that the Soviet Union continued to refuse to repatriate nationals of France. That evening the communiqué contained no information other than this simple statement of subjects discussed. It was unanimously agreed to by the members of the Press Committee. But later that night, about eleven o'clock, a Soviet representative told Mr. Walter Brown, who represented the United States on the Press Committee, that Mr. Molotov objected to the communiqué and wanted it held up. Mr. Brown replied that it had already been given out by the representative of the United Kingdom who was serving as chairman for that day.

Next morning, Mr. Molotov complained to the council. Mr. Bevin stated that the chairman of the committee had issued the communiqué as a result of unanimous agreement. Mr. Molotov replied, "My actions cannot be controlled by any secretary or representative on a committee." He insisted that the council should issue another communiqué eliminating reference to France's complaint that the Soviets failed to repatriate French nationals. Mr. Bidault objected. Mr. Bevin and I maintained that it would be an incorrect statement of the proceedings; that the communiqué had correctly stated the facts and that we would not agree to issue a second one. Mr. Molotov stated that under such circumstances he would put out a communiqué of his own. And he did so.

Later I learned that it was important to him to issue another communiqué because the previous night he had wired Moscow to prohibit the publication of the committee's communiqué in any newspaper in the Soviet Union. Consequently, Moscow expected a substitute communiqué. Mr. Molotov's personal communiqué, therefore, was the only statement on the proceedings of the council that was released to the Soviet press.

The London press arrangements greatly embarrassed me because I had known many of the correspondents covering the conference during much of my public life. Some of them I knew from my days in the Senate, while others I had come to know since I had been in the White House and the State Department.

One day I met a group of them in the lobby. An old friend addressed me as "Senator," and asked whether I wanted to be called Senator, Justice or Secretary. I told him it made little difference, because I knew at that time the press representatives were not calling me any one of those three names.

When we went to Moscow in December we had the same arrangement we had had in London. I did not like it, but the meeting in Moscow was called at my request. I wanted to progress with the peace, and I did not feel I was in a position to dictate terms on press arrangements to the government I had asked to be our host. This was particularly true since any satisfactory arrangement would necessitate the Soviet Government's altering its own censorship rules. Once again, the communiqué furnished very little news and once again the people of the world received many incorrect impressions about the proceedings of the Council and the arguments leading up to the decisions.

During the discussion of the Iranian case at the Security Council in New York, for the first time it was possible to meet freely with the correspondents and frankly tell them the problems we faced. The proceedings in the Council were opened to the public and I refused to be bound by any pledges of secrecy in the closed meetings. I met with the correspondents and explained to them, for their background information, our view of the situation. When I couldn't do it, I designated a member of my staff to do it for me. The result was that the public received accounts that were written with full knowledge and understanding. And the force of public opinion thus stimulated was a vital factor in the ultimate outcome of the case.

I decided that what was good in the Security Council would be good also in the Council of Foreign Ministers. I realized I couldn't do the task myself and that I needed an officer who was familiar with all phases of our foreign relations and whose relationship to me was close enough to enable him to be fully informed on all issues so that he could properly interpret those with news value to the press. I persuaded Charles E. Bohlen to accept the assignment. Chip was not only a veteran foreign service officer but he had spent several years in Moscow, spoke Russian fluently, and had acted as interpreter for President Roosevelt and President Truman at all their international conferences. Chip and Michael J. McDermott, who for many years has handled press relations for the State Department capably and courteously, made an effective team.

When the Council of Foreign Ministers met in Paris, I told the Ministers that I would not again agree to the previous press arrangements and that I would insist on our right to give the press the American point of view on every proposal before the council. I was determined that, if the meetings of the council were to continue to be closed, so far as the American delegation was concerned, they would not be secret meetings.

After every session, Chip and Mike would meet with the press and "brief" them on everything of importance that had taken place. The newspapermen, of course, would have preferred to be present at the meetings but they soon learned that they were receiving objective, accurate and constructive reports. They recognized that closed meetings sometimes were helpful in reaching agreement; most of them were willing to sacrifice attendance at the meetings, particularly since they soon realized that our action was forcing other delegations to take similar action.

During the Paris session the council held several "private" meetings at which the Minister was accompanied only by two advisers in addition to his interpreter. At the first of these, it was suggested that we withhold from the press everything that took place in these gatherings. I refused. I said, "In the first place, I think it wrong. In the second place, the agreement will not be kept. Somebody present will advise other members of his delegation of what has taken place and then the information will leak to a favorite correspondent."

I had been bitten by that dog before. I told them that at London I had tried to live up to such an agreement. Then, I had read in the New York

Herald Tribune an absolutely correct description of the events of the previous day. I was embarrassed at the next meeting, assuming I would be charged with having "leaked" the story. Upon investigation I learned that the correspondent had gotten his information from a person connected with the *Herald Tribune* office in Paris.

I told them of similar experiences in London. A true story in an American newspaper came, my press representative learned, from information supplied by an official in the British Foreign Office. Shortly thereafter, an enterprising reporter secured a story for the Chicago *Sun,* which was a correct statement of a debate in the council, from a representative of Tass, the Soviet news agency.

The London experience was enough for me, I told my colleagues, and consequently I would not again join in any agreement that would prevent me from giving the press information about the American position.

From then on, the press could give the people accurate reports on the progress, or lack of progress, in the council as it appeared from the American point of view. This stimulated the others to present their point of view. I was glad to observe this development, because it placed the position of the individual countries on the various issues precisely where they belonged—before the bar of public opinion.

Eventually, even Mr. Molotov was influenced by this example. In July, when he made his important speech announcing the Soviet program for Germany, he adopted our custom. Mimeographed copies of his speech —which was delivered in a closed session—were distributed to the press in advance. When I learned of this action, I congratulated him. Since then, both Mr. Molotov and Mr. Gromyko, in his work at the United Nations, have frequently followed this course. Mr. Gromyko, I understand, now even calls in various newspaper correspondents to explain to them, as background information, the Soviet point of view on questions before the United Nations.

When the peace conference convened in Paris, I proposed that the press and radio representatives be admitted to all meetings. My motion was seconded by Mr. Molotov, who declared he was heartily in favor of it. I felt my efforts to remove the curtain from the peace negotiations had at last succeeded. My satisfaction was not lessened by the intensive efforts of the Soviet delegation and its satellites to use the conference proceedings for propaganda purposes.

In one of Mr. Molotov's propaganda attacks, he charged that the United States and the United Kingdom were violating agreements to support the adoption of certain conference-procedure rules. This was so baseless that I replied with a very sharp speech in which I repeatedly cited the record to prove that his assertions were without foundation. And after each citation I would say: "Only Mr. Molotov would make such charges." Toward the end of the speech I referred to our free press and assured Mr. Molotov it would print his charges impugning the motives of the United States. I then added:

"I challenge him to permit publication in the Soviet Union of the statement I have now made. . . . Today we have only admiration and respect for the people of the Soviet Republics and we will not permit that admiration and respect to be lessened by any attack by Mr. Molotov."

Within forty-eight hours my speech appeared in the Soviet press. As far as I know, it was the first and last time a speech of mine was so honored. I only regret it had to be a speech criticizing Mr. Molotov.

In New York, when Mr. Molotov invited the council to meet in Moscow, I agreed, provided the press would be free to report the proceedings as they had the council sessions in Paris and New York. He agreed, saying that Moscow's serious housing shortage would impose the only limitation. In a private conversation I tried to get assurances that radio correspondents would be included. Radio, he said, presented a different problem and he would have to take it up with his government. Later he said that the radio correspondents would be allowed to report from Moscow. The correspondents agree that Mr. Molotov fulfilled his promise to keep their dispatches free from censorship.

Early in 1946, I determined to find some way of telling the Russians and the people of the Soviet satellite states the truth about our position on matters affecting world peace. In all these countries our position was being misrepresented daily. I did not want a vehicle for propaganda but we were engaged in a battle for the minds of the people and I did want a method of making factual statements to correct untruths. The only possibility seemed to be to increase the power of our radio station at Munich.

When I told General Clay of my keen interest in the subject, he went to work on it. Assistant Secretary William Benton, with his energy and resourcefulness, also became active. He sent engineers to Munich to determine what was necessary to improve the equipment and perfect an organization. Additional equipment was transported from England where we had been using it during the war.

Between the first and second sessions of the Council of Foreign Ministers in Paris, I returned to Washington. While there, I was invited by some of my former colleagues of the Senate Appropriations Committee to discuss with them my proposal to add 18 million dollars to the State Department appropriation bill to carry on the Department's information work, including the operation of "The Voice of America." Some Senators expressed doubt about the wisdom of the appropriation because they felt that the views of some of the persons engaged in the work were too liberal, if not radical.

I explained that these employees had been transferred to the State Department from wartime agencies, that they were protected by civil service and could be removed only in accordance with civil service rules. The result was the enactment of the McCarran Amendment which gave the Secretary power to remove employees for the good of the service. I assured the Senators that a thorough investigation would be made of the personnel to be sure of their sympathies and loyalties. They then granted the full appropriation.

Before returning to Paris, I issued instructions for the investigation. Believing that prosecutors should not be judges, I directed that the investigators should present to an independent committee which had nothing to do with the investigation the evidence believed sufficient to justify removal. As a result of the recommendations of this committee, a number of employees have been removed under the authority of the McCarran Amendment.

Once again, serious opposition to the continuation of this program has arisen in Congress. As this is written, the outcome still is in doubt. It will be most unfortunate if Congress does not make an adequate appropriation for this work. I spent many hours helping to develop this program because I thought it very important to have some means of answering the false charges made against the United States. It is not enough for us to be conscious of the purity of our motives and the innocence of our actions. It is necessary that we convince the world.

While we are appropriating hundreds of millions of dollars to aid other countries, it would be wise to spend a few million to protect the good name of the United States.

One small but important technical barrier to the free flow of information to the public is the desire of many officials to "overclassify" documents. Every army officer has encountered the problem and I imagine many of them have shared my experience of receiving material taken from a newspaper with "confidential" marked over it, and in some cases even "secret." I found altogether too many State Department documents that were classified "top secret" when they did not merit even a "secret" classification. Since the war was over, I issued instructions to liberalize the classification of all messages. I am afraid that I did not make much progress. It will take some time to change the habits of years, but changed they must be.

Early in 1946 I found another way to remove diplomatic exchanges from the realm of secrecy. On February 28, instead of sending a "note," I made a speech setting forth our position on existing problems. I hoped it would result in bringing into the open the discussion of those problems. I followed this with other speeches and my efforts were more successful than I had expected. Thereafter, not only did the Soviet officials speak publicly explaining their position on current problems but Generalissimo

Stalin began giving newspaper interviews to correspondents of the United States and the United Kingdom.

There are, of course, some matters between governments which should not be discussed in this manner but, after all, there are not very many of these. This decision, as well as my decision not to agree again to secret conferences, was based on a conviction I reluctantly reached on the attitude of the Soviet Government. If, at the time of the London Conference, the American people had known about the communications exchanged by President Roosevelt and President Truman with Generalissimo Stalin, which I have reported in preceding chapters, they would have better understood the difficulties I encountered at London. Certainly, the people would have been more sympathetic with my position.

After the London Conference, in justice to our position, I was forced to describe in my radio report some of the difficulties we encountered. I did not tell all that I have now told because I still hoped and wanted to believe that the Soviets were moved by the same common purpose that moved us—the desire for an early peace. Whenever persons representing their own interests or the interests of their governments meet in conference and have a common purpose, it is advisable to minimize differences on methods in order to reconcile those differences more easily. This was the thought that President Roosevelt expressed just before he died when he advised Churchill to minimize our difficulties with the Soviets in his public address.

At Moscow I still hoped that the Soviet Union and the United States had a common purpose. However, by the latter part of January 1946, there was accumulated evidence that regardless of what might be their long-term plan, certainly their immediate purpose was to delay the peace in Europe and in the Pacific.

Stalin's speech on February 9, 1946, in which he announced the new Five-Year Plan with its emphasis on rearmament instead of the production of consumer goods the Russian people need so badly, was a shock to me. But even more threatening was the Soviet attitude toward Iran, the evidence of their willingness to violate the sovereignty of their little neighbor. It confirmed the ambition Molotov had expressed to Hitler for the control of the territory south of Baku. These things inspired my speeches beginning in February 1946, speeches which were correctly interpreted as reflecting a firmer attitude toward the Soviet Government. No longer was there any wisdom in minimizing our differences because no longer was there any justification for the belief that we were animated by the common purpose of an early peace.

And no longer was it necessary to minimize our differences because of the condition of our armed forces. In the fall of 1945 the American Army was being demobilized with greater rapidity than anyone expected and the point system of discharges left us with only skeleton divisions. As Director of War Mobilization, I had approved that system because I thought it fair and because I assumed the world would want peace quickly and permanently. However, it meant that the most experienced men were among the first to be discharged. Key men in all divisions were discharged at about the same time. Some of the people who yelled the loudest for me to adopt a firm attitude toward Russia, yelled even louder for the rapid demobilization of the Army. Theodore Roosevelt once wisely said, "Uncle Sam should speak softly and carry a big stick." My critics wanted me to speak loudly and carry a twig.

With the turn of the year the reorganization of the Army was under way and there was no longer reason for withholding from the people full information as to our differences with the Soviets.

With that decision there had to be a change in our information policy. The people had to know what was going on else we could not hope for their support. Thereafter, by speeches, daily conferences between Mr. Bohlen, Mr. McDermott and the correspondents, and by the frequent meetings I held with the correspondents, we kept the people fully informed of our relations and our negotiations with the Soviet Government.

I continue to think that, if we are to have a lasting peace, it must be a people's peace. The people can exert their full influence in the conduct of foreign affairs only if they know more about them.

That basic democratic right, the right of the people to know, must be applied increasingly to the conduct of foreign affairs. If that right is essential—as I believe it is—to the functioning of democracy here at home, it is at least equally necessary to apply it in the field of foreign affairs where the need for knowledge and understanding is so much greater. To carry this policy into action involves a break with the diplomatic habits of the past. Such habits are not easily broken. Time, effort, and a constant demand by the public to know what is happening will be needed.

People cannot act intelligently if, in all matters of importance affecting our relations with other governments, they are kept in the dark.

Let there be light—and lots of it!

Chapter 13

Control of Atomic Energy

I DO NOT REMEMBER just when it was that President Roosevelt told me about the atomic bomb. I do remember that it was a hot summer afternoon and the two of us were sitting alone in his oval office discussing certain phases of the war mobilization program. Suddenly, and for no apparent reason, he began to tell me the awesome story of the Manhattan Project.

I confess I thought the story fantastic. I was sure the President was exaggerating the possibilities just to watch my amazed reaction. I didn't disappoint him. And, as he noted my amazement, he proceeded with obvious pleasure to astound me with the scientists' prediction of what atomic energy would do. He told me that, prior to 1939, the Germans had made some progress with their experiments and he knew they were continuing their efforts. It was a race between us, he said, to see who could develop the first bomb.

At that time, which I believe was the summer of 1943, the President thought the Germans were ahead of us in the atomic race. It was evident that the information on which he based his belief contained more speculation than fact. Our Intelligence agents necessarily were restricted in securing accurate information on such a highly technical matter. From what we learned after the war, it was clear that the President had overestimated the progress of the Germans in this respect. Nevertheless, such reports served to stimulate the extraordinary efforts put forth on the Manhattan Project.

After the first discussion, neither the President nor I mentioned the atomic project to each other for many months. In fact, no one ever talked about it unless it was absolutely necessary. I remember once mentioning it to Secretary of War Stimson who, from its very inception, personally supervised the Manhattan Project. His reaction indicated surprise that I knew about it.

Even if the President had not told me about the project, as Director of War Mobilization I could not have avoided noting certain aspects of an enterprise as colossal as this. It, of course, held a top priority both for men and materiel. With manpower one of our most critical shortages, a project that at its peak claimed the labor of 125,000 men could not escape my notice, particularly since so many of the workers were highly skilled technicians.

However, I was not directly concerned with the project and was too busy to be curious. Thus it was not until December 1944, when another aspect of the labor situation brought me into the picture, that I learned definitely of the great progress we had been making.

An effort was being made to organize the workers at the Oak Ridge plant; controversies over the jurisdiction of the labor organizations involved had arisen and these had been referred to the National Labor Relations Board. The public hearing required under the circumstances had been postponed four times at the War Department's request; no further postponement was possible.

Under Secretary of War Robert Patterson and Major General Leslie R. Groves came over to the White House to discuss the problem with me. General Groves pointed out that the hearing would require the presentation of evidence on such things as the number of workers employed, the number to be employed, the relationship of a particular unit to the project as a whole, and so on. Such evidence, General Groves was convinced, would necessitate disclosures that would seriously jeopardize the security of the project. They thought it would be helpful if I would arrange a meeting at the White House for the three of us and the leaders of the labor organizations involved. I agreed.

During our discussions, Mr. Patterson said that the War Department would know by April 1, 1945, whether or not they could develop the bomb. Both he and General Groves thought the effort would succeed, and they were confident they would know one way or the other by that date. It was the first time I had heard anyone venture to name a date.

The conference was arranged for the morning of December 5. The union officials were Mr. Joseph P. Clark of the International Brotherhood of Firemen and Oilers and Mr. Al Wegener of the International Brotherhood of Electrical Workers.

We took these men into our confidence. We told them that few people knew about the project. At that time, I believe, only four members of Congress had been given any concrete information. We asked the labor officials to waive their rights under the Wagner Act and to co-operate with General Groves in protecting the security of the project. They were good and patriotic men. They agreed to help and left immediately to do so. They were given authority to explain the situation to the presidents of their respective unions, Mr. John F. McNamara and Mr. Edward J. Brown; both of these leaders likewise promised their full co-operation. Their promise involved sacrificing rights given them by the law, but they kept it. They convinced the local union leaders, and the secret was protected for the duration of the war.

As a matter of fact, it was always amazing to me that the project did not become more generally known. It also was surprising that the Congress was willing to appropriate approximately two billion dollars without demanding more information on the use to which it was being put. It is a great tribute to those few congressional leaders who did have some idea of the nature of the project that they resisted the temptation to tell their colleagues and thus share the great responsibility.

The April 1 deadline came, but the result of the gigantic effort still was in doubt. Secretary Stimson, however, was confident of success. He instilled his confidence in the President. I am glad he did. But I have always regretted that President Roosevelt died without knowing definitely that the project was a success: It had been undertaken and carried to a conclusion solely because of his vision and courage in the days when the effort seemed hopeless.

Shortly after President Roosevelt's death, Secretary Stimson told President Truman that the scientists and others who had been working under his direction felt confident they would produce an atomic bomb within a very short time. He suggested the appointment of an Interim Committee to consider and make recommendations to the President on such important questions of policy as the test of the bomb, its use in the war, and the postwar use of atomic energy.

President Truman approved Mr. Stimson's suggestion and asked him to serve as chairman. The President requested me to act as his representative on the committee. The committee also included Under Secretary of the Navy Ralph Bard; Assistant Secretary of State William L. Clayton; Dr. Vannevar Bush, Director of the Office of Scientific Research and Development; Dr. James B. Conant, President of Harvard University; Dr. Karl T. Compton, President of the Massachusetts Institute of Technology; and Mr. George L. Harrison, president of the New York Life Insurance Company and special consultant to Secretary Stimson. Mr. Harrison served as chairman in Secretary Stimson's absence. We were assisted in our work by a group of scientists who had been connected with the project. They were Dr. Arthur H. Compton, Dr. Enrico Fermi, Dr. E. O. Lawrence, and Dr. J. Robert Oppenheimer.

During May and June 1945, while the attention of the country was focused on the end of the European war and on the San Francisco Conference, this group worked quietly and intensively in Washington. It was an interesting—and exciting—task. Some of the newspaper correspondents noted my presence in Washington when I was supposed to be resting in South Carolina, and were curious about my activities. Of course, I couldn't tell them, so they resorted to speculation. Most of them speculated that I was there in connection with some appointment in the government service.

During that period I made several trips to the Naval Hospital at Bethesda, Maryland, to talk with former Secretary Hull and get the benefit of his advice about the work of the Department of State, which I was to take charge of in a few weeks. On one of these trips two young sailors showed me how unimportant was my war service.

They were hitchhiking, but were not making much progress. One, in fact, was leaning against a post, slightly intoxicated. I thought he needed a ride. They got in the front seat with me. The boy who sat next to me was very alert. I got the impression that he wished to divert my attention from his friend and, therefore, was doing a lot of talking. Finally he asked me what my business was. I told him I did not have a business; that I was out of a job. He sympathized with me and then asked what had I done. Thinking to impress him, I said I had been Director of War Mobilization. His expression clearly showed he had never heard of it. After being quiet for a second or two, he made another effort to satisfy his curiosity and asked: "Well, what did you do before that?"

"I was Economic Stabilizer," I said. I saw he had never heard of that one either.

"I mean before the war," he replied.

"I was a Justice of the Supreme Court," I told him. This time he was impressed, and asked: "You mean the High Court?"

"Yes," I said.

He nudged the redheaded boy next to him: "How would you like to be a member of the Highest Court?"

The young sailor replied: "I wouldn't like it. No chance for promotion."

In the first meeting of the Interim Committee, Doctors Bush, Conant and Compton described the destructive power of the bomb. After hearing them, I was confident that, when developed, it would bring a speedy end to the war in the Pacific. I remembered that as a member of the Senate committee handling naval appropriations I had often heard naval officers say that a new defensive weapon was developed for every offensive weapon. I asked the scientists what defense there could be against the atomic bomb. But these distinguished gentlemen, who had directed the advisory work on the bomb, could think of no defense. They did anticipate the development of still larger and more destructive bombs. I asked them if I should believe the only defense against further development was to kill off all the scientists. This suggestion did not appeal to them.

After listening to the scientists discuss the development of the project, we spent a day with the industrialists and engineers who had performed the amazing task of constructing the huge plants in Tennessee and Washington, and of installing the manufacturing processes that produced the bomb. Because it was a vital point in any decision on a system of control, I asked both groups how long it might take other governments to produce atomic bombs. The question, of course, was not only one of physics, but one of materials, of engineering skills, of technical know-how, and many other factors. From all the information we received, I concluded that any other government would need from seven to ten years, at least, to produce a bomb. And I think that to accomplish the task at such speed would require a quicker return to normal conditions than has taken place in any country within the last few years.

On July 1, 1945, the Interim Committee unanimously recommended to the President that the bomb be used against Japan as soon as possible. It added that the bomb should be used only where war plants or military installations were located. With the exception of Mr. Bard, the committee recommended that it be used without warning. This last question we had carefully considered.

We feared that, if the Japanese were told that the bomb would be used on a given locality, they might bring our boys who were prisoners of war to that area. Also, the experts had warned us that the static test which was to take place in New Mexico, even if successful, would not be conclusive proof that a bomb would explode when dropped from an airplane. If we were to warn the Japanese of the new highly destructive weapon in the hope of impressing them and if the bomb then failed to explode, certainly we would have given aid and comfort to the Japanese militarists. Thereafter, the Japanese people probably would not be impressed by any statement we might make in the hope of inducing them to surrender.

Arrangements for the test in New Mexico also were a problem for the committee. Because no one could be sure what the full results of the first atomic explosion might be, arrangements had to be made to evacuate the whole area if necessary. We knew that under the best circumstances the explosion would reverberate so far that secrecy would be difficult to maintain. News releases, with stories to meet every foreseeable contingency, were prepared and were to be issued to the public only if the circumstances required.

As the President's representative on the committee, it was my duty to report to him the reasons for our various recommendations. Throughout our deliberations, I told him, we relied on the estimates of the military situation presented by the Joint Chiefs of Staff. Their plans called for an invasion of Kyushu, the southernmost island of the Japanese homeland, on November 1. This was to be followed by an invasion of the main island of Honshu in the spring of 1946. The Joint Chiefs anticipated that more than five million of our armed forces would be engaged. The Japanese armies were then estimated at about five million—an estimate we later found was quite accurate. Secretary Forrestal had told me that the Japanese air force suicide attacks were increasing our losses in ships and in human lives. These attacks gained in intensity the closer we got to Japan; it was certain that an invasion force would be attacked with far greater fury and recklessness. The military experts informed us that, from the facts at their disposal, they believed our invasion would cost us a million casualties, to say nothing of those of our Allies and of the enemy.

I reported these conclusions to the President. I also told him what the scientists, engineers and industrialists, who had come before the committee, had to say. He expressed the opinion that, regrettable as it might be, so far as he could see, the only reasonable conclusion was to use the bomb.

While we were aboard the *Augusta* en route to Potsdam, the final preparations were under way in New Mexico for the crucial test. The day the greatest blast the world had yet known was reverberating over the sands of Alamagordo, the President, Admiral Leahy and I were looking at the rubble that had been Berlin. Reports of the test, which had to be transmitted in top secret codes, did not reach us for several days. By that time, the conference was in full swing; I was so busy that I have never been able to recall the time and circumstances under which Secretary Stimson brought us the news. Another reason the moment made so little impression on me was that my work on the Interim Committee had already convinced me that the bomb would succeed. News of the test seemed simply a confirmation of a well-known fact.

Prime Minister Churchill, whose co-operation with President Roosevelt had contributed so much to the success of the great gamble, was intensely interested in the reports. He discussed the project at length with President Truman and was eager to hear from me about the work of the Interim Committee. In addition to his tremendous interest in the effect of the bomb on the war with Japan, he foresaw more clearly than many others the possibilities presented by the release of atomic energy.

We faced a terrible decision. We could not rely on Japan's inquiries to the Soviet Union about a negotiated peace as proof that Japan would surrender unconditionally without the use of the bomb. In fact, Stalin stated the last message to him had said that Japan would "fight to the death rather than accept unconditional surrender." Under those circumstances, agreement to negotiate could only arouse false hopes. Instead, we relied upon the Potsdam Declaration.

As soon as we had studied all the reports from New Mexico, the President and I concluded we should tell Generalissimo Stalin that we had developed the bomb and proposed to use it unless Japan acceded promptly to our demand for surrender. The Soviet Government was not at war with

Japan, but we had been informed of their intention to enter the war and felt, therefore, that Stalin should know.

At the close of the meeting of the Big Three on the afternoon of July 24, the President walked around the large circular table to talk to Stalin. After a brief conversation the President rejoined me and we rode back to the "Little White House" together. He said he had told Stalin that, after long experimentation, we had developed a new bomb far more destructive than any other known bomb, and that we planned to use it very soon unless Japan surrendered. Stalin's only reply was to say that he was glad to hear of the bomb and he hoped we would use it. I was surprised at Stalin's lack of interest. I concluded that he had not grasped the importance of the discovery. I thought that the following day he would ask for more information about it. He did not. Later I concluded that, because the Russians kept secret their developments in military weapons, they thought it improper to ask us about ours.

Two nights after the talk with Stalin, the Potsdam Declaration was issued. We devoutly hoped that the Japanese would heed our warning that, unless they surrendered unconditionally, the destruction of their armed forces and the devastation of their homeland was inevitable. But, on July 28, the Japanese Premier issued a statement saying the declaration was unworthy of notice. That was disheartening. There was nothing left to do but use the bomb. Secretary Stimson had selected targets of military importance and President Truman approved his plans. Shortly thereafter Secretary Stimson left for the United States.

Despite the Japanese Premier's statement, I continued to hope the Japanese Government would change its mind. I was greatly disappointed when August 2, the day of our departure from Potsdam, arrived and no further word had been received. I recognized then that our hope of avoiding use of the bomb was virtually gone.

The President had accepted an invitation from King George for a brief visit at Plymouth Harbor, where we were to meet the USS *Augusta* for the trip home. Because the law of succession placed the Secretary of State next in line for the presidency in case of the death or resignation of the President, President Truman and I traveled from Potsdam to Plymouth on separate planes. We landed at Harrowbeer, near Plymouth. Shortly thereafter Admiral Leahy and I accompanied the President aboard the battleship H. M. S. *Renown,* where King George entertained us at luncheon.

The King had learned from Churchill of the successful experiment with the bomb and was eager to know all about it. Most of our luncheon conversation was devoted to the bomb. The only one of the group who was skeptical about its success was Admiral Leahy and the King enjoyed joking with him about his pessimism. Admiral Leahy felt that the scientists greatly exaggerated the bomb's capacity to damage. Throughout the entire discussion, King George showed that, contrary to the impression of some Americans, he was well informed on the diplomatic as well as the military situation. His views on pending problems, in my opinion, were sound. Later in the afternoon, the King paid a return visit to the *Augusta;* when he departed, the *Augusta* started for home.

On August 6, the President and I had lunch with the enlisted men. A few minutes before twelve, Captain Frank H. Graham, the watch officer of the White House Map Room, hurried into the mess hall and handed the President a brief message from the Navy Department saying that Hiroshima had been bombed a few hours before. Ten minutes later Captain Graham was back with a second message, this time from Secretary Stimson. His report indicated that the results of the bomb were even more successful than the test had led us to expect. The President read the message aloud to me, and then stood and asked the crew to listen for a moment. He announced that he had just received two messages informing him of the highly successful results of our first use of a terrifically powerful new weapon with an explosive 20,000 times as powerful as TNT. As the President left the mess hall with the two messages in his hand, the crew clapped and cheered. He went to the wardroom, where he made the same announcement to the ship's officers, and again applause rang through the ship. A few minutes later, the ship's radio began to carry news bulletins from Washington about the bomb and the statement about its development, which the President had approved just before leaving Germany.

I thought that the bombing of Hiroshima, southern headquarters and depot for the homeland army, would convince the Japanese that the Allied nations meant what they said in the Potsdam Declaration. Millions of leaflets were dropped warning the Japanese that one out of ten listed cities would be the next target. We received no communication from them and so, on August 8, the second bomb was dropped on Nagasaki, a major seaport with many war plants.

As at Hiroshima, the destruction in Nagasaki was terrific. The Emperor did not wait for further evidence of our intention to carry out the Potsdam Declaration. He broke the deadlock that had existed for several days in the Japanese Cabinet; on August 10, he submitted the offer of surrender. No one should doubt that the destruction wrought by the atomic bomb influenced the action of the Emperor and the Cabinet.

Those two bombs were all we then had ready for use, but others were on the way and some were expected to be even more powerful. In these two raids there were many casualties but not nearly so many as there would have been had our air force continued to drop incendiary bombs on Japan's cities. Certainly, by bringing the war to an end, the atomic bomb saved the lives of thousands of American boys.

No one who played a part in the development of the bomb or in our decision to use it felt happy about it. It was natural and right that men should worry about performing a duty that would cost so many human lives. Most of these men were civilians, but I have no doubt that all thinking men in the armed forces felt the same way about air raids, the dropping of incendiary bombs and similar actions which cost many lives. Being soldiers, they did not write to the press about their views as did the civilians. But the truth is, war remains what General Sherman said it was.

Shortly after Japan's surrender, many people demanded that we immediately give the world all the scientific and engineering information on the atomic bomb that we possessed. Most thinking people wanted international control of atomic energy. Some, however, were not so particular about safeguards necessary to protect us against a violator of the international agreement. I agreed with the scientists who argued that inevitably some other nation would produce an atomic bomb, but I felt that we should not shorten that period unless we were fully protected. I felt that if any nation were opposed to submitting atomic energy to complete control by an international organization, with safeguards against violations, then the longer we could keep the bomb out of the hands of that nation, the better it would be for the people of the world. I still feel that way.

On November 10, 1945, Prime Minister Attlee and Prime Minister Mackenzie King came to Washington to talk with the President about our future atomic energy policy. The day of their arrival President Truman invited his guests to accompany him on Sunday on a cruise down the Potomac aboard the presidential yacht, the *Williamsburg*. The party also included Lord Halifax, Sir John Anderson, Admiral Leahy and myself. That afternoon conversations began. They continued that night and for several days. On November 15, the President, Mr. Attlee and Mr. Mackenzie King held a press conference. They announced that the three governments agreed on the need for international action, under the auspices of the United Nations, to provide controls over atomic energy to insure its use only for peaceful purposes, to outlaw atomic weapons and other major weapons capable of mass destruction, and to provide for effective safeguards through inspection.

History will not disclose action by any governments comparable to this generous offer. It was only as a result of great expenditures that we, in co-operation with our Allies, the United Kingdom and Canada, developed a weapon so destructive as to frighten all thinking people. We could have held this weapon and used it as a threat to force concessions from other governments. Instead, the three governments hastened to offer the secret of this power to an international organization in order to have it used for peaceful rather than for destructive purposes.

I was scheduled to give a speech the following day at Charleston, South Carolina, on international trade. With the announcement of this historic agreement I rewrote the first half of the speech. I did not want to neglect a single opportunity to stress to our people the importance of controlling atomic energy "so that it may be used, not for war and destruction, but for the peace and happiness of the world."

In meeting the challenge of atomic energy, I said, we must "let our minds be bold." At the same time, I cautioned, "we must not imagine wishfully that overnight there can arise full grown a world government wise and strong enough to protect all of us, and tolerant and democratic enough to command our willing loyalty.

"If we are to preserve the continuity of civilized life, we must work with the materials at hand, improving and adding to existing institutions until they can meet the stern test of our time."

I described the plan announced in Washington the day before and said we realized that it was "a very modest first step in what is certain to be a long and difficult journey." I emphasized that even though we had advanced a program, "the creation and development of safeguards to protect us all from unspeakable destruction is . . . the responsibility of all governments."

"Without the united effort and unremitting co-operation of all the nations of the world," I said, "there will be no enduring and effective protection against the atomic bomb."

A month later, when Mr. Bevin and I went to Moscow, we took with us a very definite proposal based on the Washington agreement of November 15. It called for the establishment by the United Nations of a Commission on Atomic Energy and all weapons capable of mass destruction.

I proposed that we place the atomic energy resolution at the top of the agenda. Mr. Molotov objected and asked that it be placed at the end. I agreed, although I wondered why he took such a position. At first, I thought it might be because one of Russia's most distinguished scientists, reportedly an expert on nuclear physics, was reported by the press to be in Paris. I assumed Molotov wished to have him present for the discussions and therefore had suggested deferring the item. This theory was upset, however, when the scientist returned to Moscow and still did not attend the conference. I then came to the conclusion that Molotov's request had been made solely to give us the impression that the Soviet Government did not regard the atomic energy problem as important.

At Moscow, as at Potsdam and then at the Council of Foreign Ministers meeting in London, no member of the Soviet delegation expressed any curiosity about atomic energy. At Potsdam, neither Stalin nor Molotov had mentioned the matter after the President's talk with the Generalissimo. At London, Mr. Molotov showed no interest whatever; his only references to the bomb were a few offhand remarks about my carrying an atomic bomb in my pocket. I decided that I was right in the conclusion I had come to at Potsdam, that the Russians never disclose information about such a discovery to anyone else and so thought it would be improper for them to exhibit curiosity about ours.

Postponement of the atomic energy issue, however, meant considerable inconvenience for Dr. James B. Conant, president of Harvard University, who had generously agreed to accompany me to Moscow in an advisory capacity. He had done so expecting that, as soon as the atomic energy resolution was adopted, he could return home to the urgent business that was awaiting him. Instead, he had to sit through about ten days of discussion on totally unrelated issues.

Conant sat near me during most of the meetings. After being a silent observer for nearly a week, he leaned over to me one day and said:

"I think the President of every university in the United States should be forced to attend a conference of the Council of Foreign Ministers. They might then appreciate the patience required to reach agreement with our Soviet friends."

I felt like accusing him of harboring some secret animosity toward his fellow university presidents, but I appreciated his thought.

Dr. Conant's presence in our delegation was noted at length in the Moscow press. He and I fully expected that some of the Russian scientists would call on him. They did not.

One afternoon, Mr. Molotov entertained the three delegations. He is always a good host. In talking with Dr. Conant, Mr. Molotov remarked that, during his visit in Moscow, the president of a great university like Harvard should address the University of Moscow on the subject of atomic energy. That night Dr. Conant told me about Molotov's statement and said he was willing to make such a speech. He thought it would be one way to pierce the "iron curtain" and explain our views on atomic energy, but he was not sure Molotov really meant it. The following day I mentioned the matter to Molotov, saying that, if he were serious, Dr. Conant would be glad to address the university. Mr. Molotov said he had not been serious, that he had no authority to extend an invitation on behalf of the University, and that he had been only trying to be pleasant.

When we finally reached the subject of atomic energy, Mr. Molotov offered only a few amendments to our proposed resolution. With some revisions, we accepted the Soviets' suggestions. One dealt with the relationship between the proposed Atomic Energy Commission and the Security Council of the United Nations. As revised, the resolution provided that, in view of the Security Council's primary responsibility for the maintenance of international peace and security, the Security Council should issue directions to the commission in matters affecting security. It is obvious this must be done by the Security Council, which is in continuous session and which has the power to take action. The Assembly, on the other hand, is not always in session, and even when meeting it can only make recommendations.

The only paragraph of our proposal to which Mr. Molotov raised serious objection provided: "The work of the Commission shall proceed by separate stages, the successful completion of each of which will develop the necessary confidence of the world before the next stage is undertaken."

Mr. Molotov argued that this was a matter to be determined by the commission. I told him it went to the heart of our whole proposal and that without it we would not offer the resolution. I stated that this language had been agreed upon by the President, Prime Minister Attlee and Prime Minister Mackenzie King and we would have to insist upon its retention. He withdrew his objection. As a result, the proposal that we had expected would provoke extensive discussion was agreed to with less debate than any other subject on the agenda.

At the Christmas Eve dinner given by Generalissimo Stalin, I told him about Dr. Conant's distinguished service as an educator and more particularly as one of the contributors to the success of the atomic energy project. Stalin was not so indifferent as Mr. Molotov had appeared to be. He said that, although scientists spoke a language he did not clearly understand, they did a wonderful work and he thought those American scientists responsible for the discovery of atomic energy were to be especially congratulated.

A few minutes later, Molotov, acting as toastmaster, proposed a toast to Dr. Conant and, in a good-humored way, expressed the hope the doctor did not have an atom bomb in his pocket. Dr. Conant responded in like good humor to the toast. Generalissimo Stalin, beside whom I was seated, arose and said he was not satisfied to dismiss Dr. Conant's work thus lightly. He believed, he said, that Dr. Conant and his associates had rendered a great service and he wanted to congratulate them upon their success.

During the few days between my return home from Moscow and my departure to London for the United Nations General Assembly meeting, I acted in anticipation of the adoption of our resolution. I appointed a committee to begin work upon plans to be presented to the Atomic Energy Commission when it was organized. The committee was composed of Under Secretary of State Dean Acheson, as chairman, the former Assistant Secretary of War John J. McCloy, Dr. Bush, Dr. Conant, and General Groves.

In London, the British Government presented the resolution, drafted at Moscow, to the General Assembly on behalf of all five permanent members of the Security Council and Canada. On January 24, just before the resolution was adopted without amendment by a unanimous vote, I made a short statement to the Assembly emphasizing the common responsibility for controlling atomic energy.

"The problems presented by the discovery of atomic energy and of other forces capable of mass destruction cannot be solved by any one nation," I stressed. "They are the common responsibility of all nations and each of us must do our part in meeting them. In meeting these problems we must realize that in this atomic age and in this interdependent world our common interests in preserving the peace far outweigh any possible conflict in interest that might divide us."

The day before the adoption of the General Assembly resolution, the committee I had appointed in Washington appointed a board of consultants with David E. Lilienthal as chairman. The other members were Mr. Chester I. Barnard, president of the New Jersey Telephone Company; Dr. J. Robert Oppenheimer, director of the Los Alamos atomic laboratory; Dr. Charles Allen Thomas, vice president of the Monsanto Chemical Company, and Mr. Harry A. Winne, vice president of the General Electric Company.

The so-called Acheson-Lilienthal report was the work of the committee and its Consultants. It was adopted and released to the public on March 28, 1946. In a foreword to that report, I referred to it as a "suitable starting point for the informed public discussion which is one of the essential factors in developing sound policy," and emphasized that "the document is being made public not as a statement of policy but solely as a basis for such discussion."

The report succeeded in its purpose. The discussion was nation-wide and the objectives the report set forth were received generally with approval.

The essence of the report was summed up by Undersecretary Acheson in a radio discussion on April 23, 1946, in which he said:

"In plain words, the report sets up a plan under which no nation would make atomic bombs or the materials for them. All dangerous activities would be carried on—not merely inspected—by a live functioning international authority with a real purpose in the world and capable of attracting competent personnel. This monopoly of the dangerous activities would still leave a large and tremendously productive field of safe activities open to individual nations, their industries and universities. . . . The extremely favored position with regard to atomic devices which the United States enjoys at present is only temporary. It will not last. We must use that advantage now to promote international security and to carry out our policy of building a lasting peace through international agreement . . ."

For the task of translating the various proposals stimulated by the Acheson-Lilienthal report into a workable plan, I recommended to the President the appointment of Bernard M. Baruch. During the recent war, as during World War I, he had rendered distinguished public service. He had been official adviser to me when I was Director of War Mobilization, meeting with me regularly and helping with many problems; he had been an unofficial adviser to the President and the heads of several war agencies. He had earned a rest from public service, but, appreciating the importance of the assignment, he agreed to undertake the job. The President sent his name to the Senate on March 18, 1946. The appointment was greeted by the public with deserved acclaim, and his nomination was quickly confirmed.

The law governing our membership in the United Nations stipulates that our representatives in the organization and on its commissions must follow the policy determined by the President, transmitted through the Secretary of State. Accordingly, Mr. Baruch asked for a directive giving the American policy on atomic energy control. I asked him to help draft the policy. After several conferences between Mr. Baruch, his associate, Mr. John M. Hancock, Mr. Acheson and me, we agreed upon an extensive, eleven-page statement of policy. I submitted it to the President for his consideration. Later, the President, Mr. Baruch and I discussed it further and made some changes; the President then gave it to Mr. Baruch as his directive. In doing so, he advised Mr. Baruch to exercise his own judgment on the methods most likely to accomplish the stated objectives.

The policy of the United States, as described in that directive, was presented to the United Nations Atomic Energy Commission by Mr. Baruch on June 14, 1946. It was a noteworthy speech which began with this solemn injunction to the commission:

"We are here to make a choice between the quick and the dead."

The United States proposed the creation of an International Atomic Development Authority, to which should be entrusted all phases of the development and use of atomic energy, starting with the raw material including:

1. Managerial control or ownership of all atomic-energy activities potentially dangerous to world security.
2. Power to control, inspect, and license all other atomic activities.
3. The duty of fostering the beneficial uses of atomic energy.
4. Responsibility for research and development intended to put the authority in the forefront of atomic knowledge and thus to enable it to comprehend, and therefore to detect, misuse of atomic energy.

Mr. Baruch said that when an adequate system for control, including the renunciation of the bomb as a weapon, was agreed upon and put into operation and when punishment was provided for violation of the rules of control, then the manufacture of atomic bombs should stop; existing bombs should be disposed of pursuant to the terms of the treaty; and the authority given full information concerning the know-how for producing atomic energy.

The policy further provided that penalties be fixed for such violations as the following: (1) illegal possession or use of an atomic bomb or of atomic material suitable for use in an atomic bomb; (2) the seizing of any plant or other property belonging to or licensed by the authority.

Mr. Baruch drafted a group of men of unusual ability, including Mr. Hancock, whose services during the two world wars have been invaluable; Ferdinand Eberstadt, former Vice Chairman of the War Production Board; Herbert Bayard Swope, who had been an associate of Mr. Baruch in the War Industries Board in World War I; Fred Searls, Jr., who had served with me as special assistant in the Office of War Mobilization and also in the Department of State. He also called on Mr. Thomas F. Farrell and Dr. Richard C. Tolman, to assist him in representing the United States.

From the beginning, he insisted the plan should provide that, once the treaty was ratified, any government violating its treaty obligation and developing or using atomic energy for destructive purposes should be subjected to swift and sure punishment; and in case of violation no one of the permanent members of the Security Council should be permitted to veto punitive action by the council. Our position was that the permanent members of the council should in this special situation agree in advance to waive the veto power.

The public was kept fully informed of everything that took place in the Atomic Energy Commission from June until November. When the Council of Foreign Ministers met in New York, Mr. Baruch and his associates conferred with me about the advisability of asking the Atomic Energy Commission to vote immediately on the principles of the United States proposal.

These gentlemen had been studying the problem for six months and were certain the United States proposal was generally acceptable to every member of the commission except the representatives of the Soviet Union and Poland. Their description of the tactics of the Soviet representative, Mr. Gromyko, was simply a restatement of the delaying tactics I had encountered on other questions in the Council of Foreign Ministers for over a year. They called my attention to the fact that the terms of two members of the commission would expire on December 31; if no action was taken by that date, in January Mr. Gromyko probably would move to postpone further action on the ground that the two new members should have time to study the problem. I knew they were right and agreed that they should act at once.

On December 5, Mr. Baruch presented his plea for immediate action to the commission and proposed a series of general findings and recommendations which encompassed the American plan. He pointed out that the commission and its committees had held over seventy meetings and were qualified to take this step. The commission, with the Soviet Union and Poland abstaining, agreed to act. Subsequently, on December 30, it voted to submit its first report to the Security Council with a recommendation that a comprehensive international system of control and inspection be established and its functions be defined by a treaty in which all the United Nations should be entitled to participate. Again, the vote was 10 to 0, with the Soviet Union and Poland abstaining.

The report recommended the establishment of an international agency to promote among all nations the exchange of scientific information on atomic energy for peaceful ends; prevent the use of atomic energy for destructive purposes; and to exercise the controls necessary to insure its use only for peaceful purposes. It could carry out research and developmental responsibilities in order to remain first in atomic knowledge and would have the exclusive right to carry on atomic research for destructive purposes.

Representatives of the agency would be afforded unimpeded rights of ingress, egress and access for their inspections and other duties into, from and within the territory of every participating nation. The agency should have the right to prohibit the manufacture, possession and use of atomic weapons, provide for the disposal of any existing stocks of atomic weapons and insure the proper use of nuclear fuels adaptable for use in weapons.

The commission stated that the treaty should specify how to determine violations of its terms and should define the violations which would constitute international crimes. It also should establish how to enforce its measures and how to punish violators. Serious violations, it proposed, should be reported immediately to the nations that signed the treaty, the General Assembly and the Security Council.

The commission supported our contention that once the violations had been defined and the methods of enforcement and punishment agreed to, a violator should have no legal protection by veto or otherwise, from the consequences of his act. The report also stated that a violation might be of so grave a character that the inherent right of self-defense, recognized in article 51 of the Charter of the United Nations, might be exercised.

Finally, the report provided that the treaty should embrace the entire program for putting the international system of control and inspection into effect and should provide a step-by-step schedule for the completion of the process. The commission would determine when any particular stage or stages had been completed and subsequent ones were to begin.

While Mr. Baruch was pressing for action on atomic energy, Mr. Molotov presented to the General Assembly of the United Nations a proposal for general disarmament. I did not take it seriously. What the

Soviet delegation really sought was to combine the Atomic Energy Commission with a commission on general disarmament.

The record since January 1946 shows what would happen if this effort had succeeded. The Security Council has been unable to agree upon the relatively simple question of establishing military contingents to enforce the decisions of the United Nations. It is therefore easy to guess how long it would take a commission to agree on a general disarmament program, including the reduction of naval, air and land armaments—several years certainly. Therefore, if the two commissions were combined, there would be many more excuses for delaying an agreement on atomic energy control.

Despite the clear and obvious necessity for the control of atomic energy, and despite the existence of a plan which has won approval everywhere except with the Soviet Union and its satellites, agreement still seems remote. If we cannot agree upon the control of this one major weapon, we certainly cannot agree upon the limitation of all armaments. The Soviet Union does not take into consideration the fact that the United States proposals, as presented by Mr. Baruch, offer a pattern for control of more than atomic weapons. The resolution creating the Atomic Energy Commission specifically authorized it to investigate how to control other weapons of mass destruction. The pattern developed for atomic energy could be applied to these other weapons, such as bacteriological warfare. That pattern could mark the beginning of general and genuine disarmament, but the Soviet Union chose to ignore what could have been and what still could be a fruitful possibility.

The Soviet tactic was exceedingly smart. The word "disarmament" is very attractive to a war-weary world. But disarmament, to be effective, must look to the future. It is easy to see now what folly it would have been, when gunpowder was discovered, to start disarming by limiting the use of the bow and arrow. But that is what the Soviet Union, in effect, proposed.

The General Assembly insisted that the work of the Commission for the Control of Conventional Armaments be kept distinct from that of the Atomic Energy Commission. Nevertheless, the Soviet Union's representatives have continued their efforts to merge the two.

I think I know their motives.

Through such a merger of issues they want to get away from the Atomic Energy Resolution, to which they agreed at Moscow and which was adopted by the United Nations. That resolution provides for safeguards and adequate inspection. It provides that the work should proceed by stages and that the commission must be convinced by inspection that one stage of the work is proceeding satisfactorily before it begins the next stage. This is the clause to which Mr. Molotov objected at Moscow, but finally accepted. I think he has regretted that agreement ever since. That section prevents a full exchange of information until the system of inspection and control is operating effectively. It would make it possible for representatives of the international organization, who may be nationals of another state, to inspect Soviet plants. This is in conflict with their whole system, which is based upon and sustained by secrecy.

The Atomic Energy Resolution, therefore, is an agreement the Soviet Union wants the world to forget and which it urgently desires to see superseded.

The reason for this determined resistance to effective control is equally clear. Mr. Gromyko disclosed it recently when he stated that the American plan proposes that "a system of inspection be established in such a way that it should be given unlimited powers *and the possibility of interfering with the internal economic life of nations."*

It is unfortunate but apparently true that the Soviets think capitalist interference is more to be feared than atomic bombs. And protection of the Soviet economic system from that interference seems to be more important than the protection of humanity from the scourge of atomic warfare.

This fear also explains the Soviet stand on the veto as applied to atomic energy. Mr. Gromyko has said that the Soviet Union is not willing to subject the fate of its internal economy to a majority vote. The veto, he contends, is necessary to protect the sovereignty of the states. The Soviet leaders do not yet appreciate that civilization and not state sovereignty is at stake.

No one wants to interfere in the internal economic life of their nation, but Soviet suspicion of the outsider is so deep seated that they believe that any inspection made by representatives of the international organization, adequate to satisfy the rest of the world, would interfere in their internal affairs. Every statement Mr. Gromyko has made on the subject of disarmament and atomic energy control should be read and considered in this light and in the light of what the Soviet Union has done in these postwar years. One is forced to the conclusion that the United States must not agree to any plan that will make it possible for anyone, including the Soviet Union, to avoid effective inspection.

If the United States destroyed its bombs and agreed not to make any more and then desired later to violate our treaty obligations and make bombs, our alert and uncontrolled press soon would discover it and make public the violation of our pledge. But that is not possible in the Soviet Union. Should the Soviet Government obtain from the international organization the scientific information and the engineering know-how and decide to build a plant and produce bombs, no one outside the Soviet Union would know it until the Red Army was ready to use them. That would be too late.

I know the officials of the present Soviet Government assert that they scrupulously carry out agreements. I hesitate to charge them with violating agreements, but I do say they have a very peculiar way of interpreting some of them.

What, then, shall we do in case the Soviet Union refuses to join in a treaty containing the safeguards it accepted in principle in Moscow and in London, and which clearly are essential to effective control? The answer is not a happy one, but I see no other. We must pray that the Soviet leaders will change their minds, and while we pray, we must use our best efforts to develop better bombs and more of them. For our own protection, we must continue pushing forward the boundaries of our scientific knowledge.

This is a harsh judgment, but the nature of the weapon demands that we be realistic.

We have not been, and I do not believe we ever shall be, guilty of using "atomic diplomacy." Others might suspect us of it because that is what they would do under similar circumstances. But, as I said in Charleston, South Carolina, on November 16, 1945, the suggestion that we might use the atomic bomb "as a diplomatic or military threat against any nation is not only untrue in fact but is a wholly unwarranted reflection upon the American Government and people."

It is one of the inherent characteristics of our democracy that we can fight a war only with the genuine consent of our people. No President in the absence of a declaration of war by the Congress could authorize an atomic bombing without running the risk of impeachment. No one who knows the peace-loving temper of our people can believe that our Congress would adopt a declaration of war contrary to our obligations solemnly undertaken, under the United Nations Charter. The history of 1914 to 1917 and of 1939 to 1941 is convincing proof of the slowness of Congress to declare war. There is surely no reason to believe that it would be more eager to engage in a future war more terrible than any we have ever known.

While we wait for the realities of the atomic age to penetrate the fears and suspicions of the leaders of the Soviet Union, we must not permit the magnitude of the United States initiative to become blurred in the minds of men. It is a record that clearly shows we do not wish to continue making atomic bombs.

Within one year after the successful demonstration of atomic power, the United States had done these things:

1. Secured the agreement of our collaborators in the discovery of atomic energy to place that discovery under international control.

2. Secured the co-operation of the five major powers in initiating machinery to consider plans for international control.

3. Secured the unanimous adoption of that proposal by the United Nations.

4. Devised a detailed plan for world control of nuclear energy by an Atomic Development Authority representing all the United Nations.

5. Established by act of Congress a civilian commission to exercise strict control over all fissionable materials.

6. Released radioactive materials (isotopes) for medical, biologic, and scientific research.

7. Presented to the United Nations Atomic Energy Commission our detailed plan for international control of atomic energy; and, within a few months after the end of that first year, secured approval for our plan from all but two of the members of the commission.

I do not agree with those who predict that should the Soviet Union continue to block that record of progress, mass destruction must follow in a few years. In the war just ended, the Germans and Japanese had poison gas and death-dealing germs, as did the Russians, the British and ourselves. That war was no polite tea party. It was brutal. Nevertheless, no nation dared use these terrible weapons because they knew the same weapons would be used against them.

In saying this, I do not minimize the danger. It would be unfortunate if hostile governments possessed atomic bombs. But, it would be even more unfortunate if we threw our bombs away, gave our information to an international organization with inadequate power to exercise effective control, and thus enabled another government to manufacture bombs without our knowledge far sooner than otherwise would have been possible.

The years ahead pose no greater challenge to mankind. In the time we have at our disposal, fear and suspicion may yet yield to the wisdom of insuring the use of atomic power for human welfare rather than for deadly warfare.

Chapter 14

What Are the Russians After?

THE AMERICAN PEOPLE, in their deep and abiding desire for peace, look toward the Soviet Union with many anxious questions in their hearts and minds. The two I have encountered most often are:

What are they like?

What are they after?

Both are good questions. Our ability to acquire some understanding of the leaders and the people of the Soviet Union, and some idea of their objectives will govern to a large extent our success in framing policies that will promote peace.

The best way I can approach the first question is out of my own experience. And the first conclusion clearly indicated by that experience is that Russia's leaders are stubborn and resourceful negotiators.

I have had quite a broad experience in dealing with men. My active practice as a trial lawyer was rich with such experience. In my service in the House of Representatives and in the Senate I served with over two thousand Representatives and nearly two hundred Senators. I conferred with most of them in the adjustment of differences within each branch and between the two branches of Congress. As Justice of the Supreme Court, as Director, first of Economic Stabilization, and then of War Mobilization, I met many men with many interests, and settled many issues. But through all these years I had no experience that prepared me for negotiating with Mr. Molotov.

I remember once at London one of the newspaper correspondents, reluctant to believe that Mr. Molotov would break up the conference rather than meet the views of the rest of us, asked me incredulously:

"But are you certain you have explored every avenue of approach to the problems?"

"My friend," I replied, "I've not only explored every avenue, but I've gone down every lane, byway and highway. I've tried everything I ever learned in the House and Senate. But there I worked with a majority rule. This is more like a jury. If you have one stubborn juror, all you can expect is a mistrial."

I have often thought that dealing with Mr. Molotov would be good experience for an attorney, who represents a corporation constantly being sued for damages, whose task is to play for time in the hope that the complainant will get tired of waiting for a trial and settle for a small part of his claim.

I have mentioned Molotov's tactics at the close of the Moscow Conference when the protocol of the conference had been signed and I had left the table. Mr. Molotov at that very late eleventh hour then announced that, after consideration, he had decided to accept the United States' proposal on the Balkan issue made the previous afternoon. That indicates his perseverance and patience.

If we are correctly informed about the patience exercised by Job, I am certain Mr. Molotov is one of his lineal descendants. He has unlimited patience as well as a fine mind and tremendous energy. Any exhibition of impatience or bad temper by others gives him amusement. At such times it is interesting to watch his serious, solemn expression as he protests his innocence of any provocation. These qualities were well demonstrated by Mr. Molotov's stand on the Dodecanese Islands.

At the first meeting of the Council of Foreign Ministers at London in September 1945, the other members of the council believed that the Dodecanese should be transferred from Italy to Greece and be demilitarized. But Mr. Molotov objected. He said that while he might finally agree to the transfer, he objected to the proposal for demilitarization. In view of the Soviet Union's well-known attitude toward Greece, it was certain he did not want the existing government to have the right to fortify the Dodecanese. It was evident he wanted to withhold action in the hope that the Communists would get control of Greece and would then fortify the islands, or that he could later use his consent to the transfer as a concession in driving a bargain for his territorial demands.

Every day the question was presented for action, but each time he would say he had to submit the matter to his government. We would ask if he would submit it promptly and get instructions. He would doubt that this could be done because his government would want to consider it. He still had not heard from his government when, after a month, we adjourned. When we met in Paris the following April, he could not then very well give the same excuse. He had a new one—he could not agree because Greece had never asked for the transfer of the islands. We pointed out at length and through many arguments that other transfers of territory had been made without formal requests. Finally, he said that in any event the matter should be settled in connection with the settlement of other territorial questions.

Shortly after we gathered at Paris for the second session of the council, we again reached the question of the Dodecanese. Mr. Molotov said he had hoped to be able to discuss the matter but he had been informed that morning that the Greek Ambassador was going to call on Mr. Vy-shinski and he would have to await the result of that conference! The rest of us laughed at this newest and lamest excuse. Even Molotov smiled.

After enough problems were settled to his satisfaction, Mr. Molotov then proposed that the Dodecanese be transferred to Greece and demilitarized. And he made the proposal as if the subject were being mentioned for the first time.

Mr. Molotov likes to discuss questions of procedure. In such discussions he has no equal. He will argue for hours about what subjects should be placed on an agenda. You must not only be patient but also must watch carefully even the manner in which your own proposal is stated. If you do not, you will later spend hours trying to get your complete proposal before the council for discussion. Mr. Molotov's answer will be "Nyet," the Russian word for "No," which I heard so often that I almost accept it as part of my own language. He can say in English "I agree," but so seldom does he agree that his pronunciation isn't very good.

In any conference, with or without the unanimity rule, he will win your reluctant admiration by the resourcefulness he exhibits in his delaying tactics. He will sit through it all imperturbably, stroking his mustache or spinning his pince-nez glasses as he waits for a translation and smoking Russian cigarettes in what seems to be an endless chain.

In one important respect, Mr. Molotov is typical of all Soviet representatives. When they conclude that they have exhausted their bargaining efforts, that further delay will result in no further concessions and they might as well agree, the Russians suffer no embarrassment whatever in changing their position—even if it involves a complete reversal of stands they have maintained for hours on end. As a rule, Mr. Molotov smilingly announces that the Soviet delegation, in order to bring about agreement, desires to make a proposal. He then presents your proposal, which has been the subject of controversy for weeks, with only a few unimportant changes. Having argued the question so long, the other conferees are so anxious to get rid of it that they receive the announcement with pleasure. And frequently they even express appreciation to Mr. Molotov for his doing what he should have done weeks or months before.

Another well-exercised tactic is the counteroffensive. Whenever Mr. Molotov suspects that the United States or another country is going to present a complaint about the failure of the Soviet Union to comply with an agreement such as that at Yalta on free press, free elections, and so on, he anticipates the discussion. He either makes an attack himself or gets one of the satellites to do it, and usually it is directed against Greece.

He charges the Greek Government with corruption; with aggressive intentions and unwarranted attacks upon its peaceful neighbors, Yugoslavia, Bulgaria, and Albania; he cries out against the domination of the Greek people by British imperialists who maintain troops in Greece solely to deprive the Greek people of their freedom and to support the Greek Fascists. Usually, he expresses deep regret that the United States Government should give its support to Britain and thus share responsibility for the British misconduct. He repeats his charges about Greece so often that I fear he comes to believe them.

The people of whom Mr. Molotov disapproves are always described as "Fascists." All Communists and Communist sympathizers are "democratic forces." It is a simple classification.

Senators Connally and Vandenberg were never called Fascists by Mr. Molotov directly, but the Communist press made up for his oversight. Both of them were characterized as representing the "big interests." Senator Vandenberg was selected by the Communists in Paris as the real representative of the Fascists, but Senator Connally managed to take the lead during the period when he was ably presenting the United States' position on Trieste to the peace conference. The Communist press intimated that, if left alone, I might possibly do the right thing, but these two "Fascist" Senators were always at my side to influence me against the "democratic" forces.

When I left Washington for the peace conference, the two Senators had to stay there because of some important matters pending in the Senate, but they agreed to come to Paris later. I joked with them about getting away from their "evil influence."

After the conference had been in session about a week, Molotov charged that the United States and the United Kingdom were violating agreements made in the Council of Foreign Ministers regarding the procedure for the peace conference. Knowing him by that time, I had anticipated that he would make such charges, and in the council I had consumed a lot of time making a record. In that record we reserved the right at all times to vote our views on procedural questions. The charge of bad faith was too much for me. I read the record and made some comments about Mr. Molotov which I disliked greatly having to make. It was the severest criticism I ever made of him. Members of our delegation suggested that I should send for the two "Fascists" who, they said, were peaceful individuals compared to me.

After a heated session in Paris one afternoon, Chip Bohlen remained behind talking to a member of the Soviet delegation. The Soviet representative said it was impossible for him to understand the Americans. They had a reputation for being good traders and yet Secretary Byrnes for two days had been making speeches about principles—talking, he said, like a professor.

"Why doesn't he stop this talk about principles, and get down to business and start trading?" the Soviet representative asked Chip in all sincerity.

Chip attempted most unsuccessfully to explain that there were some questions which, in the opinion of Americans, involved principle and could not be settled by bargaining.

Dealing with Generalissimo Stalin and Foreign Minister Molotov are entirely different experiences. Where Molotov is devious, Stalin is direct. But in all my dealings with Stalin, I could not forget a story President Roosevelt had told me in the early days of the war about his communications with Stalin. One day he received a message from Stalin that was very discourteous. He dictated a reply in the same vein, but decided to hold it a day. The next morning, while I was with him, he received a second message from Stalin which was couched in the most courteous language possible and contained assurances of great personal friendship. The President did not understand how such contradictory behavior was possible but it happened more than once.

When I first observed Stalin at Yalta, I also could not understand the President's experience. Stalin was unusually courteous to the President and generally appeared anxious to reach agreement with him. He was always in good humor, and enjoyed a joke. My favorable impression was not at all impaired when I would see him at an afternoon session beckon to a Red Army general who sat back of him, and send him out for a cup of tea. I knew a lot of GIs would pay good money to see a man who could order a general to wait on him.

Despite their differences in personality, one can be sure that the aims pursued by Mr. Molotov are those approved by Generalissimo Stalin. Only in the negotiations on reparations at Potsdam, and in the Soviet rejection of the forty-year treaty, have I ever felt that it was Molotov who influenced Stalin. Otherwise, it clearly has been Stalin who has called the tune—and Molotov who has made it last as long as a symphony. How much the Politbureau influences Stalin, I do not know. My guess is that he accepts Politbureau recommendations whenever he has no special interest or strong conviction. Like every successful leader, he recognizes the necessity of holding the support of his associates. However, in any matter affecting foreign relations in which he has strong convictions, I am certain the Politbureau has supported him. I have seen him make so many important decisions promptly that I do not think he worries very much about control by the Politbureau. Stalin and the gentlemen of the Politbureau realize they could not exact blind obedience to their decisions unless they gave the party workers and the people the impression of unity on all important matters.

I have said enough, I think, to indicate one cardinal fact that must be kept in mind in evaluating any Soviet action. The fact is that, to them, the ends justify any means. The question we must therefore ask is, what are the ends sought by Soviet leaders. In other words, what are the Russians after?

My experiences merely confirm an answer that actually is found in Russian history. Few Americans are well informed on Russian history. I do not profess to be. But I have learned enough to conclude that many of the problems which perplex us today have their explanation in that history. Despite the violence of the Russian revolution, the aims of Bolshevik diplomacy differ very little from those of the Czars. And the aims that Stalin and Molotov have pursued since the end of the war vary little from the demands they made of Adolf Hitler.

Russian expansionism, which has concerned us so deeply in the postwar years, was clearly exposed, and strangely enough, by the godfather of the Communist revolution, Karl Marx. In a series of articles written for the New York *Tribune* from London in 1853, Marx dealt at length with "The Eastern Question." Among his observations were these:

> As to Russia's antipathy against aggrandizement, I allege the following facts from a mass of the acquisitions of Russia since Peter the Great.

> The Russian frontier has advanced: towards Berlin, Dresden and Vienna, about 700 miles; towards Constantinople, about 500 miles; towards Stockholm, about 630 miles; towards Teheran, about one thousand miles. . . . The total acquisitions of Russia during the last 60 years are equal in extent and importance to the whole Empire she had in Europe before that time.

In another dispatch, Marx wrote:

> And as sure as conquest follows conquest, and annexation follows annexation, so sure would the conquest of Turkey by Russia be only the prelude for the annexation of Hungary, Prussia, Galicia, and for the ultimate realization of the Slavonic Empire which certain fanatical Panslavistic philosophers have dreamed of. . . . The arrest of the Russian scheme of annexation is a matter of the highest moment.

How contemporary that sounds!

Following 1853, the year of these dispatches, Russia continued to acquire territory right up to World War I. The total territorial gain of czarist Russia between 1853 and 1914 was 971,277 square miles, which brought the prewar area of the Russian empire up to 8,645,000 square miles.

The advent of Soviet power in Russia was accompanied by the loss of nearly half a million square miles of territory. The new Soviet Union excluded the areas of Finland, Estonia, Latvia, and Lithuania, which became independent states. Kars was ceded to Turkey; Bessarabia was returned to Rumania, and a large area was lost to the new Poland.

During the first twenty years of Soviet rule, the only extension of territory was the annexation in 1926 of certain islands in the Arctic. But in 1939 the Soviet Union embarked upon an active policy of expansion. Between December 4, 1939, and the end of 1945, the Soviet Union took control of the territories of Latvia, Lithuania, Estonia, Bessarabia, south Sakhalin and the Kuriles, parts of Finland and of Poland, the Königsberg area in East Prussia, the Transcarpathian Ukraine, and Tannu Tuva. It also took over Port Arthur where, although it did not acquire sovereignty, it did acquire the right for thirty years to maintain a naval base jointly with China. In all, nearly 300,000 square miles of territory have been acquired since 1939, bringing the area of the Soviet Union to 8,455,939 square miles, only slightly less than the greatest extent of czarist Russia.

It is clear, then, that expansionism is not an innovation of the Communist regime. It is rooted in Russian history. Only the personalities and the tactics have changed.

Russia's modern leaders nevertheless have given us an outstanding demonstration of the means they are quite willing to employ to achieve their ends. This is found in the story of Russo-German relations from the Munich agreement in September 1938, through the Russo-German Non-aggression Pact of August 1939, to Hitler's attack on the Soviet Union in June 1941.

In an after-dinner conversation at Yalta, Stalin said that the Soviet Government would never have entered into the Nonaggression Pact with Germany had it not been for the attempt at Munich to appease Hitler and the failure of Britain and France to consult the Soviet Union on the subject.

Certainly it is true that immediately after Munich, the Soviet press began to modify its campaign of criticism against Germany. By December 1938, when a trade agreement between the two countries was renewed, the press felt free to hail the action as a forward step in Soviet-German relations. Shortly thereafter, in an address to a Congress of the Communist Party, Stalin stated that the only differences between Germany and Soviet Russia were ideological, and these differences were exaggerated by others who wanted someone else to "pull their chestnuts out of the fire" for them.

In the spring of 1939, Stalin made known his disappointment over the results of Soviet negotiations with France and England. Foreign Minister Maxim Litvinov, known for his understanding of "the West" was removed and replaced by V. M. Molotov.

Hitler seemed indifferent to these overtures. It was not until the summer that Hitler evidently decided he would need the support of Russia to make his projected attack on Poland. Events followed so quickly that they mystified the governments of the world and frightened those of us who still hoped war might be avoided.

The history of those negotiations remained obscure until records of them were discovered among the captured archives of the Nazi government. They make an important contribution to our understanding of what it is the Soviet Union seeks. That part of the story which includes the conversations of the principal actors was reported by Gustav Hilger, counselor of the German Embassy in Moscow, who acted as interpreter for the negotiators. His report is from notes made at the time when he could have had no motive for making them inaccurate or false. The rest of the story is based upon official documents discovered in the files of the German Foreign Office.

The record, therefore, is German and has not been confirmed by Soviet sources. However, it cannot be disregarded by anyone seeking the truth about what occurred in that fateful year preceding Hitler's attack on the Soviet Union. Nor can it be disregarded by anyone seeking to understand what is in the minds of those in the Kremlin today. Do they merely desire security? To get what they regard as security, do they intend to expand their control over other states and peoples? Often it is possible to tell what is in a man's mind and heart by what he has said and done in the past in relation to the same issues. Let us, then, look at the record.

On August 15, 1939, the German Ambassador in Moscow, Graf von Schulenburg received instructions to advise Mr. Molotov: (1) ideological differences need not preclude friendly relations and there are no real conflicting interests between Germany and the Soviet Union; (2) Germany has no aggressive intentions against the Soviet Union and believes such questions as the Baltic states can be solved to their mutual satisfaction; (3) the capitalistic Western democracies would try to incite the Soviet Union to war against Germany, a fight which would benefit only the capitalistic powers; (4) English warmongering makes necessary a clarification of Soviet-German relations in order to avoid circumstances that would make German-Soviet friendship and the settlement of territorial questions in Eastern Europe impossible; and (5) therefore, Foreign Minister Ribbentrop is willing to visit Moscow to explain Hitler's views to Mr. Stalin.

When the German Ambassador presented his message, Molotov expressed keen interest, but thought there should be preparation for such a conference. He wanted to know what the attitude of the German Government would be toward a Nonaggression Pact between the two countries and whether Germany would use its influence on Japan to improve the Japanese-Soviet relations. He also wanted to make certain that the

Baltic states would be considered at the proposed conference. He immediately received affirmative replies.

Molotov expressed appreciation of the German Government's willingness to send its Foreign Minister to Moscow, in contrast to Great Britain's action in sending a civil service officer, such as Sir William Strang. He suggested that both governments prepare drafts of a Nonaggression Pact.

On August 19, a trade and commerce agreement between the two countries was signed in Berlin. On the same day Molotov transmitted to the German Ambassador a draft of a Nonaggression Pact.

Hitler was impatient. Evidently he was ready to attack Poland but was anxious to complete this pact with Stalin first. He sent a personal telegram to Stalin saying that he would accept Molotov's draft of the Nonaggression Pact. Germany, he said, was not interested in the Baltic Sea bay and the bordering countries of Finland, Estonia, Latvia and Lithuania. This assurance, he added, could be placed in a secret protocol attached to the Nonaggression Pact. The secret protocol, he suggested, also could set forth the spheres of influence to be observed by the two nations in eastern Europe.

Hitler ended his message by saying that Poland was increasing its provocative acts daily, and a crisis might occur at any moment. He therefore urged Stalin to receive, not later than August 23, Foreign Minister Ribbentrop who would have authority to sign the pact and the secret protocols.

The importance of Hitler's declaration was immediately appreciated by Molotov. Within thirty minutes after it had been delivered by the German Ambassador, the latter was asked to inform his government that the Soviet Union was ready to receive Foreign Minister Ribbentrop and discuss an agreement on the terms set forth in the telegram.

There is every reason to believe that Stalin was pleased by this unexpected turn of events. He was annoyed with Britain and France for failing to join in the pledges he desired. He wanted assurance that the Soviet Union would not be attacked by Hitler. He knew there would be war between Germany and Poland in the immediate future. He must have reasoned that, if the Nonaggression Pact prevented the Western powers from coming to Poland's aid, general warfare would be averted and the Soviet Union would have more time to develop its military strength. On the other hand, if the Western allies did go to war the balance of strength would be such that Russia would still have time to train and equip its armies. In addition, the pact would enable him to take over the Baltic states without the risk of war.

Ribbentrop arrived in Moscow on August 23. The conferees included Stalin, Molotov, Ribbentrop, Ambassador Schulenburg, and Hilger.

Stalin insisted that the secret protocol include a declaration of the

Soviet Union's special interest in Bessarabia and that the northern boundary of Lithuania be fixed as the line of demarcation between the Russian and German spheres of interest. This was accepted. The pact and the protocols were approved; the signing was celebrated; champagne was served; Stalin proposed a toast to Hitler; and Ribbentrop returned to Berlin the following day.

Only nine days had elapsed since Ambassador Schulenburg had made the first approach! The speed with which they reached agreement impresses me because I spent fifteen months trying to get Soviet agreement to five treaties of lesser importance. In the first case, they wanted to agree; in the latter case, they did not.

Although the propaganda machines in both countries had been trying to prepare the people for this about-face, the Russian and the German people must have been mystified by the sudden shift. The assumption is justified by the difficulty of the people in this hemisphere, including the Communist press, to understand what had taken place.

This pact, it seems to me, is a classical example of an agreement not worth the paper it was written on. Stalin's statement at Yalta confirms the line usually taken by Soviet representatives: the pact was entered into solely to gain time for a conflict Russia recognized was inevitable. Thus, it seems clear that the Soviet Government concluded the pact while fully intending to violate it. We have no statement of Hitler's intention, but we have his act of violation. It is therefore reasonable to doubt the good faith of either Stalin or Hitler in agreeing to this pact.

Hitler overran Poland more rapidly than Stalin had expected, and in pursuing the retreating Poles, Hitler's troops entered the Soviet sphere of influence. Stalin asked that Ribbentrop return to Moscow and make a new agreement on the line dividing Poland between them.

Ribbentrop arrived on September 27. This time Germany agreed that the Soviet Union should take over Lithuania. A boundary line was devised splitting Poland in half and Soviet plans to set up an autonomous Soviet Republic were approved. Germany permitted the Soviet Union to take over the oil sources of Drohobycz and Boryslaw, and the Soviets contracted to furnish the Nazis with 300,000 tons of raw oil from these sources. The new border and friendship pact was celebrated at a banquet given by Mr. Molotov on September 30.

Thereafter, Wagner's operas were once again heard in Moscow. The German war communiqués were featured on the front page of the official Soviet newspapers. On October 31, 1939, Molotov made a speech in which he said: "Germany is in the position of a state which is striving for the earliest possible termination of war and for peace, while Britain and France are in favor of continuing the war and are opposed to peace." And Hitler told friends that the Friendship Pact would last for years.

Estonia, Latvia and Lithuania were brought more tightly into the Soviet sphere. They were forced to cede bases to the Red Army. Finland, however, resisted similar proposals and, without the formality of a declaration of war, was invaded by the Red Army in November, 1939. The earlier concessions made by three Baltic states proved to be merely stepping stones; these nations soon were forced to join the Union of Soviet Republics. At this juncture rifts began to appear in the Hitler-Stalin partnership.

In the earlier division of territory, a small area in the southwest corner of Lithuania was allotted to Germany. But the Red Army, when it marched into the country, occupied this area. Germany protested. The Soviets admitted the protest was justified but argued that it was difficult to separate this area from the rest of Lithuania. The issue was pending for months until the Soviet Union finally agreed to pay Hitler 31,500,000 reichmarks for this Lithuanian territory.

In June 1940, the Soviet Union demanded Bessarabia from Rumania. Germany could not object because Hitler had declared he had no interest in this area. But next the Soviet Union demanded north Bukovina. This area had not figured in the earlier discussions or agreements and Germany objected. Mr. Molotov simply replied that he saw no reason for the objection since the area was settled by Ukrainians. He blandly added that the Soviet Union not only expected Germany's support for this claim but also for a claim they would make later for south Bukovina.

Hitler began to be irritated. Evidently, he felt that Germans were shedding blood for the territory they got, and the Soviet Union was insisting upon taking the spoils without the fighting. The German Ambassador in Moscow received instructions to inform Molotov that Germany was interested in guaranteeing Rumanian territory. Germany needed Rumania's food and oil. Germany felt the same way about Hungary. The Nonaggression Pact, the Ambassador added, obliged each party to consult the other on questions of mutual interest, yet Germany had not been consulted when action was taken against neighboring areas. He cited the Lithuanian area and Russia's sudden action in Bessarabia and Bukovina.

Molotov insisted (I can almost hear his words!) that the German procedure was not loyal to the agreement and Germany should have known that the Soviet Union would be interested in Rumania and Hungary.

Suspicions began to grow on both sides. On October 13, 1940, Ribbentrop wrote a nineteen-page letter to Stalin giving a detailed explanation of the steps taken by Germany in the previous months and the reasons for such steps. He invited Molotov to Berlin. Stalin's reply was noncommittal, but he agreed that an improvement in relations was entirely possible and said Molotov would arrive in Berlin on November 12.

Molotov had two conferences with Hitler, one on the twelfth of November and the other on the thirteenth, each lasting three hours. These discussions were recorded by Ambassador Paul Schmidt. In my opinion, these marked the turning point of the war. In fact, as closely as such things can be calculated, I believe these visits represent a decisive point in history. For Mr. Molotov greatly overplayed his hand. His interview with Hitler on the thirteenth, particularly, stands out as a major diplomatic blunder.

Hitler apparently was in a grandiose and expansive mood. Since Nazi victory was certain, he declared, Germany and the Soviet Union should reach agreement on the division of the British Empire which soon would fall into their hands. Germany, he thought, should look to the West and the Soviet Union should direct its attention toward the East. Russia needed an exit to a free warm sea which could be found by way of Iran, the Persian Gulf and the Arabian Sea. Hitler waxed eloquent as he described a world divided between Germany and the Soviet Union.

Mr. Molotov's precise, legalistic mind failed to respond to Hitler's grandiose scheme. He agreed that Hitler was presenting an interesting long-term program but the Soviet Government, he said, wished to discuss immediate problems. Evidently the existing arrangements between them "are not satisfactory to Germany," Molotov went on, because the agreements clearly placed Finland in Russia's sphere, yet German troops were there. They should be withdrawn promptly. Germany's guarantee of the Rumanian border the Soviet Union must protest, and he could not help but wonder at whom such a guarantee was directed.

What a let-down this must have been for Hitler's flights of fantasy! He explained that German troops had to be in Finland to protect lines of communication for the supply of Swedish ore and of oil which was of greatest importance to Germany's war effort. The troops would be withdrawn as soon as possible. Germany had interfered in Rumania because otherwise there would have been open conflict between Rumania and Hungary, which would have injured Germany's economic interests there. Rumania had suffered cessions of territory to Hungary and to the Soviet Union, Hitler went on, and the border guarantee was essential to preserve peace and order in Rumania. Germany had only a military mission in Rumania which was there at the request of its government. He emphasized that Germany had no political, only economic interest in the Balkan states; he wanted to protect the Rumanian oil sources from attack.

Molotov said bluntly that he was not satisfied with Hitler's reply. In addition, Molotov said, the Soviet Union wanted to enter into closer relations with Bulgaria and possibly sign a Mutual Assistance Pact with her, because of her position in relation to the Dardanelles. His final demand was for a new regime for the Dardanelles that would involve realistic guarantees rather than paper assurances.

Hitler replied that he was unable to give an answer without consulting the Bulgarian government and Mussolini.

It was here that Molotov made his worst blunder. He insisted upon a definite and immediate answer. The interpreter's report says that at this point Hitler showed great indignation.

I can picture the scene. Hitler had just said what he actually believed. He was certain of victory; he thought he dominated the world; and he had just painted a picture allocating an exceedingly generous portion of the world to the Soviets who had not lost a life nor spent a dollar in the war. But Molotov simply said that it was "interesting" and demanded an immediate answer to what Hitler must have regarded as relatively trivial things—Rumania's boundary, a mutual assistance pact with Bulgaria. It is easy to visualize the excitable and explosive Hitler wondering at the temerity of this man whose government, Hitler believed, was not prepared for war telling him—Hitler—that his answers were unsatisfactory.

Historians may discover when Hitler decided to make war on Russia. He may previously have considered it in a general way, but until I see other evidence, I shall believe that this interview with Molotov was the decisive moment. Certain it is that from this fateful November 13, Russo-German relations steadily declined.

Later that day, Ribbentrop read to Molotov a draft agreement and two secret protocols; he proposed the Soviet Union join the Axis powers in signing them. Evidently these were prepared before Molotov's arrival and before he saw Hitler. The agreement provided that the Soviet Union would co-operate with the other three powers, each to have a separate sphere of interest, and each to agree not to support any other power bloc directed against any one of the four. The first secret protocol set forth the territorial aspirations of the four, as envisaged by Hitler; for Germany, there would be central Africa; for Italy, north and northeast Africa; for Japan, the Asiatic area south of the Japanese islands; and for the Soviet Union, all the region south of the USSR in the direction of the Indian Ocean. The second secret protocol provided for replacing the Montreux Convention governing the Black Sea Straits with an agreement which would give the Soviet Union unrestricted rights to use the Straits; all other powers except the Black Sea states would abandon passage rights through the Dardanelles for their warships. In addition, Ribbentrop offered to mediate between Japan and the Soviet Union in an effort to promote a lasting understanding.

Molotov's response to this proposal is especially noteworthy. It should be read and considered in light of recent history.

Japan had already offered to enter into a Nonaggression Pact; the Russian Government awaited replies to some questions it had submitted, Molotov said. There would have to be "substantial" discussions about Iran, and the Soviet Union would insist on concrete guarantees for the Dardanelles. Molotov then brought up Bulgaria, Rumania, Hungary, Yugoslavia, Greece, the future of Poland, and Swedish neutrality. (When I first read this report it impressed me as sounding like an agenda for a meeting of the Council of Foreign Ministers!) He concluded with the statement that great questions of the future should not completely obscure the questions of the day.

Molotov gave no more definite answer than this during his visit. But on November 25, he asked the German Ambassador in Moscow to come to the Kremlin and he then presented a full reply to the Ribbentrop proposals of November 13. This, too, is worthy of special note in light of subsequent events.

The Soviet Government, Molotov informed the Ambassador, was ready to accept the Ribbentrop draft of the four-power agreement on four conditions: (1) that German troops be withdrawn immediately from Finland; (2) that Soviet security in the Dardanelles be guaranteed by a Mutual Assistance Pact with Bulgaria and by the establishment of a base for Soviet land and sea forces in the Straits; (3) that Soviet aspirations in the area south of Baku and Batum in the general direction of Iran and the Persian Gulf be recognized; and (4) that Japan abandon its concession rights to coal and naphtha in north Sakhalin.

Molotov apparently had not realized how ineptly he had played his hand in Berlin nor the degree of Hitler's indignation. The Soviet Government never received a reply to this message.

Both Stalin and Molotov began to worry about Hitler's silence. In January 1941, through their representatives, they negotiated a second economic agreement. The Soviet Union had scrupulously fulfilled the deliveries called for in the first agreement and now agreed to a further increase in the exchange of goods. Later in the month Molotov's concern about Hitler's failure to reply to his proposal prompted him to suggest further conversations. The German Government simply informed him that his proposal had been received, that communications had been sent to Italy and Japan regarding it, and that it was hoped discussions might be continued in the near future. Such a reply—two months after the proposal was made—showed clearly that Hitler was no longer interested. The conversations never took place.

Instead, the Germans increased their troop concentrations in the Balkans. They informed the Soviets of their action. On February 28, Ambassador Schulenburg told Molotov that Bulgaria had subscribed to the Axis three-power pact and would sign a concurring protocol on March 1.

Molotov received this communication with great concern. He emphasized that these developments in Bulgaria created a situation entirely different from that which had existed on November 25 when the Soviets made their proposal. Apparently, Molotov did not realize that his November 25 proposal represented the final divorce decree ending the strange marriage between Hitler and Stalin.

On March 1, Schulenburg informed Molotov that Germany had decided to move troops into Bulgaria. Immediately, and in the presence of the German Ambassador, Molotov wrote a note expressing regret that the German Government had violated the security interests of the Soviet Union by such a military occupation.

On April 5, a Friendship and Nonaggression Pact was concluded between the Soviet Union and Yugoslavia, almost simultaneously with the German attack on Yugoslavia. It is not clear what prompted Stalin to take this step although it was said at the time that Russia's support of Yugoslavia might keep the Germans so involved in the Balkans that there would be less danger of their attacking Russia. Within a few weeks, however, it was evident that Stalin had miscalculated Yugoslavia's strength.

Thereafter, the Soviet Government avoided doing anything that might displease Germany. Raw materials were delivered promptly. When the foreign press published reports that German troops were concentrating on Russia's borders, the Soviet Government, through the official Tass News Agency, declared that the rumors were inspired by warmongers, that relations between the two countries were pleasant and that existing treaties made it clear there was no threat to the Soviet Union. Of course they did not believe what they were saying.

Ambassador Schulenburg did not believe it. He was so concerned that late in April he personally took to Berlin a memorandum setting forth the dangers of war with the Soviet Union. I do not know whether this memorandum reached Hitler. The evidence does not disclose that he mentioned it in his talks with Schulenburg but the Ambassador is quoted as saying that Hitler, in parting with him, said he would not make war on Russia.

Weeks of suspense followed. Meetings no longer took place between Molotov and Schulenburg. Finally, in June, the German Embassy received instructions to send all German women and children back to Germany without creating excitement.

On June 22, Molotov asked Schulenburg to visit him. He stated that German planes were making an increasing number of unauthorized flights over Soviet territory and insisted that steps be taken to prevent further violations. Schulenburg promised to refer the matter to his government. Molotov then said rumors were circulating over the world that there would be war between Germany and the Soviet Union, and now he had heard that the women and children of members of the German Embassy were leaving the country. He desired an explanation. Schulenburg was embarrassed. Molotov must have known Schulenburg was not telling the truth when he replied that he knew nothing of the rumors and that the departure of the women and children was due merely to summer vacations.

The next day, June 23, 1941, Schulenburg received instructions from Berlin to see Molotov and make the following statement:

"The increasing Soviet troop concentrations at the German border have reached such a proportion that they are intolerable to the German Government. The German Government, therefore, has decided to take countermeasures."

"Is this a declaration of war?" Molotov asked.

The Ambassador made a helpless gesture with his hands.

Molotov said he could not regard the message in any other light, since German troops had already crossed the Russian border and Nazi aircraft had been bombing several Russian cities for more than an hour. He described the attacks on a country with which Germany had a Friendship and Nonaggression Pact as a breach of faith such as the world had never seen. The alleged concentrations of Soviet troops, Molotov added, could only be a pretext since the Russian forces were merely engaged in customary maneuvers. Had the German Government questioned, the Soviet Union would have given an adequate explanation.

Ambassador Schulenburg did not say that "customary maneuvers" was the customary explanation. He simply said he was unable to make any further comments on the situation.

Thus ended the "enduring" twenty-two-month-old Friendship and Nonaggression Pact between Germany and the Soviet Union. Thus began the war between the Nazis and the Soviets.

Now let us see what guidance this history holds for us. I think it reasonable to assume that Soviet ambitions still include the territory Molotov desired when he sent his message to Hitler. Some of those desires have been fulfilled. However, the flush of victory has encouraged the Soviet Government to extend its ambitions.

In the North, their demands against Finland have been satisfied. During the war, Mr. Molotov explored the possibility of extending Soviet power a little through concessions from Norway. In November 1944, he asked Norway to grant the Soviet Union greater economic privileges in the Spitsbergen group of islands. He wanted outright possession of Bear Island and the right to establish military facilities on other islands of the group.

Mr. Molotov made this request despite the fact that the 1920 treaty—by which Norwegian sovereignty over these islands was recognized and which was signed by thirty-four countries, including the Soviet Union—contained a proviso that Norway could not construct fortifications and that the islands could "never be used for warlike purposes." The Norwegian Government, after first agreeing to discuss both subjects, has since declared it would consider only the economic issue and has pointed out that the military proposal must be a subject of multilateral negotiation.

In the East, the Soviet Union now has all of Sakhalin and, in addition, has taken over the Kuriles and has acquired rights in Port Arthur, Dairen, and on the Manchurian railroad. Whether Stalin will continue to resist the temptation offered by the successes of the Chinese Communist forces in Manchuria is a question which, at this writing, remains in the balance.

Soviet aspirations south of Batum and Baku have not been realized, but the effort has been made. Turkey was asked to cede the provinces of Kars and Ardahan south of Batum. The effort to extend south of Baku into Iranian territory was blocked by the Security Council.

The familiar technique of trying to install a puppet government under the protection of the Red Army was employed. The Red Army interfered with the armed forces of little Iran. The Soviets encouraged the establishment in Azerbaijan of an independent government. The case was brought before the Security Council. When the Soviets kept their troops in Iran beyond the date of their treaty, the council acted on the complaint of Iran. Every member of the council except the Soviet Union and Poland voted to protect the integrity of Iran. The Soviet Union complied with the Security Council's decision because it was not yet ready or willing to be isolated from the rest of the world.

Now, let us compare Molotov's 1940 demands with today's situation in Europe.

The Bulgarian Government, installed and protected by the Red Army, has now made a pact unnecessary. Thus the "safety zone" between the Soviet Union and the Straits, which Molotov requested, has been achieved. In Rumania, a similar regime has been installed by tactics I described earlier. The pursuit of Soviet ambitions in Hungary is a more recent story, but the pattern is old.

Poland has been subordinated to the status of a satellite. Albania and Yugoslavia are tightly clasped in the Soviet-dominated Slav bloc. Czechoslovakia is a captive of this bloc. Out of all the European areas toward which Molotov expressed an interest, only Greece and Turkey remain free. And the struggle for them is in progress.

The reports of our able observer, Mark Ethridge, have made it clear that a small, well-organized Communist minority, based in and supplied from Greece's Soviet-dominated neighbors, would have captured Greece long ago had it not been for two things: (1) the action by the United

Nations, and (2) the Soviets' realization that, if they took over Greece, the United States and the United Kingdom would demand that the United Nations act against such aggression.

The Security Council's Balkan Investigating Committee delayed and exposed the effort. But chaos still prevails and the fate of Greece hangs in the balance while the American mission headed by former Governor Dwight Griswold seeks to promote the economic and political health which alone can kill off the disease of Communist-agitated unrest.

As for Turkey, we must remember that Stalin declared at Potsdam the continuing interest of the Soviet Union in the Straits and that subsequently a demand was made for the right to build a land and naval base in the area. Our efforts to obtain collective guarantees to maintain the freedom of the Dardanelles have been unsuccessful. We now have taken other measures to protect the sovereignty of Turkey.

Karl Marx and other historians made it plain that Soviet aspirations differ little from czarist aspirations. And certainly, Mr. Molotov's 1940 demands are a good general signpost for the immediate future.

As to whether the Soviet Union seeks security or expansion, I suppose the Soviets themselves, in analyzing their motives, would find it difficult to tell exactly where security ends and expansion begins. And if they did know the dividing line, I am certain they would not admit it. In considering this question, I keep thinking of the kind of people—and many of us know them—who buy the house or farm adjoining theirs for protection. The difficulty always is that there is another adjoining house or farm. So it is with the Soviets who think the governments adjoining the Soviet Union or its satellites must be "friendly governments" for their security. The chief difference is that the Soviets do not buy the adjoining territory and they have no scruples about violating laws and pledges to acquire the property they want for security.

Frequently people ask whether, in the name of security, the Soviets intend to dominate all of continental Europe. I think they want in all European states a sufficient number of organized Communists so that they can dictate the policies of these states. I do not think they want to take over all European governments now. They fear the people of western Europe would not accept the form of government existing in the Soviet Union. They realize also that in most of those countries they have not yet trained leaders who could make such governments succeed, and failure would impair their prestige all over the world. For the present, while developing local leaders, they are satisfied to bide their time. By the threat of strikes and by encouraging discontent, they can in many states exert power without having responsibility. Greece is apparently their first objective. They are likely to seek next, through the usual infiltration method, control of the Italian Government. This would be because of the military effect it would have on Greece and Turkey. I do not doubt that their ultimate goal is to dominate, in one way or another, all of Europe.

In determining our course of action, Karl Marx is helpful. In 1853, about the Czar's demands on Turkey, he wrote:

"It would have been impossible for Russia to make more extensive demands upon Turkey after a series of signal victories. . . . *If the other powers hold firm, Russia is sure to retire in a very decent manner.*"

Should the Soviet Government get the impression that the United States and other members of the United Nations will only voice protests and will do nothing, Russia will continue the pursuit of these historic objectives. The Soviet Government will do as it did shortly after the Yalta Conference in connection with Rumania; it will take over a government and then say the matter has been settled and there is no excuse for further discussion.

But, on the other hand, if it is made to realize now that if it commits an act of aggression, we will appeal immediately to the Security Council of the United Nations; if we make it clear that a Soviet veto in the Security Council will bring a call upon the other United Nations to act collectively to support and enforce the principles of the Charter—if these things are made clear, I do not believe the Soviets will violate the integrity of Iran, Turkey, Greece, Italy, or any other country.

For many reasons the Soviets do not want war now. They will, I believe, "retire in a very decent manner." But if the other powers do not "hold firm" then, as Marx warned us of the czarist Russians, "conquest follows conquest and annexation follows annexation."

We must not indulge in idle threats. We must not start anything we do not intend to finish. We must meet aggression and pressure with firm resistance. At the same time, we must be just and objective in our analysis of each situation. We should always keep the hand of friendship extended. And we should constantly make clear our earnest desire to live at peace with our neighbors.

Soviet policy, as it stands today, is fairly well revealed by the historic record I have cited. I should like to point to one other guidepost. It is the speech Stalin made to his Communist Party comrades at the time of the first postwar election—February 9, 1946. A speech on such an occasion and to such an audience is a far more reliable guide, I believe, than the statements made to visiting Americans and foreign correspondents. In it Stalin had this to say of the future:

I have no doubt that if we render the necessary assistance to our scientists they will be able not only to overtake but also in the very near future to surpass the achievements outside the boundaries of our country. As far as plans for a longer period are concerned, the Party intends to organize a mighty upsurge of national economy which will enable us to increase the level of our production, for instance, three-fold as compared with the prewar level.

To achieve this, we must endeavor to see that our industry produces 50 million tons of pig iron per year; 60 million tons of steel; 500 million tons of coal and 60 million tons of oil.

Only under such conditions will our country be insured against any eventuality. Perhaps three new Five-Year Plans will be required to achieve this, if not more. But it can be done and we must do it.

Time is not all on the side of the Soviet Government.

In seeking to answer the question, "What are they like?" I have said nothing of the Russian people. I have spoken only of the Russian leaders. They are the only Russians I know. Few Americans have been able to really learn much about the Russian people.

In evaluating present Russian policy, we can ignore the mass of Russians: they have no more influence on Soviet foreign policy today than they did under the Czars. But in considering future policy, we must not ignore them. They are, I believe, our hope. I cannot believe that the Russian peasant, who fought with such valor to defend his own home and land, really wants to impose foreign rule on people like himself. I cannot believe that the Russian worker, who only a few years ago emerged from conditions approaching slavery, would knowingly deprive other workers in other lands of their freedom.

I once said "there is no iron curtain that the aggregate sentiments of mankind cannot penetrate." I believe that. And I also believe there is a reasonable chance that we have enough time at our disposal to bring those sentiments to bear on the people and the leaders of the Soviet Union.

I also have said that "we must guard against the belief that delays or setbacks in achieving our objective make armed conflict inevitable." It is one of the beliefs held by the Soviet leaders that makes our task so difficult. But we will never be able to rid them or the rest of the world of that belief if we ourselves become its victims.

Neither is time necessarily on the Russian side in the non-Soviet countries.

Today the Soviets have armies in Germany, Austria, Poland, Rumania, Bulgaria, Hungary and Manchuria. An occupation army is an idle army and an idle army is a bad army. The very purpose of retaining soldiers in a foreign country is to restrict the lives and liberties of the people of that country. People who want to be free resent the presence of occupation troops and they grow to hate the country that keeps them there. They grow also to hate, perhaps even more intensely, the puppets who are kept in office by a foreign army. As long as the army is there, the people are cowed into submission. But when the Red Army leaves, the legacy of hatred it leaves behind will mean a difficult and uncertain future for the puppets in government and in the militia.

The Soviet Government cannot indefinitely find reasons for keeping troops in these states. Five treaties of peace already have been concluded. The Soviet Union has not yet ratified the treaties, but I think it will. Our Senate did not ratify them until four months after they were submitted. When they are ratified, it will be difficult for the Soviets to postpone for long the reduction in occupation forces that these treaties require. These states then become eligible for admission to the United Nations. Once they are members, it is then the obligation of all the United Nations to protect them from pressure and aggression. The sooner we prove to these countries that this obligation will be discharged, the sooner they will be encouraged to assert their independence.

I conclude that the Russians are after everything they set forth in the written statement to Hitler, together with a number of additional "aspirations" they have developed as a result of their success in the war.

The Soviets did not tell Hitler their aspirations because of their love and affection for him. They told him only because they feared that if they tried to take territory without his consent, he would use force to stop them. Today there is no military strength in Europe to restrain the Russians. Only the power of the United Nations can do it. The United Nations must make known its determination to act to protect the threatened states. And the United States must make known its determination to use all of its power to support the action of the United Nations.

Chapter 15

Where Do We Go from Here?

IN THE preceding chapters, I have tried to indicate where we are and how we got here. I have done so in the hope that it may help us to decide what to do and how to do it. Having gone thus far, I feel I should not avoid drawing out of my experience some thoughts on the question that is disturbing all of us: Where do we go from here?

There is no easy answer. For the ills of a war-torn world there are no speedy cures, no panaceas. I believe that mankind *can* build a lasting and a just peace. And I believe, also, that we must guard equally against the ready optimists who believe that only an act of faith is necessary to do it, and the reckless pessimists who are convinced that only another war can do it.

The charting of a course of action is always a hazardous enterprise. It is especially so when it is complicated by the fact that I deliver this manuscript to the publisher on July 1, 1947, and the book will not be ready for sale until mid-October. In these days of kaleidoscopic change only a prophet or a soothsayer would venture to predict what will happen in those three months. I am neither. I am keenly aware that each day brings a new crisis, and the crisis of today is frequently forgotten tomorrow. Obviously, then, opinions expressed today, based on existing facts and circumstances, may require extensive alteration or may even be entirely irrelevant in light of the facts and circumstances three months from now. With this qualification, I suggest some steps I believe we should take down the long road toward peace.

I believe we should immediately seek the early conclusion of treaties with Austria, Germany and Japan. In preceding chapters, I have suggested the course I would follow to secure those treaties and I earnestly hope the Soviet Union will see the wisdom of joining in this endeavor. But Russia's opposition must not deter the other nations from a course they know is right and indispensable to the reconstruction of the world. It is a course that requires dedication to the principle of collective action. It requires courage.

The importance of the objectives demands action. Continuation of a state of war, with its perpetuation of military governments and large armies of occupation, is a constant threat to peace and security. It jeopardizes the economic and political well-being of millions of people in Allied as well as ex-enemy states.

Even as we plan these peace settlements, many developments abroad have made us question the permanency of the peace. Ever since the war ended in Europe, we have had reason for concern in the Soviet attitude toward Greece and Turkey. The gallant Greeks, by their heroic stand against the Italians and later the Nazis, won the admiration of liberty-loving people the world over. Unfortunately, the withdrawal of enemy troops did not bring the difficulties and sufferings of the Greek people to an end. Almost immediately, they were confronted with civil war. The Greek Government believed the attacks were inspired, and certainly encouraged, by the Soviet satellites.

British troops finally took a hand and restored order. But since the summer of 1945, there has been unrest in Greece. Guerrilla warfare in the areas adjoining Albania, Yugoslavia and Bulgaria has kept the Greek Army occupied and prevented the restoration of the shattered economy of Greece. The Greek Government believes that guerrilla troops trained in Yugoslavia, Albania, and Bulgaria cross the border and, after raiding a community, return to foreign territory. This belief has been supported, in part at least, by the findings of the United Nations Balkan Commission of Investigation. The guerrillas are assisted by Greek Communists. Last year the people living in that area did not plant crops because they did not expect to be able to harvest them. Families left the farms and sought the greater protection of the city. In resisting these attacks and in protecting its citizens, the government resorted to measures that many people regarded as oppressive.

While in Paris in 1946, I frequently saw the Prime Minister of Greece, Mr. Constantin Tsaldaris, and members of his government. The Prime Minister's position was that those of us who did not receive daily reports of the killing of Greek soldiers and civilians might criticize what we considered oppressive measures, but that the problem was not easy for one with the responsibility of upholding the integrity of Greek territory.

In the election of early summer 1946, the Greeks voted for the monarchy and for the return of the King. Some persons, who were in Greece at the time of the election and whom I think well informed, believe that the people were not in favor of the monarchy but regarded it as the only alternative to Communism, to which they were genuinely opposed. After the election, the Prime Minister told me that the King was anxious, and so was he, to bring into the government representatives of liberal parties—a course which I had urged upon him. However, he did not succeed in his efforts.

During the peace conference, on about October 1, the Prime Minister told me that the need to devote a large part of the national income to military expenditures aggravated what, in any event, would be a bad economic situation. Greece, he said, needed financial assistance and its army needed additional military equipment. In response to my inquiry, he said that Britain had been furnishing them with military supplies and had agreed to continue such assistance. I told him we could help them with military equipment only to the extent that it was available from surplus property then in Europe. I requested the officer in charge of that property to assist Greece in every way possible. I also told Prime Minister Tsaldaris that in the absence of appropriations by Congress, I could not promise a financial advance for relief, but if Congress made the appropriation of 350 million dollars for relief which we intended to request, Greece would certainly receive a liberal share. I also told him I would urge favorable action by the Export-Import Bank on an application for a loan and would grant his request to appoint a commission to visit Greece and make an economic survey. This survey subsequently was made by a commission headed by Mr. Paul Porter.

Mr. Tsaldaris was in New York in December 1946, and again discussed Greece's needs with me. I invited him to Washington to talk with officials of the Export-Import Bank and Under Secretary Clayton about his request for assistance. Before his arrival, President Truman and I surveyed the situation with the directors of the Export-Import Bank. They said that, under the statute, they could not make a loan unless they had "reasonable assurance of its repayment," and they doubted whether this condition could be met for Greece considering the unsettled conditions there. They said they would consider the application, but I realized that there was little hope for a loan to Greece unless the law was changed.

While Mr. Tsaldaris was in New York, I discussed the Greek situation with Mr. Bevin. Britain, he told me, had been helping Greece both financially and militarily. His government would continue to help with military equipment but he hoped we would provide economic assistance. He said the British were anxious to withdraw their troops from Greece and several other places whenever and wherever it could properly be done. However, at no time did he indicate that, regardless of conditions in Greece, Britain would withdraw its troops on March 31, 1947, or any other specific date.

A somewhat similar situation existed in Turkey. Economic conditions in Turkey were better than in Greece, but Turkey's sovereignty was—and is—in just as much, if not greater danger. There may be some debate about the aspirations of the Soviet Union in Greece but there is no doubt about its aspirations in Turkey.

The record shows: (1) Molotov's request to Hitler in 1939 for approval of the establishment of a Soviet naval base in the Straits; (2) Stalin's reiteration of this desire at Potsdam; (3) the Soviet Government's direct request to Turkey for naval base rights and for the cession of the provinces of Kars and Ardahan. This war of nerves has required Turkey to keep under arms from 700,000 to 900,000 men. It is impossible for Turkey to maintain such an army without devoting to military expenditures the revenue needed to rehabilitate and develop its economy.

In the fall of 1946, I took the same position toward Turkey that I took toward Greece—we could not furnish military equipment but would do everything possible to help economically. I told Turkey's representatives that I would recommend that they receive a share of the 350 million dollars relief appropriation if Congress approved it, and that I would urge sympathetic consideration of a loan for reconstruction purposes.

At about the same time, the Turkish Government informed us of a communication from the Soviet Union renewing the demand for base rights in the Straits. We immediately advised Turkey that we adhered to our position of the previous November—that the revision of the Montreux Convention should be the subject of an international conference. We could not agree that control of the Straits was a matter of concern only to the Black Sea powers, or that Turkey and the Soviet Union should jointly organize for the defense of the Straits. Defense of the Straits, we said, should be based upon, and administered in accordance with, the purposes and principles of the United Nations. We asserted that we would insist upon this course.

This was the situation on January 20, 1947, when I left the Department of State. About March 1, the British Government informed the United States that it could give no further economic or military aid to Greece and Turkey after March 31.

On March 12, 1947, President Truman appeared before the Congress. He said that the United States had received from the Greek Government an urgent appeal for economic and military assistance without which Greece could not survive as a free nation. Britain, he said, was no longer able to furnish the necessary assistance.

"We must assist free peoples to work out their own destiny in their own way," President Truman declared. He urged Congress to appropriate 400 million dollars to aid Greece and Turkey with supplies and military equipment for the period ending June 30, 1948. In addition, he asked for authority to detail American military personnel to Greece and Turkey for the instruction and training of selected Turkish and Greek personnel.

Without having firsthand information, I am of the opinion that the disastrous weather conditions in Britain last winter, the labor strikes, and, particularly, the shortage of dollars, all combined to make British Treasury officials nervous, influencing the British Government to give us sudden notice of their intention to withdraw assistance from Turkey and Greece by March 31.

The financial condition of the British Government, I assumed, required it to stop financial assistance to these two countries. But I was certain, notwithstanding the statements made by some of our officials, that Britain would not withdraw its troops from Greece on March 31, or until we had an opportunity to determine our own course of action. The British do not act that way.

I did not misjudge them—their troops are still in Greece as of this date, July 1. They are reported to have approximately 8,000 troops there. We propose to send not more than seventy-five army and navy officers. Even our military authorities would admit that seventy-five American officers could not take the place of 8,000 British soldiers in protecting Greece against aggression. But the knowledge that we stand ready to do whatever is necessary to protect Greece against aggression gives comfort to the Greeks and a warning to potential aggressors.

While I think the British acted nervously in announcing withdrawal of assistance from these countries, I believe we were equally nervous—but right—in our response to this notification. I say we were "right" because, under the circumstances, we could not refuse to help. I say "nervous" because of some of the reasons given for the assistance; reasons which seemed to imply that we would oppose the efforts of Communists in any country to gain control of the government, even when they acted without the interference of a foreign government and through the free votes of their own people. That was not and should never be the position of our government. There is a vast difference between taking control of a government by honest ballots and taking control by bullets—or as a result of the threat of a foreign power. However, in a government like ours, different reasons may inspire different individuals in Congress and in the executive branch of the government to reach the same conclusion. The important thing is that the action in this case was correct—we had to give assistance.

We were justified in furnishing military supplies. We did not have to decide that the Turkish Government and the Greek monarchy were outstanding examples of free and democratic governments. We were not interfering in the internal affairs of those states. Greece had complained to the Security Council that her border was being violated by nationals of Yugoslavia, Bulgaria and Albania. If true, and if the aggression was countenanced by these governments, it constituted a threat to the peace of the world.

When Greece first asked for an investigation into this threat to the peace, the Soviet Union opposed it. The Council of Foreign Ministers was then meeting in New York. At that particular time Molotov had agreed with me on several questions and I was encouraged to ask for his co-operation. I told Mr. Molotov that the Soviet Union and the United States shared responsibility for maintaining the peace and I felt certain he could relieve the Greek situation by using his influence with Yugoslavia, Albania and Bulgaria. He said these three were not at fault; that the Greek Government was corrupt and did not have the confidence of the people. I disagreed and gave my reasons. In my second conversation with him, I told him that since his information was so different from mine, the sensible thing for us to do was to get the facts and then we might agree upon a remedy. Finally, to my surprise, he instructed his representative on the Security Council to support the resolution for an investigation. It was adopted, and I appointed Mr. Mark Ethridge to represent the United States.

From the outset, the commission met difficulties and delays—which our representative charged primarily to Greece's neighbors—even while the Greek Government continued to complain of more attacks from across its borders.

It was under these circumstances that the President addressed the Congress. He did not declare that it should become a permanent doctrine of the United States that, whenever we consider the independence of a free nation threatened, we should act unilaterally and, if necessary, use military power to prevent aggression. That is what the United Nations was created to do. The United States did not intend to by-pass the United Nations or to destroy or to cripple it. And the statement of the President does not warrant such an interpretation.

Senator Vandenberg made the position of the United States clear when he offered, and the Senate adopted, an amendment to the resolution authorizing assistance, which recognizes the right of the United Nations to assume jurisdiction over the situation in Greece and Turkey whenever it considers such action desirable.

Today the United Nations has no military force—owing again to the delaying tactics of the Soviet representative on the Military Staff Committee of the Security Council. The United States as one of the sponsors of the United Nations was compelled to let the Soviet Government and the world know that while the Security Council was investigating alleged acts of aggression against the Greek Government, we would act to maintain the status quo until the council could reach a decision, or had the military strength to control the situation. We were helping, not harming, the United Nations. And until it has such strength we must maintain the status quo in Turkey.

My belief that firmness brings results is also fortified by the Iranian case. There, as in Greece and in Turkey, the Soviet Union was seeking to fulfill one of its historic aims. The pattern was the same. Under the protection of the Red Army a puppet government had been installed in the province of Azerbaijan. We repeatedly warned the Soviet Union that the United States, as well as the Soviet Government, was pledged by the Teheran Declaration signed by Roosevelt, Stalin and Churchill to protect the sovereignty of Iran. I personally stressed to Stalin that, if Iran protested to the United Nations, we would support Iran. But all our efforts failed to convince the Soviet Government that we would fulfill our Teheran pledge. Therefore, when Iran appealed to the Security Council, we acted.

As so often happens in public affairs, the main battle was fought over a subsidiary issue; the right of Iran to present its case to the Security Council. I felt that if a precedent was established that denied any country the right of speedy access to the Security Council, the United Nations would be crippled from birth. I felt so strongly, in fact, about both the issue of Iran's sovereignty and the issue of ready access to the Security Council, that I personally argued the American case before the Security Council. Soviet resistance extended even to the point where Mr. Gromyko "walked out" on the Security Council. But firmness and the United Nations won.

Generalissimo Stalin announced the withdrawal of his troops in a telegram to the president of a news agency rather than to the Security Council. And then, last December, the puppet regime collapsed. The people of Iran were not fooled by Soviet propaganda. When Allied observers went into Azerbaijan with the Iranian authorities they were greeted with cries of "Long Live the United Nations." It is a cheer we should not forget in the months and years ahead.

The Security Council never took action in a formal sense, but it was the forum which made it possible for Iran to appeal to the conscience of the world. The Soviet Government may make renewed efforts to fulfill its aims toward Iran. Nevertheless, we can take heart from this example of firm and positive action within the framework of the United Nations.

Similar firmness is required in the case of Hungary. There, the Soviets have deliberately caused the removal of Hungarian government officials who received 57 per cent of the votes cast in an election which Stalin and Molotov have heretofore called free. The Hungarian Prime Minister has been driven from office and the Communists have taken charge. The Prime Minister declares that this action was dictated by the Soviet Government. There is corroborating evidence. If the Prime Minister's charges are true, the action in Hungary is a violation of the pledges made by the Soviet Union to its Allies at Yalta. I do not know what action the United States and the United Kingdom will take. But I know what I think they should do. They should call upon the Security Council to investigate and determine whether or not the facts constitute aggression. If the council makes that finding, it should require that the government be turned back to the political party that received 57 per cent of the votes of the people; or it should take some similar action that would assure the Hungarians their right to an independent existence free of the coercion of the Soviet Government.

We expect to act if there is aggression against Turkey and Greece. Why should we not act in the case of Hungary when there is evidence that the Soviets have already done there what we say will make us act in Turkey and Greece? Because of the events in Hungary, our government has canceled a credit of approximately 15 million dollars to buy our surplus property. If we have evidence to justify the suspension of credit and the filing of protests, we certainly have evidence sufficient to justify a request for an investigation.

We can not sit idly by simply because the Soviets have not formally ratified the treaty with Hungary. That treaty was agreed to by Foreign Minister Molotov and ratified by Great Britain, France and the United States. The Soviets should not be allowed to profit by their own delay. If, by the same methods, the Soviets tomorrow should take control of the Italian Government, we certainly would do more than protest, even though the Italian Treaty has not been ratified. I think the case of Hungary comes within the spirit of the declaration of policy made to Congress by President Truman on Greece and Turkey. Therefore, we should not now establish a precedent of inaction.

At all these points of present danger to the peace of the world—Iran, Greece, Turkey, Hungary and the other Balkan states—it can be argued that the national interest of the Soviet Union is involved or that fear and suspicion prompt her action. That may be true, but the unilateral pursuit of national interest, plus fear and suspicion, can lead to conflict—conflict that is contrary to the interest of all peoples.

Changes in power relations always tend to create uneasiness in the world. Russia long has been an important power, but never before has it been so clearly the dominant power on the European continent. When the power of any state has greatly increased, there naturally is concern regarding its possible further expansion. This is particularly true when the leaders of the expanding state have an aggressive ideology.

There is particular uneasiness in the world when a power—like the Soviet Union—acquires great strength in relation to others, but lags behind them in its own internal standard of living.

Other governments besides the Soviet Union seek territory. France wants the Saar. Greece has expressed a desire to annex Epirus. The Netherlands desires a slice of German territory adjoining its border. Belgium also may ask for adjoining German territory. The difference is that these governments seek changes through international machinery, either the peace conference or the Council of Foreign Ministers, whereas the Soviets apparently prefer to seek changes through unilateral action. That action frequently takes the course of political infiltration.

The Charter of the United Nations pledges all members to "refrain from the threat or use of force against the territorial integrity or political independence of any state." The definition is not restricted to armed invasion. It can mean coercion, pressure or subterfuge such as political infiltration.

The threat of political infiltration is especially grave in the countries whose political and economic structures were shattered by the war. Inevitably, it provokes countermeasures in retaliation. A situation can readily develop where all concerned come to believe they are acting in self-defense. Soon it becomes possible for a spark to start a fire that may engulf the whole world.

If we are to prevent such a holocaust, not only must we halt acts of aggression, but we must seek to eradicate the causes of those acts. In many countries, as a result of the war, the people are without adequate shelter and without adequate nourishment, and become easy prey to aggressive ideologies which offer them the illusion of escape from the hard realities of their daily existence. If we want these people to value freedom and respect law, we must give them at least the chance to feed, clothe and shelter themselves and their families, and give them the necessary means to keep internal order. We must give them the feeling that they can have an independent life without becoming satellites of Russia, the United States or any other power.

In extending economic aid, we must not seek to control the people of a country, but rather we must seek to make them free. We must have confidence that if we give people the opportunity to be free, they will not wish to be dependent upon us or upon any other power. Where there is no freedom, we must make sure that our economic aid is not turned against us.

We must make it unmistakably plain that we are not competing with the Soviet Union for the control of other states. Rather, we should stress that we would welcome a real and bona fide willingness on the part of the Soviet Union to collaborate in rebuilding and protecting political and economic independence.

I would not be speaking frankly, however, if I did not repeat that thus far our efforts to collaborate with the Soviet Union have met with little or no success. My efforts in this direction are told in the preceding chapters. And today we have before us Mr. Molotov's rejection of the plans advanced by Mr. Bevin and Mr. Bidault in response to the proposal made by Secretary Marshall on June 5. In his speech at Harvard University, Secretary Marshall called upon European nations to agree on "the requirements of the situation and the part those countries themselves will take in order to give proper effect to whatever action might be undertaken by this Government."

Secretary Marshall did not say the United States would furnish any specified amount to aid the program agreed upon. He said simply that we would support "such a program as far as it may be practical for us to do so." But other officials of the government have made statements which are quoted abroad, estimating that such a program would cost us from five to six billion dollars a year for four or five years. These estimates were made even before the European governments met, indicating that our officials have some idea of what the over-all program should be. Certainly the estimates have whetted the appetites of many European officials.

I welcome the initiative of Mr. Bevin and Mr. Bidault, but political realities demand that in welcoming this program to advance Europe's economic recovery, we should also express some words of caution. It should be made clear that the United States will determine, in the light of its resources, the amount of aid to be extended, where the money will be spent, and what conditions, if any, will be attached to its expenditure.

Some European governments and peoples do not understand that a member of the executive branch of our government cannot make a financial commitment until Congress actually appropriates the funds. We should make sure they do not proceed in the belief that any program agreed to by them will automatically be paid for by us. Unless this is done, a subsequent refusal by Congress to provide money for the agreed program will cause misunderstandings and disappointments which will dangerously affect our relations with European states.

In considering what the Congress may do, we must not overlook what has been done recently. We did not try to extend the life of UNRRA because it was decided that, instead of other governments allocating funds appropriated by us for relief, the United States should make the allocation. When the Congress authorized 350 million dollars for relief, it did not leave it to the executive department to determine where it should be spent. It specified that 335 million dollars would be available only in Austria, Greece, Hungary, Italy, Poland, Trieste and China, and only 15 million dollars should be available for relief in other states. It also provided for supervision and control of expenditures in every country by missions of American citizens.

And again, the recent legislation authorizing 400 million dollars for military and economic aid to Greece and Turkey, which was passed by Congress and approved by the President, provides that the money should be spent under the supervision of an American committee, the chairman of which must be approved by the Senate.

Mr. Molotov's action in late June in refusing to attend the Paris Economic Conference unless he could first know the terms and conditions under which the United States would furnish financial aid, and could receive certain assurances that the sovereignty of states would not be interfered with, was disappointing to all who favor world co-operation. However, I do not agree with some officials and editors who think this refusal is conclusive proof that the Soviets want chaotic conditions to continue in Europe.

Judging by the Soviets' refusal to co-operate in other matters, it is entirely possible that they may not object to a continuance of unrest in Europe. Nevertheless, Mr. Molotov's action in this matter is open to a different interpretation. The invitation of Britain and France placed him in an embarrassing position. The satellite states, like all people in financial distress, must have welcomed the invitation to inform the United States of the financial assistance they needed, particularly when the news reports indicated that the assistance would be a gift instead of a loan. If the Soviets now bring pressure on them not to accept financial help from the United States, the Soviets themselves will have to help the satellites economically, and consequently they will retard their own reconstruction projects.

I think that Mr. Molotov's refusal to participate is influenced by the same fear that has made him refuse to co-operate in our atomic energy proposal and many other proposals—the fear that they would be forced to agree to inspection by representatives of other governments who could demand the right to freely travel in the Soviet Union.

Mr. Molotov has consistently objected to every proposal that involves inspection by representatives of other powers in areas under Soviet control. Evidently, Molotov now thinks that if we require supervision or inspection in giving economic aid to friendly countries like Greece and Turkey, we shall insist upon similar arrangements in helping other countries. My guess is that the Soviets will continue to refuse to co-operate in the Paris Conference unless they have some assurance that there will be no inspection and supervision in the Soviet Union or in areas under Soviet control by representatives of the United States.

On this July 1, my opinion is that Mr. Molotov, by refusing to co-operate, has without intending to, settled a difficult problem for the United States Government. Had the Soviets and its satellites attended the Paris Conference, it is fair to assume that Britain and France, who are certain to recommend financial assistance for themselves, would also have recommended that we advance large sums for reconstruction in the Soviet Union and in its satellites. That would have posed for our Congress a question as embarrassing to it as the invitation of Britain and France was to Molotov. The proposal to help all needy European countries was, I assume, submitted to the leaders of both political parties before it was made. But even so, we can only speculate about the action of the Congress under those circumstances.

If Congress required the same supervision of expenditures that is required in the cases of Turkey and Greece and the relief appropriations, the Soviets and the satellites would have refused to accept the assistance. They would have declared that they should have been informed of those conditions when the offer of assistance was made. On the other hand, if Congress was asked to make a large appropriation for the Soviet Union and its satellite states without any supervision, the chances are that Congress would not make the appropriation. By refusing to attend the Paris Conference, Mr. Molotov has saved the Congress this difficult decision. He has assumed the burden of dividing Europe into two economic and political spheres.

The American people and the Congress realize that we must deal with the causes of unrest in the world and not merely with its symptoms. The need for help has proved greater than expected. And the rise in the American price level since the war makes necessary larger grants and credits than previously were thought necessary. Nevertheless, I am convinced they will make the sacrifices necessary to build the peace. But the program must be a reasonable one. If it is not, I fear the Congress will not appropriate adequate funds. Should that happen, it would have been better if aid had never been proposed.

As a first step toward restoring Europe's economy, we should concentrate on projects that will help to remove the economic bottlenecks which keep the individual states from increasing their trade and production. It does not require the agreement of all European governments or even an extensive inquiry to determine those bottlenecks—we know them.

First of all, we should use not only our money but our brains to devise means of increasing Europe's coal production. The need for coal is at the heart of nearly every European nation's economic problem. And the heart of Europe's coal problem lies in the Ruhr.

In the peacetime years before 1939, the mines of the Ruhr produced about 440,000 tons of hard coal per day. In May 1947, two years after the end of the war in Europe, those mines produced only 214,000 tons per day. Some of the shortage is being offset by purchases from the mines of the United States. But coal produced in the Ruhr region costs ten dollars a ton while West Virginia coal laid down in Naples, for example, costs twenty-two dollars a ton. This year, European states will pay approximately 600 million dollars for coal from the United States. The money will come in part from funds loaned to them by the United States. This is an uneconomic and wasteful process. It should be stopped at the earliest possible moment.

Disorganization and faulty administration of the Ruhr's production and distribution is a factor in this situation. Lack of improved machinery is another. But the main reason is much more understandable. A miner needs to work only two days a week to earn the money necessary for the limit of his rations. There is nothing else in the Ruhr for him to purchase. The future of his country is so uncertain that there is no incentive to save, and he has no confidence in the money he is paid. Improving the lot of the German coal miner may raise storms of protests from those who want to punish the Germans. But without such action, not only the Germans will be punished, but all Europeans.

We can start work on this problem now without waiting for other countries to agree. A substantial increase in the ration of the Ruhr miner, improved mine machinery from the United States, and some plan to provide more consumer goods for the miner and his family would be reflected almost immediately in an increased output of coal.

The coal mines of Silesia also are important producers. We should consider means of increasing production there. But our aid should be advanced only on the condition that a portion of the coal is made available to those countries of western Europe which prior to the war relied on Silesia for their coal. Even though Poland does not attend the Economic Conference at Paris, we can confer with its representative and try to solve this problem.

After coal, we should consider how to increase the production and availability of electric power. The last time I saw President Roosevelt, I introduced to him General Clay who was leaving for Germany. I told the President that Clay, who is an engineer, had built a great power project in Texas. The President immediately told us of his pet project—the building of a power project in Central Europe. He foresaw that fuel would be the main European problem.

We must be careful not to become preoccupied with the economic problems of Europe alone. The reconstruction of Asia's economy also is vital to world stability. There, as well as in Europe, the projects we help to finance should be the kind that give hope and increasing opportunities for self-support to those who are trying to rebuild their shattered lives. The advances of science have made it possible for all nations to preserve and increase their living standards if they work together to produce what they want and need.

The mere statement of the problem shows its immensity. What we in the United States do must be done within the limits of our resources. It would not contribute to the long-range goal of world stability if, in order to meet present emergencies, we drained away our economic lifeblood.

Prosperity, like freedom, must be shared, not on the basis of "handouts," but on the basis of fair and honest exchange of the products of free men and women. If we want repayment for the help we give, we must be willing to accept goods and services as part of that repayment. But we cannot realistically expect repayment until Europe's economy is placed on a self-supporting basis.

A world with working economies able to provide its people with food, shelter, clothing, schools and other necessities, will be a much easier world with which to deal. But while we are working toward economic recovery, we must continue working in other fields as well. Equally important is the building of a system of collective security.

Through collective action, Germany and Japan have been decisively defeated. Neither of them has the capacity to wage war. Neither of them will have the capacity to wage war for a generation unless the Allies, choosing to use them as pawns or as partners in a struggle for power, permit them to rebuild their armaments. Surely, we have learned enough from our experience following World War I to know that if the peace terms are to be changed it is better to revise them ourselves than to permit our former enemies to acquire the arms with which to dictate revision.

As a concrete demonstration of our desire to see that these countries stay demilitarized, I have proposed that the four great powers join in a forty-year treaty with provisions to insure that neither Germany nor Japan again threaten the peace of the world. The treaty provides for swift punishment if there is violation of its terms. And it provides for certain punishment by denying to any one of the four powers the right to veto action.

Acceptance of this treaty is a clear test of the sincerity of any nation's intentions of keeping these countries disarmed. Britain and France have endorsed it. It was agreed to in principle by Generalissimo Stalin but since has been opposed stoutly by Mr. Molotov. We should again call for acceptance of this treaty. If the Soviet Government continues to reject our offer, we will have reason to fear the future.

I still have hope that the treaty will be adopted. I believe that when the Soviets realize we are going to maintain American armed forces in Germany as long as there are occupation armies there, they will accept the treaty. It will take them a long time to get over the rapid disintegration of our military power in Europe after V-E Day. They were then inspired to hope that the United States was withdrawing its power from Europe. A conclusion nurtured by a desire is slow in changing, but this is one conclusion that the Soviet leaders, sooner or later and whether they like it or not, will have to change. As I stated at Stuttgart—"We are in Europe to stay."

Adoption of this forty-year treaty would be additional testimony of our belief in the principle of collective security which has reached its culmination in the Charter of the United Nations. I do not agree with those who declare that Russia's failure to co-operate has destroyed the United Nations. I still think our greatest hope for peace lies in supporting and developing the United Nations. It has much greater potentialities than is generally realized. And it gives us the opportunity to advance the co-operative ventures which alone can assure peace.

It has been said that the success of the United Nations depends upon the ability of the great powers to work together. Such a statement is only partly true. It is true that if the great powers co-operate to maintain peace, there is little chance that any one power will take the risk of breaking the peace. But co-operation of all the great powers, while devoutly to be hoped for and worked for, is not indispensable. I deny that the Charter of the United Nations—which unqualifiedly commits the member states to settle their disputes by peaceful means and to refrain from the use of force except in defense of the principles of the Charter—can be nullified by a single vote of a permanent member of the Security Council.

It is a fact that the Security Council can not *require* the member states to take action unless there is unanimity among the permanent members. But that does not mean that the members are not free to act, and should not regard themselves as morally bound to act, if there is a clear violation of the Charter.

Of course, a state in honest doubt about whether there has been a violation of the Charter ought not to be bound, morally or otherwise, to take action simply because one side or the other happens to get a certain number of votes in the council. But there are principles of law incorporated in the Charter which should be regarded as the law of all lands. These principles *will* be regarded as the law of all lands if we and all other members of the United Nations make it clear that we are determined, if need be, to defend them by force.

If we and the other powers are prepared to act in defense of law, the United Nations can prevent war. We must make it clear, also, that we will not use force for any other purpose.

But it follows, then, that if we are going to do our part to defend these principles, we must maintain our power to do so. We must not further reduce the appropriations for the Army and Navy. We must encourage and promote continued scientific research, and we must adopt some plan of universal military training. The force of an argument in an international conference is not lessened by the existence of military power at home.

Making clear that we are ready to enforce the Charter is not a threat or a hostile act against any nation. It is rather the spirit and vitality that will give strength to the rule of law among nations. It is the attitude toward the law that must be evident if law is to be respected.

I do not believe the Soviet Union wants war. But Soviet statesmen seem to believe it is their duty to struggle to the utmost to advance their power and interest. We must make it absolutely clear that, if they carry the struggle beyond definite limits, the law will be enforced against them. Otherwise, they may transgress those limits in the mistaken belief that we will not challenge their transgressions.

We must be ready to recognize, however, that many issues admit of honest differences of opinion. We cannot and must not claim infallibility for our policy decisions. We certainly must not expect less warmth in the arguments in the United Nations than we have in our own Congress, our own legislatures, and our own city halls.

Diversity of thought and competition in ideas can make both for progress and for peace if we are willing to meet one indispensable condition—respect for the right of others to ideas, opinions and ways of life we do not share. Others must equally respect our right to ideas, opinions and ways of life they do not share.

There is and always has been room in this world for more than one ideology and more than one way of life. There is room for the Soviet way of life and for the American way of life. The belief in the inevitability of conflict between ideologies is more likely to produce conflict than it is to enshrine any single ideology or way of life in this world. Even the unfortunate division of Europe into two economic and political spheres does not justify talk of the inevitability of conflict. There is too much talk of war and too little of peace. We need not fear the result if we use our power but we must fear the unnecessary use of our power. Should all our efforts for peace fail, we want to be sure in our own minds that the fault is not ours.

Even in these chaotic postwar years, the United Nations has been a powerful instrument for peace.

The Charter of the United Nations came into force as a fundamental law for the peoples of the world on October 24, 1945, when as Secretary of State I announced that the necessary number of ratifications had been obtained. As I look back over the events which have crowded the life of the United Nations since that date, I recall that the League of Nations was in existence nearly eleven months before its Assembly had its first meeting. The United Nations General Assembly, on the other hand, convened for the first time in London in January 1946. In October 1946, it met again in regular session and, in May 1947, in special session.

At its first meeting it brought into being the Security Council, the Economic and Social Council, the International Court of Justice, and it elected a Secretary General to begin the task of organizing a Secretariat—civil servants to the world.

The United Nations Security Council—unlike the Council of the League which met but four times a year—has been in almost continuous session. The clash of interests among the permanent members of the council has hampered its efficiency but has not yet sapped its vitality. The influence of the Council in the Iranian case I have cited. The integrity of Greece has been protected by the presence of a Security Council Commission of Investigation. British and French troops were withdrawn from Syria and Lebanon in accordance with a majority decision of the council. The negotiated settlement of the territorial dispute between France and Siam, and the prompt compliance by Yugoslavia with United States' demands in connection with attacks on our airplanes are examples where the *possi-*

bility of Security Council action stimulated peaceful adjustment of the situations.

We should not overlook these positive contributions in the midst of disappointment over the lack of progress in the Security Council's related agencies—the Atomic Energy Commission, the Commission on Conventional Armaments and the Military Staff Committee. To these agencies, the people of the world have entrusted the supreme task of building a system of collective security that will *develop and enforce* the rule of law. The principal reason they have not made the progress that their task demands is the Soviet Union's reluctance to accept the international controls, and the delegations of national sovereignty, that the overwhelming majority of the nations believe are essential.

The United States took the first step toward an effective system of international control of atomic energy and all other weapons of mass destruction. We should maintain our initiative. If such a system can be established, we then shall have safeguards that will enable the world to disarm with security. Until that is done, we cannot and must not disarm.

Meanwhile, we should press tirelessly for the special agreements, still to be prepared by the Military Staff Committee, which would give the Security Council adequate military strength to enforce its decisions.

We must continue building on the other structural foundations which have been laid. These include not only the principal organs of the United Nations established by the Charter—the General Assembly, the Security Council, the Economic and Social Council, the Trusteeship Council, and the International Court of Justice—but also the various specialized agencies, many of which have international operating functions. These specialized agencies include such bodies as the Food and Agricultural Organization, the International Labor Organization, the United Nations Educational, Scientific and Cultural Organization, the International Civil Aviation Organization, the International Bank for Reconstruction and Development, the International Monetary Fund, the International Refugee Organization, the proposed World Health Organization, and International Trade Organization. There is, in fact, scarcely a field of activity having a common interest for the peoples of the world for which continuing instruments of international co-operation have not been developed during the past two years.

The United States, the United Kingdom and Canada are the only countries which, by the summer of 1947, had become members of all the specialized agencies. The Soviet Union, on the other hand, had thus far announced its adherence only to one—the World Health Organization.

Notwithstanding all that I have said about the difficulty of getting along with the representatives of the Soviet Union, it is my firm conviction that we must continue our efforts to bring about world co-operation. We must do it in full recognition that the Soviets may not co-operate. Should our efforts fail, we must let the world know who is responsible for the failure. Experience has shown that Soviet policy is flexible and at any time Soviet spokesmen may change their views. We must let them know we are sincere in wanting their co-operation but nevertheless firm in the determination that if we do not get it, we will go ahead anyway with all those states that will co-operate.

In our efforts at world co-operation, we must be careful that we are not guilty of the offenses we charge to others. In international conferences we meet as equals, and there is no place for a "take it or leave it" attitude. For two years our patience has favorably impressed all fair-minded observers. Too much is at stake for us to lose our patience. Negotiating with the Soviets may affect the nerves of a few statesmen but another world war would more seriously affect the lives of millions of people. We must continue our efforts to develop through the United Nations a common law of nations to provide definite and agreed standards of conduct. It must rest upon something more than rules, something more than force, and something more than fear. It must be made to rest upon the growth of a common fellowship, common interests and common ideas among the peoples of the world.

In seeking the many-sided answer to the question, "Where do we go from here?" there is one course of action which I regard as the most important of all. That course is to take stock of our country and of ourselves. The leadership the modern world demands of us requires that we work from strong foundations here at home. We must enter international conference rooms with the firm but humble assurance that can come only from complete confidence in ourselves and our way of life.

If my public service has taught me anything, it is that the teachings of Thomas Jefferson and Abraham Lincoln can bring greater happiness and satisfaction to greater numbers of people than the teachings of Karl Marx and Nikolay Lenin. Nowhere is there an ideology that surpasses in its power and in its potential appeal to all peoples the ideology contained in such a statement as this:

"We hold these truths to be self-evident; that all men are created equal; that they are endowed by their creator with certain inalienable rights, and among these rights are life, liberty, and the pursuit of happiness."

No one has devised a system of government more lofty in concept or more responsive to the common good than "government of the people, by the people and for the people."

These ideals are part of our way of life. If we give evidence that we are striving unceasingly and progressing steadily toward their fulfillment, I have no fear of the outcome.

We are the world's greatest industrial nation. If we keep our own house in order, proving to the world that we learn from past mistakes; that our country is not one that booms and busts; and that we provide our people with the opportunity to live in expanding freedom and increased well-being, we can contribute immeasurably to the building of a politically free and economically stable world.

During the past two years, there were many times when I was deeply discouraged. Our repeated efforts to achieve co-operation in a peaceful world seemed to be meeting only with constant rebuff. But we persisted in our efforts with patience and firmness. I have not lost hope, but today I would reverse the order and alter the emphasis. I would say that our policy should be one of *firmness* and *patience*.

I remain confident that we can achieve a just peace by co-operative effort if we persist "with firmness in the right as God gives us the power to see the right."

To the goal of a just peace, freedom's past inspires us, and freedom's future calls us.

Index

A BASIC HISTORY OF THE UNITED STATES

A BASIC HISTORY
OF THE
UNITED STATES

BY

Charles A. Beard

AND

Mary R. Beard

The New Home Library

THE BLAKISTON COMPANY—PHILADELPHIA

An original publication of THE NEW HOME LIBRARY

THE NEW HOME LIBRARY is a series published by
The Blakiston Company, 1012 Walnut St., Philadelphia 5, Pa.

CL

PRINTED IN THE UNITED STATES OF AMERICA

Prefatory Note

With this book we bring to a close our many years of co-operative efforts in seeking to interpret the long course of American history. As its title indicates, the volume deals with fundamental activities, ideas, and interests which have entered into the development of American society from the colonial period to the contemporary age. Whatever may be added to the record here presented, a consideration of these activities, ideas, and interests is basic, we believe, to any understanding of American history.

Although compact in form and directed to the general public, the book is no mere summary or digest of our previous works. Nor is it a collection of excerpts from any or all of them. On the contrary it is newly designed and newly written to express the historical judgment which we have reached after more than forty years devoted to the study of documents and the observation of life at first hand in all parts of the United States, rural and urban, and in parts of the Old World and the Orient.

CHARLES A. BEARD
MARY R. BEARD

New Milford,
Connecticut.

Contents

Maps and Charts

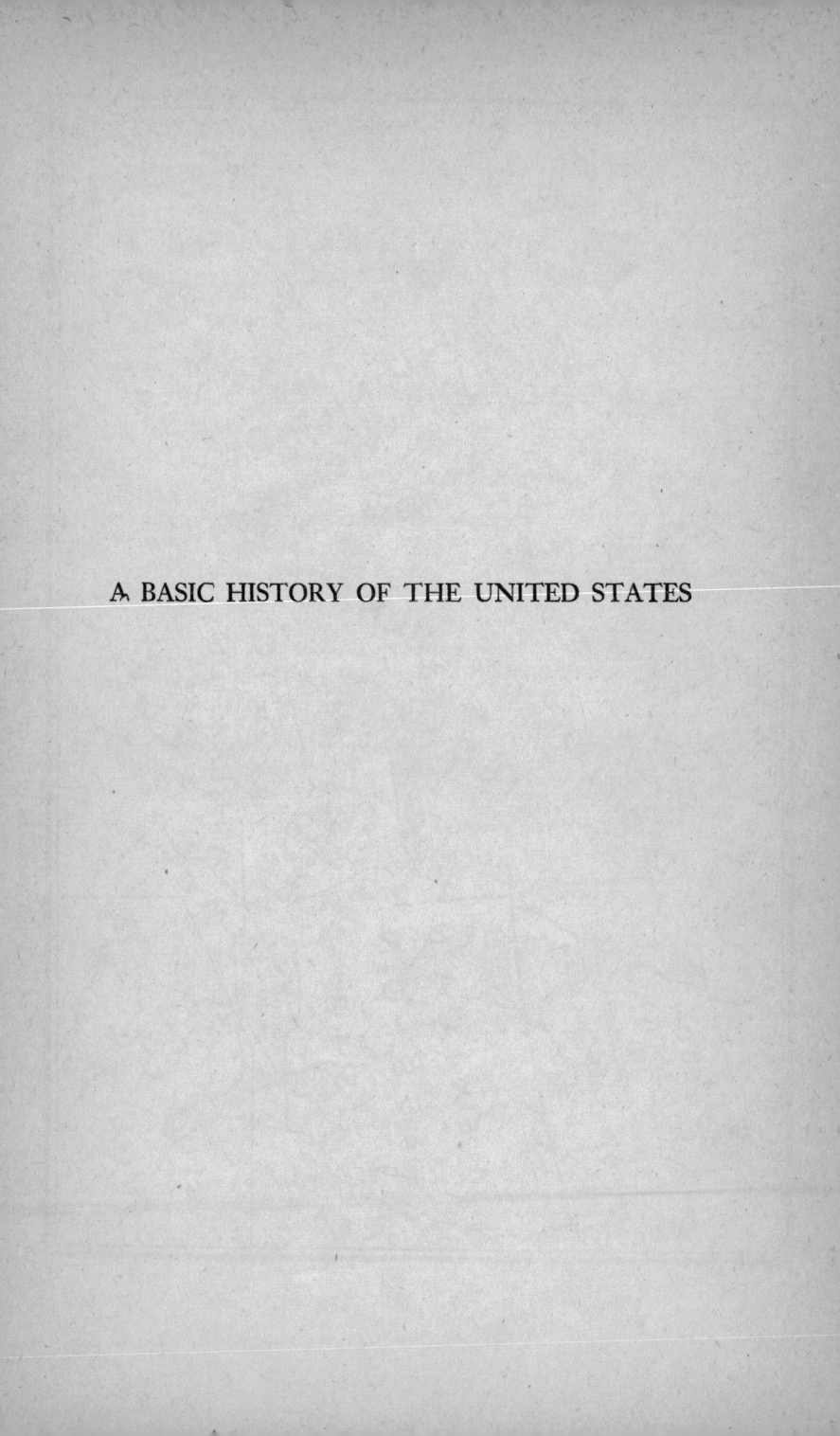

A BASIC HISTORY OF THE UNITED STATES

TERRITORIAL GROWTH OF THE UNITED STATES 1783–1867

CHAPTER I

English Territorial Claims and Colonial Beginnings

IN FAR-OFF TIMES it had been written: "Blessed are the meek for they shall inherit the earth." As if to fulfill the law, Henry VII, King of England, established in 1497 a claim to the continental domain in which the history of the United States was to unfold. Thus he took title to a great portion of the earth for the English people long before anyone, even in England, knew that the voyage of Columbus from Spain across the sea to the West Indies in 1492 had broken the path to a vast new world.

The claim which brought such good fortune to the English nation was based on the voyages of John Cabot, an Italian sea captain. Cabot, with his three sons, was commissioned by Henry VII to seek and find "whatsoever islands, countries, regions or provinces of the heathen and infidels, which before this time have been unknown to Christians." The King and the seamen in his service assumed that heathen and infidels might be found on the way to Cipango [Japan] and China by the coveted but as yet undiscovered all-water route to the trade of the Orient.

Cabot reached Cape Breton Island in 1497 and there planted the standard of the English King, supposing that he had come upon the east coast of Asia. With news of this discovery he went back to England. The next year Cabot was sent out again, on a second voyage, to explore further. This time Cabot sighted the east coast of Greenland but his sailors mutinied against pushing as far north as he wished to go. Turning south, he scouted the shore to a point in the neighborhood of Chesapeake Bay. Unable, however, to find a rich people with goods for profitable trade, he returned to England deeply disappointed.

Nevertheless Henry VII appreciated Cabot's services. Pleased by the result of the first voyage, the King made him a present of ten pounds in cash, entered the item in his account book, and granted Cabot a pension of twenty pounds. For his subjects, the King did more. He claimed a dominion of unknown size that eventually opened for the English the greatest real estate and investment opportunity in the history of Western civilization.

But nearly a century passed before the English began to take full advantage of that opportunity. In the interval numerous and wide voyages by Portuguese, Italian, Spanish, French, and English explorers led to mapping, if roughly, the contours of a large part of the two Americas. And as an outcome Spanish, Portuguese, and French rulers also laid claims to large shares of land in the Western Hemisphere. International rivalry for power over the newly discovered continents lying between the Atlantic and the Pacific oceans was to be a spur to English action in developing the King's claim.

Intrepid explorers under the flag of Spain, by innumerable journeys, were the first to penetrate the mainlands. Spanish conquerors led by Hernando Cortes and Francisco Pizarro invaded Mexico and Peru, robbed them of gold, silver, and precious stones, and excited all Europe by reports of wealth in the New World. Between 1539 and 1542 Hernando de Soto traveled overland from the coast of Florida, with his mounted companions, to the Mississippi River and some distance beyond. During those years Francisco Vásquez de Coronado, with an armed band of horsemen, toiled his way northward from Mexico into the heart of the region lying west of the Mississippi, looking for more treasure in the rumored Indian cities of Cibola. In 1565 the Spanish planted the settlement of St. Augustine in Florida.

By the middle of the sixteenth century the Spaniards seemed about to take possession of the newly discovered world. Though they had not found more gold and silver in regions above Mexico or the elixir of youth sought in Florida by Ponce de Leon, by 1550 the ruler of Spain, Charles V, could claim as his property many islands in the Caribbean; Mexico by right of conquest; all of South America except Brazil, which the Portuguese had seized; and an immense area, if indefinite as to boundaries, north of the Gulf of Mexico and the Rio Grande. To back up his claim he had at his command a big navy, a large merchant marine, and many hardy soldiers. With his conquering hosts were associated dauntless Catholic priests to aid in establishing a New Spain in the New World—a state, church, and feudal aristocracy all resting on the labor of subject peoples.

Before the English government began to develop its territorial rights by occupation the monarchs of France had also become interested in the New World. Francis I laughed at Spain and Portu-

FAMOUS VOYAGES OF COLUMBUS, CABOT, AND CARTIER

gal for pretending to own so much of it, and declared that he wanted to see the will of Father Adam, the first proprietor, bequeathing to them the inheritance they claimed. In 1524, while Henry VIII, who had succeeded his father in 1509, was neglecting the patrimony won by Cabot's voyages, Francis sent an Italian seaman, John Verrazano, across the Atlantic to hunt for a northwest passage to the Orient. Verrazano did not find the passage, but he did sail along the coast of North America and gave Francis good grounds for asserting that he too owned a big share of the new continent. Several years later Francis sent Jacques Cartier forth on two successive voyages. They resulted in explorations of the St.

Lawrence River region, the bestowal of the name Montreal on an Indian village, and a more definite claim to a huge area in that neighborhood.

Such were the rights asserted by England, Spain, and France to enormous masses of land in the New World when Queen Elizabeth came to the throne of England in 1558. Her father, Henry VIII, had done nothing to develop the real estate nominally acquired through the voyages of Cabot. Busy with intrigues on the continent of Europe, his marital troubles, and his quarrels with the Pope, he had continued to neglect his opportunities in the New World. During the reigns of his son Edward VI and his daughter Mary, England had been torn by religious disputes, and the exploitation of land over the sea had been slighted by English statesmen.

With the accession of Queen Elizabeth, however, many things incited English enterprisers to develop the real estate and investment opportunity opened to them by the voyages of Cabot under Henry VII. Elizabeth was high-spirited, well educated in the secular learning of the Renaissance, and greatly interested in adding to the riches and power of her realm. She was determined that her people should be kept Protestant in religion under the Church of England, firmly united, and strong enough to break the dominion of her Catholic rival, the King of Spain, in the Atlantic Ocean. Elizabeth gathered around her Protestant statesmen of the same mind, fostered the growth of the English navy, and encouraged her sea captains to plunder Spanish ships and colonies wherever they could.

The new temper of the Elizabethan age was imperiously displayed in 1577–80 when the English "sea dog," Francis Drake, sailed around the world plundering cities and Spanish ships laden with treasure as he went—down along the east coast of South America, up along the west coast, to the shores of California, and all the way home.

From this exploit English capitalists got an inkling of the investment opportunity before them, on and across the seas. Money for Drake's expedition had been supplied by a corporation in which Elizabeth held shares. The company's original investment was £5000. In return for the stockholders' risk, Drake's treasure ships brought them £600,000 in profits—enough to satisfy the most expectant investor. As a prudent ruler Elizabeth used her portion of the proceeds to pay off the debts owed by the Crown. According to careful estimates, the numerous raids on Spanish ships and colonies during Elizabeth's reign netted the handsome sum of £12,000,000.

With news of splendid returns on investment undertakings at sea ringing in their ears, English merchant capitalists, including investors among fair ladies, began to take a serious interest in the real estate of the English Crown in the New World. Since it was undeveloped real estate—not land occupied by peoples abounding in wealth—its exploitation demanded colonization by the English people themselves and the founding of a "New England" under the Crown of the old England. Having this project in view, Queen Elizabeth gave Sir Walter Raleigh, one of the favorites at her court, a patent to all the territory he might colonize, on condition that he pay to the Crown one fifth of the returns from the mining of precious metals.

Under this patent Raleigh sent out in 1584 an expedition which visited the island of Roanoke off the coast of North Carolina and brought back reports of a favorable climate and country—"the most plentiful, sweet, fruitful, and wholesome of all the world." The next year Raleigh dispatched seven ships and 108 colonists to Roanoke, but the colonial experiment was a failure. Raleigh made another attempt in 1587, only to fail again. The colonists who shared in that venture utterly disappeared from the scene, leaving behind them not even a clue to their fate. The sixteenth century came to a close without the creation of a single permanent English settlement in America.

But the century did not close until the English navy, aided by a terrible storm at sea, had destroyed in 1588 the Spanish Armada, a mighty fleet sent by the King of Spain to crush the rising power of England. This victory for the English helped to clear the way for the development of their real estate when they were ready to go about it again in earnest.

Yet before the English could demonstrate their ability to occupy the territory nominally under the English Crown, other claimants disputed their ownership. In 1609 Henry Hudson, an English navigator in the service of Holland, sailed up the river which now bears his name and thereupon the Dutch government asserted its authority over an immense area in the neighborhood. For a time the Dutch were allowed to develop plantations in their colony of "New Netherland." For a time also the Spaniards were permitted to keep their land in Florida; and the French to hold regions of the St. Lawrence and Great Lakes. It was not until the English had created large and prosperous colonies on the Atlantic seaboard that they were prepared to deal effectively with the three rival claimants to lands on the northern continent.

The establishment of large, permanent, and prosperous colonies was a tremendous task, new in English experience. Beside this complicated undertaking the spectacular dispatch of Drake on a voyage of exploration and the sensational robbery of Spanish vessels were mere theatrical displays of power and daring. To arm a few ships, shoot up Spanish galleons, loot them, and send them to the bottom of the ocean was an operation that required little money—mainly skill in navigation and the fighting spirit. The defeat of the Spanish Armada merely helped to clear the seas for colonizing expeditions.

Qualities and courage of a different sort were necessary to create large and orderly societies in a wilderness. This business demanded huge capital. It was more than men's work: women in great numbers had to be associated with it. All the ideals, arts, and sciences of civilization were involved in it.

LAND GRANTS BY JAMES I IN 1606

Great pieces of real estate were granted to the London Company and the Plymouth Company. In the shaded portion of the map both Companies could make settlements provided their plantations were at least 100 miles apart.

Not fully aware of all that colonization implied but eager to exploit the real estate in America, English merchant capitalists sought that privilege from the Crown at the beginning of the seventeenth century. They had already formed trading companies to engage in commerce with Russia, the Levant, and the East Indies. In corporate enterprises of that type they had demonstrated their ingenuity. Besides they had accumulated much capital for investment. This capital they now proposed to use in colonial enterprise, about which they knew so little. Only one aspect of it was clear to them: individual farmers, merchants, artisans, and their families, with small savings or none at all, could not embark unaided on any such undertaking as large-scale colonization.

Under English law all the territory claimed in America belonged to the Crown. The monarch could withhold it from use, keep any part of it as a royal domain, or grant it, by charter or patent, in large or small blocks, to privileged companies or private persons. It was to the Crown, therefore, that English enterprisers bent on colonizing America turned for grants of land and powers of government. And in making such grants by charter or patent, the Crown created two types of legal agencies for colonization: the corporation and the proprietary.

The corporate type of colonizing agency was the company, or group of individuals merged into a single "person" at law by a royal charter. The charter named the original members of the company and gave them the right to elect officers, frame bylaws, raise money, and act as a body. It granted to the company an area of territory and conferred upon it certain powers: to transport emigrants, govern its settlements, dispose of its land and other resources, and carry on commerce, subject to the laws of England. Such a corporation was akin to the modern joint-stock company organized for profit-making purposes.

The proprietary agency for colonizing consisted of one or more persons to whom were given a grant of territory and various powers of government by the Crown. The proprietor or proprietors thus endowed with special privileges had authority to found a particular colony and enjoy property, commercial, governing, and other rights similar in character to those vested in a company by royal charter.

Companies and proprietors did not, however, have a completely free hand in managing their colonial affairs. They were limited by the terms of their charters or patents and were compelled to confer upon free settlers certain liberties and immunities enjoyed by English people at home, including a share in the making of local laws.

Various motives inspired English leaders to form companies or embark on careers as proprietors in America. Among the motives was the desire to extend English power, to make money out of trading privileges and land sales, and to convert the Indians to Christianity. For some companies and proprietors the idea of establishing religious liberty in America for members of persecuted sects was also among the primary considerations in their colonizing activities. Still another purpose entering into the plans of companies or proprietors was that of giving poor and otherwise unfortunate persons in England a chance to work and live better in a new country so open to opportunity. In other words, political, economic, religious, and charitable motives induced English leaders to devote their energies to the business of colonization.

The systematic beginnings of all the American colonies were made by companies or proprietors or under their jurisdiction. By 1733, the year in which the last colony, Georgia, was started at Savannah, there were thirteen colonies under the Crown at London, legally known as the British Crown after the Union of England and Scotland in 1707. These colonies, taken arbitrarily in geographical order, with references to origins, were:

New Hampshire—partly an offshoot of Massachusetts, given a separate status in 1679.

Massachusetts—founded in 1630 by Puritans under the Massachusetts Bay Company; with it became associated in 1691 the colony of Plymouth, established by the Pilgrims in 1620 on land belonging to the Plymouth Company chartered by James I in 1606.

Rhode Island—incorporating two offshoots from Massachusetts, Rhode Island and Providence Plantations, to which, as a single colony, a royal charter was given in 1663.

Connecticut—originating partly in offshoots from Massachusetts planted in the Connecticut River valley in 1635 and partly in settlements on the shore, united under a royal charter in 1662.

New York—founded as New Netherland under the Dutch West India Company in 1624; seized by the English in 1664 and given the name of New York.

New Jersey—founded under Dutch auspices, seized by the English in 1664, and afterward named New Jersey.

Delaware—first settled by the Dutch under the Dutch West India Company and by Swedes under the Swedish South Company; taken by the English in 1664 and placed under the proprietorship of William Penn in 1682.

Pennsylvania—granted to William Penn as proprietary by Charles II in 1681; first settlement at Philadelphia in 1682.

Maryland—granted to Lord Baltimore as proprietary in 1632 and started by settlements on Chesapeake Bay in 1634.

Virginia—founded by settlement at Jamestown in 1607, made under the London Company chartered by James I in 1606.

North Carolina—early settlements made by pioneers from other colonies; passed under an association of proprietors in 1665 by a royal grant covering all the Carolina region, formerly within the jurisdiction of the Virginia Company; given a separate status as the royal province of North Carolina in 1729.

South Carolina—granted to proprietors in 1665; settlements made at Albemarle Point in 1670 and near Charleston in 1672; an independent royal province after 1729.

Georgia—granted to a board of trustees, or company, by George II in 1732; Savannah founded in 1733.

This table, indicating the corporate and proprietary agencies under which English colonization took place, does not give an adequate impression of the amount of free movement by individuals and groups in America, especially after the first settlements had been planted. Nothing less than an encyclopedia could do that.

Take for example North Carolina. Virginians had made a permanent settlement in that region at least five years before it was granted to proprietors in 1665, and other pioneers, mainly Scotch, Scotch-Irish, and Germans from Pennsylvania, went down into North Carolina on their own motion.

Again, take New Hampshire in the far north. An independent settlement was established there as early as 1623 under a royal grant. Other beginnings in New Hampshire had been made before the Puritans came to Massachusetts Bay in 1630. When Puritans pushed over into the New Hampshire region and claimed it as a part of their grant, they encountered stout opposition from the forerunners. Only after many disputes was a final separation from Massachusetts effected by New Hampshire in 1679.

But independent undertakings and individual or group migrations from colony to colony, significant as they were in colonial beginnings, had relatively little influence on the rise of self-governing colonies. It was under companies and proprietors holding grants of land subject to the English Crown that systematic colonization on a large scale was made possible. It was under companies and proprietors that the foundations of all the colonies, except New York, were securely laid, and the old Dutch settlement was developed under the auspices of the English Crown after 1664. Crown, companies, and proprietors—their work in colonization was to have from the outset a profound influence on the course of affairs which eventuated in the formation of the continental United States.

CHAPTER II

Backgrounds of Migration and Settlement

OCCUPATION OF THE TERRITORY claimed by England in America, building "the New England" in the wilderness, required the transfer of thousands upon thousands of men and women from the Old World to the New World. This meant a resettlement on an enormous scale. Trading corporations and proprietors alike confronted that problem. They had titles to great areas of land. They had money. They could buy ships, tools, stock, seeds, and other things necessary to starting agriculture on the virgin continent. But empty lands in America were in themselves worth no more to their nominal owners than lands in the moon. Money in their hands was in itself just so much dead metal. Stock, tools, and implements in storage were equally inert.

Only labor could put the material capital and the vacant lands to use. Only able-bodied men and women possessing many skills and crafts, many arts and sciences, could produce the food, clothing, shelter, and other necessities of a civilized social order, could build prosperous and self-sustaining societies on the territory claimed by England.

But trading corporations and proprietors, even aided by the English government, could not simply commandeer farmers, mechanics, artisans, and managers for colonial adventures. In the nature of things, most of the men and women for the undertaking had to be persons who were willing, even eager, to cross the sea. They had to be volunteers moved by one reason or many reasons to tear up their roots in the Old World and brave the perils and toil of transplanting themselves across the wide ocean into the lonely territory claimed by the English Crown.

The bulk of the white men and women who came to North

11

America between the founding of Jamestown in Virginia in 1607 and the eve of the American revolt against Great Britain came voluntarily. Even those who indentured, or bound, themselves by contract to labor for a term of years as servants, in order to pay their passage, were in the main volunteers.

It is true that many white laborers were kidnaped in England for shipment to the American colonies and that Negroes were dragged out of Africa for that purpose by slave traders. Forced migration of laborers was undoubtedly extensive. Yet the overwhelming majority of immigrants came to America of their own choice.

☆

What lay behind this choice? The whole history of Europe. The long struggle between barbarism and civilization since the beginning of human societies in the Old World. Immediately influential were the convulsions of the age in which the emigrants lived. From the opening of the seventeenth century to the close of the colonial period the Old World was in turmoil—physical, intellectual, moral, religious, military, economic, and political. The feudal order of the Middle Ages was breaking up amid fierce resistance to change.

The years of the great migration from the Old World to the English colonies in the New World were marked by international wars, civil wars, religious controversies and persecutions, political disputes, displays of royal despotism, and social dislocation, accompanied by growing poverty and the enactment of barbaric criminal laws against the poor.

None of these events was sharply separated from others. All were interrelated. For example, wars were connected with national jealousies, ambitions of monarchs, religious hatreds, and rivalries over trade and territory. Religious clashes were associated with the political interests of kings and queens, Catholic and Protestant, with the conflicts of nations over commerce and empire in the Old World and beyond the seas, and with the struggles of classes.

An impression of the almost endless wars waged in Europe between 1618 and 1776 may be derived from the following list of the major wars:

1618–48—The Thirty Years' War, involving Bohemia, Denmark, Sweden, France, German princes, Spain, and other Powers; large parts of Germany were devastated by battles, burnings, and lootings; Protestants and Catholics both engaged in it.

1648–59—France and Spain, two Catholic monarchies, continued the Thirty Years' War, between themselves.

1667–68—The War of Devolution; the King of France, Louis XIV, waged war to wrest neighboring territories from Spain.

1672–78—France waged war on Holland.

1689–97—War of the Palatinate; French, Dutch, and English struggled for power on the Continent; called in America King William's War.

1702–14—War of the Spanish Succession; France, England, Spain, Holland, and other Powers fought over territory on the Continent and over colonial possessions; known in American colonies as Queen Anne's War.

1739–48—War of Jenkins' Ear, between England and France; widened out into the War of the Austrian Succession, involving England, France, Spain, Austria, Prussia, and other Powers; known in the American colonies as King George's War.

1756–63—The Seven Years' War, involving England, France, Spain, Prussia, and other countries; contest between England and France over dominion in Canada, India, and other places; known in America as the French and Indian War.

These major wars, covering in all more than eighty years between 1618 and 1776, to say nothing of many local wars such as short fights between the English and the Dutch, spread ruin in several parts of western Europe. And one reason for the extent of this ruin was a revolution in the "art of war."

In the Middle Ages wars almost endless had been fought largely by a relatively few feudal lords and their retainers—by dukes, earls, barons, knights, and esquires. Into feudal armies workers on the land and merchants in the towns had not been drafted wholesale. With the discovery of gunpowder and the invention of cannon, muskets, and other powerful implements of destruction, however, a new kind of army—the standing army—was organized in Europe.

The standing army could be extended by summoning tens of thousands of men to its ranks, thus far exceeding in size any feudal army. To fill the ranks of the new and bigger armies sturdy young men were caught and dragged to the barracks for training if they could not be got otherwise. Princes drafted their subjects en masse for their own wars and sometimes sold them in large blocks, as mercenaries, to other princes in need of soldiers.

With this transformation in the character of armies, the actual snatching of men for wars and the fear of being snatched made life a genuine terror for innumerable men of military age, their families, and young marriageable women. Moreover the death and destruction spread by wars on a large scale made the "art of war" so practiced more terrible to non-combatants. For all such reasons British and European workers in town and country, as well as yeomen and merchants, could regard the perils and hardships of re-settlement in America, in a strange land, as offering trials slight in comparison.

To wars between nations were added conflicts within nations arising from religious and political sources. In the Middle Ages the people of all countries in western Europe were members of one church—the Catholic Church, and belonged to one faith—the Catholic faith. Dissent from that faith, heresy, was forbidden and if it appeared was put down by Church and State.

But during the opening years of the sixteenth century a revolt, known as the Protestant Reformation, broke out against the Pope and the Catholic Church of which he was the head. In southern Germany, Italy, and Spain, the Church and the princes managed to suppress religious uprisings and keep most of the people loyal to the Catholic religion. France, long torn by religious wars, found peace for a time when the King was able to make a truce in 1598 —by granting a limited toleration to the Huguenots, Protestant followers of John Calvin. In Holland, Scandinavia, and the countries of northern Germany, the revolt against the Pope ended in the establishment of independent Protestant churches under the various rulers.

The religious quarrels in England took a peculiar turn. After the power of the Pope was finally cast off under Queen Elizabeth, a state church—the Church of England—was established by act of Parliament and everybody in the realm was ordered to become a member of it under pain of fine or physical punishment. But this official church had scarcely been set up, and Catholics had barely been suppressed, when more religious protests arose among the people.

Some of the new objectors merely wanted to reform, or "purify," the English Church; they were known as Puritans. Others, generally called Dissenters, spurned the English Church entirely and asserted the right of individuals and groups of individuals to form churches of their own and worship God according to their consciences. This was the view taken by Presbyterians, Baptists, and Quakers, for example.

Nowhere in the Old World at the beginning of American colonization was there anything like religious toleration in the modern sense of the term: that is, the right of every person to join any church he or she pleases, or none at all, and to express his or her opinions freely on matters of religion. In the Catholic countries, except France, Protestantism was forbidden and Protestants were persecuted. Even in France the limited toleration of Huguenots was abolished by the King in 1685, and they were subjected to persecution. On the other hand, in Protestant countries Catholicism was forbidden and Catholics were persecuted. In England persecution cut two ways. The government of that country meted out stern punishment to Catholics who clung to their faith and also to Protestants who wanted to "purify" the English Church or to found independent churches. As far as the strict letter of English law was concerned there could be no Catholics at all in England or any Protestants outside the Church of England. Although many religious objectors defied or winked at the law, they were liable at any time to be arrested and fined, imprisoned, mutilated, or put to death.

Religious disputes in England were embittered by a political struggle which broke out between the Parliament and James I, shortly after his accession in 1603. High-tempered and arrogant, James tried to make laws and lay taxes without the consent of Parliament, and Parliament resisted his encroachments on its rights.

Under his successor, Charles I, the quarrel developed into a civil war and a revolution, led by Oliver Cromwell with the general support of the Puritans. The struggle ended temporarily in the execution of Charles, the exile of his son, the flight of many members of the aristocracy, and the establishment of a dictatorship by Cromwell.

In the course of the civil conflict a flood of radical, or "leveling," ideas was let loose in England. It was boldly said that no King or House of Lords was needed at all; that every man should have the right to vote for members of the House of Commons; that all the people had "natural rights" which no government could take away from them.

Shortly after the death of Cromwell the monarchy was restored by the coronation of Charles II, in 1660. But this brought only a few years of internal peace to England. Even then religious and political unrest continued beneath the surface of social peace. It emerged in a revolt soon after Charles II died and his brother, James II, an avowed Catholic, came to the throne. James tried to rule England as autocratically as his grandfather had done, and in 1688 he was driven out in a popular uprising.

The following year, William, the Prince of Orange, and his

wife, Mary, the elder daughter of James II, were called to England. Under an act of Parliament they were crowned king and queen of the realm. In the general settlement which went with the revolution of 1688 the supremacy of Parliament as the lawmaking body of England was acknowledged, a bill of rights for English subjects was proclaimed, and a limited tolerance was granted to Protestant Dissenters—though not to Catholics.

During the many years of this strife in England migration to America was stimulated; and the colonies that had already been founded were deeply affected by rapid changes in the mother country. Resenting the autocratic rule of James I and Charles I, thousands of Puritans and Dissenters fled from the kingdom in search of more political and religious freedom for themselves. While the Puritans under Cromwell's leadership were in power in England, hundreds of their opponents, loosely called "Cavaliers," took refuge in America, especially in Virginia. And all the while news of the disputes in England over the political rights of the people and over religious toleration circulated from one end of the colonial settlements to the other, affecting judgments respecting politics and religion on this side of the Atlantic.

Amid the wars, religious revolts, persecutions, and political upheavals which kept the Old World in convulsions, the feudal order inherited from the Middle Ages was disintegrating. In that order government had been in the hands of kings and princes, supported by the clergy and nobility, as a rule. The land of the various kingdoms and principalities had been held by great landlords, lay and clerical; and most of the earth had been tilled by serfs bound to the soil on which they labored, so that they were unable to leave it even if they desired to do so. The number of merchants was relatively small and they counted for little in the class valuations of early feudal times. Stated in another way, feudal society was a class society in which each class, from serfs at the bottom to princes at the top, had a fixed and permanent place. The mass of the people were not free to move around as they pleased, even in the region in which they lived, or to emigrate to any other country.

But wars, religious upheavals, and the growth of commerce finally shook this rigid class order apart. In England the process of dissolution began early and went forward rapidly, particularly after the Protestant revolt opened in the sixteenth century. Under

Henry VIII great landed estates held by the Catholic Church were seized by the Crown and many of them were parceled out among the King's favorites, thus increasing the number of English landlords. About the same time landlords discovered that they could make more money by raising sheep and exporting wool to the continent of Europe than they could by having the soil tilled for the production of crops. So they turned a vast acreage into sheep pastures and evicted serfs and laborers from the land, forcing them, homeless and forlorn, to search for other work in the towns.

By the beginning of Elizabeth's reign England was swarming with "free" men and women, hunting in the streets and highways for employment or begging for charity. Cruel laws were enacted against them. They were harshly punished for begging, driven into poorhouses, or forced to labor at anything they could find to do at wages fixed by government officials.

In some of the English towns at the opening of the seventeenth century as high as one third of all the inhabitants were paupers dependent for a living on the charity of their neighbors. Although paupers were unequally distributed over England, the number was enormous and their plight was nothing short of horrible.

Everywhere even those fathers and mothers who earned a fair livelihood could see that their children had slight chances of getting along at all or of bettering their condition and that their families might easily fall into the great mass of pauperism. Since most of the English land was monopolized by great landlords it was difficult for anyone to buy a farm; and the oversupply of labor in the cities made competition for jobs an agonizing struggle.

When the cry that cheap land, even free land, was offered to immigrants in America rang through the streets of English towns and cities and through the byways of the English countryside, it awakened in the imagination of multitudes of nameless men and women a dream of liberty, security, and advancement such as had never before come to toiling masses in the Old World. Even the homeless and propertyless were stirred by news from some of the colonies that, if they would bind themselves to service for a term of five years, they would receive at the end of their indenture at least fifty acres of land for their own.

☆

Such were the Old World backgrounds for migration to America. It was in these circumstances, according to estimates from fragmentary records, that about 750,000 people, for one reason or another or for many reasons, journeyed over the ocean between 1600 and 1770 to seek a way of life on this continent. Relatively few of them were from the permanent class of helpless English paupers created by the heartless eviction of peasants from the lands their ancestors had tilled; for paupers did not always have the energy or skills required for successful farming that made them desirable indentured servants. Approximately two thirds of the immigrants belonged to families able to meet the cost of the journey and make a start of some kind in the new country. The other third, composed of indentured servants, although lacking in money or property, had skills and talents which they could apply in making their way in a land of opportunity.

The motives provoking men and women to brave the perils of the sea voyage in slow sailing vessels overcrowded with passengers and to risk their lives and fortunes in a strange continent, far from their native habitats, were no doubt various. But historical records justify such a summary as the following:

A desire to get away from the devastations of the endless wars and conflicts in Europe.

A resolve to flee from the snatching and selling of men for service in the armies of kings and princes constantly engaged in wars.

A longing for an opportunity to find honest and honorable work and create better homes for themselves and their children.

An eagerness to escape religious persecutions and to found communities in which they could worship God in their own ways, free from the domination of church and government officials trying to enforce conformity to other faiths.

In addition to one or more of these motives, immigrants had a quality for which no name can be found. Countless men and women who lived amid the wars, persecutions, and poverty of the Old World and suffered from them as did the emigrants, stayed at home and continued to endure them. If the Old World backgrounds in themselves had supplied the sole motives for migration, then more millions would also have broken away and joined the voyagers bound for the New World. It follows, therefore, that there was something in the spirit of the men and women who voluntarily made the break and migrated, a force of character not simply determined by economic, political, or religious conditions—a force that made them different from their neighbors who remained in the turmoil and poverty of the Old World. That something was a quality of energy, enterprise, daring, or aspiration that was to be a power in the course of American history, immediately and by transmission through coming generations.

☆

The strength of the several motives for migration doubtless varied from immigrant to immigrant, from group to group. The assignment of specific weights to the motives is impossible. But among them a desire to win a larger religious freedom was widely acknowledged as significant and impelling by many immigrants and their descendants. Practically all the immigrants were members of some church or adherents to some religious faith. The overwhelming majority were Protestants—but Protestants who objected, as much as Catholics did, to the faith and government of the Church of England. On this point of objection Quakers, Baptists, Presbyterians, and Lutherans agreed in spite of their differences on other matters. In any event, religious considerations entered into the founding and development of every colony from New Hampshire to Georgia.

The early settlers of Virginia were members of the Church of England and it was the practices of their church which were to be observed in the colony. This church soon became and long remained the Established Church of Virginia, supported by taxation. Nevertheless, in the course of time Protestants of other denominations went into Virginia though, theoretically, they had no legal right to be there. A few Catholics also found their way quietly into the Old Dominion and officers of the law merely winked at their presence. Thus a kind of toleration grew up in practice. But it was far from universal religious liberty and was often marred by persecutions fostered by the Virginia government and Established Church.

The neighboring colony of Maryland, often spoken of as a free refuge for Catholics persecuted in England, was in fact at the outset nothing of the sort. It is true that the first Lord Baltimore, who received the grant of land from King Charles I, was a Catholic in spite of the prohibitory English law, favored and protected by the King. It is true that many Catholics from the British Isles were able to settle in Maryland and enjoy a high degree of religious liberty, although according to English law Catholics were not supposed to exist anywhere under the English Crown. But the second Lord Baltimore, who on the death of his father started the settlements on Chesapeake Bay, was interested in more than a religious refuge. He wanted to develop a prosperous colony by selling his lands to farmers, and he invited Protestants as well as Catholics to migrate to Maryland.

Within a short time the Protestants in Maryland outnumbered the Catholics and prepared to abolish the toleration that had quietly become a custom in the colony. To avoid a disruptive religious conflict, leaders in Maryland arranged for the colonial assembly to pass, in 1649, what is known as the Toleration Act. The term is inexact. It did not establish universal religious liberty in Maryland. It granted freedom of religious worship only to those who professed faith in Jesus Christ, thereby excluding Jews, unbelievers, Deists, and Unitarians from the benefit of this freedom.

In the case of the Massachusetts Bay Colony, religious affairs took a course unlike that in Virginia or Maryland. Although, like Virginians, the Puritans who settled on the bay were members of the Church of England when they arrived, they had wanted to alter some of its practices and soon they separated from it entirely in their new home. After the separation each town set up a church of its own, called Congregational, and taxpayers were required by law to support it. For a long time every voter in Massachusetts had to be a member of a Congregational church.

Strenuous efforts were made to bar immigrants belonging to other religious denominations. Dissenters and critics who appeared among the Puritans were frowned upon and sometimes severely punished, executed, or exiled into the wilderness. In short Puritans came to Massachusetts to develop, among other things, religious liberty for themselves, not to establish an ideal of toleration for all religions—a liberty utterly unknown as practice in the England they had left.

The first English colony in America to grant general religious liberty as a matter of law and principle was an offshoot from Massachusetts, at first called the Rhode Island and Providence Plantations. It was not founded by settlers coming directly from England but by inhabitants of Massachusetts who rebelled against the teachings and practices of Puritan preachers and magistrates. In 1636 Roger Williams, ordered to conform or get out, fled with a few friends into the wilderness and founded the town of Providence at the head of Narragansett Bay. Two years afterward Anne Hutchinson, also outlawed by the Puritan clergy of Boston for her religious and general independence, took refuge with her companions for a while at Portsmouth on Rhode Island.

Both Roger Williams and Anne Hutchinson believed that the government should not force any form of religion by law on anybody; that every person should be free to worship God according to his conscience. This rule of broad tolerance, extended to Quakers and Jews, was retained in the Providence and Rhode Island plantations after all the townships were united in an independent colony—by a charter from Charles II granted in 1663. It made Rhode Island unique among the colonies.

No such general religious liberty was permitted in the second offshoot from Massachusetts, the colony of Connecticut, founded about the same time as Providence. The expedition of Puritans who built the towns of Hartford, Windsor, and Wethersfield in the Connecticut River valley was led by a preacher rightly deemed broad-minded for his time, Thomas Hooker. But neither he nor his companions accepted the liberal toleration proclaimed by Roger Williams and Anne Hutchinson. Likewise strict in their views of religious discipline under government control were the Puritans who made settlements at New Haven and other places on Long Island Sound.

Before and after the two groups of towns were united in a single colony as Connecticut, under a charter granted by Charles II in 1662, the Congregational Church was the established church in each town, and it remained so established by law through the Revolution down to 1818. Catholics, Protestant dissenters of various kinds, especially Quakers, and even members of the Church of England encountered hostility in Connecticut. Immigrants who were not Congregationalists in faith filtered into the colony here and there but full toleration and equality were not accorded to them as a matter of principle and law.

A wide, though not complete, religious toleration was adopted in Pennsylvania under the leadership of the Quaker proprietor, William Penn. By his faith Penn was committed to the principle that religion is a matter for the conscience of the individual and is not to be imposed on anybody by law and government officials. But from the beginning of his settlement at Philadelphia in 1682 Penn opened his colony only to immigrants who professed belief in God. As a proprietor Penn, like Lord Baltimore, was eager to have immigrants settling in his colony, buying farms carved out of the land granted to him by the King, and engaging in lucrative commerce. In his quest for settlers he made special efforts to encourage the migration of Scotch-Irish Presbyterians and German Protestants, as hardy folk with skills and crafts.

Religious considerations entered into the rise and growth of settlements in other parts of America. It was in search of freedom for their form of religious worship as well as a livelihood that the Pilgrims, persecuted in England and for a time exiles in Holland, went to Plymouth in 1620. After the English seized the Dutch holdings in 1664 and renamed them New York, the practice of granting toleration to Protestants of all denominations was followed in New York, although the Anglican Church was established in certain counties of the colony as the official church. Quakers and Presbyterians took part in filling up New Jersey and a similar toleration became the general practice there. Under the Penn proprietorship the inhabitants of Delaware shared the almost unlimited religious freedom established by William Penn for Pennsylvania. While the proprietors of North Carolina and South Carolina were favorable to the Anglican Church, settlers of various Protestant faiths, including French Huguenots, were welcomed and allowed to worship God according to their creeds. In Georgia, founded as an experiment in philanthropy, a rule of religious liberty akin to that in South Carolina soon prevailed generally.

As long as shipping was controlled by companies and proprietors, it was relatively easy to keep people of "undesirable" religious sects out of any colony. But after ports and inland towns were well developed, owners of ships were fairly free to make independent voyages to America. Then colonial barriers crumbled and immigrants of all faiths found easier entrance into all colonies. Ship captains in search of emigrants who could pay their passage were prone to disregard laws on religion or colonial restrictions on the ingress of religious refugees.

Indeed, to promote passenger traffic ship captains offered to carry over to America emigrants who had no money to pay their way, and collected the cost, with a profit, by selling the labor and skills of their passengers to employers for a term of years. Colonists who engaged these laborers were inclined to be more interested in strong bodies and stable characters than in the theological opinions of their servants.

At all events, for one reason or another the religious restrictions that existed in the beginning slowly relaxed, in some places more than in others, but everywhere more or less. And it came about that the English plantations in America were inhabited only in part by men and women who adhered to the Church of England in religious faith. In an overwhelming majority, the colonists were Protestant dissenters from that church—Congregationalists, Presbyterians, Baptists, Quakers, and members of other sects. To these Protestants were added a large number of German Lutherans and a small number of French Protestants, or Huguenots. English and Irish Catholics, no more friendly to the Church of England than Protestant dissenters, found their way into other colonies as well as into the more hospitable Maryland.

In these circumstances no religious denomination was numerically strong enough, had it been so disposed, to force a single form of the Christian religion on all the inhabitants, even though in some colonies people were required to pay taxes to support a colonial church. Accordingly there prevailed in these American societies an amount of religious liberty hitherto unknown in England and in western Europe since the days of ancient Rome. Even Jews, severely oppressed nearly everywhere in the Old World, were able to find shelter from persecution in several seaboard towns and to erect synagogues in which to conduct their religious rites.

Throughout the colonies, therefore, in law or practice or both, a broad religious liberty was accorded to the people. But it was not universal religious freedom. Nor were the American people, by 1776, prepared in spirit to approve that freedom as the law of the land. How do we know this? From the first state constitutions adopted after the break with Great Britain.

With some exceptions those constitutions excluded Catholics, Unitarians, Deists, and Jews from the right to vote and hold office in the new state governments. Individuals, if free to choose their own forms of religious faith and worship, had to remain outside the pale of politics in case they did not conform to the law of privilege. Protestant Christians almost monopolized the powers and offices of government in the states.

Americans had gone a long way toward universal religious toleration by 1776 but they had not completed the journey. In six colonies—Virginia, Maryland, the two Carolinas, Georgia, and New York—the Church of England was an official church under colonial laws. In three other colonies—Massachusetts, Connecticut, and New Hampshire—the Congregational Church, supported in each town by taxation, remained established as the official church. The Old World heritage of religious intolerance and persecution had been severely shattered everywhere in America, even in the nine colonies with established churches, but many vestiges of religious discrimination remained to be cleared away.

CHAPTER III

Laying Foundations in Agriculture

THE WILL OF IMMIGRANTS to separate themselves from the Old World was of course an impetus to resettlement in the New World. But successful resettlement called for a still more positive force of mind and character. For shaping a new and secure life and creating societies in the wildernesses of a continent more was necessary than a feeling of revolt and separatism. This operation required an exercise of intellectual prowess, manual skills, and inventiveness—constructive abilities of a high order.

A few emigrants at the beginning of the seventeenth century, it is true, were lured by the original dream of the London Company that gold and silver for quick riches would be found in its territory. A year before the tiny settlement had been planted on the James River, an actor in the English metropolis had declared on the stage that the Indians' dripping pans were of "pure golde," that their "chaines with which they chained up their streets were of massive golde," that their prisoners were "fettered in golde," and that they "goe forth on holy days to gather rubies and diamonds by the seashore." But neither in Virginia nor anywhere in the colonies were the English to discover, conquer, and loot Indian societies fabulously rich in rare treasures, such as the Spaniards had found in Mexico and Peru. So all the pioneers had to come down to hard earth and create the real wealth which was alone valuable for life—farms, houses, food, clothing, and all the material commodities necessary for the living of civilized people. They had to cherish the values of a working society.

In the new environment the pioneers confronted primitives such as they had never seen before. All along the shores from Maine to

Georgia were scattered tribes of native Indians ranging in degrees of social organization from marauding nomads to more or less settled communities engaged in practicing the economic arts of forest, stream, field, and domesticity. With the Indians the pioneers entered into varied relations: from peace and friendship to treachery and massacre on both sides.

In terms of peace the newcomers sometimes bought lands from the Indians, giving them in exchange such English goods as cloth, beads, hoes, knives, axes, and other implements. For example, when Roger Williams founded his first plantation in Rhode Island in 1636, he displayed good will toward the Indians at once and bought from them the land on which he settled with his companions. Sometimes colonial leaders, occasionally in connection with the purchase of land, made treaties of amity with the Indians. William Penn, for instance, besides protecting the Indians of his colony from the rapacity of white traders, made treaties of friendship with them which they faithfully kept. By the marriage of John Rolfe to Pocahontas, daughter of the warlike chief, Powhatan, in 1614, peace was brought to the settlers of Virginia for eight years. More than once an English settlement was saved from starvation by timely supplies of food furnished by neighboring tribes.

From red Indians "the palefaces" recovered some of the primitive arts of survival which had been lost to the English since their own primitive times. Indian women were farmers, cooks, and practitioners of other domestic arts, and from them English women learned how to handle native foodstuffs, especially Indian corn, and provide nutritious meals. Indian men also had their arts of hunting, fishing, and woodworking, and from them English men acquired various new skills which, combined with their own, enabled them to make rapid progress in every form of economic operation. As hunters adept in the ways of wild animals, Indians knew how to procure fish, game, and furs for their own people. By studying the hunting arts of the Indians and by trading with them, white pioneers were able to get meat more quickly and stocks of furs.

Unhappily, relations with the Indians were not all confined to genial exchanges of arts and commodities. Human nature, red and white, also displayed cruelty and stupidity. From time immemorial Indian tribes had fought among themselves, the warlike nomads preying upon the tribes that tilled the soil, the settled tribes trying to defend themselves, tribes battling against other tribes for other reasons or without rationality. Under the thin veneer of their civilization the barbaric greed and brutality of innumerable whites led them to rob, murder, betray, and try to enslave Indians. White traders sold them whisky and firearms and cheated them in transactions over furs and the purchase of lands. Thus the whites incited retaliations even among Indians formerly disposed to be friendly.

So sporadic brawls, local conflicts, and general wars punctuated the relations of whites and Indians all along the line from North to South and all through the years from the early days in Virginia to the close of the colonial period. After the whites had introduced the Indians to "fire water" and guns the fighting became more desperate and bloody as the years passed and as the frontier advanced upon the Indian hunting grounds. Nothing but stockades, militiamen, and eternal vigilance prevented the Indians from exterminating many of the early settlements and keeping the frontier constantly aflame.

Besides encountering the strange aborigines, the first English settlers found themselves in the presence of new and wide variations of climate. In their old home they had been accustomed to a moderate temperature. Now they had before them a great range of climate from the cold coasts of Maine to the hot savannahs of Georgia, with all the gradations from the far North to the deep South. To the exigencies of these variations, all the immigrants, from the British Isles as well as the Continent, had to adapt their economy and ways of living. Wherever the colonists set to work in clearing land for tillage, building houses, sowing and reaping, and producing the commodities required for living, they had to take into account the conditioning element of climate.

The soil at their feet was likewise a conditioning feature of their life in America. It, too, presented variations, from the small fields in narrow valleys, the rocky ground and steep hillsides of New England, through the broad and fertile valleys of the middle colonies, to the pine barrens, swamps, clay, and shallow loam of the deep South. Yet in every colony settlers could find land on which to produce all the grains, vegetables, and fruits for their staple foodstuffs and grasses for the grazing of livestock. Nothing was needed to furnish a generous and diverse food supply from the cultivation of the earth except implements, skills, good management, and hard labor.

While the soil for the most part was favorable to multiform agricultural production, clay beds and quarries yielded bricks, stones, and marble for building purposes. Primeval forests provided additional means of a livelihood more abundant than that of workers on the land in England or Western Europe. In every section the amazing array of trees offered materials for every kind of shelter from quickly constructed cabins to carefully built great manor houses, for barns and workshops, for the making of furniture and other household equipment, and for the output of staves, barrels, and lumber to be shipped to England in payment of debts partly incurred by the purchase of the finer grades of manufactured goods.

In the forests were also wild animals in a great variety, the furs and skins of which were useful for domestic purposes and profitable for export. In the forests was wild game for food—turkeys, deer, rabbits, and squirrels, for instance—and more meat and more kinds of meat could be procured than the plain peoples had ever enjoyed in the Old World, at first without asking the permission of any lord or gamekeeper or poaching secretly on private preserves. In the forests were nuts, berries, grapes, and other wild fruits available to agile climbers and pickers, aids to a balanced diet and free as the air.

Moreover the rivers, brooks, ponds, and lakes teemed with fish easy even for children to catch, while off the long coast were deep-sea fish accessible to professional fishermen.

Most of the immigrants who came to the colonies, rich and poor alike, knew more about agriculture than about any other practical art; and in turning to the creation of real wealth, by inclination and necessity, they found ways and means of applying this knowledge in old and new forms. At home the English had been accustomed to the production of a few standard commodities—a few grains, fruits, vegetables, and meats. In the colonies, owing to the variations in climate and soil, they were able to produce new and special crops. In many respects this very fact had decisive influences on the branches of agriculture which they developed, on types of commodities entering into the trade with the mother country, on the growth of wealth in America, and on the social characteristics of the several regions from Maine to Georgia.

Besides possessing extraordinary resources for the food, clothing, and shelter required in daily living, the South from Maryland to Georgia had climate and soil especially suitable for the raising of certain staples which supplemented the agricultural economy of England, provided cargoes for English vessels, and business for

English merchants. First among these staples was tobacco. While Virginia was still an infant settlement the raising of tobacco became almost a mania.

Zeal for tobacco production quickly spread all along the Southern coastal plains as new colonies were founded and as supplies of indentured white laborers and servile laborers—Negro slaves—increased. Planters gathered great fortunes from tobacco and the prospect of larger fortunes led them to push into the interior even up into the foothills. News of the prosperity to be won by tobacco growing stimulated the immigration of capitalistic planters and merchants ever ready to handle cargoes. Tobacco planters became land speculators and engrossers of small freehold plots. Until the eve of the American Revolution, Southern riches rested largely on this crop.

A second Southern staple from which flowed new wealth was rice. The settlement near Charleston, South Carolina, founded in 1672, was little more than ten years old when it was discovered that rice could be grown luxuriantly in the swampy lands of the coast and along the rivers. In favorable years planters could make as high as a forty per cent return on their capital invested in rice fields and slave labor. Here, too, was a staple which England and European countries did not produce and hence it furnished a profitable article of export for which there was a large demand. Between 1713 and 1724 exports of rice through Charleston rose from 3000 barrels a year to 124,000 barrels. As the death rate of slaves in the rice swamps was high, rice production fostered the importation of slaves and furnished business for British and New England shippers, adding to their wealth.

Near the middle of the eighteenth century a third staple was added to Southern economy—indigo. This was a precious dyestuff, one of the most important until the rise of modern chemistry, and indispensable to the English textile industry. The successful production of this staple was due to the perseverance of Eliza Lucas, who in her youth took over the management of three plantations owned by her father, then governor of Antigua.

Securing indigo seeds from her father in the West Indies, Miss Lucas tested them on her own land. Previous attempts by others had been failures, but by persistence she demonstrated that crops could be produced successfully in South Carolina. Indigo grown on one of her plantations served as a wedding dower when she married Charles Pinckney, of Charleston, in 1744. Pinckney encouraged his neighbors to go into the business. Four years later the

British Parliament voted a bounty of sixpence per pound to producers. With this aid and a fair price in England, planters could make a profit ranging from thirty to fifty per cent a year. So valuable did indigo become that small cubes of it were used for money during the Revolution when all forms of paper currency became worthless.

Far to the North, in New England, climate and soil confined colonists to the production of agricultural commodities practically identical with those which could be raised in England. Moreover the narrow valleys, rocky hills, and stony yet often fertile land were unfavorable to the establishment of plantations or great landed estates of any type. There were, in truth, many extensive land holdings in parts of New England, especially in early days, but there was available no cheap and adequate supply of labor by which they could be tilled with large profits to owners. Besides, New England was peopled mainly by yeomen used to owning and tilling small farms and by farm laborers eager to get possession of land in their own right.

So in respect of agriculture New England became a region of small holdings on which farming families produced for their own use nearly all the commodities necessary to a comfortable living. Although iron, salt, some tools, and finer cloths, if any were bought, had to come from the towns, practically everything else was grown or made on the farm. Life on such farms was hard—toil from sun to sun. Out of it came no large accumulations of wealth or cargoes of grain, flour, or meat for export. Yet it yielded a high degree of economic well-being and freedom from dependence on the fortunes of British commerce. With it went a spirit of impatience at most forms of official control from above which interfered with the course of farm and community affairs. If New England agriculture produced no great riches for English merchants or investors, it did produce wealth for the support of a large farming population, sturdy, educated, and owing neither rents nor obeisance to overlords.

In the middle colonies between New England and the South, agriculture took other forms. The soil, more level and fertile than that of New England, was adapted to the production of similar crops on a larger scale, but the climate was not favorable to the establishment of plantations for raising tobacco, rice, or indigo in the Southern style. There were many great estates in New York, tilled by tenants under terms akin to feudal bondage. Landlords and speculators—Dutch, English, and American—managed, by investment, chicanery, and corruption, to engross from one half to two thirds of the land in the colony. Enormous holdings, comparable in size to great plantations in the South, were in the hands of a relatively few families, for example, the Van Rensselaers, the Van Cortlandts, the Schuylers, the Phillipses, the Beekmans, the Livingstons, and the Morrises. The estate of the Beekmans embraced 240,000 acres, that of the Van Cortlandts 140,000 acres, and the holdings of the Van Rensselaers about Albany no less than 700,000 acres.

Often the landed families of New York combined agriculture with shipping and merchandising, sometimes by intermarriage. For instance, Frederick Phillipse, a rich Dutch landlord of the Hudson Valley, while traveling at sea on a packet line operated by Margaret Hardenbroeck, a Dutch landowner and merchant, was captivated by her personality and enterprise. Soon afterward, in 1662, they were married, and united in a single household landlordism with zeal for commercial undertakings. While Frederick looked after his estates and later engaged in shipping so irregularly that he was charged with being involved in the piratical activities of Captain Kidd, Margaret attended principally to regular mercantile undertakings and proved to be "a very desirable business partner."

After New Jersey was taken from the Dutch in 1664 and turned over to English proprietors, efforts were made to create large estates there. The proprietors themselves engaged in land speculation, established titles to huge areas in their own names, and in their eagerness to sell land in large blocks carved out many holdings of considerable size. But the inhabitants of New Jersey, especially of the western part, almost rose in arms against this land policy. Even the proprietors came to see, at least dimly, that to increase the population and wealth of the colony provision must be made for selling, even giving, land in small plots to actual settlers prepared to cultivate them.

In Pennsylvania the proprietor had the right, like the proprietor of Maryland, under his charter, to lay out and sell great estates, manors, in his colony and he did in fact lend some encouragement to great landlordism. But most of Pennsylvania was divided into farms that could be tilled by their owners aided only by one or a few extra laborers, if any. Furthermore large numbers of pioneers simply settled on the frontier without asking the permission of Penn or anybody else. Thus farming on a small or moderate scale became the general rule in Pennsylvania agriculture.

With agriculture the population of all the colonies became self-sustaining as regards food products; and by the tens of thousands farmers grew prosperous, as prosperity was rated, in tilling their own soil; not rich in gold coins or paper claims, but secure in real wealth—houses, barns, stock, tools, and all the means of commodious living. The great areas of level land in the middle colonies, free from stones and covered by a fertile topsoil, enabled them to produce a surplus of grains, beef, pork, and bacon for export. Thus they could pay for imported manufactures and enter into competition with British agriculture in respect of its principal staples.

Inasmuch as even the planters of the South usually combined the production of foodstuffs, for their slaves and for their own use, with the raising of special staples for the British market, all the colonies were, therefore, soon independent of the Old World with regard to these primary essentials of living. There were few if any landlords in New England as rich as the largest Southern planters; but from New York to the borders of Virginia there were landlords who could vie in wealth with the greatest Southern planters. Indeed as the soil on the coastal plains of the South was worn down by intensive cultivation and returns from tobacco raising diminished, the relative position of landlords in New York and Pennsylvania improved.

☆

Closely connected with the agricultural pursuits was domestic manufacturing in the strict sense of that phrase—making things by hand at home. This was especially true in the colonies north of Maryland which produced no great staples that were not also produced in Great Britain. Southern planters did raise crops, such as tobacco, rice, and indigo, that did not compete with British agriculture and could therefore be readily exchanged for British manufactured goods, since those crops were desired by British buyers. But from Pennsylvania northward and in all the back-country regions farming families, having no such staples to sell to English merchants, had to make many things themselves or go without them. And countless families refused to be deprived of necessities and comforts of a manufactured kind. Many men and women among them were Jacks-of-all-trades, meaning "artists in living," and they made living an art by their domestic manufacturing. Even great planters in the South established workshops on their estates in which commodities for household use, for supplying slaves, and for other purposes were manufactured out of materials at hand.

The extent to which manufacturing combined with agriculture could go was represented on the estates of Robert Carter, of Virginia, the grandson of a rich planter, colonial officer, land speculator, and businessman in Virginia. Carter's land holding, including his family seat in Westmoreland County, embraced about 70,000 acres (his grandfather had owned some 300,000 acres) and his slaves numbered more than five hundred. Besides raising tobacco and other agricultural produce, he maintained many shops on his properties for making cloth and salt, grinding grain, baking bread, and working iron. Agriculture and manufacturing he supplemented by selling goods as a merchant, lending money at interest like a banker, and sending ships to and fro carrying goods. At his great mansion, so large that it took twenty-eight fireplaces going full blast to warm it in wintertime, Carter whiled away his leisure hours with balls, music, reading, and dinner parties. Yet, with the aid of overseers and superintendents, and his wife's co-operation, he managed to hold all his agricultural, manufacturing, and trading enterprises together and keep them in successful and profitable operation.

On farms and plantations from New Hampshire to Georgia men usually made and repaired farm implements—plows, sleds, wagons, and hoes. Out of furs and skins they made shoes, hats, and caps. Out of wood they fashioned furniture, churns, spinning wheels, and looms. Where wrought iron was available they manufactured nails, shovels, and chains. At the same time women generally turned their skills and wits to making cloth, rugs, soap, candles, bedding, coverlets, tablecloths, and garments. They also operated processing plants, in which bread was baked, meat was packed, fruits and vegetables were dehydrated and preserved, and butter was churned.

As a rule the products of home workshops were used on the farm or plantation but in time women developed an industry which turned out goods for community and colonial markets. With flax for linen at their command and, in the Northern colonies, wool from sheep, they set to work spinning and weaving with such vim that their output soon alarmed British merchants, who wanted the textile markets free for their own manufactures. While most of the cloth produced by women at their homes was coarse in quality and used mainly for "working clothes," the finer linens and woolens compared well with the grades offered by

British merchants. As time went on women so improved the textile art that they made it possible for Americans to clothe themselves well, if not in the finest goods, and to achieve a high degree of economic independence in one primary line of manufacturing.

For the development of agriculture and domestic manufacturing, an abundant and increasing supply of labor, skilled and unskilled, was furnished by the migration of free whites and indentured white laborers and the importation of Negro slaves. On the small farm owned and operated by the freehold family, the husband, wife, and children did all the work in fields, forest, workshops, and the house. At harvest time and on other special occasions, the family might have the co-operative help of neighbors in return for similar labor, but it carried the main burden of its own self-support.

After crossroad settlements and villages arose as centers for stores and craftsmen who made things on order, the farm family could be relieved from certain tasks at home by exchanging farm produce with the smith or woodworker for "odd jobs" or manufactured goods. As colonization proceeded, itinerant artisans —tinkers, smiths, weavers, bakers, tailors, and carpenters—wandered from community to community and worked for their board, lodging, and payments in coin. Yet even in the most populous of the rural regions there was little specialization. The farm family supplied most of the labor for agriculture and domestic manufacturing.

On the larger farms of the North the labor of the owner and his family was often supplemented by the labor of one or more indentured servants. Such a servant was a person bound by contract to work for an employer for a term of years, ranging from four to seven as a rule, in return for board, lodging, and clothing, and some gift or gifts on the expiration of the service. Many men, women, and children kidnaped by gangsters in Great Britain or taken from prisons were shipped over against their will for sale into servitude. But nearly all indentured servants were immigrants who had freely chosen their hard lot in the hope of eventual advantages. They preferred this choice to remaining in the Old World where they could either find no work at all or had to toil all their lives with no prospects of more than subsistence wages.

In all the colonies from early days there were indentured servants, mainly farmers but often household workers and craftsmen. Although the number was small in New England, it was large in Virginia and the middle colonies. Eighteen years after the founding of Jamestown in 1607 more than one third of Virginia's inhabitants were indentured servants. During the closing years of the seventeenth century more than one third of all the immigrants in Pennsylvania were of this class and the proportion did not decrease for a long time.

After they had finished their term of service indentured servants were free to make their way as best they could. Those who were skillful, industrious, and fortunate either acquired farms of their own in the neighborhood or went west to the frontier to settle on new land. Or, if they were especially ingenious in the crafts, they went to the towns and set up shops for themselves or found employment with merchants and master craftsmen. At all events no stigma of servitude rested upon them and, as far as the law was concerned, they could and often did rise to good fortune and even honors in their colony. The fact that they had started near the bottom put no bar against their advancement. Although thousands of servants, on the expiration of their indentures, joined the "poor whites," South and North, the great majority of them merged with the population of farmers and artisans and shared their labors and advantages as free citizens.

In an entirely different position were the Negroes imported from Africa and sold into bondage. As early as 1619 Negroes were brought to Virginia and soon slavery became an established institution under the law. Before many years it spread to all the colonies, and by 1770 about one sixth of the entire population were Negro slaves.

In the North, however, climate, soil, and types of agriculture made slavery on a large scale unprofitable; and, comparatively speaking, the proportion of Negro slaves remained small. In the colony of New York, for example, where it was high, it amounted to about one seventh of the population at the end of the colonial period. On the other hand the climate, soil, staple crops, and plantation system of the South favored the use of slave labor. White bond servants were often intractable, their terms of service made them impermanent laborers, and the most enterprising among them valiantly struggled to get land for themselves as soon as they became free. Negro slaves by contrast had to work for their masters as long as they lived and could be bought in great numbers as the slave traffic increased. Only by slavery, planters insisted, was it possible for them to expand rapidly the cultivation of the soil and make profits in large amounts. At all events, two thirds of the inhabitants of South Carolina were slaves at the close of the colonial period, and along the Southern seaboard the labor of Negroes underlay the wealth and power of masters.

By such means in the great rural resettlement the colonists were able to build up a strong agricultural economy that long continued to be the principal basis of American security. At the end of the colonial age at least nine tenths of the people, from New Hampshire to Georgia, lived on the land and produced for themselves the commodities necessary to a good, if often simple, living. A few thousand great landlords, North and South, grew rich on tenant and slave labor and lived luxuriously. But the overwhelming majority of the white people belonged to families that owned, frequently under mortgage it is true, small farms and worked with their own hands in fields, forests, farmhouses, and little shops.

Their life was toilsome, no doubt, but by their mode of living, their self-supporting economy, and their spirit of independence they made a rural order different from the Old World orders of tenantry, feudalism, and serfdom. In self-sustaining industry, character, and love of their freedom, they formed a body of working people such as had never appeared before in the history of Western civilization.

CHAPTER IV

The Rise of Commerce and Industry

RUNNING ALONG with the development of autonomy in agriculture was the promotion of commerce and industry. Although the population in the colonial age continued to be predominantly agricultural, the character of American life, the evolution of American society, and the total power of American economy, as it gathered force, represented a combination of agriculture, commerce, and industry.

From the beginning of colonization, commerce was integrated with agriculture. It carried over the sea certain raw materials of the colonies and brought back from England tools and other finished commodities that increased the productivity of agriculture and raised the standard of rural life. It speeded up the circulation of commodities within and among the colonies, giving outlets to surplus domestic manufactures and acquainting the people of each section with the people, customs, and economic activities of other sections. Besides pouring commodities into commercial channels, industry evoked the energies of local enterprise, enabled Americans to produce many kinds of things hitherto imported, and demonstrated to discerning persons the immense potentialities of American resources. Together, commerce and industry permitted the accumulation of large capitals in American hands, decreasing dependence on British investors.

The promotion of commerce was an essential element of the mercantilist policy under which the English government operated, and was among the purposes of the companies and proprietors that led in colonization. A provision of the Virginia charter issued in 1606 granted to the London Company special privileges in trade, by laying heavy duties on the commerce of outsiders, English and foreign, and turning the revenue into its treasury for a term of years. To meet the cost of the expedition that brought the Pilgrims to Plymouth in 1620, a large sum was borrowed from English capitalists and the debt could only be paid by gathering in articles of commerce, such as fish and furs, which could be sent back to England. The royal patent of 1681 constituting William Penn proprietor of Pennsylvania also gave him the right to build harbors and docks for commercial purposes and to lay customs duties on goods "to be laded and unladed" at such ports and places. If colonization was to be profitable to English investors, cargoes had to be provided for the return voyages of ships that transported immigrants and their goods to America.

The early newcomers to America were under obligations to look about for objects of commerce almost as soon as they landed. The first ship which deposited settlers in Virginia carried home a cargo of wooden staves prepared for it under the direction of Captain John Smith. Lumber and its by-products became commodities for export from Virginia before settlers in that colony learned to produce, cure, and pack tobacco.

☆

Long before any colonies had been started, English sailors had embarked on large-scale fishing off the coasts of Newfoundland, and the early explorers had excited English interest in this business by glowing reports of haddock, cod, mackerel, and whales in unlimited quantities in the waters of that region. The Pilgrims at Plymouth and the Puritans at Massachusetts Bay, shortly after their arrival, began to build small boats and send out fishing expeditions. In time Boston, Salem, Marblehead, and a few other towns became busy ports for the fishing industry; and all down the coast fishing became a source of lucrative trading.

Besides furnishing supplies to American markets, fishermen cured and packed huge quantities for export. But the English themselves were extensively engaged in this industry, and American fishermen had to seek other than British markets. They found them principally in France, Portugal, Spain, and the West Indies. On the basis of this exchange an immense business was built up. The fish shipped to Spain, for example, were exchanged for citrus fruits and specie, and the specie was used to pay for English manufactures. The fish sent to the West Indies were traded for sugar and specie; a part of the sugar went to the colonies and another part, with the specie, went to England to pay debts and buy manufactures.

With particular doggedness the fishermen of New England turned to whaling. At first they concentrated their efforts largely in the waters off Newfoundland, but in time they pushed their enterprise all over the Atlantic, using the ports of New Bedford and Nantucket as their chief bases of operation.

So extensive were their whaling voyages and so daring were their undertakings that Edmund Burke, when in 1775 he warned the British Parliament against "ill-considered" tampering with the strength and independence of Americans, paused to give a dramatic picture of their whaling industry: "Look at the manner in which the people of New England have of late carried on the whale fishery. Whilst we follow them among the tumbling mountains of ice, and behold them penetrating into the deepest frozen recesses of Hudson's Bay and Davis's Straits, whilst we are looking for them beneath the Arctic circle, we hear that they have pierced into the opposite region of polar cold, that they are at the antipodes, and engaged under the frozen serpent of the South. . . . Nor is the equinoctial heat more discouraging to them, than the accumulated winter of both the poles.

"We know that whilst some of them draw the line and strike the harpoon on the coast of Africa, others run the longitude, and pursue their gigantic game along the coast of Brazil. No sea but what is vexed by their fisheries. No climate that is not witness to their toils. Neither the perseverance of Holland, nor the activity of France, nor the dexterous and firm sagacity of English enterprise, ever carried this most perilous mode of hard industry to the extent to which it has been pushed by this recent people; a people who are still, as it were, but in the gristle, and not yet hardened into the bone of manhood."

Although the British at home caught plenty of fish for themselves and took relatively little from American exporters, they were short of one prime raw material which the colonies had in abundance—timber. They had exhausted many of their forest areas in building houses, shops, and ships, and in supplying charcoal for their iron industries. British shortage of timber was thus an opportunity for the colonists and they made haste to meet it. Almost at the outset of settlement they had to cut down trees in clearing land for cultivation and they saved many choice logs—especially oak, pine, and walnut—for shipment to England.

Within a few years little sawmills were built along the streams and rivers, and enterprising merchants began to produce lumber in various forms for the English market. New England, New York, Pennsylvania, and North Carolina became the main centers of such undertakings.

In time Americans were supplying finished and semifinished timber products for local, intercolonial, and English markets, such as masts and spars for ships, shingles, and staves for barrels and casks. By developing the lumber industry Americans were enabled to discharge debts in England, buy English manufactures, accumulate profits for new investments in colonial lands and business adventures.

Furs and skins furnished another immensely profitable group of articles for commerce. For some time they were readily procured by colonists near their settlements or from Indian hunters who brought them to the very doors of houses, as soon as they learned that they could exchange otter, mink, bear, fox, beaver, and deer furs or skins for beads, metal knives, hoes, hatchets, cloth, and trinkets. Able to buy furs for so little and sell them overseas at enormous prices, white traders reaped golden rewards from this business. Farmers could supplement agriculture by gathering in furs without giving much time to it. Nor did they need capital for the easy traffic. While settlers clung to the shores and forests still stood at the back doors of cabins, dealing in furs was a simpler transaction than the catching and selling of fish or the cutting and shipping of lumber.

But as forests were cleared for farming and settlements pushed inland, the fur business became more restricted for farmers who were not located on the frontier. Now organized enterprise steadily pressed into the collecting and bundling of furs for shipment. Monopolies of the trade in certain regions were sought and sometimes obtained by personal initiative or through government grants. Among the Dutch, who preceded the English as settlers in the Hudson River valley, fur monopolies were rich prizes over which merchants and officials waged many a lusty contest.

Even in favorable circumstances hunters, woodsmen, and trappers who roamed the frontiers freely in search of furs were finally at the mercy of fur merchants who usually fixed the prices at their own pleasure. As the frontier was pushed westward and forests were cleared, the fur business needed ever larger amounts of capital to pay for scouting and the maintenance of trading stations in the far backwoods. So the traffic in furs gradually became highly organized and tended to concentrate in the hands of a few merchants, British and American. By the close of the colonial period competition between them for mastery over this trade often broke out in political quarrels at colonial capitals and in London.

☆

With the expansion of agriculture and commerce, creating and enlarging markets, opportunities widened for the use and sale of ships, iron products, and other commodities that were not supplied by domestic manufacturers. Indeed the colonies were still very young when independent manufacturing industries sprang up in the neighborhood of farms and plantations, especially in the North. Three industries attained first rank: shipbuilding, iron-working, and flour milling.

So abundant in the colonies were ship timber and naval stores, including tar, that shipbuilding soon became an important business. Being British subjects, Americans enjoyed the benefits of British navigation laws; ships built in the colonies and manned by Americans belonged to the merchant marine of the mother country and had the same rights in the shipping business. And special circumstances favored American shipbuilding. It was cheaper to build vessels in the colonies, where materials were abundant, than in England, for the English had to import a large part of their ship timber and naval stores. The rapid growth of the fishing industry also made a local demand for ships.

In response to these opportunities and needs, shipyards sprang up all along the coast, especially north of Maryland; a lucrative industry gave employment to ship carpenters and yielded profits to investors. Before long Americans were building ships as stout and swift as any that sailed the seas.

In its turn shipbuilding spurred other industries, particularly the production of ship timber, tar, chains, rope, anchors, and nails. Now there was a demand for ironworking on a scope larger than that needed for making the few types of agricultural implements then in use.

Here again the state of things in England had to be considered. The English had iron ore in abundance and their iron industry had reached a high stage of development. But they used charcoal for smelting ore and were exhausting their local wood supply. On the other hand, Americans had iron ore in almost every colony and their charcoal sources were practically unlimited.

In these circumstances English interest called for the importation of pig, or rough, iron to be transformed in English foundries into finished products for English usage and for export to the colonies. The Americans could, of course, supply the pig iron to English merchants. But they also had skill for working iron into products necessary to their own agriculture and industry and could approach self-sufficiency in that line.

Iron ore was discovered by the first settlers in Virginia and they sent a large quantity of it to England in 1608. Within a few years they were smelting ore and working iron in the colony and might have gone far with it if tobacco raising had not proved to be a quicker way of making large profits. Puritans also early unearthed iron ore. By 1644 Massachusetts had an ironworks in operation. In the other New England colonies and in the middle colonies the discovery of iron deposits was quickly followed by the building of furnaces for ore smelting and mills for hammering, rolling, and slitting iron.

At the middle of the eighteenth century American ironmasters were making iron products of nearly every kind—chains, anchors, guns, kettles, axes, knives, nails, iron bars, and pipes. For fine iron products, such as the best cutlery, needles, and carpenters' tools, the colonies depended largely on imports from England. But the arts of iron manufacture were being steadily improved; so steadily, in fact, that British merchants grew worried over American competition in the colonial market.

Flour and lumber milling industries rose and flourished as agriculture and shipbuilding advanced. Right at hand was wood for water wheels and mills, and hard stone for millstones. Almost everywhere streams rushing down to the sea could be used for power. With the increase in the production of grain for home consumption, the crude labor of pounding, grinding, and bolting wheat, corn, and rye in domestic shops became so burdensome that farmers welcomed the release from it. As the export of grain from the middle colonies enlarged, merchants saw a chance to add to their profits by substituting flour in barrels for the shipment of grain in the raw state. Very early the demands of shipbuilding outran the supply of lumber which could be sawed slowly by hand, and as prospering colonists prepared to move from log cabins to frame houses local needs for lumber and shingles were multiplied.

So on the streams from New Hampshire to Georgia, mills were built to process grain and saw logs into various types of lumber. Sometimes the two processes were combined at a single mill; often they were separated. In Pennsylvania enterprising flour millers barreled their flour for shipment and even erected shops for baking bread and manufacturing the famous hardtack biscuits served to sailors on naval and merchant vessels.

☆

From the farms and plantations, from the gathering of raw materials, from the ironworks, from mills for grinding grain and sawing timber flowed a swelling stream of various commodities to be marketed in the colonies or abroad and exchanged for colonial or British manufactures. Here were expanding opportunities for specialized merchants and shippers. Often, if not usually, the merchant was a shipowner, and combined the business of buying and selling with the business of transporting. But whatever the form of operation, American commercial enterprise had a spacious theater in which to distribute goods and accumulate gains. At home it could use the coastal waters and navigable streams penetrating interior regions. Before it was the Atlantic Ocean, touching all the ports of Europe and Africa, as well as those of Great Britain.

As the population of America rose—from about 300,000 in 1700 to about 2,500,000 in 1770—trade and shipping were extended. In the beginning most of this business was in the hands of merchants resident in England, who operated personally or through agents in the colonies; but it was not long before Americans entered into a vigorous competition with them. Colonists could build and navigate ships, as well as keep accounts and handle commercial transactions. What was to hinder them from gathering more and more of the business into their own hands? As events proved, nothing could.

Five main avenues of trade were open to American merchants and shippers. One branch of their commerce was with Great Britain. Another was with European ports—French, Spanish, and Portuguese—in certain commodities. A third was with the British West Indies and, often illegally, with the French West Indies. Intercolonial trade also flourished from port to port along the Atlantic coast and from point to point along the navigable rivers reaching into the interior. In prosecuting the slave trade, merchants and shippers, particularly from New England and New York, visited the shores of Africa and carried away cargoes of Negroes for the plantations of the West Indies and the South and to supply the smaller markets of the Northern colonies. When wars were raging—frequently the case in the seventeenth and eighteenth centuries—shipowners could embark on privateering, sometimes akin to piracy, and prey upon French, Dutch, or Spanish commerce.

With the wealth garnered from transporting goods was thus combined the loot of commercial wars. When George III ascended the throne in 1760 American merchants and shippers in the great colonial ports were numerous enough, rich enough, and powerful enough to vie with the stoutest merchants of Bristol and London.

☆

The development of commerce and industry encouraged an increasing immigration of workers who specialized in the several crafts, including shipbuilding; and in the course of time the line between purely domestic artisans and industrial mechanics became sharper in the rural districts and very definite in the towns. At the end of the colonial period the colonies thus had an important, if small, body of industrial workers engaged solely in the manufacture of goods for the markets.

Carpenters, masons, smiths, and woodworkers were among the earliest immigrants in the seventeenth century. Some were freemen. Others were indentured servants. With the rise of shipbuilding, ironworking, flour milling and other industries, the stream of artisans, free and indentured, swelled in size, though it was never large enough in the opinion of business enterprisers in the colonies. Workers from the British Isles, from Germany, Holland, Sweden, Switzerland, and France crowded the incoming ships and played a vital part in the building up of industry, commerce, and the standard of living.

Besides regular workers competent in using wood, stone, and other materials for the construction of simple buildings and the manufacture of articles necessary to a commodious living, there were in all the colonies designers and artisans of special and higher skills. Among them were architects, woodcarvers, silversmiths, wheelwrights, potters, pewterers, and makers of glassware, watches, leatherware, coaches, and cabinets.

After the first years of pioneering were over, architects began to design and erect fine mansions for great landlords and merchants, stately buildings for public purposes, and handsome churches for religious worship. So solid, beautiful, indeed exquisite, was much of their work that it became the pride of discriminating colonists and their descendants. In the designing and making of elegant furniture, objects of glass, panels for walls and doors, mantels, carvings for cornices and porticoes, iron gates and grills, silver ornaments of tableware, masters of such arts could satisfy fastidious taste and at the same time supply markets with goods at prices which enabled even small farmers, storekeepers, and mechanics to incorporate some refinements into their simple ways of living.

☆

Out of the economic activities of numberless men and women, white and black, especially out of the export and import trade in all its branches, developed specialized centers of settlement on the seacoast and at favorable points on inland waters. By 1690 the foundations of flourishing cities had been laid at Boston, Newport, New York, Philadelphia, and Charleston. According to careful estimates, the population of these towns at that time was as follows:

Boston, founded in 1630, 7000.
Newport, founded in 1639, 2600.
New York, founded as New Amsterdam in 1625, 3900.
Philadelphia, founded in 1682, 4000.
Charleston, founded in 1672, 1100.

On the eve of the Revolution in 1774, Philadelphia, serving as a leading port of entry for immigrants and for the shipping of surplus produce from a great hinterland, had forged to the top. With almost 40,000 inhabitants, it stood first in population and was second only to London among the cities of the British Empire. Boston had about 20,000 inhabitants; Newport 12,000; New York between 25,000 and 30,000; and Charleston about 10,000. Except in the case of Boston these were only estimates but, however out of line on one side or the other, they corresponded roughly to the facts.

Among other growing centers of trade on the coast or inland were Salem, Providence, New Haven, Perth Amboy, Baltimore, Richmond, and Savannah. Among the minor towns, as yet little more than overgrown villages but increasing in size, were Albany, Princeton, Trenton, Germantown, Lancaster, Annapolis, Norfolk, and Wilmington in North Carolina. Although the population of all the cities having more than 8000 inhabitants was less than three per cent of the total population of the colonies, their importance in wealth and as centers of economic, social, political, and intellectual activity outweighed the mere number of their inhabitants.

☆

Of the total wealth produced by all the economic activities of men, women, and children in all the colonies from year to year between 1607, the founding of Virginia, and 1774, on the eve of the rift with Great Britain, no official census was ever taken. Nor were any figures recorded from which more than the roughest guesses could be made. The first census taken by the United States, in 1790, gave only the population—3,172,000 whites and 700,000 Negroes. Of this population, according to reckonings by family names, 75.2% were English, Scotch, and Scotch-Irish in origins; 3.7% South Irish; 8.7% Germans, and the rest Dutch, Swedish, French, and miscellaneous.

Although no economic census was taken in colonial times, two well-established facts indicate that the annual output of wealth was immense and on the increase. It was great enough to provide the main support of the rapidly growing population, particularly with regard to the primary staples of living, and a surplus for export. That the output was rising swiftly was disclosed by figures for the trade with Great Britain. In his address to the House of Commons in 1775 *On Conciliation with America*, Edmund Burke presented the following table:

The whole export trade of England, including that to colonies in 1704 ....£6,509,000.
Export to the colonies alone [including Canada and the West Indies] in 1772 ....£6,024,000.

Well could Burke exclaim: "The trade with America alone is now within less than £500,000 of being equal to what this great commercial nation, England, carried on at the beginning of this century with the whole world!"

The exact amount of the English export to the thirteen American colonies was not separated in Burke's figures from the trade with Canada and the British West Indies; but there was no doubt about its magnitude. No longer were the Americans puny colonists almost wholly dependent on Great Britain for capital, primary supplies, and manufactures. They had built up on this continent a great society and provided for it an economic underwriting of unquestionable strength. What was more: they saw extraordinary chances for the expansion of their enterprise and were determined to take advantage of them.

CHAPTER V

Growth of Social and Intellectual Autonomy

WHATEVER may have been the visions of English kings who chartered companies and granted patents to proprietors for the purpose of founding colonies in America;

Whatever may have been the intentions of the companies and proprietors who planted settlements;

Whatever may have been the dreams of the English leaders who hoped to see a New England established beyond the sea;

Whatever may have been the hopes of immigrants who acquired great estates and became mighty landlords or turned to commerce and became rich merchants able to compete with the most powerful merchants of London;

Whatever may have been the aspirations of the men and women engaged in tilling the soil and building up domestic manufactures, or of the artisans devoted to developing industries and creating the refinements of living;

However much of the Old World heritage the immigrants brought with them to the New World;

There were from the beginning social and intellectual tendencies which reinforced the separatist qualities and energies that had led to migration and worked in the direction of consolidation and autonomy in the colonies.

Giving form and force to these autonomous tendencies were certain elemental facts. In America emigrants from England did not reproduce the whole social order of England—king, lords, established church, and peasantry with no hope of owning land. Nor did they reproduce the whole intellectual outlook of England. Neither did they begin anew, from primitive origins, the history of civilization in the Old World and thus start repeating that history as it had been from the days of savagery. The overwhelming majority of the emigrants to America, from the early years to the close of the colonial period, were dissenters from the Church of England, whether they were English, Scotch, French, or German. No less opposed to that religious establishment were the English and Irish Catholics who found refuge in the colonies. Despite claims to aristocratic origins made by proud descendants, the overwhelming majority of the emigrants to America were from the "middling orders"—agricultural, mercantile, and artisan. And for their activities in America, whatever the ambitions and hopes of any or all the immigrants, there were two conditioning material realities which helped to shape their fortunes—a virgin continent vast in extent and resources, and three thousand miles of water separating them from the world they had left behind.

Helping to sustain autonomous tendencies and strengthen them as they developed were, first, the qualities of the immigrants as such and, second, the knowledge and ideas acquired from the Old World, out of which they came, and modified for their purposes, in the course of colonial evolution. This truth was firmly grasped by Mercy Otis Warren, herself a colonial, born at Barnstable, Massachusetts, in 1728 and long a resident of Plymouth. "The first emigrations to North America," she wrote, "were not composed of a strolling banditti of rude nations, like the first people of most other colonies in the history of the world." On the contrary, she declared, speaking out of direct knowledge: "The early settlers in the newly discovered continent were as far advanced in civilization, policy, and manners; in their ideas of government, the nature of compacts, and the bands of civil union, as any of their neighbors at that period among the most polished nations of Europe." While recognizing that vices of Europe had also come with virtues, Mrs. Warren maintained that "the progress of everything had there [in America] been remarkably rapid from the first settlement of the country. Learning was cultivated, knowledge disseminated, politeness and morals improved, and valor and patriotism cherished, in proportion to the rapidity of her population."

The qualities of mind and character to which Mrs. Warren referred were abundantly illustrated in the little colony of Plymouth, founded in 1620. Two outstanding leaders among the Pilgrims were Elder William Brewster and William Bradford. Brewster was the son of a local bailiff and postmaster in Yorkshire and had spent some time at Cambridge University in his youth.

His library, as a biographer has said, "proves him to have been well read in history, philosophy, and religious poetry and shows that he continued to buy books throughout his life." Bradford, brought up in his youth to follow the plow, was a self-educated man of wide learning who, in his intellectual explorations, read among other books the *Republic* by Jean Bodin, French writer on government and society—a critique of Plato's idealistic and communistic theories. Both Brewster and Bradford displayed qualities of statesmanship, if in a small community, in dealing with lawless and discontented men who made grave troubles for the Pilgrims before and after they landed.

To Massachusetts Bay, during the early years, came more than one hundred graduates of Cambridge and Oxford universities. John Winthrop, the first governor of that colony, was the son of a lawyer and had studied at Cambridge. Roger Williams, who, in rebellion against the government of Massachusetts Bay, founded a freer community at Providence, belonged to a mercantile family of London, had graduated from Cambridge with honors, and was a philosophic thinker of humanist inclinations. Some of the later colonists, notably Charles Carroll, born in Maryland in 1737, were educated at the best Catholic institutions in Europe. Among the leaders in all the colonies were men who had studied law at the Temple in London, or theology, natural philosophy, the classics, medicine, and other branches of learning at the best institutions in Great Britain, on the Continent, or in both places.

From first to last colonial women in large numbers were well educated—though not in universities. Anne Hutchinson, evicted like Roger Williams from Boston for her independence of mind, was the daughter of a Puritan clergyman and wife of a well-to-do merchant, a mother of fourteen children, known for her learning and the vigor of her intellect—the reason for her eviction. Anne Bradstreet—ancestor of Oliver Wendell Holmes and Wendell Phillips—who arrived at Massachusetts Bay in 1630, was the daughter of Thomas Dudley, deputy governor under Winthrop, and the wife of Simon Bradstreet, a graduate of Cambridge. Eight tutors had been employed by her parents in starting her education and the poetry that she composed in America displayed her familiarity with Raleigh's *History of the World*, with Plutarch, Usher, and contemporary French literature. In every colony were numerous women of English, Dutch, Huguenot, and other national origins who had been trained in the classics and modern literature—women of the planting and professional circles, women of the great landed and mercantile families. And a stream of hired tutors in the prosperous families maintained this standard of the proprieties for sons and daughters.

As the sprawling and widely separated settlements grew into populous and orderly colonies, social and intellectual changes of weighty meaning for the future took place. In every colony members of the classes drew together for social and intellectual intercourse and formed permanent ties of customs, manners, and views. In the South the planting and merchant families led in this concentration; generally, in the North, clerical and merchant families took the leadership; in New York and Pennsylvania landlord, merchant, and professional families were preëminent.

In every colony intermarriage strengthened the social ties of the respective communities and intercolonial marriages fortified the enlarging sense of continental solidarity. As generation succeeded generation, memories of family bonds with the Old World grew dimmer and sentiments of attachment to the here and now deepened in their hold upon the minds and hearts of the people. Also, among small farmers and mechanics, increasing density of population was accompanied by multiplying points of contact, and by opportunities for intermarriage and concerted thinking and action relative to common interests. While in many respects these classes were at times in conflict in their communities, in other respects they had common ideas and grew accustomed to think of themselves as Americans.

Among the problems which marked the evolution of the American mind was the question of the permanence of the social system in each colony at each period of its development and the place of that system in the greater British society of which it was a political and economic part. Was this social system impervious to changes under the impacts of changing social facts and ideas? Was it to be defended through thick and thin against encroachments from below and within, and against encroachments from Great Britain— social as well as economic, religious, and political? If its permanence was to be secured, by whom was the feat to be accomplished and under what ideas and declarations?

Arrayed on the side of permanence for the patrician features of the inherited social system was the congenial association between royal governors and proprietors or their agents and the lords of land and trade. At imitation royal courts in the capitals of royal and proprietary colonies social preferment was given to the colonial upper classes and it deepened their affection for "the seasoned culture" of the British social order deemed the best and safest of all social orders. This relationship was dual: it strengthened ties with the mother country and confirmed loyalty to a social hierarchy in America. At such courts were formed centers of resistance to the turbulence of popular demands for a break with the fixations of the class structure in the colonies and the class domination of British rule.

The fine mansions of royal governors and proprietors or their agents were matched or surpassed by the mansions of the wealthy planters and merchants. To dwellers in such mansions mutual hospitality was extended. The menial services required for lavish entertainments were performed, alike for the governors and the governed, by servants, indentured, free, or slave. Similar raiment of fine woolens, silks, and laces gave distinction to the upper circles. The same manners, customs, and pretensions tightened the cords of unity between British and colonial "aristocrats."

If a royal governor or proprietary agent and his retinue of subordinate officials asserted high prerogatives, though flamboyantly, many of the colonial courtiers accepted the assertion as a part of British security and their own security within the aristocratic political and social system. When Governor Thomas Boone, shortly after his arrival in South Carolina in 1761, installed in his mansion at Charleston a woman who was not his wife the gentlemen of Charleston accepted his invitations as a necessary recognition of his privilege and their security, though the ladies boycotted his dinners.

Of the wealthy planting class that sought permanence in the order of special privilege, yet without servility to a royal governor, William Byrd II, of Virginia, was a pungent example. He was the grandson of a London goldsmith and the son of an Englishman who had amassed a great fortune in Virginia as a tobacco planter, merchant, slave trader, and land speculator. Inheriting that fortune, he established his family at Westover, not far from Jamestown. He had spent some time in England, studying law at the Temple and making friends in the ruling circles there. On his large estate at Westover, Byrd lived the life of a leisured country gentleman in a magnificent dwelling famous throughout the colony for its size and elegance, its splendid furnishings, and its exceptionally large and well-selected library, the largest private library in Virginia if not in all the colonies, containing about four thousand volumes.

For the struggling pioneers on the Carolina border Byrd developed a strong contempt, evident in the diary which he kept and in other writings. If his scorn for the small farmers who labored with their own hands in Virginia was less, he was determined that they should submit to government by gentlemen. For his own rights and property he stood up like a landed warrior. When the royal governor, Alexander Spotswood, tried to establish a high judicial court filled with his own appointees, Byrd went to England and protested with success to the Board of Trade. It was tyranny insufferable, in his opinion, for a governor to choose judges with power "to determine concerning not only the lives and liberties, but also concerning the whole estates" of the Virginia gentlemen.

A similar attitude toward an aristocratic order—permanence and conformity—was illustrated in Massachusetts, before and after it became a royal province in 1691, by a contemporary of Byrd, Samuel Sewall, a rich merchant and public official of that Northern colony. Sewall was the grandson of an English merchant. After graduation from Harvard College he entered upon a mercantile career in which he augmented the family patrimony. Like Byrd he was an omnivorous reader and kept a diary, besides writing on various subjects.

When Massachusetts lost its independence and was compelled to bow before a royal governor, Sewall accepted the new system and wrote in defense of it. He once said that it was "intolerable" for "private persons to print reflections and censures on the highest acts of government." Though he objected to gross corruption in politics, he declared: "I was for upholding Government whether in or out of it." As Vernon Parrington has said of Sewall in his volume, *The Colonial Mind:* "He desired no innovation in church or state; established forms answered his needs and filled the measure of his ideal. The existing system was approved by all the respectable people of the community; there was everything to gain in upholding it."

While the conservatism of Byrd was tempered by a will to resist official interference with his personal interests, and the conservatism of Sewall rejected supine acceptance of corruption in government, that of Jonathan Boucher went to the extreme of advocating servile obedience to duly constituted authorities, British and American. Boucher, the son of a poor English schoolteacher, arrived in Virginia in 1759 and soon afterward was ordained a clergyman in the Anglican Church. For a time he preached in Virginia and then moved with some of his slaves to Annapolis, Maryland, where he served as rector of Saint Anne's.

To restive Americans Boucher taught this doctrine: "Obedience to Government is every man's duty, because it is every man's interest, but it is particularly incumbent on Christians, because it is enjoined by the positive commands of God." If government is mild and free, Boucher argued, the people must be grateful; if it be less liberal than it ought to be in reason, "still it is our duty not to disturb the peace of the community, by becoming refractory and rebellious subjects, and *resisting the ordinances of God*." In the sermons and writings of Boucher conservatism reached its pinnacle.

Had the order of things which Byrd, Sewall, Boucher, and men of their type defended been unchanging and unchallenged, the conformity which they taught might have been indefinitely accepted. But that order had been and was changing; it was challenged by hard facts and by bold advocates of change. In England the rapid growth of the mercantile class in numbers and wealth was weakening the hold of the old landed gentry and clergy on English government and policy. In the colonies where land was abundant, no class could monopolize all of it as the landlords of Virginia and the Hudson River valley were inclined to engross the land of their regions. On the frontiers freehold farmers who worked with their own hands were increasing in numbers and evolving ideas of their own.

Nowhere were the class lines absolutely rigid. Many, if not most, of the Southern planters had sprung from mercantile or farming families of England and new merchant immigrants were rising into their class. Farmers and artisans in the North were embarking on careers as merchants, lawyers, or clergymen. Indentured servants, as they worked out their terms of service, were becoming freehold farmers and winning elections to colonial legislatures, even in Virginia.

In other words a leveling of individuals and families proceeded rapidly in the colonies soon after the first settlements were planted. According to Voltaire, "History is full of the sound of wooden shoes going upstairs and the patter of silken slippers coming downstairs." In Great Britain and Europe this process—or its reverse—filled the seventeenth and eighteenth centuries with tumult and revolution. In the colonies wooden shoes seemed to be climbing up the stairs steadily as farms and industries multiplied and as commerce expanded.

In no way was the process better illustrated than in the case of indentured white servants. After their term of service expired some of them were able to climb the social stairs by marrying into already prosperous families. Others were able to get land by outright purchase or on mortgage or merely by going to the frontier and settling down upon it as "squatters." Indentured artisans and merchants' clerks, by the hundreds, went into industry or trade for themselves as soon as they were released from their obligations to those who had bought their labor. In the seventeenth century, it is estimated, at least 100,000 servants rose from bondage to freedom. Many, no doubt, continued to be laborers on farms or in towns, but thousands either acquired land or an established position as craftsmen or merchants; and occasionally they became planters or clergymen.

Generally speaking, this leveling up process, which intruded upon the order cherished by landlords and merchants of patrician temper, South and North, went on quietly, but at times it was accompanied by disturbances bordering on revolution. Mutterings appeared early. In the very cabin of the *Mayflower*, as it rode in the harbor of Plymouth, some of the members of the Pilgrim band made "discontented and mutinous speeches" and threatened that they "would use their own liberty" when they landed. Such mutterings had something to do with the decision to draw up the Mayflower Compact binding the Pilgrims to that plan of government.

Nearly everywhere independent pioneers and indentured workers made trouble by running off to the frontier, building homes of their own in the wilderness fringes of the colonies, and demanding from the older communities protection and equal rights in colonial government. In Virginia in 1676 frontier discontent with the policy and actions of the royal governor broke out in a rebellion led by Nathaniel Bacon; it was only suppressed, after a long struggle, by desperate measures on the part of the governor. During the spring and summer of 1766 farmers and tenants of great landlords in the Hudson River valley raised "the great rebellion" against the exactions of landed monopolists and were not put down until troops had been called out against them.

The leveling up process as facts and ideas controverted the system and ideas of government which Byrd, Sewall, and Boucher supported in their conformity to upper-class law and order of the British type. With the steady increase in the number of small farmers the representation of farmers in colonial legislatures grew in strength and the very basis of government was examined by inquiring minds in the colonies. On what did government rest—the prescriptive rights of king, lords, clergy, and merchants?

No, said John Wise, of Ipswich, Massachusetts, in 1717. Wise was the son of an indentured servant, born in 1652, while many founders of the colony were still living. Educated at Harvard College, he entered the Congregational ministry. As a young man he resisted the attempts of the temporary royal governor, Edmund Andros, to impose taxes on the people of his town, was arrested, tried, convicted, and put under bonds to keep the peace. But after Andros was ousted and until his death in 1725 Wise battled for popular rights.

With reference to government, Wise took the ground that "democracy" is "the form of government which the light of nature does highly value, and often directs to as most agreeable to the just and natural prerogatives of human beings. . . . The natural equality amongst men must be duly favored. . . . government was never established by God or nature, to give one man a prerogative to insult over another. . . . The end of all good government is to cultivate humanity, and promote the happiness of all, and the good of every man in his rights, his life, liberty, estate, honor, etc., without injury or abuse to any." In effect, as early as 1717, John Wise rejected the very basis of government by privileged classes then defended in England and the colonies by conformists in State and Church.

A few years after John Wise died a son was born to Joseph and Mary Baker Allen, at Litchfield, Connecticut, in 1738. They named him Ethan. It is said that he was preparing to enter college when the death of his father threw upon him the burden of fending for himself. After serving in the French and Indian War, he went to the frontier of New Hampshire, to the region soon to be known as Vermont, where he engaged in land speculation and farming.

Somehow, somewhere, Allen learned to read and write and acquired the habit of reading books. Writing autobiographically about his reading, he said: "Ever since I arrived at the state of manhood and acquainted myself with the general history of mankind, I have felt a sincere passion for liberty. The history of nations doomed to perpetual slavery, in consequence of yielding up to tyrants their natural-born liberties, I read with a sort of philosophical horror; so that the first systematical and bloody attempt, at Lexington, to enslave America, thoroughly electrified my mind, and fully determined me to take part with my country."

Whether the leveling process went on silently or amid uproar, it was accompanied by "subversive" ideas no less definite and positive than the conventional ideas expressed by Byrd, Sewall, Boucher, and gentlemen of their school—ideas of a different type, based not on theological mandates or the mere legal rights of Englishmen. While yeomen of New Jersey were waging a ten-year conflict between 1745 and 1754 against the claims of great landlords, they uttered provocative doctrines. "No man," they declared, "is naturally entitled to a greater proportion of the earth than another," and land "was made for the equal use of all." By what right then could any person claim the ownership of land? Their answer to this question rested not on existing "law and order" but on what they called "natural justice." A person may appropriate land, they contended, "by the improvement of any part of it lying vacant"; and after a man has thus bestowed his labor upon such a piece of land, it cannot afterward be taken away from him, "without breaking thro' the rule of natural justice; for thereby he would be actually deprived of the fruits of his industry."

☆

In the young colonial societies where the majority of the people belonged to freehold farming families and where class lines, though marked, were so fluid that former indentured servants could and did rise to membership in legislative assemblies, radical sentiments and ideas respecting life and labor, differing from those in England, gained in force. In the mother country, where land was limited in amount and all privately owned, most workers on the soil were tenants or day laborers on the estates of great landlords; and the social lines between the upper classes and the masses of the people were sharply drawn. Essentially true was an old couplet, even if there was something ironical in it:

> God bless the squire [landlord] and his relations,
> And keep us all in our proper stations.

To the majority of American farmers and artisans, who had no fixed "station," such sentiments were not only unreal but offensive.

To American merchants they were equally objectionable. Americans by the hundreds of thousands, amid different circumstances, held tenaciously to other views of themselves, their opportunities, and their duties. And as the colonies grew older—more populous, more self-sustaining in agriculture, commerce, and industry—intellectual leaders formulated American doctrines into a systematic program of thought about American affairs.

In their searching, thinking, speaking, and writing, these intellectual leaders touched upon every major theme that interested reflective colonists and had a bearing on their growth in economic, political, intellectual, and moral power. They raised and answered in their way at least four fundamental questions: What is the origin of human government and by what right does one set of men make laws for, and govern, all the rest of the people? What is the place of the colonists in the British Empire and what rights do they and should they enjoy as British subjects in America and primarily as human beings? What are the sciences, arts, and opportunities of commerce which will promote the economic and social welfare of the American people? What, after all, are the great ends of human life and how may men and women best attain them?

To these questions in one form or another American minds directed their attention and gave answers which in sum made up an American ideology that clashed with the ideology of the British governing class and their allies in the American colonies. The nature of this great American inquiry and the duty of Americans to pursue it were eloquently described by John Adams in 1765:

"Let us dare to read, think, speak and write. Let every order and degree among the people rouse their attention and animate their resolution. Let them all become attentive to the grounds and principles of government, ecclesiastical and civil. Let us study the law of nature; search into the spirit of the British constitution; read the histories of ancient ages; contemplate the great examples of Greece and Rome; set before us the conduct of our own British ancestors, who have defended for us the inherent rights of mankind against foreign and domestic tyrants and usurpers, against arbitrary kings and cruel priests; in short, against the gates of earth and hell.

"Let us read and recollect and impress upon our souls the views and ends of our own more immediate forefathers, in exchanging their native country for a dreary, inhospitable wilderness. Let us examine into the nature of that power, and the cruelty of that oppression, which drove them from their homes. Recollect their amazing fortitude, their bitter sufferings,—the hunger, the nakedness, the cold, which they patiently endured,—the severe labors of clearing their grounds, building their houses, raising their provisions, amidst dangers from wild beasts and savage men, before they had time or money or materials for commerce. Recollect the civil and religious principles and hopes and expectations which constantly supported and carried them through all hardships with patience and resignation. Let us recollect it was liberty, the hope of liberty for themselves and us and ours, which conquered all discouragements, dangers, and trials. . . .

"Let the pulpit resound with the doctrines and sentiments of religious liberty. Let us hear the danger of thralldom to our consciences from ignorance, extreme poverty, and dependence, in short, from civil and political slavery. Let us see delineated before us the true map of man. Let us hear the dignity of his nature, and the noble rank he holds among the works of God,—that consenting to slavery is a sacrilegious breach of trust, as offensive in the sight of God as it is derogatory from our own honor or interest or happiness,—and that God Almighty has promulgated from heaven, liberty, peace, and good will to man!

"Let the bar proclaim, 'the laws, the rights, the generous plan of power' delivered down from remote antiquity—inform the world of the mighty struggles and numberless sacrifices made by our ancestors in defense of freedom. Let it be known that British liberties are not the grants of princes or parliaments but original rights, conditions of original contracts, are coequal with prerogative, and coeval with government; that many of our rights are inherent and essential, agreed on as maxims, and established as preliminaries, even before a parliament existed. Let them search for the foundations of British laws and government in the frame of human nature, in the constitution of the intellectual and moral world. There let us see that truth, liberty, justice, and benevolence, are its everlasting basis; and if these could be removed, the superstructure is overthrown of course.

"Let the colleges join their harmony in the same delightful concert. Let every declamation turn upon the beauty of liberty and virtue, and the deformity, turpitude, and malignity, of slavery and vice. Let the public disputations become researches into the grounds and nature and ends of government, and the means of preserving the good and demolishing the evil. Let the dialogues, and all the exercises, become the instruments of impressing on the tender mind, and of spreading and distributing far and wide, the ideas of right and the sensations of freedom.

"In a word, let every sluice of knowledge be opened and set a-flowing. The encroachments upon liberty in the reigns of the first James and the first Charles, by turning the general attention of learned men to government, are said to have produced the greatest number of consummate statesmen which has ever been seen in any age or nation. The Brookes, Hampdens, Vanes, Seldens, Miltons, Nedhams, Harringtons, Nevilles, Sidneys, Lockes, are all said to have owed their eminence in political knowledge to the tyrannies of those reigns. The prospect now before us in America, ought in the same manner to engage the attention of every man of learning, to matters of power and of right, that we may be neither led nor driven blindfolded to irretrievable destruction."

The business of making these inquiries into fundamentals of intellectual and social life was not monopolized by any small class of persons. It was carried on, as John Adams urged, by "every order and degree among the people"—by multitudes of people in homes, taverns, churchyards, town meetings, and at crossroads stores; by men and women of humble origins and occupations as well as by those who enjoyed the advantages of leisure and higher education. Yet four groups of persons led the great inquest into American rights, duties, and problems: clergymen, lawyers, physicians, and publishers and publicists. And all members of these groups had audiences to hear what they had to say or to read what they wrote in pamphlets, books, and newspaper articles. Furthermore, in homes, in secondary schools, and in colleges, from generation to generation, new leaders were given the rudiments of learning upon which to build in carrying on inquiries and formulating answers.

Primarily charged with the care of souls, clergymen devoted themselves mainly to religious affairs. But then, as ever, no clear line was drawn between the things that belonged to God and the things assigned to Caesar. The Anglican Church, a state church in England and in several colonies, was associated with English policies of state. But the immense majority of the colonists belonged to dissenting and non-conformist denominations. Early in the history of New England, the Puritans became independents in religion and stoutly resisted all encroachments by the English Crown and Church. Presbyterians objected with equal vigor to the doctrines and methods of the Anglican Church and insisted on having liberty for their faith and worship. Besides, many of them had suffered under English legislation directed against their economic interests in their old home in the north of Ireland and had carried to the colonies piercing remembrances of that experience. Baptists and Quakers had undergone persecution in England and strove against any tightening of the English grip on the religious life of the colonies.

Outside the Anglican communion, accordingly, the clergy were concerned with increasing the dissidence of dissent, educating their flocks in dissidence, and fortifying non-conformity. While their sermons and writings were largely theological, many clergymen were interested in all the great questions of human rights, government, and social duty raised in the growth of American economy. They preached on such subjects to congregations from one end of the colonies to the other. They taught their doctrines in the schools over which they presided and wrote pamphlets for general circulation.

The eighteenth century had not advanced far when lawyers began to dispute the intellectual preëminence of the clergy. In the early stages of settlement there was little business for lawyers and dislike for their profession existed in many circles. Throughout the colonial period, in fact, Puritan divines were inclined to look down upon them as a lower order of human beings. When, for instance, the Reverend William Smith learned that his daughter was inclined toward marriage with John Adams, he was distressed; for young Adams was not only the son of a dirt farmer; he was also a lawyer. On principle, the Quakers were opposed to lawyers; they insisted that disputes among members of the meeting should always be settled by private negotiation. It was in Virginia and South Carolina that lawyers were first heartily welcomed and given high standing in the best society.

Yet as the colonies approached maturity, lawyers were prominent everywhere in the cities from Boston to Charleston, and were scattered around in the inland regions. In New England the litigation connected with commerce had become too complicated for field-stump and corner-store justice. In Philadelphia, where Quakers were growing worldly, lawyers flourished and were famous throughout the North for their learning, shrewdness, and boldness. At Williamsburg and Charleston, the Bar was crowded by distinguished attorneys.

Lawyers, if intellectually enterprising, were more than students of law and government. Engaged in litigation for their clients, they were accustomed to preparing briefs—or statements of facts and law—and making oral arguments before judges and juries.

They were acquainted with the art of public speaking and many of them studied the art as represented in the speeches of Cicero and the speeches of statesmen in the British Parliament. Wherever there was a controversy, public or private, lawyers were interested and the best of them could "make a powerful case" for the side on which they were enlisted; that is, marshal facts, lay down ruling principles applicable to the facts, and order facts and principles in a logical form, appealing to sentiments of their supporters and commanding the attention, if not always the respect, of their opponents.

For the practice of law in any case, some intellectual preparation was necessary. There was no law school in any of the colonies and there was no professorship of law at any of the colleges. But leading lawyers usually had some preliminary training at a college and often young men of wealthy families, especially in the South, studied at the Inns of Court in London. Whatever their early education, lawyers had to read one or more legal treatises and the statutes of their colony. The ablest and most intellectual among them read widely in the classics, in works on history, jurisprudence, government, and the relation of the law to the people and the economy of the society in which it was made and enforced.

As the colonial period drew toward a close physicians were also outstanding among intellectual leaders, especially at Philadelphia, the great medical center of the colonies. About 1750, it is estimated, at least eighty-two physicians and surgeons were practicing in that city, many of them trained at the medical school of Edinburgh or on the Continent. While some of them adhered strictly to the professional line, many others took a keen interest in civic affairs and allied themselves with the autonomous tendencies. The latter promoted the arts, music, higher education, the establishment of libraries, and the building of social institutions such as hospitals and homes for the impoverished. Thomas Bond, for example, who had completed his medical education abroad and long practiced with success, joined the Revolutionary Committee of Safety in 1776 and rendered service to the Revolutionary army. Benjamin Rush, distinguished in the medical profession, took an interest in most great public questions from education to the abolition of slavery, was elected to the Continental Congress, signed the Declaration of Independence, and for a time was surgeon general of the Middle Department armies.

Important as were clergy, lawyers, and physicians in shaping American opinion and forming the ideology of American au-

tomony, they had able assistants in independent editors and publicists who wrote articles for newspapers and pamphlets for
general circulation. Among all the colonists so engaged, Benjamin
Franklin, the publisher and businessman, was especially versatile,
active, and influential. For the Pennsylvania *Gazette* and for *Poor
Richard's Almanack*, which he published, he wrote articles, short
and long, on nearly every subject—scientific, moral, and economic—bearing on the affairs of the colonists. These he supplemented by pamphlets on various topics, such as the vital money
question. Although his publishing house was in Philadelphia, his
writings circulated widely in the North and the South.

Intellectual leaders in America, from those of community or
colony prestige to those of intercolonial or international reputation, had at their command, to inform, inspire, and strengthen
their minds, a growing literature on American themes. In this
literature, by 1750, there were actually thousands of printed titles,
running from large volumes to pamphlets, tracts, and broadsides.
When intellectual and social autonomy approached its maturity,
there was scarcely a nook or cranny of the seaboard region that
had not been explored and described by able writers; scarcely a
branch of American economy and social life that had not been
written up with more or less fullness; scarcely an American institution or custom on which information was lacking to inquiring
minds; scarcely an American idea or aspiration unrecorded in print
for the instruction of those who searched for enlightenment on
that score.

This immense literature included: histories of individual settlements and colonies—such as Robert Beverly, *History of Virginia*
(1705), William Smith, *History of the Province of New York*
(1757), and Thomas Prince, *A Chronological History of New
England* in two volumes (1736–55); books of travel and surveys
describing various parts of the colonial dominion—for example,
John Archdale, *A New Description . . . of Carolina* (1707), and
John Bartram, *Observations on the Inhabitants, Climate, Soil,
Rivers, Production, Animals and Other Matters Worthy of Notice*
from Pennsylvania to Canada (1751); books on natural philosophy
and the practical arts—for instance, Samuel Johnson, *An Introduction to the Study of Philosophy, Exhibiting a General View
of All the Arts and Sciences* (1743); books on social morality, in-

cluding John Woolman, *Considerations on Pure Wisdom, and Human Policy; on Labour* . . . (1768); works on phases of economy and government—as illustrations, Benjamin Franklin, *A Modest Enquiry into the Nature and Necessity of a Paper Currency* (1729) and *An Historical Review of the Constitution and Government of Pennsylvania* (1759). If, as had been said in ancient times, "knowledge is power," American colonials were fortunate in having ample stores of it within their reach.

Intellectual leaders intent on exploring theories of society in general and American relations to the government of Great Britain in particular also had at hand works which they had imported from abroad and kept in their libraries, private and public, for ready use. From these they selected germinal ideas, gave to them meaning in the light of their peculiar experiences in a New World, and applied them, so interpreted, to the accomplishment of their purposes.

Among the imported works generally read in the colonies by assiduous students and thinkers, four were of unquestioned influence on American intellectual leadership:

1628—Edward Coke, *Coke upon Littleton*. Treatise on the legal rights of English subjects, defending them against encroachments by Crown and Church. A textbook on common law for colonial students of law.

1690—John Locke, *Treatise of Government*. Philosophic justification of the Revolution of 1688 in England. Traced the origin of government to a compact among the people made for the protection of their lives and property and asserted the right of revolution to assure such protection against tyranny.

1748—Montesquieu, *Esprit des Lois*. Soon in translations. Dealt with the material and social backgrounds of law and government. An early treatise on "sociological jurisprudence."

1757—Adam Ferguson, *An Essay on the History of Civil Society*. A work on the origins and progress of civil societies (civilization), on social relations, and on human beings as active, creative, and progressive creatures.

Americans of searching intellectual curiosity also had at their command, either imported or from their own presses, books reflecting all the main tendencies of thought in the Old World respecting the nature of mankind's universe. They read, discussed, and wrote about these tendencies so widely that the chief ideas which were shaking Great Britain and Europe became common in all the colonies. And what were these chief ideas?

The rationalism in the work of Sir Isaac Newton that eliminated arbitrary interferences of God in the physical universe, the old basis of astrology and other superstitions.

Deism—rejecting the Hebraic and Miltonic interpretation of the cosmos and substituting, for Jehovah, the universal God of all mankind. As Alexander Pope expressed it:

> Father of all! in every age,
> In every clime adored,
> By saint, by savage, and by sage . . .

The idea of progress—now fortified by the new science and by Voltaire's social history, which rejected the theological view that the earth is a temporary place of misery and maintained that advance in arts, sciences, and social improvement is the supreme destiny of mankind.

The doctrine of natural rights—that all people everywhere, whatever their status, are entitled to the rights of life, liberty, property, and the pursuit of happiness.

The idea of the pursuit of happiness on earth as a legitimate and worthy aspiration of the human spirit. "O happiness! our being's end and aim! Good, pleasure, ease, content! whate'er thy name," wrote Pope in his *Essay on Man*.

The doctrine of utility—that usefulness in well-being is the test of things, institutions, and actions.

As these ideas circulating in Europe presented a revolutionary contradiction to the ideology of kings, lords, clergy, peasants, and serfs, so in America they ran counter to the conservative practices of British overlordship. Not only that. They acquired additional force in America on account of the fact that Americans, as contrasted with Europeans, were in possession of the natural resources that made possible the easier realization of these ideas.

So in America, as in the Old World, the Battle of the Books raged. If William Byrd, in Virginia, could read his *Lucian*, the Greek satirist of the second century, A.D., laugh at the follies of mankind, and learn contempt for everything except his own pleasure and interests, Thomas Jefferson in Virginia could draw from the new writers—Locke, Ferguson, and Pope—a faith in mankind and human progress that prepared him in letter and spirit to write and proclaim the declaration of complete autonomy—independence.

☆

It was not merely to a small, exclusive set of upper-class persons that writers on American matters directed their articles, pamphlets, and books. They wrote for a large audience, for a popular audience, for men and women belonging to farming and artisan classes as well as to the ranks of clergymen, lawyers, professors, physicians, schoolmasters, planters, and merchants.

No census of the number of colonists over ten years of age who could read and write was ever taken, but the number was certainly large. The extensive sale of books, pamphlets, almanacs, magazines, and newspapers was one indication that there was a wide reading public in all parts of America. Foreign travelers in the eighteenth century were deeply impressed by the amount of reading that was done in homes and in taverns "on the house," and they contrasted this mental alertness with the stolidity of the ignorant masses in their own countries. So plainly were American writers taking the people at large into account, as readers, that strangers interested in classes and masses seldom failed to make note of it as a sign of distinction in the intellectual development of the colonies.

How had the large public learned to read? To Protestantism must be attributed the main source of this wide literacy. The colonial population was overwhelmingly Protestant and a tenet of dissenting faith was the right of everyone to read the Bible for himself instead of listening merely to its exposition by priests. Hence the Protestant clergy, especially among Puritans, Baptists, and Presbyterians, made it one of their prime duties to see that children of their sects acquired the ability to read and actually carried reading forward, as they grew up, with a sense of religious obligation.

In extending literacy by means of public schools New England stood apart. Homogeneity in population and religious faith characterized that region. There legislation, beginning with the Massachusetts statute of 1642, required the towns to make some provision for giving the rudiments of learning to those children who did not get them at home. In many places this fiat was more honored in the breach than by observance, but in time all the better New England communities had public primary schools of some type. In other parts of colonial America, dissenting sects— Baptist, Quaker, Presbyterian, Lutheran, and Huguenot—also established town and field schools in which children learned elementary reading, writing, and arithmetic. Such schools were supplemented by private enterprise. Schoolmasters and schoolmistresses conducted private elementary schools, usually in their homes; and itinerant teachers journeyed about "holding school" for short periods of the year wherever a few pupils could be collected and fees obtained.

In thickly populated districts, especially in the larger towns, to elementary schools were added grammar schools and academies at which boys and girls were taught more advanced subjects. Secondary schools founded by private interests often catered to sons and daughters of the upper classes, especially boys on their way to college and girls preparing for the life of "polite society"; their curricula included the classics, mathematics, English literature, and frequently French. But secondary schools were not all of that type. Perhaps more generally, particularly in the middle colonies, they adapted their instruction to the needs of boys and girls who had to look forward early to earning a livelihood by their own efforts. At all events secondary schools gave thousands of Americans a more than elementary training for reading newspapers, pamphlets, and books; for taking part in the discussions of public affairs; and for sharing in the growth of social and intellectual autonomy.

It was mainly to religious motives that colleges, like elementary schools, owed their foundations. Massachusetts was only a few years old when, in 1636, Harvard College was established, primarily to train "learned and godly Ministers." A similar purpose led to the creation of a college at Killingworth in Connecticut in 1701—an institution afterward moved to New Haven and in 1718 given the name of Yale College. William and Mary, organized in Virginia in 1693, and King's College, founded in New York City in 1754, were intended as centers for the advanced education of Anglican men. The College of New Jersey, started in 1747 and removed to Princeton in 1756, relied mainly on Presbyterians for support and guidance. Dartmouth College began to function in 1767 as a Puritan mission to the Indians.

Two colonial colleges were less exclusive in sectarian sponsorship: Brown, founded in Rhode Island in 1764, was interdenominational; a majority of its board of trustees were Baptists, but Congregationalists, Anglicans, and Quakers were included in the membership. The Philadelphia Academy, forerunner of the University of Pennsylvania, formally opened in 1751, also admitted to its board of trustees members of various faiths; and Benjamin Franklin, its arch promoter, would have turned it into secular channels if he could have kept its control in his hands. Franklin, however, was outmaneuvered by the provost, William Smith, an invincible Anglican who gradually managed to dominate this institution.

The instruction offered by colleges included secular learning. The presidents and the professors were generally ministers of religion but, whatever their professions of faith, they opened the gateways to the accumulated knowledge of the ages and colonial writings on every theme. Young men admitted to the colleges all had an opportunity to master classical languages and were given access to the learning of antiquity, for example, to the politics and morals of Aristotle and Plato and the ethics of Seneca and Plutarch as well as the historical writings of Tacitus and the constitutional works of Cicero. Thin as they were, modeled on Oxford and Cambridge patterns, the colonial college curricula contained instruction in the elements of moral or natural philosophy, contemporary science, and a drill in logic that sharpened young men's wits for inquiry and argumentation, in the event that they made use of this drill. Within college walls leaders were trained for all the intellectual activities that marked the growth of the colonies into mature and autonomous societies.

Yet in the acquisition of learning, the development of intellectual powers, and the spread of knowledge and conceptual thought, formal education played a minor role in colonial times. Relatively speaking, only a few men had the benefit of college education and those who did gained from it only a limited body of knowledge. On entering business, professional, or political careers, college graduates often found themselves in intellectual competition with men of little formal training who were their peers, if not their superiors, in mental power. Thomas Jefferson was a graduate of William and Mary College; John Marshall was not a graduate of any college. John Adams attended Harvard; Benjamin Franklin was among the founders of a college, never a student in one. All over the country, in communities large and small, on farms and plantations as well as in towns and cities, men and women who had got the rudiments of an education from their fathers and mothers or hired tutors spent laborious days and nights lifting their education by their own efforts, inspired by their intellectual curiosities and other desires.

Self-education on the higher levels was especially the way of women, to whom the doors of colleges were closed. Eliza Pinckney, of South Carolina, which had no college, went on reading and learning, after her youthful studies in England, as the impulse of her own mind and spirit directed. Abigail Adams and Mercy Otis Warren, of Massachusetts, could not go to Harvard; and Abigail lamented the lack of equal education for women, but how well she could think and write is attested by her letters to her husband and family and friends. Mercy Otis had studied the same subjects under the same tutors as her brother, James Otis, previous to his departure for Harvard. She could not follow him there despite their close intellectual companionship, but she did follow where her mind continued to lead her, learning all the time independently. Anna Maulin Zenger, of New York, who took over the publication of John Peter Zenger's New York *Weekly Journal*, after his death in 1746, must have acquired her education and competence for editing largely by her own efforts, like the numerous other women journalists in the colonies. And even in lonely cabins on the frontiers women as well as men frequently educated themselves and opened for their children the paths leading to the knowledge that enabled them to win high places in the public service. From his mother George Wythe, born on a Virginia plantation in 1726, learned the Latin language and he eventually studied jurisprudence by himself. He was of great influence in the intellectual development of Jefferson.

Books, pamphlets, and tracts that passed from reader to reader, formal instruction in schools, the dissemination of learning by fathers and mothers, training at home by private tutors, formed only a part of the process by which Americans were equipped with knowledge and ideas for dealing with affairs private and public. After the opening of the eighteenth century, newspapers added instruction on current issues to the colonial college curriculum dealing mainly with the past. In April 1704 John Campbell at Boston brought out the first number of the first American newspaper, the Boston *News-Letter*, a periodical so hardy that it lasted till independence was declared. In 1719 Andrew Bradford established in Philadelphia the *American Mercury*. In November 1725 the New York *Gazette* came from the press of William Bradford.

From these beginnings, journalism spread to other colonies in the following order of time:

> 1727—Annapolis, Maryland.
> 1732—Charleston, South Carolina.
> 1732—Newport, Rhode Island.
> 1736—Williamsburg, Virginia.
> 1755—New Haven, Connecticut.
> 1755—New Bern, North Carolina.
> 1762—Wilmington, Delaware.
> 1763—Savannah, Georgia.
> 1777—Burlington, New Jersey.

Among the early newspapers the rate of change and mortality was high as competitors appeared in the leading cities; but this signified a growth and persistence in journalism—signs of new thinking and action for those who could see them.

In the columns of newspapers Americans could learn about many things that were going on in the colonies as well as overseas. The small pages of these papers contained brief notes on British and European "occurrences," reports of happenings in the neighborhood and in other colonies, advertisements of commodities in bewildering varieties for sale at merchants' shops, letters from pleased and irate readers on questions of public interest, and essays on events, manners, morals, customs, and politics. Always under the watchful eyes of royal governors, proprietors, or politicians, colonial editors had to be circumspect in discussing disputes among Americans or between Americans and British officials, but as time passed they became more adroit in their retreating and advancing maneuvers. From the journals of other colonies, local editors in each town clipped notices of general interest and made reports to their communities. Ship captains sailing from port to port and post-boys traveling from point to point carried news for editors to use. When, for example, the great agrarian rebellion of 1766 occurred in the Hudson Valley, accounts of it appeared in the newspapers of Boston and Philadelphia as well as in the New York press. Provincial journalism was merging into American journalism.

The dissemination of knowledge and ideas, news, information, and misinformation was facilitated by the rise and growth of a colonial postal system. As early as 1639 the legislature of Massachusetts made provision for a local post office and this example was followed by other colonies as they grew in size and population. Under a royal patent of 1692 an intercolonial postal service was established as a private enterprise. Fifteen years later it was taken over by the English government and developed under successive postmasters general, Benjamin Franklin assuming that office in 1753.

In the course of time post roads were extended, new local offices established, the speed of transmission increased, and packet lines to England and to coastal ports were started. Day and night, through the years, post riders, stages, and coastal ships kept communications throughout the colonies open. Correspondence among citizens, once local and restricted, became general. Newspapers issued for local circulation reached out in influence beyond their communities and broadened the scope of their contents accordingly. The circulation of knowledge and ideas was being enlarged. The provincial mind was becoming American in its range of interest and in the subject matter of its concern.

CHAPTER VI

Practicing the Arts of Self-Government

ACCOMPANYING THE GROWTH of autonomy in agriculture, industry, commerce, social relations, and intellectual powers, indeed mingled with every phase of it, was a training in the arts of self-government which prepared colonists for asserting their political and economic rights against British authorities and for managing their own political affairs. From the beginning government played a necessary and formative role in the founding and development of the colonies. At the outset, the Crown granted charters and privileges to companies and proprietors, bestowed upon them huge areas of land, and laid down rules as to how they should divide and sell their land and govern the people who settled in their domains. During the entire colonial period the government in London furnished military and naval assistance in protecting the colonies against Spanish and French attacks and at times against Indian raids on the frontier. Without the guardianship of the English government, therefore, individuals and groups would have been unable to cross the seas in safety and to lay on this continent the foundations of the American nation.

"The people," unaided and unprotected by government, did not put out on the sea, land on the shores of America, and establish colonies. At no moment, as the tiny settlements spread into great and prosperous colonies, was government absent from the scene. There was government in the mapping, division, and sale of the lands to be taken up and cultivated by farmers and planters. There was government in protection of the settlements against internal disorders and external foes. There was government protection and encouragement of commerce between the colonies and European countries as well as with the motherland; and without this commerce the colonies in America could not have become prosperous and powerful. However energetic, industrious, and enterprising the people might have been as individuals and groups, it would have been impossible for them to found and build up the colonies by their own efforts. Government was for them indispensable at every step in the starting and progress of the colonies.

This was true, of course, of the Spanish and French colonies but there was one fundamental difference between the policy of the French and Spanish governments and the policy of the English government. French and Spanish colonies were ruled absolutely by royal governors who held office at royal pleasure. In those colonies the inhabitants were not allowed to take an active part in making their own laws, laying taxes, choosing officials, and deciding how public affairs were otherwise to be managed. On the other hand, in all the English colonies a considerable portion of the inhabitants enjoyed a large measure of self-government; in some, from the very beginning and in others after they were securely established. To the development of independence and liberty, exercising the rights of self-government in some measure at least was as essential as the activities in agriculture, industry, business enterprise, and every other phase of autonomous unfolding.

To appreciate the importance of political privileges in the making of the American nation, it is only necessary to imagine what would have happened if every colony had been governed solely by a royal agent from London, endowed with dictatorial powers to make and enforce laws of every kind—laws for dividing and selling the lands; for laying out towns and managing farms and industries; for imposing and collecting taxes as heavy or heavier than the people could bear; for controlling speech, press, and religious worship; for regulating the kinds of work to be done and assigning people to their tasks. If wholly autocratic policies had been pursued by the English government in the colonies, the American people would have felt crushed, and liberty might have been stifled. What is more, the colonists would not have learned the arts of self-government so necessary to the establishment and maintenance of independence, the making of popular constitutions, and the management of local, national, and foreign affairs.

☆

Running through the long period from the founding of Jamestown in 1607 to the declaring of independence in 1776 were two opposing tendencies in colonial government. The first was the development of local legislatures, or lawmaking bodies, consisting in every case of one house elected by the qualified voters and in all colonies, except Pennsylvania and Delaware, of an upper chamber or council or body of assistants. The second tendency was a strengthening of royal power in America by the transformation of eight colonies into royal provinces, each headed by a royal governor appointed by the British Crown.

The Virginia colony was only a few years old when the London Company decreed that the power of its local governor and council should be limited by a local assembly, called the House of Burgesses, to be elected by the voters. In 1619 members of the House of Burgesses were chosen; and the legislature, duly assembled, began to make laws respecting the management of local affairs.

Before the Pilgrims actually set to work at Plymouth in 1620, the men of that little band met in the cabin of the *Mayflower* and drew up a document celebrated in history as the Mayflower Compact. By solemn written agreement they bound themselves together in a "civil body politic," to make "just and equal laws" for the government of the colony, and promised to obey such laws when enacted. The founders of Massachusetts Bay, who followed the Pilgrims to America ten years later, brought their charter with them. After governing themselves directly for a time by meetings of the members, they established in 1634 an assembly composed of representatives from each town.

Even proprietors could not be complete autocrats in the domains granted them by the King. The charter which gave Lord Baltimore the right to found his colony in Maryland required him in due course to seek the consent of the freemen in making laws. Within a short time after the first settlements were made, in 1635, an assembly representing the freemen was set up in Maryland.

In 1639 the men of the towns founded on the Connecticut River by emigrants from Massachusetts drew up for their colony the "Fundamental Orders of Connecticut"—a document called "the first written constitution known to history which created a government." The Orders provided for a general assembly, or "Court," composed of representatives from each of the towns, and for a governor and magistrates to be elected annually. The people of the colony were thus bound together as "one public State or Commonwealth" and they were "to be guided and governed" in their civil affairs by the laws, orders, and decrees properly made by the government so organized.

In contemplation of growth, the Orders provided that new towns were to be given representation in the assembly, reasonably proportioned to the number of their freemen. Four years later, in 1643, the settlements on Long Island Sound united with New Haven in creating a representative legislature. Finally, the royal charter of 1662, which joined the two groups of settlements in Connecticut, made provision for popular government consisting of a governor, assistants, and representatives, all elected by the qualified voters. A similar system was established in Rhode Island.

As popular assemblies came into existence in the other colonies, one after another, they were formed on a common model. Representatives were assigned to each town, city, borough or county, and they were all to be elected by the voters who had the qualifications fixed by law.

The qualifications for the suffrage varied from place to place and from time to time. But on the eve of the Revolution the right to vote was generally restricted to men who owned property of specified amounts. In New York, for instance, voters for members of the assembly had to be freeholders of land or tenements to the value of £40 free from all encumbrances, except in New York City and Albany where all men formally admitted to civic rights as "freemen" could vote. In Pennsylvania the suffrage was restricted to the owners of fifty acres of land "well seated" with twelve acres "cleared," or other property worth at least £50 in lawful money. According to Virginia law the voter had to own at least fifty acres of land if there was no house on it or twenty-five acres with a house at least twelve feet square; or if a dweller in a town, he had to own a plot of ground with a house at least twelve feet square.

As a result of the various limitations on the suffrage a large proportion of the people in each colony were deprived of the vote; and many who were entitled to that privilege failed to exercise it in elections. In the rural districts of Pennsylvania about one person in ten had the right to vote and in Philadelphia only about one in fifty owned enough property to qualify for the exercise of the suffrage. At times in Massachusetts and Connecticut, where approximately sixteen per cent of the population were enfranchised, only two per cent took the trouble to vote. Similar conditions prevailed elsewhere. It was therefore only a small proportion, even of the freemen, who actually participated in the government of their respective colonies.

Nevertheless, there were in America, at the end of the colonial period, thousands of men who were acquainted practically with voting, managing local campaigns, and taking part in elections; and there were hundreds of men who were serving, or had served, as members of legislatures, in the making of laws and the supervision of law enforcement. When important issues were up for action, campaigns were often exciting. Even men and women who could not vote formed opinions about questions under popular consideration and shared in the discussions that went on in country and town.

But as a rule, by the end of the colonial period, the popular assembly was checked by an upper house or council. In seven of the eight royal provinces, members of the council were appointed by the royal governor; in Massachusetts they were elected by the lower house. In Connecticut all high authorities—governor, assistants, and representatives in the legislature—were elected by the voters. Of the proprietary colonies, Maryland alone had a legislative council, a kind of upper chamber, composed of councilors selected by the proprietor or his deputy; the legislature in Pennsylvania and Delaware consisted of a single house based on popular election.

Generally speaking, councilors or assistants were selected from prominent and wealthy families in the colony and exercised large powers in respect of lawmaking and the conduct of executive business. In the royal provinces they were, with some exceptions, warmly attached to the royal governor and the Crown and acted as a conservative force in blocking the desires and demands of the elected representatives in the lower house.

The powers possessed by the colonial legislature in the beginning, or acquired by practice, were extensive. It could make laws respecting the general and local affairs of the colony. It could lay various kinds of taxes for the support of the colonial government. It could appropriate money for public purposes, including the salaries of the governor and other officers. Speaking broadly, it was limited only by the provision that its acts must not be contrary to the laws of England or the terms of the colony's charter. Otherwise the assembly was fairly free to legislate on all matters pertaining to life, liberty, and property, subject to the veto of the governor in the royal and proprietary colonies and ultimately of the Crown in England.

☆

The second important tendency in the history of colonial government—the transformation of company and proprietary colonies into royal provinces, with governors chosen by the King—is traced in the following table showing the steps of this development in the direction of stronger royal control over American affairs:

1624—Virginia became a royal province.
1679—New Hampshire
1685—New York
1691—Massachusetts
1702—New Jersey, with a separate governor in 1728
1729—South Carolina
1729—North Carolina
1752—Georgia

By 1752, therefore, eight of the thirteen colonies were royal provinces; three were subject to proprietors—Maryland, Pennsylvania,

ROYAL, PROPRIETARY, AND CHARTER COLONIES ON THE EVE OF THE
REVOLUTION

and Delaware; and only two had governors elected by assemblies of voters—Connecticut and Rhode Island.

The powers enjoyed and exercised by the King's governor in the royal province were both extensive and highly effective. He was really the viceroy of the King and exercised in the colony all the civil and military authority vested in him by the Crown. As chief executive he enforced the laws of England applicable to the colony and all the laws passed by the colonial legislature. He appointed, usually with the consent of the council, the important civil officers and directed them in the discharge of their duties. He acted as the head of the highest court in the colony, which tried important cases at first hand and heard appeals from the lower courts. The power of granting pardons and issuing reprieves was entrusted to him. In military affairs he was commander in chief of the colonial forces and appointed officers of high rank.

In relation to the legislature the royal governor also had many prerogatives. Not only did he choose in all the royal provinces, except Massachusetts, the members of the council which served as the upper house of the legislatures. He could summon, adjourn, and dissolve the assembly, lay before it projects of law which the Crown or he himself deemed desirable, and veto bills. He could hear and approve or reject petitions from the assembly, send messages to it, and try to influence its members by methods both public and secret.

Governors in the proprietary colonies had controls and wielded powers resembling those possessed by royal governors. When the proprietor was a resident of his colony he was in fact "a petty king" and could exercise executive authority in person. When absent or residing permanently in England, he acted through a lieutenant governor who served as his agent. In the proprietor or his deputy was vested the right to appoint high officials, summon and dissolve the legislature, approve or veto laws.

In all save two colonies, Connecticut and Rhode Island, where the governor was popularly elected, the colonial executive, royal or proprietary, was, formally at least, above responsibility to the people. If he wished or dared, he could defy public opinion.

Many of the governors at the head of royal and proprietary provinces were men of wisdom and moderation who tried to deal amicably with the colonists. Yet they were all periodically in sharp conflict with the colonial assembly. Whatever their personal merits and views, they were expected to promote, if they could, the interests of the British government or of the proprietors, and to enforce, if they could, British law applicable to the colonies. Placed as they were between two fires—British masters and local assemblies—they were fortunate if a year passed without a quarrel of some kind. If a governor was stiff-necked, the colony over which he presided was likely to be in more or less of an uproar during his entire administration. Examples of such disturbances will illustrate the nature of the difficulties that arose between British governors and the colonists bent on having the substance as well as the form of self-government.

In 1642 Charles II sent over Sir William Berkeley to serve as royal governor of Virginia and for about thirty-five years Berkeley held that post. Along many lines he labored zealously for the welfare of the colony but in other respects he was a martinet. He was almost savage in persecuting Quakers and Puritans who ventured to settle in Virginia. He was opposed to newspapers and free schools and thanked God that Virginia had neither. With an iron hand he tried to keep all branches of the government under his own control. He insulted and cursed Virginians who were brash enough to resist his actions and object to his policies.

As the years passed, things went from bad to worse. When in 1676 he failed to take effective measures against marauding Indians, Berkeley found himself in the midst of an armed rebellion led by Nathaniel Bacon and was driven out of Jamestown. Recovering power for a short time, he put to death so many leaders in the rebellion that even the King of England was disgusted with him and appointed another governor to supersede him. "The old fool," Charles II was quoted as saying, "has killed more people in that naked country than I have done for the murder of my father."

A second illustration of the kind of serious troubles that could arise between a royal governor and colonial leaders occurred in New York under Governor William Cosby, who arrived to take office in 1732. In his dealings with the colonial assembly, Cosby managed to avoid bringing on a revolution, though he was brusque in manner and profane in language. But he quarreled fiercely with some members of his council and with leaders in local politics over jobs and money. He ousted from power the chief justice of New York. The displaced man, aided by rich friends, helped John Peter Zenger, a local printer, to establish a newspaper in New York City and attack the governor's policies in print.

Angered by attacks in Zenger's paper, Cosby took steps to have Zenger arrested and brought to trial for criminal libel. To the defense of Zenger came Andrew Hamilton, of Philadelphia, a lawyer from that more liberal colony. Appealing eloquently to the jury in the name of a free press and the right to publish the truth, Hamilton won a verdict of "not guilty" amid cheers from the people who had crowded into the courtroom. Thus by an effort to curb a printer, Cosby helped to make freedom of the press a cherished privilege in the American colonies, whether he was right or wrong on his points of law.

Another type of royal governor and dispute appeared in Massachusetts in 1771 when Thomas Hutchinson was placed at the head of that province. Hutchinson was born in Boston in 1711, educated at Harvard, and, as a member of a rich and powerful family of merchants, quickly rose to an influential position in colonial politics. Though conservative in temper and loyal to the King, he opposed many acts of Parliament, such as the Stamp Act, as bad policy, and sought to pursue a moderate course. Yet he did not deny the right of Parliament to tax and govern the colonies according to its own desires; as governor he secretly encouraged British authorities to adopt strong measures in dealing with colonial agitators. He quarreled with the Massachusetts assembly and with Samuel Adams, leader in local resistance to British actions. In an address to the legislature he declared that the supremacy of Parliament must be admitted and that "the mere exercise of its authority can be no grievance." Though a man of personal honor and courage, eager to exert a moderating influence, Hutchinson added fuel to the fires of discontent in Massachusetts. In 1774, after the Boston Tea Party, he left for England and was never able to return to America.

If proprietors had, as a rule, lived in their colonies, they might have enjoyed greater powers as governors in their own right, but most of them remained in England and acted through deputies whom they chose to direct their colonial affairs. Naturally the proprietary agent in a colony had less of pomp and circumstance than a royal governor. Yet he had similar legal powers: to appoint members of the council, if there was one; to choose military and civil officers; to grant lands; to veto acts of the legislature; and to supervise the enforcement of the laws. Like the royal governor, he might be on good terms or bad terms with the colonial legislature. Usually, in the best of conditions, he was more or less in open conflict with it.

The Penns managed to hold fast to Pennsylvania and Delaware until the Revolution broke their proprietorship. Although they and their deputy governors had troubles enough, by twisting and turning and making concessions to the legislature the Penns were able to keep their property until the rupture with Great Britain.

The career of the Baltimores in Maryland was more stormy. Between 1660 and 1689 they encountered four or five open revolts among their subjects. As a result Maryland was made a royal province. Not until a Protestant heir appeared in the Baltimore family was the colony restored to that family, in 1715, and then Catholics in Maryland were disfranchised.

In South Carolina it was a revolt against the proprietors which ended in the transformation of the colony into a royal province in 1729. Proprietary agents in the North Carolina district were no happier in the executive office. Between 1674 and 1729 six of the deputy governors were ousted by turbulent actions of the colonists, amounting on two occasions to open rebellion.

In contests with royal and proprietary governors and in the ordinary management of legislative business, Americans by the hundreds learned to practice and think about the arts of government. They acquired training in drawing up bills and resolutions expressing their grievances, ideals, or demands. They could stand upon the floors of assemblies, defend the projects they favored, argue with their opponents, and carry on business in accordance with the rules of parliamentary law. They could draft petitions to the governor and appear before him to support their demands upon the executive. They could investigate the measures and deeds of officials in charge of law enforcement, and often compel the governor to remove them, by threats of withholding the money for the payment of their salaries.

No form or function of government in fact escaped their thought or experience. With the theory, practice, and arts of lawmaking and administration they became familiar. There was no work of that type in which they were wholly untrained; there were no mysteries veiled to their understanding. Thus through the years, if not wholly aware of it, Americans were equipping themselves to take over all branches of government, and to direct, as persons adept in the business, the public affairs of America.

As members of legislatures gained in political dexterity and wisdom, they insisted on having, holding, and exercising certain fundamental powers of government. Sometimes, in this respect, they gained ground; at other times they lost it. The lines of the battle with royal and proprietary governors swayed to and fro. But to many rights legislatures clung so stoutly that only a hardheaded and stubborn governor could override them for any long period. Among the claims asserted by the legislatures, nine were regarded by colonists as basic to liberty and self-government:

To introduce and enact bills on all matters of local and general interest in the colony, subject to the terms of the charter and English laws.

To fix the kinds and amounts of taxation to be laid on the people.

To pass upon the governor's actions in the nature of legislation.

To control the voting of money to pay salaries, including the governor's, and audit the disbursement of funds.

To create courts of law and regulate the salaries of judges.

To choose and pay agents charged with lobbying for or against measures pending in the Parliament or before royal officers in London.

To elect the speaker of the lower house.

To decide disputes over contested seats and check any resort to corruption on the part of the governor in elections.

To have periodical elections of members fixed by law at from two to five years.

Although members of the colonial legislature generally agreed on their rights as against the government of Great Britain, its agents, and the deputies of proprietors, they often differed violently respecting the way in which their colonial affairs were to be conducted. Representatives from districts occupied by owners of small farms were frequently at loggerheads with representatives from districts in which great landlords and merchants were numerous and powerful.

In part the roots of this conflict were sectional. From New York to Georgia, along the coastal plain and up to the headwaters of rivers emptying into the Atlantic, big landlords and merchants were usually in the ascendancy, clever enough to keep an upper hand in politics. In the frontier regions back of this coastal strip, small farmers were dominant.

Many and various were the grounds of strife between representatives of the seaboard and representatives of the frontier. As a rule the people of the seaboard had more representatives in the legislature than their numbers warranted and they wanted to run the colony to suit their ideas and interests. On the other hand, farmers from the back regions demanded more representatives in the assembly and more consideration of their ideas and interests. So within each colony, despite agreement on rights as against Great Britain, there were endless controversies over the concrete issues of representation, taxation, the disposition of Western lands, defense against the Indians, and matters of local government. In such controversies also, Americans gained experience in debating, lawmaking, and law enforcement.

In local or community affairs, Americans in each colony were steadily educated and trained in the arts of self-government if on a small scale. Most of the people were engaged in agriculture and duly qualified men in large numbers shared in the local government of rural districts—towns or counties as the case might be.

Throughout New England and parts of the middle colonies the unit of government was the town—a small rural region, usually with a village or crossroads group of houses as a center. Such a town or township was governed by a meeting of the voters who chose its officers, levied taxes, appropriated money, and passed laws pertaining to roads, schools, bridges, and other local matters. There were counties in New England but they were mainly for judicial purposes. At the county seat a court held sessions for trying important civil and criminal cases and hearing appeals from town justices of the peace.

In Pennsylvania and the colonies to the south, the county was the chief unit of local administration. There local business was carried on by sheriffs, justices of the peace, coroners, and other officials, usually chosen by the governor of the colony.

So well entrenched was the system of local government that it was generally retained during and after the Revolution; indeed, it still exists, with some modifications here and there. Thus town and county "schools of government" furnished abundant opportunities for Americans to practice the arts of lawmaking and law enforcement. In the local schools of politics, leaders acquired training for action in the larger realm, colonial or intercolonial.

At many places cities and boroughs grew up in the course of colonial development. In New England they were governed by town meetings modeled on those existing in rural districts. In the middle and southern colonies, it became a custom to incorporate populous centers, such as New York, Albany, Trenton, Philadelphia, and Norfolk; that is, to give them charters and provide a kind of independent municipal government. As a rule the city charter was granted by the colonial governor. By charters qualified voters in a majority of the cities were given the right to elect members of the council and board of aldermen, who in turn chose the mayor and other city officials. In a few places, for example Philadelphia, Annapolis, and Norfolk, members of the city council were named in the original charter and empowered to choose their own successors as vacancies occurred.

Although the suffrage in cities was limited as a rule to the well-to-do classes and in some places there were no popular elections at all, many inhabitants had some share in conducting municipal affairs. Besides, urban residents, if they owned enough property to qualify for the suffrage, took part in electing members to the colonial assembly. So, for one reason or another, townspeople became "politically minded." Nowhere were they just an inert mass ruled by agents of royal governors.

Active as thousands of Americans were in the local and central governments of their respective colonies, they had little to do with the relations of the colonies to one another. Laws regulating intercolonial commerce were made by the British government. Although a large amount of freedom to engage in such commerce was given to all colonists, dominion over it remained in the hands of superior British authorities. In addition, control over the relations of the colonies to foreign countries was a complete monopoly of the British government. As to the management of intercolonial and foreign affairs, therefore, Americans enjoyed little or no power and were relatively inexperienced during the colonial age.

Yet in regard to intercolonial relations, Americans were not wholly ignorant or indifferent. Nor were they totally without experience, or devoid of the desire to foster closer connections. Indeed many things conspired to draw the colonies closer together: the need for defense against Indians; participation in the numerous wars waged by Great Britain against France and Spain, partly on colonial frontiers; the necessity of co-operating in raising troops and supplies for such wars; and the growth of travel, trade, and intercourse along the seaboard.

As early as 1643, Massachusetts Bay, Plymouth, Connecticut, and New Haven formed the New England Confederation. They united in a "firm and perpetual league of friendship and amity for offense and defense, mutual advice and succor, upon all just occasions. both for preserving and propagating the truth and liberties of the Gospel and for their own mutual safety and welfare." For about twenty years the Confederation was active in carrying out the purposes for which it was created. Until 1685 delegates from these united colonies held meetings from time to time and dis-

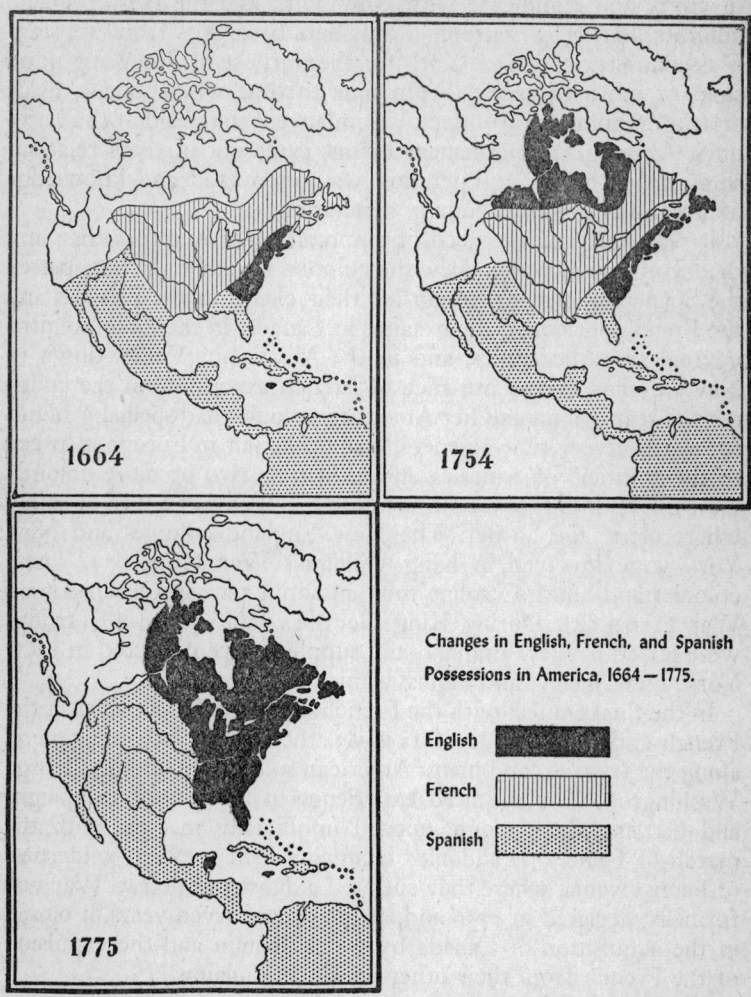

1664

1754

1775

Changes in English, French, and Spanish Possessions in America, 1664—1775.

English

French

Spanish

cussed common affairs. But as the need for defense against the Indians on their borders declined, the Confederation weakened. By the end of the seventeenth century it had completely broken down. Still it pointed the way to intercolonial action, as a precedent.

Other colonies also discovered the advantages of mutual aid. Near the middle of the seventeenth century Virginia made treaties of amity and commerce with New York and the New England colonies. In 1684 a conference was held by agents from Virginia, Massachusetts, and New York for the purpose of discussing questions of mutual interest. From time to time when Indians made attacks on Southern frontiers, Virginia went to the aid of the Carolinas. Although no permanent unions came out of these relationships, the value of co-operation was discovered and knowledge of it handed down to coming generations.

It was wars and the need of common defense, rather than any theory of union, which drew the colonies together. As time passed the Spaniards tried to strengthen their claims in the Floridas and the French developed their claims in Canada, in the Ohio country beyond the Alleghenies, and in the Mississippi Valley down to New Orleans. In the presence of French expansion on the continent, Great Britain and her American colonies had special grounds for alarm. Every time a general war broke out in Europe it spread to the frontiers of America and each time two or more colonies were drawn into the war—in the North or West or South or somewhere along the border. The New England colonies and New York were involved in King William's War (1689–97). These colonies and South Carolina took an active part in Queen Anne's War (1702–14). During King George's War (1739–48) troops were levied in New England and supplies were collected in New York, New Jersey, and Pennsylvania.

In the final contest with the French and their Indian allies in the French and Indian War of 1756–63, the conflict became general along the frontier; and many American soldiers, including George Washington, then acquired experience in the arts of campaigns and battles. The struggle opened unofficially in 1755 with the march of General Braddock's troops into the western wilderness of Pennsylvania, where they suffered a disastrous defeat. War was formally declared in 1756 and, at the end of seven years, it closed in the acquisition of Canada by Great Britain and the expulsion of the French from their other continental claims.

Hard pressed for men, money, and supplies for this long war, the British government again called on the colonies for help. Most of them were laggard in responding and a few of them did nothing at all. Massachusetts, Connecticut, and New York furnished nearly three fourths of the American troops raised; but out of the experience all the colonies learned something about the bearing of common burdens and responsibilities.

As if in anticipation of the demands to come during the French and Indian War, an ambitious attempt had been made to unite them in a permanent federation. On a suggestion from the British government, an intercolonial conference was held at Albany, New York, in 1754. Among other things its purpose was to bring the colonies under "articles of union and confederation with each other for mutual defense of his majesty's subjects and interests in North America in time of peace as well as war."

Delegates from Maryland, Pennsylvania, New York, and all the New England colonies attended the conference. Without a dissenting vote they quickly resolved that a union of the colonies was "absolutely necessary for their security and defense." A committee, headed by Benjamin Franklin, brought before the delegates a plan to effect this union. The draft was debated, adopted, and sent to the colonies and the British government for approval but, owing to indifference or hostility, it was never put into force.

Whatever the reason for its failure, the Franklin plan demonstrated that some Americans had a deep understanding of intercolonial affairs. It provided for a general council composed of forty-eight members elected by the colonial assemblies. Representation in that body was to be roughly apportioned among the colonies according to wealth and population. Meetings of the council were to be held once a year or oftener if need be. The president was to be appointed by the Crown. He was to choose the military officers with the consent of the council. The selection of civil officers was vested in the council, subject to the president's approval. As to taxation, the new government was to levy such "general duties as appear equal and just" with due regard to the circumstances in the several colonies.

According to Franklin, the Crown disapproved his scheme as "having too much weight in the democratic part of the constitution, and every [colonial] assembly as having allowed too much prerogative." Though it was rejected, the plan of union was extensively discussed at the time and in years soon to follow it served to light the way toward a permanent union.

If no union was effected by this effort or the wars in which they became involved, colonists learned many things from such experiences. They became acquainted with the pull and haul of interests in the different sections of the country and the nature of the compromises that would be necessary to bring about adjustments among the conflicting forces. In raising troops, collecting supplies, and waging wars, they acquired some rudimentary arts of intercolonial co-operation on a large scale and in difficult circumstances. From Braddock's disaster in Pennsylvania, where George Washington was present and displayed bravery under fire, they developed a suspicion that British regular troops were far from invincible, especially in the arts of wilderness warfare adapted to the American terrain. What was more, and no less significant for American autonomy, discerning leaders among the colonists gained insight into the rivalry of governments for power in the Old World as well as for imperial dominion, into their ambitions and hatreds, and into the great game of diplomacy in Europe based on the balance of power. All this, too, was enlightening and useful in developing the arts of self-government in America.

CHAPTER VII

Two Systems and Ideologies in Conflict

OVER AGAINST colonial maturity in matters political, religious, social, and intellectual on this continent stood, across the sea, the British system of politics, economy, and ecclesiasticism. The system was an oligarchy collected around the monarch—an oligarchy composed of lords and the clerical hierarchy. There was in Great Britain, to be sure, a "popular" legislative body, the House of Commons; but, under the restricted suffrage and "rotten borough" scheme of representation, the oligarchy, through personal influence, wealth, and corruption, was generally able to dominate it. In economic terms, the policy of the British system was mercantilism—the permanent subordination of the colonies to the interests of the British governing classes.

The strength of the British oligarchy was fortified by the almost universal belief in England that the colonies were as subordinate socially and intellectually as they were politically and economically. In his *Origins of the American Revolution* (1943), based on microscopic and comprehensive researches in British records, William Miller says, while taking note of exceptions: "One of the convictions most firmly planted in the minds of the eighteenth-century Englishmen was the superiority of true-born Britons to the American colonists. . . . The status of the colonies was fixed for all time: regardless of their strength and population they must remain inferior to the mother country." This inveterate attitude was expressed by Dr. Samuel Johnson in the words: "We do not put a calf into the plow, we wait until he is an ox." In other words the young colonies might play in their youth but they must wear the yoke after they grow up.

Though the British oligarchy was often divided over various questions and there were occasional popular outbursts of protest against its harsher measures of government, the ruling classes of Great Britain were fairly united on one thing: they wanted to keep the British Empire intact and to make it contribute to the wealth and power of the mother country. The American colonies furnished many offices and jobs for British lords, their younger sons, and their hangers-on; the American colonies had vast areas of unoccupied land, huge parcels of which royal favorites could obtain for a song if they had the King's approval. British merchants and shippers found American trade highly profitable and naturally sought to get and keep as much of it as they could. British manufacturers looked upon the American markets as their own and as necessary outlets for their woolen cloth, hardware, and other finished commodities. The arable lands and forests of America were the objects of great desire to British enterprisers. British capitalists, whether landlords, merchants, manufacturers, or bankers, ever hunting more advantageous places for the investment of their capital, regarded the American colonies as offering almost unlimited opportunities for money-making.

Associated with British interests in political power and economic advantage were a number of principles—an ideology—which seemed natural, right, and proper to persons who held them. The King and the members of the titled aristocracy, who formed his inner circle, deemed it their right and privilege to hold the colonies tightly and permanently under the British government which they so largely controlled. To British merchants and shippers it was perfectly "reasonable" that they should enjoy ever-enlarging opportunities in the American trade, fix the prices to be paid to American planters and farmers for their produce, and restrain the menacing competition of American merchants and shippers. For British manufacturers it was "natural" to think that Americans should stick at the business of producing grain, lumber, and other raw materials and be compelled, as far as possible, to buy British finished products at good prices. That British capitalists should have special advantages in investing in the lands, fur trade, commerce, and other lucrative enterprises in America was, in their minds, both "right and proper."

These ideas all fitted into the pattern of "mercantilism" which generally prevailed in Western Europe throughout the colonial period. In sum and substance, mercantilism meant that the government should adopt and enforce measures to accomplish the following objects: hold colonies in the status of raw-material provinces supplying the mother country with materials for its manufacturers and foodstuffs for its workers; promote export and import trade in such a way as to bring gold, silver, and other forms of wealth into its coffers; give the mother country the profits that arose from manufacturing; monopolize more or less the commerce of the colonies to the advantage of its merchants. In the theory of mercantilism, the British government in London and its supporters found "good reasons" for believing that their ideas about managing American affairs were "sound" and "patriotic."

For carrying the ideas of mercantilism into effect, certain very definite laws and practices were necessary. The bonds of union between the American colonies and Great Britain must be kept firm and made stronger as the colonies matured in wealth and power. Laws favorable to the interests of British merchants, manufacturers, and investors must be enacted; and the American colonists must be stopped from passing laws and doing other things which interfered with the enforcement of British measures. To carry British legislation into effect, the number of British officers and agents in the colonies must be increased and, if necessary, British soldiers must be stationed there to uphold British governors and agents in the performance of their duties. Given British interests and ideas of values, given the theory of mercantilism as soundly patriotic, British designs for the colonies followed logically.

But in many matters, American interests ran directly counter to British interests. Most Americans were more concerned with developing the lands and resources right at hand than they were in promoting prosperity in Great Britain or upholding the British interests in India and other distant parts of the world. American artisans and manufacturers wanted to develop their own industries and reap the profits accruing from them. American merchants and shippers longed to enlarge their share of international trade. American farmers and planters believed that they could get better prices for their produce if British merchants exercised less control over the export and import trade; if Dutch, French, and other merchants from the continent of Europe could operate more freely in American markets, offering their goods for sale and buying tobacco, grains, and other farm commodities. American capitalists and enterprisers thought they would have larger opportunities for profitable business if all the lands, forests, and minerals at hand were at the disposal of colonial governments. Farmers and planters on the seaboard looked with hungry eyes toward the vacant lands beyond the near frontier and wanted them thrown open to easy settlement or speculation. Moreover, Americans could scarcely help wanting a larger share of the lucrative offices and jobs filled with appointees of the British King and the colonial governors, whose salaries were paid out of American taxes, without colonial representation in Parliament.

To support their counter interests, Americans had a large stock of ideas. One part of the stock consisted of legal ideas, another part of political ideas, and still another of economic ideas. The whole program included the following elements: under the English "constitution" Englishmen everywhere in the realm have certain rights which cannot be taken from them, such as the right to share, through their representatives, in the making of laws and the laying of taxes; the purpose of government is to protect the life, liberty, and property of the people; when tyranny or oppression takes the place of protection, the people have a right to change the government by revolution if necessary; all human beings are equal and have a right to obtain the land necessary to a livelihood. From such legal, political, and economic theories, Americans active in the advancement of their own interests had little difficulty in choosing arguments that fitted their respective cases.

If Americans were to realize their interests and ideas in practice, they believed that two types of measures were necessary. They needed local laws providing more control over the sale of lands, over the issue of currency used in trade, and over their manufacturing and commerce. Defensive measures were also indispensable —measures directed against British regulations and their enforcement in the colonies.

Having a care for such matters, colonial legislatures, from year to year, passed laws designed to serve American interests, despite the fact that acts were often vetoed by the colonial governor, or disallowed and set aside by the British Crown on its own motion or on appeal from objectors. On the defensive side other lines of action were open to Americans who resented British regulations: they could petition the King; they could send a colonial agent to London for the purpose of lobbying on behalf of their demands; they could simply ignore or violate British laws, especially if the royal or proprietary governor was lenient or negligent, as he often was.

☆

In giving effect to mercantilism and British ideology in general, the Parliament in London enacted many laws pertaining to American economic enterprise and political affairs. In general terms such laws fell into three broad classes.

The first class affected shipbuilding and the carriage of freight by water. They were known as Navigation Acts. These acts provided that goods carried both ways between Great Britain and the colonies and between the colonies and European countries must be transported in British-built ships manned mainly by British sailors. Since, in the eyes of the law, Americans were British, the ships the Americans built were "British-built" and the sailors they furnished were also British. In many ways, therefore, the Navigation Acts worked to the advantage of the colonies as well as the mother country. On the whole, the acts stimulated American shipping and promoted American commercial interests.

To the second class of British legislation belonged the Trade Acts. By such laws certain "enumerated" commodities produced in America had to be exported to Great Britain alone. In time the enumerated list included rice, tobacco, iron, lumber, furs, hides, naval stores, and a few other types of goods. Thus many American farmers and planters had to sell their prime produce through British merchants and accept the prices fixed in the British market, subject to no competition by Dutch, French, and other foreign merchants offering better terms.

Under other trade laws, American goods passing to the continent of Europe and European goods imported into the colonies had to go through the hands of merchants in Great Britain who collected their profits on the business. A special trade law, called the Molasses Act, passed by Parliament in 1733, laid taxes on important articles in the trade of the colonists with non-British possessions in America, especially the French West Indies, for the purpose of benefiting British merchants and capitalists engaged in commerce and sugar production in the British West Indies.

But the trade laws as a rule gave Americans many advantages, while restricting their operations in certain directions. To cite an example, for the enumerated articles Americans had a virtual monopoly in the markets of Great Britain as against their foreign competitors.

It was clearly in the interests of British manufacturers, however, to have laws enacted by Parliament for the purpose of restraining colonial industries. These formed a third class of regulatory laws. In 1699 the colonists were forbidden by act of Parliament to export woolen goods anywhere, and even to trade in such goods between towns and between colonies. In 1732 colonists were deprived of the right to export hats, finished or unfinished, to any place in America or abroad. By 1750 British ironmasters were feeling the pinch of their American competitors and in that year Parliament forbade Americans to set up iron mills for working bar or pig iron and for producing finished iron manufactures.

It was not so easy for the British government to enforce laws restricting American manufactures as it was to carry into effect the Navigation and Trade acts. Strict enforcement would have required a British official in every community, for instance, where housewives were spinning and weaving or men were making hats or hardware. As a matter of fact the British government did not attempt to police the colonies in this respect and the American manufacture of the forbidden goods flourished in spite of the laws.

But a turn came in the relatively negligent methods of the British government after the Seven Years' War with France which ended in 1763. In that conflict colonists had taken an active part by supplying soldiers and supplies. A heavy burden, however, had fallen on Great Britain, for the war raged in distant places at sea and at points as far apart as the coasts of India and the frontiers of North America. Although some results of the conflict were fortunate for Britain—the capture of Canada and other territorial gains—the struggle had been expensive and had greatly increased the British debt. As an outcome also, the British government faced other problems; for instance, the administration of the Northwest Territory adjoining the Mississippi and the Ohio rivers, and the regulation of relations with the Indians in that region.

In addition, a highly controversial question arose: Who are to benefit most from the exploitation of Western territories now cleared of the French and opened to development—American or British investors, farmers, land speculators, and fur traders? The British had undoubtedly made prodigious sacrifices in the effort to oust the French from the continent. The war had likewise been costly in men and money to the colonies. Both the British and the Americans therefore had logical and legitimate claims regarding all these matters, but there was no high and impartial court above them to which they could appeal for satisfactory adjudication.

☆

Whatever the merits of the respective claims to the benefits arising from enterprise and speculation in America, the British government eventually embarked upon a program of strengthening, adding to, and enforcing laws and decrees designed to regulate American economic and political affairs. Responsibility for this departure was assumed by the British ministries that succeeded one another after George III came to the throne in 1760, in the midst of the great war between England and France.

George himself, upon whom much of the blame for the trouble was later thrown, had little to do with initiating the program, but in general he approved it. Besides, by bribery and corruption, he helped to support the ministers who formulated it in the Parliament; and he had high notions about his royal prerogatives at home as well as over his "farms," as he referred to the colonies. In no way did the new program run counter to his conceptions of government.

Briefly stated, the program included three principal elements: Americans must be taxed to pay a part of the expense incurred by Great Britain in defending, protecting, and administering her possessions in America; old trade and navigation laws must be more strictly enforced; and new laws regulating British and American commerce and enterprise in the colonies must be enacted.

Within five years after the close of the war with France the following measures had been adopted by the British government:

1763—Royal Order, reserving to the King the disposal of Western lands beyond a certain line.

1764—Sugar Act, taxing certain imports, partly with a view to bringing money into the British treasury for supporting British government in the colonies.

1764—Currency Act, forbidding the colonies to issue paper money.

1765—Stamp Act, taxing numerous articles and transactions in America to help pay the costs of British government in the colonies.

1765—Quartering Act, requiring Americans to help house and feed British regular troops stationed in the colonies.

1766—Declaratory Act, asserting the supremacy of the British Parliament in making laws for the colonies.

1767—Customs Collecting Act, establishing British commissioners in the colonies to collect customs and other duties.

1767—Revenue Act, laying taxes on lead, paint and other articles imported into the colonies.

1767—Tea Act, regulating importation of tea in British dominions in America in favor of the British East India Company.

All these measures deeply affected the American colonists: their agriculture, industries, commerce, and investment opportunities; their habits, practices, and desires respecting self-government; their freedom of elections, press, and speech. The Royal Order of 1763 forbade the colonists to buy any more land from the Indians in the West beyond a certain line, and vested in the Crown the sole power to hold and dispose of such lands. If enforced, this decree would mean that hardy pioneers, land-hungry and bent on acquiring homes for themselves, could no longer go West, take up land, and "squat" on it as their own. It would also mean that American land speculators could not acquire huge blocks of Western land in the hope of making money as land values rose with the advance of Western settlement.

The same order contained another provocative clause. It placed in the hands of royal officers the power of licensing persons engaged in trade with the Indians and thereby deciding who was to enjoy the profits of the lucrative fur traffic. In fact, the proclamation, though designed among other things to introduce order along the frontier, indicated that British officials were henceforward to dispose of large sections of the Western territory and settle the question as to who was to reap the profits of the various operations there, including the fur business. This, in turn, meant that Americans would no longer have the liberty to do very much as they pleased on the frontier—to hunt, trade with the Indians, gather up furs, and roam around at will, looking for adventures or "taking up" land.

The purpose of the Sugar Act was clearly stated in the preamble. It was to promote the business of the British sugar colonies in the West Indies, raise money toward the expenses of "defending, protecting, and securing" British colonies and plantations in America, more strictly enforce the laws against smuggling, and secure and improve the trade between Great Britain and her colonies in the New World. The act, like its predecessor in 1733, laid duties on sugar brought into the American colonies from non-British possessions. It also imposed duties on certain wines, silks, calicoes, and linens imported into the American colonies. With a view to enforcement, the act provided heavy penalties for all shippers, British and American alike, who tried to smuggle goods contrary to the terms of the law.

Explicitly, the Sugar Act taxed Americans for the purpose of raising money to pay the expenses of British officials and soldiers employed in governing the colonies and upholding British dominion over them. In itself, this was enough to rouse American ire. But the act also struck a severe blow at one branch of American commerce. Americans could no longer buy sugar cheaper from the French sugar colonies in the West Indies. They had been buying large quantities there, turning it into rum, and exchanging the rum for African slaves to be brought back to America for sale. This was a highly successful business and a tax on it in favor of British sugar growers and slave traders, if enforced, would hamper an important branch of American commerce.

The Customs Collecting Act of 1767, coupled with many provisions in other new British laws, showed that the British government was determined to stop smuggling and other violations of tax and trade laws on the part of Americans. British revenue collectors, officers of the navy and army, royal governors, and other agents were ordered to be diligent, to see that taxes were collected and regulations observed. Shipmasters engaged in the carrying trade had to be registered in official books and give bond that they would obey the laws. Patrols of British ships guarded the Atlantic coast, with power to halt, search, and hold merchant ships suspected of smuggling. Thus American liberty to trade at will was to be drastically curtailed.

By the Currency Act of 1764, American merchants, farmers, and debtors were adversely affected in numerous ways. No rich mines of gold and silver were discovered in the seaboard regions; so that Americans had no gold and silver of their own coinage with which to pay for domestic goods and meet their debts at home. For the same reason they had difficulty in finding specie to pay for imported British and foreign goods and to discharge the debts they owed British capitalists for money they had borrowed to buy land, stock, tools, and other capital supplies. In their straits, nearly all the colonies had been issuing colonial paper money at one time or another, and had made it lawful in business transactions. Now the Currency Act put a stop to this practice definitely and positively, evoking an early episode in the American battle over the "money question."

None of the British regulatory measures, however, affected large numbers of Americans seriously enough to arouse great popular opposition. It was the Stamp Act of 1765 that first set the colonies aflame. In the preamble of this act also appeared the declaration that its purpose was to provide money for the British treasury, "towards defraying the expenses of defending, protecting and securing the British colonies and plantations in America." That in itself was resented by many colonists. But the clauses of the act intended to raise the money, covering several pages of fine print, prescribed taxes which reached the pocketbooks of Americans from Massachusetts to Georgia.

Americans now had to buy stamps of various kinds, ranging in price from a few pence to several pounds each, to be placed on many classes of papers and articles. Deeds and mortgages relating to property, licenses to practice law, licenses to sell liquor, college diplomas, playing cards, dice, almanacs, and calendars all had to bear British stamps of stated values. More than this: publishers and printers of advertisements, newspapers, and other sheets had to buy stamps for their publications.

If the British Parliament had deliberately searched for taxes that would annoy as many Americans as possible, it could scarcely have improved upon the Stamp Act. The law was especially hard on two classes of Americans who spoke, wrote, and made their opinions heard: the lawyers and the publishers—both given to preaching freedom of speech and press. The very men in the streets were so angry that they instigated boycotts and riots against the act.

In itself the Stamp Act of March 1765 would have made trouble for the British government but it was quickly followed in April of the same year by the Quartering Act which gave the colonists to understand that the laws were to be enforced. Since the British ministry was preparing to send more soldiers than usual to the American colonies, with a view to upholding its authority, it faced the problem of furnishing the soldiers with quarters and supplies.

For this problem the Quartering Act provided what was deemed a solution: Americans were to lodge officers and privates in inns, taverns, uninhabited houses, barns, and other buildings; supply them with numerous articles of consumption; and furnish wagons to haul their goods. American constables, magistrates, and other civil officers in villages, towns, townships, cities, districts, and other places were charged with the duty of seeing that the buildings, candles, liquor, salt, and other articles mentioned in the act were promptly placed at the disposal of the British troops.

Consequently Americans not only had to endure the sight of British troops and the thought of military government; they had to help in housing, feeding, and serving British soldiers. Yet time was required to transport the British soldiers to the colonies and many months passed before American communities were stirred up by the necessity of finding quarters and supplies for them.

It was the Stamp Act which awakened immediate protests and

alarms. Lawyers and merchants were quick to voice their resentment against it. The cry, "No taxation without representation," was taken up in cities, towns, and country regions by artisans, mechanics, farmers, and housewives. Popular societies called the Sons of Liberty and the Daughters of Liberty were organized to resist the sale of stamps. Crowds gathered in the streets of Boston, New York, Philadelphia, and Charleston, and rioted against officers who tried to force people to buy stamps. The offices and houses of royal officials were stoned, in some cases sacked and burned. Going far beyond blocking the sale of stamps, Americans organized groups to boycott British goods of all kinds—to cut down the sale of British manufactures as well as stamps. Indeed there was so much disorder in several colonies that even the protesting merchants and lawyers became frightened and tried to restrain the torrent of popular anger.

Colonial leaders took steps to bring united pressure on Parliament for the repeal of the act. In the Virginia House of Burgesses they forced the adoption of resolutions denouncing the principles of the Stamp Act, asserting that the General Assembly alone could lay taxes on the people of the colony, and branding other methods of taxation as "illegal, unconstitutional, and unjust." It was in supporting this resolution that Patrick Henry delivered the speech which made him famous as a firebrand of the Revolution.

In the spirit of the Virginia Resolutions, the House of Representatives in Massachusetts opposed the Stamp Act and issued a circular letter inviting all the colonies to send delegates to a general congress to be held in New York for the purpose of discussing common problems and taking common action. Nine colonies responded favorably, chose their delegates amid popular excitement, and sent them to New York.

In October 1765 the Stamp Act Congress assembled. Despite some difference of opinion, it agreed on a set of resolutions and the terms of a petition calling upon Parliament to repeal the act. Members of the Congress professed their loyal allegiance to the King and their subordination to the Parliament of Great Britain. But they claimed all the inherent rights and liberties of natural-born British subjects. They declared that no taxes could be laid on the people without their consent, that the colonies were not and could not be represented in Parliament, and that no taxes could be constitutionally imposed upon them without the consent of their legislatures. They also sought to show that various acts of Parliament both burdened the colonies and interfered with trade between them and Great Britain. British merchants were tersely warned that restrictions recently placed on trade would render the people of the colonies unable to purchase British manufactures. While resolutions were respectful and moderate in tone, they were specific and firm.

In consternation over the open resistance in the colonies and under pressure from British merchants hard hit by the American boycott, Parliament in 1766 repealed the Stamp Act. In so doing, however, it did not concede the American claim that it had no right to tax the colonists. In fact, by the Declaratory Act, signed on the same day as the repeal measure, Parliament asserted that the colonies have been, are, and ought to be subordinate to the Crown and Parliament; and that the King and Parliament had, have, and of right ought to have full power and authority to make laws and statutes binding the colonies and people of America "in all cases whatsoever." This language left no loopholes through which Americans could escape admitting their subordination to the British government, but, as they rejoiced over the abolition of the Stamp Tax, they spent little time arguing about the mere legal theory of the Declaratory Act.

Evidently foreseeing the dangers in trying to collect taxes in the colonies directly, the British ministers, still determined to raise revenue in America, took another course. The very next year after the repeal of the Stamp Act, Parliament passed the Revenue Act of 1767, which laid duties on glass, red and white lead, painters' colors, paper, and tea.

At the same time Parliament informed the colonists that these duties were to be collected. It coupled with the Revenue Act a law which had "teeth" in every line. The Customs Commissioners Act of 1767 vested in the hands of British commissioners the duty of supervising the enforcement of the revenue laws. The tax commissioners were to be appointed by the King; they were to reside in the colonies; and they were to be paid from the British treasury, not out of grants of money voted by colonial legislatures. In the Revenue Act itself, Parliament also expressed its resolve to collect the duties: it gave the higher courts in the colonies, made up of British judges, power to issue "Writs of Assistance," authorizing customs officers to search houses, warehouses, shops, cellars, and other places for smuggled goods and to seize them summarily if found.

A third commercial measure passed by Parliament in 1767 was the Tea Act. This act, supplemented by another Tea Act in 1773, among other things relieved the British East India Company of the necessity of paying duties on its tea exported to America. In effect it amounted to giving the company a monopoly of the tea business in America; enforced, it would enable the company to sell tea at lower prices than were asked by other British merchants or, for that matter, even by American merchants who had bought tea from foreign merchants and smuggled it into the colonies. Not without reason did objecting colonists regard the Tea Act as a step toward setting up British monopolies for the control of all American foreign and domestic trade.

Events swiftly following the enactment of the British laws of 1767 revealed to the two parties the sharpness of the conflict. It was now obvious that the British government was determined to raise revenue in the colonies by taxation; to use this revenue toward defraying the expenses of governing the colonies; to enforce its authority through higher officers appointed by the Crown and paid out of the British treasury; to free the royal officers from control by the colonial assemblies; and definitely to subordinate the colonists to British commercial interests. It was made equally plain by events that irate Americans who opposed the British policies would stubbornly resist them by official resolves in colonial assemblies and by popular actions outside the legislative halls—even actions involving violence.

The basic animus of the colonists against British policies became manifest within a year. In 1768 the assembly of Massachusetts, inspired by Samuel Adams, approved the sending of a circular letter to the legislatures of the other colonies, calling upon them to consider their common plight, and declaring the principles of retaliation on which Massachusetts was taking her stand. For this defiance the royal governor at Boston dissolved the assembly.

When assemblies in other colonies approved the doctrines of the Circular Letter, they too were dissolved by their governors. In 1769 the Virginia House of Burgesses proclaimed that it alone had the right to lay taxes in Virginia, and petitioned the King for a redress of grievances. The governor of the colony replied by dissolving that assembly.

Meanwhile a contest especially bitter was going on in New York. In that colony the assembly had refused to make provisions for British soldiers under the Quartering Act of 1765. Parliament answered in 1767 by passing a law suspending the New York Assembly until it was ready to comply with the terms of the Quartering Act. When at length, in 1769, it bowed to British demands, it made no attempt to conceal its indignation; and the necessity of housing and supplying British soldiers stirred up wrath among the residents of the colony.

In 1770 British soldiers, stationed at Boston, jostled and stoned by a crowd of men and boys, fired on their assailants, killing five and wounding several more. News of this "Boston Massacre," as it was described, spread into other colonies, awakening both resentment and anxiety. When in 1772 a British armed vessel engaged in hunting smugglers in Narragansett Bay accidentally ran ashore, it was quickly boarded by men from Providence who seized the crew and set fire to the ship. In 1773 the House of Burgesses in Virginia, meeting in spite of the governor's prohibition, created a standing committee to correspond with leaders in other colonies and bring about combined actions against British policies and measures. Late that year a group of men, disguised as Indians, forced their way upon ships at Boston, which had brought tea for sale to the colonists under the new terms, and dumped their cargoes into the harbor. In 1774 rioters at Annapolis compelled the destruction of a British vessel, the *Peggy Stewart*, and all the tea chests on board. American resistance was taking the form of physical violence when the year 1774 opened.

If members of the Boston Tea Party thought that the British government would yield to their display of anger they were mistaken and soon disillusioned. Early in 1774 Parliament enacted five new laws intended to cure unrest in America. One of the acts closed the port of Boston to all trade by sea. Another revamped the charter of Massachusetts, made the government still more royal in nature, and even subjected town meetings to the control of the governor. A third act empowered royal officials to take to Great Britain or elsewhere in her American colonies all persons in Massachusetts accused of murder in connection with law enforcement. By a fourth act the quartering of British troops in Massachusetts towns was specifically authorized. The fifth act offended Protestants and affected other interests in the colonies: it granted toleration to Catholics in Canada, widened the boundaries of Quebec southward to the Ohio River, and provided for the government of that vast Western territory by a viceroy of the King.

More British soldiers were now sent to Massachusetts and the commander of the British armed forces in the colony, General

Gage, was installed as governor. Such actions on the part of the British government in Massachusetts served as a warning to all the colonists that British authority was not to be denied or defied with impunity. As the spring of 1774 merged into summer, leaders of the opposition to British authority, from Massachusetts to Georgia, had to face that fact and, if still stubborn in their militancy, make further decisions on the basis of it.

CHAPTER VIII

Independence Completed by Revolution

In the spring of 1774 a cry went up in the colonies for united action and for a general congress to assure such action. The assembly of Virginia, still meeting, if irregularly, in spite of the royal governor's prohibitive orders, expressed sympathy with Massachusetts and favored combined efforts in resistance to British policies and measures. Encouraged by reports from various sources, the assembly of Massachusetts, under the leadership of Samuel Adams, resolved that a continental congress was highly expedient and indeed necessary to deliberate and determine upon wise and proper steps to be taken in recovering the rights of Americans and restoring harmony with Great Britain. As proof of its intransigence it appointed delegates to attend such a congress on the first of the coming September.

In line with the action of Massachusetts, other colonies chose representatives and on September 5 the first Continental Congress met at Philadelphia. Among its members were men soon to be powerful figures in history, such as George Washington and Patrick Henry from Virginia, Samuel Adams and John Adams from Massachusetts. But they differed among themselves as to the best course to pursue. Many favored radical action verging in the direction of independence; others were cautious and conservative; on the whole, moderates held the balance of power. After tempestuous debates, the Congress agreed upon three expedients.

First, it adopted a set of resolutions, in dignified but pointed language, setting forth the rights, liberties, and immunities of the colonists and naming the measures of the British government which, in their view, violated these rights, liberties, and immunities. As to exactly what they claimed and what they were protesting against, members of the Congress left no doubt. By these resolutions they repeated and expanded the claims made by the Stamp Act Congress of 1765.

Second, while promising to support Massachusetts in her struggle against Great Britain, the Continental Congress drew up an address to King George III and another to the people of England and to the inhabitants of British America, in which it respectfully presented American grievances and called for a restoration of American rights. The resolutions and the addresses were words —firm, moderate, positive words; still they were only words.

A third expedient approved by the Continental Congress went beyond words into action. That was a decision to stop the importation of British goods into the colonies until a redress of grievances could be obtained and to vest the enforcement of the boycott in the hands of local "committees of safety and inspection." The boycott was, of course, a violation of British law. It was more than this. It was aggressive. It provided for establishing in every community a boycott committee to prevent the buying of British goods and to discover who was loyal to Great Britain and who was loyal to the American cause, as tested by their acts in buying goods. Words might be debated and hairs split indefinitely but a colonist either upheld the boycott or he was against it and bought British goods in spite of it. He was in short a Patriot or a Loyalist!

Before adjourning in October, the first Continental Congress provided for a second Congress to be held in May of 1775 in case the situation then required such an assembly.

In response to the demands of the first Continental Congress, the British government made one concession: it was willing to relieve any colony of taxation on condition that it would bear its share of imperial defense and provide money for supporting the officers of the Crown within its borders. But with this concession, such as it was, Parliament coupled a set of resolutions pledging full support to the King in the enforcement of British laws in the colonies. These resolutions it supplemented by restraining acts which practically destroyed the commerce of the colonies.

Meanwhile British officers—civil and military—in the colonies tightened, instead of relaxing, their efforts to compel obedience to British authority. It was in the fulfillment of this duty that General Gage, in Boston, dispatched a small force of soldiers toward Lexington and Concord in April 1775 for the purpose, among other things, of seizing some military supplies supposed to be stored in that neighborhood.

Warned by William Dawes and Paul Revere that British soldiers were on the march, a small number of American militiamen gathered on the green at Lexington early in the morning of April 19. With about thirty or forty onlookers the militiamen were standing there when the British forces arrived under the command of Major John Pitcairn. Seeing that armed resistance would be futile, the captain of the militiamen, John Parker, ordered his men to disperse. While they were slowly breaking ranks a shot was fired.

By whom? British who were present at the time laid the blame for the first shot on Americans; and Americans put it on the British. Since that day the question of blame has been repeatedly debated without reaching any generally accepted conclusion. Whoever cares to weigh the evidence of contemporary witnesses who saw the fray with their own eyes may find the testimony admirably summarized in the pages of Allen French's *The Day of Concord and Lexington*.

Although the person who fired the first shot that nineteenth day of April 1775 must apparently remain forever unknown, it is certain that his shot was followed by firing all day, as militiamen poured in from the surrounding country and harassed British troops on their retreat to Boston. It is also certain that this shot, "heard around the world," heralded a war.

If there had been doubts about the need for a second conference of delegates from all the colonies, they were settled by the clash at Lexington and Concord in April 1775. In the next month the second Continental Congress assembled at Philadelphia. Though blood had been shed, most of the delegates were still inclined to be conciliatory toward the British government when sessions of the Congress opened; for they seemed to hope that the American rights previously declared might yet be acknowledged by Great Britain.

But the Congress prepared for the worst—a general war. It provided for organizing the New England militiamen near Boston into a regular army and appointed one of its members, George Washington, as commander of the American forces in Massachusetts. It also resolved to raise money and supplies for an armed conflict if it came; to seek support by opening diplomatic relations with several European countries; and to carry on the struggle until the liberties claimed by Americans could be realized by British concessions or American independence.

These resolves were met in Great Britain by a proclamation from George III denouncing American leaders in the revolt as "rebels" and ordering the British military and civil agents to suppress the insurrection and punish the authors and abettors of "such traitorous designs." The war was now in full course.

In June 1775 American militiamen at Bunker Hill near Boston, though finally driven from their position, proved that they could and would fight as long as they had gunpowder. Taking command of the army at Cambridge the next month, Washington prepared to besiege Boston. In this operation he was so successful that Lord Howe, who had now supplanted General Gage, gave up the city in March 1776 and sailed for Halifax. In his flight Howe carried along, besides his troops, several hundred British officials and Boston residents who were steadfast in their loyalty to King George.

Meanwhile, late in 1775, Vermont militiamen, under Ethan Allen and Benedict Arnold, had seized Ticonderoga and Crown Point, getting possession of strongholds which might block a British drive from Canada. Still later in that year American forces invaded Canada and captured Montreal. But an assault on Quebec failed and they were forced to withdraw, thus losing their hope of bringing Canada to the support of the struggle against Great Britain.

As the war proceeded, prospects for a reconciliation with Great Britain faded and the desire for independence, which only a few Americans had hitherto entertained, flamed into a fixed resolve. On January 10, 1776, while Washington was still besieging the British in Boston, Thomas Paine gave voice to this resolution in a powerful tract called *Common Sense*, published in Philadelphia. Spurning the humble language of loyalty formerly used in petitions to George III, Paine assailed the King in acrimonious words, scorned the once praised British constitution, and demanded immediate and unconditional independence for America. "Now," he exclaimed, "is the seed-time of Continental union, faith, and honor. . . . O! ye that love mankind! Ye that dare oppose not only tyranny, but the tyrant, stand forth."

As edition after edition of *Common Sense*, totaling more than 100,000 copies, came from the press, the call to revolution swept throughout the colonies. The word "independence" had now been spoken and was echoing from New Hampshire to Georgia. The debate with Great Britain over rights claimed as just—rights treasured as the liberties of Englishmen—had become a war of ideas which could not be stopped. Reconciliation, Paine had proclaimed, is "a fallacious dream."

Doubting, wondering, and wavering men in the Continental Congress now began to accept the climax. From all the royal and proprietary colonies, British governors and officials were fleeing as from the wrath to come, accompanied by small bands of American officials and crowds of Americans who still clung to George III. In May the Congress advised every colony to form a government of its own, as if British dominion had actually come to an end. In fact Virginia and other colonies were already taking this fateful step and their example was quickly followed. In short, the colonies were assuming the powers of independent states. South Carolina, having adopted a provisional constitution in March 1776, supplanted it by a definite constitution in 1778.

Strictly speaking, the movement for the break with Great Britain was spreading upward from the colonies to the Continental Congress, rather than downward to the colonies from the Congress. On April 13, 1776, the North Carolina revolutionary assembly gave its delegates in the Congress full power to unite with the other members in boldly declaring independence. Elsewhere the idea was also approved. On May 15 the Virginia delegates at Philadelphia received instructions from a convention of that province to propose independence in the Congress and support it.

Thoroughly aroused by the surge of revolutionary temper from below and incited by daring spirits among its members, the Continental Congress girded itself for final action. On June 7, Richard Henry Lee, speaking for the Virginia delegation, moved that "these united colonies are, and ought to be, free and independent states." But cautious men prevented the immediate adoption of the resolution and the Congress did no more than authorize the appointment of a committee to draw up a declaration of independence. Yielding at length to popular demands, the Congress, by an almost unanimous vote, on July 2 approved a resolution in favor of independence.

Meanwhile the committee appointed in June, composed of five members, including Thomas Jefferson, John Adams, and Benjamin Franklin, was busy framing the document which was to express the ideas and the spirit of independence. A draft of the document was first prepared by Jefferson. It was then reviewed by his colleagues. Adams and Franklin suggested several changes. For example, Jefferson had written: "We hold these truths to be sacred and undeniable." Later it was modified, perhaps by Franklin, to read: "We hold these truths to be self-evident." Finally the draft was completed and laid before the Congress. After making other changes in it, the Congress formally adopted the document on July 4. During a period extending over several months, it was signed by members of the Congress.

The Declaration of Independence set forth in great detail the "causes" that impelled the American people to the revolutionary act of separation from Great Britain. This part of the Declaration was, of course, an American statement of the case against the British government and was directed particularly against King George III as if Parliament bore little or no responsibility for the troubles that had arisen. It put the charges in summary and pointed language which Americans could readily understand, for they had personal knowledge of many a grievance listed in the indictment against the British sovereign.

Unlike the resolutions of the Stamp Act Congress in 1765, which also proclaimed grievances but in a humble tone, the Declaration of Independence was animated by a fixed determination to cast off British dominion and furthermore by a radical theory of government. The theory was not new by any means. It had been known and discussed in the colonies for a long time among students of government and even among people at large. The framer of the Declaration, Thomas Jefferson, was well aware of this fact. Had he invented an entirely novel idea, it would have made less of an appeal to the people. With the aid of Franklin and Adams, he did, however, put all the elements of the theory together effectively and present the whole in a flowing eloquence that electrified American minds and hearts.

In the theory of the American Revolution, as Jefferson formulated it, were three principal features: (1) All men are created equal and endowed by their Creator with certain unalienable rights, among which are life, liberty, and the pursuit of happiness. (2) It is to secure these rights that governments are instituted, and they derive their just powers from the consent of the governed. (3) When any form of government becomes destructive of these ends, it is the right of the people to alter or abolish it, and to institute new government, laying its foundations on such principles and organizing its powers in such form as to them shall seem most likely to effect their safety and happiness.

It was these doctrines, the Declaration asserted, which the British government had violated and the American people were to accept as the basis of their independence and the new governments they were to institute. To all other governments then existing in the world the doctrines offered a revolutionary challenge that was to ring through the centuries. Indeed there were even many Americans who, though they were disposed toward independence, were afraid that "the people" might set up governments destructive of the privileges hitherto enjoyed by particular classes in the colonies.

To incarnate the principles of the Declaration in the life of the nation, it was necessary for the Revolutionists first to overcome the armed forces of Great Britain on land and sea; and for many months the prospects for an ultimate American victory looked gloomy. In August of 1776, less than seven weeks after the fateful July 4, the American troops under General Washington were badly mauled on Long Island by superior British regulars. Instead of capturing New York City as they had expected when they marched southward from New England, they were driven northward to White Plains, then across the Hudson River, and then southward through New Jersey.

Not until near the end of that year did a light appear in the blackness. On Christmas night, while the mercenary Hessian troops under British command were celebrating the season at Trenton, Washington made a surprise attack on them and captured about a thousand prisoners. A few days later, early in January 1777, he struck another hard blow at the British in a battle at Princeton a few miles above Trenton.

But these were merely episodes encouraging to Americans, not great victories. Later in the year Washington was defeated at Brandywine. He lost Philadelphia to the British and narrowly escaped disaster at Germantown. Forced to retire westward with his shattered troops to Valley Forge for the winter of 1777–78, he seemed to be almost at the end of his resources.

Then came news from the north which once more raised the enthusiasm of the Revolutionists to a high pitch—news of a great victory for their side. Under orders from the British war office, General John Burgoyne, at the head of a strong force, had invaded northern New York, expecting to be joined by a band of Loyalists and Indians from the west and to be aided by British troops from Lord Howe's army in lower New York. If successful this invasion would have split the country into two parts and imperiled or ruined the American cause. But it failed miserably for the British. Burgoyne was attacked on all sides, his supplies were cut off, the troops sent by Howe from New York City did not arrive to support him, and on October 17, 1777, he surrendered at Saratoga to General Horatio Gates, the American commander who had replaced General Philip Schuyler just as the American victory was in sight.

Burgoyne's surrender at Saratoga, rightly counted among "the decisive battles" of history, marked a turning point toward American independence. It demonstrated that American troops, though poorly trained and supplied, had a genius for warfare and that they could in certain circumstances cope with British regulars. The victory at Saratoga was also crucial in that news of it tipped the balance in the minds of the French ministers then advising Louis XVI and brought France into the war against Great Britain.

For tedious months Benjamin Franklin, the American minister to France, despite his extraordinary popularity in that country, had sought in vain to bring the French government into the war. Smarting under the numerous defeats and losses suffered in fights with Britain, that government had found pleasure in the prospect of a successful revolt against her in America and had secretly given help to the colonies in the form of money and supplies. It had, however, shrunk from entering into an alliance with the United States and declaring war on Britain. Such a venture might end in another disaster for France. Only after the victory at Saratoga were the French ministers induced to gamble again with fate in an open war on the ancient foe.

In February 1778 the French government made treaties of amity and commerce with the United States. It officially recognized American independence, agreed to an alliance for mutual aid and defense, declared war on Great Britain, and immediately began to take part in the military and naval operations against her. Early the next year Spain joined France in the war, hoping to recover among other things Florida, which the British had annexed in 1763 at the close of the French and Indian War. Later Holland lent support to the American cause by preying upon British commerce.

The alliance with France brought to Americans the kind of assistance they sorely needed: strong naval forces, generous loans of gold, silver, and supplies, and a large body of French officers and soldiers well trained in the arts of warfare. It also encouraged Americans in every way; but it did not immediately turn the tide of war. Nor did it mean that they could escape making more strenuous efforts and assuming burdens heavier than any they had as yet carried.

As a matter of fact Americans suffered many reverses during the three years which followed the signing of the treaty of alliance with France. Anxious about a possible blockade by a French fleet, the British evacuated Philadelphia in June 1778, but they repulsed an American attack soon afterward at the Battle of Monmouth. Late in that year the British captured Savannah and, in many campaigns, planned to conquer the whole South. They overran most of Georgia, South Carolina, and North Carolina, in spite of repeated assaults by local bands of American soldiers.

In May 1780 the British took Charleston. Under the command of Lord Cornwallis they pierced the uplands of South Carolina and defeated the Americans at the Battle of Camden. Flushed by successes, Cornwallis led his troops into the interior of North Carolina though they had been checked by American forces at King's Mountain. After shattering American lines at Guilford Courthouse in March 1781, Cornwallis headed for Virginia.

On arriving in Virginia, Cornwallis tried to capture the American troops led by the Marquis de Lafayette, "the boy," as he called the young Frenchman who had come over to help in the struggle for independence. Failing in this maneuver, Cornwallis retired to Yorktown on the Virginia coast, where he hoped to get reinforcements by sea.

While American armies were meeting misfortunes in the Eastern campaigns, a stroke was accomplished in the West that was to count in the final settlement. Under a commission from Virginia, George Rogers Clark recruited volunteers and in 1778 seized several towns on the east bank of the Mississippi in the Illinois country. The next year he captured the British garrison at Vincennes on the Wabash River. Thus an American grip was fastened on the Northwest.

None of the exploits by the British in the South, discouraging as they were to patriot leaders, proved to be decisive. The British could beat or scatter the Americans in battle but could not round them up wholesale or prevent their gathering again quickly to re-

APPROXIMATE FRONTIER LINE OF THE
COLONIES IN 1774

new the struggle. They could make marauding expeditions into the back regions of South Carolina, North Carolina, and Virginia, but they could not occupy those regions and hold them in subjection against bands of American troops skilled in guerrilla warfare. They hit hard and yet they did not conquer. This lesson Cornwallis learned at great cost in men and supplies. It was, in part, for this reason that he drew back upon the coast at Yorktown and waited for the British navy to support him from the sea.

By that action Cornwallis unwittingly prepared for his doom and the end of the war. General Washington and his French allies, then in the North planning an attack on New York, saw what seemed to be a golden opportunity for a conclusive stroke at Yorktown. So American and French troops were rushed South to pen up Cornwallis from the landward side. A French fleet, under Admiral de Grasse, arrived from the West Indies in time to beat off British naval forces and prevent an escape of the British troops by the sea. Under fire from land and sea, Cornwallis ran up the white flag and surrendered on October 19, 1781. As events were to prove, the long war was over; for the British government, stunned by the blow, either could not or would not make another gigantic effort to recover its dominion over the colonies.

Nevertheless many months passed before a treaty of peace could be concluded between the United States and Great Britain. The French were still at war with Britain and their alliance with the United States remained in force. It was not until 1782 that negotiations were opened between the British agents and the American peace commissioners in France—Franklin, John Jay, and John Adams, with whom Henry Laurens was later associated.

Now it was Britain's turn to conciliate Americans in an effort to prevent France from making great gains out of the war. Fortunately for that design, British affairs were in the hands of a new ministry, composed of men who had been sympathetic with the American cause, including Edmund Burke who had so eloquently defended it in the House of Commons. Working quietly with the British agents in Paris, keeping their plans hidden from the French government, the American commissioners won generous terms for the United States and secretly signed the draft of a treaty with Great Britain.

When the French minister, Count de Vergennes, heard about this secret settlement he reminded the American commissioners that the Congress of the United States had instructed them "to be guided by the wishes of the French court," and he charged them with violating the pledges made to France in 1778 when the alliance was formed. Eventually, however, he yielded and, after long negotiations, France also came to terms with Great Britain.

The final treaty between the United States and Great Britain was signed on September 3, 1783, and ratified by the Congress in January 1784. Under its provisions King George recognized the independence of the United States. The boundaries of the Republic were fixed, roughly, from the Atlantic Ocean to the Mississippi River and from the Great Lakes to the Floridas. The navigation of the Mississippi was declared to be open to American citizens and British subjects.

In specific clauses the treaty assured creditors on both sides that there would be no lawful impediments to the collection of just debts. It was also agreed that Congress would recommend to the state legislatures that provision be made for restoring to loyal British subjects all properties and estates that had been confiscated during the Revolution. The right of Americans to fish off the coasts of Newfoundland and in the Gulf of the St. Lawrence in the customary manner was guaranteed by a definite article of the treaty. Even the most zealous patriot in the United States could find little fault with the settlement that brought the war to a conclusion.

The numerous battles and skirmishes waged on land from Massachusetts to Georgia and the exploits of American naval forces at sea, under such officers as John Paul Jones and John Barry, were only a part of the story of the war and the Revolution. During the long contest, men, officers, and supplies had to be provided for the armies, civil government had to be carried on, and many a dispute among Americans over the conduct and aims of the war had to be adjusted or endured.

In itself the war worked havoc in colonial economy and made new economic undertakings necessary to victory. Commerce with Great Britain was practically destroyed and trade with other countries could not fully take its place. Many regions were either occupied or harried by British troops. Loyalists bent on actively aiding the British cause, often with arms, waged a civil war within the war for independence. They in turn were harassed by resentful patriots; many were harshly treated or imprisoned; thousands were driven out of the country, to England or Canada. In important respects, therefore, the revolt against Great Britain involved also a revolution in American affairs—in military power, industry, finance, diplomacy, government, and social arrangements.

In colonial times Americans had relied for their local defense mainly upon militia composed of civilians who gave a limited amount of time to drilling and were officered by men with little more experience than the privates possessed. At the opening of the war militiamen and new volunteers filled the ranks of armies that had to wage battles with trained British regulars.

A large proportion of the recruits were brave men who fought courageously, but they were accustomed to serve for short terms, were undisciplined, not inured to long and grueling campaigns. At the beginning few among them had ever seen a real battle. A majority were farmers who had homes and families and whose minds were filled with their personal cares. After the first burst of enthusiasm died away, especially when they had to go far off from their own communities, hundreds of militiamen insisted on quitting as soon as their terms of service were over, no matter how grave the danger to the American cause and despite the pleas of their officers.

Sorely tried by the conduct of militiamen and volunteers, General Washington again and again begged the Congress to provide for a regular army composed of men enlisted for a long term or the duration of the war. But it was only when failures and defeats threatened utter ruin that the civilians in the Congress, frightened at the mere thought of a standing army as dangerous to civil liberty, yielded to his pleas and offered extra pay to officers and privates pledged to see the war through to the end. At last in the closing years of the conflict Washington had at his command a large body of men so pledged and well disciplined for action in battle.

With regard to officers of all ranks, the colonies were also ill prepared for combat with British regulars. Washington had seen actual, but not extensive, fighting in the French and Indian War. Even he was in fact little equipped by firsthand knowledge for planning and executing great campaigns or coping with the disciplined armies of Britain, enlarged by mercenaries hired from German princes.

None of the high officers on whom he had to rely for help was thoroughly schooled in the arts of war. Henry Knox had been a bookseller in Boston; Nathanael Greene a farmer and blacksmith in Rhode Island; Benedict Arnold, the brave soldier who turned traitor, a merchant in New Haven; Francis Marion a shy South Carolina planter; and John Sullivan a lawyer in New Hampshire. Anthony Wayne was farming in Pennsylvania when he answered the call to arms, raised a regiment, and offered himself to his country. Daniel Morgan, who distinguished himself at Cowpens in South Carolina, had been only a teamster in General Braddock's army during the French and Indian War.

Competent for battle as many American officers proved to be after they had been tried by fire, Washington was fortunate in having the aid of several military men from Europe, who came to help the American cause, for the love of adventure, or in the hope of honors or other rewards: young Lafayette from France; Pulaski and Kosciuszko from Poland; and from Germany, Baron von Steuben, a former officer in the Prussian army, trained in the iron regimen of Frederick the Great and credited with long military service.

It was Steuben who joined Washington during the dark days at Valley Forge, prepared a drill manual for American soldiers, drilled a model company, and laid the basis for discipline throughout the American forces. Steuben's larger manual, later written for general use in giving soldiers the essentials of military instructions, became "the military Bible of the Continental Army." Besides teaching soldiers, Steuben took part in campaigns; he commanded a division under Washington at the siege and capture of Yorktown.

At all stages of the war American troops in the field needed large quantities of arms, ammunition, clothing, food, and other supplies, in addition to the goods furnished by the French and to some extent by the Dutch. Thus the demand for domestic manufactures and farm produce rose rapidly and the home market was widened to include all the states. At once iron, steel, hat, textile, and other industries, which had begun to flourish in colonial times, were expanded; new plants and forges were built; and special privileges were granted to stimulate war production. Women spun and wove more diligently; and spinning clubs were formed in town and country, turning out increasing amounts of woolen, linen, and cotton cloth to meet military and civilian requirements. Workers in iron, wood, and other materials, often from the farms, were drawn into industrial enterprises, especially in New England and the middle states. As a result of the quickened and enlarged activities, now that British restrictions were cast off and British imports materially reduced in volume, American economy advanced rapidly on the way toward emancipation from dependence on the Old World for several prime articles of manufacture.

In the same process, financial independence—of a kind—was achieved. Facing the necessity of providing funds to pay war bills, the Continental Congress and the state governments were forced to wrestle with difficult financial problems. Gold and silver coins of British, French, and Spanish mintage continued in circulation but the supply was wholly inadequate for public and private needs. So the Congress resorted to the issue of paper money—bills of credit—by the millions and, before the end of the war, it had outstanding about $210,000,000 in Continental money—all badly depreciated in value. To this large sum the states added paper notes of their own in an amount almost equal to the total Continental output.

Paper money was supplemented by interest-bearing securities, Continental and state, which were sold to patriotic bond buyers in exchange for specie or paper notes at a fixed rate. More millions were borrowed from France and Holland, yielding the specie desperately needed. Other revenues were derived from the sale of property confiscated from Loyalists who gave aid and comfort to the British. The Congress also called upon the states for quotas of money to meet the common bills, often without getting much in return. In attempts to comply with the demands of the Congress and cover their own requirements, the states laid heavy taxes on their citizens. In this fashion the Congress and the states created a "financial system" of their own or, rather, a financial disorder, for both paper money and bonds dropped rapidly in value—in many cases to a few cents or less on the dollar.

In various phases of war production and financing, as well as in revolutionary pamphleteering, in spying, in making bullets and other munitions, and in direct aid to fighters at the front, patriotic women were active in all the states. While their husbands, fathers, and sons were away under arms, farm women carried double burdens in field and domestic workshops, furnishing food and clothing for the armies. In towns they formed clubs to speed up production. When drives were made to raise money for the war, they organized committees to help, subscribed themselves, and contributed their gold and silver objects to the common treasury.

"Even in their dresses," complained a writer connected with the British army in South Carolina, "the females seem to bid us defiance; the gay toys which are imported here they despise; they wear their own homespun manufactures, and take care to have in their breast knots, and even on their shoes something that resembles their flag of the thirteen stripes. An officer told Lord Cornwallis not long ago, that he believed if he had destroyed all the men in North America, we should have enough to do to conquer the women. I am heartily tired of this country, and wish myself at home."

As colonists, Americans had been subject, in their relations with other countries, to the diplomacy and foreign policies of the government in London. In seeking a place among the independent nations of the earth, the Continental Congress was compelled, on its own responsibility, to make provision for diplomatic representation abroad and evolve the elements of an American foreign policy. As early as 1776 it sent an agent to Paris, Silas Deane, of Connecticut, to open negotiations, if possible, with the government of France. Later Benjamin Franklin and Arthur Lee were instructed to join Deane at the French capital. Other representatives went to Holland, Spain, Vienna, Berlin, and St. Petersburg in quest of recognition and support.

Only in France and Holland did American diplomacy achieve noteworthy results for some time. Spain was cold to American pleas for aid. Russia maintained an attitude of chilly indifference. Frederick the Great of Prussia expressed sympathies but would take no steps likely to involve himself in trouble with Britain. Yet in the end American ministers abroad—whether they procured aid or got no aid—gained a firsthand knowledge of European governments and their foreign policies, of their ambitions, designs, intrigues, and interests in various parts of the world, especially in the Western Hemisphere. Thrown upon their own resources, American diplomats proved ingenious in negotiations and acquired skill in managing foreign relations as they took over this important branch of government, formerly monopolized in America by the British Crown.

Through all the turmoil of war and the activities connected with it, the work of civil government, local and general, was carried on in the United States. While British governors were being driven from power or fleeing for their lives, eleven of the thirteen states set about drawing up plans for full self-government and at the end of the conflict had constitutions of their own. The other two, Connecticut and Rhode Island, made some changes in their old royal charters, under which they had enjoyed a generous liberty, and governed themselves as before. In each state was installed a legislature resting upon popular elections, and in some cases the property qualifications on the right to vote were made lower than they had been in colonial times. In each state provision was made for a governor, elected by the legislature in a majority of cases; in Massachusetts and New York, by popular vote.

Under these written constitutions, in which, except in New York and Massachusetts, the legislature was supreme, elections were held, campaigns conducted, and issues debated by the voters and by citizens who could not vote. Drawing upon colonial experiences, legislatures enacted laws, laid taxes, made provisions for administering state affairs, elected delegates to the Continental Congress, and co-operated, often faithfully, often negligently, with the Congress in the conduct of the war. Now free from British interference, the state legislatures, even during the most trying hours of the Revolution, began to revise and reform radically the laws inherited from England and from the colonial age, and to make American laws conform more closely to the spirit manifest in the Declaration of Independence.

Meanwhile, at the center of things, members of the second Continental Congress—the provisional body hastily assembled in May 1775—gave attention to the strengthening of the union. In June 1776 the Congress appointed a committee to draw up a plan of confederation for the states. The plan, called the Articles of Confederation, was duly reported to the Congress, debated from time to time amid the exigencies of the war business, finally approved late in 1777, and sent to the state legislatures for review and action. By 1779 all the states, except Maryland, had ratified the Articles and Maryland approved them at last, on March 1, 1781. The next day the Congress assembled under the terms of the Articles. Now the states were formally pledged to "a firm league of friendship" and "a perpetual union" created for "their common defense, the security of their liberties," and their "mutual and general welfare." A fateful step had been taken toward a republic, one and indivisible.

☆

As the revolt against Great Britain proceeded to its triumph, a civil revolution began in American society. In the prewar stage of the controversy over British policies Loyalists had warned conservatives in the Patriot party that the destruction of British dominion would lead to popular insurgency and attacks on the privileges of property and class. Their prophecies were more than fulfilled during the course of the Revolution.

Absorbing as the war was, heavy as were the burdens it imposed, most of the American people from 1775 to 1781 were occupied with civilian pursuits and immediately concerned with their economic and social affairs. At the beginning of the war the total population was about 2,500,000 men, women, and children. In 1776 the American army, then at its highest point in numbers, including militiamen and Continentals, had about 90,000 officers and privates—not more than one man in eight of the males able to bear arms. In the latter part of the war, it included only about one man in sixteen of the fighting age.

It would be a conservative estimate, then, to say that at least three fourths of the men, as well as all the women and young people, devoted themselves mainly to civilian affairs, though often engaged in war production. No longer under the dominion of British officials, they insisted on pursuing their interests, discussing public questions as they pleased, exalting their rights, and undermining special privileges. Spurred by the impacts of the war, they began to attack the social order developed during the colonial period.

Thus a landslide toward democracy—a state of affairs dreaded by American conservatives and British Loyalists—was started. During the Revolution a large portion of the upper class collapsed. After the British governors and their horde of officials fled from colonial capitals, thousands of merchants, clergy, landlords, and lawyers who adhered to Britain were forced to leave the country or retire from public life. As a rule Loyalists who remained outside British military lines were silenced. Often they were subjected to physical violence.

Many large estates owned by British subjects, sometimes embracing several hundred thousand acres, were confiscated and then auctioned off in blocks to Americans. Immense areas of unoccupied lands, once at the disposal of the British Crown or its agents, passed under the control of state legislatures and the Continental Congress, to be granted or sold under American laws. The right of American landlords to pass their estates intact to their eldest sons under the rule of "primogeniture" was assailed and either destroyed or materially modified in favor of the division of estates among all heirs, including daughters. Everywhere in the states the English Church was disestablished and religious liberty was generally widened, though not made complete.

Associated with these changes was a rapidly widening interest among the people in social and political issues. The number of newspapers increased despite the handicaps of the war. Thousands of Americans who had hitherto cared little about election campaigns were aroused by the stirring events of the Revolution and began to take part in public discussions and agitations, to vote, if they had the right, and to demand the right to vote, if it was denied to them under the new state laws. In the most crucial years of the war tumult and perils, differences of opinion over politics, government, and reform divided Americans into parties and factions and precipitated conflicts among the patriots themselves, often verging in the direction of physical violence. For an immense number of the American people, the Revolution in all its phases was, therefore, a great social and intellectual awakening.

CHAPTER IX

Constitutional Government for the United States

AFTER THEY HAD WON independence from Great Britain, Americans faced the problem of governing themselves and holding together the union formed during the Revolutionary War. Could they do it? From the three proprietary colonies—Pennsylvania, Delaware, and Maryland—the proprietary officials had been expelled. From the eight royal provinces—New Hampshire, Massachusetts, New York, New Jersey, Virginia, North Carolina, South Carolina, and Georgia—royal governors and their train of subordinates had been driven out. No longer could disputes within and between colonies be carried to London for settlement. No longer did loyalty to the British King or the need for common action in the war against him constitute a unifying principle for Americans. No longer did the British navy and army serve as shields against the warlike Powers of Europe, especially France and Spain, both eager to extend their dominions in the New World.

In colonial times the British government had exercised control over all the colonies in essential matters of public policy and administration. It had conducted foreign affairs and provided common defense against other nations. Foreign commerce, intercolonial commerce, and the monetary system had all been subject to British regulation. The British Crown had served as the chief executive organ for the colonies, and British courts as tribunals of appeal in cases involving the rights of person and property. Now all this central machinery of power had been swept away and each state was set free to do about as it pleased; that is to say, as the majority of the voters represented in the legislature pleased.

During the Revolution, British officials had scoffed at the idea that Americans could successfully carry on the work of government in its higher ranges where great statesmanship was required; and Tories had sneered at them as pettifogging lawyers, riotous mechanics, disorderly farmers, and lawbreaking merchants. Even patriots on the right wing of the Revolution had expressed dislike and contempt for the people and republics. Neither the Declaration of Independence nor the Articles of Confederation nor any of the first state constitutions had mentioned the word "republic." At the time it was like a red flag to conservatives everywhere.

Moreover, educated patriots knew that revolutions in history, democratic and republican, had often resulted in despotism. Again and again in the Greek states of antiquity, democracy had been supplanted by a dictatorship or tyranny. The Roman republic had disappeared in the rule of an absolute emperor. Only about a century before, the Puritan revolution in England had culminated in the military dictatorship of Oliver Cromwell, followed shortly by a restoration of the monarchy.

Reflective Americans who were confronted with the task of governing the country had read about such historic events. Loyalists who had opposed the American Revolution from start to finish expected it to end in a disaster for the patriots and the re-establishment of a monarchy in some form. Indeed a few of them cast about for a suitable prince to be made king of the United States. Many patriots, some in high places, military and civil, abhorring the very idea of popular rule, looked forward with satisfaction to the triumph of a military dictator, supreme throughout the Union.

Even before peace came, Colonel Lewis Nicola wrote to General Washington expressing scorn for republics and calling for a military government, at least in a part of the country. Washington sent him a blistering reply. But other army officers wrote to Washington more or less in the same vein. In fact, he received so many letters hinting at violent action against the government which had been set up that his brooding spirit burst forth with cries of apprehension over the future of his country.

Rumors of a reaction in the shape of a monarchy or military dictatorship were bruited here and there among the people after peace came. In Connecticut Noah Webster heard from some source that military men and merchants in New England were working at plans to overturn popular rule and establish a government of special privileges by force. In Massachusetts Mercy Warren learned from some source that many young men, "particularly students at law and youth of fortune and pleasure," were clamoring for a monarchy and a standing army to support it. She thought there was "a formidable body ready to bow to the sceptre of a king, provided they may be the lordlings who in splendid idleness may riot on the hard earnings of the peasant and mechanic." Governor George Clinton, of New York, confessed publicly in 1788 that in the closing years of the War for Independence a design had been formed in his state to establish a kind of military government.

Rumors and open threats of drastic action against "popular tumults" increased after a band of debt-burdened farmers in Massachusetts, led by Captain Daniel Shays, a soldier of the Revolution, tried to redress their grievances by an uprising in 1786. According to the constitution of that state, drafted by John Adams and put into effect in 1780, the right to vote and hold office had been limited to property owners and taxpayers; and the richer towns were given special weight in the state senate. Under this government, creditors began to sue debtors in the law courts and take property away from farmers who could not pay what they owed.

In protest Shays organized a large body of men in the western part of the state and attempted to shut up the courts by a display of armed force. It was only with difficulty and some bloodshed that the state government put down "Shays' Rebellion." Even then popular sympathies with the uprising remained so strong that the state officials did not dare to execute Shays or any of his followers. Whatever the merits of this popular revolt, it increased the fears of property owners and conservatives in general, inciting them to work harder than ever for a powerful national government.

☆

Amid efforts to substitute for the Confederation a highly centralized government, akin in some respects to the regimen Great Britain had formerly maintained over the colonies, complaints against state governments grew in number and virulence. In all the states except Massachusetts and New York, which both had strong governments, the control of public affairs was in the hands of the legislature elected by the qualified voters, among whom farmers predominated. In short, the states were controlled by popular majorities with little or no restraint from executive or judicial officers, such as British royal governors and the Crown had imposed on colonial legislatures.

In these circumstances states issued their own money in coin or paper or both and, under pressure from farmers, seven states emitted large quantities of paper money. This was done partly for the purpose of raising the prices of farm produce, making it easier for farmers to pay their debts. Before the Revolution Great Britain had stopped the practice; now Americans were at liberty to revive it.

More liberties were asserted by popular legislatures. Urged by special interests, states put tariff duties on imports from foreign countries, modified them, or repealed them, at will. Determined to protect their local interests, some states laid duties on goods coming in from other states; New York, for instance, taxed firewood from Connecticut and vegetables from New Jersey. During the Revolution states had borrowed money for war purposes and several of them were slow in paying off those debts. In short, for a time, the states acted as independent republics ruled by popular majorities represented in the legislatures; and, warmly attached to their own liberties, they went to extremes in their indifference to the fortunes of the Union.

While the states and their legislatures were coming under an increasing fire of criticism from merchants, creditors, and holders of state bonds, a storm of disapproval was gathering against the Articles of Confederation and the Congress of the United States. A part of this censure was directed to the form of that government. The Confederacy, according to the critics, was really a farce; it had no executive to enforce the laws made by the Congress; and the states and the people disregarded the laws with impunity. It also lacked a judiciary empowered to try persons accused of violating the laws of the Union, to hear cases arising under them, or to settle disputes among the states.

The Congress was disparaged as faulty in form and futile in action. In the Congress, states, not the people, were represented; its members were elected by the state legislatures; and in all important matters the states, large and small, were equal, for each had only one vote to cast. Its members were negligent in attendance and public business dragged on from year to year unfinished.

On two special counts critics disparaged the Congress in respect of its powers: the Congress lacked power to make laws necessary to the safety and welfare of the Union; and it had no authority to prevent the states from interfering with matters of common, or general, concern.

The Congress could vote money for the purposes of the Union, but it could lay no taxes directly on anybody; it had to depend upon the willingness of the state legislatures to raise money and pay it into the Confederate treasury. The Congress could provide for an army but it was compelled to rely upon each of the states to supply its quota of men voluntarily. Although the Congress could make treaties with other countries respecting foreign commerce, the states decided for themselves whether or not they would obey such treaties. The Congress could not regulate commerce among the states or establish a single and uniform system of currency for the country. Furthermore, as time passed, the states refused, despite urgent appeals from Congress, to grant it additional financial powers essential to its very existence.

On the score of power the Congress was also assailed because it could not compel the states to quit doing many things which interfered with property and comity. It could not stop their issues of paper money or their interference with interstate and foreign commerce. It had no check on their legislation designed to make it easier for debtors to pay their debts in "cheap money." It could not send troops to help put down insurrections or to enforce the laws of the Union if they encountered popular resistance.

In these circumstances agitations were started in several quarters for changes in the American system of government that had come into being as an emergency government during the Revolution and had been continued under the Articles of Confederation. Former army officers, now organized in the Order of the Cincinnati, and former soldiers of the rank and file found the paper scrip with which they had been paid off at the close of the war so reduced in value as to be almost worthless. Holders of state and Continental securities were disgruntled, for the interest on their bonds was not paid promptly, if at all, and their paper sank in the markets, sometimes to a price as low as ten cents on the dollar. Manufacturers complained that the imports of foreign goods seriously cut down their business. Merchants and shippers grumbled over the lack of protection against foreign merchants and shippers in America and distant ports. Owners of undeveloped lands in the West, including soldiers of the Revolution holding claims to tracts there as part payment for their services and speculators engaged in accumulating great areas with a view to profitable sales to settlers, deplored the lack of a national army capable of suppressing the Indians who hampered the spread of settlements. Creditors fretted over paper-money schemes and other threats to their mortgages on property.

Generally associated with one or more of these economic interests, but often rising above purely personal interests, were critics with national vision who joined the movement for drastic changes in the Articles of Confederation. Familiar with the intrigues and ambitions of European Powers, they feared that the United States might be divided by foreign plotting, might be reconquered perhaps by Great Britain, or fall a victim to France or Spain, both with territorial ambitions in the neighborhood. They were also alarmed by schemes for overturning the republican institutions and establishing a monarchy or military dictatorship. Scarcely less disturbing to them was the possibility of an upheaval from below. Worried by the outlook, these national leaders sought to find a peaceful way of setting up a stronger and yet representative government for the Union.

Among the leaders in the nationalizing movement George Washington was foremost in character and influence. As early as 1783, in a circular letter to the governors of the states, Washington, who had done so much to save the Revolution, warned them of perils ahead and recommended the adoption of a more powerful government, able to "regulate and govern the general concerns of the confederate republic." Meanwhile Alexander Hamilton, who had fought in the Revolution, launched a campaign against the Articles of Confederation and demanded the calling of a new congress or convention to draft a constitution based on different and firmer principles. Other men, well known and less well known, including Pelatiah Webster, put forth plans for amending the Articles or substituting an entirely new form of government.

But all along the line advocates of material changes met vigorous opposition. Although none of the leaders in this resistance had the prestige of Washington, many of them had been eminent in the Revolutionary cause. In the struggle against the powerful grip of the British Crown and Parliament, thousands of Americans had acquired a horror of "strong government." Some among them feared that any strong government might end in a monarchy or that it would mean, in any case, big armies, big navies, heavy taxes, mountainous debts, and interference with personal liberty, in the style of the British government. Especially among farmers, who formed a majority of the people, the idea was rigidly held that the state legislature was the best bulwark for the protection of their interests and rights.

Widespread was the conviction that full autonomy in towns,

counties, and states was the truest and best basis for the life, liberty, and pursuit of happiness proclaimed in the Declaration of Independence. To Americans who had such views nothing seemed more reasonable than the belief that "centralization" was to be dreaded and that the rights of states were to be cherished and preserved.

To change or not to change the form of government—to swing away from more authority or toward it—became by 1786 the burning issue before the American people. At firesides, in taverns, by correspondence, and in the press it was debated with a searching and enlightened intelligence, worthy of the generation that had won independence.

Out of heated discussions came decisive actions. A small group in Virginia induced the state legislature to call a general convention at Annapolis to discuss taxation and commerce. The convention met in 1786 but delegates from only five states appeared on the floor and the prospects were discouraging to its members. One of the delegates, however, Alexander Hamilton, from New York, refused to give up the struggle to realize the aims of the nationalizing movement.

Seizing time by the forelock, Hamilton persuaded the Annapolis convention to adopt a resolution urging the Congress of the United States to take leadership and summon a convention at Philadelphia, for the purpose of proposing amendments to the Articles of Confederation which, when adopted by the states, would make them "adequate to the exigencies of the Union." To this project the Congress agreed. In response, all the states except Rhode Island elected delegates. In May 1787 the new convention assembled in Philadelphia and settled down to the task of devising a stronger government for the United States.

On the roll of the convention, consisting of fifty-five members in all, were many of the most prominent names in America: for example, George Washington, Benjamin Franklin, Alexander Hamilton, James Madison, Robert Morris, Gouverneur Morris, John Dickinson, James Wilson, Roger Sherman, Oliver Ellsworth, Charles Pinckney, and Edmund Randolph. Eight of them had been among the signers of the Declaration of Independence. Nearly all had been active in the Revolution, as military officers, financiers, members of the Continental Congress, and public officials. Among them were men of wealth and influence in their communities— merchants, lawyers, and planters.

On the whole the convention was a conservative body. Thomas Jefferson, then minister to France, a liberal, was not present. Neither was John Hancock, whose name led all the signatures to the Declaration of Independence. That outstanding firebrand of the Revolution, Patrick Henry, though elected a delegate, refused to attend, saying that he "smelt a rat." Even so, great talents, wisdom, and experience in statecraft were represented at Philadelphia in 1787.

The sessions of the convention lasted from May to September 17, 1787, and were marked by many differences of opinion and long debates. Indeed it has been customary for historians to lay stress on the differences of opinion and treat the Constitution which emerged as a mere "bundle of compromises." But this view is far from the whole truth of the matter. Strictly speaking, the agreements of the convention were more numerous and important for the nation than the dissensions and the compromises.

In the course of their proceedings, a large majority easily agreed on the following fundamentals:

The Articles of Confederation must be discarded, not merely amended, and a new constitution substituted.

The new government must have three departments—legislative, executive, and judicial.

The large states must have more power in the new government than the small states, thus giving to it a popular basis.

The new Congress must have the power to legislate on all matters of national concern and all matters with which the states cannot deal competently, including the power to tax, to regulate interstate and foreign commerce, and to spend money for common defense and general welfare.

The debts of the Confederation must be binding on the new government.

Many restraints must be laid on the state governments.

The serious disputes in the convention turned mainly on details and ways and means of realizing the accepted purposes. They involved such questions as these: What shall be the composition of the new Congress? Shall the executive consist of one person or more? How shall the executive be elected? How shall the large states be given their appropriate share of power in the new government and the claims of the small states to equality be recognized? How shall the enlarged power of the new Congress be expressed in terms of specified powers? How is it possible to create a strong national legislature and a strong executive and yet prevent either from becoming all-powerful in the government of the Union? How shall direct taxes be apportioned among the states in such a way as not to burden unduly the poorer states? What qualifications shall be fixed for voters in federal elections and for places of trust in the new government? What provisions shall be made for amending the new Constitution as times change? How shall the Constitution be finally adopted and put into force?

Out of the debates that swirled around these and subsidiary questions for four months was finally evolved, on September 17, the finished document which thirty-nine delegates, a safe majority, were willing to sign. By that time several of the members had gone home, alienated by the spirit and plans of their colleagues. A few malcontents, who remained to the end, for one reason or another refused to sign the finished instrument. One of the dissenters, Luther Martin, of Maryland, was so perturbed by all he had seen and heard at Philadelphia that he wrote a long letter of denunciation to the legislature of his state and published it widely in an effort to defeat the ratification of the Constitution. Even among the signers there were doubts as to particular provisions in the document, but these were subordinated to the interest of unity on fundamentals. Washington expressed the general sentiment of his colleagues when he declared that the Constitution was about as good as could be expected and the people ought to adopt it, leaving to the future the making of corrections by amendments.

Running through the text of the Constitution from the Preamble to the last line were evidences of the fundamental propositions on which the majority of the convention agreed early in its proceedings. Interwoven with them were answers to the questions of means and details by which the essential purposes of a stronger Union were to be accomplished. Here and there were signs of the compromises and adjustments of interests that the framers found necessary to the settlement of disputes large and small. Only when so viewed does the Constitution take on the fullness of its meaning for the time and the ages.

First of all, the Preamble made it clear that the framers were creating no mere league of states. The Articles of Confederation had declared explicitly that "each state retains its sovereignty, freedom, and independence"—the high power which state legislatures had been exercising. Respecting the sovereignty, freedom, and independence of the states, as such, the Constitution contained not a word, and what it did to the pretensions of the states to full sovereignty stood out boldly in the lines imposing restraints on their powers. The announcement that the Constitution and federal laws were to be supreme over all state actions conflicting with them was unmistakable in its brevity and import.

The Preamble declared that the Constitution was a constitution ordained and established by the people of the United States —not mere articles of agreement between the thirteen states. The Articles of Confederation had called the Union "a firm league of friendship" between the states. The new order contemplated by the Constitution was more than a league of states. The government for which it provided, in the exercise of its powers, was authorized to deal directly with individuals, not states. It was authorized to go over the heads of state officials and legislatures and compel obedience to federal laws by the use of its own agencies of coercion. In fine, the Constitution worked a political revolution—a transformation—in the form of government that had been set up in the violence of the break with Britain. Its critics understood this at the time and history to come validated the fact.

In the structure of the new government this revolution was reflected. The old Congress had been little more than a conference of ambassadors from the states. In one house of the new Congress, it is true, each state, large and small, was to have two senators and the states were thus nominally equal. But each senator was given a term of six years, was to be paid out of the Treasury of the United States, and could not be retired at will or compelled to vote against his conscience by his state legislature. The Senate was given the power to pass upon treaties and nominations to certain high offices proposed by the President.

Sharing the legislative power with the Senate was the House of Representatives, based on population, not on states. Members of this chamber were apportioned among the states according to their respective numbers of free persons, excluding Indians not taxed and including three fifths of "all other persons," that is, slaves. The members of the House were to be elected directly in each state by the persons entitled to vote for members of the most numerous branch of the state legislature. That "the voice of the people" might be heard frequently, provision was made for biennial elections. To prevent state legislatures from interfering too grossly with congressional elections, Congress was given the power to alter and make laws regulating such elections.

In all ordinary legislative matters, the House of Representatives was made equal to the Senate. In one vital matter it was given the supreme weapon of political power—control over the national purse; for the Constitution provided that "all bills for raising revenue shall originate in the House of Representatives." Although in time this provision was allowed to become a dead letter, the intention behind it was indubitable; if it so decided, "the people's house" might exercise supreme power over the purse in the government of the United States.

In another essential respect the weight of the people as against the states counted in the structure of the federal government—in the Executive Department. After careful discussion the convention decided that the Executive should consist of one person, not three or more representing sections of the Union. The President was to be elected, not by Congress as at first decided, nor by popular vote as was proposed, but by electors chosen as the legislatures of the states might decide. In fixing the number of electors assigned to each state, the Constitution recognized both population and the states and so gave the people, as such, a share in the presidency; that is, it prescribed that the number of electors allowed to each state must equal the number of senators and representatives to which it may be entitled. Until a census could be taken in 1790 there were to be sixty-five representatives.

Under the Articles there had been in fact thirteen heads to the confederacy—the thirteen delegations in the Congress, which merely had a presiding officer. Under the Constitution there was to be one head, the President of the United States, endowed with great powers in peace and war. He was to symbolize the unity, not the diversity, of the country. And for strength of support, he was to depend upon numbers of people, not the pleasure of state legislatures.

The unity of the country was also symbolized by the Constitution in the creation of a Supreme Court, the members of which were to be chosen by the President with the consent of the Senate. Congress might at will establish inferior courts, district and circuit, but the Supreme Court was anchored in the Constitution. Its justices might be divided as to cases before it, but its decisions made by a majority of them were to be binding at law throughout the land. Thus in matters of federal concern the will of one high court was to be substituted for the clashing wills of thirteen or more state courts.

The judicial power conferred upon federal courts covered every issue of general interest throughout the Union. It shall extend, ran Section 2 of Article III, "to all cases in law and equity arising under this Constitution, the laws of the United States, and treaties made, or which shall be made, under their authority." That was not all. This power was to embrace all cases of admiralty and maritime jurisdiction arising on the high seas and public waters of the Union. It was to include controversies between two or more states; between a state and citizens of another state; between citizens of different states; between a state and citizens thereof and foreign states, citizens, and subjects. Thus special kinds of conflicts between private persons in the several states and between states as such were to be finally resolved by the exercise of federal judicial power, with the Supreme Court as the tribunal of ultimate appeal.

Yet, powerful as was to be the structure of the new government —Congress, Executive, and Judiciary—it was so formed that, in operation, checks could be placed on the accumulation of despotic power in any hands, even in the hands of the people who had the right to vote in elections. How to set up a government strong enough to serve the purposes of the Union and still not too strong for the maintenance of the liberties of the people? That was a prime issue in the convention. It had been in all previous history, and was to be in centuries to come, the central problem in the science and art of government.

This question the framers of the Constitution sought to settle by establishing what is known as the "system of checks and balances." First of all they founded each great branch of the government on a separate basis of political power. They provided that members of the House of Representatives should be elected for a term of two years by persons entitled to vote under certain laws of the respective states; that the senators should be elected for terms of six years by the legislatures of the states; and that the President should be elected for four years by electors chosen as the state legislatures might decide—by the legislatures themselves or by the voters or in any other appropriate manner. Members of the federal judiciary were to be selected by the President and the Senate, both one degree removed from direct popular vote.

Against the possibility of tyranny, therefore, two safeguards were set up in the Constitution. The ultimate source of power, it was recognized, was the people—the enfranchised voters in the states. But under the methods provided for the choice of representatives, senators, President, and federal judges, no political party or faction could get possession of the whole government at a single election. In the long run, through a period of years, the persistent will of the popular majority might prevail. Yet at no moment could the "snap judgment" of a popular majority prevail in all departments of the federal government.

Moreover, within the very structure of the government, power was so distributed that no branch could seize all of it, unless the others deliberately abdicated. The House and Senate were to check each other in legislation. Congress and the President were to put brakes on each other. As against both, members of the federal judiciary were given the independence of tenure for life; and yet the House could impeach them and, by the judgment of the Senate, they could be removed from office. The President was to enjoy a high degree of independent initiative; but he could do nothing unless Congress enacted laws and voted money for carrying his proposals into execution. Besides, he too could be ousted from office by the process of impeachment.

Upon the government so constructed, the Constitution conferred immense powers in terms specific and general. For convenience they may be divided into two classes: powers over domestic affairs and powers over foreign relations. But in fact these powers were so closely interwoven at many points that lines could not be drawn between them. For example, Congress was given the right to tax and appropriate money for defense and the general welfare of the United States.

Among the great powers particularly relevant to domestic affairs the following were vested in Congress in specific terms: to lay and collect taxes, duties, and excises; pay the debts of the United States; borrow money; regulate commerce among the states; establish uniform rules for the naturalization of aliens; enact laws on bankruptcies; coin money and regulate the value thereof; establish post offices and post roads; promote science and the useful arts by giving exclusive rights to authors and inventors—copyrights and patents; establish courts inferior to the Supreme Court; raise and support armed forces; provide for calling out the militia to execute the laws and suppress insurrections; establish penalties for the punishment of persons who counterfeit the coins and securities of the United States.

The powers relative to foreign affairs were not concentrated in the Executive or in Congress but were distributed among the three departments; or, to put it another way, they were vested in the whole government. To Congress was given exclusive power to provide for the common defense; to regulate commerce with foreign nations, including control over the immigration of aliens; to declare war; to raise and support armed forces; to define and punish offenses against the law of nations; and by implication, to establish and appropriate money for ministers, consuls, and other agents of the United States in foreign countries. To the President was granted the power to make treaties with other countries, but only by and with the advice and consent of at least two thirds of the senators. With the consent of the Senate also he was to appoint the consuls, ministers, and other agents to represent the United States abroad.

Since the Constitution was designed to endure for ages in which great changes were bound to come in American affairs, the framers knew that Congress would have to deal with them or be helpless in serving the purposes for which the stronger Union was established. So, besides vesting in Congress powers later called "specific," the Constitution gave it two general powers to make the instrument flexible for adaptation to changes in the needs, ideas, and interests of the American people.

It authorized Congress to raise and appropriate money for "the general welfare of the United States." It also authorized Congress "to make all laws necessary and proper for carrying into effect" its specific powers, "and all other powers vested by this Constitution in the government of the United States or any department or officer thereof." Many a conflict was to rage over these lines but in time they were accepted as giving sanction to types of legislation conceived in the general interest of the nation as distinguished from interests purely local in nature.

While creating a strong government, balanced within itself and endowed with great powers, the framers of the Constitution placed definite limits on the federal government with a view to preserving liberty. They provided, for instance, that Congress shall pass no bill of attainder, that is, no law imposing penalties on any person without a judicial trial. They likewise forbade *ex post facto* laws—measures stigmatizing as crimes actions which had been committed but were not crimes at the time of commission. The trial of all crimes against the United States, except in cases of impeachment, they declared, must be by jury and in the state where committed. "No money shall be drawn from the Treasury," ran another clause, "but in consequence of appropriations made by law; and a regular statement and account of receipts and expenditures of all public moneys shall be published from time to time."

Even a strong and limited government for the Union, the framers decided, was not sufficient to fulfill their national purposes. Hence they laid specific restraints upon the states, forbidding them to meddle with many matters of life, liberty, and property. Some of these restraints pertained to domestic affairs; others, to foreign affairs.

The states were stripped of powers to coin money, emit bills of credit, make anything but gold and silver coin legal tender in the payment of debts, pass bills of attainder and *ex post facto* laws, grant titles of nobility, and enact laws impairing the obligation of contracts. Every state was commanded to give full faith and credit to the public acts, records, and judicial proceedings of all other states; in other words, states were to place no barriers in the way of enforcing legal rights throughout the land. As a guarantee of free migration and commerce throughout the country, the Constitution provided that "the citizens of each state shall be entitled to all the privileges and immunities of citizens of the several states."

No less mandatory were the restraints laid upon the states in respect of foreign affairs. They were forbidden to enter into any treaty, alliance, or confederation. They were ordered to lay no imposts or duties on imports or exports, without the consent of Congress, except such as might be absolutely necessary for the execution of their inspection laws. To use the language of the Constitution: "No state shall, without the consent of Congress, lay any duties of tonnage, keep troops, or ships of war, in time of peace, enter into any agreement or compact with another state, or with a foreign power, or engage in war, unless actually invaded, or in such imminent danger as will not admit of delay."

In return for the many limitations imposed upon the states, the framers of the Constitution offered them pledges of protection. The Constitution provided that "the United States shall guarantee to every state in this union a republican form of government, and shall protect each of them against invasion." As if remembering

Shays' Rebellion of 1786 in Massachusetts, they offered to the states the aid of the United States against "domestic violence."

Having in mind an enduring Union, the framers of the Constitution realized that conferring general powers upon Congress might not make it competent to cope with all the problems of coming times, with formidable changes that might occur in the ideas and interests of the American people. Radical alterations might be necessary in the form and powers of the proposed government.

In recognition of this fact the framers made provision for amending the Constitution; and here, too, they overrode the sovereignty of the states. No alteration could be made in the provisions of the Articles of Confederation without the consent of every state. For this principle was substituted another rule. By Article V the Constitution provided that Congress might, by a two-thirds vote in each house, propose amendments to the Constitution or, on application from the legislatures of two thirds of the states, must call a convention for the purpose of proposing amendments.

Amendments proposed by Congress or by such a convention were to go into effect when ratified by legislatures or conventions in three fourths of the states. Only one exception was made to this plan for binding states against their wills: "No state, without its consent, shall be deprived of its equal suffrage in the Senate."

The Constitution so drawn was strong medicine for advocates of states' rights. Its framers knew this very well. Throughout their proceedings in the convention they were impressed or oppressed by fear that it would not be ratified. How to put it into effect? That was for them a specter. Many state legislatures had refused to permit any increase in the powers of the old Congress. Perhaps that Congress, still functioning under the Articles of Confederation, would reject the new plan of government. Popular opposition to any changes in the existing form of government might be insurmountable. Perhaps state legislatures would refuse to ratify the Constitution. The knot had to be cut and it was cut by the makers of the Constitution with two provisions for ratification.

First, they appealed over the heads of Congress and the state legislatures. They sent their plan to the existing Congress, with two recommendations, namely, that it be referred to the states by the Congress and that the state legislatures call special conventions, elected by the voters, to pass upon the plan. Second, they provided that the Constitution should go into effect when ratified by nine states as between the nine—leaving the other states, if they preferred, out in the cold without a national roof over their heads.

When on September 17, 1787, the secrecy of the convention was broken and the proposed plan was published, a tempest of public debate over its merits began to blow. Critics fell upon it with might and main. It was not a plan for a "federal" union, some said, but a dark plot to establish a centralized despotism and reduce the states to provinces. The President, others insisted, would become a monarch, perhaps worse than George III. It was a device, radicals claimed, by which the rich and powerful would govern the country and oppress the plain people with armies, taxes, and debts. It had no bill of rights, friends of liberty protested. In fact scarcely a line of the Constitution escaped an attack, mild or passionate. On the other hand, able defenders came to its support in pamphlets, articles, and letters. The most comprehensive and cogent defense was made by Alexander Hamilton, John Jay, and James Madison. Between October 1787 and May 1788 they wrote eighty-five long articles, most of which appeared in the press of New York, under the pen name of "Publius." Many of the articles were reprinted in the newspapers of other states. They were all brought out in the spring of 1788 in two volumes entitled *The Federalist*. From that day to this *The Federalist* has been widely regarded as the most profound single treatise on the Constitution ever written and as among the few masterly works on political science produced in all the centuries of history.

While the public debate over the plan was in full course, conventions duly elected in the states assembled to pass upon it. Within three months three states ratified it—Delaware and New Jersey unanimously, and Pennsylvania after a hot contest. Early in 1788 Georgia and Connecticut added their approval. By a close vote Massachusetts accepted it in February. Maryland and South Carolina soon followed. The New Hampshire convention, at first opposed or hesitant, decided favorably before the end of June. Nine states, the number necessary to put the Constitution into effect, had now made the fateful decision.

But two large states wavered. In New York a majority of the convention was against ratification. In Virginia tenacious opponents, including Patrick Henry, kept the result long in doubt, but in the end the supporters of the new plan triumphed there. Then, under the leadership of Alexander Hamilton, the opposition in New York was overcome and a resolution of ratification was adopted. Thus by the autumn of 1788 eleven of the thirteen states had accepted the new Union. The advocates of the revolutionary change in the loose form of government provided by the Articles of Confederation were at last victorious.

Only two states remained aloof. The convention in North Carolina withheld its approval—until November 1789. Rhode Island would have nothing to do with the new Constitution until the spring of 1790, when it added its ratification.

Exulting in their success, victors in the contest celebrated the occasion by organizing spectacular parades in the principal towns. With justification they looked upon the outcome as the triumph of reason over force. Without drawing the sword in a civil war, without shedding a drop of blood, a new plan of government had been proposed, framed, discussed, and adopted. The victors in seven states, it is true, had been forced to appease opponents distressed about dangers to civil liberties by agreeing that a bill of rights, in the form of amendments, should be joined to the Constitution when the new government got under way. But as none of the proposed amendments affected the form of that government, this pledge, fulfilled in 1791, merely confirmed the faith of Americans in the power of the people to govern themselves on a continental scale by peaceful constitutional processes.

CHAPTER X

Establishing the Republican Way of Life

WITH GRATEFUL UNANIMITY presidential electors, chosen after the adoption of the Constitution, cast their ballots for George Washington as the Chief Executive of the United States. Inaugurated on April 30, 1789, amid the plaudits of the people in New York City, the first capital of the new government, he delivered an address emphasizing the solemn nature of the republican experiment that was being launched. "The pre-eminence of free government," he said, should be "exemplified by all the attributes which can win the affections of its citizens and command the respect of the world. . . . The preservation of the sacred fire of liberty and the destiny of the republican model of government are justly considered, perhaps, as *deeply*, as *finally*, staked on the experiment entrusted to the hands of the American people."

In this declaration Washington no doubt expressed the sentiments of all Americans save those intransigent Tories who hoped for the failure of the Republic and a return to the fold of the British monarchy. A new government, republican in form, had been founded. Many Americans living under it, even some who had been ardent in support of the Revolution, feared that it might not endure. One great problem of the opening years, then, was that of making universal—in thought, sentiments, and outward signs—the spirit necessary to sustain it.

The Revolutionary generation, now embarking on the republican way of life, had all grown up under a monarchy. Accustomed to that regime, many of the patriots, some of them high in the political and military circles of the Revolution, believed, even while the fighting was going on, that a monarchical form of government was the only kind that could maintain law and order. According to rumors, private negotiations were carried on with or about possible candidates for the throne in America, including the second son of King George III. Certainly a few officers in the Revolutionary army thought that a military dictatorship of one man should be established over the people. John Adams was of the opinion that the President should be given a title as resounding as that of "His Highness" or "His Majesty" in order to excite great respect or awe among the people for the chief magistrate. Attachment to the aristocratic ideology prevalent among nations across the sea was likewise strong among a large number of Americans who sought to shape the American way of life under its republican forms. If no true aristocracy of blood and lineage could be set up, they thought an "aristocracy of wealth and talents" might be substituted for it.

But the monarchists did not have their way. Nor did an aristocracy based on mere wealth and talents attain supreme power. While members of the upper classes of the United States were proposing to take over the government and direct it according to their ideas and interests, no organized royalist movement, even as a temporary grasp at power, interrupted the transition from monarchy to republic. In the shadows was no dethroned king or queen or ambitious pretender who could form the center of a monarchist reaction. The constitutional way of governing had been widely accepted and, in rallying the people to the Constitution, the planting and mercantile interests, so dominant in the Philadelphia Convention of 1787, had to make concessions to popular, and even leveling, doctrines in efforts to make their policies prevail.

The first President was a military hero—the commander in chief of the Revolutionary army. But he was not to become a Caesar or a Napoleon and put a crown on his own head. He had refused, with wrath at the suggestion, to be a party to any conspiracy for setting up a monarch or a military dictator. Of his own choice he had returned to the old Congress the symbol of his military authority—his commission as commander—the military authority granted him by that body of civilians. Now the unanimous choice of the nation's electors, he was to wear no title superior to that of plain "Mr. President." And he was to go down in the republican tradition, not so much as General Washington as simply George Washington.

There was no impulsion to Caesarism in him. His sense of

dignity prevented hero worship from degenerating into that form of popular betrayal. Long accustomed to fine horses and equipages, Washington, as "Mr. President," rode out frequently in the first capital of the nation in his grand coach drawn by six horses driven by a slave, accompanied by outriders. But he did not think of himself as a demigod chosen to rule the United States. Nor was he moved to be a lesser divinity and wield power as a demagogue through a resort to hypnotic oratory. He had no genius for oratory.

Despite his great wealth and his social position he was essentially modest in his estimation of his political sagacity. No amount of public adulation changed his estimation of himself—not even during the journey from his home in Virginia to New York City. During that journey he passed through one triumphal arch after another amid cheering throngs to the capital, where he was welcomed by leading citizens with lavish ceremonies and by huge crowds that had come from distant places to shout acclaim and throw flowers at his feet. But nothing fired him with dangerous vanity.

However intractable the remnants of the monarchical tradition may have been, George Washington had no desire, and was not temperamentally fitted, to reinforce it. He was sincere in his profession that he lacked many qualifications for carrying the burden of presiding over the new government as its highest and most responsible official. Before he started to New York to assume that duty, he had written to General Henry Knox that his "feelings were not unlike those of a culprit going to his execution." In his diary he had recorded that his mind was "oppressed with more anxious and painful sensations than he had words to express."

It was with no mere gesture of false pride that he referred, in his first inaugural address, to his "inferior endowments from nature," his lack of experience in "the duties of civil administration," and his other "deficiencies." These were not the ideas of a man thirsting for power or eager to play the role of a demagogue. They were rather the confessions of a man prepared to take counsel with the people, his advisers, and friends, to make compromises with extremists, and rule in the constitutional manner appropriate to the republican way of life.

Moreover, he soon began to study books which might be helpful, such as Vattel's *Law of Nations* and volumes of the *Debates* in the House of Commons, making use of the Society Library in New York City. He had based his scientific plantation management on knowledge acquired in part by reading books on agriculture in his own large collection. Now he also looked for such guidance in his public work as books might afford.

Had Washington been inclined to regal or arbitrary habits of rule—and his political associate, James Madison, testified that he never was so inclined—he would have found strong opposition among the people of New York. To be sure, there were still many Tories in the city, reminders of the fact that it had been occupied by the British troops from 1776 to the end of the Revolutionary War. But monarchist loyalties were declining among them. King's College, closed during the British occupancy, had been renamed Columbia College and its learned professors were republicans now, if cautious in their political expressions. Distinguished lawyers, physicians, and surgeons, who had been eminent in the old regime, were adjusting themselves to the new regime.

Furthermore, the city had many influential residents who, while definitely republican in principles, had opposed the adoption of the Constitution. Surrounding Alexander Hamilton, prime exponent of centralization, were unswerving defenders of decentralization. Ratification of the Constitution had been literally wrung from the representatives of the New York voters at the state convention in Poughkeepsie in 1788, less than a year before Washington's inauguration. Members of the state legislature were so avid for power that they could not agree on how presidential electors were to be chosen and so New York had not even voted for Washington in the first election. The governor of the state, George Clinton, enjoying his sixth term in office, had fought ratification and had yielded in his last-ditch battle only after nine states had approved the Constitution. He was a forceful figure in New York society.

So was John Lamb, who had been so fervid in his opposition to the Constitution that he barricaded his residence against a Federalist "mob." He had been a leader of the Sons of Liberty, who had rioted against the Stamp Act in 1765, and a soldier in the Revolution. John Lamb was not inclined to approve centralizing "tyranny" in a new form.

Nor were the "plain people" of New York City likely to uphold an ambitious leader bent on "seizing power." Many of the artisans and tradesmen had supported the adoption of the Constitution in the hope that an improvement in business would follow. But memories of rioting by the Sons of Liberty lingered among them and they certainly did not belong to Alexander Hamilton's set. In meetings of Tammany Hall or in public taverns they continued to argue over public questions; and some of them, going beyond republicanism, began to use openly that more incendiary word "democracy."

Even the plays on the New York stage, which Washington and other members of the government occasionally witnessed with the people of pit and gallery, gave no encouragement to kingly or "high-toned" pretensions. For example, Royall Tyler's play, *The Contrast*, starting on its successful career in 1787, was republican in its argument. Although it dealt humorously with the vanities of small farmers and urbanites alike, it ridiculed British affectations and exalted republican dignity. If it was not agrarian in tone, neither did it lend countenance to royalist designs.

While a "republican court" soon developed among the fashionable circles at the first national capital and was emphatically high-toned in its sympathies, it could not or did not block the tendency toward republican simplicities. Some of its members, according to Jefferson's reports, had doubts whether the constitutional experiment would succeed and even secretly sighed for or expected a return to "kingly rule." Senator William Maclay, one of the earliest outspoken democrats in the country, caustically criticized, in a puritan vein, its balls and dinners, calling them a waste of time and injurious to minds, morals, and the public interest.

But, however skeptically some members of the "republican court" regarded the republican experiment or confidently expected the adoption of a still stronger form of government in case another crisis came, they all rallied to the side of President Washington's administration. They gave to it the support of the "wealth and talents" without which, Hamilton argued, the Constitution could not be successfully launched. Jefferson believed that they were actually royalist in sympathies. But in 1790, when Hamilton told him that the Union was in danger of breaking up, even Jefferson approved a financial measure advantageous to bondholders and speculators on the ground that "the preservation of the Union and concord among the states was more important" than defeating it.

The adoption of New York as the first seat of the new government was in many ways fortunate for what Washington called "the destiny of the republican model of government" on a national scale. The city lay between New England and the South. It cordially received the new government and by generous encouragement helped to make its inauguration an unquestionable success. But, to the regret of merchants, proprietors of taverns, boardinghouse keepers, and hostesses, among other beneficiaries, Congress decided against New York as the permanent capital of the nation.

That decision was the result of a "deal" between Hamilton and Jefferson at a time when Congress was badly split, in 1790, over the issue of assumption of state debts by the federal government. Threats of disunion were thus overcome. Two Southern votes and some Pennsylvania votes were brought over to the support of assumption on condition that Philadelphia was to be the capital for ten years and that the permanent seat of the government was to be located on the banks of the Potomac, as a final concession to the South. Late in 1790 the government of the United States was transferred to Philadelphia. Some New Yorkers found consolation for the loss in the huge profits they had garnered from their speculations in state evidences of indebtedness—speculations made possible by the "deal" between Hamilton and Jefferson.

Philadelphia, the second national capital and the largest city in the Union, also made its peculiar contribution to shaping the spirit and practices of the "republican model." Pennsylvania had never been a royal province. The monarchical tradition was weaker there than in New York. Neither the Penns nor their proprietary agents had imparted to their local administration the glamor that adorned the "court" of a royal governor. Moreover, the population of Philadelphia was more varied in racial stocks than that of New York, and its interests and activities were more diversified. It included some rich landlords and many merchant princes eager to reproduce the "republican court" of New York and prepared to entertain federal officials, members of Congress, and foreign envoys on a scale equally if not more extravagant. At the same time Philadelphia had more small tradesmen and artisans, more schoolmasters, music teachers, lawyers, physicians, surgeons, scientists, and philosophers of a rationalistic and secular bent. Leadership in New York, where the English Church had formerly been established, was still strongly Anglican in religious faith. Philadelphia, on the contrary, had long been the home of religious dissidence, the chief center of scientific inquiry and rationalism.

In Philadelphia there was greater political, social, and intellectual ferment than in the first capital. The state constitution of New York, despite its republican leanings, was, next to that of Massachusetts, the most aristocratic of all the documents drawn up in the early days of independence. The constitution of Pennsylvania, of 1776, on the other hand, was accounted about the most radical of the time—with a legislature composed of a single chamber and a governor subservient to that body—and the new constitution of 1790, though more conservative, was still liberal in spirit. Philadelphia had numerous clubs and societies of tradesmen and artisans addicted to free discussions—political, religious, scientific, and social. The opposition to the adoption of the federal Constitution in Pennsylvania, though not so strong as in New York State, had been bitter; and the memory of it still rankled, particularly in the western regions, which were soon to test President Washington's administrative skill by an open revolt against a federal tax on whisky—the "Whisky Rebellion." If, as the President said, the new government needed, for endurance, the affection of the people, there was ample opportunity to cultivate that attachment in Pennsylvania.

While bestowing its "affection," Philadelphia had many advanced ideas to offer members of the administration and Congress —to Puritans from New England, Anglicans from New York, and planters from the South also usually Anglican in faith. It was the center of the freest thinking in the Union on all matters, human and divine. For a city of those days, it was well laid out and ably governed. Even its wealthy inhabitants displayed a sensitivity to urban poverty and suffering, and maintained institutions of benevolence definitely progressive for the times. In Philadelphia religious toleration was peculiarly broad. Quakers, who made up a large part of the population, were for it on principle and the other denominations, whether on principle or not, accepted it. In scientific inquiries and applications, educational experiments, and civic enterprise, Philadelphia compared favorably with any city in Western civilization.

There the "utilitarian mentor," Benjamin Franklin, had kept the people astir with new adventures in ideas and, though he had died in April 1790, his spirit still enlivened the mood of that city. There the American Philosophical Society which he had promoted was creating intellectual currents that were to spread to all the shores of thought in America. Thomas Jefferson was an officer in this society during the days when he was living in Philadelphia as Vice-President of the United States. Through the port of Philadelphia came travelers, newcomers intending to make America their home, and foreign emissaries, bringing with them, among other intellectual interests, the knowledge and radical philosophy of the French.

Jefferson had become familiar with new French thinking while, from 1785 to 1789, he was minister of the United States at Paris, where he was adjudged a first-rate thinker in his own right. In Philadelphia he encountered congenial minds that fortified his determination to give the government of the United States a firmer bent in the direction of leveling republicanism. His followers in Congress, who had begun to form the nucleus of a political party before the federal government was moved to Philadelphia, were more at ease in the city of Benjamin Franklin than in the metropolis of Alexander Hamilton. In short, Philadelphia aided in smoothing the way for the Jeffersonian "revolution" in politics that attended the next transfer of the capital—to the District of Columbia in 1800.

Under the private agreement and the ensuing act of Congress that fixed the permanent capital of the federal government on the banks of the Potomac, the second President, John Adams, in the summer of 1800, ordered the removal of the administration to the District of Columbia where Congress was to assemble on the first Monday in December. The task of removal was not very burdensome. All told, the federal officers and clerks numbered only one hundred and twenty-six persons. Official papers were boxed and shipped by boat. The officers and clerks made the trip by various routes. President Adams went to see the place in June and later he and his wife Abigail were installed in the "President's House." In a report on the official residence, then unfinished and full of litter, she said that she was using the great "audience room" in the "President's Palace" as "a drying room . . . to hang the clothes in."

In 1801 the District of Columbia was a profusion of forests, hills, and streams interspersed with a few farms, the little village of George Town, some newly laid out streets for the city of Washington, and a few public and private buildings just completed or under construction. Land speculators and real estate promoters swarmed over the place buying and selling lots with little or no respect for community plans of any kind. Good houses dotted the landscape, but the roads between them, in the "city of magnificent distances," were axle deep in summer dust or winter mud. "An awful contrast to the public buildings," exclaimed Oliver Wolcott, Secretary of the Treasury, were the many "small, miserable huts." The inhabitants of the huts, he declared, "are poor, and as far as I can judge, they live like fishes, by eating one another." There were no fine churches, no schools, no colleges, no seasoned residents to extend hospitality at balls and dinners to members of the incoming government. Laborers' shanties and brick kilns stood out starkly in the scene—more vividly than the habitations of the laboring poor in New York or Philadelphia. A slave market, with its pens and auction block, gave obtrusive notice that the capital of the Republic had been located in a region where the "peculiar institution" flourished. The outlook for republican grandeur did not seem brilliant.

But behind the confusion lay the dream of a splendid city worthy of the Republic. Major Pierre Charles L'Enfant, a French engineer and soldier of the American Revolution, whose services President Washington had enlisted, had drawn a grandiose plan for the permanent capital, with broad avenues, spacious plazas, and long vistas, in anticipation of a time when the wealth of the nation would permit an orderly and full development of his design. Having regard for the republican principles of Thomas Jefferson, whom he consulted in making his sketches, L'Enfant was careful to avoid a mere duplication of any European pattern, whatever might have been his personal preference, and to make room for the originality of simplicity. It is true that, for the time being, L'Enfant's plan was largely defeated by real estate speculators and that he retired from further activity, discouraged and ruined. Late in the nineteenth century, however, his dream was to be revived and honor paid to his memory.

Notwithstanding the disputes and divided councils that attended the laying out of the new city, the architecture of the two outstanding public buildings in process of completion was in keeping with Jefferson's republican aspirations. For the Congress House, or Capitol, William Thornton's sketches, with provision for a great central rotunda, were accepted by President Washington and, subject to modifications, were used as the basis of construction. The President's House, designed by James Hoban, was modest in lines and proportions. Both buildings represented a departure from Georgian and other purely colonial architecture and a tendency toward the severity of classical models set by the Greek and Roman republics of antiquity.

As if symbolizing this simplicity, the first President to be inaugurated in the new capital of the nation was Thomas Jefferson himself. His party had wrested the federal administration from the "aristocrats" and "monocrats" in the party founded by Hamilton and Washington. Despite his "simplicity," ridiculed as "affected" by his political foes, he was one of the most sophisticated persons of his time in the New World or the Old World. By virtue of

THE UNITED STATES IN THE EARLY DAYS OF THE REPUBLIC

his wide knowledge, his interest in natural science, art, and learning, his geniality, humor, and readiness to listen as well as pronounce, he was exceptionally equipped to assume the leadership of the political community in Washington. Though familiar with cities of Western Europe as with New York and Philadelphia, he loved the country, and Washington was then little more than a village. Though treated as a philosopher among the intellectuals who gathered in the home of Condorcet and his high-minded wife in Paris, he had been snubbed by the socially pretentious landlords and merchants of New York and Philadelphia, and felt happier in the White House at Washington.

According to the custom followed at his Virginia country place, Monticello, Jefferson made the President's House in the permanent capital of the Republic a center of social and intellectual leadership, while he presided as Executive over the young nation. At the dinner table, where conversation among Americans from all sections of the country and foreign diplomats was made easy and informal, he was cordial, skillful, and deeply interested in evoking diversities of opinions and tastes. In this way at the crude capital of the young Republic, he attached all sorts and conditions of people, high and low, to the republican experiment. And fortunately, in this wide-open though experienced hospitality, he was aided by his daughter, Martha Jefferson Randolph, whose education, after the death of his wife, he had carefully and thoughtfully supervised.

It was significant for the future that Thomas Jefferson, with his strong faith in the people, took over in 1801 the administration of the republican system of government which had been framed in deep distrust of the people; that as President he strengthened it before the rising tide of Jacksonian democracy began to beat upon it. The very fact that the seat of the government was then in a mere village, frontier in its physical appearance and isolated as a political community, no doubt was a factor in enlarging Jefferson's influence in Congress and public councils generally.

Distrust of cities had been a cardinal feature of agrarian republicanism. Even John Adams had feared the aggressions of plutocratic merchants and speculators as much as he had feared an uprising of the poor. At all events the presence of Jefferson at the head of the Republic in the village of Washington, though his election had evoked the fury of haughty Federalists, increased "the affections of its citizens" for "the republican model of government," as George Washington had called it, and gave vigor to the republican way of life in the United States.

☆

Influential as was the work of Washington, Adams, and Jefferson in fortifying republican government, their work was only one phase of the transition from monarchy to the republican way of life. To the new order was brought the support of intellectual and artistic talents among the citizens, made manifest in forms of written and oral expression, such as books and dramas, and in visible symbols, such as paintings and engravings. Through the press, the theater, and popular education—formal and informal— the results of these activities became known and appreciated among multitudes of people upon whose thought, aspirations, labors, and character the republican experiment ultimately depended for its success.

By the intellectual and artistic activities of private citizens the doctrine was formulated that the Revolution and the Republic were worthy of the highest esteem in themselves, and admirable in the history of humanity. By the same processes were widened and deepened knowledge and thought respecting the new nation whose fortunes were involved in the republican way of life, with all that it signified in terms of civilization. With increasing interest in society, economy, and the people went inquiries, ever more microscopic, into the physical geography and the natural resources of the continental domain as expansion and settlement proceeded —the material setting in which the republican experiment was being carried on.

During the transition from monarchy to the republican type of life, writers gave expression to the revolution in literally thousands of books on the United States—on its government, people, institutions, and resources. By classes, somewhat arbitrary, these books came under the heads of government, law, economy, geography, travel, public policies, and conditions of the people from the poorest slave at the bottom to the richest merchant or planter at the top. Some of them, however, were so comprehensive that they took in all or nearly all the themes then engaging American interests. Collectively, the books contained knowledge and thought bearing upon almost everything human and material that was germane to the republican experiment, its policies and its possibilities, its ideals and its resources. The scope of this literature is merely indicated, rather than adequately illustrated, by the following selected titles and comments:

1787—Thomas Jefferson, *Notes on Virginia*. A model survey of the government, laws, economy, climate, resources, and people of Virginia—the forerunner of many such treatises on individual states.

1787—John Adams, *Defence of the Constitutions of the United States* (Vols. I–III). A historical study of the science of politics in which the principles of the first state constitutions were defended with great learning.

1788—Jay, Hamilton, and Madison, *The Federalist*, essays written in support of the Constitution, published in book form. Frequently republished. French edition in 1792. A treatise on the sociology, economics, and strategy of republican government which formed the primary textbook for the education of the American people in republican ways of government.

1789—William Gordon, *History of the Rise, Progress and Establishment of the Independence of the United States* (Vols. I–III). Published previously in London. Displeased the English by its American sympathies and was regarded in America as scarcely patriotic enough. Gordon copied wholesale from other writings.

1789—David Ramsay, *History of the American Revolution* (Vols. I, II). More favorable to the American cause than Gordon's work.

1791–92—Thomas Paine, *Rights of Man*. Textbook of republican principles. Sold by the tens of thousands in the two hemispheres.

1805—Mercy Warren, *History of the Rise, Progress and Termination of the American Revolution* (Vols. I–III). Far more original than Gordon or Ramsay. Based extensively on personal knowledge; Northern in emphasis. Discussed the conditions from which the Revolution sprang, leading characters and events of the Revolution. Democratic in sympathies and a warning against monarchical tendencies and the greed for riches that might undermine the Republic and restore tyranny.

1805–07—John Marshall, *Life of George Washington* (Vols. I–V). Based on extensive researches. An eloquent defense and vindication of Washington; Federalist in tone; and did more than any other work to set the tradition of Washington as "the father of his country." Severely criticized by Jefferson and his followers, but remained powerful in influence.

1814—Lewis and Clark, *History of the Expedition . . . to the Pacific Ocean* (Vols. I, II). Summary description of a famous journey and the country through which the explorers passed.

1814—Tench Coxe, *A Statement of the Arts and Manufactures of the United States of America for the year 1810*. Based on a federal census taken in 1810.

1814—John Taylor, *An Inquiry into the Principles and Policy of the Government of the United States*. A philosophical treatise on politics, following the Anti-Federalist or agrarian party line in opposition to the "aristocracy of riches."

1817—William Wirt, *Sketches of the Life and Character of Patrick Henry*. Eulogy on the fiery leader of the Revolution.

1819—David Ramsay, *Universal History Americanized* (Vols. I–IX). Three additional volumes unfinished on the death of the author. A grand design to put the United States in the setting of great history.

How many Americans burned midnight oil studying the histories of Gordon, Ramsay, and Mercy Warren was not entered in the records of the time but there can be no doubt that thousands upon thousands saw, as originals or reproductions, the paintings which celebrated in visible form the Revolution and its leaders. The task of such delineation was deliberately assumed by John Trumbull, who had a vision of the "vast consequences" to flow from the establishment of independence. A former colonel in the Revolution, Trumbull had the spirit of the new age and he gave vivid expression to it on his canvases representing the "Battle of Bunker's Hill," the "Signing of the Declaration of Independence," the "Capture of the Hessians at Trenton," the "Surrender of Cornwallis at Yorktown," and in his portraits of leaders, such as Washington and Hamilton.

Two contemporaries of Trumbull, Gilbert Stuart, of Rhode Island, and Charles Wilson Peale, of Maryland, also painted portraits of the outstanding personalities of the Revolutionary generation. Stuart's portrait of Washington, soon to become the most widely accepted for technical competence, depicted the hero as a polished aristocrat of Virginia. Truer to life, Peale portrayed him in his rugged character as outdoor planter, soldier, and stalwart manager of men. The chief paintings of Trumbull, Stuart, and Peale, reproduced by lithographic processes, soon ornamented public buildings and private homes, great and humble, making lifelike, to all who could see, characters and events connected with the making of the independent Republic.

Moved by a kindred spirit, poets joined in the same celebration. Joel Barlow, of Connecticut, for example, dreamed of a great creative future for America. "The American Republic," he told a friend, "is a fine theater for the display of merit of every kind. If ever virtue is to be rewarded, it is in America." In this mood, Barlow wrote and published in 1787 *The Vision of Columbus*, an epic poem of more than five thousand lines on the real significance of the discovery of America. Recognizing, with his critics, some of the youthful exaggerations of this venture, Barlow later worked over and reworked the theme and republished it in 1807 in two sumptuous volumes as *The Columbiad*. Barlow's object, he declared in his preface, was to demonstrate that Columbus "had opened the way to the most extensive career of civilization and public happiness," to inculcate the spirit of liberty, to discountenance violence and war, and "to show that on the basis of republican principles all good morals, as well as good government and hopes of permanent peace, must be founded."

The convulsive changes which marked the transition to the republican way of life were dramatized by playwrights. Following the success of Tyler's comedy, *The Contrast*, in New York, the play was presented in Baltimore, Philadephia, Charleston, and Boston; and it was published in 1790, with a subscription list at the head of which stood George Washington, the President of the Republic. From year to year in far-scattered places it was reproduced by players both professional and amateur.

Tyler's success encouraged William Dunlap to enter seriously upon a career as a dramatist, dedicating his talents to the service of the Republic, as he believed American artists of every type should do. Knowing that monarchies had been made glamorous by the aid of painters, poets, historians, architects, dramatists, musicians, and novelists, Dunlap felt that the Republic was far more worthy of devotion and should be made attractive to the people by all such forms of art. His father had been a Loyalist during the Revolution and had sent William to Europe to be trained as a painter. But in London William became enamored of the theater; his sympathies with the struggle of the people for liberty were awakened; and on his return home he composed plays and wrote works on the drama and the arts of design.

Dunlap's long career as an important and productive playwright of the Republic opened in 1789 with a drama entitled *The Father; or American Shandy-ism*, in which he presented his view of the "contrast" in the following lines:

> *Now I see in this new world*
> *A resting spot for man, if he can stand*
> *Firm in his place, while Europe howls around him. . . .*
> *Then might, perhaps, one land on earth be found,*
> *Free from the extremes of poverty and riches;*
> *Where ne'er a scepter'd tyrant should be known,*
> *Or tyrant lordling, curses of creation.*

Other forms of literature expressed the ideas, interests, and ideals of the people in the republican era. The novels and tracts of Charles Brockden Brown contained flashes of discussion which illuminated the wrongs of yeomen and the "rights" of women, as well as nearly every other current theme of democratic interest. James Fenimore Cooper, whose first novel came out in 1820, chose to tell stories of the struggle for liberty in the Revolution, and to portray all kinds of Americans from Indians and pioneers to planters and sailors. Poets, such as Philip Freneau, "the poet of the Revolution," tried their lyrical talents on the aspirations of the Republic. Noah Webster wrote to George Washington in 1786: "I am encouraged by the prospect of rendering my country some service, to proceed with my design of refining the language & improving our general system of education." So he went ahead compiling dictionaries on the basis of American usages for scholarly and popular purposes and making plans for giving the children of the people an education that would inspire a devotion to the Republic and prepare them for citizenship in it.

Newspapers for the distribution of knowledge and ideas, true or false, multiplied in the republican era. Forty-three colonial newspapers, it was estimated, lived through the Revolution; in 1810 Isaiah Thomas recorded, in his *History of Printing*, the existence of 366 newspapers scattered all the way from New Hampshire to the Louisiana Territory, with no less than fourteen in Ohio and one on the frontier of Michigan. In this period the daily press entered the journalistic arena, exciting readers every day instead of every week. Philadelphia printers supplied the first daily—in 1784; and by 1809, the end of Jefferson's second administration, there were twenty-seven dailies in the flourishing cities from Boston to New Orleans.

As the party division into Federalists and Republicans deepened, practically all the newspapers, weekly and daily, became ferociously partisan and outdid in the passion of their language anything the colonial age had experienced. But they distributed news, or at all events selections and versions of news, reported on the great public questions and policies of the day, and supplied topics for discussion at dinner tables, in taverns, at corner stores, and by firesides throughout the land.

All the pressures of thought in the new society struggling to establish the republican way of life—insurgent interests and traditional tastes—found outlets in new magazines which burst forth luxuriantly. In their pages, taken collectively, readers were supplied with polite letters, fragments of creative fiction, patriotic boasting, practical philosophies of daily living, scientific information, codes of etiquette, poetic effusions mawkish or brave, essays on humble ambitions and national aspirations, old and new bigotries with their simplicities of dogma, and solid articles on actions and policies directed to the advantages of classes or the progressive attainment of general welfare. Magazine editors seemed to labor hard at meeting every demand, real or imagined, from the supposed needs of gentlewomen eager for "culture" to the requirements, actual or alleged, of popular success in upholding the Republic.

Among the more substantial periodicals was the *Columbian Magazine*, founded by Mathew Carey at Philadelphia in 1786, a miscellany of original and selected articles on government, currency, industries, agriculture, and science. Its pages carried articles by some of the most distinguished writers of the early Republic, for example, Benjamin Rush, physician; David Ramsay, historian; Charles Brockden Brown, novelist; and Joel Barlow, pamphleteer and poet. It started bravely and seemed destined to have a long career, but after four years of struggle it gave up the ghost.

Other magazines tried to fill the void left by its death, only to meet a similar fate. Yet at no time in the early republican era was the country without an ambitious monthly of the general type. At last, in 1815, when the *North American Review* was launched at Boston, a magazine editor received the support necessary to long endurance. Of the flock of magazines founded between 1776 and 1815 that *Review* alone survived the buffets of fortune into the twentieth century.

On no subject were the leaders of the Revolutionary generation more thoroughly united than on the advancement of popular education and science as indispensable to permanence in the republican way of life. The old Congress under the Articles of Confederation had demonstrated its faith by dedicating to public education regular blocks of land in the Northwest Territory. Then President Washington, in his first annual address to Congress, sounded a national note: "Nor am I less persuaded that you will agree with me in opinion that there is nothing which can better deserve your patronage than the promotion of science and literature. Knowledge is in every country the surest basis of public happiness. In one in which the measures of government receive their impressions so immediately from the sense of the community as in ours it is proportionably essential. To the security of a free constitution it contributes in various ways." To Congress at the moment he left the choice of ways for accomplishing this end but later he recommended the establishment of a national university. This recommendation Thomas Jefferson renewed as President.

Although Congress did not adopt the proposal, one state after another made the beginnings of state colleges and universities; and Jefferson, after he retired from the presidency, set an example of fidelity to conviction by taking the lead in founding the University of Virginia at Charlottesville. This university was not projected as merely a college with a classical curriculum. It was designed as a true modern institution of higher learning, dedicated to freedom of thought, inquiry, and teaching, especially in natural science and the humanities.

Lack of interest among the rank and file of politicians—even hostility—did not deter advocates of public education from planning for the future. Some of their programs, notably that of Robert Coram, a brave seaman in the war of the Revolution and an intellectual leader in Delaware, called for the training of all children in the practical arts as means of assuring personal independence and overcoming the poverty which belied civilization. Other plans, especially that of Noah Webster, while pleading for general education, insisted upon the training of women in the philosophy of republicanism, on the ground that women exercise a major influence through their training of the young and must be taught how to bring up the generations in republican ways of living and thinking.

James Sullivan in Massachusetts produced still another plan for a system of republican education. Sullivan was active in public affairs before, during, and after the Revolution—a justice of the Supreme Court in his state, a member of Congress in 1783, a publicist, one of the "richest, ablest, and most powerful" of the Jeffersonians. In his writings on government, politics, and society in America, Sullivan declared that a system of national education was absolutely necessary if the morals of the people were to be shaped according to the genius of republican government and if the people were to realize the ideals of liberty, happiness, and general welfare that had been proclaimed as the objectives of the republican experiment.

In the voluminous literature on education and the advancement of science, stress was placed on the practical aspects of living. Research in the natural sciences was to be promoted and useful inventions encouraged. Yet the moral sciences of community and national living were also to be emphasized to prepare the nation for its opportunities and destiny. The people, Jefferson insisted, must not only be trained in the practical arts; they must be instructed in those branches of learning, especially history, which would enable them to discharge their duties as citizens while maintaining a vigilant watch against the tendencies of government to encroach on human liberty, including the liberty of free inquiry, thought, and speech.

It was, no doubt, this concern with practical and earthly affairs in educational programs that helped to arouse opposition among the clergy, then the chief leaders in such popular education as prevailed, and to arrest the progress of universal and non-sectarian education until the nineteenth century was well advanced. Yet before the Revolutionary generation passed from the scene, its pioneers in thought had worked out and formulated essential principles for the advancement of science and the education of the people—all with a view to making the nation strong and wise in the use of its resources, solicitous for social improvements, and competent in the arts of republican government.

CHAPTER XI

The Revolutionary Generation in Charge of the Federal Government

FOR THIRTY-SIX YEARS after the Constitution went into force—from 1789 to 1825—the new government was headed by Presidents who belonged to the generation of revolutionists: by five men, George Washington, John Adams, Thomas Jefferson, James Madison, and James Monroe.

What a roll of services and honors, what varieties of experiences in war and peace, in domestic and foreign affairs, these five men represented!

Washington had been a member of the Virginia Assembly in colonial times, a soldier in the French and Indian War, a member of the Continental Congress, commander of the Revolutionary armies, a member of the convention that drafted the Constitution, the presiding officer of that body, and was literally "first in war and first in peace."

John Adams had spent laborious years in the Continental Congress during the War for Independence, had led in framing the Massachusetts Constitution of 1780, had represented his country in continental capitals and in London, had written a powerful work, the *Defence of the Constitutions of the United States,* and had been Vice-President under Washington.

Like Adams, Thomas Jefferson belonged to the civilian wing of the Revolutionary generation. He had been a member of the Virginia legislature and the Continental Congress. He had drawn up the Declaration of Independence. He had been governor of Virginia, minister of the United States to France, Secretary of State under Washington, and Vice-President during the administration of President Adams.

Before he became the fourth President, James Madison's lines had also fallen in the field of civilian leadership. He had been an active member of the old Congress. He had been a delegate to the convention of 1787 and, in that assembly, had brought to bear in the framing of the Constitution a profound knowledge of history and statecraft, besides an exceptional talent for negotiation. After the adoption of the Constitution he had been a member of the House of Representatives. For eight years he had served as Secretary of State under President Jefferson.

As in the case of Washington, so in the case of James Monroe the experiences of war and peace were combined. In the war of the Revolution, Monroe had learned the perils of the battlefield. He had represented the United States abroad. Under the presidency of Madison he had been Secretary of State and then Secretary of War. Although neither his talents nor his achievements measured up to those of his predecessors, he had qualities which gave him a place of distinction among the leaders of the Revolutionary generation.

Through all these years American citizens generally agreed that the executive leadership of the nation should be vested in outstanding figures of the Revolution. But they by no means agreed on the policies to be adopted and the measures to be enforced by the government of the United States. Americans had been divided into conservative and radical factions during the Revolution as in the preceding colonial order. This division was still evident during the framing and adoption of the Constitution. For a brief time, however, after the Constitution had been ratified, its opponents, accepting their defeat with good grace, permitted a lull in partisanship. Not until the first Congress under the new Constitution revealed its intentions in a program of legislation and the President began to appoint officials and indicate his domestic and foreign policies did serious dissensions reappear among the people.

To both houses of the first Congress many men were elected who had helped to draft the Constitution or who had worked for its adoption in their several states. In choosing the members of his Cabinet and high officials in his administration, Washington was careful to appoint men known as stanch advocates of the new plan. His Secretary of the Treasury, Alexander Hamilton, his Attorney General, Edmund Randolph, and General Henry Knox, his Secretary of War, belonged to that group.

Perhaps with a view to conciliating an expected opposition,

Washington gave to Thomas Jefferson the important post of Secretary of State. Jefferson had been in France as minister of the United States during the contest over the drafting and ratification of the Constitution. It was known to his intimates that he had at first thought a few amendments to the Articles of Confederation would suffice and had criticized the Constitution in several respects, especially the lack of a bill of rights. But Jefferson had rallied to the Constitution after 1789.

When the first Congress assembled in New York City and Washington was inaugurated as President, in the spring of 1789, the new government of the Republic was in the hands of its friends, experienced leaders, men long outstanding in public life. The cold text of the written Constitution had become flesh and blood. The time for action had arrived. But what actions in domestic affairs and in foreign affairs? That was the question which aroused expectancy among members of Congress and the people of the states.

Soon answers began to come, first in respect of domestic matters. In response to a popular demand for a bill of rights, Congress early proposed a series of amendments to the Constitution; and ten of them, ratified by state legislatures, went into effect in 1791. Still these involved no alteration whatever in the form of government.

Immediately pertinent to the support of the government were the measures, affecting the property and incomes of the people, that began to flow from Washington's administration and Congress. Revenues from taxation were necessary to the very existence of the government. All knew that. But what kind of taxes? On whom and what were they to fall? Taxation had been a sore point with the people since the Stamp Act of 1765. Well aware of it, Congress resorted to indirect taxation at the outset. The first revenue law, in 1789, laid duties on foreign goods imported into the United States. Both Washington and Hamilton thought that such duties should favor American manufacturers, especially of goods required for national defense. So did many members of Congress from the manufacturing states. In subsequent revenue acts "protection" was given to manufacturers of iron and several other commodities. To provide further revenues Congress laid an excise tax on whisky, a liquor distilled in thousands of farmhouses in various parts of the country.

Other measures affecting special interests were passed by Congress, one after the other, during the administrations of Washington and Adams. High on the list were provisions for paying off the big debt owed by the United States to its creditors—in the main to Americans, but in part to bankers in Holland and to the government of France.

This debt had been incurred by the Continental Congress largely for the purpose of carrying on the War for Independence. Interest on it had long remained in arrears. The prices of the bonds and other securities representing the debt had fallen, at times as low as to ten or fifteen cents on the dollar. Discouraged by the prospect of a total loss or needing money, hundreds of Americans had sold their bonds for almost nothing, to speculators who gambled on the chance that the cheap paper would someday be paid off in full by the government.

Should it be paid in full or at a sum below face value? If paid in full, should discrimination be made between the rate paid to persons who had originally bought the bonds from the Continental government and the rate paid to speculators who had bought the bonds from the original subscribers at low prices?

These points became storm centers of public discussion. The Secretary of the Treasury, Hamilton, proposed that the Continental securities be paid, ultimately, dollar for dollar and that no distinction be made between the persons who had bought their bonds directly from the government at the regular price and speculators who had bought theirs from original holders, second or third hand, for mere pittances. After exhaustive debates marked by thoughtfulness as well as passion, Congress adopted Hamilton's proposal. The Continental debt was thus "funded" and all bondholders were given new bonds for their old paper, dollar for dollar.

The states also had big debts incurred in the War for Independence. Some of the states were making payments on interest and principal; other states were delaying. In any case the bonds of the states had fallen in value, many of them to a low price, and speculators had been buying the state bonds too, at various price levels, in the hope of a rise in values.

That the state debts ought to be paid, people generally recognized. But by whom? Hamilton proposed that the federal Treasury assume the burden of paying them all and at face value. He argued that such a course was just, since the debts had been incurred in a common cause, and that it would strengthen the new government by making all bondholders look to its Treasury, instead of state treasuries, for payment of interest and principal. But on that point Hamilton encountered a still hotter opposition than had been raised against funding the Continental debt at face value. Even so, he managed by a close squeeze to win the approval of Congress for this plan, and the state debts were assumed by the federal government. New federal bonds were then exchanged for old state bonds, dollar for dollar, no distinction being made between the original subscribers and the speculators.

Another thing, Hamilton believed, was necessary to strengthen the Union. That was a national currency stable from one end of the country to the other. But the question of money was likewise vexatious. No great mines of gold and silver had been found along the Atlantic seaboard. During the Revolution the states and the Congress had poured out paper money by the bale and the country was full of notes "not worth a Continental," as the saying went. Now the Constitution had forbidden the states to emit bills of credit and had given Congress the power to coin money and regulate the value thereof—not to issue paper money. The only "sound money" in circulation consisted of metallic coins, mostly British, Spanish, and French; and they were being clipped, filed, and shorn by the money-changers.

Soon after Washington's inauguration, Congress made provision for minting new United States coins, but the precious metals available were small in quantity. For the purpose of expanding the amount of money in circulation, Hamilton devised and induced Congress to adopt a plan for a United States Bank. As set up in 1791, the bank was a joint-stock concern, with the United States Government among the holders of shares. The major portion of the stock, however, was subscribed by private investors, partly in specie money and partly in certain new bonds floated under Hamilton's funding and assumption schemes.

Little specie was actually paid in by private investors. So the "capital" of the bank rested principally on the paper bonds of the government. The bank, thus formed, was empowered to receive deposits, issue paper notes of its own, establish branches in various parts of the country, handle government accounts, and lend money at interest. The central office was established in Philadelphia. In time it had a network of branches scattered from Portsmouth, New Hampshire, to Savannah, Georgia. Through the agency of the United States Bank, paper notes of uniform value were put into circulation everywhere in the states; and merchants could now buy, sell, and make exchanges, assured that the bank currency would be both safe and stable.

With a view to promoting other branches of business enterprise,

Congress voted bounties to encourage the growth of American fisheries and granted special favors to American shipping interests. Great Britain and other Old World countries were helping their own shippers and discriminating against American shippers in their ports, according to accepted mercantilist theories. Under a strong government the United States was following suit.

To all such American measures Washington lent the support of his great name. The Constitution, he felt, warranted his doing this. He had been president of the convention which drafted it, had heard the debates, and was familiar with the purposes of the men who framed it. He knew more about those purposes than any of his critics, such as Thomas Jefferson, who had not been members of the convention and were less acquainted with the broad conceptions of government written into the Constitution. Giving expression to them, Washington recommended to Congress the enactment of laws promoting not only commerce and industry, but also agriculture, science, and education, with emphasis on the establishment of a national university for the training of young men for public life under the sway of American principles.

The growing body of federal officers engaged in enforcing the new laws under Washington's executive direction was supplemented by a new federal judiciary. By the Judiciary Act of 1789, Congress established the Supreme Court prescribed by the Constitution and a federal district court in each state, with a set of officials and agents for each court. Washington appointed as Chief Justice John Jay, who had battled for the ratification of the Constitution; and all the other judgeships he filled with men having a similar attitude toward the new order.

As soon as the new courts went into operation, citizens everywhere could look to federal judges for the protection and enforcement of their rights under the Constitution. If they felt that their rights were violated by state legislatures or state courts, they could appeal to federal judges independent of both. For example if a merchant of New York City wished to collect a debt from a citizen in North Carolina, he was no longer at the mercy of a local judge and jury; he could take his case into a United States district court. For interstate commerce and general business transactions, therefore, the federal judicial system was no less important than the United States Bank.

With the rise of party conflicts, the significance of the federal judiciary for the Union increased. Federal judges held office for life and could not be ousted except by impeachment. Presidents and members of Congress could come and go. Federal judges could remain on the bench throughout their lifetimes. Nobody understood this better than John Adams. Just before he left the White House in 1801, Adams made John Marshall, of Virginia, Chief Justice of the United States, and also appointed judges to the new circuit courts which Congress had just created. For about thirty-five years, until after Jefferson, Madison, and Monroe were all dead, Marshall kept at his post. A fervent advocate of a strong national Union from the days when he had fought for independence on the battlefield, Marshall welcomed the opportunity to make his views of the Constitution prevail in law. In case after case he declared acts of state legislatures null and void, as contrary to the Constitution. With the same firmness he upheld the power of Congress to enact laws broadly conceived in the general interest of the United States.

The national program of domestic measures, instituted under Washington and continued under Adams, was thoroughgoing. It was designed to, and did, strike deeply into the life, industry, habits, and sentiments of the American people. It set precedents for ages to come. All this it would have done, if Europe had remained at peace and American foreign relations had been undisturbed. But agitations in the United States over the French Revolution and war in Europe beat against the domestic policies of Washington's first administration. They broke in with such force that he and his successors were compelled to develop, also, a program of actions coming under the head of foreign policy.

A few weeks after Washington was inaugurated in 1789, the once powerful French monarchy began to crumble, revealing its decrepitude as popular demands for liberty and self-government increased in vehemence. At first it made concessions which seemed to promise a peaceful transition to a new political order. The authority of the French aristocracy and clergy was shattered; and the King, Louis XVI, was compelled to grant his subjects a constitution, including a national legislature, elected by the voters, and a bill of rights known as "The Rights of Man."

Soon reform merged into revolutionary violence. The constitution was overturned; a republic was proclaimed. The King was put to death in January 1793. In the autumn of the same year, the Queen, Marie Antoinette, was borne to the scaffold. One group of radicals after another seized power. A "reign of terror," accompanied by executions and a civil war, spread from Paris to the provinces. Before many years had passed the struggle closed in the military dictatorship of the warrior and demagogue, Napoleon Bonaparte, as First Consul, then as Consul for life, and finally as Emperor of the French in 1804.

The turmoil in France would have raised questions for the government of the United States to decide in dealing with the rulers who succeeded one another in that country, even if the revolution had not extended beyond French borders. But it spread far and wide beyond the Rhine; and, terrified by events in Paris, the despotic monarchs of Prussia and Austria started a war on revolutionary France, with the diplomatic support of the British government. In 1793 France declared war on Great Britain.

Then country after country in Europe became involved in the fight. Victorious French armies overran Italy, Belgium, Holland, Scandinavia, the western regions of Germany, and Spain, disseminating doctrines of "liberty" as they marched. For twenty-two years, with a brief intermission (1801–03), the wars of the great European Powers raged in nearly every part of the Continent, on the high seas, in Africa, even creating uproars as far away as India. Since the war between France and Britain on the oceans was a war on commerce, both belligerents preyed upon the ships and trade of American citizens, searching for munitions carriers and blockade runners.

As soon as the war broke out between France and Great Britain in 1793, President Washington faced a question that could not be avoided. In the treaty of 1778, under which France came to the aid of the American cause with money and arms, the United States promised to help France in defending her remaining American possessions if, at some time in the future, she again became involved in a war with the British. Recalling this pledge, the government of France in 1793 asked Washington for aid in its new war.

The dilemma was embarrassing for Washington. The promise had been made. There was no doubt about that, and American sympathies in general were on the side of the French. But getting into another war meant laying heavy taxes, raising armies, building war vessels, and increasing the already large national debt. Furthermore it might, Washington thought, completely disrupt the government just established under the Constitution. After consulting his advisers, including Hamilton and Jefferson, he refused to comply with French demands and proclaimed the neutrality of the United States in the European conflict.

More than this, President Washington decided to get on a better footing with the British government. Several sources of ill-feeling still lingered from the War of Independence. Americans had not paid all the debts they had incurred in dealings with British merchants in colonial times. Loyalists in America whose property had been confiscated still waited for the compensation that had been promised them. The British had not removed their troops from forts in the western part of the United States. And other matters interfered with the development of amicable relations between the two nations.

To promote this development, Washington sent John Jay to London, commissioned to make a treaty with Great Britain that would remove some of the worst irritations. Jay managed to wring very few concessions out of the British government. But Washington approved the treaty Jay had negotiated and persuaded the Senate to ratify it in 1795. The United States, he resolved, was to stay out of the war; to pursue the policy of neutrality toward all the belligerents.

The moment Washington and Hamilton began to frame and put into force domestic and foreign policies, they confronted critics and formidable opponents in Congress and outside. Working as individuals and in groups, some objectors picked at one policy and some at others. But practically all of Hamilton's program encountered protests from members of Congress, pamphleteers, and editors of newspapers. At firesides and in taverns knots of citizens debating his program expressed strong opinions for or against it. Even within Washington's Cabinet the conflict raged. Hamilton and Jefferson engaged in such fierce controversies over the proper course to pursue that Washington could not mollify them, hard though he tried. Within a few years the country was flaming with the polemics of a great dispute.

In a little while two well-knit political parties gave concentration to the scattered fire of the opposing forces. Supporters of Washington's administration, led by Hamilton, called themselves Federalists. Opponents, who at length rallied around Jefferson, were generally known as Anti-Federalists in the beginning—as mere oppositionists. Later they assumed the title of Republicans. In the House of Representatives, in the Senate, in the cities, and in the country districts far and wide, Federalists formed committees or caucuses for the purpose of uniting their forces. The Republicans did likewise. Thus party organizations cutting across state lines spread from New Hampshire to Georgia.

Each of the parties was mixed in membership. But Hamilton appealed particularly to the business interests—to holders of government securities, financiers, manufacturers, shipowners, and speculators in Western lands; and around him gathered advocates of strong and stable government. Since he was sympathetic with Great Britain and hostile to France after the revolution flared up in Paris and the European war opened, former Tories who had remained in America and were now American citizens flocked to his standard. In effect the Federalist party could lay claim to representing "the wealth and talents" of the conservative classes in the United States. "Your people," Hamilton was reported to have said, "is a great beast." In any event, he and Washington resented popular agitations at home, as they abhorred such agitation in France, and they thought that the "democratic societies" springing up in towns and country districts ought to be suppressed before they got out of bounds.

For the agricultural interests, especially for the small farmers who owned and tilled their lands themselves, Jefferson became the prime spokesman—leader of the Republican party. Freehold farmers, he declared, were the best and truest support for republican government. He charged Hamilton and his close friends with being monarchists and British sympathizers. He applauded the rights of man proclaimed by the French reformers and rejoiced in their efforts to erect a republic in France. To his partisans Jefferson, author of the Declaration of Independence, was the American Revolution incarnate—the foe of monarchy and the whole British social system in peace and war. After the French Revolution ended in the Napoleonic dictatorship, Jefferson's ardor for France cooled, but his dislike of British policies and actions long remained intense. He stood like a rock for "the people," against "rich and well-born" aristocrats and "monocrats."

By the time the election of 1796 approached, the Republicans were ready for a campaign to get possession of the government. Distressed by attacks on his policies and pained by assaults on his character despite his long public service, Washington refused to run for a third term as President. Rejecting every plea that he stand again for election, he wrote a farewell message to all his countrymen warning them against party passions at home and against becoming involved in the frequent quarrels, combinations, and collisions of European friendships and enmities.

Unable to persuade Washington to lead them again, the Federalists turned to John Adams, the Vice-President, whose conservatism they approved. Yet Adams was no abject disciple of Hamilton, and the Federalists found it hard to forgive his independence in politics. Though the Revolutionary generation respected his talents, his fidelity to the patriot cause, and his important services, he was not a magnetic figure for a popular campaign.

Yet the Republicans were not strong enough to defeat Adams, although they gave him and his party a fright. When the electoral votes were counted, it was found that Adams had seventy-one and Jefferson had sixty-eight. The narrow victory added nothing to Adams' popularity and his conduct as President reduced it. He did his best to win public favor, but his four years in office were full of troubles and his best was not enough to make him a national hero.

The financial and commercial policies started by Hamilton were continued by President Adams. With regard to Great Britain, he maintained the sympathetic neutrality initiated by Washington. In the case of France, however, affairs were more complicated. The French government in power when Adams became President had denounced President Washington for refusing to aid France in the war against Great Britain and for making terms with the British government in the Jay Treaty. To put it mildly, the relations of France and the United States were strained.

The first efforts of President Adams to ease the strain with France eventuated in an undeclared war between the two nations. In his desire to resolve the difficulties, he sent three envoys to Paris empowered to reach a settlement with the French government. Their reception was frigid. Indeed French agents demanded an apology from the United States, a loan of money, and a bribe to be paid to members of their government.

Exceedingly indignant when he heard about the chilly reception of the American mission and the demand for a bribe, Adams, naming the French agents only as X, Y, Z, reported the affair to Congress and the public. The public response was a cry that ran throughout the United States: "Millions for defense, but not one cent for tribute!" Washington was summoned from his plantation to take charge of the armed forces again. Fighting started at sea. With alacrity Federalists gave their support to Adams while Republicans moderated their criticisms of him. For a moment his leadership seemed to be gaining popularity. Then suddenly in 1799, Bonaparte, who had become dictator in France, proposed a peace with the United States on fair terms and Adams accepted it. Now the war excitement died away and with its disappearance attacks on the Adams administration were renewed.

Bent on suppressing their opponents and keeping power if they could, Federalist leaders rushed through Congress, in 1798, two laws directed to those ends.

The first, the Alien Act, gave the President power for two years to expel from the country any alien whom he might deem "dangerous to the peace and safety of the United States." Although Adams did not deport a single person under the act, the mere passage of the law aroused the ire of many Americans as a violation of liberty. Moreover it frightened unnaturalized Irish and French persons in America, who did not like the foreign policy that favored Great Britain.

The second measure, the Sedition Act, placed heavy penalties on every person, alien or citizen, found guilty of trying to stir up "sedition" or who wrote or published anything "false, scandalous, or malicious" against either house of Congress, the President, or the government. This act, opponents contended, transgressed the first amendment to the Constitution forbidding Congress to make any law abridging freedom of speech or of the press. But the Federalists, in power, brushed aside all objections; and under the Sedition Act several Republican writers and publishers were indicted, fined, or imprisoned for criticizing the President and his administration.

These two acts, instead of fastening the grip of the Federalists on the government, laid them open to attacks in the name of American liberty. Republicans interpreted the conduct of the Federalists as revealing their true colors—their liking for arbitrary government. Back in Washington's second administration that kind of "high-toned" government had been displayed when disorders, described as the "Whisky Rebellion," had occurred during efforts to collect an excise tax on whisky in 1794.

On that occasion Washington and Hamilton had called out 13,-000 militiamen to overcome a few rioters. In his excitement over the riots, Washington had ascribed them to subversive agitations and had privately expressed his belief that the young "Democratic Societies" should be exterminated.

Shocked by the attitude of the government in that affair, Jefferson had helped to turn Washington and his Federalist advisers away from that aggression against civil liberties. Now, four years later, the passage of the Sedition Act confirmed Jefferson's suspicion that Federalists were resolved to destroy critics by fine and imprisonment, after the fashion of Old World despots.

Adopting underground political tactics, Jefferson wrote an indictment of the Alien and Sedition Acts which was sent quietly to a friend in the state of Kentucky, recently admitted to the Union. On the basis of this document the Kentucky legislature formulated and passed, in 1798, a set of resolutions branding the acts as contrary to the Constitution, as null and void. It declared that, when the federal government exceeded its powers, the states had a right to interpose; and it called upon other states to join in demanding a repeal of the laws in question. Receiving little aid and comfort from other states, the Kentucky legislature then passed, in 1799, a second set of resolutions proclaiming the right of states to nullify "unconstitutional" acts of Congress.

Rejecting the doctrine of nullification as likely to endanger the Union, James Madison, now affiliated with the Republican party, induced the legislature of Virginia to pass milder resolutions while joining in the protest against the objectionable acts. In fact Jefferson himself later avowed that he had no intention at the time of encouraging action that might lead to a dissolution of the bonds established by the Constitution. Both he and Madison regarded their tactics as only calculated to fan discontent with the Alien and Sedition Acts and weaken the hold of the sponsors, the Federalists, on the nation.

Just how much effect the arguments over the Alien and Sedition Acts had on the voters cannot be determined precisely. Certainly they contributed little or nothing to the popularity of the Federalist party. Nor did they assure an easy triumph for the Republican party in the ensuing election of 1800. In fact, though the political campaign was bitterly waged, the shift of a few votes in New York, where Aaron Burr was especially strong, would have given John Adams a second term as President. Sixty-five votes were cast for Adams, seventy-three for Jefferson, and seventy-three for Burr.

The tie between Jefferson and Burr threw the election into the House of Representatives as provided by the Constitution in such cases. Only with the aid of Federalists in that House was the deadlock resolved in favor of Jefferson. Although Jefferson called his victory a "revolution," the Federalists were still powerful in Congress and he had to walk warily in exercising his powers as Chief Executive.

On March 4, 1801, when John Adams had left the White House

in a huff over his defeat, Thomas Jefferson took the oath of office as President. In his inaugural address he spoke softly if positively. Federalists had called him an atheist, a Jacobin, the foe of order and property; but from start to finish he refrained from retaliation in abusive epithets and was conciliatory. We are all Republicans, he said at his inauguration; we are all Federalists; the majority has expressed its will at the polls according to the forms of the Constitution and must be obeyed; for resort to the sword, the parent of despotism, is the only alternative to such obedience. But the minority, he proceeded, has its rights and they must be respected. If any citizen would change our form of government, Jefferson pleaded, let him be heard and let truth combat his error. The rights and liberties guaranteed by the Constitution, he insisted, are to be preserved; the Union is to be strong and the states protected in their rightful powers.

Not even Washington had expressed a greater attachment to the nation and its unity under the Constitution than was displayed on that occasion by the author of the Kentucky Resolutions. Despite his talk about his "revolution," Jefferson made no demand for an overthrow of the financial and foreign policies initiated by Washington and Hamilton.

Jefferson had made several pledges, however, in the name of his party, and they were redeemed. The Sedition Act was allowed to expire; men imprisoned under it were released; and the fines collected were repaid. The tax on whisky, which had stirred farmers to revolt, was repealed. Reductions were made in outlays for the Army, the Navy, and federal officers. Judge Samuel Chase, who had denounced Republicans from the bench, was impeached by the House of Representatives and only the Federalists in the higher court, the Senate, saved him from conviction. The formalities and ceremonials observed by Washington and Adams were modified. Like the British king who delivered his speech from the throne to Parliament, they had read their messages to Congress in person. Jefferson quit the practice and sent his message to the two houses in written form.

While he was operating merely as a critic of the Federalists, Jefferson had adhered to the view that the government of the Union was limited to the exercise of specific powers to be literally, or narrowly, construed. Nevertheless, during his eight years as President he did and approved many things not specifically mentioned in the Constitution, thus taking in fact a broad view of the document.

The Constitution, for instance, did not, in exact words, empower the United States to acquire more territory. Yet Jefferson bought from Napoleon in 1803 the vast Louisiana Territory for $15,000,000, and Congress, on his insistence, sanctioned the purchase. By this single stroke, more than doubling the domain of the United States, Jefferson helped to assure the strength and perpetuity of the Union. Perhaps he accomplished as much in that direction as Washington and Hamilton had achieved by the financial and banking measures that he had once opposed.

The Constitution had said nothing about the power of the federal government to build national highways or canals or improve harbors or found a national university. Nevertheless in Jefferson's first administration Congress appropriated part of the money received from the sale of public lands to the construction of highways into the West. In this way it provided for the building of the Cumberland Road, or national highway, extending from the edge of Maryland through Pennsylvania, Ohio, Indiana, and Illinois, into Missouri. With Jefferson's approval, his Secretary of the Treasury, Albert Gallatin, a statesman of broad outlook, made grand plans for a national network of river, harbor, and canal improvements. Following Washington's example, Jefferson recommended to Congress the creation of a national university. He likewise approved the idea of using surplus revenues of the government to promote the interests of commerce, industry, agriculture, and education, even if a constitutional amendment should be needed to accomplish such national purposes.

In foreign affairs Jefferson continued the general policy framed by Washington; and in his efforts to keep the United States out of the European war he interpreted the Constitution liberally. British naval officers were searching and seizing American merchant ships on the high seas at their pleasure and often carrying off sailors alleged to be British subjects. The French navy was likewise preying on American commerce. From year to year British and French actions grew more and more aggressive until at length nearly all American ships bound to and from Europe were liable to be seized by the one belligerent or the other. In vain did Jefferson assert and insist that American rights on the seas must be observed.

Driven into a dilemma by his resolve to avoid getting into war, Jefferson proposed and Congress approved, in 1807, an embargo forbidding all ships to leave American ports except with the President's permission. By this measure, by cutting off all their American supplies, he thought the British or the French or both might be forced to respect American commercial rights. The Constitution empowered Congress to "regulate" foreign commerce; now Congress had prohibited it altogether on the high seas. Yet this measure failed to bring the British and the French to terms, while it infuriated American merchants and shippers. In response to outcries against it, Congress substituted in 1809 a Non-Intercourse Act directed against Great Britain and France alone. It too was more than a mere "regulation" of commerce but Jefferson supported it in his anxiety to uphold American rights and at the same time keep the United States out of the war.

Notwithstanding the dissatisfaction over his handling of foreign relations, Jefferson could have had a third term if he had so desired. In his second campaign, of 1804, he had carried every state in the Union, except Delaware, Maryland, and Connecticut, against his Federalist opponent, Charles C. Pinckney. If his popularity had somewhat diminished by 1808, it was still very great. Instead of playing upon it, however, Jefferson voluntarily promoted the election of his Secretary of State, James Madison, in whom he had implicit confidence. He declared that two terms were enough; that repeated re-elections of a President might lead to election for life. Thus he set a tradition inimical to a third term for anybody.

Madison was victorious in the campaign and then he had to face the preservation of peace which Jefferson had entrusted to him. But the rise in Congress of a war party, called "War Hawks," led by John C. Calhoun, of South Carolina, and Henry Clay, of Kentucky, both young men of the post-Revolutionary generation, took the issue out of his hands. Some members of the war party were for war on Great Britain; others for war on France; and almost a majority for war on both countries.

Nominally the quarrel with Britain was over her preying on American commerce, her seizures of American sailors, and her support of restless Indians on the northwest frontiers of the United States. In large part war actually grew out of a resolve of Southern politicians to conquer Florida and of Western politicians to subdue and annex Canada. At all events, in June 1812 Congress declared war on Great Britain, and Madison set forth the war aims mainly in commercial terms, saying nothing about either Florida or Canada.

For more than two years the war was waged on land and sea. American sailors and soldiers proved their valor by many ex-

THE UNITED STATES IN 1812

ploits—under Oliver Perry on Lake Erie, under Thomas Macdonough on Lake Champlain, under Andrew Jackson at New Orleans, for example. Even so, the invasion of Canada was a failure; whereas the British invaded the United States and applied the torch to public buildings in Washington.

To make matters worse for Madison, the war was decidedly unpopular in the Northeast where, presumably, a war proclaimed in behalf of free commerce would have been welcomed. In the House of Representatives, Daniel Webster, of Massachusetts, denounced the draft of men as unconstitutional. Federalists decried the conflict as merely "Mr. Madison's war." The governor of Connecticut refused to obey the President's call for troops and the Connecticut assembly declared the state to be "free, sovereign and independent." A convention of delegates from various parts of New England, assembled in Hartford in October 1814, adopted resolutions akin in spirit, if not in letter, to those put forth by Kentucky and Virginia in 1798.

In the meantime negotiations for peace with Great Britain were proceeding at Ghent. On Christmas Eve, 1814, a few days before Jackson's victory at New Orleans, the draft of the treaty of peace was signed in Ghent. It contained not a word about British seizure of American sailors, about British preying on American trade, about British searching of American ships, or British support of Indians on the frontier. But when the news of the peace arrived early in 1815, Americans, passing "from gloom to glory," shouted with joy, rang bells, and held holiday parades.

None of the war aims was realized, neither those publicly announced by President Madison nor those unofficially cherished by the "War Hawks." Moreover Madison and his fellow Republicans were in "a sea of troubles" over domestic problems in the aftermath of war. The war had cost a huge sum of money and business was badly deranged. Hamilton's big national debt had been condemned by Republicans; now they confronted a bigger debt. Even the currency was in disorder, the dollar fluctuating violently in value. Manufacturers who had built up industries to furnish the armies with munitions and other supplies clamored for protection against the inrush of cheap British goods. Soon veterans by the thousands were demanding pensions for their services. From day to day the perplexities of the Republicans increased.

In their dilemma the Republicans resorted to the very measures of Alexander Hamilton, which they had so long assailed. His

United States Bank had perished when its charter expired in 1811; they established a second United States Bank on the principles of the old one. They funded the scattered government debts into a consolidated debt, larger than the debt they had once condemned. Hamilton had fostered a tariff designed to protect American manufacturers. In 1816 the Republicans passed a tariff measure outstripping in its high protectionism the tariff projects of Washington and Hamilton. Even Jefferson, the champion of agricultural interests, endorsed protectionism, thus joining hands with Calhoun and Clay. In 1819 the first great business panic in the history of modern industrialism burst upon the country, and the Republicans did not know what to do about that.

President Madison closed his second term in 1817 with relief at the thought of turning the office of Chief Executive over to someone else. He proposed James Monroe as his successor and his choice was approved by his party. In the election of 1816 the Republicans had a landslide, the Federalists carrying only three states. Some Federalists had lost ground on account of their opposition to the war. Other Federalists refrained from activity in the campaign in view of the fact that the Republican party had put their program and their principles into effect. For a time the two-party system appeared to be at an end—in the "era of good feeling." Yet a new party was really coming into existence. Monroe was re-elected in 1820 but that was the last act in the short-lived, one-party play.

Three great measures of Monroe's administrations added to the strength of the Union and the feeling of attachment to it. In adopting them Monroe went counter to his former views. He had opposed the ratification of the Constitution in 1788 and had sided with Jefferson in his strict interpretation of that document. But on these three measures Monroe took a broad view of the Constitution—as Jefferson had done on many occasions during his tenure as President. Although he did not renew Jefferson's proposal for a national university, he abandoned his strict constructionism when he had to deal with issues involving the fortunes of the nation.

Among the first problems before President Monroe was that of the Floridas, East and West, which Great Britain had given back to Spain in 1783. Owing to the uncertainties of the Florida boundaries, the United States had some claims to West Florida. Moreover, the swamps of the Floridas were the hiding places of Indian marauders who emerged from time to time to harass American settlements. Ordered by Monroe, after one of these attacks, to pursue a band of Indian raiders to their retreat, General Andrew Jackson marched after them into East Florida, where he did more than fight them; he took possession of the region. Now the Spanish King, who claimed the ownership of this coveted territory, faced what is called in diplomacy a *fait accompli*—a dead certain fact; namely, occupation by Americans.

Caught in a jam, the King ceded his Florida land to the United States in 1819, in exchange for not more than $5,000,000, to be paid to American citizens who had damage claims against his government. As Jefferson had done on the constitutional issue, President Monroe simply overlooked the question as to whether the government of the United States had any express power under the Constitution to buy more territory. In this instance "strict construction" was not allowed to interfere with the transaction.

The second outstanding measure of Monroe's administration also involved an interpretation of the Constitution. Under its power to make "all needful rules and regulations" respecting territory belonging to the United States, could Congress lawfully exclude slavery from such territory? That subject was not mentioned in the document, but it was squarely raised in 1818–20 during a dispute over the admission of Missouri to the Union as a slave state. By that time Northern states had abolished slavery within their borders, or had provided for gradual abolition, and anti-slavery sentiment was growing insistent in the country.

Opposition to the admission of another slave state was outspoken in Congress and a deadlock occurred on the issue. After many angry words had been uttered, the standstill was broken by a compromise: Missouri was to be admitted with slavery, and the balance of political power maintained by the admission of Maine as a free state. In addition, as a part of the compromise, slavery was to be prohibited in the rest of the Louisiana Territory north of the line 36° 30'.

On the one side it was claimed that Congress had no authority to prohibit slavery in this territory. On the other, attention was called to the fact that the Northwest Ordinance, adopted in 1787 and ratified by Congress in 1789, had excluded slavery from the Northwest Territory; so it was argued that Congress could lawfully do this under the Constitution.

While the constitutional point was being argued, President

Monroe laid it before members of his Cabinet. They agreed that Congress could prohibit slavery in the territories; and, with their approval, he signed the bill on March 6, 1820, dedicating the major part of the Louisiana Territory to freedom.

Following Washington's example, President Monroe, in 1823, formulated a momentous declaration of foreign policy for the United States—the third notable measure of his administrations. Recently Spain's colonies in the New World had nearly all declared their independence, and President Monroe, like other Americans, was troubled in mind lest European monarchs help the Spanish King in his efforts to recover control over them. From such schemes Great Britain, however, held aloof. British merchants, winning a profitable trade in Latin America, were reluctant to see Spain's commercial monopoly restored. Fully appreciating their situation, the British government proposed to the minister of the United States in London that the two countries join in upholding the independence of the Latin American republics.

On receipt of the news President Monroe turned to Jefferson, Madison, and John Quincy Adams, the Secretary of State, for advice. They all agreed on the desirability of backing up the freedom of the Latin American republics. Jefferson welcomed the assistance of Great Britain in such a project—one so clearly advantageous for the security of the United States in the Western Hemisphere. With the aid of Adams, Monroe framed a message on the question and sent it to Congress in December 1823.

In this message, which was to bear his name in coming times as the Monroe Doctrine, the President made four clear-cut assertions. First, the United States did not propose to interfere with any colonies still owned by European Powers in the New World. Second, any effort on the part of monarchs in Europe "to extend their system to any portion of this hemisphere" would be regarded as "dangerous to our peace and safety." Third, the attempt of a European government to oppress or control colonies that had declared their independence would be viewed as showing "an unfriendly disposition toward the United States."

With reference to a claim to a part of the Pacific coast which the Czar of Russia had lately put forward, Monroe made the fourth assertion: "The American continents . . . are henceforth not to be considered as subjects for future colonization by any European powers." While proclaiming freedom for the Western Hemisphere, however, he informed European governments that in turn the United States would not interfere in European affairs.

Coupled with Washington's Farewell Address to the nation, the Monroe Doctrine was long a main "cornerstone" of American foreign policy. Thus the last, as well as the first, of the Presidents belonging to the Revolutionary generation fortified the independence of the United States and the security of the Republic.

CHAPTER XII

Expansion to the Pacific

It took American people one hundred and seventy-five years to build up and achieve independence for thirteen colonies with about three million inhabitants. In less than one third that span of years seven new states were established in the region immediately westward and occupied by a population larger than that of the whole United States when the census of 1790 was taken. In less than half that number of years five additional states were formed in the Louisiana Territory still further west, Texas was brought into the Union, a vast area to the southwest wrested from Mexico, and California admitted to statehood.

Events in this westward expansion followed one another in no regular order. For example, when the Louisiana Territory was acquired in 1803, Indiana and Illinois, to the east of the Mississippi, had only a few inhabitants. Louisiana and Missouri, in the Louisiana Territory, reached statehood before Michigan. Texas was admitted to the Union three years before Wisconsin; and Wisconsin had been a state only two years when California, on the Pacific coast, became a full-fledged member of the federation. But for the sake of convenience, the expansion to the West may be treated in three stages: settlement of the region between the old seaboard states and the Mississippi River; exploration and settlement in the Louisiana Territory; and occupation of the far Southwest.

When independence was won several Eastern states had claims to territory in the region stretching westward to the Mississippi —claims based on royal charters and colonial grants. But by 1786

they had all surrendered to the Union their rights in the territory north of the Ohio. In a short time the territories south of the Ohio were separated from the seaboard claimants—Virginia, North Carolina, South Carolina, and Georgia. Thus the Western lands were cut loose from the overlordship of individual states, put into a national pool, and thrown open for settlement to emigrants from all parts of the seaboard region and also from the Old World.

More than this, it was decided that settlers on the Western lands were not to be held permanently under the dominance of the United States Government. They were to be allowed, subject to certain rules, to form governments in their respective territories, draw up constitutions of their own, and at length, as states, join the Union as partners in every respect equal to the thirteen original states. Thus a promise of self-government preceded the great westward migration.

Both in character of settlement and in form of government, therefore, the occupation and management of the region westward to the Mississippi diverged fundamentally from that process in colonial times on the seaboard. The authority in general charge of the operations was at first the old Congress under the Articles of Confederation and then the new government established under the Constitution of 1787. It was an American and a republican government, not a British monarchy located in distant London. No companies chartered by the British Crown, such as the Virginia Company, no great proprietors holding patents from the Crown, such as Lord Baltimore or William Penn, got permanent possession of immense areas in this Western region. Huge blocks of land, it is true, were granted to companies of American citizens; but no company had the right to govern as well as own the district assigned to it, or to hold the district indefinitely as a semi-feudal principality. A few American companies which acquired large holdings did assist in outfitting and transporting emigrants to the West; but in the main the work of occupation was effected by individuals, families, and small groups of pioneers, on their own initiative.

The spirit of the new enterprise in land settlement appeared in the Northwest Ordinance, adopted in 1787 by the old Congress under the Articles of Confederation and continued in force by the first Congress under the Constitution. This ordinance applied to the territory north of the Ohio River. Other congressional acts provided for official surveys of the Northwest Territory. By such surveys the region was laid out into townships each six miles square, and each township was subdivided into sections, each containing 640 acres, readily divisible into half sections, quarter sections, and even a smaller acreage. The surveys furnished definite maps and facilitated the location and purchase of lands. At first the price of land was fixed at two dollars an acre, but this was cut in 1820 to one dollar and a quarter.

The Northwest Ordinance itself made provision for temporary territorial government under governors chosen first by the Congress and later by the President of the United States. As soon as there were 5000 free male adults in a particular territory they could establish a local legislature under the supervision of the federal governor. A territorial government so formed consisted of the federal governor, federal judges, a legislative council, and a house of representatives. When a territory acquired 60,000 free residents its people were entitled to a constitution of their own making and to be admitted to the Union "on an equal footing with the original states, in all respects whatever."

The Northwest Ordinance contained more than a plan of government. It stipulated that religious freedom should prevail throughout the region, that the inhabitants should enjoy the right of trial by jury, and that other forms of liberty should be observed. It declared that "schools and the means of education shall forever be encouraged." And this declaration was more than a verbal pledge. Land laws, already passed in connection with the surveys, set aside a section of land in every township to be devoted to the support of schools. A crowning provision of the ordinance, so vital to the growth of liberty, was the article which read: "There shall be neither slavery nor involuntary servitude in the said [Northwest] territory, otherwise than in the punishment of crimes, whereof the party shall have been duly convicted."

Under the generous provisions of the ordinance, pioneers poured into the Northwest Territory. One stream sprang from the South, especially from Virginia, North Carolina, and Kentucky, and flowed into the southern counties of Ohio, Indiana, and Illinois. Other streams sprang from Pennsylvania, New York, and New England. With the westward-moving Americans were mingled newcomers from the Old World—British, Germans, Swiss, and immigrants of other nationalities. Nearly all the families quickly settled down to tilling lands which they had bought either outright or on installments. They built log cabins and cottages, cleared the forests, and prepared fields for crops.

Clues to the swiftness of this movement and the scale of the settlement can be gleaned from the following table showing the dates on which states were admitted to the Union, and the population in the year 1820:

Admission to Union	Population 1820
1803—Ohio	581,400
1816—Indiana	147,100
1818—Illinois	55,200
1837—Michigan	8,800
1848—Wisconsin	

The occupation of the Western territory south of the Ohio River differed in several respects from that of the Northwest. Long before the close of the eighteenth century the Kentucky region of western Virginia was dotted with settlements. By 1792 it had more inhabitants than either Delaware or Rhode Island. Separating itself from Virginia in that year, Kentucky entered the Union as an equal state, with the full consent of Virginia. The Tennessee region, to which North Carolina had claims lasting from the colonial era, was ceded to the Union by the parent state; and for a little while was governed as a territory of the United States. But in 1795, when a census showed that Tennessee had more than 60,000 inhabitants, a local constitution was drafted and the following year, in 1796, Tennessee became a state in the Union.

In regions surrendered by South Carolina and Georgia the remainder of the Southern land was organized under the acts of Congress as a territory of the United States. In 1817 this territory was divided. The western part was admitted to the Union as the state of Mississippi. The eastern part, after two years of territorial status, was given statehood as Alabama.

By 1819 all the divisions of the territory between the original seaboard states and the Mississippi River, except the districts of Michigan and Wisconsin in the north central part, had become equal partners in the Union, as states with their own constitutions. To the list was added, in 1845, the state of Florida in territory acquired from Spain in 1819.

In the meantime expansion beyond the Mississippi was under way. Shortly after Jefferson was inaugurated President in 1801 news reached him that Spain had ceded to France the huge Louisiana Territory extending from the Mississippi River to the Far West. American pioneers over the Appalachians now feared that

Napoleon, the head of the French government, would close New Orleans to their shipment of grain and other farm produce by water to the Eastern seaboard and to the Old World. So they urged Jefferson to prevent that misfortune, and he sent a special agent to France with a commission to buy New Orleans and West Florida if possible.

Before the agent arrived Napoleon had concluded that he might lose his American possessions in a war with Great Britain, and had informed the American minister at Paris that he would sell the whole territory to the United States for $15,000,000, from which certain American claims against France could be deducted. Surprised at the size of the territory offered so cheaply, Jefferson at first hesitated. But at length the purchase was completed in 1803, despite laments from Federalists on the Atlantic coast. Thus at one stroke and without warfare the territory of the United States was more than doubled, though the boundaries of the Louisiana Purchase were vague.

To collect information on the new territory, Jefferson sponsored an expedition headed by Meriwether Lewis and William Clark to explore it, find an overland route to the Pacific, and report on its resources. Under their leadership a party of hardy adventurers was formed near St. Louis. Special boats were built and a traveling outfit was assembled. On May 14, 1804, they set out on the Missouri River for the Northwest. A year later they reached the great falls of the Missouri in Montana. From that point they made their hazardous way across the mountains, with the guidance in part of an Indian woman named Sacawajea. Over the mountains they arrived at the headwaters of the Columbia River, where they built new boats, embarked on the river, and floated swiftly to the Pacific Ocean, reaching their goal in November 1805.

Having blazed the way, the explorers were able to make the return trip more quickly, and in less than a year they were safely back at St. Louis, having completed a long and dangerous journey of about eight thousand miles in two years and four months. From the records kept by Lewis and Clark a report was soon compiled and published. As a result Americans who felt cramped in the East had at their command considerable knowledge of the newest West and could make plans for going where there was more elbow room.

In the same year that Lewis and Clark started from St. Louis on their journey, Zebulon Pike, leading another party, explored the headwaters of the Mississippi. When Pike had finished that

EXPLORATIONS OF LEWIS AND CLARK AND ZEBULON PIKE IN THE FAR WEST task he was sent on an expedition into the region west and south of St. Louis. He kept on his way until he came to the mountain now known as Pike's Peak in the Rockies. Shortly afterward he turned south and journeyed in that direction until he reached the Rio Grande. Finding himself then in territory occupied by Spaniards, Pike retraced his steps. But in 1810 he published reports on the regions he had covered and persons inclined to adventure in the Southwest thus had access to more information of many kinds about that frontier.

At the time of the Louisiana Purchase the white population of the territory was estimated at figures running from 50,000 to 80,000. The great majority of the inhabitants were French—mainly descendants of the French pioneers who had long before settled at important trading centers, particularly at St. Louis and New Orleans, under the King of France. Among them were many Spanish residents, who had moved up from Spanish territories or from Spain itself, after Louisiana had been turned over to the Spanish King in 1763, at the close of the Seven Years' War. Here and there were also Americans who had crossed the Mississippi even while the west bank was under a foreign flag.

To all the inhabitants of the Louisiana Territory, however, were guaranteed by the treaty of cession "all the rights, advantages, and immunities of citizens of the United States." By act of Congress the territory was divided into two districts later known as the territory of Louisiana and the territory of Missouri.

The more thickly populated region to the south was granted statehood as Louisiana in 1812. As Americans poured across the river into the Missouri district to the north, they began to seek admission to the Union. But a national agitation over slavery delayed admission. In 1819 there were twenty-two states in the Union— half of them slave states and half committed to freedom. If Missouri came in with slavery the balance of power in the Senate of the United States would be upset.

In the North, anti-slavery sentiment was growing. Slavery had been abolished or was rapidly on the way to extinction in all the original states north of Delaware. Ohio, Indiana, and Illinois were free states as required by the Northwest Ordinance. In the House of Representatives, based on population, counting three fifths of the slaves, the strength of the free states was rapidly increasing.

On the other hand, with the spread of cotton planting, proslavery sentiment was becoming stronger in the South. Old Southern statesmen, such as Washington, Jefferson, and George Mason, had looked upon slavery as an evil and hoped that in time it could be uprooted. But a new generation of Southerners was beginning to regard slavery as good for both whites and blacks, and to speak of it as a permanent institution to be extended wherever climate and soil were suitable. In these circumstances the admission of Missouri as a slave state was hotly opposed in Congress by Northern men and championed with no less heat by Southern men.

As we have seen, a compromise was reached. Under a congressional act of 1820 Missouri was admitted with slavery; but it was balanced by the admission of Maine, a free state, formerly a part of Massachusetts, now given a separate status by mutual consent. Accompanying this settlement was another compromise destined to be the subject of political agitation in years to come. Slavery was prohibited "forever" in all the territory ceded by France to the United States, under the name of Louisiana, lying north of 36° 30' north latitude, except Missouri. As to slavery in the rest of that territory, nothing was said in the law; silence merely gave consent to its existence in that region.

Another balancing act was performed in 1836. The territory of Arkansas, definitely laid out at the time of the Missouri Compromise, had been filling up with pioneers, many of them planters with their slaves, and others working farmers. By 1836 the Arkansas settlers numbered more than 47,000 and, in the customary way of Americans from the early days of colonization on the seaboard, they demanded self-government. Acceding to their demand, Congress admitted Arkansas to the Union as a slave state, with the provision that the sixteenth section of land in every township be set aside for the support of schools. Far to the northeast, the people of Michigan, with equal zeal, were putting forth their claims to greater autonomy; and the following year, 1837, they entered the Union as a free state. The voting power of slave-owning planters in the Louisiana Territory was thus offset by the voting power of free farmers in the Northwest Territory.

Long before Arkansas and Michigan were "balanced" in the Union, farmers from New England, New York, Ohio, and other Eastern states were moving in long wagon trains into the region known as Iowa. There they staked out for themselves freehold farms in every direction. Three prosperous trading centers sprang up on the Mississippi: Dubuque, Davenport, and Burlington. Academies and colleges were established. In 1846 Iowa won self-government as the fourth state to be erected in the Louisiana Territory, balancing Florida (1845). The fifth state to be carved out of Jefferson's great land purchase was Minnesota, admitted in 1858, without slavery.

☆

Meanwhile, at the extreme western end of the Louisiana Purchase—in the Oregon country—fur traders, missionaries, and farmers from the East were building a new free colony, in the American style. In 1843 Oregon settlers, feeling the need of mutual aid, held a meeting at Champoeg and, after listening to a Fourth of July oration, drew up a compact for governing themselves "until such time as the United States of America extend their jurisdiction over us."

As a matter of fact the United States Government had been in trouble over Oregon and was still in trouble. The northern boundary of the country was vague. Under the obscure terms of the Louisiana Purchase and rights of exploration, the United States claimed all the territory up to the line of 54° 40′ north latitude—to the borders of the Russian territory of Alaska. But that claim was stoutly contested by the government of Great Britain, and in 1818 the two governments made a kind of truce providing for temporary joint occupation. This agreement was renewed in 1827 for an indefinite period. Yet it was unsatisfactory to British as well as American fur traders; and settlers insisted that an end be put to joint occupation by drawing a definite boundary line between the British and the American parts.

For years neither side would surrender to this demand. In the presidential campaign of 1844 the Democrats declared for "Fifty-four Forty or Fight"; that is, announced that they would, if necessary, wage war rather than give up the old claim. No fighting ensued, however. The victorious candidate of the Democrats, James K. Polk, had not been long in the office of President when he made, in 1846, a treaty with Great Britain fixing the Oregon boundary at the forty-ninth parallel, not the fifty-fourth. In 1859 the southern part of the Oregon country, the most thickly settled, was admitted to the Union as the sixth state in the Western territory. Many other sections in that territory were also filling up with settlers, and meanwhile the United States had entered upon the third phase of its westward expansion—into the far Southwest.

☆

Under the terms of the purchase from France the boundaries of the Louisiana Territory in the Southwest were also indefinite. At first the United States, on good grounds as later evidence proved, claimed that the boundary ran from near the mouth of the Rio Grande on the Gulf of Mexico in a northerly direction along the course of that river to about the forty-second parallel of north latitude, and thence west to the Pacific Ocean. Spain rejected this claim as encroaching upon her territory, and after long negotiations the boundary was fixed, in 1819, in such a way as to cut off a part of the Louisiana Territory in the Southwest.

The line as then defined started on the gulf at the western border of the state of Louisiana, ran northward along that border, and thence northwesterly and westerly in such a fashion as to leave the Texas country and adjoining regions in the hands of Spain. It was in connection with this settlement of 1819 that the Spanish King ceded to the United States all his claims to the territory east of the Mississippi, known as East and West Florida.

For years before the signing of the treaty of 1819 that established the new boundary for the Louisiana Territory, Spain had been involved in struggles with revolutionists in Mexico; and two years later, in 1821, the last Spanish viceroy to Mexico was forced to recognize the independence of that country. Consequently it was the republic of Mexico, now in the disorders of revolution, with which the United States had to deal in the Southwest.

From the border of Louisiana to the Pacific, especially in the region later known as New Mexico and California, Spanish settlements and missions had been established. But the Southwest as a whole was sparsely settled. In 1821 it was estimated that, excluding the Indians, there were about 4000 Mexicans or Spanish in the Texas country, not more than 3000 or 4000 in Upper California, and perhaps 15,000 or 20,000 in the vast intervening area. The size of the Indian population was unknown, but, unlike that of Mexico proper, it was small and thinly dispersed. In other words, the great Southwest was mostly unoccupied and there were no signs that colonists from Mexico, owner of the territory, would soon, if ever, people that region.

To encourage the settlement of this territory by Americans and other alien immigrants, the government of Mexico granted large blocks of land to contractors who would bring in colonists. In 1820, for example, it arranged with Moses Austin, of Connecticut, to found an American settlement near Bexar, in Texas, and the undertaking was carried out by his son, Stephen F. Austin. By 1830 at least 20,000 American farmers, planters, and traders had established themselves in Texas and more were on the way.

Then, frightened by the deluge, Mexico abandoned the policy of granting land to aliens, declared invalid many grants already in effect, abolished slavery, and otherwise sought to check immigration.

Besides being futile, these actions irritated the Americans already in Texas and ensuing conflicts culminated in an American revolt in 1836. The Mexican army sent to quell the rebels was defeated by American forces under General Sam Houston; and Santa Ana, the Mexican general, was taken prisoner. Texas was now in effect an independent country.

Having achieved their independence, Texans organized a government of their own and sought admission to the United States as a slave state. Owing to the strength of the anti-slavery opinion in the North and in the House of Representatives, admission was long postponed. Andrew Jackson was sympathetic with the Texan appeal but he did not push the matter. Nor did his successor, Martin Van Buren, who was at heart opposed to slavery.

But when John Tyler became President on the death of William H. Harrison in 1841 the outlook for the Texans improved. Yet even Tyler, a pro-slavery man from Virginia, moved slowly in the affair. At last in 1844, near the end of his term, a treaty of annexation was concluded with Texas, only to be rejected in the Senate where the two-thirds vote for ratification could not be mustered.

In their political campaign of that year the Democrats joined with the Oregon slogan, "Fifty-four Forty or Fight," another slogan, "The Reannexation of Texas." Under these battle cries they were successful in the election. Tyler and his supporters now took a new course. Before the new President, James K. Polk, was inaugurated, they gave up the idea of a treaty and in February 1845 Congress adopted, by a simple majority vote, a resolution admitting Texas to the Union.

Texas was in the Union but what was its southwestern boundary? Texans claimed that it was the Rio Grande. Mexicans insisted that it was the Nueces River. President Polk ordered American troops under General Zachary Taylor to cross the Nueces and hold the disputed territory. Soon they were attacked by Mexican forces and President Polk responded by declaring that war had begun "by act of Mexico." With the support of Congress he carried it forward. While General Taylor drove southward into Mexico an expedition, sent by sea and overland under General Winfield Scott, captured Mexico City; and Americans on the

Pacific coast, with aid from American naval commanders, raised the Stars and Stripes in California.

In February 1848, Mexico gave up the unequal fight. New Mexico, Arizona, California, and other districts were ceded to the victor. To this huge domain the United States, by treaty with Mexico five years later, added a small strip known as the Gadsden Purchase in the Gila Valley along the southern border of Arizona. The enormous region between Texas and California, bounded on the north by the Oregon country, was soon divided into two organized territories, Utah and New Mexico, clearing the way for occupation.

Long before war broke out between the United States and Mexico in 1846, a migration of Americans to California had started. For many years shipmasters and merchants from the Atlantic seaboard had been sailing around Cape Horn, visiting California, and trading pots, pans, shoes, and other manufactures with Spanish owners of great estates and with trappers for hides, furs, and other raw materials. News of the mild climate, the fertile soil, and the resources of the region attracted other fortune hunters. By 1830 a trail was opened to Los Angeles from Independence, Kansas, by way of Santa Fé. In 1844 John C. Frémont, intrepid Western explorer, went over the mountains into Sacramento Valley. By 1846 at least one fifth of the people in the little town of San Francisco were citizens of the United States; and Americans were taking part in the quarrels between the Mexican governor of the province and his distant superiors in Mexico City. Trouble was already brewing and had there been no war with Mexico the American colonization of California would have become ominous to its Mexican owners.

In fact the government of the United States already had an eye on the rich prize of California. As early as 1845 the Secretary of State in Washington secretly informed an American agent in Monterey that he could count on help in case difficulties occurred. The Secretary told him that the United States would not foment a revolution there, but it would protect Californians if they revolted against Mexico. The next year some Americans in upper California flung out a flag on which was painted a bear, and began to shout for independence. The Bear Flag movement was quickly submerged when the war with Mexico opened; but Frémont, with the aid of Commodore John Sloat, Commodore Robert Stockton, and General Stephen Kearny, clinched American possession of the whole region. On July 7, 1846, Commodore Sloat raised the American flag over Monterey and proclaimed the annexation of California to the United States.

The war with Mexico had just closed in 1848 when gold was discovered at Sutter's Mill in the Sacramento Valley, and the gold rush to California began—along the overland trails, around Cape Horn, and by way of the Isthmus of Panama. Within two years, it was estimated, about 100,000 immigrants from all parts of the United States and the world had crowded into the gold regions and neighboring towns. With prospective miners were associated merchants, farmers, doctors, teachers, mechanics, lawyers, and laborers, all seeking good luck in the latest Eldorado.

For the future of California the character of the immigrants was decisive. Planters with droves of slaves were not to occupy the territory and add another slave state to the Union. Without waiting for action by Congress, Californians held a convention in 1849, drafted a constitution, put a prohibition on slavery, and demanded statehood. That was a shock to the pro-slavery politicians in the South and the East, but as a part of a general compromise reached by Congress in 1850 California was admitted to the Union as a free state.

The territorial settlement at the close of the Mexican War and the rapid progress of California in population and wealth affected the career of one of the strangest communities in the whole story of American pioneering. This was the Mormon colony in Utah. The Mormon sect had started on its course under the leadership of Joseph Smith, of New York, in 1830, and had been pushed from place to place by hostile neighbors before it settled finally in Utah. Its members had tried living in Missouri. From Missouri they moved to Illinois. Having now adopted the practice of polygamy, or "plural marriage," and given it an elaborate religious sanction, the Mormons seemed to multiply their enemies on every hand. When Brigham Young became their second leader, they decided to go to some remote region where they might live and work in their own fashion with no interference from outsiders. After inquiring about the distant West, Young selected a spot so far away and so arid, he supposed, as to invite few if any intruders; and in 1847 he led his flock to the Salt Lake Valley.

By hard labor and efficient management, the Mormons in Utah made that desert blossom like a rose, as Young had said they would, and built up a prosperous society. Their freedom in the wilds of the West was, nevertheless, soon curtailed. In organizing the territory of Utah the government of the United States brought them under its control; and the gold rush to California over the trail running through Salt Lake City introduced "foreigners" and the lure of gold into their midst. Moreover, many Gentiles insisted on settling down in Utah. Thus the Mormons' longed-for escape from the difficulties of relations with other people proved to be no escape at all. They were destined to be merged in the great Union as the tide of immigration rolled westward toward the Pacific.

CHAPTER XIII

The Industrial Revolution

THE WESTERN SETTLEMENT—from the Appalachians to the Mississippi, beyond the Mississippi, and to the Far West—had great repercussions in the politics and economy of the original thirteen states based on the British colonies. The West broke the Eastern monopoly over the choice of candidates for the presidency of the United States and assumed the right to have its share in making party platforms. The West also affected the economy of the East in both its commercial and planting aspects. It opened more domestic markets for seaboard merchants, enlarged their export business, augmented the demand for capital to invest in lands and industries, and created new demands for manufactured goods. Its spreading plantations in the Southwest brought severe competition to the planters in Virginia, the Carolinas, and Georgia as producers of cotton and other staples.

On the other hand an economic revolution in the East had immense repercussions in the West. This was the Industrial Revolution wrought in manufacturing and social life by the invention and use of steam engines and power-driven machines.

All through the years from the enactment of the Northwest Ordinance in 1787 to the admission of California to the Union in 1850, announcements of inventions and mechanical experiments synchronized with great events in westward expansion.

The following table of events in the history of inventions and applications is merely illustrative in selection but gives an impression of parallels in time between steps in the Industrial Revolution and the westward expansion:

1787—John Fitch's steamboat made a successful demonstration on the Delaware River.

The Northwest Ordinance was enacted.

1791—Samuel Slater put a spinning mill in operation in Rhode Island.

Congress authorized Kentucky to form a new state.

1793—Eli Whitney's cotton gin was patented.

General Anthony Wayne was placed in command of troops in Ohio to protect settlements against Indians.

1797—A solid cast-iron moldboard for plows was introduced.

Andrew Jackson took his seat in Congress as senator from Tennessee.

1798—David Wilkinson patented a machine, with slide rule, for making machines.

Kentucky protested against the Alien and Sedition Acts.

1802—Oliver Evans completed a high-pressure steam engine of greater efficiency than James Watt's engine.

Ohio drafted a constitution for self-government.

1807—Robert Fulton's steamboat, the *Clermont*, made its successful trip from New York City to Albany and back.

Meriwether Lewis reported to President Jefferson on his exploration of the Louisiana Territory to the Pacific Ocean.

1825—Erie Canal connected New York City with the Great Lakes.

The Mexican legislature of Texas-Coahuila opened the door of Texas to American colonists.

1831—Steam trains began to run from Charleston to Hamburg, South Carolina.

Steamboat *Yellowstone* made its first trip on the upper Missouri River.

1833—Patents were taken out for automatic reapers by Obed Hussey and Cyrus McCormick.

Abraham Lincoln began to read Blackstone's *Commentaries* at Salem, Illinois.

1844—Samuel Morse's electric telegraph line opened between Washington and Baltimore.

John C. Frémont's expedition reached Sacramento Valley, California.

1847—Richard Hoe's printing press was printing 8000 copies of the Philadelphia *Public Ledger* per hour.

American army occupied Mexico City.

1849—McCormick reaper works were established in Chicago.

Great exodus to California gold mines began.

1851—William Kelly started developing "air-boiling" process of making steel, anticipating the discoveries of Bessemer.

The territorial legislature of Oregon created the county of Umpqua.

1852—First railway train ran from Philadelphia to Pittsburgh.
Leland Stanford settled in California.

1853—Baltimore and Ohio Railway entered Ohio.
Chicago and St. Louis Railway line opened.

In application the thousands of inventions, major and minor, made between 1790 and 1850, utterly transformed methods that had been employed almost unchanged for hundreds of years in manufacture, transportation, mining, communications, and agriculture. Considered in its largest terms, this revolution meant releasing the production and transport of goods from the limitations of human hands and strength, supplemented by animal, wind, and water power. No longer was the amount of goods produced to be determined by the number of human beings employed in the process. Henceforward production could be expanded indefinitely by the substitution of mechanical fingers for human fingers and mechanical power for human power. For the first time in the history of the human race the possibility of an abundant production, freed from the leash of mere human energy, loomed on the horizon of peoples capable of developing the Industrial Revolution toward the goal set by the potentials of technology.

Slowly in the beginning but steadily gaining momentum, machinery, driven first by water power and after about 1810 by steam engines, was used to produce commodities in great factories, swiftly and on a large scale. In 1807 only fifteen cotton mills existed in the United States and they were operating only 8000 spindles. Four years later the number of mills had increased to eighty-seven and the number of spindles to 80,000. Within four years, more than 500,000 spindles were whirring under the watchful eyes of 76,000 tenders, becoming known as "industrial workers."

When the eighth census was taken in 1860, the leading commodities used for food, clothing, and shelter had been caught up in the Industrial Revolution with astounding results in output. For the year ending June 1, 1860, the total value of machine and hand manufactures, including fisheries and mining, and excluding very small shops, was placed at $1,900,000,000, nearly twice the output of 1850 and more than four times the total national wealth in 1787.

In order of respective values of output the following commodities were highest on the list: flour and meal, cotton goods, lumber, boots and shoes, leather, clothing, woolen goods, machinery, steam engines, etc., books, newspapers, sugar, spiritous liquors, cabinet furniture, bar and other rolled iron, malt liquors, agricultural implements, paper, soap, and candles. The very list of articles and amounts of each exhibited the advance Americans had made on the road to the manufacturing independence foreshadowed in colonial times.

America was ceasing to be a mere raw-material country for manufacturing nations in the Old World. Census takers of 1860 reported that 1,385,000 persons were employed in American manufacturing establishments and enterprises; they estimated that, counting the dependents of these persons, about one sixth of the whole population was directly supported by manufactures. Adding to this number all the persons engaged in the production of raw materials for manufacturing and in the distribution of manufactured goods—capitalists, transportation workers, merchants, and clerks, for instance—the census reporters declared: "It is safe to assume, then, that one third of the whole population is supported, directly or indirectly, by manufacturing industry. . . . The nation seemed speedily approaching a period of complete independence in respect to the products of skilled labor."

A mechanical revolution in the carriage of goods and passengers by water and land went along with the swift advance of manufacturing. In 1807, sixteen years after Samuel Slater put his spinning mill in operation, Robert Fulton's steamboat made a successful trip from New York City to Albany and back. In 1819 an American ship driven by steam and sail crossed the Atlantic Ocean. By that time steamships were plying the coastal waters of the Eastern seaboard, the navigable streams of the Mississippi River system, and the Great Lakes. Between 1840 and 1850 the tonnage on lakes, rivers, and coastal waters more than doubled. Already steam navigation to California by way of Cape Horn and the Isthmus of Panama had been opened. In 1829 the number of steamboats on the Mississippi system was 200; in 1836 it was 240.

The Erie Canal, establishing water connections between New York City and the Great Lakes in 1825, and the Pennsylvania Canal to the West, completed in 1834, had scarcely started the promotion of rapid and long-distance transportation when they were challenged by the railway, which completely emancipated the carriage of passengers and freight from bondage to water-courses. Before the Pennsylvania Canal was finished, steam trains were running between Charleston and Hamburg, South Carolina, and the railway era had dawned.

Soon there were railway connections between the chief cities of the Northern seaboard. By 1860 trains were running regularly between Baltimore, Philadelphia, New York, and Boston; those cities were linked by rail with Cleveland, Cincinnati, Chicago, and St. Louis. Meanwhile the chief cities of the South were joined by railways, and connections were established between them and the Northern network. The time of travel for passengers had been cut from weeks to days and the cost of carrying freight from dollars to cents per ton-mile.

In the train of the mechanical revolution followed a rapid growth of population in old cities and the appearance of new cities, even in the Western wildernesses. In 1790 only five towns —Boston, New York, Philadelphia, Baltimore, and Charleston—had more than 8000 inhabitants each and their combined population was under 135,000, a little above three per cent of the total population of the United States. Thirty years later there were thirteen communities having 8000 inhabitants or more, with a combined population of almost 500,000. New York alone in 1830 had as many people as all the five towns of 1790 put together; and in 1860 the population of New York, including surrounding districts later drawn under its jurisdiction, had passed the 1,000,000 mark.

In the eight industrial states of the seaboard—from Massachusetts to Maryland, inclusive—there were in 1840 eleven cities with over 20,000 inhabitants; by 1860 the number of cities in that class had increased to twenty-four; and the twenty-four had more than twenty-seven per cent of the total population of the eight states. In 1840 nine towns to the west of the mountains had a combined population of about 150,000—Pittsburgh, Cincinnati, Louisville, Chicago, St. Louis, Milwaukee, Detroit, Cleveland, and Buffalo; within twenty years their aggregate population had risen to about 800,000.

To the factories and shops in the cities moved a steady procession of young people from American farms and small towns. In New England it was led by the daughters of farmers in the neighborhood of the spinning mills, who had been taught that it was their

moral and patriotic duty to be as useful as possible in such industries. Indeed to a large extent young women "manned" the first
textile mills of that section. Wherever machine industries appeared
men and women from the rural regions flocked to them in search
of work; and the number of "mill hands" was swelled by child
laborers—socially an uprooting phase of the new production
methods.

In the growth of manufacturing centers, as in the settlement of
the West, immigrants from the Old World became factors of increasing importance. The Industrial Revolution was in reality a
new spur to immigration and its effects in this relation were soon
manifest in the shipping records. Between 1820 and 1860 more
than 5,000,000 alien passengers arrived at the ports of the United
States on ships from foreign countries. In 1820 they numbered
8385; in 1850, 310,004; in 1854, 427,833. This inflow of labor forces
was stimulated by steamship companies, by employers of labor
seeking a plentiful supply to keep wages as low as possible, as well
as by other influences within the United States and in the lands
of the emigrants.

Reckoning the immigrants of the period by economic classes,
the most numerous were as follows:

Laborers	872,000
Farmers	764,000
Mechanics	407,000
Merchants	231,800
Miners	39,900
Textile workers	11,500

In the list of callings and occupations that classified other immigrants who entered the country between 1820 and 1860, the census reported: mariners, shoemakers, tailors, milliners, actors, clergymen, lawyers, clerks, physicians, engineers, artists, teachers,
musicians, printers, painters, masons, hatters, millers, butchers,
bakers, and servants.

More than twenty countries were recorded as supplying quotas
of immigrants during those forty-one years of American expansion. The United Kingdom furnished the largest of all, 2,750,000,
of whom 967,000 came from Ireland. Germany stood next with
1,486,000; France third with 208,000; British America fourth, with
117,000. Among the other countries represented were Spain, Prussia, Norway, Sweden, Poland, Italy, China, Mexico and other
Latin American nations. To the population of the United States—

in 1790 about three-fourths British in origin—were thus added national strains more diverse in origins, languages, and customs.

Although thousands of aliens moved into the West seeking farms to own and till, other thousands stayed in the rising industrial towns on the seaboard and furnished skill, enterprise, and labor for manufacturing, transportation, and commerce. If George Washington could have journeyed again from Virginia northward in 1860, as he had done in 1789 by carriage and on horse, he would scarcely have known the land to whose independence he had dedicated his talents.

Apart from the farmers and great landed proprietors in 1790, the chief economic class among the owners of property had been the merchants who handled exports and imports and interstate commerce. After the Industrial Revolution got under way the role of manufacturers was magnified in American society. Often, if not generally, at first, the manufacturer who assembled machinery and workers for industries came from the old class of mechanics and craftsmen. Frequently he developed his little hand-labor shop into a factory, using machines and steam power. Sometimes, like Samuel Slater in Rhode Island, he began anew by building a great mill, frequently with the financial aid of merchants who had capital to invest.

As opportunities for manufacturing multiplied, individual enterprisers, finding their own resources inadequate, banded together in corporations to raise larger capital. These concerns sold stock to the public and borrowed money from banks. Long before 1850 corporations had become numerous and powerful in every branch of industry, transportation, and commerce.

As industries expanded in size and number, manufacturers became more closely associated with inventors engaged in devising new machines and processes and with capitalists seeking opportunities for profitable investment. In the early days of the factory system manufacturers usually managed their own plants, aided by foremen; but with the rise of corporations they often turned this responsibility over to deputies. Out of the varied development of machine economy six groups of enterprisers emerged; manufacturers, specialized inventors, industrial bankers, capitalists pure and simple, corporation lawyers, and industrial managers.

For building and operating machine industries large bodies of skilled and unskilled workers were necessary. They were procured from two principal sources: first, from the mechanics of the towns and the men, women, and children of the farms, that is, Americans of the old stock; and then from the new immigrants. From whatever source they came industrial workers were generally dislocated in respect of their historic status and their historic opportunities.

In the handicraft economy of earlier times, manufacturing was carried on extensively in connection with agriculture, in the households and in small outside shops; and the workers were not solely dependent upon the sale of sheer labor power for a livelihood. Furthermore, as owners of their tools and their time, they had direct control over their hours of labor and working conditions, onerous as those might be. Even master mechanics who lived in towns, and worked apart from the land, were likewise owners of their tools and shops; and their employees were often apprentices who expected in due time to be their own masters.

Under the new machine economy, on the other hand, few workers personally owned their tools and implements of production; nor, in the nature of things, could any large proportion of them look forward confidently to becoming mill owners. Their wages, hours of labor per day, and even employment on any terms were largely or wholly beyond their control—in the hands of employers, subject to the invisible but imperious conditions of the market for the manufactures produced by capital and labor.

From the point of view of labor and its prospects, therefore, a striking feature of the Industrial Revolution was the immense increase in the proportion of workers dependent wholly upon wages for their subsistence and upon the fluctuations in the market for employment. In former days, on account of the abundance of land open for settlement on easy terms, industrious farm workers including indentured servants had good prospects of acquiring farms of their own. Labor was arduous on the land but families that tilled it could usually count on having some food, clothing, and shelter in the worst of times.

In a different situation were workers connected with machine industries. Thousands of them rose, it is true, into the employing and professional classes, owing to economic opportunities and the fluidity of American society. But the vast majority of them were destined to remain wage workers throughout their lives, and to be subject to the vicissitudes of the panics and depressions which afflicted machine industries. Not only did this destiny present a strange problem to individual men and women in the disruption of the old family economy. It brought to the nation unprecedented problems in class relations and in public policies.

As a result of the Industrial Revolution, a new conflict over the balance of power took form. From the early days of colonization freehold farmers had clashed with seaboard landlords, merchants, and money-lenders. They had struggled to get power, first in the colonial and then in the state legislatures. They had constituted a substantial part of the opposition to the adoption of the Constitution and had rallied in politics to the support of the Republican party under the leadership of Jefferson. Now wage workers in machine industries by the thousands surged into the political arena and began to form organizations for the promotion of their interests.

In large numbers they flocked to the party of Jacksonian democracy, although it was largely a farmers' party. But their interests did not exactly coincide with agrarian interests. They had needs, demands, and methods of their own. Crowded together, as they were, in cities, they could easily create associations of their own to voice their interests and bring pressure to bear on employers, politicians, and on society in general, for the redress of their grievances real or alleged.

The associations organized by or for industrial workers after the rise of machine industries were numerous and varied in nature and purposes. But the most persistent type was the trade union. Between the end of the eighteenth century and the middle of the nineteenth century the trade-union movement went through four rather definite stages, as to forms of organization.

The first stage was the creation of local unions in single crafts or trades, for the purpose of influencing wages and the length of the working day. As early as 1792 the shoemakers of Philadelphia formed a union. Two years later the printers of New York and Philadelphia organized typographical societies. By the end of Jackson's second administration in 1837 workers in the leading trades of Boston, New York, Philadelphia, Baltimore, and several other towns had established local unions. Among them were unions of bookbinders, machinists, ironworkers, hatmakers, jewelers, type founders, glassmakers, millwrights, ship joiners, furriers, leather dressers, shoemakers, printers, boilermakers, loom weavers, and plumbers.

As local unions in single trades multiplied they showed a tendency to draw together in their respective cities, and this marked the second phase of their evolution. New York led off with the establishment of a central or city trades union, a union of trades, in 1833. Within five years there were similar city organizations in Baltimore, Philadelphia, Boston, Newark, Albany, Troy, and Pittsburgh, and also in the Western towns of Cincinnati and Louisville.

During these very years trade unionism entered the third stage in its development: the federation of local craft unions in a national association representing a single trade, an industry, or a craft. For this movement the journeymen cordwainers, or shoe and leather workers, were pathbreakers. In March 1836 they held a convention in New York City, composed of delegates from cordwainers' unions in New York, New Haven, Brooklyn, Newark, Paterson, Philadelphia, Washington, and several other places. Then and there they formed a constitution for the National Co-operative Association of Journeymen Cordwainers and framed a platform pledging mutual assistance. In the same year unionist printers, after many exchanges of letters, sent delegates to a general convention in Washington and entered into a loose national federation. Other trades followed these examples, with ups and downs in fortune, until within twenty years each of the principal crafts had a national organization of some kind.

The fourth step in the organization of labor—the union of all unions in a national federation—was the most difficult of all and was not permanently effected until more than fifty years after the cordwainers had formed their national craft federation in 1836. But the project had been planned in the early stages of trade-union development and efforts had been made to realize it as soon as local unionism had gained its first strength.

An experiment in general organization was attempted in New England in 1831, with the formation of the New England Association of Farmers, Mechanics, and Other Working Men. Although some unionists were represented in its meetings, the association was as much concerned with politics and social reforms as with hours, wages, and working conditions. Within three years it went to pieces.

A stronger effort at national federation on a unionist basis in respect of membership was made in 1834 at a convention of delegates from trades unions held in New York City. After extended debates the National Trades Union was formed under a constitution which declared its purposes to be moral, intellectual, and pecuniary. This national union held conventions in 1835 and 1836 and then collapsed in the panic of 1837. The foundations for such a national union of unions had not yet been securely laid and nearly thirty years were to pass before another undertaking of the kind was even attempted.

Amid the uprush of factories and cities, the multiplication of wage workers, the relative decline of handicraft production, and the growth of trade unions, a thoroughly dislocating force broke into the economy of the nation. That was the periodical panic followed by a widespread industrial collapse. Such crises had often occurred in the past but as long as the overwhelming majority of the people tilled the soil for a livelihood depressions did not create destitution for the masses. Now, however, hundreds of thousands of people were concentrated in great industrial centers and divorced from the soil with its food-giving crops, its raw materials for clothing and shelter, and its enduring opportunities for productive employment. Now a breakdown in industry and business enterprise meant, for such urbanized workers, unemployment, no wages, actual lack of the vital necessities—food, clothing, and shelter.

The first terrific smash in the machine-production age occurred in 1819; another in 1829; the third and most severe in the history of the United States up to that date opened in 1837 and lasted for about five years. A brief recovery was only a prelude to a fourth collapse in 1847. Ten years later, in 1857, another depression settled over the nation and almost crushed the labor movement entirely.

Even in the intervals called prosperous, poverty and distress haunted the working-class districts of the great cities. Famines and misery had marked the course of all history in the Old World and the Orient, but slaves and serfs had usually had some shelter and some bread even in hard times. There had been poverty in colonial times in America and in the early days of the Republic, but it had been widely dispersed and its evils mitigated in considerable measure by charity and poor relief.

Whether the Industrial Revolution increased the relative amount of poverty or not, it made the position of mere wage workers more precarious than that of the serf or the farmer; and it concentrated poverty-stricken persons in urban masses so large that only the blind could fail to see their plight. Such poverty, on a scale so

enormous and so obtruding, so contrasted in the cities with flaunting riches, was a new thing; and it aroused consternation among
American citizens who had social sympathies and cared about the
security of the Republic. Their interest was heightened by the
agitations and protests of labor leaders, charity workers, and political reformers.

In a land where the objectives of society and government were
declared to be life, liberty, equality, the pursuit of happiness, and
the general welfare, what was to be done about such poverty?
Were the institutions and ideas derived from the great Revolutionary age of the Republic sufficient to meet the new problems?
Fifty years after the Declaration of Independence Americans were
impelled to thinking more comprehensively than their forebears
had done in the days of the Revolution itself.

Before the industrial upheaval had gone far the American stock
of ideas on society and government, on industry and agriculture,
on the rights of men and women, was reviewed, reinterpreted,
modified, and augmented. Reforms bewildering in number were
proposed. They were forced upon the attention of political parties. They were written up in books, pamphlets, and newspaper
articles, and made subjects of discussion in circles high and low,
from one end of the country to the other. During the advance of
the Western frontier, the contests of politicians, the westward
sweep into the Louisiana Territory and the Southwest, the upsurge of cities and industries, the building of canals and railways,
the celebration of a growing population and mounting wealth—
amid all this—plans for recasting the heritage received from the
founders of the Republic were forced into the thought of reflective people concerned with the future of the United States. In
nature these ideas and plans ranged from specific reforms to an
overhauling of the entire social order.

Reformers who spoke from the ranks of labor or in the name of
labor presented a long bill of specific demands: equal suffrage for
all white men and, sometimes, for women; free and equal public
education; the abolition of imprisonment for debt, which especially oppressed the poor; an independent labor press; the dissolution of monopolies; full right of labor to organize, strike, and
bargain collectively with employers; a ten-hour day, with hints of
an eight-hour day; payment of wages in cash instead of "store
goods"; restriction of immigration; sound money for wages, instead of fluctuating bank paper; regulation of factories and mines
in the interests of safety and health; and the division of the public

domain into small homesteads to be given, not sold, to persons willing to occupy and develop them.

Other reformers, including many men and women distinguished for their idealistic leadership, declared that such schemes were not enough to cure the ills of poverty or release the full productive force of machine economy; and they offered a variety of panaceas. One of the earliest of such reforming groups advocated a peaceful reconstruction of American society, especially that type expounded by the French idealist, Charles Fourier, under a theory of utopian socialism. The utopists of this school were generally called "associationists." They proposed to abandon the capitalist factory system, found colonies of associated workers on the land, and combine farming with manufacturing. In colonies of the kind, they believed, workers could be self-sufficing, share their wealth on equal terms, and acquire economic stability and independence.

One school of American associationists, in their thinking, used extensively the ideals propagated by the British utopian socialist, Robert Owen, who made lecture tours in the United States and, with his son, Robert Dale Owen, founded a socialist colony at New Harmony in Indiana. They were especially impressed by Robert Owen's three revolutionary propositions: the enormously increased productive powers which man in modern times has acquired involve, and in a measure necessitate, great changes in the social and industrial structure of society; the world has reached a point of progress at which co-operative industry should replace competitive labor; society, discarding large cities and solitary homes, should resolve itself into associations—communities uniting agriculture and manufacturing. If in theory Owen's propositions were revolutionary, in practice his program was intended to be pacific, for the independent communities were to be established by the voluntary co-operation of capital and labor.

Convinced that they were on the right line, American associationists made experimental tests of their doctrines. They established several colonies in different parts of the country; but only those motivated by religious fervor and sacrifice managed to survive for more than a few years.

Also revolutionary but at an opposite pole of thought from utopian socialism, and violent rather than peaceful in its implications, was the interpretation of recent industrial events proclaimed by disciples of Karl Marx, whose *Communist Manifesto* was issued in Europe in 1848. Three years later a German apostle of Marx, Joseph Weydemeyer, landed in America and founded a newspaper to spread the doctrine that the historical role of the working class was to overthrow the whole capitalist system and usher in a "co-operative commonwealth." But Weydemeyer did not make much headway with his propaganda in the American labor movement. When the Civil War started he enlisted as a captain in the Union army and by valiant service rose to the rank of general. Though his call for a revolutionary labor party gained no material support in the American labor movement, Marxism was thrust into the ferment of the new industrial age in the United States.

The influence of the mechanical revolution was not confined to urban centers. Indeed one great machine industry, railway transportation, coupled with the electric telegraph, ran out in every direction until at length it spanned the continent. Railways cut channels from the seaboard to the West, through which manufactures flowed to farmers and planters and farm produce flowed back in exchange. One striking feature of the trunk lines was the close economic union effected between the Northeast and the old Northwest Territory before the sixth decade of the nineteenth century closed.

By that time enterprisers of the North and the South were projecting trunk lines to the Pacific. Had it not been for a dispute over the route—whether it was to go through the Southwest or the Central West—and the political struggle over slavery, beginnings of construction would have been made before 1860.

Rapid transportation between the manufacturing regions of the East and the farming regions of the West did not prevent Westerners, however, from developing industries of their own. Cleveland, Chicago, Cincinnati, Milwaukee, St. Louis, and Louisville early became manufacturing as well as merchandising centers. A survey of American economy published in 1854 reported: "Cincinnati, Ohio, appears to be a great central depot of ready-made clothing, and its manufacture for the Western markets may be said to be one of the great trades of that city. . . . Latterly sewing machines, of varied construction, have been largely employed. . . . At Louisville, Kentucky, and St. Louis, Missouri, the manufacture of clothing is extensively carried on; but Cincinnati may be considered as the great mart of ready-made clothing for the Western states, and, in a measure, for those of the South also. In 1851 there were in the latter city 108 establishments, employing 950 hands in their own workshops, and upwards of 9000 females either at their own homes or under 'bosses.' The proprietors are chiefly German Jews, and most of the operatives are Germans."

A petty village with a few inhabitants when Cook County, Illinois, was organized in 1831, Chicago soon became a focus for shipping on the Great Lakes and for distributing Eastern manufactures brought by water and rail. Then its enterprisers turned to manufacturing. After the establishment of the McCormick reaper works in 1849, Chicago rose to be the leading center for the manufacture of plows, reapers, threshers, and other machinery needed for the expansion of farm production as vast areas of level Western land were opened up for cultivation, especially enormous corn- and wheat-growing regions.

Although many men in the South saw the immense potentialities of machine industry for economic welfare and sought to balance the agriculture of that region by the introduction of manufacturing, their efforts, for one reason or another, met with only slight success. It is true that by 1840 Virginia, North Carolina, Georgia, Tennessee, and Kentucky had many cotton mills in operation, but these factories were small in size and in their growth fell far behind Northern competitors. In 1850 the annual value of manufactures produced in the free states was more than four times the output of manufactures in the slave states. Omitting Maryland, Kentucky, and Missouri from the list of slave states, it was more than eight times the Southern output. In 1857 the free states had 17,800 miles of railway lines; the slave states only 6800 miles.

By the middle of the century four portentous facts stood out in the economy of the United States. First, the capital value of industrial and urban property overtopped the capital value of all the farms and plantations from the Atlantic to the Pacific. Second, the Northeast and the Northwest, linked together by common interests, greatly surpassed in manufacturing wealth and production all the Southern states, especially the slave belt below Maryland, Kentucky, and Missouri. Third, the iron products and leather goods, including boots and shoes, alone equaled in value of annual output all the cotton grown in Southern fields. Fourth, by similarity of freehold agricultural practices, the people of a vast section between the Southern seaboard and the Mississippi—in western Virginia and North Carolina, and in eastern Kentucky and Tennessee—were affiliated by economic habits and kindred sentiments with Northern farmers, rather than with the planters of the coastal plain who used chattel slaves to till their soil.

Over continuously larger areas of the continental domain the interests and ideologies of the early Republic were undergoing changes and transformations fundamental in character. Inherited productive methods of agriculture and manufacturing were being outmoded. The American population was becoming increasingly urban. The family system of economic and cultural unity was giving way to the factory system which drew even young children into its fold. An organized movement was beginning to assert the claims of labor to a larger share of the profits of capitalistic enterprise; and revolutionary social theories were competing with loyalty to capitalism in the ranks of labor. Localism was yielding ground before the invasion of new laws, customs, institutions, and social problems national in scope. The trend of thought and interest was toward a more consolidated national Union and a fuller realization of the opportunities for the life commodious and abundant on this continent.

CHAPTER XIV

Rise of National Democracy

ATTENDING the expansion of the American nation to the Pacific Ocean and the transformation wrought in economy by steam and machinery was the decimation of the governing elite, in the name of democracy. Previously the very word "democracy" had been terrifying to ruling classes throughout the world. In America only a few groups of persons belonging to the Revolutionary generation of the eighteenth century had used the word "democracy" as a symbol for their political and social ideals and programs. Such groups had been regarded with horror by those men and women of the times who believed with Chief Justice Oliver Ellsworth that Jeffersonians were the "apostles of anarchy, bloodshed, and atheism"; or with Elbridge Gerry that "the evils we experience flow from the excess of democracy. The people do not want virtue, but are the dupes of pretended patriots."

This fright at the thought of democracy was illustrated in the systems of government set up in the states by the leaders of the Revolution. Those systems in a majority of cases limited the right to vote to men who owned property or paid taxes, and put high property qualifications on the right to serve in legislatures and important offices. In this way they excluded from government a substantial proportion of white males. But since the number of white male property owners and taxpayers was large, the suffrage was widely extended. And in fact, with the abolition of British control, legislatures became very powerful in all the states, representing a positive tendency in the direction of democracy.

On the eve of the revolt against Great Britain the Americans, possibly with some exceptions, were wholehearted monarchists.

During the Revolution the word "democracy" was little used. It did not appear in any of the great public documents of the age— neither in the Declaration of Independence, nor in any of the first state constitutions, nor in the Constitution of the United States. In the convention which framed the Constitution powerful statesmen expressed aversion to democracy and sought to put checks on majority rule by the people. Thomas Jefferson did not publicly call himself a democrat or use the term in any of his public addresses and messages. He was convinced that government by a simple majority—even of farmers—could be as despotic as a one-man tyranny and he especially distrusted "the mobs of the great cities."

Indeed even the word "republic" frightened timid souls. None of the first state constitutions mentioned the word. The Constitution of the United States did not officially declare the new nation to be a republic. Only gradually did that term come into official use. Jefferson was really promoting the idea when he called his party Republican.

During the Revolution, however, multitudes of disfranchised people thought and acted in the domain of public affairs. Throngs who were excluded from the privilege of voting and holding office took part in boycotting British goods. Many men who could not vote fought in the War of Independence. After the new governments were established local, state, and national elections were held periodically and struggles over public questions and for political power quickened the minds of thousands who had no actual share in the government. Elections and campaigns also stimulated political interest among men entitled to vote but hitherto indifferent to their rights and duties as citizens. Political newspapers multiplied. Books, pamphlets, leaflets, and broadsides on politics and government rolled from presses in swelling streams, helping to make citizens more alert to the importance of public questions for themselves and their country.

In this political awakening the advocacy of democracy spread rapidly, especially after the opening of the French Revolution in 1789. Democratic agitations accompanied the outburst of American sympathy for the French Republic when it became involved in war with Great Britain in 1793. During those years of excitement local societies were organized in nearly every state in the Union for the purpose of carrying on political education and propaganda—from Addison County in Vermont to Charleston, South Carolina; from Philadelphia to Lexington in Kentucky.

Forty-two such societies are reported by E. P. Link in his *Democratic-Republican Societies, 1790–1800,* published in 1942. Of this number at least fifteen called themselves "Democratic" societies; others chose the more conservative word "Republican" as their title; two adopted the hyphenated title, "Democratic-Republican."

So active were the societies that conservatives, such as Hamilton and Washington, saw the specter of a revolution from below and considered ways and means of suppressing it. In fact the Alien and Sedition Acts, pushed through Congress by the Federalists in 1798, were aimed at such agitations fomented by the popular societies. Nevertheless, respectable leaders in local affairs, apparently in ever larger numbers, were boldly speaking of their political aspirations as "democratic."

The outcome of the French Revolution in the dictatorship of Napoleon Bonaparte cooled the ardors of the democratic and republican societies and most of them as distinct organizations seem to have disappeared by the opening of the nineteenth century. But their places were taken by local party machines which had been growing up in every state and populous community. For the fateful election of 1800 both the Federalists and the Anti-Federalists, or Republicans, were well organized.

Each of the two parties in Congress formed a separate group, or caucus, to promote its political interests. In cities, towns, and counties, from New Hampshire to Georgia, from Pennsylvania to Tennessee, members of the opposition to the Federalists held local conventions and established local committees, each free to choose its name. Most of them adopted the name "Republican"; some preferred the title "Democratic-Republican"; a few candidly called themselves "Democrats."

As the decades of the nineteenth century passed, more and more members of the Republican party appropriated the Democratic label. But national leaders of that party continued to insist they were simply Republicans. State and local committees of the party used the one or the other title, according to their degree of sympathy with popular demands. Since no national party convention was held until 1831, there was no official body empowered to fix the party name.

Madison, Monroe, and even Andrew Jackson clung to the name "Republican." In no state paper or official address did Jackson proclaim himself a Democrat or refer to the United States as a democracy, although in private letters he occasionally used the words with approval. Nor did the early national conventions of the party desert the name given to it by Jefferson. The national convention of 1840 spoke of "cardinal principles in the Democratic faith"; but not until 1844 was its national convention ready to discard officially all references to the "Republican" brethren and declare the party to be "the American Democracy"—"the Democratic party of this Union."

☆

Intimately related to the spread of the democratic ideal were changes in political and social arrangements which registered the growth of democratic practices. All the states admitted to the original Union between 1789 and 1840—New Hampshire, Kentucky, Tennessee, Ohio, Indiana, Illinois, Louisiana, Mississippi, Alabama, Florida, Missouri, Maine, Michigan, and Arkansas—differed in several features of their social structure from the old seaboard states with their colonial backgrounds. In none of them was there an upper class of wealth and political power comparable to that represented by the great landlords or the rich merchants of the original thirteen states. In short, there was more equality in wealth and social condition in the new agricultural states than in the old.

Furthermore the constitutions of the new states were more democratic in many respects than the constitutions of some older states. The new states all adopted white manhood suffrage or at most slight qualifications on the right to vote. They also opened places in legislatures and public administrations to adult males in general. As the number of senators and representatives from new states increased in Congress, as Western states acquired more voting power in presidential elections, even seaboard politicians who had no natural liking for democracy were forced to accept some of it as a hard fact or retire from public life.

At the same time the old East was undergoing a transformation which favored the growth of democracy there. The number of freehold farmers was increasing in the regions behind the seaboard, from Maine to Georgia. Popular agitations were making more farmers politically conscious, and changing them from negligent into active voters. New industrial cities were springing up. The population of the older cities was rising rapidly. Immigrants were flooding in from the Old World and acquiring American citizenship. Industrial workers were forming trade unions and labor parties.

These events helped to erode the prevailing class structures of

the Eastern states and promote the growth of political democracy
—a vote for every white man at least and the opening of all public
places to white men of every rank in society. Far and wide, people
of democratic inclinations were recalling that the Declaration of
Independence had declared all men born equal and pointing the
logic that all men ought to have the right to vote and hold office.

So the democratic changes did not all occur in the Western
states. As a matter of fact low suffrage qualifications were adopted
in several Eastern states before many Western states had come into
existence. This was in line with the principles of 1776, reinforced
by agrarian and labor agitations in the East since the establishment
of the Republic. It had little or nothing to do with the so-called
"frontier."

Step by step, seaboard states altered their constitutions, in
various parts, in such a way as to abolish or qualify the rule that
only owners of property could vote and to confer the suffrage
on nearly all adult white males. The property requirement for
voting was removed among the original thirteen states in the following order of time:

1778—South Carolina	1821—Massachusetts, New York
1784—New Hampshire	1842—Rhode Island
1789—Georgia	1844—New Jersey
1792—Delaware	1850—Virginia
1810—Maryland	1856—North Carolina
1818—Connecticut	

In several cases, when the property-ownership qualification on
the right to vote was abandoned, the payment of a small tax, on
the Pennsylvania model of 1776, was substituted or continued; but
in time that tax was also generally abolished. By the middle of the
nineteenth century practically all white male citizens in the original states could vote. Thus two movements between 1776 and 1850
—one in the East and the other in the West—converged to make
white manhood suffrage prevail generally in the country.

In the same span of years property qualifications on the right
to hold office were removed, along with various religious qualifications. Under many of the first state constitutions public officials
and members of the legislatures had to be the owners of property
in fixed amounts. For example, according to the Massachusetts
constitution of 1780, the governor had to own freehold property
worth at least £1000; under the South Carolina constitution of 1778
the governor's property qualification was at least £10,000 freehold.

Many of the first state constitutions also contained provisions which limited the suffrage or office-holding or both to Christians or to Protestants alone. But with the spread of democracy the restriction of offices to men of wealth and members of specific religious denominations was destroyed.

Coupled with the extension of the suffrage and the removal of property and religious qualifications on office-holding were two other practices also called democratic. The first was the custom of giving short terms to public officers, known as "rotation in office"; the second was the rule that the victors in an election should take over the political jobs held by their predecessors—"to the victors belong the spoils of office."

Democrats early resented the tendency to keep men of old and rich families in office from generation to generation. They maintained, moreover, that long service in places of power was likely to make men arbitrary and aristocratic in the management of public business. A change of officers every few years, they insisted, was necessary in a democracy and conducive to the right conduct of administration. Short terms, frequent elections, and rotation in office, therefore, became popular watchwords.

To them was added one less theoretical: "Turn the rascals out and give the jobs to our 'boys.'" By 1840 "the spoils system" had become general throughout the Union, even in the federal government at Washington. After every election crowds of public officials, including clerks, accountants, and doorkeepers, were removed to make room for men belonging to the victorious party or faction.

Another feature of the democratic tendency was the adoption of the rule that presidential electors must be chosen by popular vote. The original Constitution provided that each state shall appoint in such manner as the legislature thereof may direct the number of electors to which it may be entitled—that is, the number equal to its whole number of senators and representatives. This method of election had been adopted by the convention of 1787 instead of other plans presented, such as election by Congress or by direct popular vote. It was intended to remove the selection of the President from the heats of political campaigns. Presidential electors so chosen, it was thought, would be free to review all the candidates, pass careful judgments on the merits of the men available for the office, and cast their votes according to their best opinions.

In the beginning presidential electors were chosen by the state legislatures themselves in several states, but five states established popular election at the very outset. By 1824, when twenty-four states participated in the election, eighteen had provided that the presidential electors must be chosen by the voters; in only six states were they selected by the legislatures. In the next election, 1828, electors were popularly chosen in all states except Delaware and South Carolina. Meanwhile presidential electors had lost their freedom of choice; they had become "dummies," bound to vote for the candidate for the presidency duly nominated by their political party. Thus popular election had been substituted for the deliberative electoral process contemplated by the framers of the Constitution.

In another respect the election of the President was made still more popular—by the rise of the national party convention as a machine for selecting candidates prior to the election. After the retirement of Washington, whose election had been unanimous, Federalist members of Congress organized a caucus or unofficial committee to select their candidate. The Republicans soon followed their example. Until 1828, one or more candidates were regularly nominated by congressional caucuses. But in that year "King Caucus met his death." Jackson's supporters had outlawed the practice as aristocratic and contrary to the Constitution besides. For a short time there was no national party assembly for nominating purposes.

In 1831, however, a new machine was created—the national nominating convention. In that year the Anti-Masons and the National Republicans, or Whigs, held conventions to choose their candidates for the coming election. The following year the Jacksonian Republicans also summoned a convention, at which Martin Van Buren was nominated to run for Vice-President with Jackson their presidential nominee. By 1840 the national party convention had become an established political institution in the United States.

Delegates to the national convention of each party were chosen by party committees or conventions, state or local or both, in each state. They were, Jacksonians alleged, "fresh from the people." Yet in reality every national convention was dominated by officeholders and professional politicians, including senators and representatives from the Congress of the United States. Nevertheless it was not as secret and autocratic as the congressional nominating caucus which had met and carried on its negotiations behind closed doors. Moreover it was a national assembly which drew together partisans from all sections of the country. It was both more democratic and more national than the caucus.

Besides serving as an assembly for the selection of candidates, the national convention, soon after its appearance, adopted the practice of framing and publishing a platform, or declaration of the party principles, that helped to define and fix the issues of the campaign for public discussion. Hitherto in presidential elections there had been no party statement giving the public any official information respecting the policies for which the candidate stood and which he might carry into effect if given his chance by voters at the polls.

After the election of 1840 the voters had for use in every campaign the national platforms of the rival parties; and the speeches of the campaign could be focused on the doctrines and planks of the platforms. As a wag once said, the platform was often "a thing to get on by and not a thing to ride on." But, vague and elusive as it frequently was, it was usually more definite than the rumors, private letters, and newspaper stories which had formed the chief basis for popular information and judgment in the campaigns held prior to the appearance of the national nominating convention. Henceforward the people had before them in campaigns, besides the personalities of the candidates, statements of party purposes which they could criticize, approve, or reject. Whatever its shortcomings, the practice of issuing platforms was an advance in the democratic process and political education.

During this democratic development women asserted claims to rights and privileges denied them in law and custom. From early colonial times women had been active in public as well as private affairs. They had not only carried on domestic industries that fostered national independence; they had edited and published newspapers, written and printed pamphlets, tracts, poems, and plays in support of the Revolution; they had organized boycotts against British goods and participated in essential work throughout the war against Britain. They had expressed their opinions respecting the course of events at the conclusion of that war; and forceful women had objected to the way in which men proposed to monopolize voting and lawmaking in the nation whose interests women were promoting and defending. Now in the Jacksonian age women were banding together to demand equal rights with men as fellow citizens of the United States. They were applying the principles proclaimed in the Declaration of Independence to their own legal and social status.

Following their excursions into reforming fields, leaders among women came to feel the need of an organized and directed movement for overcoming discriminations against women in law and practice. With the sympathy and aid of several prominent men that movement was formally launched by the holding of a convention at Seneca Falls, New York, in 1848. Lucretia Mott, of Philadelphia, and Elizabeth Cady Stanton, of Seneca Falls, were the prime instigators of this undertaking. After a long debate the convention drafted and adopted a Declaration of Sentiments, or principles, on which to base appeals for united and nationwide action.

Almost in the language of the Declaration of Independence, the women's declaration opened: "When, in the course of human events, it becomes necessary for one portion of the family of man to assume among the people of the earth a position different from that which they have hitherto occupied, but one to which the laws of nature and of nature's God entitle them, a decent respect to the opinions of mankind requires that they should declare the causes that impel them to such a course. We hold these truths to be self-evident: that all men and women are created equal . . ."

Then, after the style of that earlier declaration which had asserted the natural equality and rights of man, there followed a long list of "repeated injuries and usurpations on the part of man toward woman": among other things, man has denied to her the right to vote, compelled her to submit to laws in the making of which she has no voice, taken from her rights in property and the wages she earns, denied to her the facilities for obtaining a thorough education, and monopolized "nearly all the profitable employments."

Having set forth the grounds of women's revolt in the clear terms of the Declaration of Independence and cited the grievances to be remedied, the Seneca Falls convention demanded that women "have immediate admission to all the rights and privileges which belong to them as citizens of the United States." To the Declaration of Sentiments the convention added a set of resolutions dealing with these rights and privileges, and affirming specifically that "it is the duty of the women of this country to secure to themselves their sacred right to the elective franchise."

In demanding equal civil and political rights and in carrying on discussions of public questions women now had a broad program for inspiration and guidance. It was greeted with abuse and derision in many quarters; but, despite rebuffs and setbacks, women pressed forward with their agitation for "the rights and privileges" which they claimed as citizens of the United States.

Equal suffragists were rapidly gaining adherents when the excitement of the slavery crisis broke over the land. Then leaders in the woman movement concentrated largely on the cause of freedom for slaves and the preservation of the Union. But after those causes had triumphed in 1865 they renewed their agitation and started with invincible resolve on the course that led, first, to gains in communities and states and, finally, to national triumph in the Nineteenth Amendment of 1920 which provided that the right to vote shall not be denied or abridged on account of sex.

With the forward surge of democracy the idea took firmer root that free public schools supported by taxation should be established for the education of the children of the people, not otherwise educated. In this school movement many purposes and forms of advocacy were commingled. Large numbers of radicals regarded education as a cure for many social ills and as a means of preparing the people to win more privileges by reducing the power of the educated minority to dictate the terms on which the masses were to work and live. Only an educated people, reformers avowed, can govern themselves, supply competent officials all over the huge continent, and assure the safety of the Republic. On the other hand conservatives thought that public education would be useful in preventing the spread of "wild ideas" among the people and make them less responsive to appeals for their support from "agitators" and "demagogues."

Immigration was likewise brought into the pleas for free and universal education. Swarming thousands of men, women, and children were arriving in America from foreign lands. Many of them were unacquainted with the English language and with the arts of self-government. Among them was a large proportion of Catholics; and Protestants feared that the Catholics would gain too much power in politics and public affairs generally if they were not "Americanized." In this situation it was argued by educational reformers that free schools were needed to start the children of immigrants on the way to citizenship in the Republic and offset the feudal heritage brought from Europe.

Under the impulse of varied motives the movement for free public schools made headway against opposition and indifference. But by no single master stroke throughout the land was universal education established. On the contrary, progress in popular education took the form of local gains slowly accumulated in towns, cities, and states.

Horace Mann was active in formulating the comprehensive program of education finally adopted in Massachusetts; it encompassed, with elementary public schools, training schools for teachers, and free libraries in towns. Henry Barnard was the prime leader of a similar development in Connecticut. Besides working in their own communities, Mann and Barnard labored in other parts of the country for the establishment of free schools. Able men and women by the thousands in many communities and states, including governors, legislators, town councilors, and other officials, gave time and strength to this cause, by speaking and writing, by framing plans and drafting laws.

Grudgingly, stone by stone, amid the grumblings of taxpayers, the foundations of the system of free public education were laid in all the Northern states and in several Southern states by 1860. According to official estimates for that year every white inhabitant of the country received, in public or private schools, on the average, more than five times as many days of schooling as such inhabitants received in 1800.

In this attack on ignorance the following phases were salient:

Grants of public funds to aid charity, church, and private schools, all free from public control.

Laws permitting cities, counties, towns, and other districts to lay taxes for schools if the voters so decided.

Laws making special provisions for the education of the indigent poor.

Laws *requiring* communities to make provision of some kind for education, occasionally with grants from the state treasury, supplemented by small tuition fees.

The abolition of all tuition fees, thus making instruction free.

Equalization of education by abolition of pauper schools and of grants to schools maintained by churches.

Creation of normal schools for the training of teachers.

Organization of regular boards of education, state and local, for the establishment and management of schools.

Mandatory and statewide laws requiring the establishment of elementary, free, and compulsory education in every district.

Limited measures providing for the creation of public high schools to furnish advanced education.

Establishment of state colleges and universities, crowning the system of lower schools.

Yet the phases did not follow one another exactly in order of time. For example, the University of Virginia, designed by Thomas Jefferson, was organized in 1819, but not until 1846 did the Virginia legislature enact a comprehensive law providing for school districts, regular taxation for the support of elementary schools, and county school commissioners. By 1860 only Massachusetts, Connecticut, New Jersey, New York, Pennsylvania, Michigan, Rhode Island, Illinois, and Minnesota had normal schools for the training of teachers.

Tendencies toward continental unity coursed under and through the ferment of the democratic interests and ideas expressed in the widening of the suffrage and provisions for popular education, in the erection of new states in the West with liberal constitutions, and in the entry of women's organizations into agitations for egalitarian laws and practices. Emphasis on the rights of individuals to their own personalities and political privileges by no means dissolved the nation into anarchy. On the contrary bonds were forged among the people by visible and invisible relations tending to weld the democracy into a national unity.

Better methods of communication speeded the process of nationalization. The development of post roads was almost unbelievable in its rapidity. In 1774 there was only one great post line—the shore road from Portsmouth, New Hampshire, to Savannah, Georgia; except for the road from New York City to Albany there were practically no regular post connections with the interior. Sixty years later, in 1834, there was a large network of post roads from the Atlantic Ocean to the Mississippi River, from the Great Lakes to the Gulf of Mexico, with three lines running beyond the Mississippi to forts on the far frontier. The great Cumberland Road, or national highway, started in 1811 under a congressional act of 1806, had penetrated the heart of Ohio and regular stagecoaches were running over it to and from the seaboard. The Erie Canal linked the regions of the Great Lakes with New York City and intervening points. The Pennsylvania Canal joined Philadelphia to the headwaters of the Ohio and the whole Mississippi basin. Steamboats plying along the Atlantic shore quickened communications between seaboard cities; they were running from seaboard towns to New Orleans and to all settled centers on the Mississippi and its navigable tributaries.

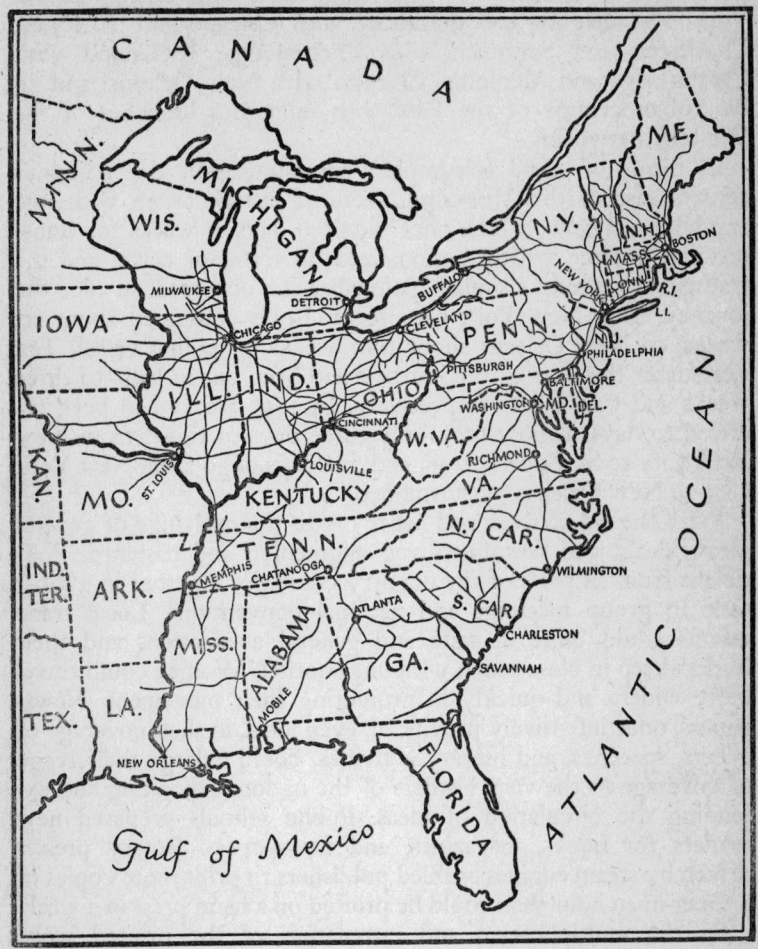

RAILROADS OF THE UNITED STATES IN 1860

Before Andrew Jackson left the White House in 1837 the building of railways had begun and a few years later the first message by electric telegraph was flashed between Washington and Baltimore. By the close of the sixth decade all the main regions between the Atlantic and the Mississippi were bound together by telegraph wires, over which news as well as private messages could be transmitted in a few minutes. In 1860 telegraph lines as well as railways connected Boston and New York with Chicago; New York, Philadelphia, and Baltimore with Chicago and St. Louis; Charleston and Savannah with Chattanooga; Richmond with Chattanooga and Memphis; Chicago with New Orleans; and all the urban centers of the East with numerous branches of the Western network.

In terms of rapid telegraphic communication the populous centers east of the Mississippi were in instant touch with one another; and news, which once required days or weeks for transmission, became swiftly nationalized. In terms of travel and the transport of goods, a similar nationalization occurred. In 1800 the journey from New York City to St. Louis consumed about six weeks; to New Orleans about four weeks by sailing vessel. Ten years later the time of the journey had been cut in half—to three weeks and two weeks respectively. In 1857 weeks had been reduced to days: it now took only three days to travel from New York City to St. Louis by rail, and five days to go from New York City to New Orleans by steamboat.

With the aid of these and other means the exchange of general ideas, ideals, and sentiments was augmented and hastened. Politicians from all parts of the country could get together in a short time in group meetings and national conventions. Local trade unions could unite in state and general associations and their leaders keep in close touch with one another. Women could travel more widely and quickly in promoting their movement. Newspapers, once intensively provincial, even local, in their coverage of events, speeches, and literary activities, could enlarge their range of coverage to the very borders of the nation, expediting and extending the circulation of ideas. Public schools prepared new readers for books, magazines, and newspapers. Rotary presses driven by steam engines enabled publishers to print more copies of a paper in an hour than could be printed on a hand press in a week.

So the multiplication and circulation of the printed word reached immense proportions. In 1839 a report of the Post Office placed the number of newspapers and periodicals in the United States at 1555. Eleven years later a special census fixed the number of dailies, weeklies, and other periodicals at 2800 and the number of copies printed annually at 422,600,000. Into this outpouring flooded books, pamphlets, leaflets, and broadsides.

The web of unity, while becoming more complex, was growing tighter. Regions, sections, and states remained, but sentiments and loyalties were becoming more uniform. Democratic customs and a public opinion accepting them were spreading without regard to physical boundaries.

In this transfusion of thought and interests the press played an active role. An intimation of its strength may be gathered from the following table for the year 1839, showing the number and the distribution of newspapers and periodicals over selected settled regions of the continent:

Massachusetts	124
New York	274
Pennsylvania	253
Ohio	164
Indiana	69
Illinois	33
Missouri	25
Michigan	31
Virginia	52
South Carolina	20
Georgia	33
Louisiana	26

It is evident from this table that in 1839 New York had twice as many newspapers and periodicals as Virginia, South Carolina, Georgia, and Louisiana combined; a single new state in the West, Ohio, had more than all of the four Southern states combined. Indiana had more than Virginia; and the frontier state of Illinois, in which Abraham Lincoln was growing up, had more than South Carolina, the home of John C. Calhoun. Even so, there were now more newspapers in Virginia in 1839 than there had been in all the states when their independence was declared in 1776.

As an outcome of the stirring and converging forces at work in the United States the little Union formed by the original thirteen states on the seaboard—the Union now continental in extent—was becoming national in its ideas and feelings, even in the South as pro-slavery secessionists learned from the number and vigor of their opponents in their very midst. It is true that nowhere in the Constitution of the United States did the word "nation" or the word "national" appear. In their secret convention at Philadelphia in 1787 the framers of the Constitution at first resolved that they were seeking to establish a government "national" in all departments; but they struck out the word "national" from their resolutions, thinking, no doubt, that it would disturb advocates of states' rights. Nevertheless Madison, Jay, and Hamilton used the fateful and prophetic words in *The Federalist*. Washington, Jefferson, and Jackson repeatedly referred to the United States as a "nation" and to its great interests as "national." Although as late as 1850 it was still customary in popular usage and in prayers for divine blessing to speak of "these" United States, events were outrunning the language. In the travail of the democratic insurgency these states were fusing into an American nation—one and indivisible.

CHAPTER XV

A Broadening and Deepening Sense of Civilization

BLENDED WITH the insurgency of democratic thought and action as expressions of individual rights was concern with American society as a whole and on the continental scale. This concern involved a search for the bonds of social, economic, intellectual, and spiritual loyalty cutting across the variations of states, regions, and classes. It raised such fundamental questions for exploration and treatment as these:

What is the social mission of this nation in its continental home?
What duties and virtues are necessary to the fulfilment of its historic mission?
What opportunities for action lie open to the people?
What knowledge is necessary for the accomplishment of their highest purposes?
What principles, inherited or newly devised, should be applied for progress toward the goal called American?

This interest in American society as a whole, more comprehensive than interest in republican or democratic politics, was affirmed with growing frequency under the covering word "civilization."

The word was new in all the history of thought and represented a new idea or ideal. It first appeared in French and English writings, it seems, about the middle of the eighteenth century and was first used in America, apparently, by writers of the Revolutionary age; by Thomas Jefferson, Thomas Paine, Mercy Warren, John Adams, and Joel Barlow, for example. Amid the upheavals of the democratic age it came into wider usage among orators, writers, and publicists, who employed it to distinguish the ways of rational, ethical, and progressively more refined human relations from the

225

ways of barbarism. "The exact measure of the progress of civilization," said the historian, George Bancroft, in an address before the New York Historical Society in 1854, "is the degree in which the intelligence of the common mind has prevailed over wealth and brute force; in other words, the measure of the progress of civilization is the progress of the people."

Thought about popular progress had entered into the daily work of men and women who by labors of mind and hand had brought American society into being and given it a stable government, wealth, and strength. In the democratic era special circumstances favored the rise of thinkers dedicated to the business of speaking and writing, and more or less freed from the tasks associated directly with domestic, agricultural, or industrial enterprises. With the reading public enlarged by popular and secular education, publishers of newspapers, books, and magazines reached out for its patronage. The opportunities to earn a living by studying and writing expanded correspondingly. In other words, there was now a widening market for essays, articles, and books written in a popular style and dealing with every theme of human interest —economic, scientific, political, historical, social, religious, and philosophical.

Avenues opened to abilities in writing for a democratic public by the invention of machines for cheaper printing were paralleled by avenues opened to public speakers by the rise of the platform. In this democratic age auditoriums of many kinds for general assemblies were constructed in the leading cities and many smaller platforms were made available for smaller meetings. A Lyceum Lecture Bureau was organized to furnish speakers on various subjects to clubs and societies on a circuit reaching from the seaboard to the frontier. In Lyceum lecture rooms thousands of Americans heard letters, art, science, and the issues of the time discussed by "the best minds" of the nation. Mass meetings came into vogue, organized by men and women who wished to put before the people at large their proposals for innovations and to ask for popular support.

Though liberty of speech, as well as of press, was guaranteed by federal and state constitutions, free speech from public platforms had not been a general practice before the advent of democracy; and when first attempted it encountered sore trials and tribulations. Unruly elements hissed, booed, and often stoned orators engaged in analyzing traditional theories and practices, pleading for new rights, and demanding reforms, mild or radical, in customary ways of thinking and acting. Yet against opposition and disorder the platform grew in influence as audiences were disciplined by eloquence or were moved to reason by the power of argument. Public speaking became a practice of increasing importance in agitation and the formation of public opinion. In time hundreds of women from the middle class, self-educated by intensive or wide reading and activated by experiences in public life, were addressing audiences with pleas for social improvement.

As platform facilities multiplied and public speaking became an accepted way of distributing knowledge or disseminating ideas, innumerable organizations for education and propaganda sprang up like mushrooms, in communities large and small. Scarcely a proposal, from the amelioration of prison conditions to temperance reform, from the revision of marital relations and family life to easier divorce and woman suffrage, from modifications in the wage system to the abolition of slavery, was without a society devoted to promoting it by concerted efforts.

When Alexis de Tocqueville traveled in the United States during Jackson's administration, studying American habits and customs, he was astounded by the number of civic societies; and in his *Democracy in America* he wrote: "In no country in the world has the principle of association been more successfully used, or applied to a greater multitude of objects, than in America. . . . In the United States, associations are established to promote the public safety, commerce, industry, morality, and religion. There is no end which the human will despairs of attaining through the combined power of individuals combined in a society."

As the idea of civilization in the United States broadened and deepened in the consciousness of the people it became more generally recognized that the destiny and opportunity of the American people lay first of all in their own development. Political independence had signalized that fact. As industries flourished an increasing economic independence corroborated it. Multiplying presses for the publication of books and other writings invited consideration of it. Thought confirmed it, sometimes in boastful arrogance and at other times in calm, rational admission of intellectual and moral obligations.

In an essay published in 1837, Ralph Waldo Emerson acclaimed the growth of national consciousness: "Our day of independence, our long apprenticeship to the learning of other lands, draws to a close. The millions, that around us are rushing into life, cannot always be fed on the sere remains of foreign harvests. Events, actions arise, that must be sung, that will sing themselves. . . . There are creative manners, there are creative actions and creative words. . . . That is, indicative of no custom or authority but springing spontaneous from the mind's own sense of the good and fair."

Was political democracy, into which millions were rushing in America, among the things which Emerson called "good and fair" and a sure promise of advance in civilization? Followers of Andrew Jackson and politicians who were beneficiaries of popular suffrage thought that it was. Walt Whitman agreed that it was with the ardor of a poet, while finding in democracy more than votes to be counted on election days and the spoils of office to be captured. He accepted joyfully as brothers and sisters all sorts, conditions, and classes of people from the sidewalks of New York to California's shores. He rejoiced in their "companionship as thick as trees," and gave his pledge to it: "For you these, from me, O Democracy, to serve you. . . . For you! for you, I am trilling these songs."

Here on this continent Whitman envisaged the making of "the most splendid race the sun has yet shone upon; . . . with the love of comrades"—America linked to humanity by mystic bonds and yet emancipated from many ties to Europe. "Nothing," he declared, "merely copied from and following out the feudal world will do. . . . The entire stock in trade of rhyme-talking heroes and heroines" must be discarded and the songs of a free people sung. Here, in Whitman's vistas, democracy was to build a civilization of greater freedom, equality, and fellowship than the world had ever known.

But the Federalists surviving from Hamilton's era, still clinging to Hamilton's social outlook, and new Federalists bearing the name of Whig were openly skeptical. Josiah Quincy, of Massachusetts, who had been an "insurgent" among the Federalists in the election of 1820, concluded, after he had witnessed the Jacksonian upheaval, that this democracy would fall into anarchy, try revolution, and end in despotism, unless the children of the people could be educated to respect the law, defy demagogues, and play a better role as citizens. And as to that he was by no means optimistic.

Among the Whigs of the South similar views of democracy were stoutly defended. Alexander Stephens, of Georgia, publicly said that the equalitarian ideas espoused by Jefferson and other early leaders of the Republic were simply wrong—"fundamentally wrong" as applied to slavery. Indeed the wealth and talents of the Southern planters were largely enlisted in the opposition to Jacksonian democracy. Whether applied to white men or to slaves, the free and equal doctrines of the Declaration of Independence were regarded by most of their spokesmen as dangerous—to property and prestige.

Writing in a philosophic vein, Emerson took a middle course with respect to the issue of democracy. Many reforms championed by democracy he approved. "The philosopher, the poet, or the religious man," he said, "will, of course, wish to cast his vote with the democrat." The spirit of equality, the spread of popular education, the refinement and elevation of society in all its parts, the opening of opportunities to all the people—these he praised as desirable features of democracy. Such progress was in many ways inevitable in the United States, he thought, and worthy of universal support.

But Emerson refused to admit that the Democratic party was synonymous with democracy. He insisted that it was "the party of the Poor marshalled against the Rich" and was directed by "a few self-seeking deserters from the Rich or Whig party," who misled the people by seeming to be their spokesmen while loving to dine and wine with the wealthy and privileged. In saying this, however, he disclaimed any intention of endorsing Whig denunciations of democracy. "From neither party, when in power," he lamented, "has the world any benefit to expect in science, art, or humanity, at all commensurate with the resources of the nation." In other words political democracy, in Emerson's opinion, was one necessary phase of civilization in the United States and yet not without its gloomy prospects.

For the advancement of civilization, speakers and writers argued, innumerable reforms must be undertaken in order to bring practice more closely into harmony with the humane ideals professed by and for the American people. High among the needed reforms, perhaps the most generally advocated, they listed the revision of laws inherited from colonial times and reproduced to some extent in the new states admitted to the Union. The inherited laws had been heavily freighted with feudal customs, with cruel and barbaric punishments, and with English class doctrines respecting property, crimes, and punishments. When, for example, the leader of the agrarian uprising against the Hudson Valley land-lords in 1766 was caught and tried, he was condemned to be hanged, disemboweled, and otherwise mutilated; and nothing but the mercy of the King of England saved him from this horrible fate. At the opening of the nineteenth century the laws of England still prescribed the death penalty for about two hundred and fifty offences, ranging from petty stealing to such high crimes as murder and treason.

Under the statutory and common law of England, from which the colonists had derived many legal principles applicable to property and domestic relations, innumerable rules upheld personal and class discriminations. The English law governing the inheritance of landed property tended to concentrate it in the hands of a few families through transmission to the eldest sons, leaving younger sons and the daughters to fare as best they could. In the absence of prenuptial contracts and other private arrangements the personal property of a married woman, even her wages, according to common law, became the possession of her husband and her landed property passed under his management.

According to this old law children were almost the property of their parents, particularly the father. Savage treatment could be and was at times meted out to them.

By no means all of those harsh English legal principles had been adopted in the colonies. Colonial legislatures had abolished or amended many of them. A further renovation took place during the Revolutionary period and, amid the upswing of democracy, reformers began even to advocate a revolt against the whole English legal heritage, including the common law. After all, it was asked, what is the intellectual and moral foundation of the law in America?

Speaking to this point, a judge in Connecticut in 1819 declared that it was the purpose of "our ancestors" to found a pure government in church and commonwealth, "bottomed on the word of God," and that they "brought with them no more affection for the common law than the canon law, the court of star chamber, and high commission, from which they fled with horror and detestation."

This was an extreme view, not universally entertained. But twenty years before it was expressed, the legislature of New Jersey had by law forbidden lawyers to cite in the courts of that state any treatise, decision, or opinion made or written in Great Britain since July 1776. With some modifications this principle had been incorporated in the laws of Kentucky and Pennsylvania. Such extremes were in many ways unworkable. Nevertheless the concept of founding American law, criminal and civil, on the humanizing ideals of the Republic exerted a powerful influence on popular thinking about law and on legislation in the United States.

Reforms in law, proposed and in part realized in practice, followed specific lines of the new thinking. The law of landed property, it was contended, should assure equality of inheritance rights to all children, daughters as well as sons. Equality of legal privileges for women, respecting their personal liberty, their property and wages, their children, and control of their own affairs, was deemed in accord with the principles of the Republic and a progressive civilization. Children, it was argued, are not property to be used or abused at pleasure by their parents but should be protected by the government in the interests of their development and community welfare. Imprisonment for debt, so burdensome to the poor, was stigmatized as a relic of barbarism. The horrible punishments meted out under old laws were condemned as brutal; and a call was made for further reduction in the number of capital crimes—to a very few, such as treason and murder. In this general overhauling of the law the idea of punishment as a mere retribution for evil action—an eye for an eye—was steadily modified by the introduction of practices shaped by the thesis that the true purpose of punishment is to protect society and reform the criminal if possible.

The reforming zeal of the age struck at the slave codes in the name of civilization and at the institution of slavery itself. The codes Lydia Maria Child analyzed acutely with a historical retrospect, in her *Appeal in Favor of That Class of Americans Called Africans*, published in 1833 while Andrew Jackson, a slave owner, resided in the White House. And her carefully formulated attack on slavery became a veritable textbook for those political leaders in the North who adopted the anti-slavery cause.

In other works by succeeding writers slavery was assailed in the name of civilization—as violating all the rights of persons upon which liberty and democracy rested for justification, as the very antithesis of civilization. Defenders of slavery, it is true, also appealed to the idea of civilization and maintained that Negroes as a race were devoid of the capacities and character necessary to help carry civilization forward. But within a few years after William Lloyd Garrison founded his anti-slavery paper, the *Liberator*, in 1831, the intellectual and moral crusade against slavery had gained such momentum that it ripped into the discussion of almost every national question.

So wide-ranging was the reforming thought of the time that it reached all phases of human misery which challenged pretensions to civilization in the United States. "I come to present the strong claims of suffering humanity," wrote Dorothea Lynde Dix in a memorial to the legislature of Massachusetts in 1843, ". . . I proceed, Gentlemen, briefly to call your attention to the state of Insane persons confined within this Commonwealth, in *cages, closets, cellars, stalls, pens: Chained, naked, beaten with rods* and lashed into obedience!" At last the mentally ill, long treated cruelly even in the most enlightened communities, were to be brought within the circle of humanity.

In three years Dorothea Dix, with tireless spirit, traveled more than ten thousand miles, studying prisons, poorhouses, county jails, and houses of refuge. For long years afterward she journeyed, spoke, and wrote in behalf of the unfortunates who had done no wrong and yet suffered so grievously at the hands of people called civilized. Though President Franklin Pierce vetoed a bill granting federal aid for the care of the mentally ill which she had finally persuaded a reluctant Congress to pass, Miss Dix toiled on and on in aid of her wards. Before her death in 1887 she had wrought an irrevocable change in American thought and practice relative to these helpless and burdensome members of society, and paved the way for much prevention of mental illness through the study and promotion of mental hygiene.

☆

Of the many contradictions to civilization in the United States which troubled humanitarians and enlisted reforming efforts, none was more obtrusive and persistent than the misery of poverty—the poverty of strong and active men and women who sought work and bread without finding them.

Scattered poverty Americans had always known, and sensitive persons from colonial times had tried to deal with it by private charity and public relief. Social derelicts, often sodden by drink, had evoked the solicitude of temperance workers. But as the Industrial Revolution swept forward in the great cities of the North, another kind of poverty assumed congested and more morbid forms. During the economic crashes which periodically reverberated throughout the country, from the great thundercrack of 1819 to the milder storm of 1857, the poverty of the strong and unemployed was aggravated beyond the silent endurance of the victims or of the comfortable citizens who cared about the making of civilization in the United States.

Nor was the "perfect civilization" of the South, as planter apologists called it, immune from the scourge. If Horace Greeley, in the terrible winter of 1837–38, found unbearable the "filth, squalor, rags, dissipation, want, and misery" of the sixth ward in New York City, William Gregg, of Charleston, South Carolina, was scarcely less distressed by the perennial squalor and misery of the "poor whites" of the Southern uplands.

The problem of poverty in its manifold forms, this contradiction to civilization, was viewed from various angles. Theologians might regard it as a mysterious ordinance of God—an opportunity for the faithful to display the virtue of charity and make the best of two worlds. But numerous intellectual leaders of the democratic age refused to accept it with complacency. They inquired into the nature of private property, the industrial system, and social as well as individual responsibilities. For some inquirers education seemed to be the remedy, especially vocational training. Others looked to collective bargaining between employers and employees for an escape from poverty due to low wages even in times of business prosperity. Many offered as a solution free lands in the West. Defenders of industrialism relied on an expansion of capitalist enterprise to extirpate poverty in a triumphant and universal prosperity; utopists on voluntary co-operation, productive and consumer; and radicals on a thoroughgoing reconstruction of society with reference to the potentials of the new technology.

In his *Recollections of a Busy Life*, Horace Greeley, the great New York editor, gave his explanation of the existence of poverty in the midst of plenty:

"I. I believe that there need be, and should be, no paupers who are not infantile, idiotic, or disabled; and that civilized society pays more for the support of able-bodied pauperism than the necessary cost of its extirpation.

"II. I believe that they babble idly and libel Providence who talk of surplus Labor, or the inadequacy of Capital to supply employment to all who need it. . . . Where Labor stands idle, save in the presence of some great public calamity, there is demonstrated deficiency, not of Capital, but of brains.

"III. I believe that the efficiency of human effort is enormously, ruinously diminished by what I term Social Anarchy. . . . It is quite within the truth to estimate the annual product of our National Industry at less than half what it might be if better applied and directed.

"IV. Inefficiency in production is paralleled by waste in consumption. . . .

"V. Youth should be a season of Instruction in Industry and the Useful Arts, as well as in Letters and the Sciences mastered by their aid. . . .

"VI. Isolation [of workers] is at war with efficiency and with progress. . . ."

Writing from Europe as a correspondent of Horace Greeley's *Tribune*, Charles A. Dana expressed the conviction that radical changes in the social order were necessary to progress in civilization. "The antique civilization . . . reached its climax and then perished," Dana recalled. "It is for us to take a lesson from its fate. It perished because it was based on slavery. . . . The basis of the social structure is industry. If there is wrong in the relations of industry—that is, of property and labor—the time will arrive when they must be reformed, or the whole structure will go to pieces. . . . Under the existing system of labor, modern society has reached the utmost development which that system will allow. New methods of industry must be established, as much superior to the wages system as that is superior to slavery, or else the doom will be pronounced and executed."

Having offered his clue to the crisis in civilization, Dana then addressed himself to the question whether that doom could be avoided and arrived at an optimistic conclusion: "It should not be forgotten that the civilization of modern times is fortified against an overthrow as that of the antique world was not; the railroads, the steamships, the manufactories, the wealth more abundant and more generally divided, which exists now, are so many substantial guarantees that society is to go forward to higher forms without the sad necessity of beginning the circle anew with barbarism and ignorance for its elements. . . . The principle of co-operation is surely, I believe, supplanting that of competition."

On methods of eliminating poverty and waste, of assuring employment and plenty, writers and speakers of the time ran the gamut of reforming speculations. At one extreme Greeley and Dana held that the answer to the riddle lay in the establishment of co-operative communities owning land, machines, and tools in common and practicing communal industry and agriculture. At the other extreme George Fitzhugh, of Virginia, in his volume

Cannibals All! or, Slaves without Masters, advocated the creation of a fixed class system in which each owner of property would be compelled to act as a guardian of a number of paupers proportioned to his wealth. As their guardian, the owner could command their labor, while assuring them a livelihood. But, argued Fitzhugh, they "would work no harder than they do now . . . would be relieved of most of the cares of life. . . . What would they lose in liberty and equality? Just nothing!"

Most reformers, though aware of the immense potentialities in technology, thrust aside as visionary the formation of co-operative colonies proposed by associationists, especially after so many experiments of that kind ended in failure. Fitzhugh's plan for establishing the class servitude of a new feudalism they dismissed as simply fantastic. Nor did they esteem more highly the Marxian scheme for a spring into freedom by means of a sudden proletarian revolution.

Threats of a mass revolt against special privilege had flared up in American history from time to time since Bacon's Rebellion in colonial Virginia; and slogans of revolutionary defiance ran through the speeches and writings of many labor champions in the age of the Jacksonian uprising against "the money power." But the great majority of American reformers and most labor leaders preferred pragmatic programs, embracing many lines of attack on poverty—through the organization of labor and political action in support of specific measures directed to the redress of specific grievances. The freedom of speech and press enjoyed under the American constitutional system permitted them to express their discontents openly and obtain a hearing for their indictment of poverty and their proposals to overcome it. The privilege of the vote, won in state after state for white males, enabled agricultural and industrial workers to engage frankly and above ground in political action for a redress of grievances—a uniquely American liberty and form of power in that time.

Sensitive to the agitations of democracy and the demands for reform in every direction, many clergymen of various denominations inquired into the relation of the Christian religion to the unrest around them. From time immemorial Christian leaders had taught the worth of every human being and the spiritual equality of all persons in the sight of God. They had advocated charity and care for the needy and suffering. What was the bearing of such doctrines on the new tendencies of democracy and reform, both of which rested their justification on moral grounds?

To Protestant clergymen especially this question was immediately challenging. They were the most numerous of the clergy and they gave it the most attention. Catholics, of course, were not indifferent to it; but, despite the rich store of ethical writings in Catholic literature, including the emphasis on the "just price" and the "just wage," no Pope had as yet issued an encyclical on labor and reform. Moreover the Catholic priests who had accompanied the new immigrants to the United States had come principally from agricultural countries in which feudal traditions and practices were still strong and the problems of the Industrial Revolution had not yet become so acute as in the United States. At all events, for various reasons opinion among the Catholic clergy did not endorse reforms as drastic as those proposed in American democracy. On the whole, as Charles A. Dana said at the time, Catholics did not seem to sympathize with "a radical improvement in the social relations of mankind."

To Protestants and Catholics alike, it was one thing to write into constitutions, state and federal, provisions for religious freedom and seek to remove all signs of the intolerance which had been so cruelly manifested through the centuries. It was another thing to make the ethical teachings of religion real in the life and industry of every community and the nation. Yet to this effort at the realization of Christian ethics in human relations—in social theory and practice—numerous religious leaders devoted abilities and energies. Some stopped short at mild measures of legislation and gentle admonitions to the rich. Others went as far as Horace Greeley and Charles A. Dana in demanding a thorough renovation of American society and made acceptance of this program a duty for Christians.

The age, exclaimed William E. Channing, distinguished Boston preacher, "requires an enlightened ministry. . . . A new spirit of improvement is abroad." In a sermon delivered at Philadelphia in 1841, Channing amplified his meaning: "The multitude is rising from the dust. Once we heard of the few, now we hear of the many; once of the prerogatives of a part, now of the rights of all. . . . Even the most abject portions of society are visited by some dreams of a better condition for which they were designed. The grand doctrine, that every human being should have the means of self-culture, of progress in knowledge and virtue, of health, comfort, and happiness, of exercising the powers and affections of a man, this is slowly taking place as the highest social truth. . . . That the great end of government is to spread a shield over the rights of all—these propositions are growing into axioms, and the spirit of them is coming forth in all departments of life."

While the struggle for the public schools went forward, slowly but steadily, against protests of taxpayers and religious sectarians, an educational philosophy befitting the spirit of the democratic age was formulated by leaders in the battle for free schools. They generally agreed upon several propositions. The vote had been given to nearly all white men, and women were demanding it in the name of the equality and human rights proclaimed in the Declaration of Independence. Multiplying factories using technology were demanding greater knowledge and skill on the part of workers in industry. Poverty was a blight on American civilization. People were commonly lacking in knowledge of the simplest rules for health and healthful living. Illiteracy barred the way to that knowledge as well as to the treasures of the world's best thought.

Therefore, said the philosophers of educational progress, public education must prepare pupils for citizenship in the Republic. It must train them in the elements of the arts and sciences used in industry and agriculture, and necessary for earning a livelihood. It must inculcate the habits and manners of civility as values in themselves conducive to happiness and as indispensable to the practice of self-government in the community and the nation. Education, in sum, is to advance civilization in all its phases.

"Its general purpose," said Horace Mann, indefatigable leader in the public-school movement, speaking of education, "is to preserve the good and to repudiate the evil which now exists, and to give scope to the sublime law of progression." Training for citizenship Mann placed high among the specific aims of education: "Since the achievement of American independence, the universal and ever-repeated argument in favor of free schools has been that the general intelligence which they are capable of diffusing, and which can be imparted by no other human instrumentality, is indispensable to the continuance of a republican government."

While Mann thought that children should be taught respect for property, law, and order, he did not regard everything in this relation settled for all time. "Our advanced state of civilization," he admonished his readers, "has evolved many complicated questions respecting social duties. . . . We want no more of those patriots who exhaust their patriotism in lauding the past; but we want patriots who will do for the future what the past has done for us." By this he meant, bring wisdom, knowledge, and virtue to bear upon the improvements of the conditions of the people. "To diffuse a knowledge of improvements" he made a primary function of education.

To the grand end of a happy and virtuous life for the individual and the progress of civilization in American society Horace Mann subordinated all other aims of education. He advocated strict training in the arts and sciences of industry, in civil habits, and in care of the physical body, but no American, he insisted, can claim the elevated rank of a statesman, "unless he speaks, plans, labors, at all times and in all places, for the culture and edification of the whole people."

☆

The debates over the merits of democracy and innumerable reforms in laws and customs were accompanied by efforts to work out a system of political economy corresponding to the peculiar conditions of the United States. A primary issue was raised by these efforts: Are the conditions of the United States really peculiar or does the British system of economic theory apply precisely to this country as well as all others? A large number of American writers and teachers who dealt with economic theory seemed to think that the "laws" of the British economy were universal and thus reigned in the United States as well as in Great Britain.

In the British theory, especially as it had been worked out by David Ricardo and Thomas Malthus, two principles were firmly fixed: (1) each country, in the division of labor among nations, should produce the things which its natural circumstances enable it to produce the cheapest and all nations should adopt a policy of free trade; (2) large-scale poverty is due to overpopulation, the improvidence of the poor, and the decline in the amount of fertile land available for cultivation.

As applied to the United States by economists, these principles required this country to concentrate on agriculture and continue to be, as in colonial times, mainly a raw-material province for nations far advanced in mechanical industries. They also decreed that large-scale poverty is inevitable and that little or nothing can be done to reduce its area or its miseries.

In various respects British economic theory fitted very well into some beliefs already current in the United States. Many Americans still clung to the doctrine, once asserted by Thomas Jefferson, that popular government must depend for its success on a population composed chiefly of freehold farming families. Farmers alone, ran the dogma, possess the independence and virtue necessary to liberty and self-government. Jefferson had in fact given up the doctrine later, and had endorsed the introduction of manufacturing in order that the United States could become economically independent of Europe, especially in the production of arms and other things imperative for the national defense, necessary to assure political independence.

But representatives of planters and farmers held fast on practical grounds to Jefferson's emphasis on agriculture as the surest basis for a republic. They argued that producers of agricultural commodities would be more prosperous if they could sell their produce abroad, and import manufactures freely from Great Britain where labor was cheap and machine industries were further developed than in the United States at that time. As to poverty, they were often disposed to make that evil the inevitable outcome of manufacturing by the machine process.

Though the British theory of America as a raw-material producing country had been challenged on this side of the water from colonial times, first by manufacturers and then by political leaders such as Washington and Hamilton, it was not until near the middle of the nineteenth century that writers developed a countervailing theory better fitted to the peculiar conditions and potentialities of the United States. The outstanding personality associated with this trend of thought was Henry C. Carey, the son of Mathew C. Carey, a Catholic refugee from Ireland who had taken part in the intellectual battles of the early Republic.

In numerous writings, including his *Harmony of Interests* published in 1851, Henry Carey broke completely away from several fundamentals of British theory. The abundance of land and natural resources in the United States, he maintained, made possible the most prosperous society mankind had ever created. The way to advance civilization here, in his opinion, was to diversify the economy of every region by building factories and workshops in the very midst of the farms. This would reduce the cost of hauling goods long distances, open up various employments to workers of all kinds in their own communities, spread science, art, education, and literature everywhere, and enrich the life of every community throughout the land. If such a policy were adopted, Carey contended, American talents would be encouraged and rewarded and poverty would be materially reduced if not entirely eliminated. In his plans for implementing his industrial program he incorporated a proposal for a government-managed currency, as distinct from Hamilton's system of bank currency managed by capitalists.

Although American economic theorists generally repudiated Carey's doctrines as unsound, several of his proposals were followed in practice by American governments, state and federal. And they were destined to have a great influence on the economic thinking of coming years.

Writings which might be classified as "political science," as distinguished from the more comprehensive political economy, were mainly legalistic in form and spirit. That is, they were primarily concerned with the mere forms and powers of government, particularly the nature of the federal Union and the interpretation of the functions of the federal government. But writings on political science sometimes bore the stamp of the great constitutional controversy then rife among politicians and the people. Is the Union perpetual and are the powers of the federal government to be construed broadly in the interest of general welfare or narrowly in the interest of states' rights?

The answer of Joseph Story, justice of the Supreme Court, in his *Commentaries on the Constitution*, three volumes published in 1833, was unmistakable. The Union, he claimed, cannot be lawfully dissolved by state action; Congress may provide for the common defense and for the general welfare. On the other hand, Nathaniel Beverley Tucker, professor of law at William and Mary College in Virginia, enemy of Jacksonian democracy and friend of aristocratic government, argued with great learning in favor of the right of secession and a strict interpretation of the Constitution. This theme he elaborated in *A Discourse on the Importance of the Study of Political Science as a Branch of Academic Education in the United States* (1840) and other writings, including novels of which *The Partisan Leader* was the most argumentative.

Two treatises dealing with political questions, however, went beyond legalistic theorizing to the substance of politics, as *The Federalist* had done. According to that ever-memorable work, which continued in circulation, political science encompassed geography, economic interests, common customs, laws, and practices, and great functions of government, domestic and foreign. To these subjects Story and Tucker gave little heed.

But John C. Calhoun, in his *Disquisition on Government*, published after his death in 1850, after examining the theory of majority rule under equal suffrage, drew an unglossed picture of the clash of economic interests in the operation of government and sought ways and means of defeating the logic of democracy in the interest of economic privilege. Eager to protect the planting interests founded on slavery against the growing population of the North, Calhoun's treatise bore the stamp of political controversy. Nevertheless it dealt with enduring fundamentals in politics.

So, too, did another volume, on the other side of the slavery debate, Hinton Rowan Helper's *The Impending Crisis*, a prophetic attack on slavery published in 1857. Although by no means academic in tone, it took into account, even more than *The Federalist* had done, all important branches of economy, the arts, sciences, letters, education, manners, customs, and habits of the people, as presenting vivid contrasts between the South and the North. Though greeted as fiercely partisan, Helper's volume went deeper than law and theory, to the sources of the social conflicts amid which government was carried on, and took the whole range of civilization within its compass.

Into the ferment of opinions and judgments pertinent to the direction of American aims and activities, historians injected their interpretations of American life. The publication of new works on the history of the whole United States, not merely histories of colonies and separate states, signified an enlarging consciousness of the time process in which the American Union was developing into a consolidated society. George Bancroft, of Massachusetts, trained in scholarship at Harvard and in European universities, especially in Germany, author of a many-volume work, the *History of the United States*, frankly ranged himself and God on the side of the people. He made the march of the people heroic, from oppression to independence; identified civilization with the progress of the people in all civilian modes of refinement; and, to the horror of New England conservatives, declared himself a Democrat and accepted offices under Democratic presidents. The spirit of his conviction gleamed through the pages of his writings. The first three volumes of his *History* were issued between 1834 and 1840, right in the middle of the Jacksonian upheaval. Originally he had intended to bring it to "the present time," but his last volumes, not published until 1882, ended with the formation of the Constitution.

While Bancroft was developing his interpretation of American history, Richard Hildreth, also of Massachusetts and a graduate of Harvard, published between 1849 and 1852 a six-volume history of the United States covering the period from 1497, the year in which King Henry VII established his claim on this continent, to 1820, the year of the Missouri Compromise. Hildreth was a Whig and had no deep affection for democracy itself or the Democratic party as he observed its practical operations in defense of slavery and machine politics. And his pages, cold and dry in style, contrasting starkly with the purple flourishes of Bancroft, disclosed not the jubilant march of democracy but the struggles and clashes of economic interests that had entered into the making of the American nation.

Neither Bancroft nor Hildreth, however, departed far from political, military, and diplomatic history—not even Bancroft with all his professed interest in democracy. As one of their contemporaries, George Perkins Marsh, said: "History has been written for the ruler, not for the people." On this ground Marsh made an eloquent plea at Union College in 1847 for a new kind of history —a history of the people, adapted to civilization in the United States and to "a commonwealth where government is recognized as being both for and from the people." This was in the temper of Nathaniel Chipman, of Connecticut, a philosopher of the American Revolution and a soldier in it who, in his *Principles of Government*, published first in 1793, had declared that the civil and political institutions of the United States "differ in principles and construction very essentially from all that have preceded them."

A history faithful to the realities of American life, Marsh pleaded, should deal with the condition of the people at different periods; in a word, should be social history broadly conceived. It should cover, besides traditional subjects, the work of city governments, the course and character of commerce, the methods and purposes of education, arts, sciences, industries, ceremonies, festivities, family life, "the sanitary and economic condition of the people, the position of the learned professions, the correspondence of families and confidential friends, the character and tendency of public amusements, the ephemeral popular literature of different periods, and the private biographies of the humble as well as the great." History of this kind, Marsh thought, would furnish guidance to citizens and to statesmen in the conduct of private and public affairs. Still, he did not attempt to write that social history. The task he left to others and no one in his time undertook it.

☆

To the broadening of the American outlook natural scientists brought the force of free inquiries and supplied factual knowledge for industrialists and workers in the practical arts and for reformers concerned with programs for the welfare and happiness of the people. Natural science was the monopoly of no section or class. In that respect it was completely democratic. It could escape domination by any special interest in American society and elude the ill-tempers of political conflicts. As a person, a scientist could be partisan. As a scientist, if a genuine scientist, he was above and beyond partisanship in his researches and reports on his findings.

Reformers could of course use the results of scientific inquiries for their own purposes. Indeed they knew that if there was to be progress in national well-being, increasing study of the physical world was one of the imperatives. Yet the scientific spirit in itself was concerned with a search for exact knowledge and not with a quest for reform. Scientists might long to conquer such ills as chronic diseases and epidemics, for instance, but only by gaining precise knowledge could they realize their longing, and they had to start on that basis.

So fruitful and varied was progress in knowledge of the natural sciences in the democratic era that it opened up visions of human welfare never before imagined. In every domain inquiries were pursued and discoveries were reported. Writers of history took little note of the scientists and their achievements. Books on history seldom if ever mentioned so much as their names. Nevertheless, scientists made history—great history as revelation and aspiration.

Among their numbers were John James Audubon in ornithology; Benjamin Silliman, Sr., at Yale College, in chemistry, geology, and mineralogy, and as founder of the *American Journal of Science and Arts* in 1818; Matthew Maury, in the physical geography of the sea; Joseph Henry in physics, meteorology, electricity, and electrical transmission by wire; Constantine Rafinesque in botany and general natural science; Asa Gray in botany; Richard Harlan in zoology and vertebrate paleontology; Josiah Willard Gibbs, one of the world's greatest scientists, in mathematics, physics, and chemistry; Parker Cleaveland in mineralogy and geography; Benjamin Silliman, Jr., in chemistry, with notable achievements in the chemistry of petroleum.

Besides working as individuals, scientists formed organizations to pool their knowledge and promote research in particular fields. Special societies were supplemented in this work of promotion by the establishment in 1847 of a general society—the American Association for the Advancement of Science. National support was also given to scientific inquiries by the founding of the Smithsonian Institution in Washington in 1846 on the basis of a gift by James Smithson, a British chemist who bequeathed a large fortune to the United States for the encouragement of science.

Scientists made advances no less striking and useful in medicine and surgery than those achieved in the physical sciences strictly defined. In general terms the medical advances included more careful and accurate descriptions of human diseases, especially those epidemic in nature; demonstrations in daring surgical operations not hitherto attempted; more precise knowledge of the composition of chemicals in relation to their curative and other properties as applied to disease and suffering; the founding of new medical schools, for example, at Yale in 1810, at Transylvania in Kentucky in 1817, and at Chicago in 1837; scientific writings on surgery, materia medica, dentistry, obstetrics, insanity, diseases of the eye, and medical jurisprudence; and the beginning of popular education in human physiology and anatomy.

In many branches of medical and surgical research hundreds of scientific inquiries were pressed and marvelous results came out of the labor. With the early use of anesthetics, to deaden pain and permit otherwise impossible operations in surgery, were associated Crawford Long, Charles T. Jackson, John Warren, Horace Wells, and W. T. Morton. William Beaumont, of Michigan, did original research in gastric digestion; his book describing his experiments, published in 1833, has been called "the greatest contribution ever made to the knowledge of gastric digestion." Daniel Drake, of Kentucky, was a pioneer in raising the standards of medical education, and wrote a path-breaking work on the *Diseases of the Interior Valley of North America* (1850–54). William Gerhard, of Philadelphia, specialized in the identification and diagnosis of diseases, and differentiated between typhus and typhoid fever, both age-old destroyers of humanity. In South Carolina, James M. Sims made bold experiments in the surgery of gynecology and founded a school of disciples in that field. At Boston, Oliver Wendell Holmes, Sr., employed his fine mind in studying the infectious nature of puerperal fever and discovered ways and means of reducing the death rate of mothers in childbirth.

Appalled by the amount of ignorance among women respecting their own bodies—an ignorance so serious for personal and maternal health—Paulina Kellogg Wright Davis studied anatomy and physiology with a view to helping them overcome their ignorance. Medical men were lecturing to selected audiences on those subjects. She lectured in a more popular way to groups of women, using a manikin in her demonstrations, much to the disgust and alarm of prudists but no doubt with much value to women. She further shocked even male doctors by demanding that medical schools be opened to the training of women in the profession of medicine. Women had been doctors and surgeons since the dawn of human history, but licenses were now being required for the practice of the healing arts. Hence formal training, preliminary to the obtaining of a license, had to be won if women were to continue in their historic relation to these arts and carry them on with the aid of the most modern learning and skills. By demanding medical training for women Mrs. Davis and other forceful women helped to cleave the stolidity of minds reluctant to recognize the role and function of women in the arts of healing and living.

All in all the epoch of "Jacksonian democracy," the "era of the common man," the "fabulous forties" and the fermenting fifties, was a time of dramatic mental activity and creative thinking in respect of everything human.

CHAPTER XVI

Party Strife over Control of the Federal Government

THE RISE of democracy in a nation continent-wide, undergoing a transformation by steam and machinery and charged with the turbulence of old and new kinds of thinking about society in the United States, was accompanied by the struggles of political parties, under old and new names, for the possession of the government of the country. The "era of good feeling," associated with the one-party system of the "Virginia dynasty," began to fade in the second term of Monroe—the last member of the Revolutionary generation to occupy the White House. A new era of fierce party battling burst forth. New personalities, of the younger generation, strode upstage as leaders of political cohorts, and employed novel methods of reaching popular audiences and arousing devotion to factional and party interests.

As the party strife grew in intensity, as travel and communication became easier and swifter, candidates for public office started the practice of making direct personal appeals to the people. In the early days of the Republic, Washington, John Adams, and Jefferson made no open bid for popular support. They conducted their campaigns quietly by writing letters or negotiating with friends. But after the democratic march got into full swing, especially after the campaign of 1840, candidates "went to the people." They made public speeches from platforms; they "took to the stump"; they toured whole regions delivering addresses; and sometimes rival candidates for the Senate of the United States joined in debating publicly the issues that divided them and their parties.

This was the era of monster political parades, torchlight processions, popular campaign songs, and huge barbecues, or picnics, attended by thousands of men, women, and youths who swarmed to "camp grounds" in wagons, buggies, and carts to see and hear the candidates. To aged Federalists all this uproar seemed to be the full and natural outcome of sheer demagogy gone insane; but to members of the younger generation it was an appropriate way of organizing parties, conducting campaigns, and letting the people share actively in the determination of public affairs.

In the campaign for a successor to Monroe four candidates were offered to the voters: two from the new West, one from the Northeast, and one from the deep South. The candidates from the West were General Andrew Jackson, of Tennessee, a popular military hero, victor in the Battle of New Orleans; and Henry Clay, of Kentucky, one of the "War Hawks" who had helped to bring on the second armed struggle against Great Britain in 1812 in which Jackson won the accolade for heroism. W. H. Crawford, an upland planter of Georgia with a frontier outlook, who had held high offices in the federal administration, was the presidential aspirant from the South. John Quincy Adams, of Massachusetts, son of the second President, was the candidate from the Northeast.

The strong figures in the campaign were Jackson and Adams, about as unlike as two men could be, but neither won a majority of the votes. So the election of the President was thrown again into the House of Representatives, as it had been in the case of Aaron Burr and Thomas Jefferson in 1800. After a long contest in the House, in which Clay was especially active, John Quincy Adams was chosen as the Chief Executive. When Adams appointed Clay as his Secretary of State, the angry followers of Jackson, who had polled the largest popular vote, shouted that a "corrupt bargain" had brought about the victory of Adams.

Though John Quincy Adams was the son of John Adams, he had moved further in his thinking, amid the social changes of his time. Yet his personality, like that of his father, did not appeal to the people at large and he was no more popular than his father had been during his term of office. A Federalist by birth, John Quincy Adams had pained elder Federalists by joining the Republican party, largely from sympathy with Jefferson's foreign policy—a heresy in their ranks. He had served Madison faithfully as minister to Russia. He had supported Monroe with equal fidelity as his

Secretary of State. He had been pleased over the adoption of Hamilton's major financial policies by the Republicans in 1816. But he was not a mere disciple in any school of politics.

His view of the Constitution was a broad view, broad enough to take account of the revolution being wrought by science and invention in industry and agriculture. He felt a deep admiration for Washington as a public character and statesman; and he wished to work in the tradition of great nation-making. Indeed his conception of that task took in the whole range of civilization in America and the long future before it.

With a frankness and a fullness rare in politics, Adams laid his national policies before the country in his inaugural address and in messages to Congress. He insisted that Congress had ample powers under the Constitution to enact laws for the general welfare of the country. Above all he believed that the heritage of land, forests, and minerals should be held by the government in trust for the nation and used for the common good—to employ labor, build highways and canals, support education, and advance science.

To administer this heritage honestly and efficiently, Adams maintained, the nation needed a permanent body of trained and competent public servants, enjoying tenure of office during good behavior. In short, he looked upon the national government as an agency for economic, intellectual, and moral improvement. In his political philosophy government was not a mere police force to keep order while politicians scrambled for the "spoils of office," while businessmen intrigued for special favors, while speculators snatched at and gambled in public lands, while everybody sought to feather his own nest.

But in holding that the great object of government was to improve the condition of the people by well-considered and positive measures, John Quincy Adams was out of harmony with current political and economic avarice. Thousands of politicians were merely hungry for offices and jobs. Land grabbers, including many members of Congress, wanted to seize the public lands, as he said, "with the thirst of a tiger for blood."

And Adams was not the man to educate the country into accepting his policies. He had no genius for drawing multitudes to the support of his ideals. He was cold in manner, suspicious of his foes and critics, and hot in temper. At the end of four years in the White House he was, if anything, less popular than in the beginning. The one important measure that came from Congress during his administration was an act of 1828 raising the protective tariff on manufactures, and his approval of it offended agrarians.

Against everything that Adams stood for, the tide of a new "people's party" was setting in. In membership and doctrines this new party stemmed from the left wing of the revolutionary movement that had won independence for America.

Though merged for a while with conservatives in Jefferson's party, several of the leaders in the faction out of which it sprang had even criticized his policies as too "high-toned." After a Republican Congress had re-enacted Hamilton's chief measures into law in 1816, dissidents in the Republican camp declared that the Republican party managers had swallowed Federalism whole and by so doing had betrayed the people. An increasing number of the objectors began to call themselves "Democrats" publicly or "Democratic-Republicans."

With the crowding into Washington of farmers, planters, and lawyers elected to Congress from the new states of the West and South, the dissidents grew in strength; and attacks on the Republicanism which had absorbed Federalism became irrepressible. Then the new people's party arose. It found its leader in "Andy Jackson"—in a "son of the soil," a "man of the people," also a war hero. Born on a small farm somewhere near the border between North Carolina and South Carolina, he had gone into Tennessee in his youth and there had made his way to a fortune by old Southern methods—as a planter, merchant, and slaveowner.

Daring by nature and intrepid in action when quarrels were involved, Jackson had won distinction in the Tennessee militia and as a general in the Army of the United States. His education was meager but by the exercise of his wits he had risen to prominence in local politics and served in the national Congress. His attachment to the Union was emphatic and steadfast; his followers could be sure of that. But his attitude toward such issues as the tariff, the United States Bank, the management of public lands, and public improvements was obscure. He had never publicly proclaimed himself a "democrat," or a "Democrat." Yet through the shimmer of hero worship he was represented as a champion of the people.

With Jackson as their banner bearer his admirers swept him into office in 1828 and again in 1832. This party, later adopting officially the name "Democratic party," carried every presidential election between 1828 and 1856 inclusive, with two exceptions in 1840 and 1848. Thus the party now commonly described as the party of Jacksonian democracy held the presidency from 1829 to

1861 save for two interludes of four years each. After two terms in office Jackson passed his mantle to Martin Van Buren, of New York, elected as his successor in 1836. Though Van Buren had held high offices in his state and in the federal government, he had

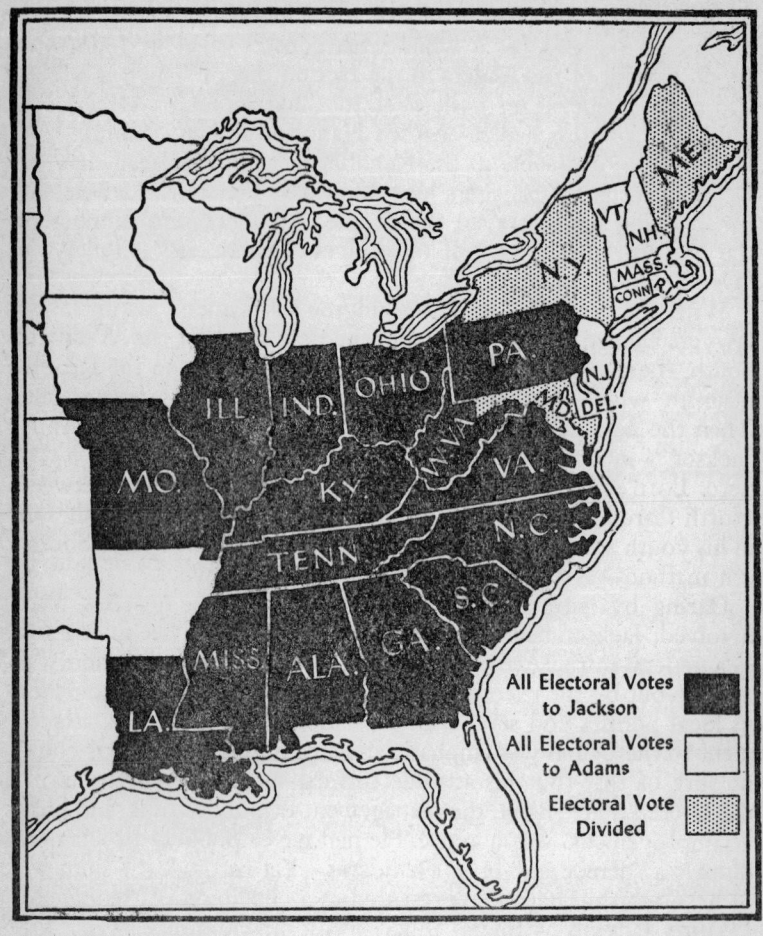

SWEEP OF THE NATIONAL DEMOCRACY. THE ELECTORAL VOTE IN 1828.

also sprung from the people—the "plain people." He had learned the art of popular politics as a taproom boy in a tavern at Kinderhook, New York, before he began to steer his own course in the world; and it was said of him that as a politician he rowed toward every objective with muffled oars.

The interludes in the Democratic sway over the federal government were brief enjoyments of power by another new party calling itself the Whig party. The title, borrowed from the Whig party in England, celebrated for its resistance to high royal prerogatives, fitted very well the American opposition to the autocratic operations of Jackson. Before Jackson's first term expired men adhering to Federalist principles and discontented Republicans, spurred by Henry Clay, of Kentucky, and Daniel Webster, of Massachusetts, had formed a combination against his re-election.

They did not call themselves Whigs immediately. In the beginning they were generally known as National Republicans, as if to deny any taint of states' rights and yet capture Republican voters. They gave no hint of the exact policies they would pursue if installed in power, any more than Jackson had done in his first campaign; but it was understood that both Northern and Southern members of this new party were, as a rule, disciples of Hamilton and incensed at the people's party for which Jackson spoke. Although Clay and Webster veiled none of the political views they personally held, the Whig party was largely a negative party—against Jacksonism rather than for anything definite as a substitute.

The Whigs came into the campaign of 1840 with a military hero of their own as their candidate—William Henry Harrison, of Ohio, who, like Jackson, had fought in the War of 1812 and had been victorious over Indians at Tippecanoe in Indiana. They boasted that Harrison had a wing to his house made of logs. They sang campaign songs in praise of log cabins, coonskins, and hard cider, to demonstrate that Harrison was as close to the people as Jackson. They accused Van Buren of putting cologne on his whiskers and taking his meals in the White House from massive gold and silver plate. In their propaganda the Whigs promised the voters "two dollars a day and roast beef," instead of Van Buren's "policy, fifty cents a day and French soup." On such flimsy pledges the Whigs carried the election and William Henry Harrison served as President for one brief month. Then death ended his career and the Vice-President, John Tyler, of Virginia, succeeded him.

In the next election, of 1844, the Whigs were defeated and the Democrats made their way back to power under the leadership of James K. Polk, a kind of heir to Jackson in that he also lived in

Tennessee and was a son of the soil. Whigs tried their luck again in 1848 and found it with another military hero, General Zachary Taylor of Mexican War fame, a Louisiana planter whose political ideas were as nebulous as those of Harrison. That success was their last presidential triumph. Though often strong in Congress after 1840, the Whigs, as an organized party, finally disappeared from presidential campaigns like the Federalists before them. In 1860 they adopted the name "Constitutional Unionists" but the name did not save them from defeat in that last grasp at power.

Amid the clashes, personalities, and rhetorical flourishes of the political campaigns waged by Democrats and Whigs, five primary issues remained fairly constant as sources of their differences. All these issues had arisen in the early days of the Republic, but changing circumstances led to varying degrees of emphasis:

Low tariffs in the interests of planters and farmers vs. high tariffs for the protection of American "infant industries."

State banks and state paper money vs. a national bank and national currency.

Federal aid to internal improvements—highways, canals, and railways vs. state aid, or none at all, to such enterprises.

Free land vs. sale for revenue purposes.

Freedom vs. slavery in the territories.

The division between Democrats and Whigs over these issues was by no means clear-cut. On some of them both parties were split. On none of them was the Northeast, the Northwest, or the South actually "solid." Neither of the great political parties was purely sectional. Whigs and Democrats throve in every state. The South furnished great Whig leaders, such as Alexander H. Stephens and Henry Clay, who ranked in learning and eloquence with Northern men, such as Daniel Webster and Edward Everett. The same was true of the Democrats. Yet in time these parties showed a marked tendency to line up on one side or the other of these paramount questions of the age.

Not long after Southern Republicans had agreed to the tariff of 1816, they began to change their minds and oppose the very idea of protection for American industries. Within a few years they formulated a well-rounded argument against it and began to denounce it as a form of robbery under government auspices. Special duties on imported manufactures, they claimed, are contrary to the interests of all agricultural states, North and South; such protection raises the prices of goods which planters and farmers must buy; it is, in effect, a tax on them for the benefit of manufacturers; planters and farmers can prosper best by selling their produce abroad and buying their manufactures from the industrial nations of the Old World with their cheaper labor. On such grounds Southern politicians sought to make an alliance with politicians in the farming regions of the North, especially the Northwest.

It took nearly forty years, however, for advocates of low tariffs, "for revenue only," to win a substantial victory, and it was transient when it came. While Jeffersonian Republicans were still nominally in power, Congress raised the duties on imports twice—in 1824 and in 1828. The second act, decried as "the tariff of abominations," though modified later in details, produced a revolt in South Carolina. In 1832 the state legislature called a convention, and that assembly, duly elected, condemned the protective tariff as contrary to the Constitution of the United States and hence null and void. The delegates further resolved that, if the federal government tried to coerce the people of the state into obeying the law, they would withdraw from the Union and establish an independent state. This was the doctrine of nullification in an extreme form.

Infuriated by the threat of South Carolina, President Jackson issued a proclamation denouncing its action from start to finish. He branded nullification as a violation of the letter and spirit of the Constitution. He exalted the Union as supreme and perpetual and spurned the thesis that it was a mere league of sovereign states from which they could withdraw at will. He informed South Carolina that he would enforce federal laws with all the agencies of power at his disposal and that, if any blood was shed in opposition to the national laws, he would hang the first guilty persons he could catch in the act. To back up his words, he prepared to mobilize the necessary military forces.

Yet Jackson also strove for peace. He advised Congress to alter the tariff that had made the trouble and lay protective duties only on manufactures required for national defense. Then he asked Congress to pass a "force bill," a measure giving him more power in executing federal laws.

Under the leadership of Henry Clay a compromise was reached in 1833. Congress provided that the tariff should be gradually reduced until by 1842 it would be about on a level with the rates set in 1816. It also enacted the force bill into law. Thus both sides could make a show of claiming the laurels. South Carolina repealed her nullification ordinance and a truce reigned for a time.

It was only a truce. Fired by their victory in 1840, the Whigs broke the compromise of 1833 and raised the protective duties on imported manufactures. They made it clear that Clay's "American system" of protection for manufacturing industries was to be a fixed part of their domestic policy. The battle line was thus firmly drawn and Democrats accepted the challenge. In their platform of 1856 they endorsed the idea of progressive free trade throughout the world. Their triumph at the polls they followed up by enacting the law of 1857 which, though far from a free-trade act, made substantial cuts in many protective duties.

The second primary issue of politics—banking and currency—also had sectional aspects. Planters in the new Southwest, often heavily in debt for the purchase of land, slaves, and implements, had a partiality for inflation—an abundance of paper money—to raise the prices of their produce. Farmers in the new Northwest, likewise often in debt for their lands and equipment, were inclined to concur. It was mainly, though not entirely, in the seaboard regions of the East that the United States Bank, re-established in 1816 by the Republicans, and the currency it issued were considered "good for the country."

Appealing especially to farmers and mechanics, President Jackson, the pride of the West, opened a war on the United States Bank soon after he entered the White House. He declared that it was contrary to the Constitution, gave special privileges to the rich, and was against the interests of the plain people. Congress answered in 1832 by passing a bill to renew the bank on the expiration of its charter in 1836. Jackson vetoed the bill. By executive order he removed federal deposits from the vaults of the bank. And as the number of his supporters increased in the Senate and House of Representatives he had the pleasure of seeing the bank utterly destroyed before he retired to his beloved Hermitage in Tennessee in 1837.

Then with no national bank to interfere, state banks, chartered under state laws, burgeoned everywhere more luxuriantly than ever. In the Mississippi Valley such banks, sometimes owned entirely by state governments, sprang up like weeds and issued torrents of paper money based on little or no gold and silver coins. The notes of the worst of these institutions, derided as "wildcat banks," usually fell rapidly in value and often became worthless as the issuing banks blew up in bankruptcy.

Once more in its history, as in Revolutionary times, the United States had fluctuating paper currencies—dollars worth one hundred cents in coin in conservative states and anywhere from ninety-nine cents to almost nothing in the wildcat-banking states. Once more commerce among the states was impeded by paper notes of varying values. But in spite of determined and unremitting efforts, the Whigs were unable to carry through Congress any kind of a bill for establishing another United States Bank.

Over internal improvements—the third leading question of the time—the ranks of both parties were badly broken. Yet, in general, Democratic presidents were inclined to the view that Congress had no constitutional power to build great national roads and should not engage in the business anyway. In taking this position they reversed precedents set under President Jefferson, their political godfather; but consistency had never been a law with politicians. So for a brief period zeal for internal improvements by federal action cooled off.

Not until the success of railways was fully demonstrated did it flare up again. Then Southern Democrats and Northern Whigs agreed that a continental railway should unite the Atlantic coast with the Pacific coast and that federal aid should be provided for the construction of the line. They disagreed, however, over the route to be chosen. Should it be through the Southern or the Northern part of the country? That question was still in dispute when the fateful campaign of 1860 opened.

As railroads were extended from the East into the Mississippi Valley and gave easier access to the Western territories, the fourth political issue became more acute—the disposition of the unoccupied land in the national domain. For a long time after the adoption of the Constitution, Congress had followed the policy of selling this land, either in small plots to settlers or in large blocks to speculators. The price fixed for the land—at first two dollars an acre and later a dollar and a quarter—though low was largely designed to bring revenue into the federal Treasury.

Low as it was, the figure made it hard for poor farmers and city workers in the East to "take up" lands in the West and establish homesteads there. Having to pay for public land at all was deemed contrary to the spirit of democracy and a hindrance to the abolition of poverty in industrial centers. Hence a clamor went up for a sharp reduction in the price of government land, and finally for a law giving it away to settlers in lots of one hundred and sixty acres.

For leaders in both parties this proposal made trouble. Whig manufacturers in the North were inclined to believe that free land in the West would entice workers away from their mills, or at least force the payment of higher wages to employees as an inducement for them to stay in the factories. Whig planters in the South could reason that free land would mean a more rapid growth of the Northwest, more free states, and the supremacy of free states over slave states in Congress and the Union. Yet the Whigs of neither section were in complete harmony on the point. Nor were the Democrats.

The division among Democrats over federal land policies deepened as the agitation over the slavery question grew more intense and reached a climax in 1859. Free land for the poor was eloquently and steadfastly championed in Congress by a Democrat from the farming regions of Tennessee, Andrew Johnson, an outspoken friend of farmers and workingmen; and around his standard many Democratic senators and representatives collected.

On the other hand, under the inspiration of Horace Greeley, a Whig, but also a friend of farmers and urban workers, many Whigs flocked to the free-land cause.

At length a combination of Democrats and Whigs was formed; a bill granting free homesteads to settlers was pushed through Congress and sent to President Buchanan for his signature in 1860. Buchanan was on a ticklish spot. The bill was unquestionably popular, but a host of pro-slavery Democrats were against it. After making his political calculations, Buchanan vetoed the bill, thus leaving the free-land issue to be settled at some indefinite time in the future.

☆

Entangled with the free homestead problem was the question of slavery or freedom in the territories. Twice before the advent of Jacksonian democracy answers had been made in the form of compromises. By acts of Congress slavery had been excluded from the Northwest Territory and permitted in the territories below the Ohio River. Again, by act of Congress, at the time of the Missouri Compromise in 1820, the major portion of the Louisiana Territory had been dedicated to freedom and the smaller portion tacitly left open for slavery. After a great region had been wrested from Mexico by war the issue was revived and brought on a spirited contest in Congress and outside.

Once more an adjustment resulted—the Compromise of 1850—in which both sides sought peace, the Whigs under the leadership of Henry Clay and Daniel Webster, now old men on the verge of the grave. The slave trade, not slavery itself, was abolished in the District of Columbia. That was a concession to freedom if a slight one. It was more than offset, however, by a new and drastic law making it easier for masters to secure the return of slaves who had run away to the North. Under its terms a master merely had to claim a Negro as his slave before the proper federal agent; the Negro so claimed had no right to have a jury trial, to call witnesses, or be heard in his own behalf in open court. If the agent ruled that the claimant was the master, the slave was handed over to him. As to the new territories, the Compromise of 1850 provided that they could come into the Union in the future with or without slavery as their constitutions might provide at the time of their admission.

One-sided as the Compromise of 1850 was in fact, the voters seemed to approve it, for they gave an emphatic majority to the Democratic candidate, Franklin Pierce, in the presidential election of 1852. Had Democrats been content, the issue of slavery in the new territories might have been allowed to languish. But under the leadership of a restless and ambitious Democrat from Illinois, Stephen A. Douglas, the old Missouri Compromise on slavery was abrogated in 1854 by an act of Congress for the organization of the Kansas and Nebraska territories.

These districts were in that part of the Louisiana Purchase where slavery had been abolished by the agreement of 1820. Nevertheless, the new law of 1854 provided that the people of the two territories, or territories formed out of them, might come into the Union with or without slavery as their constitutions prescribed at the time—in short might have slavery if they wanted it. To ring the death knell of the Missouri Compromise on slavery the law expressly repealed it. Settlers, or "squatters," who went into these territories were thus to decide for themselves by popular vote whether they would have slavery or not. In this way the vast interior of the continent, dedicated to freedom in 1820, was thrown open to slavery under the doctrine of what was called "squatter sovereignty." A question long regarded as closed became again the subject of a nation-wide clash.

According to outward signs the repeal of the Missouri Compromise and the opening of all territories to slavery seemed to mean that the Democrats would command the power of the United States Government indefinitely. The tempest of protest that flashed out against the repeal was apparently without avail, for two years later, in 1856, the Democratic candidate for President, James Buchanan, was triumphantly elected. A Virginia editor had once exclaimed that the South nominated candidates and the Northern Democracy elected them. Judging by the election returns, it was still true. A great barrier to the spread of slavery in Western territories had been removed—the Missouri Compromise prohibiting it—and the people at the polls had apparently approved that concession to slave-owners.

Two days after the inauguration of Buchanan on March 4, 1857, the Supreme Court of the United States seemed to clinch the Democratic grip on the government forever. In the Dred Scott case it declared, in effect, that the Missouri Compromise had been null and void from the beginning and that Congress had no power under the Constitution to exclude slavery from the territories.

A majority of the justices in the court were loyal Democrats and in their decision they followed the party line. They had done this with some hesitation but the upshot was clear. Now slavery could be banned from the territories only by an amendment to the Constitution; and, given the number of slave states, the three-fourths majority of the states necessary to ratify it could not be secured. Besides being successful at the polls, pro-slavery Democrats seemed to be permanently entrenched under the Constitution by Supreme Court sanction.

As a matter of fact all the five primary issues, over which Whigs and Democrats struggled for possession of the United States Government, were debated in the form of constitutional interpretations. Whatever the Whigs demanded, some Democratic orator was almost certain to declare unconstitutional. At length, in the Democratic view, a protective tariff was unconstitutional. So was a national bank and a sound bank currency. So were internal improvements and subsidies for shipping, as well as the exclusion of slavery from the territories. John C. Calhoun was so extreme as to maintain that Congress could not constitutionally accept a gift of money to establish the Smithsonian Institution in Washington for the advancement and diffusion of knowledge.

On the other hand, to Whig orators, everything they wanted the government to do was thoroughly constitutional. Daniel Webster took the position that, in letter and spirit, the Constitution empowered Congress to promote commerce, industry, and "sound practices" in banking. Henry Clay supported him with an eloquence scarcely less impressive. As arguments, they cited precedents set by George Washington and Alexander Hamilton, who, as members of the convention of 1787, presumably knew the primary purposes of the Constitution.

In the course of the constitutional debates over the details of the five specific issues two well-rounded theories as to the very nature of the Constitution were formulated. These theories were given definite shape during a great debate in the Senate in 1830 between Robert Y. Hayne, of South Carolina, and Daniel Webster, of Massachusetts. The Union established by the Constitution, Hayne asserted, is merely a compact between sovereign states; it is simply a league of independent states; and states may at their pleasure lawfully withdraw from the Union. On the other side, Webster protested that the Constitution is ordained and established by the people of the United States; the Union is perpetual; its laws are binding on the states; and states cannot lawfully leave the Union.

Enmeshed with these theories respecting the nature of the Constitution were two theories bearing on the powers of the federal government under the Constitution. By 1850 Democratic leaders in general had committed themselves to the proposition that the powers were confined within narrow bounds: to what they themselves called the explicit, specific, and enumerated purposes set forth in the Constitution. To this fixation Whig leaders opposed the doctrine that the powers conferred on the federal government were, in the very language of the Constitution, broad enough to cover all matters of "general welfare"; that Congress, as the Constitution declared, could make laws on many matters not mentioned at all in the Constitution because Congress was authorized to make all laws necessary and proper for carrying all its powers into effect.

When the dispute over the nature of the Constitution and the powers of the federal government was culminating in a deadlock of interpretations, all the men who had taken part in the framing of the Constitution were dead. James Madison lived long enough to protest against the South Carolina doctrine of nullification, but even his long life had been closed in 1836. Moreover, the debates in the secret sessions of the convention of 1787, as Madison had recorded them, were still sealed in his private papers, utterly unknown to the public. While airing their theories in 1830, neither Hayne nor Webster knew the purposes and intentions of the framers of the Constitution as written down in Madison's notes taken in the Philadelphia convention of 1787. Even after Madison's notes were published in 1840 Calhoun and his disciples went on arguing as before in defense of their narrow interpretation of the Constitution. Nor did the public pay much attention to the revelations contained in Madison's papers. Democrats in power at the national capital continued to claim the sanction of the Constitution for their political program, no matter what their opponents said to the contrary.

At the height of their power, in 1857, the Democrats had a majority in the Senate and House of Representatives. The presidency was in their hands. And a majority of the Supreme Court had come from their ranks. On such good grounds they could exult.

Yet over the bright horizon a tornado was brewing. Dissensions were rising even among the Democrats. Critics were assailing their program and the institution of human slavery associated with it. Public protest was mounting, and an opposition party was preparing to drive slavery out of the territories, despite the repeal of the Missouri Compromise and the decision of the Supreme Court.

In many ways, apart from its merits or demerits, slavery was involved in Democratic measures, actions, and successes. Slaves furnished the labor for the plantations of the agricultural South; and planters were powerful in the councils of the Democratic party. If as planters they took issue with Whigs over protective tariffs, banking, or the currency, Whigs could reply by attacking them as slaveowners. If slavery was to be preserved and the planting interests promoted by federal laws, it was necessary for Southern planters to have more slave states to maintain a balance of power in the Senate against the growing number of free states in the North. Giving free homesteads to free farmers forecast the destruction of that balance. For various reasons, therefore, slavery entered naturally or was deliberately drawn into the debates over all the major political issues of the age.

Meanwhile slavery, the source of economic and political power for planters, was being attacked increasingly and more emotionally as a moral evil, as a violation of the human rights proclaimed in the Declaration of Independence. In 1776 slavery had been lawful in the North, as well as in the South. But it was neither popular nor profitable there. One after another Northern states either abolished slavery or made provisions for gradual emancipation. Massachusetts outlawed it in 1780. New York eradicated in 1827 the last vestiges of slavery within its borders. In Southern states strong sentiments against it were expressed. Great Virginian slave-owners themselves, such as Washington, Jefferson, and George Mason, had condemned it as injurious to both slaves and masters, and had voiced the hope that in coming years it might be abolished. Washington's will provided for freeing his slaves after the death of his wife. Slavery was not mentioned in the Constitution; but Congress, given power to stop the importation of slaves in or after 1808, had exercised that authority at the earliest opportunity. Relatively few leaders of the Revolutionary generation ever undertook to defend slavery through thick and thin.

It was an easy thing, however, to dislike slavery and to hope that in some manner it might pass away. It was possible to give up one's own human chattels and feel more comfortable in conscience. It was really revolutionary to demand the instant and wholesale extirpation of slavery, root and branch. That was what William Lloyd Garrison did when, in 1831, he started publishing at Boston his anti-slavery paper, the *Liberator*. Garrison scorned "gradual emancipation," and called for immediate and unconditional abolition. In vitriolic language he denounced slavery and slaveowners alike, declaring that he would be harsh as truth and would be heard. Stoned and otherwise assaulted by mobs in the streets of Boston, he kept up his agitation with unwavering fervor, powerfully aided by Theodore Weld, a Christian evangelist, pamphleteer, and organizer.

In many parts of the North, from the seaboard to the Mississippi Valley, abolitionists formed groups to work with Garrison or to carry on the crusade against slavery in their own ways. Sarah and Angelina Grimké, of South Carolina, did more than give up their slaves, as many other Southerners did; they also dedicated themselves to the cause of general abolition by going North to join in the agitation against slavery. Their example of conviction and action was an inspiration in the abolition movement.

Negroes who had escaped from bondage told of their tragic experiences and gave firsthand knowledge of slavery to audiences far and wide in the North, helping to inflame antagonism to that system—especially Frederick Douglass, Sojourner Truth, and Harriet Tubman, "the Moses of her people," who led some three hundred Negroes out of the South by hazardous exploits, one after the other. Dramatizing the worst features of slavery in a novel, *Uncle Tom's Cabin*, Harriet Beecher Stowe startled at least a million readers with her selected pictures of its sorrows and cruelties, making slavery odious to an immense number of persons in the North who had thought little about that labor system below the Mason and Dixon border.

In 1859, John Brown, with a few backers, invaded Virginia and at the risk of his life tried to start a general slave insurrection. Like uprisings previously made by slaves, it did not succeed, but it threw fuel into the fire. Higher and higher rose the flame of resentment as political struggles for power over the possession of the federal government engaged the voters in successive campaigns.

Criticisms of slavery, in the North, at length found political expression in the creation of the Free Soil party. Yet this party, which put forward a candidate first in 1844, did not demand immediate abolition. The central point of its program was the exclusion of slavery from the territories. On that program alone, however, the Free Soilers made little progress. In their first campaign in 1844 they polled only about 62,000 votes out of over 2,500,000. Free Soilers made gains in 1848 but in 1852 their vote fell off more than one third. The mere exclusion of slavery from the territories did not then seem to be the issue on which a candidate could ever carry the country.

Nevertheless the repeal of the Missouri Compromise by Congress in 1854 and the opening of all the territories to slavery changed the temper of many voters with respect to the issue. By this action Congress dispelled the hope that slavery would die out gradually or could be confined to the states where it existed. It indicated the possibility that slavery might become dominant in vast regions of the West and in fact spread throughout the nation.

Unwilling to accept such prospects, many citizens in the North demanded a new party squarely committed to shutting slavery out of the territories; that is, to preventing its expansion. At a public meeting in Wisconsin, called shortly after Congress repealed the Missouri Compromise, a committee composed of Whigs, Democrats, and Free Soilers was appointed to start the organization of this party.

In selecting a name for it, the managers were shrewd. The Federalist party had long been dead. The Whig party was dying. Some other and more attractive title was necessary to capture public interest. Recalling their party memories, the leaders in the new movement at last chose the name "Republican party"—the old but still appealing title that had been adopted by Jefferson for the popular party that overwhelmed the "monocrats" and "aristocrats" of Hamilton's following in 1800. Under the long shadow cast by Jefferson's fame, the new Republicans nominated as their candidate for President in 1856 John C. Frémont, famous as an explorer of California, and adopted as their campaign motto, "Free labor, free speech, free men, free Kansas, and Frémont!" They were defeated in the election but the size of their vote, 1,340,000, encouraged them to expect victory in the next presidential contest.

☆

Watching the tides of public opinion flowing and ebbing through these turbulent years was a Whig of Illinois who had long been active in the politics of that state—Abraham Lincoln. Born in a log cabin in Kentucky in 1809, brought up in log cabins in Indiana and Illinois, Lincoln was certainly "a man of the people." He was poor enough and humble enough to suit any "democrat" in all the land. But, given only the barest rudiments of learning in his boyhood, Lincoln, like Franklin and Washington of the Revolution, educated himself, and well, by reading, besides a few law books, many classics in the English tongue, including the Bible, Shakespeare, and Aesop's Fables.

After a tough struggle against poverty Lincoln won some local renown as a lawyer and as a Whig member of the Illinois legislature. For a brief period, 1847–49, he served as a member of the House of Representatives in Washington. Still, as he approached the age of fifty, Lincoln was little known except as a local politician in Illinois.

With regard to the slavery issue, Lincoln was no abolitionist. Yet he believed slavery was an evil and was opposed to its extension in the territories. To abolitionists he was thus "a trimmer"; while to pro-slavery Whigs and Democrats he was "unsafe," if not "dangerous."

Lincoln's faith in the people was as stanch as that of any Democrat. Indeed Lincoln confessed that he had learned the first principles of popular government from Jefferson. Even so, he was cautious. He did not leave the Whig party until 1854. Four years later he was nominated by the Republicans as a candidate for the United States Senate.

He was defeated at the senatorial election but during the campaign he became a national figure. In a series of debates with Stephen A. Douglas, the opposing Democratic candidate, Lincoln manifested qualities of greatness—an exceptional knowledge of American history and government, genius as an orator, barbed analytical skill, and a clear conviction on a paramount issue of the times—the exclusion of slavery from the territories.

From the debates with Douglas, Lincoln emerged as a thoughtful leader commanding the confidence and admiration of throngs of citizens. To the discussions men and women had flocked on horseback, in farm wagons, in carriages, and on foot. Amid a fanfare of banner waving, band playing, and parading, however, they had demonstrated that they had serious purposes. They followed the arguments of the debaters and weighed the clashing opinions, soberly, with due recognition of their significance. At the same time newspapers had carried far and wide full reports of the debates; and citizens all the way from Maine to California could make up their minds on the merits of the arguments and the plans for meeting the impending crisis. So cutting and lasting was the impression which Lincoln made on the country by his speeches against Douglas and others delivered subsequently that the new Republican party nominated him for the presidency in 1860. In Southern eyes he was radical on the slavery question, but he was not too radical for the public in the North.

In choosing Lincoln the Republicans elbowed aside William H. Seward, of New York, who had long been prominent in public affairs. Seward was in some respects more radical than Lincoln and in other respects more conservative. He had gone beyond Lincoln by condemning the system of slavery itself. He had also spoken the ominous words: "the irrepressible conflict." Yet Seward had been associated with the "money power" centralized in the East and hence was no favorite in the Democratic strongholds of the West.

Remembering that they had been beaten at the last election when they had adopted the exclusion of slavery from the territories as the main plank in their platform, the Republicans in 1860 drafted a platform that made a wider appeal to voters. They renewed their pledge to shut slavery out of the territories but they inserted two new planks. One of these endorsed the device of a protective tariff to encourage the development of "the industrial interests of the whole country." That was gratifying to Whigs in the North. Another new plank advocated a homestead law giving a farm of moderate size to anybody who was inclined to go out and till it. That pleased thousands of Democrats, especially in the Middle West, who had supported the homestead bill which the Democratic President, James Buchanan, had vetoed. In other words, Republicans in 1860 "had three strings to their bow"— opposition to slavery in the territories, protection for American industries, and free homesteads for people discontented with their lot in the East.

Over these issues the Democratic party split asunder. One wing, dominated by Southern leaders, nominated for President John C. Breckinridge, of Kentucky, and declared that slavery must be permitted in the territories and protected there by the government of the United States. A second wing held a separate convention and nominated Stephen A. Douglas on a platform of "squatter sovereignty," that is, letting the voters of the territories decide whether they wanted slavery or not. A number of Whigs, clinging to the Clay-Webster program of compromise, took a fresh title, Constitutional Unionists, and selected as candidates for President and Vice-President John Bell, of Tennessee, and Edward Everett, of Massachusetts. In their platform, as if no slavery question tormented the land, they called upon the voters to support the Constitution, the Union, and the enforcement of the laws.

Consequently four parties were in the field for the campaign of 1860. In these circumstances Lincoln carried all the free states except New Jersey. But the number of popular ballots cast for him was smaller by about a million than the number received by his three opponents. In fact, the candidates of the two relatively conservative parties, Bell and Douglas, together received more votes than were polled by the Republicans. Still Lincoln's popular vote was so distributed among the states that he won a majority of all the electoral votes and under the Constitution was lawfully elected to the presidency. Aware that he represented only a minority of the people, though duly chosen for the office of Chief Executive, he looked forward with anxiety to the day of his inauguration.

CHAPTER XVII

National Unity Sealed in an Armed Contest

NEWS OF LINCOLN'S ELECTION in November 1860 was taken as a signal for secession in South Carolina. The state legislature called upon the voters to elect delegates to a convention endowed with full powers of action on that issue. In December the convention assembled and by unanimous resolution it withdrew South Carolina from the Union. Early the next year other Southern states followed this example: Florida, Georgia, Alabama, Mississippi, Louisiana, and Texas.

In February delegates from six of the states met at Montgomery, Alabama, formed a new union called the Confederate States of America, drew up a provisional constitution, and chose as provisional President Jefferson Davis, a Mississippi planter who had formerly served the national Union with distinction in war and peace. A few weeks later a permanent constitution was framed for the Confederacy. It was ratified by the seceded states; members of the Confederate Senate and House were chosen; and Davis was elected as regular President of the Confederacy.

In taking this action secessionists based their expectations on one or both of two theories. The first was that the North would permit the Confederate States to secede in peace and establish friendly relations with their government. The second was that, if permission was denied and war came, the South could maintain its independence by arms.

Though the Southern states were outnumbered by the Northern states in population, wealth, and all the great industries necessary to provide the sinews of war, there were at the time several reasons for Southern confidence in victory. It was assumed that Great

Britain would need cotton to keep her mill wheels turning and would intervene in support of the Confederacy; and that Napoleon III, Emperor of the French, would sympathize with the planting aristocracy and co-operate with Britain in aiding the Confederate government. It was widely believed in the South that Northern farmers and mechanics would not fight; or, if they did, that they would be outmatched by Southern valor. Another source of Confederate optimism was the faith that all the other slave states, except Delaware, would join in secession; and that blocking the mouth of the Mississippi River to the commerce of the Northwest would make states in that region eager to come to terms with the Confederacy. In the opening months of 1861 few if any Confederates could foresee how vain such expectations would turn out to be.

When Lincoln was inaugurated on March 4, 1861, he faced a hard dilemma: the Union seemed to be dissolving; the Confederacy must be allowed to go in peace; a compromise must be reached; or the Union must be maintained by arms. Between his election and his inauguration, Lincoln had refrained from the use of inflammatory language in speaking of the South. By letters and in other ways he let Southern leaders know that he had no intention or power to interfere with slavery in their states. Before his inauguration Congress passed a resolution for amending the Constitution in such a manner as to guarantee that the federal government could never attack slavery in the states where it existed. To this position Lincoln gave his personal approval.

On behalf of the South a proposal was made that the old Missouri Compromise line be drawn through the Western territories—with slavery on one side and freedom on the other. But Lincoln had been elected on a platform promising that slavery would be abolished in the territories. On that point he was adamant and he rejected the proposal.

Lincoln's inaugural address was an appeal for solving the problem within the limits of the Constitution. He declared that the Union was older than the states and that no state could lawfully secede. Under the Constitution slavery was legal in the states where it was established. This fact he recognized and again assured the South that he had neither the right nor the intention to disturb slavery there. The law providing for the return of fugitive slaves to their masters was on the statute books and Lincoln promised to enforce it. To this attitude respecting the Fugitive Slave Act the stoutest slaveowner in the Confederacy could scarcely object.

Lincoln also said clearly, however, that to him was entrusted the power to hold, occupy, and possess the property and places belonging to the government and to collect the duties and imposts; and he added that he was under a solemn oath to "preserve, protect, and defend" the government of the United States. Still he closed on a note of hope—that "the better angels of our nature" would in the end keep the bonds of Union unbroken.

As yet neither side had committed an act of violence. Only words had been spoken, papers written, and pacific measures employed. For more than a month uncertainty as to the outcome of secession prevailed, while representatives of the Union and of the Confederacy feverishly sought, more or less unofficially, to reach a compromise or a settlement of some kind. But a straight-out test of power was in the offing.

On a little island in the harbor before the city of Charleston stood Fort Sumter—a spot of land which belonged by law to the government of the United States and was garrisoned by a small Federal force in command of Major Robert Anderson. Without fresh supplies this garrison could not long hold out. The Confederate government demanded a surrender of the fort but refrained at the moment from any overt act. Its officials merely stopped the flow of provisions to Major Anderson, reckoning that he would soon be compelled to yield.

For Lincoln the plight of Fort Sumter created a delicate situation but after many delays he decided to send supplies to Major Anderson by sea. Having received news of this decision, President Davis, thinking that the garrison would quickly be starved out, issued only vague orders to General P. G. T. Beauregard, in command of troops at Charleston, instructing him to continue negotiations.

Beauregard dispatched agents to consult with Major Anderson and they received from him a pledge to surrender on April 15, if no contrary orders came to him from the national capital in the meantime. Deeming this reply unsatisfactory, the agents, without consulting Beauregard or any superior authority, reported their views on the next procedure to a Confederate artillery commander; and at half-past four on the morning of April 12 the bombardment of Fort Sumter began. After a spirited defense Major Anderson surrendered about sunset on the evening of the next day and formally evacuated the fort on Sunday, April 14.

Among many uncertainties one thing was now certain: the first act of violence had been committed by Confederates—the flag of the United States flying above Federal troops had been fired upon. The effect was electric. Millions of people in the North who had been lukewarm or hesitant now declared their unequivocal readiness to defend the Union. On April 15, Lincoln issued a call for 75,000 soldiers—not to wage a general war on the Confederacy but first of all "probably" to repossess the forts, places, and property which had been taken away from the Union—a purpose to be accomplished with the least possible disturbance to peaceful citizens in any part of the country. In the same proclamation he summoned both houses of Congress in special session for July 4, "then and there to consider and determine such measures as, in their wisdom, the public safety and interest may seem to demand."

In the South the firing on Fort Sumter and Lincoln's call for troops were also followed by swift and drastic measures. On April 17, Virginia seceded from the Union. Soon Arkansas, Tennessee, and North Carolina likewise went over to the Confederate side. Then prompt military intervention on the part of Lincoln stifled attempts to withdraw Maryland, Kentucky, and Missouri from the Union.

But the South was far from "solid" in the desire to leave the Union. As a matter of fact in Georgia, Alabama, Mississippi, and Louisiana a strong opposition to secession had appeared in a large minority vote against it. In Virginia western counties were so opposed to it that they withdrew from the Old Dominion and later entered the Union as the state of West Virginia. In the western part of North Carolina, Unionist loyalty widely prevailed. In the eastern parts of Kentucky and Tennessee, Unionists were undoubtedly in a majority and thousands of them joined the Federal army. Although opinion in Maryland and Kentucky was sharply divided, little force was needed to keep those states in the Union. Secessionists in Missouri were numerous enough to create a civil war in that state but at length they were driven out or suppressed, after several pitched battles. Less than a year after the firing on Fort Sumter the hope of Confederates that the border states would come to their aid in the struggle for independence had been dispelled.

☆

When war began in full force the Confederacy had only eleven states on its side as against twenty-three states in the North. Nine million people in the South, more than one third of them slaves, were aligned against 22,000,000 people in the North, nearly all

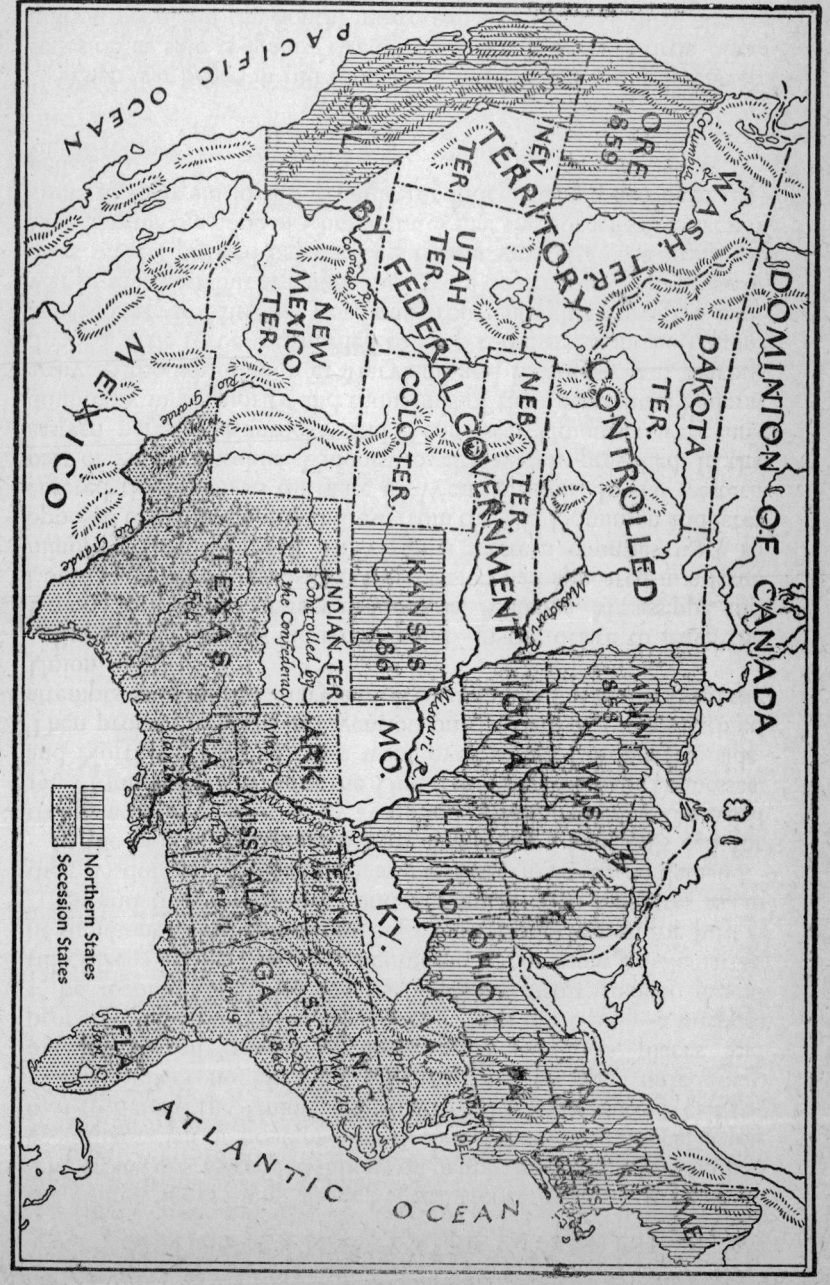

THE DIVIDED UNION IN 1861

free. States predominantly agricultural were arrayed in mortal combat with states rich in manufacturing as well as agricultural resources, reinforced by gold and silver from Western mines. Considered merely in terms of men and metal, Southern strength was inferior; but the South soon demonstrated ingenuity and enterprise in mobilizing materials and high competence in the art of warfare.

As the war got under way the Federal government at Washington and the Confederate government installed at Richmond, Virginia, confronted immense tasks for which neither was well prepared. Armies had to be raised and organized, munitions and other supplies furnished in staggering amounts, and commanding officers chosen to direct military and naval operations. The treasuries of both governments were almost empty and funds had to be provided to pay bills which aggregated before the close of the war far more than all the money the United States Government had spent since the establishment of the Republic. Relations with European governments had to be conducted with a view to securing support and warding off unfriendly acts. Problems of domestic economy and civilian affairs, numerous and perplexing, had to be considered and handled in a manner to preserve internal harmony and promote unison in arms. Finally it was necessary, among all these trials, for both governments to plan campaigns and direct fighting over immense areas of land and water. To these tasks, on their respective sides, Lincoln and Davis, aided by their advisers and legislatures, devoted their minds and energies from the spring of 1861 to the spring of 1865—for four terrible years of civil war.

During the early months of the armed conflict both governments relied for soldiers upon volunteers who at first rushed to enlist. Soon, however, enthusiasm waned. By special acts passed in April and September 1862, the Confederate Congress authorized President Davis to draft soldiers from among able-bodied males between eighteen and forty-five years of age, with many exemptions including owners or overseers of large plantations. In the last days of the war the Confederacy even made provisions for enrolling slaves; and plans for emancipating slaves in a general conscription were under its serious consideration. In August 1862, Lincoln ordered a draft of militiamen, which turned out to be disappointing as to numbers. In March of the next year the Congress of the United States enacted a law making all able-bodied males, with some exceptions, liable to military duty; and the practice of drafting men continued till the fighting ceased.

On both sides conscription encountered bitter animosity, and desertions from the armies were so numerous as to be serious in effects. When drawings began in New York City on July 13, 1863, a general riot broke out and was not subdued until many people had been killed and a large amount of property burned or otherwise destroyed. The troubles of Davis were equally great if not greater. His recruiting officers met resistance in many places. Governors in some Confederate states, especially Georgia and North Carolina, refused to aid in the strict enforcement of the draft laws. A cry, "rich man's war and poor man's fight," reverberated through the South and men deserted the Confederate ranks in shoals. Nevertheless great and powerful armies were raised by both parties to the conflict and fought valiantly in battles that never seemed to end.

Respecting munitions and other war supplies, the North had a clear superiority of productive power in the beginning and increased its facilities as the war went forward. Able to keep the seas open for Northern shipping, the Union could supplement its domestic output with heavy importations from Great Britain and the Continent. Though the South started with more limited resources, it displayed remarkable energy in building new mills and turning out quantities of war materials. Its achievements were all the more extraordinary by reason of the fact that the Federal blockade of its harbors almost cut off imports of iron, steel, munitions, and other goods. But as the blockade grew tighter, Confederate armies and the civilian population in the South sank into dire distress from the want of adequate supplies.

With regard to financial resources the two governments locked in war were decidedly unequal. At the outset the Union had a Treasury Department and a monetary system; the South had neither and was compelled to create both. The North could command enormous outputs of gold and silver; the South had little hard money and early exported a large portion of what it had to buy military supplies. For raising money both governments resorted to the ancient devices of public finance: taxes, bond sales, and issues of paper notes.

On the Federal side repeated increases were made in customs duties on imports and in excises on tobacco, liquor, other commodities, and occupations; and to these were added taxes on inheritances and incomes. By the sale of bonds and notes the Union Treasury collected a total of $2,600,000,000 during the war. It adopted the third expedient, paper currency, in 1862; and before the conflict closed it issued $450,000,000 in "greenbacks," supplemented by $50,000,000 worth of fractional currency, with notes as low as three cents in face value.

Similar measures were put into force in the Confederacy, coupled with calls upon its states for quotas of money to be raised by direct taxes on property. Confederate bonds were exchanged for specie, produce, and state and Confederate notes. Altogether, about $1,000,000,000 worth of paper currency was emitted, in addition to notes floated by the states, banks, and business concerns.

While Federal bonds dropped in value during the darker days of the war and greenbacks once fell as low as thirty-nine cents on the dollar, Federal financing was, comparatively speaking, sound and stable. In the Confederacy, on the other hand, the course of bonds and notes was on the whole steadily downward as new issues poured out and consumers' goods became scarcer. In the summer of 1862 tea sold in the South at five dollars a pound and boots at twenty-five dollars a pair. In 1862 one dollar in gold was worth twenty-two dollars in Confederate currency; shoes were selling at a hundred and fifty dollars a pair and flour at three hundred dollars a barrel. Early in 1865 beef was six dollars a pound, flour a thousand dollars a barrel, and firewood five dollars a stick. After the surrender at Appomattox in the spring of 1865 Confederate bonds and paper currency dropped dead in the hands of the possessors. According to a current saying of the people, a Confederate dollar was "not worth a Continental," in memory of the paper money issued by the Continental Congress during the Revolution, which hit bottom long before the War for Independence was over.

Especially with reference to foreign relations, the problems of the two governments differed. The government at Washington was already recognized by foreign countries as the lawful government of the United States. Its prime cares were to keep this status unimpaired, to prevent the recognition of the Confederacy as independent, to ward off intervention in the war by Great Britain and France, and to hold the channels of commerce open. On its part the Confederacy struggled to achieve recognition as an independent government, to win financial assistance, to break the blockade on its commerce, and if possible to gain direct intervention on its behalf by Great Britain and France. In this situation Northern measures were essentially protective—against radical changes in foreign relations. Those of the South were essentially exploratory—directed to securing a position as an independent nation among the nations of the earth.

During the first year of the war the Confederacy was recognized as a belligerent by Great Britain and France, though not as an independent state; and it sent two agents abroad, James Mason and John Slidell, to represent it at London and Paris respectively. When the two men were taken from a British steamer by Captain Wilkes, in command of a Union vessel, Great Britain protested against this act of search and seizure. To avoid worse perils, perhaps a foreign war on top of the civil war, Lincoln ordered the Confederate agents released and they went on to Europe to appeal for a recognition of Southern independence and for aid to the Confederacy.

Confederate bonds to the face value of about $15,000,000 were sold in Britain and France. British shipyards, defying an old rule of international law, built war vessels for the Confederacy and the British government allowed them to escape to sea, where they preyed on the commerce of the United States. The sympathies of the British aristocracy and government, of the ruling classes in France, and of Napoleon III, Emperor of the French, were overwhelmingly on the side of the South. In both countries aristocrats hoped that "the upstart Yankee Republic" would be destroyed in the war and many British and French newspapers rejoiced in the prospect. But working people in English cities held mass meetings in protest against giving assistance to slaveowners; and Queen Victoria counseled her Cabinet to be cautious.

Napoleon III attempted to form a European coalition for intervention in the war. In 1861 he suggested to the Czar of Russia that certain great Powers take joint action respecting America, but he met a firm if polite refusal. Meanwhile the British government was toying with the idea. Yet when Napoleon proposed intervention to the British in 1862 he was told that the time was not ripe. One member of the British Cabinet openly declared that the Confederacy was in effect a success; but the Prime Minister, who was watching closely the course of the war in America, was unwilling to take the plunge in aid of the South.

Unable to restrain his meddlesome spirit, Napoleon sent a message to Lincoln offering his services as a mediator between the North and the South. Lincoln responded courteously, declining the offer. In language less urbane Congress replied by passing a resolution telling the French Emperor, in effect, that he should keep his nose out of American affairs.

If it had not been for the decisive Northern victories at Gettysburg and Vicksburg in the summer of 1863, British and French intervention might have come. Those triumphs in arms, however, seemed to assure the future of "the upstart Yankee Republic" and serve as a warning to impertinent foreign Powers. At all events Great Britain and France never recognized the independence of the Confederacy. Nor did they officially intervene in the war.

While raising and supplying armies, providing financial support for the war, and conducting foreign relations, both governments in America framed and tried to enforce complicated measures in direct aid of their respective battle fronts. Acting under war powers conferred upon him as commander in chief by the Constitution, Lincoln struck out vigorously in the spring of 1861. He declared a blockade of Southern ports and ordered the Union navy to halt all vessels, Confederate and foreign, endeavoring to enter or leave those waters. In effect this blockade almost destroyed all Southern commerce. Although some blockade runners escaped the net, the number was not large enough to prevent a growing paralysis of the Confederate export and import business. The trade in cotton, the prime reliance of the South, was for practical purposes completely ruined.

To check Northern citizens who wanted to help the Confederacy and critics who might weaken Federal war efforts, Lincoln resorted to two forms of stringent action. He suspended the writ of habeas corpus and empowered military authorities to arrest, hold, and try persons accused of giving assistance to the South or of interfering with the movements of Federal troops. In the name of military necessity he authorized the arrest and imprisonment of many newspaper publishers, orators, and agitators who printed or uttered severe criticisms of the Federal government and its war activities. The exact number of arrests under those orders is not known, but it was large.

The most celebrated of all Lincoln's war measures was the Proclamation of Emancipation on January 1, 1863. His resolve to effect this historic stroke of state had matured slowly. At the outbreak of the war idealistic men and women in the North urged him to do it and continued their insistence from month to month, rolling monster petitions into the national capital to reinforce their pressure. But for various reasons Lincoln long hesitated. Weighty among them, no doubt, was his fear of losing the support of the slave states which remained in the Union, and his knowledge that the North was seriously divided over abolitionism in every form. He was aware also that a declaration of emancipation would be futile unless confirmed by victory at arms.

It was not until the summer of 1862 that Lincoln decided to act. In July of that year he read to his Cabinet the draft of a proclamation of emancipation which he had written and might issue when occasion seemed to make it feasible. Encouraged by the Federal victory at the battle of Antietam in September, he announced his resolve to the world. He gave notice that unless the states in arms against the Union returned to their allegiance he would, on January 1, 1863, deliver a blow directly at slavery. When the New Year arrived he fulfilled the promise.

In the Proclamation of Emancipation, issued under his war powers, Lincoln declared thenceforward and forever free all the slaves in all the districts of the United States then in arms against the Union. From one point of view this was an empty threat. It freed no slaves in fact. In the loyal districts of the Union slaves remained slaves and, in the districts still controlled by Confederate arms, slaves also remained slaves. But the Proclamation electrified the imagination of all who loved liberty and was indeed a move toward the abolition of slavery throughout the United States.

Even in the South, supposed to be solid, rigorous means were adopted in efforts to stamp out criticisms and crush overt actions interfering with its war program. Early in 1862 the Confederate Congress authorized President Davis to suspend for a term of months the writ of habeas corpus and proclaim martial law in regions where open resistance occurred. Under this act, from time to time, martial law was declared in Richmond, the very capital of the Confederacy, in several Virginia counties, in parts of South Carolina, including Charleston, the hotbed of the secession movement, and in other places in the South.

When this law expired it was not immediately renewed, partly on account of the outcries against it. But in 1864 another temporary act of the kind was passed by the Confederate Congress, in response to a message from President Davis asserting that "disloyalty and hostility to our cause" existed in certain localities and that deserters were being protected by the civil courts.

Actions under such Confederate statutes were numerous and often stern, but apparently fewer and less drastic than similar actions by the Union government in the North. If President Davis had found ample support in the Confederate Congress he might have used martial law mercilessly in trying to prevent the dissolution of the Confederacy during the closing months of the war, but such support was never granted to him.

For Jefferson Davis, as well as Abraham Lincoln, emancipation became a practical issue before the close of the conflict. In desperate straits for soldiers to fight its battles, the Confederate Congress, near the end of the war, passed an act for the employment of slaves in military services. That law had the approval of General Robert E. Lee, as well as of President Davis, and he aided in recruiting Negroes as soldiers. While the language of the statute and of the orders issued under it was vague, it was interpreted to mean that a slave acquired freedom by joining the Confederate army.

Even plans for complete emancipation were discussed at the Confederate capital. In 1864, Duncan Kenner, a member of the Confederate Congress, proposed to President Davis that an agent be sent abroad with power to offer to the British and French governments the emancipation of slaves in exchange for their official recognition of the Confederacy. Davis acceded to the plan. He appointed Kenner as minister plenipotentiary to carry out the project; and Kenner was abroad working at the scheme early in 1865—too late. Had the war continued, real emancipation might have been a Southern act of war.

Armies, supplies, finances, foreign policies, and specific measures in support of war were auxiliaries in the contest at arms. In final analysis the appeal had been made to the ultimate arbiter, force, and the decision had to be rendered on battlefields. After Fort Sumter had fallen and war had become a fact, what war plans, what systems of strategy were to be devised and followed? That was a major problem for both President Lincoln and President Davis. Having withdrawn from the Union and fired the first gun, the Confederacy confronted the task of making real by arms the independence it had asserted. If the Union was to be saved, Lincoln and his advisers had to prepare for an invasion of the South and make decisions respecting the routes to be chosen and the strategy of each movement.

At the start the Confederacy had about 400,000 men and large stores at its command and was better prepared for war than the Union in respect of those details. Some of its military officers advocated immediate offensive action against the North, especially an assault on Washington and the seizure of the capital. Such tactics, it was argued, would quickly bring the government of the United States to its knees.

Other Confederates were more wary. The idea of a possible compromise and a peaceful separation lingered among them even after blood had been shed. A blend of caution and hopes finally fixed for them the nature of their strategy. The invasion of the North was not given up; attempts at it were made, too late and with too little strength. So the South was irrevocably committed to fighting a defensive war, on the theory that the Northern armies might thus be beaten or worn down and forced to accept the independence of the Confederacy.

For the military strategists of the Union geography was of course an element to be reckoned with in planning warfare. The Appalachian Mountains separated the South into two great areas—the East, with Virginia as the bulwark; and the West, divided by the Mississippi River. Victory in either area would be more than a local success. If achieved in the West, it would split the Confederacy to the Gulf of Mexico. If it occurred in Virginia and was crowned by the capture of Richmond, it would weaken the prestige of the Confederacy at home and abroad.

Spurred to immediate decision by armchair strategists, shouting "On to Richmond!" in July 1861 an attack was made by a Union army under General McDowell on Confederate forces under General Beauregard near Centreville, Virginia, close to a little stream called Bull Run. The battle ended in a disaster for the Northern troops, and from this awful lesson President Lincoln learned that the conquest of Virginia would not be a simple affair.

It was in the Western region that military events of decisive significance for a Union victory first occurred. During the summer and autumn of 1861 small engagements in Missouri clinched the grip of the Union on that state. Early the next year Federal forces under Ulysses S. Grant started a drive into Tennessee, by way of the Tennessee River from its outlet in the Ohio. By gunboats on the river and by infantry on the landward side, Grant attacked the Confederates at Fort McHenry in upper Tennessee and forced them to surrender, on February 6.

Dispatching some of his men by gunboats around to Fort Donelson on the Cumberland River, Grant marched eastward with the rest of his soldiers. On February 16 that fortress fell before the assaults of his troops. At many subsequent battles in western Tennessee the Confederates were defeated or seriously crippled and pushed aside; by the opening of 1863 Federal forces had penetrated upper Mississippi and Alabama.

Leaving other officers to cope with the Confederate forces still intact in Tennessee, Grant began to move on Vicksburg, the great stronghold on the Mississippi River. With the aid of gunboats and transports on the river, he besieged the city and starved General John B. Pemberton, the Confederate general, into surrender on July 4. A few days later Port Hudson on the banks of the Mississippi, over the border in Louisiana, was taken by General Banks, one of Grant's aides.

As a naval detachment under Captain David Farragut had opened up the lower Mississippi River and seized New Orleans in the spring of the previous year, the "Father of Waters," as Lincoln said, now flowed "unvexed to the sea." On July 16, 1863, a steamer from St. Louis arrived with a cargo of goods at the docks in New Orleans. More serious battles were yet to be fought in Tennessee and Georgia, but the Confederacy was cut in twain by the summer of 1863 and never reunited.

Federal forces in the Eastern theater of war had accomplished nothing decisive when news of the capture of Vicksburg reached Lincoln in July 1863. Battle after battle, often long, desperate, and costly in lives, had been fought in the East: at Antietam, Fredericksburg, and Chancellorsville, for example. Lincoln had tried general after general in a vain search for a man who could win battles there—McClellan, Hooker, and Burnside, among them.

Meanwhile the army of Virginia under General Robert E. Lee, though repelled at Antietam in September 1862, remained powerful and confident. Indeed Lee felt so sure of his strength that he invaded Pennsylvania, by way of the Shenandoah Valley, in 1863. At Gettysburg, in the early days of July, his advance was stopped, but after receiving a terrible punishment he managed to retire successfully into Virginia. When the year 1864 opened, Lee's army, apparently invincible in defense, barred the roads along which Union armies would have to march if they tried to plunge into the eastern stronghold of the Confederacy.

Two master feats for the Union cause were put through, however, in 1864. In May, General Grant, in command of all the Federal armies, took personal charge of the Virginia campaign and started a relentless drive on Richmond, sparing neither men nor resources in his determination to capture it. That same month Grant's trusted companion in arms, General William T. Sherman, began his march from Chattanooga to Atlanta.

While Grant slashed his way southward, undeterred by heavy losses, crossed the James River, and laid siege to Petersburg, near Richmond, Sherman advanced on Atlanta. In September Sherman took the city. After a delay of a few weeks he led his army off on a march across Georgia, foraging, burning, destroying as he went. On December 20, Savannah crumpled up. From that scene of victory Sherman's army turned northward and pursued its course across Georgia and South Carolina, leaving ruins in its wake, into North Carolina and onward toward Virginia.

The last phase of the war was drawing to a finish. On April 2, 1865, Grant took Petersburg. The next day the Union flag floated over the Confederate capital at Richmond, abandoned by President Davis in a hurried flight. At the head of a shaken if as yet unbeaten army, Lee moved rapidly westward in the direction of Lynchburg, with Grant racing at his heels and General Philip Sheridan on his flank.

For a time Lee seemed to think that he might escape into North Carolina, join forces there with General Joseph E. Johnston, and continue the war. But on April 9, finding that hope forlorn, he gave up, and at Appomattox handed his sword to General Grant. About two weeks later General Johnston laid down his arms. Far away in the West, General Kirby Smith, commanding Confederate troops beyond the Mississippi River, surrendered; and the last fragment of the Confederate army was dissolved during the first days of June. The war, launched with the bombardment of Fort Sumter in 1861, had at last run its course.

Soon it was possible to reckon some of the cost. A careful estimate placed the number of enlistments in the Federal army at 2,898,304 and in the Confederate army at about 1,300,000. The total number of deaths from all causes in the Federal forces was placed at 359,528 and in the Confederate army at approximately 258,000. This was exclusive of the hundreds of thousands of men wounded or made invalids for the remainder of their lives. Estimates of the cost in terms of the money spent on war by the two parties depended on the time fixed—whether up to April 1, 1865, or some later date to cover pensions paid to veterans on both sides. As of April 1, 1865, calculations reported the cost to the Union at about $3,250,000,000 and to the Confederacy at approximately $1,500,000,000; or $4,750,000,000 in all. After pensions, interest on the Federal debt, and the value of property destroyed were added, a conservative computation established the total cost of preserving the Union and abolishing slavery at above $10,000,000,000.

For less than half this amount freedom could have been bought for all the 3,953,857 slaves recorded in the census of 1860—the compensated emancipation which Congress and President Lincoln had proposed in 1862.

☆

Consuming as were the events of the war and the measures of public policy immediately connected with it, the thought and activity of the people on both sides of the struggle were by no means wholly monopolized by it. The life and work of millions in both sections continued to be civilian in nature and emphasis.

The South was disturbed by complaints that civilians gave too much attention and energy to their own interests and too little to the prosecution of the war. Governors of Southern states, members of state legislatures, and members of the Confederate Congress concerned themselves continually with the protection of local and civil rights against the encroachments of military power under the leadership of President Davis. All departments of the Confederate government, amid the distractions of war, considered plans and took actions with reference to economic interests, and with a view to the reordering of affairs after independence was secured. But with the collapse of the Confederate system, legal and financial, and the occupation of the South by Federal armies, such plans and actions in respect of Southern economy and social policy came to naught or at least to little if anything.

On the other hand, in the North, untrampled by invading armies and free from the devastation of battles, the civilian way of life was less upset. There debates over political issues that had shaken the country before the war went on; and significant laws bearing on these issues were enacted by Congress. In response to the increasing demands created by government buying for war purposes, industry and agriculture flourished and the Industrial Revolution drove forward. Out of war profits prodigious masses of capital were accumulated in private hands for new investments in business. Additional millions of acres were brought under the plow by freehold farmers in the West. During the war years the supremacy of manufacturing and commercial interests over the planting interests, in wealth and the number of workers employed, became indisputable.

With senators and representatives accustomed to speak for the planting interests absent from the national capital, the Federal Congress was of course freer to enact laws long demanded by industrialists, financiers, farmers, and reformers. In providing revenues for war purposes it increased again and again the duties levied on imports and raised the discriminative protection accorded to American manufacturers to the highest point yet attained in American history. For example, the tariff on pig iron, which stood at six dollars a ton in 1861, was pushed to nine dollars a ton in 1864, and the tariff of twelve cents a pound on general woolen manufactures was doubled by the act of 1864. Neither the old Federalists nor the Whigs had ever dreamed of favors to industry so generous. Nor were the farmers overlooked in the tariff bills. The duty of three cents per pound for imported raw wool of the lower grade, imposed by the law of 1861, was lifted to six cents a pound in 1864. At the close of the war the free trade which Democrats had once advocated in their national platform seemed as dead as a doornail.

The second great issue over which politicians and statesmen had argued since the days of Hamilton and Jefferson—a national banking system—was likewise settled for a time in connection with efforts to raise money for military expenditures. Hamilton's United States Bank had lapsed in 1811. The second United States Bank established in 1816 had been abolished by Jacksonian Democrats. From 1836 to the outbreak of the war state banks had dominated banking and inundated the country with their paper notes, some sound, some unsound, others fluctuating wildly in value. To cope with financial disorders and help the sale of bonds, Congress in 1863 established a new banking system. It centered the system in the Treasury Department of the Federal government, rather than in a banking corporation such as had been set up in 1791 and 1816, only to be repudiated.

The new law authorized the formation of local banking associations or companies. It empowered them to engage in the general banking business and to issue paper money based on the Federal bonds they bought and deposited with the Treasurer of the United States. The next year, in 1864, Congress made provision for forcing all state banks entirely out of the currency business by laying a prohibitive annual tax of ten per cent on state bank notes, beginning July 1, 1866. Even after they returned to power in Washington, the Democrats, hitherto sworn foes of national banking, did not dare to overthrow it and restore state bank currency. Hamilton had truly triumphed over Jefferson.

During this distribution of national largess by legislative acts, the agrarians got a portion, in the form of free homesteads on the public domain. In their platform of 1860 the Republicans promised free land as well as protection for manufactures. This pledge Congress redeemed two years later by passing the Homestead Act, which President Lincoln gladly signed.

Under the act any person, man or woman, head of a family or twenty-one years old, either a citizen or an alien who had declared his intention of becoming a citizen, could enter a claim to 160 acres on the public domain; and by occupying it for five years, besides making certain improvements on it, the entrant was to have full possession of the property. One vital exception was made, however: excluded from this right to free land were all persons who had borne arms against the United States or given aid and comfort to the enemy. The free land was to go to loyal Unionists including soldiers in the Union army and immigrants from foreign countries.

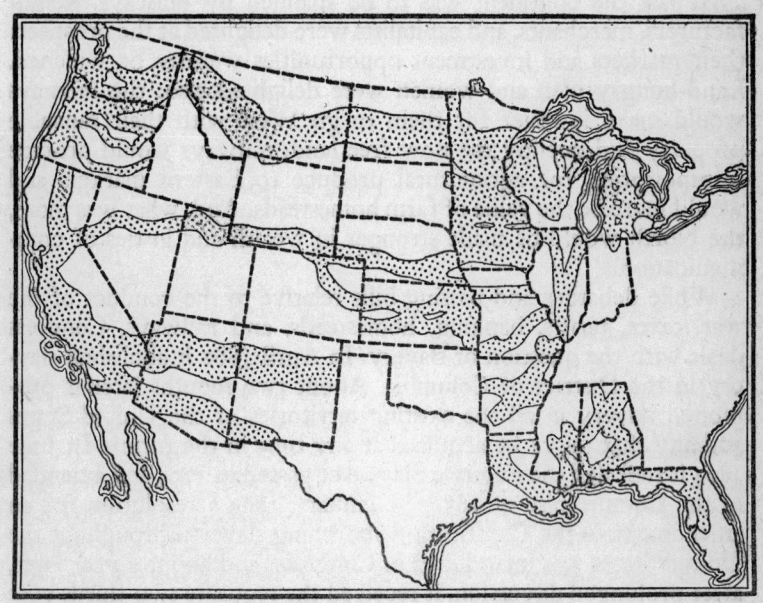

LANDS GRANTED BY THE GOVERNMENT TO RAILWAYS COMPANIES
BETWEEN 1850 AND 1871

Other momentous measures passed by Congress during the war years included laws chartering companies to build railway lines to the Pacific coast. By acts of 1862 and 1864 provision was made for a line in the central region, serving Federal interests. The

Union Pacific Company was to start from a point in Nebraska, later fixed at Omaha, and build westward. The Central Pacific Company was to begin at San Francisco or a place on the navigable waters of the Sacramento River and build eastward. At some spot, to be determined by speed of construction, the two lines were to meet, thus completing the overland route. In 1864 the Northern Pacific Company was authorized to construct a railway from Lake Superior to Puget Sound by a northern route.

To speed up the work of the Union and Central Pacific Companies, Congress granted them an enormous acreage of land in the form of free rights of way and alternate sections on each side of their lines. In addition it lent them a large sum of money for every mile of track laid—a sum varying according to the difficulties of construction.

At last the continent was to be spanned by railways. Manufacturers, merchants, and capitalists were delighted at the prospect: their markets and investment opportunities were to be widened. Land-hungry men and women were delighted also: the railways would make it easier for them to go West with their movable property and occupy the now free land; railways would provide transportation for agricultural produce to Eastern markets and would increase the value of farm homesteads. And, what was more, the North would be made stronger in wealth and in ties of communication.

While debating and passing bills relative to the conduct of the war, taxes, tariffs, banking, homesteads, and railways, Congress dealt with the question of slavery. In April 1862 it abolished slavery in the District of Columbia. About two months later it prohibited slavery in all the existing territories of the United States and any that might be acquired at any time in the future. In June 1864 it repealed the Fugitive Slave Act passed in 1793 and amended in the Compromise of 1850. In January 1864 a resolution for an amendment to the Constitution abolishing slavery throughout the United States was introduced in Congress; and about a year later, after prolonged discussion, it received the requisite two-thirds vote in both houses. It was sent to the states for consideration, ratified, and put into effect in December 1865. Thus the verbal emancipation which Lincoln had proclaimed in 1863 under his war power was extended to include all slaves and implemented by the Thirteenth Amendment.

☆

Although amid the drastic actions taken by President Lincoln and Congress the North presented a firm war front to the Confederacy, the government in Washington and the people of the North were far from united over the merits of the conflict and the measures adopted during the war years. No more than the South was the North actually "solid." From his first inauguration in 1861 until his death in April 1865, Lincoln was involved in controversies with members of his Cabinet, members of Congress, and leaders in his own party. Congress was dissatisfied with his management of the war and created a committee to investigate and supervise it. Senators and representatives bent on destroying slavery at the earliest possible moment protested against his cautious and hesitating methods.

As soon as any former Confederate state was occupied by Union troops advancing into the South, members of Congress began to take issue with Lincoln over the treatment to be meted out to that state—its relation to the Union and the kind of government it was to have. Abolitionists fumed impatiently at his delays in dealing with slavery. Nor were they all content with the elusive emancipation in his Proclamation. "Radical Republicans" in Congress and even members of Lincoln's Cabinet intrigued against him, belittled his character, and attacked many of his measures.

Behind the armed front of the Union, Northern civilians were also engaged in political struggles with one another during the war years. In the congressional elections of 1862 the Democrats gained so many seats in Congress that it looked as if Lincoln and his party might be thrown out of power at the next election. In fact the Republicans were so perturbed in 1864 that they generally dropped their name and called themselves the Union party. And for the purpose of conciliating Democrats, they nominated, as their candidate for Vice-President, Andrew Johnson, a stanch Democrat from Tennessee who had courageously demonstrated his fidelity to the Union from the beginning of the war.

During the presidential campaign of 1864 Lincoln foresaw probable defeat and for a time the outlook for his re-election was indeed dark. In their platform of that year Northern Democrats denounced the war as a failure and called for a conference to restore the old Union under the Constitution. But this defiance alienated voters in their party. The very candidate whom they nominated, General George B. McClellan, insisted in his speech, accepting the nomination, that the war was not a failure, thereby confounding the confusion. At the polls the Democrats carried only three states: New Jersey, Delaware, and Kentucky.

With gratitude to the people for their confidence in him, expressed by re-electing him, Lincoln pushed the war to a conclusion. He was preparing for a peace of reconciliation when, on April 15, 1865, he died at the hands of an assassin—John Wilkes Booth—a martyr to the cause he had served so singleheartedly.

The executive burden passed to the Vice-President, Andrew Johnson. With the office went much of the ferocious criticism that had been directed against Lincoln on account of his conciliatory attitude toward the defeated Confederates and his liberal proposals for restoring the Confederate states to the Union. With Johnson's assumption of his high office the heat of criticism rose and was intensified in many quarters on other scores. Early in 1868 animosity reached such a pitch that the House of Representatives impeached President Johnson before the Senate and he escaped conviction with removal from the presidency only by the margin of a single vote in the Senate.

CHAPTER XVIII

Reconstruction and Economic Expansion

WITH THE SHIELD of the Union assured and the issue of chattel slavery finally settled, the people of the United States turned in the spring of 1865 to peacetime tasks. The tasks were, as usual, in the main political, economic, and moral. The setting for actions was now the unbroken continental domain. But grave problems lay before the people: the rights of the Southern states in the Union, the economic advancement of the South, civil liberties for Negroes, the payment of the huge national debt, the formulation of public policies for general economic expansion, the disposition of natural resources, the development of territories into states.

In respect of these problems the government of the United States played a leading role in the framing of policies and the determination of actions. Imperative among its first obligations was Southern rehabilitation—economic and legal—amid the lingering passions of the war and in circumstances painful to both sides. Southern farms, plantations, and cities had been the scenes of battles. Over large areas buildings and fences had been destroyed, cattle driven off, and implements of production smashed. Miles of Southern railways had been torn up; rolling stock had been wrecked; railway stations and offices had been burned. Families that had led in business and agricultural development were impoverished. The financial system lay in ruins. Confederate bonds were worthless and all thought of reviving them was blasted by the Fourteenth Amendment to the Constitution of the United States adopted in 1868. Confederate paper money was valueless and specie had almost disappeared from circulation. From the ashes of war a new start had to be made in the South.

To complicate the situation, a revolution had been wrought in Southern society by the abolition of slavery. Millions of Negroes, hitherto held in bondage, generally illiterate, little experienced in management if often skilled in the arts of industry, without property, were now "free." Most of them in the Confederate states had been loyal and helpful to their masters and mistresses during the war and had not deliberately sought their freedom.

There were exceptions, to be sure, thousands of exceptions. At least 100,000 Negroes had served in the Union armies as soldiers and laborers. As the Union armies advanced in the South, other thousands of Negroes gave them aid and support in the hope of forwarding their own liberation. In the South as well as the North, hundreds of Negroes, intelligent and educated, furnished some leadership for their bewildered people.

But from the economic point of view, emancipation in general deprived Negroes of their assured livelihood on plantations and set them adrift in the world, homeless, toolless, and penniless, like the evicted peasants of England in the seventeenth century, ill equipped to enter the fierce competition for existence about them, still wearing the color badge of servitude. At the same time slaveowners, besides losing property valued at about $4,000,000,000, lost their supremacy over the labor supply for their farms and plantations. Old laws pertaining to labor relations had expired on the statute books. Old practices of slave days were forbidden. What new laws and practices were to be devised? How much power of self-determination remained in the South?

Now the old ruling class was subject to the military power of the Union and deprived of representation in the Congress of the United States. In this plight that class could do little except wait for the end of the armed occupation and political action by the President and Congress of the United States. Meanwhile small white farmers of the South were jostling it in the contest for power. Upland farmers had long struggled with the seaboard planters in attempts to secure representations in the state legislatures proportioned to their superior numbers; and in the aftermath of the war among the states they were seeking, with more confidence of success, the power hitherto denied them. But neither former slaveowners nor freehold farmers could make any basic decisions in matters of government until their states were restored to the Union in one form or another.

The position to be accorded to the Southern states had become a major question for the government at Washington as soon as its armies had permanently occupied a large area of the South; and it continued to be a primary problem for the President and Congress for many years after the war. Plans proposed in Washington for the treatment of the South, almost endless in number, fell into a few broad patterns. Utopians who had wanted to make the whole war a war for liberty yearned to hold the Southern states down, utterly destroy the great landlord class by the confiscation of its estates, divide the land among Negroes and poor white farmers who had been loyal to the Union, give the suffrage and full civil rights to the hitherto dispossessed, and force upon the defeated Confederacy the principles of liberty that Thomas Jefferson had celebrated as the perfect good.

Astute Republican politicians, knowing that their party represented a minority in the nation, had a care for measures that would keep themselves in power. Some of them encouraged and made use of the utopians; but all along they fixed their minds on the instant need of things and made plans adapted to their interests.

All the plans, whatever their source, rested on theories about the nature of the Union, the Confederate revolt, and the power of the President and Congress of the United States.

If Lincoln's theory was right—namely, that the states could not lawfully withdraw from the Union—then none of them was ever out of the Union, even during the height of Southern military strength. If this theory was sound, as the Confederate states came under Federal authority with the progress of Federal arms the loyal citizens in each were entitled to restore loyal state governments. But against Lincoln's theory it was argued that the Confederate states, by armed rebellion, had actually left the Union, were bound to come back as "conquered provinces," and in instituting governments must submit to the decrees of the conquerors.

Who was to make decisions about the restoration of the Southern states? The President or Congress? And what plans were to be followed in the process of restoration? As events developed the process was divided into two stages: "presidential" reconstruction, as it was called, and "congressional" reconstruction. Lincoln's proposals were, relatively speaking, moderate and generous; those of Congress were severe and punitive.

Under his war power Lincoln claimed the right to prescribe the terms on which military government was to be withdrawn from the states of the Confederacy as, one after another, they came under Federal authority again. When the Union forces drove southward in the Mississippi Valley, in 1862–63, he appointed military governors—in Tennessee, Arkansas, and Louisiana—and instructed them to take charge while loyal governments were being formed in those states.

Late in 1863, Lincoln issued a proclamation of amnesty memorable for its conciliatory tone. The decree offered, in the first place, to restore the suffrage to all voters who would take the prescribed oath of loyalty to the United States, with exceptions excluding practically all leaders in the Confederacy. It then provided that, as soon as ten per cent of the voters in any state had taken the oath of loyalty, they could form their own government and, having done so, would be entitled to the recognition of their state by the President of the United States. This plan, which Lincoln amplified in some respects in 1864, was, in its general outlines, followed by his successor Andrew Johnson.

Under the presidential plan of reconstruction, which did not force Negro suffrage on Southern states, new state governments were established as the Confederacy crumbled. By 1866 all of the Southern states had conformed to the terms of the plan and were ready to take their places in the Union again. But in the course of their operations the new Southern legislatures undertook to deal with the "Negro problem," and many of them enacted laws imposing severe restrictions on the rights of freedmen. These laws, known as new "black codes," excited great opposition in the North and were attacked there as attempts to restore slavery under another name.

In these circumstances reconstruction passed into its second, or congressional, stage. The war had ended and the war power of the President had been curtailed. Whatever the President might do about governments in the states that had seceded, the Senate and the House of Representatives claimed the right, by constitutional provisions, each for itself, to admit or exclude men from the South who, duly elected, were ready to take their seats.

With this weapon in their hands, radical Republicans in Congress took charge of reconstruction. In June 1866, Congress adopted a resolution to alter the federal Constitution by adding a fourteenth amendment. This proposal was intended to confer citizenship on all Negroes, establish the right of all persons to life, liberty, and property, and reduce the representation in Congress of any state which deprived adult male citizens of the right to vote in major elections. On April 9, 1866, Congress passed the first Civil Rights Act, a measure designed to assure to Negroes the full civil equality before the law enjoyed by other American citizens. In July of the same year Congress extended the life of the Freedmen's Bureau, established the previous year for the purpose of giving material relief to the emancipated slaves, and enlarged the power of the Bureau to cover protection of civil rights.

While the Fourteenth Amendment was pending before state legislatures for ratification, Congress overrode the presidential plan for reconstruction and enacted a series of bills based on different principles. These laws, the first passed on March 2, 1867, constituted a plan that was almost, if not entirely, arbitrary in nature. All the former Confederate states, except Tennessee, were divided into five military districts and each was put under the control of a Northern army officer invested with full power to keep order and supervise the process of reconstruction.

In each state a large class of former Confederate leaders was temporarily deprived of the suffrage; and the vote was given to other white men and to Negro men on equal terms. The voters so enfranchised in each state were to hold an election for the purpose of choosing delegates to a state convention authorized to frame a new constitution, including a provision for Negro manhood suffrage. On completion this constitution was to be submitted to the voters for approval or rejection. As soon as a new constitution was established by this process, the state legislature held under it was to ratify the Fourteenth Amendment. After all these steps had been taken and the Fourteenth Amendment had been proclaimed a part of the Constitution of the United States, the state thus reorganized was to be restored to the Union and its people entitled to representation in the national Congress.

The congressional plan of reconstruction was indeed a bitter pill for the former Confederates. It outlawed their recent efforts at recovering a place in the Union on other terms. But, supported by Northern arms, it was carried out. One after another Southern states yielded to its dictates. In 1868, Arkansas, Louisiana, Alabama, Georgia, Florida, South Carolina, and North Carolina complied with the terms of the plan and were restored to the Union. Texas, Mississippi, and Virginia completed the return journey in 1870. Except for Federal troops stationed in a few localities, and subject to the new conditions imposed upon all states by the Thirteenth and the Fourteenth amendments, the South had been "reconstructed."

As if not yet sure that its designs would finally prevail, Congress in 1869 submitted to the states for ratification the Fifteenth Amendment, which provided that the right of citizens of the United States to vote shall not be denied or abridged by the United States or any state on account of race, color, or previous condition of servitude. Just as the last of the states were returning to the Union in 1870 the Fifteenth Amendment was proclaimed in force.

For a brief period the governments of Southern states were in the hands of Negro men and the white men who had not been disfranchised for supporting the Confederacy. That is, in the main, voters who owned small farms or had no property at all held the reins of government. With delight, of course, they accepted the power entrusted to them and began to make laws and distribute offices with a view to their own interests. Many of their laws, for example those providing for free public education, measured up to enlightened conceptions of the age. Others fell far beneath that standard. Corruption and waste of public funds were common in the legislatures, sometimes in the grossest forms. Disgust spread among the disfranchised whites, to crown their resentment at being deprived of their former power.

Whatever the merits or demerits of the new Southern governments, disfranchised white men and white voters otherwise indignant at the new regime quickly set about overthrowing it by methods open and covert. They employed arguments and threats to keep Negroes away from the polls. Secret societies, such as the Ku Klux Klan, terrorized Negroes and their white sympathizers. In state after state "white supremacy" was re-established: in Tennessee in 1869; in Virginia and North Carolina in 1870; in Georgia the next year; in Arkansas, Alabama, and Texas in 1874; in Mississippi in 1875; and in Louisiana, Florida, and South Carolina in 1877—the year in which the withdrawal of the last Federal soldiers of occupation took place.

While Southern people were groping among social and economic ruins for economic security and reorganizing state governments, Northern economy was expanding with unprecedented speed. In the decade after the war nearly 7,000,000 persons were added to the population of the country, counting new immigrants; but the increase in the North and the West was far greater than in the South. By 1870 the population in the United States had risen to 38,500,000; by 1880, to 50,100,000; by 1900, to 76,100,000. Augmented by immigration from foreign countries, the nation now had more energies, stout hearts, and willing hands to subdue the rest of the continental domain and raise the production of wealth to heights undreamed of in the fancies of the Republic's founders.

With millions of dollars at their command for investment, captains of industry leaped forward to build more factories and railways, open up and develop additional resources, and enlarge the output of machine industries in every direction. At their disposal inventors and searchers, besides improving old machines, placed new machines, materials, and processes, on which new industries of gigantic proportions were constructed. Among the discoveries and mechanical inventions of the period the following were so important as to herald the coming of a second industrial revolution:

1859—Great "strike" of petroleum in western Pennsylvania.
1868—C. L. Sholes's typewriter ready for production.
1875—G. F. Swift's refrigerator freight car in use.
1876—Alexander G. Bell sends first telephone message.
1877—Thomas Edison has a phonograph playing.
1879—George Selden's patent for a "gasoline carriage."
1882—Edison's electric power plant starts operation in New York City.
1896—Langley's airplane makes experimental flight.
1901—The Wright brothers finish an airplane glider.

Two of the machines put into use in this period meant an industrial transformation all along the line. The first was the "gas engine," the internal-combustion engine, which emancipated manufacturing and farming from the limitations of the cumbersome steam engine, and furnished an immense market for petroleum products. The second was the electric dynamo and the transmission of power by wire for use in running machines as well as lighting houses, factories, and city streets.

The extension of facilities for the transport of passengers, farm produce, and manufactures kept pace with rising industries. Between 1860 and 1890 the railway mileage increased from 30,000 miles to 166,000 miles. At the opening of the century it stood at 240,000 miles. In 1869 the last spike was driven on the central line to the Pacific and rail communications were opened from the Atlantic to the Pacific, with way stations. Within twenty years three other transcontinental lines were completed, to the north and the south of the central line. Meanwhile new railways were built in the East and the South, short lines were combined into systems, and countless little towns and villages in far-scattered rural regions were linked to the great cities and with one another. On navigable rivers, on the Great Lakes, and in coastal waters, steamships supplemented railway transportation, increasing in some waters and declining in others according to the nature of rail competition.

To the westward rush of pioneers, which had continued even during the Civil War, a powerful new impetus was now given. Northern soldiers and citizens released from the strain of war crowded to the frontier by the thousands. They were joined by thousands of aliens—German, British, Irish, and Scandinavian—fresh from the Old World. Railways facilitated the rush.

Between the tier of states on the west bank of the Mississippi River and Oregon and California on the Pacific coast, only two states had been admitted to the Union during the war period—Kansas in 1861 and Nevada in 1864. All the rest of that vast region was still sparsely settled and under territorial government when the army of Virginia laid down its arms in 1865. But the Homestead Act of 1862, the grants of land to railway companies, and laws providing for the quick sale of timber and mineral lands prepared the way for rapid settlement and for the upswing of mining, lumber, and other industries.

Never before in the history of mankind had agricultural and industrial enterprise, so well equipped with capital and machines, enjoyed such a bounteous opportunity for exploitation. Before the close of the nineteenth century practically all the arable land in the Western regions of rainfall and nearly all the grazing lands in dry or semiarid regions had passed into the hands of farmers, railway companies, stock raisers, purchasers of Spanish grants sometimes embracing hundreds of thousands of acres, land speculators, and engrossers native and foreign. The public domain, especially in Alaska, was still large. It embraced 730,000,000 acres in 1909 and included valuable forest and mineral lands.

But by 1893 it could be officially announced that the frontier hardly existed any longer; that the best of the farming lands had all been given away or sold. The America of cheap or free land had vanished forever. An epoch of nearly three hundred years had closed. The "escape valve" through which millions from the old East and from Europe had moved from poverty and unemployment to home-owning and independence on the frontier was shut. One sensational phase of economic enterprise in America was at an end.

In the lavish parceling out of the national domain, a large acreage went directly to men and women who entered lands under the Homestead Act. Relatively speaking, however, it was small in size. By 1923 approximately 213,860,000 acres had been given away to settlers real and pretended since 1868. The word "pretended" is important, for homestead entries were honeycombed with frauds; individual entrants had often acted as dummies for land and mining companies. In the course of the years at least 620,-000,000 acres had been sold directly to companies and individuals, granted for the purpose of making internal improvements and building railways, or turned over to states in aid of education and other public functions.

Millions of acres of valuable timber, mineral, and grazing lands were literally stolen under the eyes of dishonest or negligent officials in the federal land office; and other millions were wrested from the government by chicanery of one kind or another. In the history of political corruption, seldom, if ever, had there been transactions on a scale so prodigious or conducted with more brazen effrontery. Thousands of great fortunes in the East as well as in the West were built out of resources wrung from the government for a pittance or for a bribe to its officials, if not actually stolen.

Nevertheless, in the process of dividing the national domain millions of new farms were staked out in the West; grazing lands fabulous in extent were brought into use and overuse by cattlemen and ranchers; and other resources were exploited by mining and manufacturing concerns. Between 1865 and 1900 billions of new wealth were added annually to the national output.

As farmers, miners, prospectors, cattlemen, and lumbermen, with or without families, poured into the Western territories, demands for statehood went up from every region. In 1867 the territory of Nebraska, reduced in size, was admitted to the Union. By 1875, Colorado claimed a population of about 100,000, largely composed of miners, farmers, cattle raisers, and prospectors. The following year it was granted statehood by Congress.

By this time the territories along the northern border of the United States were filling up and boasting of their progress. Within ten years their political leaders were knocking at the doors of Congress. In 1889 the pleas of North Dakota, South Dakota, Washington, and Montana were favorably heard and they were admitted to the Union. The next year Idaho and Wyoming took their places among the states. Having prohibited polygamy and forced the Mormons to adopt a constitution incorporating that prohibition, Congress finally conferred statehood on Utah in 1896.

This left only three regions, besides Alaska, under a territorial form of government, and they were soon given statehood. Oklahoma came into the Union in 1907 and Arizona and New Mexico in 1912.

At last the continental domain was fully organized, in forty-eight states, all presumed to be "free and equal" under the Constitution of the United States. Each now had a constitution of its own making and a government resting upon popular, if not universal, suffrage.

☆

The swift industrial development and westward expansion were made possible, in a large measure, by the stream of immigrants that flooded into the United States, subject to no retarding legal restrictions of any moment until the Chinese Exclusion Act was passed in 1882. Although the number coming into the country rose or fell from year to year, the general tendency was upward. In 1864 it was 193,000; in 1874, 313,000; in 1884, 518,000; in 1891, 560,000; in 1907, 1,285,000.

During these years striking shifts appeared in the national origins of immigrants. For a short time after 1865 the flow was still mainly from Great Britain, Ireland, Germany, and Scandinavia. Then the number of immigrants from northern Europe diminished relatively, and immigration from Italy, Russia, and Austria-Hungary increased. At the opening of the twentieth century these three countries furnished more than three fourths of all the immigrants. Polish, Hungarian, Czech, Slovak, Croat, Russian, and Jewish immigrants then far exceeded in number all the British, Irish, and Germans making their way into the United States. To give exact figures, between 1871 and 1880 the total number of immigrants from western Europe was 2,000,000, and that from eastern and southern Europe was 181,000. Between 1901 and 1910 the numbers from the two European regions were 2,000,000 and 6,100,000 respectively.

The striking shifts in the national origins of immigrants corresponded roughly to the disappearance of free land in the West and the diverting of immigrants to industries in the cities. In the urban centers immigrants of each nationality formed large colonies, or quarters, of their own, with separate languages, newspapers, and customs. Similar conditions prevailed to some extent among immigrants who settled on farms in the West; but the rise of "foreign cities" within American cities was an extraordinary characteristic of the period that followed the Civil War.

From decade to decade, as the following table shows, the number of foreign-born inhabitants in the United States rose rapidly:

1860, total, 31,400,000; foreign-born, 4,100,000
1880, total, 50,100,000; foreign-born, 6,600,000
1900, total, 76,100,000; foreign-born, 10,300,000

At the end of the century, according to these figures, about fourteen per cent of the total population was foreign-born. But the cities showed different proportions. In the cities of more than

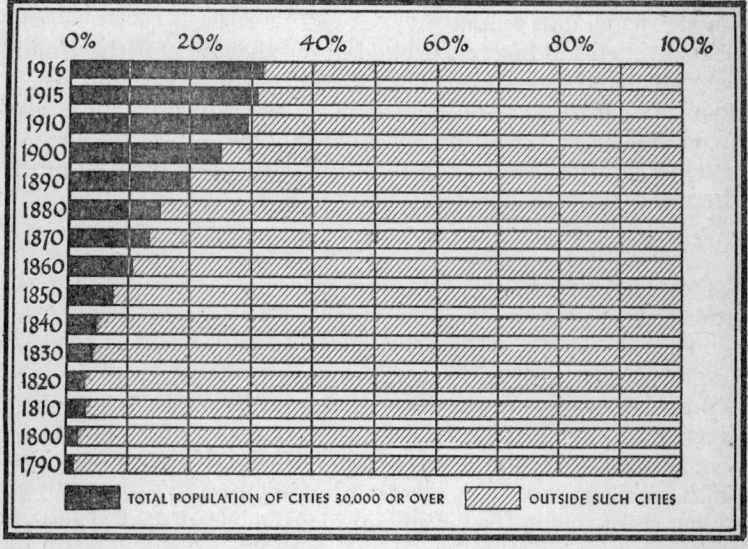

PER CENT OF POPULATION IN CITIES HAVING OVER 30,000 INHABITANTS AND OUTSIDE SUCH CITIES FOR SPECIFIED YEARS: 1790–1916.

25,000 inhabitants in 1900, approximately twenty-six per cent were foreign-born. For cities of over 100,000 inhabitants the proportion of foreign-born was about thirty-five per cent, and in a few of the largest cities it was fifty per cent or more. At that time the rapid inflow of immigrants indicated that the percentage of foreign-born in the cities at the next census would be still larger.

As Americans from farming regions and immigrants from abroad turned increasingly to industries and commerce for employment, the growth of urbanism destroyed the almost undisputed supremacy of the rural regions that had characterized the American past. In 1789 only about three per cent of the inhabitants were city dwellers and there were only five cities of more than 8000 inhabitants. By 1890 about one third of the people lived in towns of 4000 inhabitants or more.

Even more remarkable was the growth of great cities. In 1890 New York and Brooklyn combined had 2,300,000 inhabitants; Philadelphia and Chicago had crossed the 1,000,000 line; and Boston, Baltimore, and Washington each laid claim to 500,000. In Massachusetts, Rhode Island, and Connecticut the urban concentration of population was highest. Four fifths of the Massachusetts population lived in urban towns of 4000 or more; and in Rhode Island, nine tenths.

On every hand boasters exulted in the thought that the United States would soon outstrip, in respect of urbanism, England, where about four fifths of the people were living in towns of more than 10,000 inhabitants, as if urbanization was the crowning glory of national achievement. In fact for many years the fulfillment of the prophecy seemed a possibility.

Deeply engaged, as Southerners were, in the struggle for existence among the wreckage of the war and for emancipation from the rule of Northern officials supported by arms, many of them forged ahead energetically with activities which entered into the productive expansion that covered the continent. At first planters faced the burden of getting their fields into production again. Though deprived of their chattel labor supply, they still held their lands; all the radical proposals for breaking up their estates and dividing them among freedmen and landless whites failed of realization.

Dismayed by the prospects of defeat under the new labor system, numerous planting families fled to the cities, South and North, where they went into the professions or business pursuits. Those who remained on their estates usually resorted to one or all of three devices for carrying on production: allowing the former slaves to live in their old cabins and work as before, but for wages or payment in goods; "letting" small blocks of land to freedmen or whites in return for a cash rental or a share of the crops; and selling plots outright while continuing to operate the remainder on a wage or rental basis.

The dilemma of the planters afforded opportunities to many poor whites and freedmen for acquiring land. Since colonial times small farmers had been pressed back into the uplands by the apparently relentless advance of large plantation economy from the seaboard. Now, as many great plantations dissolved, small farmers were often able to buy better land and raise their standard of living. Generally the white farmer and his family supplied all or most of the labor on his freehold; if his acreage was large he hired a few workers at wages. The more thrifty or fortunate Negroes, likewise sharing in this opportunity, were frequently able to buy land and establish homesteads.

Two figures indicate the tendency. In 1860 the average land holding in the Southern states was 335.4 acres; in 1880 it was 153.4; and in 1900 it was 138.2. Yet the tendency to dissolution was checked by the end of the century, leaving many large estates intact. Furthermore, especially in times of depression, urban bankers, lawyers, merchants, investors, and corporations acquired extensive holdings of Southern land and frequently demonstrated the efficiency of large-scale farming as against small-farming, for which skill or capital was lacking.

It was in relation to the system of land economy that emancipated Negro men and women had to find footholds for themselves. If planters had been able to furnish adequate capital and pay wages regularly, many more Negroes would have become permanent wage workers on the land. But the planters after the war were usually handicapped by lack of money. Often they obtained credit for supplies from merchants and furnished the Negroes who worked for them with food, clothing, and shelter as they had done in the slave system; but at the end of the year, in the settlement, the Negroes were likely to have no balance coming to them as wages. They were apt to be in debt to the planter, even when the books were honestly kept by their employers.

Under the wage system Negroes grew discouraged and restless. Thousands left the land for neighboring or distant towns and sought employment as domestic or casual laborers. The more determined among those who remained in the country struggled hard to procure land to be worked on other than wage terms—to achieve an economic underwriting. Many became renters of small farms, paying their rent in a share of the crops—the "sharecroppers." Others by dint of exacting labor and thrift became owners of land, either outright or on mortgage. In 1874, nine years after emancipation, Negroes owned 338,769 acres of land in Georgia alone, either outright or subject to mortgage. By the end of the century, it was estimated, about one fourth of the Negro workers on the land had become freeholders of the one type or the other.

On the whole, particularly as to the production of cotton, none of these schemes for land use proved to be highly efficient. It was not until 1880 that the Southern cotton crop, measured in bales, rose again to the figure of 1860. It is true that twenty years later, in 1900, the output of cotton was about three fourths larger than it had been in 1860, but that was in part due to the extension of the cotton belt in Texas where white labor and management predominated.

If Southern economy had been compelled to depend as largely on cotton production as in the ante-bellum days, its prospects would have been dismal. But diversification in agriculture offered other sources of wealth. To the old staples—cotton, tobacco, rice, and sugar—new products were added: apples, peaches, oranges, lemons, pineapples, peanuts, watermelons, and vegetables in a large variety. As the mileage of railways increased and rapid transportation by refrigerator cars developed, Southern agriculture found large home markets for these commodities in neighboring cities and in the distant North. Thus the subordination of the South as a raw-material province utterly dependent on the world cotton market at Liverpool was mitigated by diversification and by the creation of special ties with the national market.

The stresses and strains of the struggle for existence on the land were also relieved by the growth of manufacturing in the South —an economic enterprise which contributed materially to the expansion of the national productive activities so typical of the period between 1865 and 1900. Leadership in Southern manufacturing enterprise, as Arthur M. Schlesinger has pointed out in *The Rise of the City*, was taken by industrialists who came, in overwhelming proportions, from Southern families outside the former slave-owning groups. During the early stages of its development both capital and management also sprang principally from Southern sources. Thus history seemed to vindicate Southern writers who had claimed before 1860 that the slave system hampered the direction of Southern energies to the industrial use of rich natural resources right at hand.

Scarcely had the brazen clangor of the fratricidal war subsided when Southern promoters exclaimed: "Bring the mills to the cotton!" By 1880 Southern cotton mills were turning out a volume of goods equal to almost one fourth the output of New England's mills. Between 1860 and 1900 the number of Southern spindles increased from 298,000 to 4,300,000. The rise of tobacco manufactures was hardly less spectacular, especially in Virginia, North Carolina, and Kentucky.

In the expansion of capitalist enterprise great coal beds were opened and worked in the Appalachian regions from Maryland to northern Alabama. All the way from Virginia through Alabama to Arkansas and Texas immense deposits of iron ore were unearthed and forced to yield supplies for iron mills; in a few years Birmingham, Alabama, took pride in being "the Pittsburgh of the South." In Kentucky, Tennessee, Louisiana, Arkansas, and Texas petroleum was discovered and the products of the oil industry were added to Southern wealth. Cotton, tobacco, coal, iron, and oil industries were supplemented by the lumber and cottonseed industries. At the opening of the new century the output of Southern lumber mills more than equaled that of the mills in the huge forests of the Great Lakes region.

In the train of the Southern industrial revolution followed the manifold consequences of such an economic upheaval. Around mines, factories, mills, and other scenes of operation congregated armies of industrial workers. Since immigrants from foreign countries generally preferred to settle in the North and West, Southern enterprise had to draw mainly on local sources for its labor supply. Into its industries were lured men, women, and children from rural communities—thousands of "poor whites" from the pine barrens, the uplands, and the mountains, where they had lived on the very margin of subsistence. Now they were to have some cash and be drawn into the social movements of the nation.

As in the North long before, new factory towns shot up in Southern rural scenes, and old towns grew rapidly in population. Richmond, Atlanta, Birmingham, Dallas, Houston, and San Antonio became thriving centers of manufacturing and commerce. To cope with the demands for transportation additional railway lines were built, old lines improved, and consolidations made among short lines. Between 1865 and 1880 the mileage was more than doubled. By 1900 it had been more than doubled again.

Before Hinton Rowan Helper, author of the prophetic *Impending Crisis,* died in 1909 the planters and merchants who had led the South in the days of slavery had been challenged and undermined by white farmers, by great industrialists, by high-powered merchants, and by industrial workers—with their persistent and special interests. Although in national elections the South as a rule seemed "solid," it was in fact divided into strong factions over the problems that went with the swift transformation of its economy—as it was drawn tighter and tighter into the expanding economy of other sections, North and West.

CHAPTER XIX

Centralization of Economy

BEFORE THE PROCESS of economic expansion had reached the continental borders, economic centralization was setting in; that is, the self-sufficiency and independence of families and communities were diminishing, and their insufficiency and interdependence were increasing. If, as Brooks Adams declared in *The Law of Civilization and Decay*, published in 1895, the movement of energies in society is inexorably toward centralization, the course of economic and political affairs in the United States certainly provided illustrations. Indeed the swiftness of the economic expansion had been made possible in a large measure by centralizing activities of private enterprise and the federal government.

Without the lavish aids from the federal Treasury the continental railways, facilitating the westward expansion, could not have been built so rapidly. Without the protection against the Indians afforded by the United States Army the frontier settlements could not have been pushed to the Pacific within such a short time. Without the investment and speculative activities of Eastern capitalists and corporations, often aided by foreign loans, the resources of the West would have lain dormant for many years to come if not permanently.

In turn the very nature of the dispersion of economic activities over the continental domain in itself worked for centralization. Above all it was marked by intense specialization. Colonization between the Mississippi Valley and the Pacific Ocean, unlike that in the old Northwest Territory, was not principally colonization by farming families whose homesteads were at first made largely self-sufficing by domestic manufacturing as well as by food production. By climate, soil, and resources each region in the Far West was fitted for one or more particular lines of production—wheat, corn, cattle, lumber, or minerals. For a long time Western industries were limited to a few specialties, such as the milling of grains and minerals or the manufacture of timber products. It was only by specialization that settlers could make the highest profits.

If these special interests in agriculture and industry had not been furnished outlets by railway lines into the national markets, they would have proceeded at a slow pace, comparable perhaps to the languid ways of Spanish landlords in the early history of the Southwest. It was the rapid communication with the larger markets that enabled special agricultural interests to flourish so luxuriantly and in such a short time. Similar conditions made possible the rapid advance of the South in agriculture and industry after the war at the middle of the nineteenth century.

Specialization and integration, of course, were indispensable features of the mechanical revolution in industry. Their rise and growth rested on the extension of markets and the protection of the government that assured the unity of the American markets. In short, as the Industrial Revolution spread, as farming pioneers between 1865 and 1890 pushed into the regions of the Far West, where climate, soil, and resources were peculiar, a higher degree of centralization became necessary to the lucrative expansion of production.

Indeed the settlement itself on a large scale was associated with the building and operation of railway lines—the arteries of commerce which made local specialties profitable. Amounts of capital relatively monumental were required to construct and operate even short lines of fifty or a hundred miles. Only companies or corporations of limited liability were likely to take the original risk or could have raised the money required to make the venture a reality, as had been the case in early English colonization. The longer the lines, the greater the capital needed, the more certain the reliance on corporate enterprise. To cross and encompass the continental domain called for sums of money which made the outlays of the New England factory builders look trifling.

After the principal long and short lines were completed, consolidations among them into systems and trunk lines, advantageous to the rapid and efficient movement of freight and passengers, were effected. They were engineered by actual mergers and physical connections, or by agreements for pooling and routing trains. This process was marred by frauds, gambling ventures, and

CENTRALIZATION BY RAILWAY CONNECTIONS AT THE END OF THE NINETEENTH CENTURY exorbitant charges at the expense of the public. But these were temporary incidents in the centralization of railway management and operation which for a time facilitated dispersion and then made integration essential to the existence and prosperity of regions and special industries—to the whole network of national economy.

While by its very nature railway expansion facilitated concentrations in capital, other forces pushed manufacturing industries in the same co-ordinative direction. The amount of money needed for the building of great plants ran against the dispersion of individual ownership characteristic of handicraft days. In the tendency to overbuild, competition among manufacturers became keen, sometimes sanguinary; and often in sheer self-protection they sought escape from low returns or even bankruptcy by forming combinations or agreements.

Frankly confessing that the profit motive was high among his incentives, the manufacturer who saw his profits wiped out by competition could turn the profit motive to the making of trusts and pools with his competitors, thereby reaping some returns, perhaps more than he had been reaping. Or, finding his profits injured by the high prices he had to pay for his raw materials, the keen-sighted manufacturer could increase his gains by buying raw-material sources and concentrating them under his own direction. Efficiency in production also smoothed the way to large-scale production. Within limits, according to the processes used, the bigger the plant and the operations, the lower the cost of production per unit of output, and the firmer the defense against cutthroat rivalry.

☆

The immense profits made by leaders in industrial enterprises connected with continental expansion speeded up concentration. As profits had to be reinvested if returns were to be obtained from them, the accumulators of profits had to pour them back into their own industries, thus enlarging them, or into the stocks and bonds of other industries, thus buying into the control of those industries.

Soon after its formation, for example, the first Standard Oil Company in Ohio began to pay annual dividends amounting to about twenty million dollars. A part of their earnings directors of the company invested in their oil business, adding to its magnitude, and another part they placed in other industries such as railways and iron mining. By 1887, William Rockefeller had become a director of the Chicago, Milwaukee, and St. Paul Railroad, and John D. Rockefeller had bought his way into a number of railways and into a great company engaged in opening up the iron resources of Minnesota. About the same time Andrew Carnegie was extending the area of his control by investing profits from iron manufactures in railways, mining, and Great Lakes shipping. In the course of time, as concentration proceeded, the same industrialist might be serving as a director in ten or fifteen highly diversified manufacturing concerns.

A similar expansion. and concentration occurred in nearly all the great staple manufacturing industries as the Industrial Revolution advanced after 1865. In 1873 a group of capitalists headed by Andrew Carnegie, who had accumulated the necessary means in iron, coal, railways, oil, and bridgemaking, started a monster steel mill on the banks of the Monongahela near Pittsburgh. A few years later this group acquired the Homestead Works in the same neighborhood. In the next decade the Carnegie interests became affiliated with the coal and coke business of H. C. Frick and Company; and several other works were united in the huge Carnegie Steel Corporation.

Now firmly established, the Carnegie concern branched out by buying beds of iron ore in the Lake Superior region. To cut freight charges it opened a railway line from Pittsburgh to Lake Erie and, putting a fleet of ore carriers on the Great Lakes, it established direct and cheaper connections between mines and mills. Then, to the dismay of competitors, it proposed, partly as a threat to the J. P. Morgan interests, to diversify its operations by manufacturing many other iron products, such as wire, hitherto beyond its scope of activities.

At this point in the development of the Carnegie interests, iron and steel men and their bankers began to fear that the competition of the new facilities would end in overproduction and the ruin of many companies. Manufacturers of raw iron were invading the field of finished products already occupied by independent producers. They were closing in on the coal, ore mining, and transport business. It looked as if a battle of the giants might end in disaster for the weaker men.

Put on guard by these tendencies and seeing a chance to make more money, the J. P. Morgan banking company in New York City took the lead in forming the first billion-dollar corporation in the history of the country. Under its direction in 1901 a consolidation of many concerns was effected in the United States Steel Company, and $1,400,000,000 in stocks and bonds was issued to the parties in the transaction. To the Morgan underwriting syndicate, stock having the cash value of $62,500,000 was given in the form of a commission for its services.

Later the Federal Bureau of Corporations estimated that the tangible value of the property of the corporation in 1901, the year of its establishment, was $682,000,000, against which $1,400,000,000 in stocks and bonds had been issued. How correct was this estimate became a matter of dispute, but at all events the common stock of the concern soon fell with a crash, and many outsiders who had risked their money in the venture lost heavily.

While Andrew Carnegie was operating in iron and coal resources which, as he afterward said, he got for little outlay of money, John D. Rockefeller was working in the new petroleum industry, first at Cleveland, Ohio. Having hoarded his earnings as a clerk and small merchant, he began to invest in the construction of oil refineries. Soon he found competition keen and, for self-protection as well as for the sake of gain, he set about forming a combination to "stabilize" if not control the local oil business.

After experimenting with small undertakings of this kind, Rockefeller united, in 1870, a group of capitalists in the Standard Oil Company of Ohio and embarked on oil refining on a mammoth scale. With a view to increasing its power, the Rockefeller group took over the South Improvement Company two years later and used it as a means of securing from railway companies rebates or special rates on its shipments of oil, and other favors profitable to the oil company. By extending its operations to the production of oil in the fields, and the transport of oil by pipe lines to the Atlantic coast, the Standard Oil Company of Ohio and its subsidiaries got control over about nine tenths of the refining business within ten years after its formation.

In 1882 the Rockefeller group centralized its many concerns in the form of a trust; that is, the stocks of its concerns were placed in the hands of a few trustees, including John D. Rockefeller, in exchange for "trust certificates of ownership." A few years later the Standard Oil Company of New Jersey, one of its concerns already doing business in New Jersey, was enlarged and in effect assumed responsibility for the management of the trust.

This step was taken under a New Jersey law empowering companies duly incorporated to buy, hold, and vote stock in any other corporation or corporations in New Jersey or any other state—in other words, permitting it to form a "holding company" for the purpose of centralizing control in one industry or many industries. Under this device the Standard Oil Company of New Jersey was able, within a year, to dominate from two thirds to three fourths of the national business in oil and oil products; and to pay its stockholders annually, for several years, from thirty to forty-eight per cent in dividends.

With perhaps even more speed concentration was brought about in the new electrical industry. To secure capital and aid in developing his patents for electric motors, dynamos, lamps, and other products, Thomas Edison, with the help of J. P. Morgan and other financiers, established the Edison Electric Light Company in 1878. After several competing concerns had appeared in the industry, a combination of the Edison and other interests was brought about by the formation of the General Electric Company in 1892. About the same time another consolidation of electrical interests was made by George Westinghouse and his friends, with the incorporation of the Westinghouse Electric and Manufacturing Company. Soon the two companies reached working agreements as to the joint use of patents and divided between them the major portion of the manufacturing business in the chief lines, despite the rise, especially in subsidiary lines, of many independent manufacturers.

Efforts equally determined, if often less successful, were made during this age of industrial expansion to get control over the production of other staple articles of manufacture and mining—sugar, copper, linseed oil, cottonseed oil, whisky, plate glass, and coal, for instance. In 1884 a combination appeared in cottonseed oil; in 1885 in linseed oil; in 1887 in sugar, lead, whisky, cordage, plate glass, and wire nails; in 1899 smelters and coal producers drew together; in 1900 the sugar "trust" was established.

Some of these companies were short-lived and their careers were marked by dubious if not corrupt practices. Others suffered from bad luck and were merged in larger organizations. But by the end of the century the major portion of manufacturing in each of several great lines was concentrated in the hands of corporations—in some lines, a few corporations.

Although not many of these gigantic concerns had complete monopolies in their fields of business, they had a power so great that they could often exercise a decisive influence over the cost of raw materials, the prices of finished products, and the fortunes of independent competitors. Besides wielding the control over their particular areas of the national economy such as oil or steel, corporation promoters built up a wider dominion over economy in general, over politics, and over public opinion by creating interlocking directorates among corporations and other forms of affiliation with business interests.

Concentration in industrial enterprise was facilitated by concentration in the banking business. A vast amount of money was needed for the construction of plants and for current operations. Special agencies were necessary to sell stocks and bonds to investors in large blocks. Here strong banks proved to be valuable adjuncts, and bankers found opportunities to harvest mounting profits. They made loans to corporations, aided in forming combinations among them, and took part in the sale of their securities.

For carrying on the more extensive operations several banks often joined to form an "underwriting syndicate." In the division of financial business certain banks became associated with particular enterprises; for example, the J. P. Morgan Company with the New York Central Railroad Company and the United States Steel Company. In many cases, even early in the process of centralization, bankers took the initiative or actively participated in the creation of trusts, corporations, and combinations.

Since bankers usually acquired vital interests in the companies they financed, it became a common practice to put bank presidents and directors on the boards of trustees in charge of railway and manufacturing companies. By way of reciprocity, heads of industrial corporations were also installed among the directors of banks. Through various banking activities a substantial part of the control over industry passed from the original magnates of manufacturing to magnates of finance. So industrial capitalism was transformed into what was called "finance capitalism."

Inasmuch as the greatest banks, the headquarters of numerous corporations, and the chief stock exchange for dealing in corporation securities were in New York City, that metropolis became the principal center of consolidation in the United States. There bankers and corporation presidents mingled freely with one another. Often they engaged in spectacular battles over power and wealth. Often they united in the exercise of control over finance and industry, adding personal union to legal and economic union.

In his book, *The Truth about the Trusts* (1904), a contemporary expert in financial affairs, John Moody, described the situation in the following language: "Around these two groups [the Morgan-Rockefeller interests], or what must ultimately become one greater group, all other smaller groups of capitalists congregate. They are all allied and intertwined by their various mutual interests. For instance, the Pennsylvania Railroad interests are on the one hand allied with the Vanderbilts and on the other hand with the Rockefellers. The Vanderbilts are closely allied with the Morgan group, and both the Pennsylvania and the Vanderbilt interests have recently become the dominating factors in the Reading system, a former Morgan road and the most important part of the anthracite coal combine which had always been dominated by the Morgan people. . . . Viewed as a whole, we find the dominating influences in the trusts to be made up of an intricate network of large and small capitalists, many allied to another by ties of more or less importance, but all being appendages to or parts of the greater groups which are themselves dependent on and allied with the two mammoth, or Rockefeller and Morgan groups. These two mammoth groups jointly . . . constitute the heart of the business and commercial life of the nation." At this state had American economy arrived thirty years after the death of Abraham Lincoln, whose life had been sacrificed to the preservation of the Union and the emancipation of slaves.

Paralleling in time, though not in power, the expansion, diversification, and concentration in manufacturing, transportation, and finance were efforts to effect a consolidation among dispersed industrial workers. Unlike capitalists who throve on profits from war industries during the civil conflict, industrial workers found it difficult, if not impossible in that wartime, to force an upturn in wages equal to the rise in the cost of living. Yet they sought to make advances in that direction by increasing the number of trade unions; and they came out of the war with many gains in organization.

At its close the number of local unions existing in 1860 had about trebled and to the national craft unions already formed had been added at least ten new national unions of that type. But the membership of all the unions, local and national, was small; under 250,000, it is reckoned. Even so, in 1865 nearly every large industrial city had, besides its local craft unions, a city trades assembly representing the crafts. Certain labor leaders considered the time ripe to renew the attempt, made back in 1834, to effect a permanent consolidation of unions on a national scale.

Leadership in this undertaking was assumed by W. H. Sylvis, a veteran idealist in the labor movement. In 1864, largely at his instigation, a convention called the Industrial Assembly of North America was held at Louisville, Kentucky, and a plan was framed for establishing a continent-wide association of labor organizations. At a following convention, in Baltimore in 1866, the plan was carried out by the formation of the National Labor Union.

Based mainly on the representation of local unions and city trades assemblies, not directly on national craft unions, the new organization was one degree removed from strictly craft interests. It strove, it is true, to secure the recognition of unions by employers, to raise wages, to reduce hours, and to establish the practice of adjusting labor relations by agreements between employers and employees. Yet the National Labor Union also tried to promote various political and social reforms, including the establishment of workshops owned and managed co-operatively by the workers.

Some of its demands, such as an eight-hour day for certain federal employees, were granted, but its main projects for social reform fell by the wayside. Gradually "pure and simple" trade unionists, interested primarily in wages and hours of work, began to desert the organization. After a troubled existence of six years the National Labor Union perished for lack of support.

Meanwhile another project for uniting industrial workers in a single national organization was taking shape on broader organizational lines. The germ of this movement was the Noble Order of the Knights of Labor, a local union formed among garment workers at Philadelphia by Uriah Stephens in 1869. By much agitation several unions of the kind were established in that city and in other industrial cities of the East.

Believing that the hour had struck for a concentration of forces, leaders in these unions called, in 1875, a national convention to which they invited representatives of other associations as well as their own. Out of this assembly the Knights of Labor expanded into a national organization capable of exerting for more than ten years a powerful influence in the industrial world and in labor debate and opinion.

In form and policy the Knights of Labor made departures from the attempts to federate the craft unions composed of skilled workers. It is true that the Knights sought the co-operation of local and national craft unions as fellow members of its order; but its aspiration was broader than theirs in that it tried to unite all laborers, skilled and unskilled, men and women, white and colored, with the castes of trades and crafts, in one big union. While it campaigned for higher standards of labor conditions and rewards within industrial plants and carried on many strikes, local and general, in efforts to gain these ends it did more. Like the National Labor Union, it sponsored co-operative workshops among industrial workers. Still more: it cherished a dream of transforming the capitalist system into a socialist commonwealth. As a step in that direction it advocated the public ownership of utilities such as railways and waterworks.

By its effective battles for higher wages and extensive social reforms, the Order of Knights of Labor for some time drew into its ranks thousands of actual industrial workers and thousands of sympathizers belonging to the middle class not gainfully employed in industry. At the height of its vigor, about 1880, when Terence V. Powderly was at its head as "Master Workman," it claimed an enrollment of approximately 700,000 men and women; and employers then felt themselves in the presence of an ominous challenge to capitalism. But rather suddenly a rapid decline of the Order and its power set in, due in part to the failure of mass strikes, to the strong desire of workers for immediate advances in wages and a reduction of hours, and to the disdain of craft unionists for the methods and ideals of the Knights.

Strong as it proved to be for about ten years, the Knights of Labor movement did not submerge the local craft unions, the city trades assemblies, or the national organization of crafts, from many of which it received aid. On the contrary, such unions were growing in numbers and power while the Knights were still apparently dominant. From year to year new federal unions of crafts were formed: for example cigar makers in 1864; railroad conductors in 1868; locomotive firemen in 1873; iron and steel workers in 1876; and cotton spinners in 1878.

By 1884 the national craft unions, claiming 300,000 members in good standing, showed signs of permanence despite their vicissitudes. Several of the national craft unions were led by capable men and had money in their treasuries. This was especially true of the cigar makers, with whom were associated Adolph Strasser and Samuel Gompers, both hardheaded and skillful in the work of organization and administration. In their national organization the central officers had full authority over local unions, and a part of the dues were set aside to build up benefit funds for members in distress for various reasons or unemployed. Here in firmly knit national craft unions were solid materials for the next and more successful step in concentration—a federation of all unions in one national association, with strong treasuries for tiding the members over the hazards of strikes, competently managed by directors loyal to the interests of the members.

Labor leaders of the "practical" type, quick to appreciate the opportunity before them, now urged the creation of a national organization more limited in structure and purpose than the Order of the Knights of Labor with its miscellaneous membership and its broad program of social reconstruction. At Pittsburgh in 1881 the new labor leaders took action by forming the Federation of Organized Trades and Labor Unions at a convention representing national unions, local unions, and Knights of Labor assemblies in the United States and Canada. Yet even the newest federation did not prosper at once.

Unbeaten, however, its sponsors summoned another conference of delegates, at Columbus, Ohio, in 1886; and after searching debates they merged their organizations in an association called the American Federation of Labor. This federation they grounded squarely on strong national unions of crafts already in existence, state federations of unions, and city assemblies. Representation of mere local craft unions they allowed only in cases where such unions were not federated into national craft organizations.

Under the leadership of Samuel Gompers, who served as president until his death in 1924, except for one year, the American Federation of Labor pursued a utilitarian policy—trade unionism "pure and simple." Gompers had been associated with socialism but now he avoided radical theories, defeating efforts of socialists to capture the federation. The organization clung steadfastly to a simple program: standard hours and wages; fair conditions of labor; collective bargaining with employers; and the accumulation of benefit funds for meeting emergencies. It accepted the capitalistic system of production and ownership and sought to improve the position of labor, especially skilled labor, within that framework. Refraining from declarations of unmitigated class warfare, the federation co-operated where it could with associations of employers and citizens interested in securing to labor bargaining privileges in the industrial world; with the National Civic Federation, for instance.

The success of the American Federation of Labor soon gave wide currency to three rather obvious interpretations of history: first, the Industrial Revolution had brought into being a numerous and permanent body of working men and women, despite the fluidity of class lines; second, the individual worker, with little or no savings between himself and want, was not "equal" in a wage negotiation—under "freedom of contract"—to a million-dollar corporation ruled by industrial magnates; and, third, only by unions of workers could a "fair balance" in wage negotiations be attained.

It was hard for Americans, who were still thinking in terms of handicrafts and freehold farming, to accept facts so "foreign" to old American experience. But in time many citizens acknowledged the changed situation and began to be active in bringing about fundamental modifications in the laws respecting the right of labor to organize, deal collectively with employers, procure better working conditions, and have recognition as one of the great interests of the nation. In the program, tactics, and gains of American organized labor and its middle-class sympathizers the thesis of the unmitigated class war, evolved on the continent of feudal Europe, was completely disavowed.

Though stoutly opposed to the formation of a separate labor party with a blanket program of radical reforms, the American Federation of Labor did, nonetheless, put forward at its annual conventions specific demands for new laws to be won by political action. It called for legislation to provide safety in industries and mines, compensation for workers injured in the course of their duties, the abolition of child labor, equal pay for men and women engaged in equal work, the regulation of the use of injunctions in labor disputes, and indeed a long list of definite proposals. At elections leaders of the federation resorted to the political tactics of "rewarding our friends and punishing our enemies." In presidential elections they often tried to throw the labor vote to the Democrats in return for concessions of one kind or another.

Starting with a membership of about 150,000 in 1886, the American Federation of Labor soon doubled it and by 1904 reported that 1,670,000 workers were on its union rolls. Outside its jurisdiction, but usually co-operative, were other powerful national unions. Among the independent unions the four railway brotherhoods—engineers, firemen, conductors, and maintenance men—had first rank.

Fifty years after the close of the Civil War approximately 3,000,000 industrial workers had been organized on a national scale, centralized through federation, and bound together on a program that presaged not only permanence but growth in numbers and power, economic and political. Although they demanded no overthrow of capitalism, likewise in the process of centralization, they were determined to dictate some of the terms on which capitalism was to function. Whether or not by their actions they increased the proportion of the total annual output that went to labor as a whole, they had certainly wrung favorable laws from legislatures and raised wages for the highly organized craft unionists. Though they spurned independent labor party action, they were active in politics and made labor increasingly conscious of its political strength, actual and potential.

Accompanying and promoting centralization in the sphere of industrial ownership and operation was a centralization of legal power provided mainly by the federal judiciary. Under the Constitution of the United States as it stood in 1860, the ownership of property and the conduct of industrial enterprises were wholly within the authority of the several states, except insofar as interstate and foreign commerce were involved. Each state by law defined property for itself and determined what should be the limits imposed on the use of property. The power to charter corporations and control their management also belonged to the states. Therefore capitalists, corporations, and other industrial concerns that had grounds, real or imaginary, for complaining against state laws and the actions of state officials had to resort, as a rule, to state legislatures and state courts for relief. Only in a narrow range of cases could the federal courts accept appeals, intervene on their behalf, and afford them protection. But in 1868 the Fourteenth Amendment became a part of the federal Constitution. Henceforward the ultimate protection of life, liberty, property, privileges, and immunities was to be a function of the federal judiciary, with the United States Supreme Court as the final tribunal of appeal.

Although many advocates of the Fourteenth Amendment insisted that it "nationalized civil liberty"—put everything affecting liberty and property under national authority—the Supreme Court of the United States refused to accept that view for several years after the adoption of this amendment. It held that the amendment was mainly, though not exclusively, designed to sustain the civil rights of the newly emancipated slaves, and not to reduce the historic power of the states over personal and property rights.

At that stage in its interpretation of the amendment, the Court ruled that each state could regulate, for example, the rates of railways within its borders; and when railway companies complained that they were deprived of their property by such regulations the Court told them that they must look to the state legislatures for help, not to the federal courts. Judicial decisions of this type thus continued the dispersion of legal power over property, corporations, and industry among the states, that had prevailed in the days of agricultural supremacy in 1787 when about ninety per cent of the people were engaged in farming.

Under such judicial rulings business corporations operating throughout the country were subject to the varied and often conflicting regulations of as many legislatures as there were states in the Union. Efficient centralization in corporate management became difficult if not impossible. Endless lawsuits over regulations and taxation in states and endless conflicts with state politicians harassed and impeded the formation and operations of corporations, trusts, and combines, as concentration proceeded in industry and transportation. Not without reason did lawyers for dissatisfied capitalists insist that such "anarchy," such a dispersion of legal authority to regulate and control the use of property, if appropriate for earlier times, was unfitted to the prosecution of industrial enterprise on a national scale. Well paid for their advice, lawyers for corporations kept appealing to the Supreme Court of the United States for protection against state legislation adversely affecting the property interests of their clients.

Eventually they were successful in getting a reinterpretation of the Fourteenth Amendment. Under that amendment corporations were "persons" at law and no "person" could be deprived of life, liberty, or property without due process of law. As justices of the Supreme Court died or resigned and new justices were appointed, judicial opinions respecting the rights of corporate persons changed.

In 1889 the Supreme Court decided that, while state authorities could regulate the rates of railway companies, they could not fix rates so low as to deprive the companies of their property without due process. "If the company," said the Court, "is deprived of the power of charging reasonable rates for the use of its property, and such deprivation takes place in the absence of investigation by judicial machinery, it is deprived of the lawful use of its property, and thus, in substance and effect, of the property itself without due process of law and in violation of the Constitution of the United States." Under ruling of this type state regulations of property had to be of such a nature as to allow for a "reasonable" profit to the owners; and the question of reasonableness was a matter to be finally determined by the Supreme Court of the United States in cases duly brought before it.

By this and many other cases decided before the end of the nineteenth century the once almost sovereign powers of the states over property and business within their borders were reduced to mere shadows of their former greatness. Now all laws and actions by state authorities that seriously affected the property rights of corporations and industrial concerns throughout the country were subject to review and possible annulment by a single authority— the Supreme Court at Washington. This was a centralization of legal power practically ultimate in nature; for beyond that tribunal lay no formal appeal, save to the latent power of the people to amend the Constitution by an extraordinary majority in Congress and of the states.

Under the Fourteenth Amendment, so interpreted, innumerable laws and decrees by state, municipal, and county legislatures and officials were declared void. Everywhere state authorities were notified in effect that they could no longer pursue "populistic" or "communistic" policies in dealing with business enterprises; that they must observe the fundamental rights of property as taught in capitalistic economics. According to the letter of the Constitution, the power to make civil and criminal laws yet remained with the states, but that power was in fact strictly limited by the new jurisprudence created by the Supreme Court.

Another practice sanctioned by the Supreme Court gave additional impetus to economic centralization. According to the Constitution, actions at law between citizens of different states could be taken, on certain conditions, into the federal courts. Corporations, besides being persons, were "citizens" within the meaning of the word so used. They were often engaged in interstate commerce which was also subject to federal authority.

As the labor movement grew in strength, and strikes became more frequent, often tying up the trunk lines of railway companies, lawyers adopted the practice of appealing to federal judges for aid against strikers. One form of relief for which they asked was a writ of injunction, forbidding strikers to picket the property of their former employers and otherwise interfere with the operation of their employers' business.

Recourse to the injunction by employers became increasingly frequent during and after the great railway strikes which broke out in the depression of 1873–78. A climax in this development was reached in 1894 on the occasion of a strike ordered by the

American Railway Union in Chicago in sympathetic support of strikers against the Pullman Company. In the midst of that labor contest the federal district court in the city issued a blanket injunction forbidding all persons engaged in the strike to interfere with the movement of trains. The president of the American Railway Union, Eugene V. Debs, manager of the strike, was accused of violating the injunction, arrested, and imprisoned for contempt by the federal court from which the injunction issued. On appeal the Supreme Court of the United States upheld the lower tribunal at Chicago and declared that summary imprisonment, without jury trial, for contempt of court in such cases did not violate the federal Constitution.

Having the full sanction of the highest court in the land for the free use of injunctions in labor disputes, lawyers for industrial concerns availed themselves of this legal weapon in every direction to crush strikes and block the efforts of trade unions to force their terms on employers. Thus a new instrument of control was added to the decisions of the Supreme Court, subjecting all state authorities to its dominion in respect of their actions seriously affecting the rights of property. Now the practice of issuing injunctions freely in labor disputes gave to centralizing industry a powerful weapon against coercive measures of the centralizing labor movement.

Therefore, in contests between capital and state governments and between capital and labor, while economic concentration advanced, the balance of legal power was weighted on the side of capital. Insofar as government was involved in its operations, industrial enterprise could now turn with confidence to the federal judiciary for negative relief and for positive assistance in gaining all the profits that, as one lawyer put it, "the traffic will bear." It was after observing such history in the making that Henry Adams was led to wonder in 1895 whether the country was "on the edge of a new and last great centralization, or of a first great movement of disintegration."

CHAPTER XX

Centralization as Involved in the Political Struggle

THE LAST HALF of the nineteenth century was crowded with events that shook from center to circumference the economic system handed down from the age of Andrew Jackson. The chief events were a civil war and the abolition of slavery—the very basis of the Southern plantation system; an upheaval in the race and class relations of the South; occupation of the great West; the disappearance of free land for farming families and the transference of natural resources to private persons or corporations; expansion and concentration in industry and transportation; increase in immigration and in the number and size of cities; the creation of a plutocracy, or money aristocracy, flaunting its wealth in the brazen display of new riches; a powerful labor movement; and judicial backing for business enterprise.

This age was also characterized by panics and depressions, nationwide in scope, unprecedented in extent, unemployment, poverty, violence, and the destruction of property. Of the span between 1870 and 1910 about two thirds of the years were years of depressions, long or short in duration: for example, 1873–78; 1884–87; 1893–98. Certainly during half the time farmers, industrialists, and industrial workers were outside the range of what was boastfully called "prosperity."

Every depression season was punctuated by strikes, local and general. The great railway strike of 1877 was accompanied by so many disorders and so much bloodshed as to make Daniel Shays' rebellion in 1786 appear like a mere argument at a garden party. Before it was over the Pennsylvania railway station in Pittsburgh had been seized by rioters and burned. Shortly afterward a railway strike in the Southwest, led by Martin Irons for the Knights of Labor, tied up more than 5000 miles of lines in Missouri, Arkansas, Kansas, Indian Territory, and Nebraska. It too was attended by the seizure of railway property and the sabotage of engines. So disturbing was the railway strike of 1894, in connection with the labor dispute at the Pullman Works in Chicago, that President Cleveland used the troops of the United States to suppress it.

If disruptive strikes could be set down to "the evil spirit" or "ignorance" of American working people, "misled by foreign agitators," the numerous politico-economic scandals which exploded in rapid succession during these eventful years could not all be laid at their doors. In New York City, William Marcy Tweed and a gang of Tammany politicians were exposed to public scorn in 1871 as robbers and bribers who had looted the city treasury and corrupted judges in the highest courts of the state. The next year the New York *Sun* "scooped" the news of a still greater scandal—the Crédit Mobilier peculations in the recent construction of the Union Pacific Railroad. Before this sensation was over the people learned that members of Congress had accepted "favors" which were in effect bribes, and that no less a person than the Vice-President of the United States, if not guilty of gross misconduct in connection with the "deal," was at least by no means impeccable.

While the Crédit Mobilier affair was on the public stage, another inquiry showed that the "Whisky Ring" had been cheating the government of taxes. The trail of that scandal led to the very doors of the White House—to President Grant's private secretary. Another ring, the Star Route gang, including federal officials and members of Congress, was caught defrauding the government in connection with the carriage of mails. It was indeed a rare year that did not produce a fresh exposure in high places.

Among the revelations of the period was the disclosure of monstrous poverty in urban quarters. As foreign immigrants by the millions and native workers from the least prosperous rural districts rolled into the centers of industry and commerce, areas of congestion, the "slums," swelled into huge proportions. Every city had its large districts of poverty, overcrowding, misery, and crime.

Americans had read in their histories about the proletariat of ancient Rome. Now they could actually see a proletariat in every urban region of their own Republic. "It is the city," exclaimed the

Congregationalist home missionary, Josiah Strong, in *Our Country*, published in 1891, "where . . . the Sway of Mammon is the widest, and his worship the most constant and eager. Here luxuries are gathered . . . here is the most extravagant expenditure. Here also is the *congestion* of wealth the severest. Dives and Lazarus are brought face to face; here, in sharp contrast, are the *ennui* of surfeit and the desperation of starvation. . . . As a rule, the greater the city, the greater are the riches of the rich and the poverty of the poor. . . . Is it strange that such conditions arouse a blind and bitter hatred of our social system?"

No longer did an abundance of free land offer an escape from this poverty. No longer could politicians delude the poor by proclaiming that "free land" was the solution for the problem of poverty. Nor were all farmers actually on the land becoming stalwart freeholders. When the census takers of 1880 had collected the figures of farm ownership, they reported that twenty-five per cent of all farmers were already tenants. Twenty years later the proportion had increased to thirty-five per cent and was on an upward climb.

To many American observers of these social earthquakes, including such prominent figures as James Russell Lowell, Walt Whitman, and E. L. Godkin, the situation was appalling. Yet throughout most of the period neither of the two major political parties, which contended for power and in one season or another governed the nation, took much account of the volcanic upheavals in American life and labor or made any substantial alterations in the form, methods, or concepts of their obligations. Nominating conventions, "fresh from the people," were held as in the good old days of Andrew Jackson. Amid open convention uproars or back-room negotiations among politicians, candidates were chosen for approval by the voters. On the morning after a triumph at the polls the spoils of office were distributed among the victors, in the style consecrated by long custom. "What are we here for?" a convention delegate once exclaimed when a reformer asked his party colleagues to endorse a civil-service proposal for removing a few hundred jobs from the grip of politicians. At party conventions political experts drafted platforms in the customary manner, praising themselves, damning their opponents, and making vague promises savoring of the millennium.

As in the past, professional politicians controlled conventions and committees, were nominated to high offices, directed party affairs, and, if elected, administered the machinery of government, local and national, with an eye to party advantage. After the overthrow of the planters in the Southern revolution, the monopoly of the professional politicians, mostly lawyers, became more complete. Businessmen, farmers, and industrial workers left to this "elite" the ostensible function of ruling the nation.

In the struggle of the two major parties for power the Republicans gained strength for some time. They had been a minority in 1860 but they emerged from the civil conflict augmented in numbers and influence. During the period of reconstruction in the South they were able to count on the support of the new Negro voters grateful for emancipation and for the civil rights accorded to their race by the party of Abraham Lincoln. To that party bankers and investors in United States bonds looked for the payment of interest and principal and for security against the inflation menace of paper currency. Railway promoters, mining prospectors, cattle kings, timber hunters, and land speculators, already enriched by government bounties, preferred to see the national government in Republican hands. To the Republicans the beneficiaries of the higher tariffs turned with eager expectancy for continued protection. Industrial workers were told that only under such protection could they enjoy higher wages than the "pauper labor of Europe" received. Farmers who were getting free homesteads in the West and Union veterans of the war entitled to land and pensions had reasons for allegiance to Republican leadership. As possessors of the Executive Department in Washington, Republicans dispensed the spoils of office among the faithful.

With these material considerations were united moral advantages in aid of the Republicans. It was under their auspices that the Union had been saved, that the perpetuity of the Republic had been assured. Theirs was the party of Lincoln, which had struck the shackles from four million bondmen—the greatest act of liberation in the tragic history of chattel slavery. The "twin relics of barbarism—slavery and polygamy," orators could say, had been abolished throughout the land by courageous and enlightened Republicans. To whom except Republicans, it was asked, can the liberty of the people and the fortunes of the Republic be safely entrusted?

On the other hand the Democrats long lay under a cloud. They were deprived of the able and powerful leadership once afforded by Southern planters and their lawyers and they were now vilified by Republicans as the abettors of slavery and disunion. They had been split into two factions in 1860. They had officially proclaimed the war a failure in the platform of 1864. What glittering program could they now offer to the voters? Their old pledges of lower tariffs with hints of free trade ahead and their doctrine of states' rights had less popular appeal during the distractions that followed the collapse of the Confederacy.

Besides, their ranks were wavering. They had lost to the Republicans many farmers in the West who had once rallied around their flag, and they were further weakened by the subjection of their fellow Democrats in the South. Thus badly crippled, they seemed to have poor prospects of ever recovering the proud dominion over national affairs previously exercised. Even South Carolina, where secession had started, went Republican in 1868! The main prospect of the Democrats for a reconquest of power, even temporarily, appeared to lie in the mistakes or corruption of the Republicans or in taking advantage of business panics and depressions to urge stricken and distressed farmers and industrial workers to turn away from Republican leadership.

Of the nine presidential elections between 1868 and 1900 inclusive, the Republicans carried all but two and in every instance with a military hero, large or small, as a candidate. General Ulysses S. Grant had exhibited little interest in politics and had voted only once in his life—the Democratic ticket in 1856; but he was perhaps the outstanding figure in national life after the death of Lincoln in 1865. Capitalizing on Grant's popular strength, the Republicans chose him as their candidate for President in 1868, elected him, and then renewed his term in 1872. During the depression which cast gloom over Grant's last years, they picked for the presidency Rutherford B. Hayes, of Ohio, a former general in the Union army, to pit against the Democratic nominee, Samuel J. Tilden, an able lawyer and politician from New York. The contest was close and the returns were disputed, but a special commission, in which the Republicans had a majority, awarded the palm to Hayes. Although Hayes had qualities, character, and intelligence, the Republicans turned from him in 1880, nominated another general, James A. Garfield, also of Ohio, and won that election. When Garfield was cut down in his first year by an assassin's bullet, the presidency passed to the Vice-President, Chester A. Arthur, a colorless man, unable to provoke national enthusiasm.

Republican fortunes were ebbing. War passions were cooling. The services of the party in saving the Union and freeing the slaves were being forgotten in the fleeting years, amid the sensational scandals of the Republican administrations at Washington. Yet Republican leaders were still so confident about their position that they thought they could elect a civilian at last. Instead of gathering around a military hero in 1884, they nominated James G. Blaine, of Maine, who had served in Congress, not on battlefields, during the war. But Blaine had been singed if not scorched by the Crédit Mobilier scandal.

Taking his selection as an "affront," disgruntled Republicans, called "Mugwumps," deserted their party in large numbers and cast in their lot with the Democrats, who had pinned their faith in victory on Grover Cleveland, governor of New York, as their candidate. Cleveland was no war hero either. Indeed, he had hired a substitute to fight for him in the war. But though intellectually complacent and incapable of emulating a fiery Andrew Jackson in his popular appeals, Cleveland had been an efficient public administrator at Albany and had the reputation of being an honest man and a trustworthy official. Despite unparalleled vituperation in the campaign, Cleveland slipped through—by a narrow margin. The switch of a few hundred votes in New York City, or perhaps an accurate count of the votes cast there, would have sent his competitor, Blaine, to the White House in his stead.

Having read their lesson in that outcome, the Republicans then returned to the practice of going to the voters with a military hero. In 1888 they chose as their candidate Benjamin Harrison, of Indiana, who, like Grant, Hayes, and Garfield, had been an officer in the Union army during the war. A cold personality and a rather drab figure in every way, Harrison nevertheless managed to whip up enough support on his military record and other grounds to carry the day against President Cleveland, renominated for a second term by the Democrats.

If there was anything heroic in the stature of Harrison after he became the Chief Executive, the people failed to appreciate it. After four years' experience with him, they retired him to private life in 1892 and restored to the presidency Grover Cleveland, the civilian, nominated again by the Democrats. Once more, and for the last time, in 1896, the Republicans staked their chance of winning an election on a former soldier of the Union army, Major William McKinley, of Ohio. Under his leadership, promoted by a shrewd political financier, Marcus A. Hanna, they recovered their control over the national administration. When the new century opened they thought themselves firmly buttressed in power—though signs of a revolt against historic methods in party politics loomed on the horizon.

While the presidential elections in those years revealed a numerical weakness in the Democratic party, they were not the sole tests of its vitality. In the congressional elections, where the great funds and pressures of the national campaign were less available, the story was different. Except for two bienniums, the Democrats had possession of the House of Representatives during all the years from 1875–95; for four of those years they had a majority in the Senate as well as in the House. During Cleveland's first administration, 1885–89, they controlled the House, while the Republicans held the Senate. For two years in Cleveland's second administration the Democrats marshaled a majority in both Houses of Congress. At no time did they despair of capturing the presidency.

Their anticipation of final triumph was energized by the fact that after the restoration of white dominion the South was really "solid." Before the civil conflict it had been politically divided and indeed it was badly split in the election of 1860. Hundreds of the richest and most powerful planters had feared, if not despised, the democracy of Thomas Jefferson, for they saw in its gospel of human equality a peril to their labor system. But after the emancipation of slaves and the rise of the Republican mastery, all the South below the border states became firmly Democratic. Furthermore, its strength in the House of Representatives was actually increased by emancipation. Before that event a slave had been treated as only three fifths of a person in the apportionment of representatives under the Constitution; after it, all Negroes were counted in fixing the number of representatives accorded to the Southern states. The Negroes now counted in representation; the whites chose the representatives and had more in Congress.

At every presidential election between 1868 and 1892 each of the two major parties put forth an official platform—a declaration of its views respecting the national needs and a statement of its program for reform or conservatism if victorious at the polls. In these successive documents were mirrored the intelligence and thought of the governing elite and its popular supporters.

In the main the platforms dealt with issues that had been uppermost since 1789: tariffs, banking, currency, taxation, internal improvements, and the disposal of the public domain. The hatred of monopolies, the great animus of Jacksonian Democrats, now and then still blazed out in platform attacks on railway corporations, "trusts," and "combines." But on the whole both parties passed over with slight recognition the basic changes that were taking place in American economy under their very eyes. For several years, it is true, Republicans laid stress on promises to uphold the civil rights of Negroes in the South but as time passed that issue relaxed its hold on public interest and on theirs.

From season to season, while pointing fingers of scorn at Democrats, Republicans stood on their record, claiming it as sufficient proof that they merited an indefinite tenure of power. In assailing that record Democrats emphasized Republican corruption and mismanagement and made much of the popular slogan: "Turn the rascals out!" Of course the charges were occasionally reversed. When the Democrats were in power briefly, they too gloated on their "achievements," and the Republicans took their turn at urging the voters to eject the rascals. Thus praise of their own virtues and abuse of their opponents furnished a major part of the stock in trade drawn upon for campaigns by the leaders of both parties.

"We charge the Democratic party," proclaimed the Republicans in their platform of 1876, "with being the same in character and spirit as when it sympathized with treason . . . With reasserting and applauding in the national Capitol the sentiments of unrepentant rebellion; with sending Union soldiers to the rear, and promoting Confederate soldiers to the front; with deliberately proposing to repudiate the plighted faith of the government; with being equally false and imbecile upon the overshadowing financial questions. . . . With proving itself, through the period of its ascendancy in the lower House of Congress, utterly incompetent to administer the government; and we warn the country against trusting a party thus alike unworthy, recreant, and incapable." Treason, imbecility, incompetence, unworthiness, and incapacity! These were Republican words supposed to describe the qualities of the Democratic party.

The Democrats retaliated in kind. In their platform of 1884 they paid their respects to their opponents in similar terms: "The Republican party, so far as principle is concerned, is a reminiscence. In practice it is an organization for enriching those who control its machinery. . . . The Republican party, during its legal, its stolen, and its bought tenures of power, has steadily decayed in moral character and political capacity. . . . Honeycombed with corruption, outbreaking exposures no longer shock its moral sense. Its honest members, its independent journals, no longer maintain a successful contest for authority in its canvasses or a veto upon bad nominations. . . . We denounce the Republican party for having failed to relieve the people from crushing war taxes, which have paralyzed business, crippled industry, and deprived labor of employment and its just reward." Thievery, moral decay, corruption, incapacity! These were Democratic words supposed to describe the qualities of the Republican party.

☆

Performances—as distinguished from professions and denunciations—registered, on the statute books of the United States, the measures which the two parties deemed appropriate and necessary in the age of economic transformation. Five times between 1868 and 1900 the tariff rates on imports were altered, generally in the form of more protection for manufacturers. In 1872 and 1883 minor modifications were made. In 1890 the Republicans, by the McKinley Act, ventured upon a substantial increase in protectionism. In 1894, Democrats, for the moment in control of the presidency and both houses of Congress, juggled the rates again and passed a bill also so protectionist in nature that President Cleveland, unwilling to approve it, allowed it to become a law without his signature.

On the currency question Republicans and Democrats blew hot and cold. In 1875, Congress passed the Resumption Act providing for the redemption of the paper currency, or "greenbacks," in gold, beginning in 1879. But to please the paper-money factions in both parties, Congress in 1878 and in 1890 passed silver-purchase laws authorizing the Treasury to buy annually certain quantities of silver for coinage. Mindful of outbursts against the spoils system in both parties, it enacted in 1883 a civil-service law under which appointments to a few federal offices were removed from the system and made subject to an examination of candidates for efficiency, held under a civil-service commission. At the discretion of the President other offices could be placed, according to this law, under the new "merit system." Judged by such performances, the two major parties were becoming as much alike in their interests and sentiments as two bottles of the same size and shape, differing only in their labels.

During the entire period from 1868 to 1900 only three notable measures passed by Congress were designed to cope with complicated problems raised by industrial concentration and the spoliation of natural resources. The first of these, the Interstate Commerce Act of 1887, forbade interstate railway companies to engage in such practices as pooling freight and giving rebates to shippers "on the inside." It also provided for the Interstate Commerce Commission, empowered to regulate and supervise railways in limited respects. The act had imposing features but no teeth. For many years it was little more than a dead letter.

The second major law bearing on recent developments in American economy was directed against concentration in industry. It was the Sherman Antitrust Act of 1890 which prohibited trusts and combinations "in restraint of trade" and imposed penalties for violations. This act was neither imposing nor effective. For a long time presidents allowed it to sleep in the statute book.

The third law, far from imposing but foreshadowing crucial actions relative to natural resources, was a mere amendment attached to another bill in 1891—a few lines authorizing the President to set aside and hold as national forests certain areas of the public domain. The process of despoiling the national heritage was not stopped by this act but a change in policy was implied.

To the list of the three measures might have been added the provision for a federal income tax incorporated in the tariff bill enacted by Democrats in 1894. This was supposed to make the rich bear their share of taxation. But most of it was declared unconstitutional by the Supreme Court of the United States the very next year.

Such, according to the official platforms and the major pieces of legislation, was the insight of the political elite of the two major parties into the meaning of the catastrophic events in American economy between 1868 and the end of the century. Such were the ideas and actions which they deemed sufficient to meet the challenge of basic changes and to assure what they were fond of calling the prosperity, liberty, and perpetuity of the Republic. Such was their vision of the future, their appreciation of the "shape of things to come," the Americanism they thought adequate for transmission to rising generations, to be maintained forever.

While Republicans and Democrats, each party pleased with itself and displeased with its opponent, thus conducted politics according to their conceptions of fitness or their power, they were all along bothered by critics in their own ranks and by minor political parties that appeared from time to time. If a disturbance was small within their own coteries or among the people in general, they could ignore it. If it was large, as indicated by the number of protests made at the ballot box, they sought to conciliate it by promises of mild reforms and political jobs. For nearly thirty years they were able to prevent revolts started by discontented people from seriously upsetting party calculations—party use and wont.

Not until 1896 did one of the major parties fall a victim to an uprising from below. Then it was the Democrats whose national machine, captured by agrarians under William Jennings Bryan, of the young generation, ceased for a time to function as of old. More years passed. Then the Republican machine was disrupted by Theodore Roosevelt, also of the young generation. But the storms which made these wrecks were slow in gathering. Their beginnings were small and for many years could be lightly disregarded by men occupied with "large and practical" affairs.

Judged by their programs and the economic interests to which they appealed, the critics who protested against the offerings of the major parties and demanded a different order of things belonged mainly to two groups: labor reformers and agrarians. The first group was concerned primarily with industrial workers and their claims; the second with farmers and tenants on the land who had not received all the blessings of prosperity to which they thought themselves entitled. Yet no deep gulf separated these two groups and their ideas about public policies. Their demands often coincided, and members of both groups looked upon the political struggle as involving farmers and industrial workers alike as in Jackson's day. Sometimes they were able to unite. At others they pursued separate courses and no effort at co-operation brought about a permanent union.

The first break with regular political affiliations after 1865 was made in the name of industrial labor. In 1872 a convention of delegates from seventeen states, calling themselves Labor Reformers, met at Columbus, Ohio, and adopted a platform on issues which the major parties had ignored. As to doctrines, they declared, in the American tradition, that all political power is inherent in the people and that government is established for their benefit; that all citizens are entitled to the use and enjoyment of the fruits of their labor and skills; that no man or set of men is entitled to special privileges from government except in consideration of public services rendered.

As to practical proposals, the Labor Reformers demanded a national currency issued to the people without the intervention of banking corporations; restriction of the sale of public lands to bona fide homeseekers; exclusion of Chinese laborers; an eight-hour day in all government employment; abolition of contract labor in prisons; government regulation of railway and telegraph corporations to assure equitable rates; civil-service reform; modification of patent laws in the interests of inventors; and the subordination of military power to the civil power. The Reformers' candidate for President, Charles O'Connor, of New York, polled a vote of less than 30,000—more in Texas than in New York, and more in Georgia than in Illinois.

Discouraged by the outcome, Labor Reformers gave up the political battle or merged temporarily with the agrarians. But in 1888 another labor party sprang up—the Union Labor party. It held a convention in Cincinnati and adopted the chief principles put forth by the Labor Reformers, adding an endorsement of woman suffrage and the popular election of United States senators. In the same city at the same time another convention of delegates assembled, the United Labor party, and displayed more radical propensities. These Laborites denounced both Republicans and Democrats as "hopelessly and shamelessly corrupt," and among other things approved an increased taxation of land values and government ownership and control of railway and telegraph lines. But the new Laborites also polled a small vote.

Then in 1892, after local beginnings, the Socialist Labor party launched an independent national campaign, appealing especially to industrial workers for support. Its platform in this campaign was reformist. It advocated government ownership of public utilities, progressive inheritance and income taxes, universal and equal suffrage, free education, municipal home rule, abolition of child labor, employers' liability legislation, and the secret ballot. It also proposed to reconstruct the federal government by abolishing the presidency and the Senate, and setting up an executive board to be elected and subject to recall by the House of Representatives.

At the end of the century, in 1900, a second socialist party, the Social Democratic party, entered the lists with a complete program for nationalizing all the major instruments of production. As an evidence of its militancy, the new party placed at the head of its ticket Eugene V. Debs, who had been imprisoned for his labor activities during the Pullman strike of 1894. In the election Debs received only 94,800 votes.

None of the labor or socialist parties made heavy inroads upon the monopoly of politics possessed by the Republicans and Democrats. But agrarian agitations, persistent since early colonial times, threatened in the closing years of the nineteenth century to fracture that monopoly. In 1876 farmers entered the national campaign with their own organization, the Independent National party, advocating the historic remedy of farmers for their distresses, namely paper money. The "Greenbackers" now proposed to suppress all bank currency and have the federal government issue notes directly to the people on the basis of its own credit and obligations. This demand for national inflation, instead of the state inflation adopted in Jacksonian times, was a striking note in the long effort of American farmers to defend themselves against deflation and get control over the national medium of exchange. Yet agrarians made little progress with a party of their own until 1892 when they invited industrial workers to unite with them and, at a national convention in Omaha that year, formally launched a farmer-labor party named the People's party, shortened by the public to the "Populists."

RAPID RISE OF TENANCY IN THE UNITED STATES, 1880–1900

Increasing percentage of farmers who were tenants between 1880, when the first census of tenancy was taken, and 1910. From report of President Franklin D. Roosevelt's Committee on Tenancy, 1937.

Before 1892 labor reformers and agrarians had spoken contemptuously of the two major parties, but the Populists at Omaha in 1892 blew against Republicans and Democrats such a blast as had never before come from a political convention. "Corruption," they declared, "dominates the ballot box, the legislature, the Congress, and touches even the ermine of the bench. The people are demoralized. . . . The newspapers are largely subsidized or muzzled; public opinion silenced; business prostrated; our homes covered with mortgages; labor impoverished; and the land concentrating in the hands of capitalists. The urban workmen are denied the right of organization for self-protection; imported pauperized labor beats down their wages; a hireling standing army, unrecognized by our laws, is established to shoot them down, and they are rapidly degenerating into European conditions. The fruits of the toil of millions are boldly stolen to build up colossal fortunes for a few, unprecedented in the history of mankind. . . . We have witnessed for more than a quarter of a century the struggle of the two great political parties for power and plunder, while grievous wrongs have been inflicted upon the suffering people. . . . They propose to drown the outcries of a plundered people with the uproar of a sham battle over the tariff. . . . The interests of rural and civic labor are the same; their enemies are identical." Then followed a long list of demands for radical changes in the law, the currency, the government, and the economy of the United States. On that platform, with General James B. Weaver, a veteran of the Civil War, a former Democrat who had become a Republican in 1860, as their candidate, the Populists polled more than 1,000,000 votes. Signs of an upheaval in party politics were visible.

Despite their appeal to industrial workers in 1892 and notwithstanding the large national vote they received, the Populists polled, relatively speaking, only a handful of votes in the great industrial regions of the country. For example, out of nearly 1,000,000 votes cast in Pennsylvania, only 8700 went to their candidate; out of about 400,000 in Massachusetts, only 3200 bore the Populist mark. Thus the Populist party proved to be mainly agrarian in character and its power lay principally, though not entirely, in Democratic strongholds.

Capitalizing on the panic, depression, strikes, unemployment, and increasing economic distress of the next four years, the Populists and their sympathizers captured the Democratic convention at Chicago in 1896. There the Democratic President in the White House, Grover Cleveland, was unequivocally spurned, conservatives in the party were treated with derision, a radical platform was adopted, and the young politician from Nebraska,

William Jennings Bryan, was nominated as the Democratic candidate for President.

From beginning to end the Democratic convention of 1896 vibrated with revolutionary fervor. Bryan lifted the delegates to their feet with a cry that the toiling masses were not to be crowned with thorns and crucified upon a cross of gold! The platform adopted at Chicago denounced the Supreme Court for invalidating the income tax law of the previous year and demanded a reconstruction of the Court so that the burden of taxation could be equally apportioned and wealth forced to bear its due share. The use of injunctions in labor disputes was condemned as highly dangerous to the rights of the people; and the employment of federal troops in the recent strike at Chicago was branded as an unconstitutional and violent interference with the rights of states. "As labor creates the wealth of the country," ran one plank, "we demand the passage of such laws as may be necessary to protect it in all its rights." To farmers in particular, this Democratic platform promised the free coinage of gold and silver at the ratio of sixteen to one. This was a demand for an inflation of the currency in favor of debtors, that vociferous historic class of rebellious Americans, as against the contraction in favor of creditors—a contraction brought about, it was charged, by using as the monetary standard of the United States the gold controlled by private bankers.

Warned that a crisis impended, the Republicans, led by an astute manager, Marcus A. Hanna, an industrial magnate of Cleveland, Ohio, had prepared to meet it at their convention, held previously at St. Louis. Having picked as his candidate William McKinley, of Ohio, Hanna at first hoped to make protection for industries the main issue, thus playing down the fact that McKinley himself had once been an advocate of free silver.

But conservatives at the convention met the issue head on, even at the price of losing the support of the free-silver faction in Republican ranks. They committed the party unreservedly to "sound money" and opposed the free coinage of silver except by international agreement with the leading commercial nations of the world —"which we pledge ourselves to promote."

Speaking on the floor of the convention, Henry Cabot Lodge arrayed his party against "not only that organized failure, the Democratic party, but all the wandering forces of political chaos and social disorder . . . in these bitter times when the forces of disorder are loose and the wreckers with their false lights gather at the shore to lure the ship of state upon the rocks." With McKinley as their candidate, the Republicans raised a great fund and launched their campaign on an extraordinary scale.

The battle between Bryan and McKinley, accompanied by censorious charges and terroristic threats, aroused the country from coast to coast, as it had not been moved since 1860. Bryan defended his cause and his followers against what he called "English toadies and the pampered minions of corporate rapacity." His party, he declared, represented "the masses of the people, the great industrial and producing masses of the people . . . the men who plow and plant, who fatten herds, who toil in shops, who fell forests, and delve in mines . . . who produce the wealth of the republic, who bear the heaviest burdens in time of peace; who are ready always to give their lifeblood for their country's flag."

The Democratic program and movement McKinley countered by declaring that Republicans would squarely face this "sudden, dangerous, and revolutionary assault upon law and order and upon those to whom is confided by the Constitution and the laws the authority to uphold and maintain them." Bryanism, the editor of the New York *Tribune* assured his readers, had sprung from "the assiduous culture of the basest passions of the least worthy members of the community." Bryan himself the editor portrayed as the willing puppet "in the blood-imbued hands of Altgeld, the anarchist, and Debs, the revolutionist, and other desperadoes of that stripe."

On the side of Bryan was aligned nearly all the discontent with the course of national affairs that had been made manifest by Labor Reformers, Greenbackers, Single Taxers, and Socialists in recent years—all the inveterate hostility to concentrated wealth. No doubt millions of Democrats voted for him out of party habit, as unreflecting partisans, but in so doing they gave sanction to his attack and program. At the election Bryan polled about 1,000,000 more votes than Cleveland had received in 1892—a larger vote than the party was to muster when it elected Woodrow Wilson in 1912. Nevertheless, Bryan was defeated by the new or hitherto lethargic voters who flocked to McKinley's banners—2,000,000 more than had voted the Republican ticket four years previously.

Though victorious in the contest for power, Republicans confronted the fact that 6,500,000 Americans had planted themselves on the side of Bryanism against the 7,100,000 committed to "McKinleyism," as Henry Adams called it. If the Republicans' victory was "glorious," as orators were wont to say, it was narrow enough

to make them realize that their avenue to power was not to be the
same in time to come as it had been since the election of Grant in
1868. It was precarious enough to set them wondering how the
ghost of Bryanism could be laid—by frontal assault, concession, or
diversion?

CHAPTER XXI

The Breach with Historic Continentalism

NEARLY THREE CENTURIES lay between the founding of the English colony of Jamestown in Virginia and the inauguration of McKinley in 1897. Through this long procession of years the energies of the people, of many national origins, called Americans, had been concentrated on expansion and development in this continental theater. Here their labor, interests, and affections centered, as under a sense of great history, often embodied in the somewhat mystical concept of "manifest destiny," as they advanced to the shore of the Pacific. By 1897 the continental domain had been rounded out. All the territories, save three, had been admitted to the Union as equal states possessing self-government under the federal Constitution.

This is not to say that no Americans—in thought, ambition, and enterprise—had gone beyond the continental borders. Keels of American ships had plowed the waters of all seas bearing masters and merchants in search of foreign markets and opportunities to garner in large profits from foreign trade. American warships had bombarded many ports in distant foreign lands in retaliation for native interference with the operations of American traders. Ambitious naval officers, such as Commodore Matthew C. Perry, who opened to American commerce the barred gates of Japan, had dreamed of and proposed the seizure of islands and territories in far-off lands; and indeed a hold was established in the Samoan Islands by 1889.

In the days of slavery, politicians among the planters had contemplated the seizure of Cuba and advances far into Mexico with a view to adding more territory for planters and their slaves. A few Northern politicians had also imagined further expansion. For example, William Seward, Lincoln's Secretary of State, had proclaimed a different type of "manifest destiny" to include all of North America and war with Russia, on the plains of Manchuria, over dominion in the Far East. In 1867, Seward bought Alaska from Russia and, by methods none too nice, forced Congress to approve his action. General Grant, as President, had tried to annex Santo Domingo in the Caribbean and would have done it if the Senate had not stood foursquare against it. But most of these plans and activities, even when fostered by the United States Government, did little to divert the interests, treasure, and affections of the people from the task of developing their continental home.

Indeed the foreign policy of the United States, prescribed in Washington's Farewell Address, in Jefferson's messages, and in the Monroe Doctrine, rested on the proposition that the fundamental interest of the American people was, and should be, concentrated on their continental opportunities—for many reasons, political, economic, and moral. According to that definite policy this hemisphere, the seat of American power, was to be kept independent and protected against further colonization and conquest by European Powers; the United States was not to intervene in the eternal vicissitudes of European power politics; territories outside the easy reach of effective defense were not to be acquired; and the protection and advance of American civilization in this continental arena was to be the primary and indefeasible objective of the United States Government in all its relations with foreign Powers, near or distant. Not until about 1890 did American politicians begin seriously to plan and publicly to advocate a reversal of this positive policy, propose active intervention in the affairs of Asia and Europe, and urge the transformation of the United States into a "great world Power"—the goal to which European imperialists had been vaingloriously leading their countries.

Like every scheme in politics, the scheme of world power for the United States had its formulators and plans for application. High in the ranks of the men who made the new world image for Americans to live and die by was an American naval officer, Alfred Thayer Mahan, author of large books on sea power. Openly and covertly Mahan labored to steer American politicians out into the new course—of building a big navy, pushing commerce everywhere in the world, and seeking positive power, physical and moral, in the ancient and perpetual controversies of Europe and Asia.

Nominally a naval officer dedicated to the defense of his country, Mahan was actually an amateur historian and a vigorous politician, publicist, and negotiator. He realized in the beginning that his self-appointed task of converting the nation to world-power politics would be difficult; there was, he said, "no aggressive action in our pious souls." Though he confessed that American citizens did not understand what was going on in his line, he told them that they would soon be deeply involved in European and Asiatic politics whether they liked it or not.

A second agitator for the plunge into world-power politics was Josiah Strong, a militant Protestant missionary who lectured and wrote unctuously on the subject. In his book, *Our Country*, published first in 1886 and in an enlarged form in 1891, Strong declared that the United States was in peril of socialism and social upheavals; that the Anglo-Saxon race was chosen by God to civilize the world; and that the major responsibility for running this crusade belonged to the people of the United States.

Associated with the school of aggressive adventurers were two young members of the Republican party then seeking political careers. One was Theodore Roosevelt, of New York, a man of moderate wealth, leisure, and ambition, full of egotism and bluster. To him Mahan's wine of imperialism was little short of a godsend as he cast about for a big role in politics. The other was Henry Cabot Lodge, son of a Boston merchant made wealthy in the China trade, who had battled his way from Massachusetts into the United States Senate in 1893. Bosom friend of Roosevelt and Mahan, Lodge spared no time or strength in preaching the new gospel of world-power politics and in striving to force it upon balky Republicans of the older generation.

In many respects the times were auspicious for the young agitators' designs on America and the world. European Powers, with Great Britain at the head, were then going into imperialism on a vaster scale than ever. They were building bigger navies, raising bigger armies, seizing territories in Asia, Africa, and the islands of the seas, forming secret alliances, carrying on undercover diplomatic maneuvers, and preparing for the climax—the World War which opened in 1914. The sight of this "grand strategy" in Europe filled the American world-power politicians with envy and a burning desire to get into it. Besides, they well knew as expert politicians that a diversion of the people's thought from domestic discontent over plutocracy and poverty, such as embroiled the land in the campaign of 1896, to world politics and wars would damp if not extinguish radicalism at home. It would smother, they trusted, those other agitators: Bryan, Debs, John P. Altgeld, and all such "incendiaries," as they were described in conservative circles.

Another consideration entered into the world-power design of young Theodore Roosevelt. For about thirty years the American people had been at peace. The bloodshed, sufferings, and destruction of the Civil War had almost been forgotten—in the North at least. The country, he said, was growing "soft," martial virtue was on a decline, and another war would be "a good thing" to tone up the people. In 1895, while President Cleveland was engaged in a vehement quarrel with Great Britain over her alleged encroachment on the territory of Venezuela, Roosevelt wrote to Lodge: "Personally I rather hope the fight will come soon. The clamor of the peace faction has convinced me that the country needs a war." The efforts of fellow citizens, particularly at Harvard University, to encourage a pacific settlement with Great Britain filled him with disgust. He asked Lodge whether he should not write to the Harvard magazine, the *Crimson*, "a smashing letter . . . giving my views and saying a word for Patriotism and Americanism."

Within a short time the agitators' program for America's thrust into world-power politics was well formulated and contained the following propositions. The United States, long an infant nation, had "grown up," had become "adult," must cast off the provincialism of its youth and, as a grown man, press into the grand game of power politics played by the grown men—the "big men"—of Europe and Asia. To continue in the old ways at home would be childish. All the free land and natural resources in the United States had passed into private hands and been developed; there was no more living room for Americans on this continent. Hence Americans must look far away for room in which to expand.

Americans, said an Indiana recruit to world-power politics, Albert J. Beveridge, produced more agricultural commodities and manufactures than they could consume; they must have new markets and colonies to exploit or American economy would be paralyzed with surplus wealth. Nations, argued Mahan in the language of Darwinism, must struggle with one another for existence and unless the United States was strong in the struggle it would perish. Millions of brown, yellow, and black men, lamented Josiah Strong, sat in the shadows, outside the blessings of Christianity, and by conquering those benighted multitudes, the United States would spread the helpful gospel of Jesus. Therefore, ran the "practical" side of the argument, the United States must build a big navy, seize new naval bases and colonies, force distant markets open, and enter full-panoplied into the competition of the great nations for the possession and domination of the earth.

In summation, the prophecy of the imperialists embraced the features deemed good politics and likely to allay domestic outbreaks against special privileges. The two great expedients of the preceding fifty years had failed to obliterate popular unrest and the will to self-expression. Free homesteads had been bestowed bountifully on settlers in the West; now those very settlers were filling the country with the uproar of a populist revolt against conditions objectionable to them in respect of government. The protective tariff had been tried as a device to assure full employment at good wages for industrial workers, but the McKinley tariff of 1890, the highest yet in American history, had been followed by the devastating panic of 1893–98, with its riots, hunger marches, and threats of revolution.

If politicians were to hold power or to get it if out of office, some new instrument was necessary and they found it in imperialist prophecy. The economic tenets of that prophecy boiled down to two mass appeals: imperial expansion would provide better markets for farmers, outlets for their "surpluses" of produce at prices profitable to them; and it would create jobs for industrial workers, fill their dinner pails.

No less important in imperialist calculations was a realization among the shrewder politicians that a foreign war and a "strong" foreign policy would in themselves divert the attention of the people from their domestic tribulations and programs of reform. In 1895, when a war with Great Britain seemed impending, Thomas Pascal, a Democratic politician of Texas, wrote privately to President Cleveland's Secretary of State that such a war would knock more pus out of the "anarchistic, socialistic, and populistic boil" than "would suffice to inoculate and corrupt our people for the next two centuries."

To the politicians of imperialism this outlook was charming; with no disturbance whatever to vested interests at home a panacea for their troubles could be offered to dissatisfied farmers and industrial workers and public attention distracted from politics on the home front.

☆

An occasion to put the plan for world-power politics into effect was afforded by a dispute with Spain about her island of Cuba, rampant when McKinley was inaugurated in 1897. For years Cuba had been torn periodically by revolts against Spanish dominion, and in 1895 a new rebellion had flamed up. Opposed to imperialism on principle, President Cleveland had studiously sought to pursue a policy of neutrality in the war between Spain and the Cubans. Personally pacific in spirit, President McKinley at first seemed inclined to follow that precedent.

But the American people were deeply moved by the stories of cruelties practiced by the Spanish generals in Cuba especially as narrated by William Randolph Hearst and Joseph Pulitzer in their "yellow journals." To the stories of atrocities were joined pleas for American aid to the "brave Cubans fighting for liberty and independence" and demands for help from American capitalists whose plantations and sugar mills in Cuba were being destroyed in the civil war.

In the midst of the excitement early in 1898 an American battleship, the *Maine*, which had been sent to the harbor of Havana "to safeguard American interests," was blown up by an explosion. Two officers and 258 members of the crew lost their lives in the disaster. Spanish officials were accused of committing the deed, but they denied it and the mystery of its origin was never solved.

For seeming to rely on pacific measures in respect of Cuba and the *Maine* affair, President McKinley was accused by impatient Americans of being weak-kneed. Theodore Roosevelt declared that he had the backbone of a chocolate éclair. Still McKinley persisted in his negotiations with Spain and was able to wring from the government in Madrid a promise to restore peace in Cuba and grant Cubans a form of self-government amounting to autonomy, if not independence. Then suddenly, on April 11, 1898, without fully revealing to the public the Spanish promise, the President sent a message to Congress calling for a resolution authorizing him to expel Spanish forces from the island of Cuba.

Although an overwhelming majority of the representatives and a safe majority of the senators were hot for war on Spain, the form of the resolution recognizing the independence of Cuba, then under consideration, became the subject of analytical debate. Among the senators especially a dread was voiced that the war would lead to unknown adventures; that the McKinley party would take advantage of it to annex Cuba and accomplish other designs than the expulsion of Spanish authorities from that island.

A leading question, therefore, was raised: What was to be the status of Cuba after Spanish dominion was destroyed? Some Americans believed that the Cubans were not fit for self-government and that the island should be annexed or in some way put under American hegemony. But Congress declared in the war resolution that the people of Cuba were, and of right ought to be, free and independent.

For the most cautious senators, suspecting ulterior purposes, that was not enough. On motion of Senator Henry M. Teller, who had bolted the Republicans in 1896 as a free-silver reformer, another provision, more precise, was added to the resolution: "The United States hereby disclaims any disposition or intention to exercise sovereignty, jurisdiction, or control over said island except for the pacification thereof, and asserts its determination, when that is accomplished, to leave the government and control of the island to its people." This prescription seemed to leave no loophole for imperialists and annexationists of the Mahan school.

With the Teller Amendment added, Congress passed on April 19 the resolution for Cuban independence, empowering the President to use the armed forces of the United States, if necessary, to expel the Spanish government from the island. That was in effect a declaration of war, and under it war began. It was supplemented, however, on April 25, by another resolution declaring war to exist in fact and directing the President to employ the land and naval forces in waging it. War had begun, without any official reference to Spain's island of Puerto Rico or her possessions in the Far East —the Philippines. To all appearances it was a war for the liberation of Cuba from Spanish dominion—an altruistic, moral war.

The hour had come for the planners of world-power politics to steer the country out on the course of imperialism. In a few weeks the naval and land forces of the United States disposed of the Spanish navy and troops in and about Cuba. Then American forces occupied Puerto Rico without having to fight a battle. Meanwhile, as American naval authorities had planned it, the American fleet in the Far East, under Admiral George Dewey, destroyed the Spanish war vessels in the harbor of Manila on May 1, and in effect ended Spanish rule in the Philippines. In August when Spain made overtures for peace, Cuba was freed from her dominion and Puerto Rico and the Philippines were at the command of the United States. Although most Americans had not thought of the war as a war for imperial expansion according to the Mahan-Lodge-Roosevelt formula, they now faced the issue of turning the war for the liberation of Cubans into a triumph for imperialism.

They had a foretaste of what was coming, moreover, in the annexation of the Hawaiian Islands on July 7, 1898, by a joint resolution of Congress. The Hawaiian Islands had long been coveted by several European Powers and by Japan. American missionaries had gone there early in the nineteenth century and Americans had taken part in the development of Hawaiian sugar interests. Before the close of the century Americans in the islands had grown restless under the government by native rulers. In 1893 they had revolted against Queen Liliuokalani, compelled her to abdicate, and established a republic. Under the administration of President Benjamin Harrison they had negotiated a treaty with the United States providing for annexation; but not long after he was inaugurated President on March 4, 1893, Grover Cleveland deliberately blocked the project.

The Republicans simply bided their time. In June 1897 the McKinley administration made a second treaty of annexation with the government of Hawaii controlled by Americans, and its ratification by the United States Senate was pending when the war with Spain broke out. Fearing endless delay, if not defeat, sponsors of annexation then substituted for the treaty a joint resolution of Congress, which required only a majority vote in each house for passage. The resolution was carried. On August 12 the islands were formally annexed and in 1900 they were given a territorial form of government.

In the preliminary peace settlement with Spain in August 1898 it was agreed that Cuba should be free, that Puerto Rico should be ceded to the United States, and that Manila should be occupied by American troops until the terms of the formal peace were determined.

For weeks McKinley withheld his decision on the fate of the Philippines. Meanwhile advocates of annexation, on the platform and in the press, worked hard to convince the American people that it was their opportunity and duty to annex the distant islands and spread American civilization among the natives.

At length McKinley made up his mind in favor of annexation and Spain was compelled to yield. In the final treaty drawn up at Paris, independence was granted to Cuba; Puerto Rico and Guam were ceded to the United States; and the Philippines were transferred to the United States in exchange for a payment of $20,000,000.

When the treaty of peace, including provisions for the annexation of the Philippines, was placed before the Senate for ratification, senators of the anti-imperialist school felt that their worst forebodings were to be justified. In war resolutions of April 1898 they had barred all plans for the annexation of Cuba and repudiated in stern and specific language every imperialist ambition in that connection. Now they realized that, by the treaty, the United States was to be thrust into the eternal wars of the Orient and into the endless intrigues of the great Powers of Europe.

As they understood the departure from the traditional foreign policy, America was henceforth to be one of the imperialist empires of the world, following the course of Spain and Great Britain in conquering and ruling subject peoples, forever warring for more territory, commerce, and dominion over other races. Immediately there was formed in the Senate an opposition so determined that the McKinley administration, backed by Theodore Roosevelt, Lodge, Mahan, and their followers, was greatly worried lest ambitions for world power be thwarted.

Soon the politicians of the McKinley school discovered that they might not be able to secure even a bare majority of the senators for the approval of the annexationist treaty, to say nothing of the two-thirds majority required by the Constitution. Exasperated by the prospect of losing their prize, they denounced the proposal to reject or recast the treaty as shameless effrontery, a reckless repudiation of national honor. In their perplexity and quest for backing they even welcomed William J. Bryan, so recently described by Republicans as an addlepated criminal, when he came to Washington and urged his followers in the Senate to vote for ratification on grounds of national honor; for without the support of Democrats and Populists defeat was certain. By strenuous efforts enough senators personally antagonistic to imperialism were at last rounded up by party whips, and the treaty was ratified with a declaration to the effect that the question of the future of the Philippines was to be left indeterminate. The fateful commitment had been made. Two years later Cuba was forced to accept the so-called Platt Amendment establishing an American protectorate over the island.

Before the conflict over the treaty with Spain was settled in 1899, news arrived that a rebellion had started in the Philippines. For years these islands had seethed with resentment against Spanish rule. The leader of the opposition, Emilio Aguinaldo, was in open revolt when the United States declared war on Spain and his aid had been sought by American army officers in defeating Spanish forces in the Philippines. When this object had been achieved he and his supporters hoped or assumed that at last independence was to be established for the Philippines, as it had been promised to Cuba.

Their expectation of freedom was soon dispelled. On February 4, 1899, a slight collision occurred between Aguinaldo's men and American soldiers and several lives were lost. Ignoring his efforts to arrange an amicable settlement, American authorities pressed the war against the "insurrectionists," who regarded themselves as "patriots." This war went on for more than three years. Early in 1901, with the assistance of Filipinos who had been loyal to the Spanish regime, Aguinaldo was captured and forced to take an oath of allegiance to the United States. But guerrilla fighting continued until July 1902, when President Theodore Roosevelt officially declared it to be at an end.

While the Philippine war was in full blast during the summer of 1900, members of a secret society in China, called the "Boxers," started an organized rout of foreigners. They murdered missionaries in the provinces, killed the German minister in the streets of Peking, and besieged the British quarters in Peking to which hundreds of aliens of various nationalities had fled for safety. At once the United States joined Japan, Russia, Great Britain, France, and Germany—the great imperialist Powers—in sending troops to the Chinese capital, where they broke the siege of the British quarters and put down the Chinese "insurrection" against foreigners.

In connection with the settlement at the close of this conflict, John Hay, the American Secretary of State, adhered to a policy for the Far East, now known as the "Open Door." He proposed that the rights already guaranteed to foreign Powers in China by treaty and international law be protected; but he urged that "Chinese territorial and administrative entity" be preserved and that "the principle of equal and impartial trade with all parts of the Chinese Empire" be safeguarded for the world. For the damage to foreign lives and property, done by the Boxers, heavy indemnities were imposed on the Chinese government, and Hay's doctrine was conveniently ignored by the great Powers engaged in seizing and dividing the spoils of China.

☆

Against the background of these war events the presidential campaign of 1900 was carried on. The Republicans renominated McKinley and associated with him Theodore Roosevelt, now ac-

THE AMERICAN EMPIRE AT THE END OF THE NINETEENTH CENTURY

claimed a hero of the Spanish War in which he had done a little fighting, as candidate for Vice-President. In their platform they took a firm position in support of the gold standard, celebrated the "splendid triumphs" of business and commerce under the McKinley administration, and stood fast against everything that smacked of Bryanism in 1896. Concerning foreign affairs, they declared that the war with Spain had been "unsought and patiently resisted," but had been "triumphantly waged" when it came. As a result of the war, "to ten millions of the human race there was given a new birth of freedom," and to the American people "a new and noble responsibility." With respect to the Philippine insurrection against this birth of freedom, the Republicans proposed to put it down and "to confer the blessings of liberty and civilization upon all the rescued peoples." In other words, they advanced confidently in defense of their domestic program and their foreign policies.

In response to this challenge on domestic and foreign policies, the Democrats renominated Bryan and, besides reaffirming their faith in their principles of 1896, declared their belief that imperialism was a curse to the nation. They lashed it as a new and dangerous threat to the American Republic. They asserted that the Filipinos could not be made citizens without undermining our civilization or subjects without imperiling our form of government. Since the United States now had these wards, however, the Democrats promised them a stable form of government, independence, and then protection against outside interference. They condemned "the greedy commercialism" which dictated the Philippine policy of the Republican administration and impugned the war against the Filipinos as a war of "criminal aggression." "Militarism" they decried as meaning "conquest abroad and intimidation and oppression at home." They were not willing, they declared, "to surrender our civilization or to convert the Republic into an empire." While assailing imperialism, Bryan insisted on upholding his program for the home front that had been formulated for the campaign of 1896.

In justifying their new course Republican orators bore down hard on two types of argument. The first was that of "our responsibility." Their policy, they insisted, was not imperialism; it was the fulfillment of duty to the peoples that had been brought under American jurisdiction as if by an "accident" of history. The Philippines had come to the United States unexpectedly, amid the fortunes of a war fought to free Cuba, and it was our moral obligation to protect these helpless peoples, to civilize them, to educate them, to raise their standard of life, and to confer on them the blessing of liberty.

The second argument of the Republicans pertained to the insurrection in the Philippines, and they shaped it into a question of American patriotism. "Don't haul down the flag!" Theodore Roosevelt shouted as he toured the country in the campaign. It had been raised in the Philippines, enemies had fired on it, every patriot must defend it, and only "copperheads" and traitors sympathized with Filipinos who wanted to pull it down and substitute their banner of independence.

Against imperialism, from the very inception of the war with Spain, a strong opposition was presented by publicists; and in the campaign Democratic politicians contributed their denunciations. William Graham Sumner at Yale University, in an article entitled "The Conquest of the United States by Spain," portrayed the United States as adopting the very course that had led to the downfall of Spain. Imperialism and its works, he contended, would result in bigger armies and navies, bigger debts, a contempt for the Constitution, and more wars whenever the politicians decided that the country needed them. Mark Twain ridiculed the program "for giving civilization to the man who sits in darkness," and condemned the whole imperialist business as a pious fraud devised to conceal commercial greed and lust for power. Andrew Carnegie inveighed against imperialism so fervently that John Hay declared the ironmaster to be "off his head." Bryan crowned it all by proposing to stop the bloodshed in the Philippines at once and make immediate arrangements to prepare the Filipinos for independence.

By the popular decision at the polls in November, McKinley remained President of the United States. He received 100,000 more votes than in 1896; while Bryan, with his program for concentration on the domestic front, dropped below his record of 1896 by nearly 130,000. Imperialists interpreted McKinley's re-election as a final approval of their quest for world power. As in other elections, however, it was impossible wholly to separate the influence of foreign policies in the campaign from the influence of domestic policies.

In any event McKinley's victory, substantial though it was, did not obscure the existence of a powerful opposition. The balloting by counties revealed a pronounced shift of party loyalties, especially in the West where agricultural prices had improved materially after 1896. That signified a return of many farmers to the Republican fold but not necessarily an endorsement of imperialism. Still committed to measures which Republicans attacked as radical and dangerous, the Democratic party was far from death's door and there were many signs that the apparent endorsement of imperialism might not be real, especially in the farming regions of the West and South.

Nevertheless the Republicans were preparing for a rapid advance along their line of world-power politics when President McKinley was assassinated in September 1901. Although his successor, Vice-President Theodore Roosevelt, promised to uphold McKinley's policies unbroken, he had ideas and purposes of his own. McKinley had been timid about foreign adventures, in spite of all that had happened in recent years. He had belonged to the old generation brought up in the belief that the foreign policy of Washington, Jefferson, and Monroe was the correct policy for the Republic. The plans of Lodge, Mahan, and Roosevelt for world imperialism had been alien to his outlook upon national destiny.

Theodore Roosevelt, on the other hand, was of the new generation and, besides loving power for its own sake, he insisted that the nation should pursue a course of power politics in dealing with foreign governments. At the same time he was far less conservative in declaring new domestic policies than were the older leaders of his party. With his imperialism, he coupled pledges of reform on the home front almost in the spirit of Bryanism. He assailed trusts, combines, concentrated wealth, and plutocrats as fiercely as Bryan and the Populists had done. He spoke openly of a more equitable distribution of wealth, of the poverty in great cities, and of social perils within the United States, due to inequalities of wealth.

In fact as President, Theodore Roosevelt, by uniting world-power politics and domestic social reform—pomp and prestige in world affairs with the conciliation of discontented farmers and industrial workers at home—formed a combination of policies that made a strong appeal to the American electorate. He "took the wind out of Bryan's sails," as the saying went, by his operations on the home front, by his "square deal," and provided the people simultaneously with almost daily excitement in his handling of foreign relations. His versatility in this type of statesmanship, or "demagogy" as his opponents defined it, was conclusively demonstrated in the presidential election of 1904.

For that test the Democrats shoved Bryan aside at last, nominated Alton B. Parker, a conservative New York judge, and jettisoned most of the Populist program of reform. Nominated by the Republicans to succeed himself, President Roosevelt came back to the White House in a whirlwind. His popular vote was larger by about 400,000 than McKinley's poll in 1900; Parker fell below Bryan's last vote by more than 1,000,000 and below Roosevelt's by more than 2,000,000. About half a million voters went over to the Socialists and the Populists, but in the Republican avalanche of November 1904 their protests against imperialism and capitalism could be ignored by the Republicans.

Under the leadership of President Roosevelt for nearly eight years a "vigorous" foreign policy was pursued. The insurrection in the Philippines was crushed. An organic law, modeled on that enacted for Puerto Rico in 1900, was put into force in the Philippines in 1902, with provisions for giving the Filipinos self-government piece by piece. The policy of the "Open Door," which was presumed to give American capitalists equal trading rights in China with the British and other capitalists, was upheld and highly praised as indicating something permanent. When Russia and Japan approached a deadlock in a frightful war in 1905, President Roosevelt offered his services in bringing the belligerents together, opened their peace conference at Portsmouth, New Hampshire, and filled the newspapers with blazing headlines about that conference for several days. He negotiated the "Gentlemen's Agreement" with Japan, which forbade the immigration of Japanese laborers to compete with American laborers. With the idea of exhibiting the naval strength of the United States, he sent a fleet around the world in 1907–09. By this action, in defiance of opposition in Congress, he sought to demonstrate to Americans and the rest of mankind that the Navy of the United States was ready for what the diplomats of world-power politics called "eventualities."

In the sphere of action nearer home President Roosevelt pressed for the construction of a canal across the Isthmus of Panama which, in addition to promoting water-borne commerce, would make possible the movement of American naval forces between the two oceans. When he came to the presidency a treaty had been negotiated with Great Britain, permitting the United States to go ahead with the canal. That arrangement set aside an old treaty of 1850 providing for joint construction and authorized the United

States to proceed alone, on condition that there was to be no discrimination among nations in rates fixed for the use of the canal.

Two routes for the canal were then being discussed: one through Nicaragua and the other through Panama. After a heated argument the second was chosen and Roosevelt set about making terms for its construction with the government of Colombia, of which Panama was a part. A draft of the treaty was framed but the Senate of Colombia rejected it. Annoyed by the delay, a few men in Panama, feeling certain that the government of the United States would support them, provoked a revolt against Colombia in 1903. Within a few days President Roosevelt recognized their independence and made a treaty with the new Panama government that granted the United States the right to build the canal through its territory.

Soon "the dirt began to fly," as Roosevelt expressed it, and in 1913 the waters of the Atlantic and the Pacific were joined; the voyage between New York and San Francisco was shortened by nearly 8000 miles. Roosevelt was criticized for his "highhanded action" in dealing with Colombia and he later confessed that he simply "took" Panama to stop endless talk and get the work done.

Just as the building of the canal began Roosevelt resorted to another action in the Caribbean region, also deplored by his critics as autocratic. Santo Domingo had long been heavily in debt to European investors, and their respective governments were considering the use of naval forces to collect the debts. Interpreting it as an omen of possible occupation of the island, President Roosevelt intervened and made a treaty with Santo Domingo authorizing the United States to supervise its finances and the payment of its debts.

When this treaty was rejected by the United States Senate, Roosevelt went forward with his plans anyway. He had an American put in charge of the customs-house in Santo Domingo and sent warships there as a sign that he had force at his command. Senators accused him of violating the Constitution and acting arrogantly, besides ignoring Congress and the rights of the people in Santo Domingo. No doubt some of the European claims against that little country were more than tinged with fraud, but Roosevelt insisted that he was conducting the foreign affairs of the United States and would not be hampered by opponents.

During the conflict over Santo Domingo, Theodore Roosevelt gave to the world a new interpretation of the Monroe Doctrine thoroughly imperialistic in letter and spirit. Was the United States, under that doctrine, to prevent European Powers from using battleships to collect debts in the Latin American countries? If so, what was to prevent them from seizing territory in defiance of the doctrine? Or was the United States to see that such debts were paid? Or should these matters be submitted to arbitration by an international tribunal?

On the issues Roosevelt took a positive stand. Foreign Powers, he declared, are not to seize any more territory in this hemisphere, as the old Monroe Doctrine affirmed; moreover controversies of the kind are not to be submitted to any international tribunal. Then he also proclaimed a new doctrine all his own: if governments in Latin America cannot keep order and pay their debts the United States, having prevented other Powers from acting, must intervene, stop disorders, and make sure that just debts are paid. This pronouncement by the President of the United States was immediately characterized in Latin America as crass "Yankee imperialism." Nevertheless, on this theory, presidential actions in the Caribbean region were multiplied.

Under Roosevelt's successor, William Howard Taft, who had beaten William Jennings Bryan in the election of 1908, imperialistic activity by the President received another name. Republicans now simply called it "dollar diplomacy." The rose under a new name meant that it was the duty and right of the United States Government to seek out and protect opportunities that would allow American businessmen to operate freely in foreign countries and American bankers to make profitable loans abroad. "The diplomacy of the present administration," President Taft explained in 1912, "has sought to respond to modern ideas of commercial intercourse. This policy has been characterized as substituting dollars for bullets. . . . It is an effort frankly directed to the increase of American trade upon the axiomatic principle that the government of the United States shall extend all proper support to every legitimate and beneficial American enterprise abroad."

In conformity with this axiom foreign policy was conducted during Taft's administration. He intervened personally, for example, in China, and tried to secure for American bankers a share of a loan that was being floated in Peking under the auspices of European financiers. Under his leadership advantages were taken of a disturbance in Nicaragua to land American marines in that country and establish there an American "protectorate."

When Woodrow Wilson, after defeating President Taft in the election of 1912, assumed the presidency in Washington, he officially renounced imperialism as theory, but as practice it was by no means entirely discarded. Although President Wilson refused to support Taft's plans for American bankers in China, he adopted strong measures in the Caribbean. The protectorate in Nicaragua was continued. In 1914, Wilson landed marines in Santo Domingo. Two years later he ordered a full military occupation of that country, suppressed its government, set up American military authority, and had a new constitution for Santo Domingo drawn up in Washington.

In 1915, during a revolution in Haiti, American marines were dispatched to the scene, order was restored at a heavy cost of lives, and Haiti put under the control of American military authorities. On this occasion the Secretary of State explained the action in sanctimonious language reminiscent of McKinley: "The United States Government has no purpose of aggression and is entirely disinterested in promoting this protectorate." As a part of the program for strengthening American power in the Caribbean, President Wilson negotiated a treaty with Denmark by which, in 1917, the Danish West Indies, not far from Puerto Rico, were transferred to the United States. Not without reason it could be boasted that the Caribbean had become an "American lake." The phrase was not exactly pleasing to Latin Americans but it rather closely fitted the facts in the case.

Meanwhile troubles had been seething in Mexico and the pot was boiling over when Wilson was inaugurated President. In 1911 its President, Porfirio Diaz, who had long ruled his country with an iron rod, was confronted by a threat of revolution. Too old to fight back as he had hitherto done on such occasions, Diaz resigned and fled to Europe. His flight was followed by one uprising after another. President Taft, then near the end of his administration, was urged to intervene, and "restore order." He refused, however, and left the thorny problem to President Wilson.

For a time Wilson pursued a policy described as "watchful waiting." But in fact he did intervene in Mexico. He declined to recognize the government of a new military dictator, Huerta, who rose to power in the confusion. In so doing Wilson took the position, revolutionary in the history of America's foreign policy, that it was his duty and right to withhold recognition from any government which did not measure up to the moral, political, and commercial standards of the United States. This made the American government a kind of censor over all governments established in foreign countries and seeking recognition in Washington.

Acting on events in Mexico, President Wilson ordered the landing of American marines in Vera Cruz and the seizure of that city in 1914. After Huerta gave up his office a settlement was made and the marines were withdrawn. Again, in 1916, after a Mexican bandit had raided a neighboring town in New Mexico, President Wilson sent American troops under General John Pershing on an expedition into Mexico in search of the marauder. Such was the state of American-Mexican relations when the energies of the United States became engaged in the war on Germany in 1917.

By this time imperialism everywhere was in a crisis. Indeed the United States had scarcely embarked on the new course of seeking world power when even leaders of imperialism in the Old World began to profess anxiety over the growing armaments and darkening perils of universal war. For various reasons, some hidden from public view, the Czar of Russia called upon other governments to hold a general conference on peace. The assembly, including delegates from the United States, met at The Hague in 1899, but did little or nothing to reduce the dangers of war. It adopted a rule that any neutral country could rightfully offer its services as a mediator between nations at war; and it established at The Hague a court for hearing international disputes voluntarily submitted to it.

After two more wars had intervened—the Russo-Japanese War and the war between the British and the Boers in South Africa—the Czar called a second "peace conference" at The Hague, in 1907. Like the first, it did nothing to reduce the growing armaments of the world and was, if anything, a more obvious failure. As later revelations respecting the proceedings of the two conferences disclosed, both were dominated by men holding imperialist doctrines, all bent on gaining advantages for their respective countries. Certainly it could be said with truth that the adventure of the United States in world-power politics had not brightened the outlook for world peace.

CHAPTER XXII

Widening Knowledge and Thought

With more or less relation to the ambitions and energies that rounded out the continent and directed political strife, yet not wholly swayed by them, a quest was carried on for more exact knowledge and a better understanding of the physical universe, biology, human history, and the society made by human beings in the United States. Knowledge and thought, of course, had been mingled with the life and labor of men and women from colonial times; and through the years, as American society afforded increasing opportunities and leisure, individuals had devoted themselves, partly or entirely, to searches for more knowledge and to inquiries into the meaning of knowledge and the use of it.

Until near the end of the nineteenth century the American people had depended for the advancement of knowledge and thought, beyond the necessities of working routines, on the sporadic inquiries of curious persons who studied particular subjects and wrote about or taught them. Governments, it is true, often looked into such topics as population, wealth, natural resources, and the output of farms and factories, and issued bulky reports; but knowledge of other matters and theories respecting them were mainly provided by private persons who hunted for facts and figures, made observations, thought about their findings, and published articles, pamphlets, and books.

As the nineteenth century drew to a close and the twentieth century advanced toward its meridian, individuals, as hitherto, continued to enlarge knowledge and bring thought to bear on its meaning and uses. Seekers after precise information and its significance for American society still worked alone, at their own expense and on their own initiative, and their findings were often so important for the advancement of American civilization as to be epoch-making. But to the explorations of self-directed individuals were now added the explorations of individuals and groups of workers, financed by mammoth sums of money dedicated to research, who made inquiries in every domain of knowledge, physical and human. They labored under the auspices of governments, federal, state, and local; of civic societies concerned with the humanities and civilization; and of special interests desiring information useful to their designs. In other words, to a considerable and an increasing extent, searching and thinking became more specialized, more organized, and more heavily financed.

For the simple economy of farms, handicrafts, and small towns the old method of acquiring and extending knowledge by individual and haphazard research met fairly well the needs of the people. At all events it was the method generally employed. But after the Civil War new and vast industries rose in all parts of the country from ocean to ocean; markets widened from communities to the national borders and beyond them to the outer world; trade unions, local and national, were organized; conflicts of capital and labor upset social peace; and the business of government, state and federal, became more and more complicated. For a long time government had been confined mainly to keeping order, building roads, collecting taxes, and administering poor relief. Now its officials encountered new and more intricate responsibilities, such as the regulation of railways and utilities, the adjustment of relations between capitalists and industrial workers, and other problems not to be "solved" by rule of thumb.

On the impacts and problems of this crucial transformation in economy and politics individual inquirers, as in previous times, concentrated intellectual energies. The huge collection of American books, articles, and pamphlets dealing with the physical and human universe, accumulated during the eighteenth century and enlarged in the age of Jacksonian democracy, was now expanded by literally millions of publications, general and special, covering the physical resources of the continent, every branch of economy to its minutest details, every tendency in action, thought, and aspiration.

The findings and reports ranged so far and wide that nothing short of the great rooms of the Congressional Library filled with card catalogues could indicate their sweep. Any selection of titles minimizes their magnitude. Was it the matter of a better understanding of social beginnings in prehistoric ages won by a long and intensive study of the American Indians? Lewis Henry Morgan, in his *Ancient Society*, published in 1877, illuminated the history of all civilization. The labor movement? John R. Commons and his associates gave a portrayal of it in their *History of Labour in the United States* (1918). The woman movement? A three-volume *History of Woman Suffrage* (1881–87) unfolded that story. A more comprehensive history of the nation? John B. McMaster began to make an answer with his *History of the American People*, the first volume of which came out in 1883. Was it the nature of American intellectual interests? Vernon Parrington dealt with that in his *Main Currents of American Thought*, published in 1927–30. Did citizens seek knowledge of anything else? Vast libraries managed by technical competence furnished bibliographies of specialized writings on a moment's notice.

But mingled with the work of individuals and enlarging it in every direction were the researches of persons and groups set apart for that purpose and financed from public and private funds. Systematic research for knowledge was fostered by the founding and expansion of universities, public and private. State institutions created in earlier times were granted more money by legislatures with which to build laboratories, assemble great libraries, and conduct graduate schools for advanced studies in the sciences, letters, and arts. Old private colleges, such as Harvard and Columbia, were transformed into universities, with research and publication as a primary aim. New universities were established on the basis of gifts by men who had accumulated wealth mainly in the manipulation of natural resources or the expansion of industrial enterprise.

The Johns Hopkins University at Baltimore, endowed by a leading capitalist of that city and named for him, opened its doors in 1876—one hundred years after the Declaration of Independence. About ten years later Stanford University was founded in California by Leland Stanford, a pioneer capitalist on the Pacific coast. In 1892 the University of Chicago, endowed with funds from the oil magnate, John D. Rockefeller, also began the promotion of research and instruction in almost everything under the sun.

By the opening of the twentieth century there were few colleges in the country, new or old, which were still content to teach routine subjects from books in the traditional style. The smallest and poorest of such institutions made efforts to extend the boundaries of knowledge and to teach the new learning that was coming from private inquiries and the graduate schools of the universities.

Systematic research for scientific knowledge and discovery was also carried on by many other agencies. Large industrial corporations built their own laboratories and engaged experts in physics, chemistry, and mechanics to invent new machines and devise new commodities for manufacture. During the opening decades of the twentieth century it became a practice for rich men and women to establish foundations for the promotion of research in the sciences and the humanities directed toward the welfare of mankind, the Carnegie Corporation, the Rockefeller Foundation, and the Russell Sage Foundation being conspicuous examples. In endowed institutions able minds concentrated on medical research that might lead to the conquest of pain and disease or on pure science from which might flow practical results in the physical and moral universe.

In 1916 the National Industrial Conference Board was organized by industrialists and supplied with funds for making studies of industrial and economic questions. Independent institutes of special types, such as the Brookings Institution in Washington, D.C., and the Bureau of Economic Research in New York were created to conduct research in the fundamental problems of economy and government. Trade unions, discovering that matters of collective bargaining were complicated, adopted the practice of employing experts in law, economics, and finance to furnish them information for guidance in policy making and action.

Governments, federal and local, more and more realized the need for organized continuous research. Earlier they had relied mainly upon the knowledge of persons who happened to be in office or upon hasty inquiries by legislative committees in emergencies. Now, confronting new and perplexing problems in administration, they established one after another, often as a result of popular or special demands, bureaus or other agencies of research, frequently in connection with the matter of expenditures and the laying of taxes—that is, in budgetary operations. By the second decade of the twentieth century research and planning agencies, associated with governments, had been set up in all parts of the United States. By that time it had also become a practice for Congress and state legislatures to appoint special committees authorized to employ experts and carry on extensive investigations, before undertaking the business of lawmaking relative to such intricate matters as the regulation of railways, conservation of natural resources, and the provision of social security.

As a result of such inquiries and reports the American people had available an increasing amount of knowledge for use in their private pursuits and callings, in the shaping of their own character and purposes, and in reaching decisions respecting policies of government and social improvement. They could either buy, or read at the swiftly multiplying libraries, books on every subject of historical or current interest; for example, business, industry, agriculture, labor organization, wealth, taxation, politics, natural science, religion, psychology, sociology, anthropology, archaeology, technology, the arts, health, home ownership, crime, poverty, the family, the relation of the individual to society, foreign commerce, international affairs, and the changes which were taking place in national affairs.

Though American life was not so complicated in his day, the first President of the United States had been conscious of the role that knowledge must play in a progressive society. In his first annual address to Congress, President Washington had said: "There is nothing which can better deserve your patronage than the promotion of science and literature. Knowledge is in every country the surest basis of public happiness. In one in which the measures of government receive their impressions so immediately from the sense of the community as in ours it is proportionately essential. To the security of a free constitution it contributes in various ways." When the two-hundredth anniversary of his birth was celebrated in 1932 his desire was being realized in part: the people of the United States had at their disposal a wealth of knowledge of things physical and human—science and literature— to use for the purposes of civilization if they could.

More or less affected by the new knowledge ran currents of thought about its implications, as the continent was rounded out and the inherited society of farms and small towns was transformed into a continental nation of closely integrated parts. In these trends of thought two theories or interpretations competed for supremacy. One placed the individual at the center of interest and made individual enterprise the primary source of invention, progress, wealth, and national greatness. The other emphasized society and general welfare as the controlling concern and insisted that the individual, however enlightened and powerful, owed his existence, his language, most of his knowledge, and his opportunities to the society in which he lived and worked. Both were used by powerful interests in American society.

To the first line of thought the name "individualism" was given. This was a new word that first came into play in the nineteenth century. It was used by Tocqueville in his book, *Democracy in America*, published in an English translation in 1835. As he employed the word, it meant a kind of individual anarchy—the conduct of any person who arbitrarily cut himself off from his family, friends, and society. Near the middle of the nineteenth century economists took up the new idea, individualism, and built a whole system of thought around it.

About the same time reinforcement of the idea came from natural science. In 1859 the English scientist, Charles Darwin, published the *Origin of Species*, mainly emphasizing biology and the struggle of the individual animal for existence—a kind of biological war of each against all. In his later work, *The Descent of Man*, published in 1871, Darwin definitely connected man with the kingdom of lower animals and again laid stress on the struggle for individual existence.

Darwin himself was cautious in his statements respecting the role of the individual in evolution, but the "Darwinians" in the United States and other countries made dogmas of his speculations, maintaining that they were truths beyond argument. Consequently when Americans, released from the strain of their Civil War, rushed to the conquest of the continent and impetuously went into the business of trying to get rich quickly, they had ready for use a theory, an ideology, that justified the strong in accumulating all the wealth they could in any way not too outrageous and in doing what they liked with their possessions.

Between 1865 and 1900 this theory of individualism was worked out by many American writers of marked intellectual power, who published articles and big books on the subject. Soon after he became a professor of political and social science at Yale University in 1872, William Graham Sumner sought to show that all civilization had come from free individual initiative; that all hope of progress and improvement lay in giving the fullest liberty to individuals; and that government interference with this liberty was injurious to mankind. As a sociologist, Sumner gave the support of his branch of learning to the individualist argument.

A contemporary at Columbia University, John William Burgess, a professor of political science, wrote brief articles and large treatises on government and liberty in which he made political science serve the cause of individualism. In the department of economics at Columbia, one of Burgess' colleagues, John Bates Clark, building on the work of other writers, American and European, constructed a whole system of economics out of individualism. At the University of Chicago another economist, J. Laurence Laughlin, taught a version of the theory about as extreme as imagination could make it, short of sheer anarchy.

Meanwhile Charles A. Dana, who had been a kind of utopian socialist in the days of Jacksonian democracy but was now a conservative editor of the New York *Sun*, daily preached individualism with withering scorn for all doubters; and as editor of the *Nation*, E. L. Godkin gave weekly versions of the same doctrine to his readers. In 1893 Frederick Jackson Turner, a professor of history in the University of Wisconsin, published a paper on "The Frontier in American History," which made individualism an interpretation of American history, by ignoring families and communities—that is, mutual aid—and tracing the secret of American uniqueness to the stoutest of all alleged individualists—the man of the frontier, as if there had been no women or families or communities or books or schools or churches there.

When the twentieth century opened, the doctrine of individualism had become a potent influence in American thought. Thousands of men and women, who knew little or nothing of its origins or were indifferent to its one-sided nature, had accepted it as a law of nature in private affairs and public policy. In fact the history of the preceding twenty-five years—the rapid opening up of the West, the swift rise of industries, and the increase of national wealth—seemed to them proof that the theory was in accord with reality.

To coming generations it was transmitted by instruction in universities, colleges, and lower schools as if it had never been analyzed and controverted by minds as able as those by which it had been formulated. So thoroughly intrenched was it in places high and low that President Hoover won rounds of popular applause when he prefixed an adjective to it and spoke of "rugged" individualism. Judging by the fervor of that applause, rugged individualism was the supreme characteristic of the American life, character, and purposes.

The thesis that human beings are actuated merely by a competitive struggle for existence and that society is a product of such individualism was countered by a thesis directing attention to the co-operative nature of human beings and the power of mutual aid in the origin and evolution of society. The sponsors of the associative principle in human life insisted that the creed of individualism, pushed to the extreme of dogmatism, was false to the facts of history, including the history of the United States; or at least so false as to be a gross distortion of reality. They pointed out, with copious illustrations, the heavy debt of all the individuals in the United States to American society for all the tools they worked with, for education, for opportunity, for the protection and benefits bestowed by the government as the representative of society. To ruthless individualism they traced much of the poverty and misery, ugliness and waste, which had marked the years of the uprushing business enterprise. To social action by groups and agencies of government they looked for the measures necessary to master these evils and bring about a greater equality of condition—a higher standard of life for all the people. The ideal of these "humanitarians" was best expressed by their own term "social meliorism"—gradual but effective improvement by social action.

If William Graham Sumner was the sociologist of individualism, Lester Ward was the sociologist of social meliorism. For leadership of this kind Ward was prepared by varied experiences and studies. After serving during the Civil War in the Union army, from which he was honorably discharged on account of wounds, Ward entered the employment of the United States Government and achieved distinction in scientific inquiry and reporting. While pursuing his work in natural science he took up the study of social evolution and in 1883 published the first volume of his *Dynamic Sociology*.

In this and other works Ward dwelt on the co-operative nature of human societies from the earliest times and on the opportunities, devices, and services provided by society for individual happiness and advancement. He marshaled a mass of countervailing knowledge against the individualist, or laissez faire, doctrine of Sumner and his school, and contended that co-operation among individuals, rather than a merciless and unfeeling competition for wealth and power, is the secret of human progress toward welfare for each and all. From his intensive study of the past Ward moved to the conclusion that government, representing society, should be positive not negative in policy and should adopt measures deliberately directed to social improvement. On the constructive side, therefore, Ward chose a middle way between individualism and socialism. By writing and lecturing in this median line of thought until his death in 1913, he helped to give social meliorism a firmer hold on American minds.

Building upon the work of the sociologists and independent inquiries, Anna Garlin Spencer, in *Woman's Share in Social Culture* (1913), dealt systematically with the role of women in social evolution from primitive times to the modern age. In this book she described the important part played by women in the original invention of the domestic, or civilian, arts; in the long development of the productive activities by which the family and society are sustained; and in the formation of the social sentiments necessary for the harmony and welfare of society.

Taking up the conditions of her own times, Dr. Spencer examined the varieties of activities carried on by women in all branches of national life, from industry to education. She demonstrated that women had been energetic in every kind of social improvement and argued cogently that, since in the modern age government was assuming positive duties in raising the standards of welfare, it was a logical and necessary step to grant equal suffrage to women—an equal share in the government. In this contribution to knowledge and thought Anna Garlin Spencer furnished a broader social philosophy for the woman movement then rapidly gaining in force and influence. She also vitalized the whole case for social meliorism by teaching and lecturing on the subject from the pulpit and in leading universities and public halls.

In the domain of economic thought the doctrine of individualism was likewise questioned, especially after about 1880, by several university economists, including Richard T. Ely, Simon Patten, and Edmund J. James. These critics attacked the doctrine on many grounds. They declared that it did not correspond to innumerable facts of human experience. They said it was simply an armchair theory and advised students of economics to go out into the real world, make observations, examine the ways in which industry and labor actually operated, and adjust theories to the facts of economy.

By setting everyone against his neighbor individualism, these critical economists declared, was contrary, moreover, to good morals, especially Christian morals. Poverty, they maintained, was due in part to legislation; not solely to individual idleness, improvidence, and incompetence. Great riches heaped up by individuals they ascribed in part to favors conferred by society, and in part to special privileges bestowed by government. According to their views it was therefore the duty of government to change unjust laws, bring about a more equitable distribution of wealth, and take an active part in improving the lot of the people.

Among the economists who refused to take individualism as the ultimate word was Thorstein Veblen, for a time a teacher at the University of Chicago. He did not concern himself, however, with meliorist reforms. What he did especially was to compare the actual conduct of American capitalists with the theories about their conduct promulgated in the works of the orthodox economists and taken by capitalists at face value. After studying court records and legislative reports on the methods of trusts, combinations, and financiers, so often ignored by theorists, Veblen presented a conclusion startling to defenders of apologetic economics.

In summary, he pointed out that modern business was carried on largely by corporations, not by individuals; that great fortunes had accrued to individuals by the formation of trusts and combines which closed many competitive plants and raised prices; that other great fortunes had been accumulated by selling pieces of paper, called stocks and bonds, to investors at prices far above their true value; that instead of increasing the production of wealth, in innumerable cases big business operations actually reduced the production of wealth.

In a way this was what populists had been saying for years but Veblen expounded the criticism, in his treatise, *The Theory of Business Enterprise*, in 1904, in an ingenious form of learning that made it more palatable to economists in universities and to other persons interested in public behavior and general welfare. This book made no case for social meliorism but it helped to blunt the edge of individualism conceived as guaranteeing the utmost production of wealth and a distribution of wealth according to "merits."

The theory of individualism as applied to political science by John W. Burgess and his school was also countered by other political scientists. According to the individualist thesis recently built up in American books on political science, government represented "the people" and its primary duty was to keep order, defend life and property, and refrain from interfering with economic enterprise. By numerous writers this thesis was attacked as in part contrary to historical facts and in part contrary to the professed ideals of the Republic. They asserted that the government of the United States from the beginning had in fact represented powerful economic classes—manufacturers, financiers, bankers, and planters—actually opposed to the interests of the people at large, and that it had constantly interfered with agriculture and small economic enterprises in order to benefit the holders of special privileges. Even justices of the Supreme Court in Washington, publicists charged, did not merely enforce the Constitution, as some theorists declared, but read into it opinions favorable to "big business."

The meliorist revolt conducted against individualism by political scientists was concisely described by J. Allen Smith at the University of Washington, in *The Spirit of American Government,* published in 1907. In a few words Smith characterized the Constitution as a "scheme of government . . . planned and set up to perpetuate the ascendancy of the property-holding class leavened with democratic ideas." The major political parties he represented as dominated by corporations and men of great wealth. The sources of many evils, such as corruption, he found "not in the slums . . . but in the selfishness and greed of those who are the recognized leaders in commercial and industrial affairs."

Individualism as "no government interference with business," Smith described as merely "the selfish view" of a "relatively small class which, though it controls the industrial system, feels the rein of political control slipping out of its hands." By way of remedies for the situation so described, he proposed the breaking up of big trusts, government ownership of many public utilities, progressive taxes on incomes and inheritances, and other measures included in the program of social meliorism.

By the ferment of critical thought respecting the nature of society historians were the least affected. Busy as a rule with writing stories of political and military events narrowly construed, they paid little attention to social and economic events or to the general ideas entertained by the people. John Bach McMaster's *History of the People of the United States,* the first volume of which came out in 1883, was a notable exception, but it was more of a catalogue or chronicle than a social history as its name implied. History, it was often said, provides the lamp of experience for guidance in the present, but the histories written merely as professional exercises or for the edification of the public dealt with only a small part of the human experience and even with that in a very limited fashion. It was even declared that scholarship must narrate events or meticulously analyze documents and avoid interpretation.

Not until 1895, when Brooks Adams' *The Law of Civilization and Decay* appeared, was much recognition given to the fact that written history in every form had a bearing on what was taking place in the United States and on what would probably come to pass in the future of the nation.

Although Brooks Adams' volume dealt with history in Europe, it set forth a theory covering history in general. His theory was that all human societies pass from a stage of wide dispersion on the land to a stage of high concentration; that they fall under the sway of capitalistic usurers; and that they then enter a period of decay and dissolution.

The theory, whether true or false, was applicable to the United States as well as to ancient Rome and modern Europe. While apparently remote from American politics in 1895, it crashed into the free and easy optimism of many editors, including Charles A. Dana of the New York *Sun*, and of many politicians, especially young Theodore Roosevelt, then at the beginning of his public career, who commented on it in a long review.

At any rate Adams' book was an evidence that some Americans of intellectual attainments were not convinced by the rosy exposition of individualism or of social meliorism either. They did not believe that all was well in the United States and were expecting serious troubles in the years ahead. Indeed, Henry Adams, a brother of Brooks, who had read the manuscript of *The Law of Civilization and Decay* two years before it was published, said in an open letter to the American Historical Association that the big social explosion would come in about fifty years—that is, about 1944.

☆

The changing conditions of American life and the new knowledge and thought were also mirrored in imaginative letters. Authors of novels dealing with the eternal triangle—one man and two women or one woman and two men—even when "historical" in pretensions, were more or less influenced by their times. Imaginative letters after 1865 carried descriptions and interpretations of the swift changes—continental and regional—which had occurred as the national domain was rounded out, industries were expanded, and concentration set in.

Nearly everything human and material seemed to be noted in the myriad pages of "fiction," turned out from year to year: reconstruction in the South; westward pioneering and settlement;

regional customs and practices; conflicts between capital and labor; strikes, riots, and disorders in industry; struggles of immigrants for footholds and social places; the grievances that flared up in populistic and socialistic revolts; every shade of opinion from Puritan distress over the poverty and grime of factory towns to communistic resentments at the whole course of capitalism; variations and clashes of opinion from decade to decade; all phases of the strife for social improvement in every direction; efforts to apply Christian teachings to the perils within the Republic.

Support for the broad statement that imaginative letters were sensitive to all phases of American history is supplied by at least two comprehensive works on American literature: the third volume of Vernon L. Parrington's *Main Currents in American Thought*, published in unfinished form in 1930 shortly after the death of the author, and Alfred Kazin's *On Native Grounds*, published in 1942. Literary critics took account of the fact in current reviews. They generally agreed, of course, that the quality of a novel depended upon the genius, skill, and discipline of the author rather than on the mere quantity or nature of the facts in his pages. But they also held that accuracy of portrayal, whether of regions or characters, and accuracy in representing ideas, whether conservative or radical, were necessary to the creation of "great" literature.

The volume, continuity, and variety of the imaginative literature which depicted the many phases of American life in all parts of the country is illustrated by the following list of twenty-two works selected from two or three hundred novels of recognized quality written between 1870 and 1940:

1871—Elizabeth Stuart Phelps, *The Silent Partner*. A Puritan protest against factory conditions in New England and a plea for better treatment of labor.

1873—Mark Twain and Charles Dudley Warner, *The Gilded Age*. Political corruption and greedy citizens in the age of President Grant.

1880—Henry Adams, *Democracy*. A defense of democracy against the indifference, contempt, and pessimism of the rich.

1881—Helen Hunt Jackson, *A Century of Dishonor*. Cruel treatment of the Indians by the United States Government.

1884—John Hay, *The Bread-Winners*. An attack on labor leaders in the spirit of individualistic capitalism.

1888—Edward Bellamy, *Looking Backward*. Utopian picture of abundance and a good life under a socialistic regime in the year 2000.

1890–98—Hamlin Garland, *Main-Travelled Roads*. Hard-bitten and impoverished farming families of the Middle West struggling for a livelihood.

1894—W. D. Howells, *A Traveler from Altruria*. Conflict between classes and masses in the light of a democratic and socialistic ideal.

1900—Theodore Dreiser, *Sister Carrie*. Cruel fate of the poor and humble in the land of great riches and prosperity.

1901—Frank Norris, *The Octopus*. An epic of great wheat production in California.

1905—David Graham Phillips, *The Deluge*. For democracy against corruption and oppression by the privileged few—financial manipulators.

1905—Edith Wharton, *The House of Mirth*. The new plutocracy against a background of seasoned riches.

1906—Upton Sinclair, *The Jungle*. Poverty, filth, and suffering in a great industrial center.

1910—Jack London, *Revolution*. Industrial strife at a high pitch and in a revolutionary temper.

1911—Edith Wharton, *Ethan Frome*. Cold fate of the poor in New England farming community.

1920—Sinclair Lewis, *Main Street*. Drab, small-town culture in the West—and almost anywhere else in the United States.

1925—Ellen Glasgow, *Barren Ground*. Struggles against poverty and defeat in a rural community of the South.

1933—Jessie Fauset, *Comedy American Style*. Follies of Negroes and whites.

1934—Stark Young, *So Red the Rose*. The South of romance.

1935—Sinclair Lewis, *It Can't Happen Here*. Fascist tendencies in conflict with American ideals of liberty.

1936—James Farrell, *A World I Never Made*. Irish working-class family in a harsh struggle for existence in the urban world of industry and business.

1938—John Dos Passos, *U.S.A.* Graphic pictures of suffering and struggling among victims of misfortune during the great depression, contrasted with the pomp and pretensions of politicians and the rich.

While knowledge in every field, much of it microscopic in detail, was being accumulated, and thought about American society was finding expression in various media, facilities for distributing facts and ideas among the people were multiplying or enlarging. A major facility was the system of education. The principle of free and compulsory education in primary subjects for all children, widely accepted by 1860, was applied in every part of the country, with variations according to the wealth of states and communities and their social composition. By 1910 it was a poor district indeed which had made no provision whatever for primary education.

As the extension and improvement of primary schools proceeded, American people were being induced to accept the idea that even higher education should be opened more freely to the youth of the land and were voting fabulous sums of money for realizing it. Evidence of the advance in higher education is afforded by the following table showing the growth in the number of high schools between 1880 and 1910:

In 1880	800
1890	2,526
1900	6,005
1910	10,213

After the high school had achieved a secure position came a demand to bring college education nearer to the people. In part this demand was met by university extension work and in part by the creation of "junior colleges" in communities able to pay for them through taxation. In 1917 there were 39 such colleges in the United States; by 1932 the number had risen to 181.

With the growth of educational facilities illiteracy declined, despite the mounting immigration of persons who could not read. In 1880 17% of the people ten years of age or more were reported as illiterate; thirty years later, in 1910, the percentage of such illiterates had fallen to 7.7; and, among the white population, to 4.9. At the same time the proportion of boys and girls pursuing higher learning rose. In 1930 one half of all the children of secondary school age were attending a secondary school of some kind, and one person in every seven of college age was enrolled in a college. Nevertheless in 1940 3,000,000 Americans twenty years of age or more had never completed as much as one year of formal schooling.

Popular interest in education was partly measurable in terms of the money spent for it. In 1925 the total annual outlay for all public and private schools, colleges, and various institutions of higher learning amounted to more than $2,000,000,000.

The distribution of knowledge and ideas was widened and

accelerated by the increase in the number and kinds of newspapers, magazines, and books, ranging from the solid volumes of individuals and learned societies to a growing flood of simple comics and "salacious literature" appealing to the lowest common denominators of interest: sex and crime. Improvements in the technology of printing made possible the publication of books, even the classics, at figures ranging from five cents to fifty and sixty-odd cents a copy and such books at low cost were turned out and sold by the millions. A rapid growth in rural free delivery under the United States Post Office, coupled with highway improvement and the automobile, brought the metropolitan daily to the doors of farmers who had hitherto relied mainly upon rural weeklies for news of the country and the world.

Given such opportunities for public education and self-education, only the most unfortunate or the most indifferent and shiftless in the American population remained outside the circle of widening knowledge and thought. If as an outcome of this development there was to be a degradation of American democracy in the coming years, as Brooks Adams prophesied, a share of responsibility would have to be laid at the door of those who sought financial profits in the literature of degradation as well as those who chose to buy it in the market place.

As progress in facilities for distributing knowledge and ideas gathered momentum, the radio appeared, producing an upheaval in education, the results of which were immeasurable. As early as 1916 the electrical transmission of sounds by wireless methods had reached such a stage that Lee de Forest could begin experiments with the broadcasting of music. A few years later, in 1921, the KDKA broadcasting station was opened in Pittsburgh. By 1925 so many stations were in operation that they interfered with one another and the federal government had to intervene and apportion among them "time and space on the air." In 1941 there were 915 licensed broadcasting stations in the United States and the number of receiving sets was at least 56,000,000.

The country had become a vast radio auditorium. In that auditorium the people, literate and illiterate alike, who had ears could hear, amid the confusion of advertising, music, and other "entertainment," speeches by the men and women who thought they had anything to say, on every conceivable subject from canning fruits and vegetables to ways and means of running the whole world.

As to the effects of all this broadcasting, there were acute discrepancies of opinion. Optimists called it progress. Doubting

Thomases suspected that it would lead to a demoralization in both knowledge and thought, with consequences disastrous to the Republic. But at all events, for good or ill, the radio was distributing information and misinformation, ideas useful or pernicious, to millions of people who did not have the brains or the energy or the competence or access to facilities necessary to educate themselves in the old and hard way, or who preferred the new form of instruction.

Into this "educational" tumult the motion picture likewise thrust its power with incalculable effects. What has been claimed to be the "first motion-picture feature" was shown publicly at Richmond, Indiana, in 1894, by the inventor of the machine, C. F. Jenkins. His contrivance was built on the basis of experiments by other inventors extending back in time more than fifty years and was soon improved beyond recognition. In 1905 the first motion-picture theater was opened at Pittsburgh. In 1927 sound-reproduction devices made possible the "talking picture."

By 1942 every town of any size from Maine to California had its film theater—and the combined capacity of the "palaces" was 10,000,000 lookers and hearers. In that year the estimated weekly attendance was approximately 85,000,000. Quickly adopted by colleges, universities, and lower schools, the motion and talking picture was used to supplement and enliven by visual education the customary methods of education.

All the forms of noise that the radio diffused could be utilized by motion pictures, and more too. Now the people, high and low, everywhere, could not only listen to the speeches, lectures, and addresses of talkative men and women on every kind of subject, hear music in all its ranges from symphonies to the syncopations of Tin Pan Alley, and catch the roar and clatter of mass assemblies; they could see animated pictures of persons directing "messages" to them and asking them to support every sort of program, panacea, or scheme of full salvation.

In short, the American people now had at their command agencies almost illimitable in range and speed for the distribution of knowledge and the circulation of ideas true, false, or simply nonsensical. What the consequences of this revolution in communication would be was a theme of emotional debate and sober examination throughout the nation. Would intelligence be stimulated or arrested or destroyed? Certainly mere facilities afforded no guarantee that the information distributed so swiftly and widely was founded on accurate knowledge or that the general ideas put before the people were valid in themselves or good for practical applications. Reports formulated by psychologists who explored the new types of human behavior seemed to indicate that neither mere knowledge nor general ideas nor instruments for their diffusion could add anything to that elusive quality of the human spirit known as intelligence. Opinions respecting the probable outcome, near and distant, of the new agencies and the uses to which they were put varied as widely as the ideas themselves which were shot forth through the air or on paper or on the silver screen to the public at large.

CHAPTER XXIII

Revolts against Plutocracy Grow in Political Power

If the glittering prophecy of benefits offered by proponents of imperialism had been fulfilled to the pecuniary advantage of everybody, if capitalists, farmers, and industrial workers had been satisfied with what they received, complaints of populists, trust busters, socialists, muckrakers, and systematic critics of American economy might have fallen on deaf ears. It was not realized. Like all wars, the war with Spain and in the Philippines furnished an immediate boom; but that boom was far from full and permanent prosperity. Dazzling strokes in war and diplomacy gave diversion to many people, especially Republican editors and propagandists. But the public was either fickle or the diversion was incomplete. Protests against the imperialist excursion, during the war with Spain and in the Philippines, grew in volume and intensity as the years passed, especially as the mirage of universal prosperity vanished and public interest converged again on fundamental domestic issues.

In the nature of things there were limits to imperialist ambitions. Territorial expansion could not go on indefinitely without incurring awful war hazards for which the American people were in no mood. By 1900 the world had nearly all been parceled out among the imperialist Powers of Europe and Asia and only petty fragments of territory remained for Americans to acquire if they could. Gone were the huge unexploited spaces around the globe, such as had existed in 1800 and could be easily wrested from defenseless natives. There were no more spoils to be seized by Americans without fights with Great Britain, France, Germany, Japan, or Russia.

In view of the opposition at home to expansion in the Philippines, even the most forthright imperialist scarcely dared to propose more war of that kind, at least candidly, as a policy likely to awaken great popular enthusiasm. John Hay made plans for seizing some territory in China but they were official secrets, and he drew back when Japan suggested that they did not comport with the noble professions of the "Open Door." Besides, the official thesis of the Republicans held that they had intended no imperialism in 1898 and that the Philippines had come to the United States inadvertently during the discharge of a duty imposed upon the country, by an accident or an act of God. Though the Republicans were successful in the elections of 1900, 1904, and 1908, they encountered a formidable antipathy even to that version of their purposes. A similar animosity was displayed by the Democrats against imperialism in the Caribbean region—until their own leader, President Woodrow Wilson, embarked upon it in Haiti and Santo Domingo.

Moreover, from the "empire" acquired in 1899 no streams of riches flowed into the United States, such as Great Britain had drawn from India. No endlessly expanding markets for the "surpluses" of American factories and farms were found. Instead of garnering wealth from their empire, American taxpayers had to face increasing levies by the government of the United States for military and naval outlays and for subduing the guerrilla warfare in the Philippines.

A cold balance sheet of the imperialist undertaking showed a large net loss to the nation as a whole. Filipinos and Puerto Ricans, most of them in wretched poverty, could not buy American goods in billion-dollar lots. Furthermore the agricultural products imported from the "empire" soon entered into competition with the surpluses of American farms. As for increasing the relative export of American goods, that proved to be another delusion—a political romance confuted by experience. There was no relative increase in fact. The export of goods in 1900 amounted to about 10% of the exportable goods produced in the United States. In 1914 the percentage was 9.7; in 1929, 9.8.

Soon after the first flush of war excitement passed it was discovered even by philosophers of the Mahan school that the current naval expenditures, though many times larger than ever, would not provide adequate defense for the Philippines if powerful aggressors chose to operate against them from land bases in the neighborhood. Before he died in 1919, Theodore Roosevelt himself realized this and exclaimed that the Philippines were the Achilles' heel of the American Republic. Only swivel-chair strategists in the Navy Department continued to imagine that American dreadnaughts with superior fire power could easily destroy the Japanese navy and effect American supremacy in the Far East. By no form of economic or military calculation could the imperialism of 1898 be called a blessing to the American nation; or, indeed, from any point of view, an unqualified success. Moreover it failed to divert Americans from their primary interests at home or to quell completely the political uprising against centralized capitalism that had grown to ominous proportions in 1896.

For a time after 1898, it is true, newspaper headlines daily shrieked sensational news of the war with Spain and then sensational news of the war for suppression of the native revolt in the Philippines. Magazines carried solemn articles on "our new obligations" in the dependencies and descriptions of the lands occupied by "our" new subjects. Professors wrote bragging books on America as a "world Power," on colonial administration, and on foreign affairs. Protestant ministers preached sermons on "our new opportunities to save souls." The same newspapers, magazines, professors, and preachers, as a rule, paid slight regard to populist complaints at home about either domestic or foreign affairs, except to curse them as the fruits of evil minds. Judging by such literary appearances, the American people were absorbed in "great" world politics and blind and deaf to the agitations of men and women, now called "mollycoddles," "calamity howlers," and "ignoramuses," who insisted on going forward with Bryan's "battle," or with other kinds of reforms on the home front.

Yet in time the throbs of the war drums were silenced, veterans of the Cuban and the Philippine wars were granted pensions, and the furor over "our new wards" faded out. After all the American people could not live on newspaper headlines, books, magazine articles, or sermons about Christianizing people in remote places. Nor, as events indicated, did many Americans take more than a transient interest in the emotional diversions created by and in the name of imperialism. If millions seemed to approve it in the elections of 1900, 1904, and 1908, with varying intensity of conviction, other millions voted with the Democrats, who denounced every feature of it.

As a matter of fact, in June 1898, while the war with Spain was at its height, Congress, though dominated by Republicans, created an Industrial Commission, composed of senators, representatives, and eminent private citizens, and charged it with studying the disturbing problems of capital and labor. In 1900, while the Philippine war was still in progress, the commission made a report that filled many large volumes and carried recommendations for reforms in capitalist methods.

Indeed, at no stage in the development of political insurgency against centralized capitalism had Republicans been wholly untouched by it. In its origin the very Republican party was itself an expression of insurgency against the supremacy of what it called the "slave power" in the government and politics of the United States. Its hero, Abraham Lincoln, had confessed that he owed the first principles of his policy to Thomas Jefferson, who in 1776 had announced the philosophy of revolutionary equalitarianism, and by destroying slavery Lincoln had dared to commit a revolutionary act himself. Not without justification could Theodore Roosevelt, in an hour of concern with domestic politics, claim that the Republican party "in the days of Abraham Lincoln was founded as the radical progressive party of the Nation."

During the agitations of the subsequent years, that party was harassed by a left wing and supplied recruits to the Greenbackers and Populists. It was a former Republican, Senator Teller, who had tried to strike a blow at incipient imperialism by imposing a self-denying ordinance on the resolution that led to war against Spain. It was a Republican, Senator Hoar, who believed that, had it not been for the intervention of Bryan on McKinley's side, he could have stopped the imperialist adventure in 1900. It was in Republican states and under Republican auspices that the most enlightened labor and social legislation had been inaugurated as the great industrial expansion proceeded.

Insurgency in Republican ranks was accelerated soon after Theodore Roosevelt had settled down in the White House as the successor of McKinley. The high Republican manager, Marcus A. Hanna, sensitive to trends of popular opinion, had insisted on the nomination of Roosevelt as Vice-President in 1900 partly with a view to capturing votes in the West, so deeply infected by agrarianism, and at a time when Republican bosses in New York wanted to get him out of the state on the ground that he was a political "troublemaker." Now this young man of impulses deemed "radical" by his party colleagues had possession of the greatest citadel of political power in the country.

By training, experience, and private reading Theodore Roosevelt was a variant from his predecessors who had come up to power through the pull and haul of politics and had given little thought to the great historical process in which they pulled and hauled. Although, as he said, he learned nothing but orthodox laissez-faire economics at Harvard College, young Roosevelt had studied some history and had early formed some decided views on social conflicts in history and the ways of plutocracy.

In 1897 Roosevelt had published, in the *Forum* magazine, a long review of Brooks Adams' *The Law of Civilization and Decay*—a prophecy of the death of civilization under the heel of capitalistic usury. While he distinctly repudiated Adams' gloomy verdict, Roosevelt confessed that "there is in it a very ugly element of truth. . . . That there is grave reason for some of Mr. Adams' melancholy forebodings, no serious student of the times, no sociologist or reformer, and no practical politician who is interested in more than momentary success, will deny. . . . The rich have undoubtedly grown richer; . . . there has been a large absolute, though not relative, increase in poverty and . . . the very poor tend to huddle in immense masses in the cities. Even though these masses are, relatively to the rest of the population, smaller than they formerly were, they constitute a standing menace, not merely to our prosperity but to our existence." Cautious and qualified as this statement was, it referred to matters which Republican party managers had not noticed, officially at least. They were the matters over which farmer and labor insurgency was highly articulate.

As President, Theodore Roosevelt abated none of his zest for his "big stick" policy in "extraterritorial," that is, extracontinental, affairs. He indulged in feverish exchanges with European diplomats, supported the Open Door in China, and almost daily provided "hot news" for the press by "strokes of state" in foreign policy. In this sphere his constant activities fretted many old Republicans of the Hanna school as well as social actionists who wanted to concentrate on political and economic reforms at home. Those old Republicans felt that they had been hustled into the imperialist adventure by the young "war hawks" of the twentieth century and they were deeply troubled over the possibility that Theodore Roosevelt might involve the nation in a foreign war really perilous to taxpayers, domestic finances and economy, and the management of business in the customary manner.

While Theodore Roosevelt worried conservative Republicans by his lunges into foreign affairs, he won enthusiastic support among liberals and radicals by his domestic policies. When business as usual was threatened by a big coal strike in 1902, President Roosevelt manifested sympathies with the miners. Instead of sending Federal troops to suppress strikers, as the Republican President Hayes had done in the railway strike of 1877, and the Democratic President Cleveland had done in the Pullman strike of 1894, he prepared to use the troops to keep the mines open and productive. He forced the mine owners to accept the arbitration which they had rejected; and he was instrumental in bringing about a settlement advantageous to labor. He also sought to stop the spoliation of natural resources by adopting a policy of conservation—withholding timber and other lands from the grasp of private interests and speculators. Moreover he introduced "righteousness" into politics. While praising "good trusts" and "sound labor leaders," he denounced the "bad" trusts, "malefactors of great wealth," and "anarchistic labor leaders." He also publicly censured many a conservative representative and senator in Congress, while he was careful not to alienate the most powerful men of his party in that body.

Meanwhile reinforcements for progressive insurgency, political and economic, came from many directions in articles, books, and magazines. For example:

Henry George's *Progress and Poverty*, issued first in 1879, grew in influence, spreading the doctrine that many millionaires owed their wealth to the "unearned increment" arising merely from increases in land values.

In 1889, Andrew Carnegie began to publish articles on wealth and labor in which he demonstrated that, while in part great fortunes had grown out of inventions and management, also in large part they had sprung from mere land ownership and speculation, from the markets developed by the social growth of the country, and from easy opportunities afforded manufacturers to acquire immense natural resources at nominal prices, or for nothing.

In 1894, H. D. Lloyd issued his *Wealth against Commonwealth*, assailing the Standard Oil Company, challenging the whole system of individualistic acquisition, and calling for a new order of cooperation.

In 1902, Ida Tarbell began the serialization of her critical articles in *McClure's* magazine, "The History of the Standard Oil Company."

In 1902, W. J. Ghent's *Our Benevolent Feudalism* portrayed

American society as a hierarchy of classes dominated by men of wealth at the top.

In 1901, W. J. Bryan started publishing the *Commoner*, a weekly journal, which soon attained a large national circulation.

In 1906, David Graham Phillips commenced a series, entitled "The Treason of the Senate," in the *Cosmopolitan* magazine, attacking it as a body of rich men who legislated for the rich and defeated the aspirations of the people.

A large school of reformers from right to left attributed most if not all the evils of the Republic to the control of party machinery and all branches of government by Theodore Roosevelt's "malefactors of great wealth," operating through political bosses, local and national. Their proposal for breaking this control was to "restore the government to the people"; and one of the first points of their attack was the Senate of the United States elected not by the people but by the state legislatures—in fact by party caucuses and bosses behind the scenes.

Back in the age of Andrew Jackson, when the Senate of the United States was under fire from popular strongholds, it had been proposed that senators should thereafter be elected directly by the voters of the state—no longer indirectly. In 1893 the House of Representatives mustered a two-thirds majority for a resolution authorizing this change by an amendment to the Constitution. Satisfied with things as they were, the Senate, however, refused to concur and so repelled this attack on its position. Beaten in Washington, advocates of direct election turned to the states and sought to circumvent the Constitution by ingenious devices for having candidates for the Senate nominated at popular primaries.

To make the popular choice at the polls binding on the state legislature, Oregon in 1901 established a system by which the voters could name the United States senator at a regular election and the candidates for the state legislature could pledge themselves to vote for the "people's choice," no matter to what party he belonged. Soon Oregon witnessed the extraordinary spectacle of a Republican legislature electing a Democrat to represent the state in the national Senate.

By 1910 at least twenty-eight states, mainly in the West and South, had in force one scheme or another compelling state legislatures to elect senators actually chosen, previously, at a primary or popular election. Thus the personnel of the national Senate and its temper were gradually altered between 1893 and 1910. In this period also the legislatures of two thirds of the states passed resolutions calling upon Congress to submit to the people an amendment providing for popular election of senators in a regular and constitutional manner.

At length, "softened up" by the arrival of new senators "fresh from the people," the Senate yielded to the House in 1912 and approved a resolution of amendment. It was sent to the states for action. With alacrity the states replied by ratifying the Seventeenth Amendment and the very next year it went into effect. As if derisively timed, the amendment was proclaimed in force by William Jennings Bryan, then Secretary of State. Only sixteen years previously he had been cursed as an anarchist for proposing to lay his rude hands on this bulwark of conservatism, placed in the Constitution by the fathers of the Republic. So swiftly had insurgency advanced in the intervening years that Bryan himself, arch-critic of the plutocracy, had become the chief cabinet officer in the Democratic administration of Woodrow Wilson.

Running along with the movement to expel "plutocrats" from the Senate was an agitation for taking the nomination of all major candidates—local, state, and federal—out of the hands of conventions ruled by professional politicians and entrusting it to the people at the polls. This action was also undertaken by states, one after another.

The instrument chosen for it was known as the direct primary. Laws applying it varied in form from state to state, but their purpose was to force all seekers after nomination for important places in government—local, state, and federal—to offer themselves to the voters of their respective parties in a party election called the primary. By 1910 at least twenty-one states, chiefly in the West and South, had direct primary laws stringent in nature.

These laws by no means eliminated the power of professional politicians over the nomination of candidates, but they disconcerted the "old-line bosses" for a time; they made it possible for many energetic young leaders to appeal immediately to the voters and ride to high places of power in government, in spite of the bosses. For years insurgents had inveighed against the "corrupt machines" of both major parties. Now they had a strong weapon in their hands if they could use it.

Another protest against the machines operated by professional politicians had represented the ballot system in vogue as permitting them to buy votes and watch the voters deliver the "stolen goods" at the polls. This system had been created by politicians themselves. Under it each party printed its own ticket or list of candidates for each election and on paper of a distinctive color. At the polls on election day the agents of each party handed out its ballots—red, white or blue, as the case might be—and kept their eyes on each voter until he dropped his colored ticket into the ballot box.

In many places a practice of "straight-arm voting" had been adopted; that is, party voters were lined up, a party ticket was put into the hand of each, and they were then marched to the polls in formation, keeping ranks until their ballots were deposited. Not only was it easy for party managers thus to lead their henchmen to the polls: they could see who was voting the opposite ticket and, if strong enough, could intimidate men who refused to vote "right." It was an almost perfect system for exposing workingmen and insurgents to surveillance, oppression, and even violence if they refused to follow the party line.

The device adopted for breaking this tyranny over voters was the Australian ballot, containing the names of all the candidates of all the parties, printed at public expense, and distributed only at the polls by public officers. Where it was used the voter indicated his own choice by marking the column of his party himself or the names of persons for whom he wished to cast his ballot. A closed booth was provided so that ballots could be marked secretly and ballots were folded so that no one could discover for whom citizens voted.

This reform was introduced first in Massachusetts, and in Kentucky in a limited fashion, in the year 1888. Within eight years thirty-six other states had adopted it. Additional legislation improved the system, and by the opening of the century such secret balloting had become a general rule in the United States. Thus intimidation at the polls was reduced and the political independence of voters increased. Money provided by the campaign funds of the parties and threats of retaliation, or even physical injury, could no longer be as effective as in the "good old days of open voting."

While the revolt against established political methods was drawing the governing power closer to voting men, the demand of women for the right to vote was renewed and gained strength. A national suffrage organization was formed. A proposed amendment enfranchising women throughout the nation was introduced in Congress in 1869. Three years later women pressed their claims on the Republicans and in doing so reminded them of the services rendered by women in the recent war for the preservation of the Union. Republican leaders still wanted the aid of women, especially help from the magnetic orator, Anna Dickinson—the "American Joan of Arc"—in the campaign of 1872, and the Republican party declared that it welcomed women to spheres of wider usefulness; that their demand for additional rights deserved "respectful consideration."

But women soon learned that they were to have no automatic victory in the national capital and they took the hard road to their goal by winning the suffrage, step by step, in the states, under the nationwide leadership of such indomitable citizens as Elizabeth Cady Stanton, Lillie Devereux Blake, Mathilda Joslyn Gage, and Susan B. Anthony. These women and others traveled up and down the land and appealed for the enfranchisement of women to voting men in the cities, villages, distant rural districts, and on outlying farms. They argued their case before members of state legislatures and constitutional conventions, published journals of agitation, wrote articles and letters to the newspapers, issued books on the subject, and spared no labor in their efforts to persuade the hostile or indifferent that their cause was just and vital to the advancement of democracy.

For some years their gains in the states were discouragingly small. Wyoming, which had established equal suffrage while still a territory, continued the practice after admission to the Union in 1889, despite strenuous objections in Congress. Four years later women won the ballot in Colorado. In 1896 they were victorious in Utah and Idaho. During the furor over imperialism and conferring the blessings of liberty on "our brown brothers" in distant dependencies, no advances were made, though women carried on their agitation with unremitting tenacity. After that militant outburst had lost its glamor women began to win victories rapidly: in Washington, 1910; California, 1911; Oregon, Kansas, and Arizona, 1912; Nevada and Montana, 1914. At length the ice was broken on the middle border: Illinois in 1913 conferred on women the right to vote for presidential electors and so gave them a greater leverage in national elections.

After older leaders had procured the ballot in several states, younger women, mostly college graduates, turned to the weapon of political power to shorten the struggle for full national enfranchisement. They built a backfire against obstinate members of Congress and Eastern politicians who aspired to the presidency. Led by Alice Paul and Lucy Burns, women organized, in the states

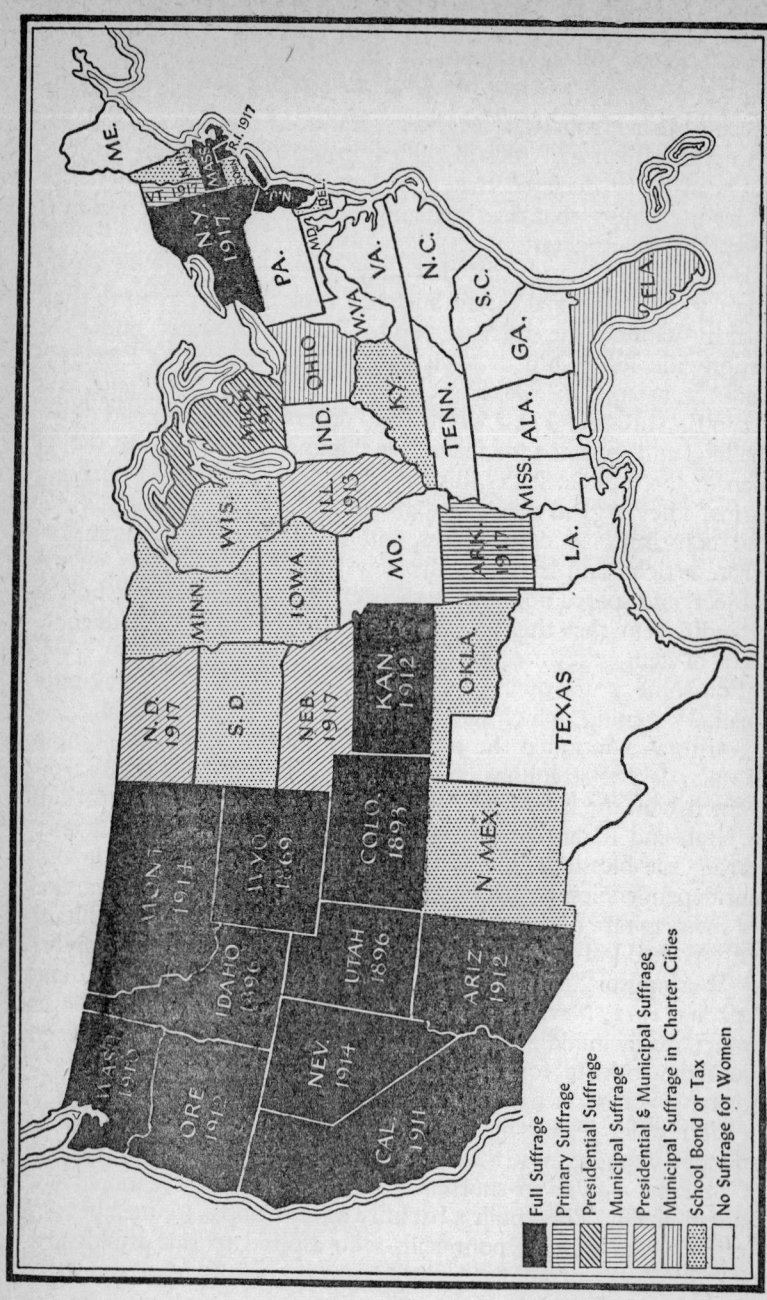

STATUS OF WOMAN SUFFRAGE IN 1918

having equal suffrage, thousands of enfranchised women who pledged themselves to cast their ballots only for candidates openly favorable to the adoption of equal suffrage on a national scale—by an amendment to the federal Constitution.

Although these new tacticians were unable to move Woodrow Wilson from his rigid opposition to such an amendment during the campaign of 1916, they secured the endorsement of the Republican candidate, Charles E. Hughes, and a helpful support from Theodore Roosevelt. On a referendum the next year, 1917, women won the vote in the great state of New York, and in 1918 they were successful in Oklahoma, South Dakota, and Michigan.

With so much power already in the hands of women voters it was difficult for any politician in Washington to treat their demands with historic ridicule or indifference. Indeed President Wilson was finally moved to call upon Congress in September 1918 to pass the suffrage amendment to the Constitution. With the aid of Republicans, who secured possession of both houses in the elections of the following November, the requisite two-thirds majority was won for the Nineteenth Amendment—in the following June. Quickly ratified by three fourths of the state legislatures, it went into effect in time for the presidential election of 1920. Equal suffrage had been made the law of the land.

☆

As insurgency flourished in the form of verbal criticism and new methods for making it effective by direct elections were brought into use, conservative managers in both the major parties were finding it harder to keep a tight rein on candidates, legislatures, executives, and courts in the former style. In seeking to escape the perils of defeat they had to make concessions to this growing independence. King Canute had to move his throne.

Aware in 1908 that the Republicans would have to meet again the resolute Bryan running on a platform of revolt in the spirit of 1896, President Theodore Roosevelt planned to take at least some of the wind out of the "Great Commoner's" sails. Having decided not to run for a "second election," he fixed upon his Secretary of War, William Howard Taft, as his successor and presented him to the country as a progressive, as a man who would follow "my policies." Roosevelt then threw the weight of executive influence and patronage on the side of Taft and had the pleasure of seeing the Republican convention bow to his will. Conservatives in the convention did it with a wry face, but they yielded as gracefully as they could.

Yet the Republican platform of 1908 gave little recognition to the unrest abroad in the land. The platform was "safe" enough to please even the followers of the late Marcus A. Hanna. After consultations with President Roosevelt, however, the candidate, Taft, made several gestures to the left in his campaign speeches. He declared himself in favor of the popular election of United States senators, which stalwarts in his party had long opposed as an assault upon the Constitution. The taxation of incomes, execrated in 1895 by Joseph Choate as communistic and populistic, Taft endorsed in 1912 mildly, not enthusiastically. Labor, he said, had a legal right to organize, strike, and bargain collectively; and in some cases, he admitted, the courts had oppressed labor by the use of injunctions.

The methods of modern business, Taft thought, were generally sound, but since there had been too much speculation, stock watering, and fraud, reforms were needed in this relation also. The currency system, assailed by Bryan, was, in Taft's opinion, defective in various respects and should be made more flexible. As for socialism, he spoke gently of its "very humane and kindly theories," while dismissing it as wholly impracticable. In other words, from the Republican view of 1896, Taft was tainted with insurgency, but with the aid of the doughty Roosevelt and his followers he defeated Bryan, who stood fast on his populistic principles and made another vehement campaign that terrified conservatives.

Reflecting changes of the intervening years, President Taft translated some progressive policies into action. He supported the adoption of the resolution by Congress which provided for the income-tax amendment to the Constitution. He pressed for a revision of the tariff, a thorny question carefully avoided by Roosevelt. He urged upon Congress, in defiance of express companies, a bill for the establishment of a parcels post and Congress complied with his recommendation.

Many bankers had long opposed a plan for creating a postal savings system in the Post Office Department. Under Taft's leadership the plan was enacted into law by Congress. Since the passage of the Sherman Antitrust Act in 1890 the prosecution of trusts and combinations in restraint of trade had been neglected. President Taft launched an active campaign against them and the Supreme Court responded by ordering the Standard Oil Company and the American Tobacco Company to dissolve. Compared measure by measure with Theodore Roosevelt's regime, President Taft's administration, though less spectacular, could be correctly characterized as on the whole more "progressive."

Nevertheless soon after Taft's term opened a rebellion broke out against him within his own party. Several Republican senators and representatives, including Senator Robert M. La Follette, of Wisconsin, and Senator Albert J. Beveridge, of Indiana, were enraged by the high rates in the tariff bill of 1909, voted against it, and took the stump against it. On his return home from a hunting trip to Africa and a visit to Europe, Theodore Roosevelt expressed irritation over Taft's policies and measures, accused him of taking a reactionary tack on the tariff, conservation, and other issues, and launched an opposition in the Republican camp in 1910.

Hints of a general insurrection were received when the voters in the congressional election of that autumn sent a Democratic majority to the House of Representatives. In 1910, also, insurgent Republicans and Democrats in the House overthrew the system by which the Speaker, Joseph Cannon, and a few chairmen of committees were permitted to determine whether any bill was to be debated or passed. Populists had condemned this system, in season and out, and now a Republican House had annihilated it. The next year a group of Republicans, up in arms against Taft's policies, met at the home of Senator La Follette in Washington and formed a Progressive Republican League to unite all the forces of insurgency within the party.

As the campaign of 1912 drew near, Democratic managers were all agog with excitement. In Republican dissensions they saw at last a chance to carry the election—the first since 1892 when Cleveland had won his second term and then, by his conservative policies, had split his own party asunder. The only question among the Democrats was whether they were to turn right or left in this golden opportunity. Three times they had failed with Bryan as their leader and radicalism as their inspiration. But they had failed far more miserably in 1904 when they veered over to the gold standard and conservatism.

Even with the Republicans divided, the prospects were clouded. Would Bryan run again—for the fourth time? If so, could he be elected? If he withdrew or could be pushed aside, what man and what policies were most likely to bring the triumph at the polls for which Democratic hearts panted? It took a shrewd calculation to discover the person and the appeal that would carry the Democratic banner to victory in a time when the historic patterns of both parties were being badly shaken along a broad front.

For years an influential journalist in the East, George Harvey, long closely associated with powerful men in the "plutocratic" wing of the Democratic party, had been thinking that Woodrow Wilson, president of Princeton University, had the right character and the right ideas for a successful career as a Democratic politician. As a professor Wilson had taught politics and government, and from his youth he had nursed political ambitions. While professor and president at Princeton he had always taken a conservative position on public questions. He had despised Bryan and everything connected with Bryanism. He had angrily opposed Bryan in 1896, had even refused to sit on a platform with him, had attacked his theories as "foolish and dangerous," and in a private letter had expressed the hope that Bryan might be "knocked into a cocked hat."

For the policies of Theodore Roosevelt, Wilson had a dislike almost as intense. He had denounced government regulation of railways and assailed federal regulation of corporations. As late as 1909 he had upbraided trade unions for interfering with individual liberty. In fact there was scarcely an item in the populist or progressive program which Wilson had not frowned upon in public addresses and in private letters. From the standpoint of Harvey and his Wall Street friends, therefore, Woodrow Wilson seemed to be the ideal candidate to swing the Democratic party back to the conservatism of Grover Cleveland, and capture control over the government of the United States.

After some astute negotiations Harvey induced the Democratic boss of New Jersey, James Smith, to nominate Wilson as the party candidate for governor of the state in 1910. Weakened by the factional fights in their ranks, the New Jersey Republicans were ill prepared for the fray; and Wilson, without going beyond generalities in his campaign speeches, won the election with little difficulty. The first step in Harvey's plan to make Woodrow Wilson President of the United States had been achieved, and now the President-maker turned to the final act of his play. At the masthead of *Harper's Weekly*, which he edited, he flung out a sign reading: "For President, Woodrow Wilson."

But it was known that the J. P. Morgan Company had once come to the financial aid of the Harper publishing firm and, besides, Woodrow Wilson had plans of his own. With keen discernment he decided that Harvey's conservative designs did not comport with the progressive temper of the country and would bring disaster in the election. So he brusquely told Harvey that his open support was no longer desired. Wilson's name was taken from the masthead of *Harper's Weekly* and he assumed direction of his own campaign for nomination and election.

Having severed ties with "reactionaries" in his party, Wilson set about securing the Democratic prize. He toured the country, even to the Far West, and made numerous speeches in the progressive vein. He repudiated conservative doctrines he once had espoused; he approved nearly all the items that had long been listed in the populist program. He sought the friendship of Bryan whom, a few years before, he had wanted to see knocked into a cocked hat, and declared in his presence at a great public dinner: "There has been an interesting fixed point in the history of the Democratic party, and the fixed point has been the character, and the devotion, and the preachings of William Jennings Bryan." To the horror of incredulous Democrats he endorsed direct democracy—the initiative and referendum—although he did not press that issue. With the support of Bryan at last secured, Wilson won the nomination for President at the Democratic convention in Baltimore after a hard tug of war among the politicians.

Aware that progressive interests were laying hold of the country, Theodore Roosevelt threw his hat into the ring for the Republican nomination. But he was rejected in favor of President Taft at the party convention in Chicago. Declaring that the nomination had been "stolen" from him, Roosevelt and his followers then formed an independent party and adopted for it the name "Progressive." At a separate convention he was nominated as the Progressive party candidate for President.

The platform of the new party endorsed practically all the insurgent political reforms, such as direct primaries, popular election of senators, the initiative, referendum, and recall, woman suffrage, and recall of judicial decisions annulling social legislation. It approved the regulation of corporations, conservation of natural resources, income and inheritance taxes, and limitations on the use of injunctions in labor disputes. In fact William Jennings Bryan was delighted with the doctrines enunciated by Roosevelt and the Progressives. He declared, ironically, if wistfully, that they were a long time coming around to the propositions for which he had battled for the last twenty years.

In his campaign Wilson expounded many views of economic and political affairs that squared with the assertions made by laborites, populists, and socialists during the previous thirty or forty years. While rejecting their remedies he agreed with their contention that the Industrial Revolution had fundamentally altered the economic scene, that old political theories did not fit the new order, and that the government of the United States had long been run by concentrated business interests in their own behalf.

"Our life has broken away from the past," Wilson exclaimed. "We have changed our economic conditions, absolutely, from top to bottom; and, with our economic society, the organization of our life. The old political formulas do not fit present problems; they read now like documents taken out of a forgotten age. . . . The government of the United States at present is a foster child of the special interests. It is not allowed to have a will of its own. . . . The government of the United States in recent years has not been administered by the common people." Continuing in the spirit of the revolt against the plutocracy, Wilson maintained that "the masters of the government of the United States are the combined capitalists and manufacturers of the United States"—"the big bankers, the big manufacturers, the big masters of commerce, the heads of railroad corporations and of steamship corporations."

Theodore Roosevelt's speeches vibrated with similar denunciations of the "big interests" and similar promises to restore the government to the people. Caught between the fire of Roosevelt and the fire of Wilson, President Taft, in a sober and dignified manner, defended his administration against their charges and sought to show that in fact it was both progressive and enlightened. Having again nominated Eugene V. Debs as their candidate, the Socialists contended that if big capitalists did rule the country, as the politicians were now agreeing, it was time to break their dominion by nationalizing the means of production from which they derived their money and their power.

The votes in the election of 1912 revealed unmistakably the growing revolt within the two major parties and outside. They also disclosed sharp differences of opinion as to what must be done about the problems brought to the front by American thought respecting the Industrial Revolution, especially the accusation that the country was dominated by plutocratic interests. Wilson was elected but his popular vote was smaller than that given to Bryan in either 1896 or 1908. Indeed it fell short by nearly 2,500,000 of the total vote cast against him. Roosevelt polled about 700,000 more votes than Taft but the combined Progressive and Republican vote was below that polled by Roosevelt in 1904 and even below that received by Taft in 1908.

There was no better evidence of the strength of the political revolt than the number of ballots cast for the Socialist candidate, Eugene V. Debs. Notwithstanding the radical talk of Wilson and Roosevelt against "big business," the vote for Debs was more than double the Socialist vote of 1908. It approached the million mark —that point which hitherto in American history had indicated an impending explosion.

Despite the clashes of opinion over what was to be done about the problems of domestic economy, one thing seemed verified: the glittering promises of prosperity to be won by imperialism and the expansion of foreign trade made little appeal to the voters. Indeed Republicans did not make much of their "dollar diplomacy" in the campaign; and Democrats spurned imperialism as they had in previous years. The glories of empire and aggressive foreign policies had not, as prophesied by populists, extinguished progressive insurgency on the home front. Nor had they eased the clashes of interests on the home front.

As if in recognition of a national uprising against imperialism and all its works, Theodore Roosevelt veered back to domestic issues. Not long before, he had declared that the country needed a war and that everybody who opposed it was a "mollycoddle"; but he was compelled at the Progressive convention in Chicago to come to terms with Jane Addams, an invincible pacifist and anti-imperialist. There he joined in castigating the "barbaric system of warfare among nations, with its enormous waste of resources even in time of peace and the consequent impoverishment of the life of the toiling masses"; and in advocating an international agreement to limit naval forces, with the proviso that two battleships should be built a year until such agreement was reached. There at Chicago he gave up the gospel of imperialism and united with the Progressives in a declaration proclaiming the responsibilities of the Americans at home: "Unhampered by tradition, uncorrupted by power, undismayed by the magnitude of the task, the new party offers itself as the instrument of the people to sweep away old abuses, to build a new and nobler commonwealth."

Confident that he had a popular mandate to act forcefully, Wilson as President assumed the leadership of his party; and during his first term in office, with the aid of progressives and dissidents from both parties in Congress, the following program of legislation was enacted:

The tariff was reduced, not to free trade or a revenue basis, but to a lower level than the country had seen for years.

A new banking law set up the Federal Reserve System, in which old Federalist ideas of centralized banking were combined with more flexibility for the currency and more government control over banking administration.

Laws against trusts and combinations were strengthened and efforts were made by administrative action to tear apart interlocking relations of banks, corporations, and business concerns in the interest of free enterprise—if with little effect.

To organized labor three offerings were made: provisions presumed to liberate trade unions from prosecution as combinations in restraint of trade and to limit the use of injunction in labor disputes; a law fixing eight hours as the standard day for trainmen employed on interstate railways; and the La Follette Seamen's Act assuring better treatment to sailors on board American merchant ships.

Farmers, who had complained about the extortions of Eastern bankers, were conciliated by the establishment of federal land banks empowered to lend them money at a lower rate of interest.

With a view to formulating and enforcing "fair" trade practices for commerce and industry, the Federal Trade Commission was created and endowed with powers to inquire into "unfair" actions in business and make recommendations for legislation to stop them. Though vague in its phrasing, the Federal Trade Commission Act of 1914 departed from the old faith that sharp competition would of itself bring prosperity, and indicated a trend toward a new faith—in government regulation of business enterprises for the public interest.

CHAPTER XXIV

Realizations in Social Improvement

OLDER than the political insurgency that went by the name of Progressive, related to it, and yet in many respects fundamentally independent of political partisanship, were efforts of humanitarians to realize ideals social in nature that transcended personal desires for self-perfection, wealth, prestige, and power. The humanitarians worked in the spirit of civilization which had found expression in colonial times, the Revolution, the early Republic, the democratic awakening, the Civil War, and the preceding age of the rising plutocracy. Now they took advantage of the new knowledge and thought evolved at the turn of the nineteenth century. They sought to apply the theories of social meliorism developed by the economists, sociologists, and political scientists who analyzed and pointed out inadequacies in the doctrines of individualism. The humanitarians were more than students, theorists, and writers, though some of them were all those persons; they were primarily activists anxious to get reforms established. They made minute surveys of blighted areas in national life and searched for ways and means of integrating social theory and social practice.

Literally millions of men and women participated in this wider movement of thought, program making, and implementation. The sources of the movement were broken into special activities by groups of citizens, such as the Association for Labor Legislation, the National Consumers' League, the National Housing Association, and the Association for the Improvement of the Condition of the Colored People, which worked for the realization of special programs. But the movement as a whole was inspired by the common purpose of raising the standards of living, promoting physical and mental health, enlarging the concept of social justice and its applications—in short, advancing civilization in the United States. In social origins and continuous support this movement was mainly, though by no means entirely, instigated by the middle class. It gave effect to aesthetic, ethical, and humane impulses in the democratic way—by proposal, discussion, adoption—within the limits of a reforming, socializing capitalism.

Few of the men and women who carried this movement forward received during their lives the newspaper publicity accorded to warriors, politicians, plutocrats, and criminals. Nor in their death were many of them given revealing obituaries or places in the twenty volumes entitled Dictionary of American Biography. Nevertheless their force of character, intellectual powers, steadfastness in research, in educating the public, in drafting legislation and advocating it before committees of government, municipal, state, and federal, so influenced the thought of the nation that ideas once "dangerous" became commonplaces, accepted by persons who had formerly fought to the last ditch the new proposals put up to the country. The humanitarians not only broke down the resistance of private interests and legislatures. They also compelled a reconstruction or re-education of the United States Supreme Court which for more than forty years had been reading into the federal Constitution, as Justice Oliver Wendell Holmes remarked, the laissez-faire doctrines of Mr. Herbert Spencer, English individualist.

Chief among the labors of the humanitarians were attempts to overcome, by public and private collective actions, the poverty, diseases, misery, and hazards of ill-fortune which millions of Americans suffered. It was their thesis that such adversities mocked the liberty, equality, pursuit of happiness, and general welfare professed as American ideals at the establishment of national independence.

In the struggle over social improvement advocates and opponents were aligned as groups and organizations. The alignment was not as wholesale or always as sharp as in the strife of political parties, but conservatism and insurgency appeared within it as in political struggles for power.

In the run-of-the-mill opinion social conservatism signified the support of measures and practices which protected concentrated wealth, and the methods of acquiring wealth, against interference on the part of government. "We have among us," wrote the economist, Richard T. Ely, in 1894, "a class of mammon worshippers, whose one test of conservatism, or radicalism, is the attitude one takes with respect to accumulated wealth. Whatever tends to preserve the wealth of the wealthy is called conservatism, and whatever favors anything else, no matter what, they call socialism." A person may love old ways and draw his ideals from a past which he deems saner in its views of wealth, Ely went on; yet if he would, "by social action," endeavor to change certain tendencies and conserve the treasures of the past, "he is still a radical in the eyes of those men whose one and sole test is money."

This was not, however, the whole creed of social conservatism. Many elements entered into it—some of them inherited from the days when America was a country of free land and immense natural resources open to energetic individuals capable of improving their condition by initiative and persistent labor. Other features were newly formulated under the head of individualism—a theory which, as we have said but repeat for remembrance, enclosed four main propositions as follows. It is individuals struggling to make a living and acquire property who set productive activities in motion and create the wealth which makes the country great and prosperous. In this struggle each individual is rewarded according to his personal contribution to the stock of wealth; his wages or profits are the measure of his contribution. Poverty is the "natural" outcome of individual idleness, lack of enterprise, imprudence, improvidence, and in many cases drunkenness. Although Christian charity may relieve poverty here and there, nothing vital can be done to prevent or remove its mass. Efforts to overcome it by government action—that is, by collective action—will merely hurt the capable portion of the population and pauperize the poor.

The theories advanced by the activist humanitarians against the thesis of conservatism were not closely knit into a single argument or philosophy, as a rule. Yet, however formulated, the theories of the activist humanitarians denied the truth of the conservative assertion that gross inequalities of wealth, signifying poverty, are decreed by any iron law of nature; that the riches of the rich are merely the rewards of their thrift and enterprise; that the poverty of the poor is solely due to indolence and improvidence. They accepted the contention of the sociologists such as Lester Ward and Anna Garlin Spencer to the effect that the individual, no matter how enterprising, derives the knowledge, the inventions he makes and uses, and the security he enjoys from the common life of society and the government that holds it together.

The active meliorists insisted that ills in society have various origins—such as accidents in industry, insanitary and congested conditions of labor and living, contagious diseases, and other adverse factors which can be removed or prevented or diminished by special measures. These changes, they argued, can be brought about peacefully, by group and public action, and this dire poverty can be abolished, misfortunes mitigated, special privileges inimical to the interests of society destroyed, and the quality of the common life improved.

A summary of the concrete proposals for social improvement conceived in the meliorist spirit was presented to the country in two works issued near the turn of the nineteenth century. The first was *Socialism, Its Nature, Strength and Weakness*, published in 1894 by Richard T. Ely, a teacher of economics who combined studying, observation, and theorizing with the formulation of programs for social action. The second was *Poverty*, published in 1904 by Robert Hunter, a student of economics who turned to social work in the slums of New York City and witnessed the making of poverty at first hand. Taken collectively, the proposals for action offered by Ely and Hunter included these:

Taxation of incomes and inheritances, and application of the revenues to social purposes.

Making all factories and tenements sanitary and safe.

Stamping out contagious diseases by public-health measures.

Shortening hours of work, especially in dangerous and laborious industries and for women and young people.

Public care of defectives and dependents, separating them from the body of employable and industrious workers.

Insurance against sickness, unemployment, and accidents in industry.

Compensation to workers injured in industries through no fault of their own—a great source of poverty and family distress.

Old-age pensions.

Establishment of minimum hours and wages in "sweated" industries and enforcement of sanitary standards by public authority.

Regulation of tenements, planning and improvement of cities with provision for parks, playgrounds, and other recreational facilities.

Conservation and wise use of natural resources.

Raising standards of physical well-being by compulsory public-health measures.

Extension and improvement of public education for all the children of all the people.

Long before the nineteenth century came to a close practically all the ideas of social improvement which Americans of later generations were to debate, modify, amplify, and apply had been formulated and thoroughly discussed by reflective persons from one end of the country to the other. Moreover for the first time serious studies had been made of the actual distribution of wealth in the United States. For a hundred years or more that subject had been talked about but few facts had been available as a basis for informed talk. Social reformers made guesses respecting the amount of wealth and poverty that existed. Conservatives admitted that there was some poverty in the United States but they declared that it did not amount to much or was deserved; that in any case America was the most prosperous nation in the world and good enough for anybody. At length statisticians tried to reduce the loose talk about concentrated wealth and poverty to something like a statement of facts.

In 1893 George K. Holmes, of the United States Census Office, formulated the following estimate: "Twenty per cent of the wealth of the United States is owned by three-one-hundredths of one per cent of the population; seventy-one per cent is owned by nine per cent of the families, and twenty-nine per cent of the wealth is all that falls to ninety-one per cent of the population." Holmes' generalization was immediately attacked as inaccurate. Richard T. Ely, in using it, admitted that, owing to the backward state of the American census, calculations respecting the distribution of wealth in the United States were "extremely uncertain." But he added: "All estimates agree in one respect, and that is in attributing a greater concentration of wealth to the United States than to any other modern country." This did not mean that a larger proportion of the people in the United States than in European countries were in poverty. Such was not a fact, Ely conceded. Yet there was no doubt in his mind that America was cursed by widespread poverty in spite of all that could be truly said about prosperity.

Determined to find out with as high a degree of exactness as possible just how much poverty there was in the United States, Robert Hunter made an extensive study of the subject, using the various kinds of available figures. In 1904 he reported the results of his work in his book bearing the plain title, *Poverty*. This was his summary: "There are probably in fairly prosperous years no less than 10,000,000 persons in poverty; that is to say, underfed, underclothed, and poorly housed. Of these about 4,000,000 persons are public paupers. Over 2,000,000 working men are unemployed from four to six months in the year. . . . Probably no less than 1,000,000 workers are injured or killed each year while doing their

PERCENTAGE OF ORGANIZED WORKERS IN MASSACHUSETTS
UNEMPLOYED, 1908–1921

work . . . We know that many workmen are overworked and underpaid. We know in a general way that unnecessary disease is far too prevalent. We know some of the insanitary evils of tenements and factories."

If Hunter had examined conditions in rural regions as carefully as in the cities, he could have noted that a special census of 1900 reported more than thirty-five per cent of American farmers as tenants—an increase over 1880 and 1890. He did state, however, that over fifty per cent of the farmers were either tenants or held their land under mortgages—propertyless or only partial owners of their homes.

Hunter's estimates were in turn attacked and shown to be in some respects lacking in accuracy if not exaggerated. Owing to the indifference or hostility of certain officials nothing approaching precise and comprehensive figures on poverty was accessible to the people of the "greatest nation on earth." Though precision as to the total picture was impossible in these circumstances, it was certain that there were millions of persons on some form of relief and that millions of self-respecting workers were from time to time unemployed or received wages which were too small or too irregular to keep them from the uncertainty of livelihood and the pinching want known as poverty. At all events, while statisticians disputed, Americans who observed poverty at first hand or suf- fered from it personally protested against it and demanded amelio- ration by concerted efforts, private and public; and leaders in the labor movement, who had direct contact with social conditions in industrial cities, promoted what was frequently called the "war on poverty."

Since one of the first needs in the quest for social improve- ment was the facts in the case of wages, hours, employment, un- employment, industrial accidents, and similar matters pertaining to the actual condition of the people, a demand went up for two immediate actions for meeting this need: the creation of labor bureaus to collect such figures; and the addition of questions to those already used in the decennial census taken by the govern- ment of the United States. Massachusetts replied to the first de- mand in 1869 by establishing the first bureau of labor statistics in America. Between 1869 and 1885 similar bureaus were set up in several other states. In the latter year provision was made for a federal Bureau of Labor in the Department of the Interior. Sub- sequently the bureau was transferred to the Department of Com- merce and Labor and in 1913 it became a separate Department of Labor in the federal administration. Among its duties the Depart- ment of Labor was to "foster, promote, and develop the welfare of wage earners, to improve their working conditions, and to advance their opportunities for profitable employment."

The year before the separate department was established, Con- gress created the Children's Bureau "to investigate and report upon all matters pertaining to the welfare of children and child life." In 1920 the Women's Bureau was set up in the Department and charged with "formulating standards and policies for promoting the welfare of wage-earning women, improving their working

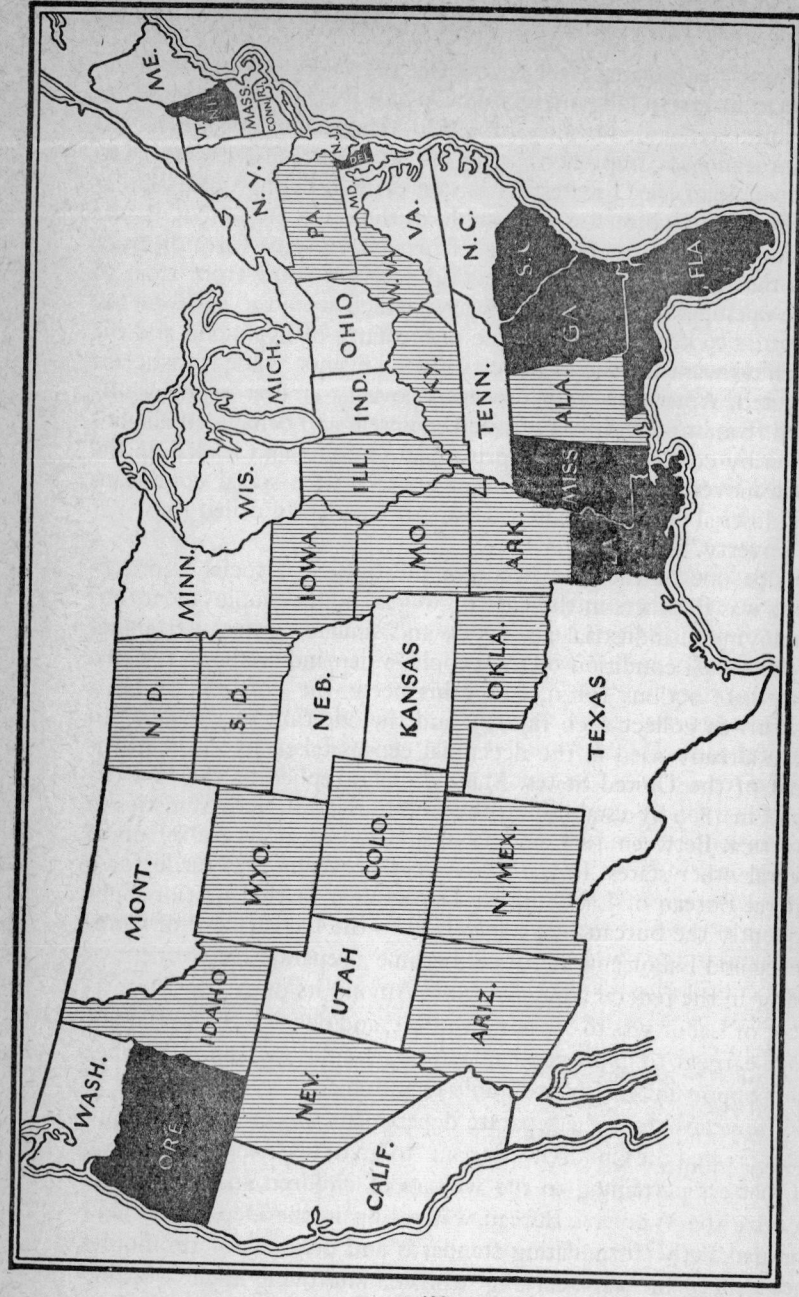

STATE INSPECTION OF MINES AND QUARRIES FOR SAFETY IN 1936

Twenty-three states (white) empower state labor departments to inspect mines and quarries to enforce safety and sanitation laws. Seventeen states, (vertical lines) assign this duty to independent state mine departments. Eight states, (black) do not provide for state inspection of mines and quarries by any of their departments.

conditions, increasing their efficiency, and advancing their opportunities for profitable employment."

Meanwhile the census takers of the United States were ordered to ask more questions of the people; various departments and bureaus of the federal government collected additional figures relative to all great branches of American economy; and state governments increased their annual output of figures and descriptions bearing on the health, employment, wages, home-ownership, and welfare of the people under their jurisdictions. These reports were supplemented by special studies of all the major phases of American life, from overcrowding in city tenements to tenancy and poverty in the most backward country districts. Eventually Americans, who cared and wanted to know realities, could acquire solid information on the conditions of the people everywhere in the United States.

In practice social improvement advanced along many lines as men and women, individually and in organizations, moved against what they conceived to be specific evils in the general situation of substandard living. The march toward these objectives was uneven and the gains varied from place to place.

Massachusetts, for example, led the attack on factory conditions harmful to industrial workers. Building upon a law of 1842 which fixed a ten-hour day in industries for children under twelve years of age—itself eloquent of the "good old times"—Massachusetts established a system of factory inspection in 1867; a state labor department in 1869; an effective ten-hour law for women in 1874; and a general law respecting industrial safety in 1877.

Soon statutes of this type began to flow in a large volume from the legislatures of the most highly industrialized states. In special occupations and industries the working hours of men were curtailed by legislation. By 1910 nearly a third of the states had fixed an eight-hour day for labor on public works. In the single year of 1907 twenty-three states enacted laws reducing the hours of toil for men in mines, smelters, and underground work generally, on trains and in other occupations where the strains and dangers of industry were peculiarly severe. Although the courts were early inclined to hold that men would have to look after themselves, the principle was finally established that the hours of labor for men, as well as women, could be regulated by law; the old idea that endless drudgery was the unavoidable lot of all workers had been widely abandoned and the doctrine of shorter hours both to relieve fatigue and enable workers to have the benefits of some leisure, in which to develop their other powers, was fairly well established.

A second type of labor legislation pertained to sanitation and safety in factories and mines. The Massachusetts general law on this subject, enacted in 1877, was followed by amendments in that state which steadily elaborated the details of public control over the building and operating of factories once regarded as a purely private matter for owners and managers. Other states soon framed laws based on the Massachusetts model and within twenty-five years such regulations were in force in nearly all great industrial regions.

Henceforward in progressive communities it was necessary for factories to be built with more regard to safety and ventilation; for dangerous machinery to be guarded by protective devices; for heat to be supplied in cold weather; for boilers to be maintained in good order and regularly inspected; for certain standards of cleanliness to be observed; and for sanitary appliances to be installed. Henceforward it was necessary for mine owners to provide their mines with arrangements for ventilation, safety, and the escape of workers in cases of explosions and other accidents if such escape was at all possible. Henceforward manufacturing in tenements was restricted and in the case of many commodities wholly forbidden for reasons of sanitation and general welfare. From year to year the early laws were supplemented by amendments and new statutes which made tighter and tighter the public control over the material surroundings in which industrial workers labored—a control of vital importance for the safety, health, comfort, and well-being of millions engaged in industry and mining.

Lagging far behind legislation respecting sanitation, safety, and hours was the extension of aid to working people injured in the course of duty. Here the traditions of the common law were used by lawyers and employers to throw the burden of accidents mainly on the workers. Under those traditions the employer was not liable for damages unless he was personally responsible for an accident; he was not liable at all for accidents due to "unpreventable causes" or to the negligence of the injured employee or a fellow employee. And any person injured in an industry could secure damages only by a lawsuit which might be long, expensive, and futile. Thus employers were under no economic compulsion to take every possible care against accidents by providing safety appliances; and the poverty of the poor was increased by the necessity of meeting the costs of most injuries incurred in mills, factories, mines, and transportation industries.

Proposals to shift the burden of accidents to industry itself were made early in the rise of the factory system but they were fiercely and effectively combatted by employers. This reform, it was said, would take money unjustly from employers and give it to workmen guilty of carelessness or malicious negligence. Judges and lawyers usually adopted this view respecting life, liberty, and property.

As machine industries multiplied, accidents increased. "Fourth of July orators," declared H. R. Seager, the social economist, in 1910, "delight to point out the various fields in which we excel, but there is one field of which they say very little, and that is that we kill and injure more workingmen in proportion to the number employed on our railroads, in our mines, and factories than any other country in the world." Statistics of accidents, like those of poverty, were far from complete, but there were enough to show that in the number of accidents America certainly led the whole world.

To extirpate this source of pain and poverty men and women from coast to coast held meetings of protest, drafted remedial laws, and besieged the halls of Congress and the state legislatures. Two schemes were proposed, one mild, the other thoroughgoing. The first modified the old common-law rule and compelled the employer to pay compensation for injuries whenever accidents were due to his negligence, that of his employees, or to the necessary risks of the industry. The second was a system of accident insurance. It required employers to insure their employees against accidents just as they insured their buildings against fires, cyclones, and explosions; it provided for easy and inexpensive methods of compensating injured persons, or their families in case of death, without requiring them to engage in tedious and costly lawsuits.

In 1913 the state of New York, by constitutional amendment, authorized legislation of both types and the backbone of the resistance to industrial insurance was broken. Some men and women who had begun the struggle for this social improvement, amid the din of "great party battles" in the eighties and nineties, lived to see the principle of accident insurance well established in every enlightened state in the Union.

Even more devastating than dangerous machinery as a source of poverty and misery was chronic disease or intermittent sickness.

Through the long centuries bad health had been looked upon as a necessary evil or an act of God or as a private matter between the individual and his doctor, if he could afford a doctor. But with the advance of medical knowledge mankind discovered that, while many diseases seemed to be hereditary or due to personal faults, others were social in origin—sprang from contagion and from methods of working and living in society. Indeed a large number of them were new "occupational diseases," arising from the use of chemicals and materials in certain processes, such as the making of matches and pottery, or from sheer fatigue.

Slowly it also dawned in the public mind that even those diseases due to heredity or personal faults constituted a costly burden for industry and society. They reduced the efficiency of workers and the number of working days in industry. They increased the heavy public expenditures to maintain hospitals and institutions for the sick, injured, and defective. In short, besides direct cost for care running into millions of dollars each year, diseases reduced the productive power of the people to a degree calculated in terms of money at billions of dollars annually.

Here then was another recognized problem, partly individual and yet involved in factory management beyond the control of individual workers. Operating as single investigators and in groups, men and women concerned with raising the standards and values of life in the United States studied this problem. They made careful surveys and devised remedial plans to be enacted into law and enforced by public agents.

Near the middle of the nineteenth century their activities were accelerated as epidemics of smallpox and cholera aroused national interest in a new subject, "public health," or social health. Amid the terror over epidemics Massachusetts created in 1849 a commission to investigate the sanitary conditions in the state and the report of that body served as the basis for extensive legislation directed against the social sources of disease. In 1853, shortly after cholera had spread death and fright in the city of New Orleans, the State of Louisiana, at the insistence of public-spirited men and women, organized a department of public health and began a public attack on the roots of disease with a view to prevention. As research enlarged medical knowledge during the closing years of the nineteenth century, a public-health movement, led by enlightened citizens and many special societies, professional and lay, carried on agitations in favor of "social medicine." They forced city councils and state legislatures to act in the interest of public health and gained victory after victory over indifference, ignorance, and often virulent opposition.

Before the twentieth century had advanced far the death rate in the country beginning with infant mortality had been materially reduced; great codes of law incorporating the latest discoveries of preventive medicine had been enacted; every state and every city had a department or office of public health charged with carrying the laws into effect. The war on disease, and on the poverty and misery accompanying disease, had won impressive victories. Not only this. The strategy of new public-health campaigns had been laid out and ideas for achievements hitherto beyond the sweep of imagination had been formulated. Moreover a young generation of doctors and health workers was being trained to carry on through the years of the twentieth century. In summarizing her years' labors in the movement for public health, Dr. S. Josephine Baker, head of the Bureau of Child Hygiene in New York City, symbolized those labors in the title of her autobiography, *Fighting for Life*.

Related to the attacks on conditions partly responsible for disease, but also connected with concern for comfort, beauty, mental hygiene, and social stability, was a collateral drive on the evils of ill-housing, the congestion of people in tenements, the spreading slums, hideous and crime-breeding. As the right of the individual to look after his own diseases had once been deemed sacred, so the right of property owners to herd tenants like cattle into buildings, and yet wrench exorbitant rents from them as human beings, had been regarded as a vested privilege, never to be invaded by government—to be protected in fact to the last penny.

Out of the exercise of this privilege came housing conditions "indescribable in print," as a New York tenement-house report of 1903 put the case: "vile privies and vile sinks; foul cellars full of rubbish; . . . dilapidated and dangerous stairs; plumbing pipes containing large holes emitting sewer gas throughout the houses; rooms so dark that one cannot see the people in them; cellars occupied as sleeping places; . . . pigs, goats, horses, and other animals kept in cellars; dangerous old fire traps without fire escapes; . . . buildings without adequate water supply—the list might be added to almost indefinitely."

In such places lived thousands of industrial workers in the United States; into them crowded new immigrants from Europe. What was to be done about them? They furnished millions of dollars annually to owners in rents and increased land values. One of the most opulent and fashionable religious bodies in New York City had large investments in such property. Thus powerful private interests were arrayed against change and denounced change as subversive and revolutionary.

But men and women of the age lightly called "gilded" declared war on American "rack-renting" and slums, and advanced inch by inch against the vested "rights" of landlords. Campaigns were made and laws drafted to cut away first this evil and then that evil. Windowless rooms were forbidden here; the installation of toilets instead of block privies was ordered there; dangerous firetraps were condemned to repair or destruction. While McKinley and Bryan were arguing about the currency and imperialism, the complaint that reformers would be next demanding bathtubs for the people rose in the land. In 1902 the state of New York enacted a comprehensive and detailed housing law applicable to the tenements of its great cities. Resistance, though by no means broken, was wavering, and the idea of decent housing for the people was competing in the market place of opinion for recognition as a necessity of civilization in America.

From exercising public control over houses and buildings in the interest of public safety, health, and welfare, it was a logical step to the concept of planning whole cities in the general interest. American cities, with a few exceptions, had grown up rapidly and in a haphazard fashion under the stimulus of free enterprise, including the acquisitive instinct. Landowners and real estate speculators had encouraged urban anarchy, with the barest reference if any to the convenience of industry and commerce, to comfort for the residents, to recreation, beauty, and wholesome living. Only here and there, and largely by accident, parks and breathing spaces had been reserved among square miles of brick and mortar and wooden buildings.

But many men and women were thinking about this outcome of greed and carelessness and ignorance. They realized that every social improvement—in factory legislation, health protection, and tenement-house control—was in some way connected with city life as a whole. In response to a growing interest in municipal affairs, a city planning movement came into being. All reflective persons admitted that some city planning seemed necessary. The question was: how much? Engineers and economists studied the subject and wrote on it. In 1907 the city of Hartford, Connecticut, created a city planning commission empowered to make, though not enforce, general plans for the control of building in the community. The example was soon followed in other municipalities. In 1909 the National City Planning Association was founded and began to hold annual conferences. Another field of social improvement was to be occupied.

In the general uprising against poverty, misery, and the inequality of wealth and opportunity, another proposal for curtailing exploitation and effecting a more equitable distribution of wealth gained headway. Corporations holding franchises for operating public utilities in cities had long insisted that they were entitled to earn "all the traffic will bear," and to determine the kind of services they were to render within the usually loose terms of their charters. Next to the large landholders in cities they had profited most from urban development. They had garnered for their stockholders and managers millions of dollars more than a "reasonable return" on prudent investment would have yielded. But efforts were made in cities and states, as well as at the national capital, to reduce and hold within reasonable limits the rates charged by public utilities for supplying water, transportation, electricity, and other services to the public.

By hundreds of state statutes and municipal ordinances enacted during the early years of the twentieth century, the granting of loose and perpetual franchises to utility corporations was definitely ended in American practice; the rates and services of such corporations were subjected to minute regulations in the public interest; and exploitation by corruption and manipulation was curtailed. Even the directors of utilities themselves were so affected by the movement of thought and action that they began to style their companies "public-service corporations." By that time the principle was being firmly established that such corporations were entitled to charge rates no higher than those yielding a fair return on prudent investment.

A primary foundation of the enormous wealth accumulated in the hands of a few thousand families in the United States had been the natural resources of the states and the national domain, bought at low prices and in many cases acquired by fraud and manipulation. As natural resources were diminished through almost unrestrained exploitation, and the glaring waste committed by the exploiters was exposed by investigations, a movement was launched for the conservation of the national heritage in forests, lands, minerals, water power, and other natural riches. Here too a contest was waged against resolute vested interests determined to get possession of the remaining resources still in public ownership, while handling as they pleased the property they already had. In this crusade progress was slow and halting. Yet progress was made.

While General Grant was still occupying the White House a committee of the Association for the Advancement of Science recommended, in cautious language, a change of national policy in disposing of the national forests. Scientists, engineers, economists, and other citizens concerned with the conservation of resources gave thought to the problem, wrote about it, and delivered speeches on it. Gradually they built up a body of exact knowledge and a strong public opinion in favor of protecting and making a wise use of the nation's physical heritage.

Governments in states, such as New York, that still held public lands, began to safeguard them and even to legislate respecting the use of resources in private hands. In 1891 the Congress of the United States, at last affected by the growing demand from conservationists, empowered the President to withdraw forest lands on the national domain from sale. President Harrison and President Cleveland took action under the law, though in no spectacular spirit, and established enormous forest reserves. In 1882, under the inspiration of Bernhard Fernow, the American Forestry Congress was organized to promote the study of forestry and the conservation of forests.

Four years later Fernow was appointed head of the forestry division in the federal Department of Agriculture and inaugurated a systematic study and administration of the national forests. Gifford Pinchot, an associate of Fernow in the movement, became head of the division. From him Theodore Roosevelt caught an enthusiasm for ·conservation and, as President, by innumerable addresses, conferences, and actions, he dramatized it as a great national obligation.

Hard-driven by the pressure of public opinion, Congress grudgingly enacted new laws for withdrawing resources from sale and making better use of the lands in public ownership. In 1910 it provided for the separation of the subsurface from the surface of coal-bearing lands and for the retention of coal deposits in public hands, while disposing of the surface for agricultural uses. The same year it authorized the President to reserve lands "for water-power sites, irrigation . . . or other public purposes." In 1911, Congress made a radical departure by beginning the policy of buying great areas of forest land in Eastern states where there was no national domain and placing them under federal authorities. Meanwhile other acts made provision for the more efficient control and

administration of forests, minerals, grazing lands, and other resources under the jurisdiction of the federal government. Before
President Taft retired in 1913 the foundations for the development
of national conservation had been securely laid.

All these measures of social improvement merely affected the
distribution of wealth more or less indirectly, despite the fact that
they were continuously assailed as undermining the vested rights
of property owners. But at length they were supplemented by a
direct attack on concentrated wealth through the use of income
and inheritance taxes. Neither tax was exactly new to American
fiscal policy. The income tax and inheritance tax had been employed by Congress in its desperate search for additional revenues
during the Civil War. A light inheritance tax, also for revenue
purposes, had been adopted by the Republicans in connection with
financing the war on Spain. When, however, the Democrats in
1894 attempted to renew the income tax, for the avowed object of
making the rich bear their share of national burdens, the Supreme
Court declared nearly every feature of the tax unconstitutional.

Defeat only spurred its advocates to more determined efforts;
and so impressive was the agitation that a Republican Congress
in 1909 submitted to the states an income-tax amendment to the
Constitution. Duly ratified in 1913, the Sixteenth Amendment
allowed the Democrats, under the presidency of Woodrow Wilson, to make the taxing of incomes a regular part of federal
financing. By this time a large number of states had also begun to
lay progressive taxes on incomes and inheritances.

Against protests of conservatives that it was communistic,
populistic, or socialistic, the principle of apportioning taxes according to riches—ability to pay—was now generally accepted as
just. What was more, the use of other forms of taxation for
social as well as revenue purposes was securely established in the
law of the land.

To utopians—those eternal dreamers and prodders of mankind,
always testing practice by purely ideal concepts of life, labor, and
government—the achievements of the humanitarians seemed excessively prolonged; meager in proportion to the magnitude of the
problems thrown up by the Industrial Revolution; painfully
limited in view of the potentials for the production of all the goods
deemed necessary to an ideal standard of living; and complacent
respecting a possible abundance for the people in the forms of

leisure and meditation and work in the creative arts. Notwithstanding such strictures, however, the achievements of the humanitarians, by contrast with the state of things in 1865, certainly represented substantial progress—*Ethical Gains through Legislation*, as Florence Kelley conceived their movement, in which she was herself a national leader. Moreover these accomplishments, in the face of the venomous opposition from individualists, kept alive the spirit of civilization, augmented its force, and prepared the way for grappling with still greater social problems.

CHAPTER XXV

Gates of Old Opportunities Closing

"A FEW GENERATIONS AGO," wrote Theodore Roosevelt with reference to the great coal strike of 1902, "an American workman could have saved money, gone West, and taken up a homestead. Now the free lands were gone. In earlier days a man who began with pick and shovel might have come to own a mine. That outlet too was now closed, as regards the immense majority, and few, if any, of the one hundred and fifty thousand mine workers could ever aspire to enter the small circle of men who held in their grasp the great anthracite industry. The majority of the men who earned wages in the coal industry, if they wished to progress at all, were compelled to progress not by ceasing to be wage earners, but by improving the conditions under which all the wage earners in all the industries of the country lived and worked, as well, of course, as improving their own individual efficiency."

In an autobiography, the story of his long struggle as a labor leader to uphold and improve American standards of life and work, Samuel Gompers dealt with changed conditions of national economy near the end of the nineteenth century and gave his reasons for believing that the unlimited flood of immigrants was threatening to "submerge standards of life and work that we had established." "The majority of immigrants," he explained, "no longer came from western Europe where language, customs, and industrial organization were similar to those of the United States but from the countries of eastern Europe where lower standards of life and work prevailed. As these immigrants flooded basic industries, they threatened to destroy our standards. . . . In the early days, boundless and undeveloped resources made possible and expedient a policy of stimulating immigration. It was not until industrialism developed and there were evidences that the newer immigration was not being assimilated that as a nation we began to consider policies of regulation. The labor movement was among the first organizations to urge such policies. . . . Although I realized that the American people in their generosity wished to maintain the United States as an open, free asylum to the oppressed of the whole world, yet we realized also that the United States could not solve all the problems of the world and that the struggle for human freedom and advancement would largely have to be worked out by each country for itself."

Whatever faults could be found with these pronouncements by Theodore Roosevelt and Samuel Gompers, both statements pointed to an indubitable fact: an epoch in the history of the United States—and the Old World—had come to an end. For four hundred years European adventurers, conquerors, capitalists, and emigrants had been operating in huge regions of the earth's surface, always with open spaces before them—in North America, South America, Australia, the vastness of the African continent below the northern shoulder, and in islands of the seas. There they had enjoyed elbowroom and opportunities for acquiring a living or riches by crude labor processes or exploitation. Into those spaces European countries could dump their surplus population and their "surplus manufactures." As the nineteenth century drew to a close practically all the "waste spaces" had been seized, carved out, and divided up among old and new nations.

After the founding of the English colonies in America, especially after the launching of the American Republic and the opening of the West, venturesome men and women by the millions had crowded into the United States in search of more liberty and wider opportunities for earning a livelihood, for trade, for acquiring land, and for working natural resources. For a full century this immigration had been practically unimpeded by legal restrictions. On the contrary, it had been actively encouraged, by federal laws, state laws, shipping concerns, land speculators, industries in search of abundant, cheap, and docile labor, and by sympathizers with refugees from European tyranny.

With sturdy, able-bodied, industrious, skilled, intelligent, and talented men and women had come criminals, paupers, paralytics, prostitutes, persons suffering from loathsome and contagious diseases, imbeciles utterly unable to take care of themselves, and cripples—all without let or hindrance. European governments had swept up paupers from their poorhouses and paid their way to

PERCENTAGE OF FOREIGN-BORN WHITE PEOPLE IN EACH STATE IN 1920

Less than 1 percent
1 to 5 percent
5 to 10 percent
10 to 15 percent
15 to 25 percent
25 to 35 percent

America so that their taxpayers could escape the burden of supporting the unfortunates of their own lower orders. Furthermore they had expelled from the countries under their control—often to America—liberals, democrats, labor leaders, reformers, and socialists in efforts to evade social problems and agitations in their own societies.

The magnitude of the migration to the United States from the Old World is indicated by the following tables, giving the number of immigrants in four selected decades:

1821–30	106,508
1851–60	2,452,660
1881–90	4,737,046
1901–10	8,136,016

Changes in the sources of this migration are revealed by the following table showing the percentage of the total immigration from three countries in successive periods:

From Austria-Hungary, in 1861–70, percentage of total, 0.33; in 1901–10, 24.4 of the total.

From Italy, in 1861–70, percentage of the total, 0.51; in 1901–10, 23.3 of the total.

From Russia, in 1861–70, percentage of total, 0.10; in 1901–10, 18.0 of the total.

When the trickle of immigration expanded after the establishment of independence, the United States had at its disposal an immense domain of Western lands and resources. Other territories were added at each stage of the westward movement. In all, between 1781 and 1853, the year of the last continental extension made by the Gadsden Purchase, the public domain of the United States had amounted to approximately 1,400,000,000 acres—an area about five times as large as the combined areas of Germany, France, and Italy.

Of this vast public domain all except a mere fragment had passed into private hands by 1900. Of the 1,400,000,000 acres only 186,000,000 acres remained in public possession in 1924; and that domain consisted mainly of mountains, deserts, arid regions, and forest lands not suitable for cultivation. The dearth of more land for cultivation and exploitation was now a fact as indisputable as the existence of the Rocky Mountains. The shrinkage of free or cheap land was a stubborn reality.

It was also portentous for the economy of the United States and the rest of the world. Every informed and thoughtful citizen of the Republic became aware of its implication in terms of diminished opportunity for economic anarchy. No longer was it possible for industrious, prudent, and determined persons of any nationality to make a living or a fortune by exploiting free or cheap natural resources in the crude manner long followed in agriculture, cattle raising, mining, and industry. Newcomers would now have to compete for a livelihood with the industrial, business, and professional classes in America—classes that were becoming "overcrowded." Even Alaska, which had been added in 1867, was nearly all staked out within fifty years and offered little escape from the occupied continental domain.

Not only had the bulk of the arable, grazing, forest, and mineral lands passed into private hands, shutting off such easy acquisition to individuals and corporations. In exploitation the land and mineral resources in private hands were being denuded and depleted in the most extraordinary carnival of waste yet recorded in all history. Arable land by the millions of acres was stripped of topsoil and eroded into ruins by greedy and ignorant cultivators. Grasslands were plowed up and turned into dust storms or overgrazed into deserts. Forests were slashed without regard to future growth, and magnificent trees by the millions were lost in forest fires. Oil, iron, and other mineral resources were exploited so recklessly and swiftly that by 1940 experts in this field of "economics" were justified in announcing that the "richest nation on earth" would be deprived within an appreciable time of the prime raw materials essential to its welfare and defense. It was with the support of confirming facts and figures that young Henry Cabot Lodge could declare on the floor of the Senate in 1943 that the United States was now in some essential aspects to be included among the "have not" nations of the earth.

Equally meaningful was the closing of the American gates against manufactures from the Old World. When the overwhelming majority of the people of the United States had been engaged in agriculture, practically all their exports to the Old World consisted of foodstuffs and other raw materials. With the opening of the Far West, the very soil of America was literally "mined" and sent to Europe in the form of wheat, corn, and other products, at prices actually below the cost of production, counting in the cost the value of the wasted soil. American exports supplied food for millions of industrial workers in Great Britain and on the continent of Europe and raw materials for innumerable industries there. In those days Americans took in exchange an immense volume of manufactured products annually, thereby contributing to the unprecedented prosperity of the Old World.

As the final decades of the nineteenth century passed, however, the percentage of raw materials and foodstuffs included in the total export of the United States declined, while the percentage of manufactured goods in that export increased. Either on account of or despite the protective tariff, the United States as a manufacturing nation was becoming a stiffer competitor of Great Britain and Europe in all the world markets. For the years 1926–30 crude materials, crude foodstuffs, and manufactured foodstuffs amounted in dollar values to only 40.5% of the total export of the United States; while semimanufactures and finished manufactures amounted to 59.4% of the total. That too was a stubborn fact: the gates of the United States were closing on the once wide-open American market for Old World manufactures, and the gates for the outflow of American agricultural commodities were drawing closer together.

Nor did even the Democrats at any time venture to destroy the protective tariffs under which the relative export of foodstuffs and raw materials was falling and the relative export of manufactures was rising. In 1856 they had announced in their platform that "the time has come for the people of the United States to declare themselves in favor of free seas, and progressive free trade throughout the world." But never thereafter did they officially repeat that declaration or even attempt to make a slashing reduction of the protective rates to a mere revenue basis.

Their President, Cleveland, in 1887 severely criticized the existing rates of duty and called for modifications. But he was careful to declare: "In a readjustment of our tariff, the interests of American labor engaged in manufacture should be carefully considered, as well as the preservation of our manufactures. . . . The question of free trade is absolutely irrelevant."

From time to time Democratic platforms condemned the tariff as the "mother of the trusts" or as the cause of various economic distresses. Yet they contained no planks demanding free trade. When in 1913 the Democrats, led by President Wilson, got possession of both houses of Congress and had the legal power to cut tariff rates to a low point, they enacted a tariff bill that was strongly protective, despite many substantial reductions in rates.

Though they returned to power again in 1933, with Franklin

D. Roosevelt as President and a still larger majority, the Democrats refrained from a frontal attack on the tariff duties raised in the meantime by the Republicans to the highest point in American history. In fact President Roosevelt rather brusquely broke up the London Conference of 1933 at which experts had hoped to reduce tariff barriers and reach an agreement on a monetary standard of international trade. He slammed the door on all such undertakings, cut loose from the countries which still clung to the gold standard, and adopted a managed currency for the United States.

Although the Democrats in Congress later authorized President Roosevelt to make "reciprocal" trade treaties with other nations and modify tariff rates, they set limits to the modifications and to the term of his powers under the Reciprocal Trade Act. The act shifted the making of specific rates from Congress to the State Department, over which presided a free-trader, Cordell Hull. But the treaties made under the law, while favoring certain American productive interests as against others, were by no means free-trade treaties.

With endless reiteration the slogan of "lower trade barriers" was repeated, and professors of economics continued to recite the free-trade formulas of their "science," borrowed largely from Mid-Victorian England. Nevertheless the force of stubborn fact was working against projects for wide-open free trade throughout the world. Indeed all the other great nations went over to some form of managed economy, some in the direction of socialism—managed economy in full form.

While agriculture was rapidly expanding as virgin soil was brought under cultivation, while industries were multiplying as resources were exploited by crude methods, protests against the swelling torrent of immigration were ineffective. George Washington, Thomas Jefferson, and John Adams had warned their countrymen against free migration from countries whose people were wholly inexperienced in self-government; but the second generation of Americans mostly ignored their warnings.

It is true that by 1840 immigration had become so extensive that loud objections were raised against it. Protestants were alarmed by the great influx of Catholics. Old-stock Americans were incensed at seeing recently naturalized foreigners flocking to the polls "under bosses" in the cities, and taking possession of municipal governments. In fact opposition to the foreign vote took an aggressive form in the organization of the Native American party in 1848; and later, of the United American, or Know-Nothing, party.

Such protests were largely confined to the East, however, and leaders of the major political parties were skittish about listening to them. Often a presidential election turned on a few thousand votes and candidates quailed at the thought of offending any minority of voters that might have political influence.

At no time before the end of the nineteenth century did either of the major political parties officially call for closing the gates to any immigrants, except oriental coolies. On the contrary, the Republicans in 1864, for the moment styling themselves the Union party, actually endorsed the encouragement of immigration and enacted a law providing for the importation of immigrants bound to labor by contract in such a way as to ensure the payment of their passage.

Although sporadic criticism of untrammeled immigration continued, it was not until organized labor in the United States began a national struggle to maintain and improve standards of work and wages—standards of living—that effective pressure for restrictions on immigration appeared in Congress. Then candidates for the House and the Senate in many districts or states had to calculate whether they had better chances in appealing to the "labor vote" or to the "foreign vote." Other interests were enlisted on the side of restriction, but the labor interest was the best organized and the most persistent. In time its demands were heeded.

Excepting an act of Congress passed in 1875, forbidding the importation of prostitutes and alien convicts, and an act of 1882 excluding idiots, convicts, and persons obviously unable to take care of themselves, the first material restriction imposed on immigration by federal legislation was the Chinese Exclusion Act of 1882. States, to be sure, had attempted to bar paupers. Massachusetts in 1820, New York in 1824, and Maryland in 1833 had enacted laws directed to this end. But such efforts did not cut down immigration, for shipmasters who brought over human derelicts could land them at ports in other states.

It was only at the worst of pauper immigration that Congress struck in 1875 and 1882. The very nature of the two statutes indicated the reckless practices that had prevailed for nearly a hundred years. Prostitutes, criminals, persons likely to become public charges in poorhouses soon after their arrival, and other defectives had been entering the country freely. Now at last the gates were to be closed against such persons from foreign lands. Americans were feeling that they had all the burden they could bear in caring for defectives and delinquents.

The Chinese Exclusion Act of 1882 was the outcome of a long agitation against cheap Chinese labor, in the East as well as on the Pacific coast. In connection with early efforts of the United States to force open the ports of China to American merchants and adventurers, the ports of the United States had been opened to Chinese immigrants by treaty provisions. Americans apparently could not, with a straight face, declare to the Chinese government that they had full freedom to enter China at their pleasure, without granting the Chinese similar rights in the United States. At all events in the treaty of 1868 between the United States and China, the high contracting parties "cordially" recognized "the mutual advantage of the free migration and emigration of their citizens and subjects . . . for purposes of curiosity, of trade or as permanent residents." Taking the cordiality of the American invitation as genuine, and stimulated by appeals of American employers for cheap labor, especially in railway construction, Chinese immigrants soon began to press into the states of the Pacific coast, and many found their way as far east as the factories of Massachusetts.

Very soon conflicts arose between American workers and their Chinese competitors, on many grounds, and as early as 1879 Congress passed a bill virtually providing for the exclusion of Chinese immigrants, in defiance of the treaty with China. President Hayes vetoed the bill. As an act of courtesy a commission was sent to China for the purpose of revising treaty relations. A new treaty was negotiated in 1880 and finally under its terms Congress in 1882 suspended the admission of Chinese laborers for a term of years—later making exclusion permanent.

The enforcement of this law led to constant friction with the Chinese government but efforts to weaken its categorical terms were in vain. The treaty of 1868 had definitely stated that nothing in its provisions should be held to confer the right of naturalization on the Chinese in the United States or on Americans in China. That provision for "reciprocity" could be kept by both parties; and it came about that there was no large "Chinese vote" to worry American politicians.

Responding also to demands from organized labor, Congress passed in 1885 the Contract Labor law—a blow at the importation of any cheap labor by employers seeking to break strikes or cut wages. The act forbade persons, companies, partnerships, and corporations to prepay the passage of aliens or in any way to encourage their immigration under a contract—written, oral, or implied—to perform services or service of any kind in the United States.

Employers soon found a vulnerable spot in the law. They evaded the act by issuing notices that laborers entering the country could find employment at specific places on their arrival. Steamship companies, nearly all of them owned in foreign countries, aided American employers by distributing such notices in Europe and bringing over shiploads of laborers who had full knowledge that they were to work at certain shops, factories, or mines. On renewed petition from organized labor, Congress made the alien Contract Labor law stricter by amendments passed in 1887 and 1888.

It was in connection with efforts to check the practice of drumming up and importing strike-breaking and wage-cutting laborers that Congress, in the act of 1888, introduced a new principle into immigration legislation. As early as 1850 demands had arisen in Eastern cities for the deportation of alien paupers who, soon after their arrival, had to be put into American poorhouses and supported at public expense. Against such demands the government of Württemberg in Germany had protested. It had been sending paupers to the United States to get rid of them and avoid its own responsibility; and it now objected to the idea that the United States could send them back. But at that time American politicians were so intimidated by the foreign vote that they enacted no laws to prevent even such flagrant abuses by foreign interests.

Not until 1888 did Congress provide for the deportation of aliens who had unlawfully entered the United States. In that year it served notice on employers, steamship companies, and foreign governments that the United States had the right and intended to deport aliens at will; that steamship companies or employers guilty of abetting the unlawful entry of aliens would have to pay the expense of carrying them back to their native countries.

Agitation over the exclusion of the Chinese, who unlike Europeans were few in numbers in the United States and so without political power, was accompanied by growing objections to free immigration from all quarters. By 1888, Chinese laborers, contract laborers, insane persons, idiots, and persons likely to become public charges had been denied entrance to the United States. The laws were loosely enforced, but they were at least written in the books. Then, in 1891, Congress grew sterner.

To the list of classes excluded it now added paupers specifically, polygamists, persons suffering from loathsome or dangerous contagious diseases, and, subject to qualifications, persons whose passage had been paid in whole or in part by others. The law also stiffened the enforcement of restrictions imposed by prior acts, especially the prohibition forbidding employers, steamship companies, and their agents to recruit immigrants abroad by advertisements, inducements, and promises of any kind.

In a careful revision of immigration restrictions, in 1903, after the assassination of President McKinley by Leon Czolgosz, a German Pole, Congress increased the list of persons excluded. It proscribed, among others, anarchists and persons believing in and advocating the overthrow of all governments by violence and the assassination of public officials. Again, in 1907, Congress added to the roll of persons excluded. By this time it was bold enough to shut out consumptives, unmistakable imbeciles, and feeble-minded persons in general.

☆

As the gates against free and easy immigration were pushed together inch by inch, opposition to additional restrictions and to the full enforcement of existing laws became consolidated; and it was strengthened by the support of the vested interests. Many American citizens insisted that the old doctrine of the United States as an asylum for the oppressed of all lands was still valid and should never be infringed. They could point, in confirmation of their view, to the inscription on the Statue of Liberty, unveiled in 1886, four years after the passage of the Chinese Exclusion Act:

> Give me your tired, your poor,
> Your huddled masses yearning to breathe free,
> The wretched refuse of your teeming shore.
> Send those, the homeless, tempest-tost to me,
> I lift my lamp beside the golden door!

They argued that sturdy sons and daughters of toil from other lands helped to promote the rapid development of the nation's resources, added to its wealth, enriched its culture, and fortified the love of liberty.

Other opponents of restriction were neither so tenderhearted nor so disinterested as the advocates of liberty in the abstract. At the turn of the century when a new immigration bill was up in Washington, the general agent of the North German Lloyd Steamship Company, then engaged in carrying immigrants from various European ports, wrote to his local agents all over the United States: "Immigration bill comes up in the House Wednesday. Wire your congressman, our expense, protesting against proposed exclusion and requesting bill be defeated, informing him that vote in favor means defeat in next election." Editors of newspapers in which the steamship company carried advertising were also informed by wire that they were expected to oppose the bill.

To such vested interests in the opposition were joined others: American railway interests which transported trainloads of immigrants to the West; employers ever struggling to keep wages low; and a horde of "labor bosses" who profited by supplying laborers of their national origins to big industries, often in the process robbing and cheating their own people in the United States.

The situation was complicated for advocates of additional restrictions and for immigrants themselves, by immigration agents operating alone or in connection with steamship companies and American employers of cheap labor. In Europe these agents gave to prospective emigrants a rosy view of the money they could quickly make in the United States, aided them in evading the immigration laws, and offered them all kinds of inducements for the adventure. In the United States they herded immigrants into blocs according to their national origins, found employment for them, supplied strikebreakers on occasion, and despoiled them of their earnings.

Deluded by the promises and frequently finding their new conditions harsher than those they had suffered at home, many immigrants turned upon the country of adoption in a natural wrath, aggravating the discontent and radical agitations among Americans themselves and evoking more resentment against the influx of foreigners. Extreme radicals joined the hue and cry against restrictions, on a Marxian theory that the worse the plight of workers became, in the United States as well as everywhere else, the sooner would be the revolutionary spring into their kingdom of heaven. On such grounds they harried the American Federation of Labor in its efforts to maintain and raise the standards of life for industrial workers by limiting immigration. Thus, while seeking to keep the gates open, they played into the hands of the very interests which exploited immigrants.

The United States Immigration Commission, appointed to make extensive inquiries into various aspects of immigration, reported in 1911 that economic interests deliberately organized were mainly responsible for the tremendous inflow of Europeans: "The present emigration from Europe to the United States is in the largest measure due to economic causes." Immigrants already here, it conceded, incited immigration by writing enthusiastic letters home to relatives and friends and by sending money to bring them over; but a considerable portion of it was artificially stimulated by "quasi labor agents" and by the "many thousands of steamship ticket agents and subagents operating in the emigrant-furnishing districts of southern and eastern Europe." In other words, the commission found that, apart from the actions of former immigrants settled in the United States, the promotion of immigration had become a money-making game highly profitable to those engaged in it.

☆

Now an old cry, which had been little heeded in the political din of the Jacksonian era, was revived and reinforced: "Immigration is a peril to the Republic, to the institutions of self-government and liberty." Henry Cabot Lodge the elder, senator from Massachusetts, took it up, despite his affiliation with Republican industrialists in search of workers at low wages. Though opposed by many members of his party, especially by Joseph Cannon, Speaker of the House of Representatives, Senator Lodge organized a new drive against immigration. The only question with him was the formula under which it was to be effected. What new and large class of immigrants was to be excluded?

An answer was provided by a proposed literacy test. So far Congress had excluded the Chinese coolies, contract laborers, paupers, idiots, polygamists, anarchists, and other special classes, but no barrier had been erected against persons totally illiterate, such as were now coming from southern and eastern Europe in enormous numbers. A literacy test would push the gates closer together. And on this proposal both Senator Lodge and Samuel Gompers agreed. "So far as I remember," wrote Gompers, "this is the only issue upon which I have ever found myself in accord with Senator Lodge."

Late in 1912, Congress passed a bill designed to shut the gates on illiterates from Europe. Early the next year President Taft vetoed it, and its supporters in Congress could not muster enough votes to carry it over executive disapproval. The succeeding Congress passed another bill similar in principle. President Wilson vetoed it, regarding it as a serious departure from traditional policies. Again Congress failed to muster the two-thirds majority necessary to make it a law in spite of the presidential opposition.

In the following session Congress renewed the battle by passing another bill embodying the literacy test. When President Wilson also vetoed this one Congress defied him by rolling up a huge majority and making it a law without his signature, on February 5, 1917. At this time a great war was raging in Europe, immigration was curtailed anyhow, and there was no opportunity to measure its results in "normal" conditions; but the intentions of the act were clearly and firmly expressed in its provisions.

With certain exceptions, especially affecting persons fleeing from religious persecution, the law of 1917 excluded "all [European] aliens over sixteen years of age, physically capable of reading, who cannot read the English language, or some other language or dialect, including Hebrew and Yiddish." Besides this barrier raised particularly against immigration from southern and eastern Europe, the law of 1917 added to the number of classes of persons already excluded under previous legislation and plugged up many crannies through which evasions had been effected. Moreover, it supplemented the Chinese Exclusion Act by placing an absolute bar against practically all immigration from Asia, except from Japan. Immigration from that country, however, had been cut down since 1907 under the Gentlemen's Agreement between President Theodore Roosevelt and the Japanese government.

Designed to curtail immigration from southern and eastern Europe, two great areas of illiteracy, the law of 1917 by no means guaranteed a reduction in the total number of immigrants admitted annually to the United States. Like other "qualitative" laws, it merely defined the character or quality of persons to be deemed admissible. In legal terms the gates were still wide open to any number of qualified immigrants.

At the close of the first World War all signs pointed to an enormous increase in the annual migration from Europe to America. Then Congress struck at it decisively by putting numerical limits on immigration. By an emergency act in 1921 it fixed the number of aliens of any nationality, to be admitted annually, at three per cent of the number of the foreign-born persons of such nationality actually resident in the United States in 1910 as determined by the census of that year. This cut the total immigration from Europe to 309,556 for the fiscal year 1921–22, to about one fourth the number of immigrants admitted in 1913. As a positive quantitative cut in immigration, the act showed a determination on the part of Congress to put an end to free and easy immigration for all time.

Having made this provision, in the face of an outburst of objections, Congress elaborated it in 1924. In the act of that year it placed a maximum limit on the total annual immigration from Europe—temporarily at 150,000. This number it apportioned among various European countries on the basis of two per cent of the number of foreign-born persons of the respective nationalities, as determined by the census of 1890, with a maximum quota of 100. The return to the census of 1890, which meant a clear discrimination against the countries of southern and eastern Europe, raised a storm of protest from people affected by it. But Congress refused to bow to the tempest. It insisted on making the drastic cut, with its discrimination against southern and eastern Europe. And, responding to labor and other demands from the Pacific coast, Congress in the act of 1924 also placed an absolute bar on the immigration of laborers from Japan; it overthrew the Gentlemen's Agreement of 1907 and assigned to Japan the same position as other oriental countries, in respect of immigration.

Subsequently, as provided in the act of 1924 and later amendments, the total number of quota immigrants for each year was fixed at 154,000 and the quota to be allowed to each foreign country coming under the law was established by a complicated process of calculation. The census of 1920 was taken as the basis. The number of persons in the United States belonging to each nationality in that year was estimated. The ratio of such number to the total number of inhabitants in the United States was then ascertained—as amounting to a certain percentage of the whole. Finally, to each nation entitled to send emigrants under the act was given a number—a quota equal to this percentage of the total number, 154,000, to be annually admitted. That is, for example, if the number of persons of a given national origin in the United States was two per cent of the American population in 1920, the immigrant quota of their country in Europe was two per cent of 154,000, or 3080.

The spirit of the national resolve against free immigration was expressed in the House of Representatives by Knud Wefall, of Minnesota, when, referring to the bill of 1924, he said: "The question [of immigration] is our own to solve in the manner we see fit to solve it. . . . We do not intend to close the door because we were here first but because it is our door. We are now under a reaction of the effects of the first World War. . . . We now want to close the door more tightly while we take stock of ourselves."

The die was cast. The proportion of foreign-born Americans was to decline swiftly. The continent had been rounded out. No more free land beckoned pioneers to the West. Crude exploitation of the continental domain by crude labor and crude capitalism had come to an end. Science might raise visions of wider opportunities for the production of wealth by other methods. But whether such visions were to be realized or not depended upon the competence of the people in the United States to order their economy and govern themselves. There could be no return to the state of things existing in 1900 or 1880 or 1870. And as threats were made in Congress from time to time to reduce immigration to a bare trickle or stop it entirely, prospects of removing the restrictions faded. Only immigrants from Canada, Newfoundland, Mexico, Cuba, Haiti, the Dominican Republic, and the independent countries of Central and South America were exempted from the quota restrictions; even they were subject to numerous restrictions. The gates of the once wide-open "asylum for the oppressed of all lands" had been brought together with a bang that awakened repercussions throughout Europe and Asia. Not even the war gesture to China in 1943, repealing total exclusion and allotting her a quota of 105 immigrants a year, altered this situation.

CHAPTER XXVI

World War and Aftermath

IN THE SUMMER of 1914 the interests of the American people were especially directed to pressing domestic problems. The presidency and Congress were under the control of the Democrats, committed to the reforms of the "New Freedom"—and to the emancipation of the country from its "masters . . . the combined capitalists and manufacturers of the United States," as the Chief Executive of the nation phrased the issue. Since 1899 the Democrats had fumed against imperialism and the entanglements in world politics which imperialism of necessity involves. Now the Department of State was headed by William Jennings Bryan, who had so intransigently combined advocacy of world peace, through treaties renouncing war, with opposition to imperialism.

Despite this concern with urgent domestic affairs, the rivalry of imperialist Powers in Europe and Asia was widely known in the United States. For years the news from Europe and Asia had carried stories respecting the alliance of Germany, Austria, and Italy on the one side; and working agreements between Britain, Japan, France, and Russia on the other side. News reports, books, articles, and essays in increasing volume had made it clear in America that all those Powers were engaged in a frantic race to build up their armaments for war, piling taxes and debts upon peoples already groaning under heavy financial burdens. Observers of world operations along such lines, including President Wilson, suspected that this rivalry among the foreign Powers, if it continued unabated, would end in a holocaust of war, the most destructive that mankind had ever experienced. And yet all that distant quarreling among great nations had not diverted the

American people from concern with their domestic problems.

☆

It was upon a people largely intent upon their own purposes that the calamity of European war burst during the first days of August 1914. When the news of the war came, shocking though it was, the general sentiment of Americans was undoubtedly opposed to participation in the conflict. On August 4 President Wilson issued a proclamation declaring the neutrality of the United States and the following day he supplemented it by another in the same vein. Two weeks later he made a special appeal to the American people to observe the letter and spirit of neutrality: "The effect of the war upon the United States will depend upon what American citizens say or do. Every man who really loves America will act and speak in the true spirit of neutrality."

Despite the President's admonition, the American public was soon deeply agitated by the war and the course of its events, especially as propagandists from both parties to the conflict in Europe descended in hordes upon the country to elicit American support. Many Americans of English descent frankly sympathized with the Entente Allies. On the other hand many Americans of German descent publicly professed their attachment to the Fatherland. Irish, remembering their own history, could scarcely conceal their satisfaction over the thought of a British defeat in the war. Jews, recalling the terrible persecutions which had recently befallen their people in Russia, as a rule deemed the Germans more civilized and more worthy of victory. On the whole, however, the sympathy of a popular majority was on the side of the Allies. Even so, that did not mean that the Americans wanted or expected to become actual fighters in the war.

But as neutrals Americans had certain historic rights under international law and were carrying on activities that were seriously affected by the war in Europe on land and on the high seas. Among the long-established rights of neutrals were the following:

1. Neutrals may sell goods to, and trade with, belligerents in a war—both munitions and goods of peace, or non-contraband goods.

2. Belligerents may lawfully suppress this trade by imposing a blockade on each other to stop the passage of ships carrying such goods; but a blockade to be lawful must be effective, that is, carried out by a sufficient number of patrolling war vessels.

3. If a peaceful merchant ship, whether belonging to a neutral

or an enemy, is caught by a belligerent, it may be seized and confiscated in certain circumstances, but it must not be sunk or destroyed without provision for the safety of the crew and passengers.

Under international law and the laws and policies of the United States, it was the duty of President Wilson to see that these rights of Americans to engage in commerce as citizens of a neutral Power were enforced against both the belligerents in Europe. Thus he was compelled, as the Chief Executive of the nation, to consider American complaints against violations of neutral rights and to act on violations by the parties to the war.

At the outset of the conflict, the government of Great Britain made two decisions affecting the rights of Americans as neutrals. It proclaimed an iron blockade on the ports of the Central Powers and the ports of neighboring neutrals through which goods might pass to those Powers. The perils from German submarines made it impossible for Great Britain to sustain an effective blockade by keeping rings of ships near the blockaded ports; yet in spite of this fact, she declared her blockade effective. The second British decision reduced the number of non-contraband goods which neutrals had a right to sell to belligerents and other neutrals, if they could get them through the blockade. In time the British government included in the list of forbidden goods nearly every important article of commerce, including grain, other foodstuffs, and cotton, hitherto regarded as non-contraband.

Numerous British actions invaded the rights of Americans as neutrals to trade and travel. Great Britain insisted on stopping and seizing American ships bound for neutral countries bordering on Germany, such as Holland, Denmark, Norway, and Sweden. This she did on the ground that the goods they carried would eventually go to Germany or release goods in those neutral countries for sale to Germany. In November 1914 the British government declared that Germans were sowing mines in the open seas and proclaimed the whole North Sea a war zone closed to neutral shippers, subject to British orders.

Against these decisions by the British government, the State Department at Washington made strong objections. It asserted that they were unlawful, violated American rights, and were not necessary to British self-preservation.

Meanwhile the German government was also defying international law and endangering American lives as well as property on the high seas. In 1915, Germany proclaimed all the waters around

Great Britain a war zone and announced that German ships, meaning her submarines now in use, would sink every enemy vessel found within that zone. Under the established international law Americans had the right to travel all the seas on their own merchant ships, on British ships, or on the ships of other countries. If such a merchant ship was caught by an enemy war vessel, the safety and lives of passengers were to be protected by the captor. But a submarine ordinarily could not take on board the passengers and crew of a captured ship about to be sunk. Hence a new instrument of war entered into the extension of the war and helped to destroy the code of international law built up by agreements among the nations.

Against the German threat to merchant shipping in the zone marked out, President Wilson lodged a protest in February 1915. In very clear language he informed the German government that it would be held accountable for American lives destroyed in its submarine campaign. Nevertheless, on May 7, a great British ship, the *Lusitania*, with American passengers and some munitions on board, was torpedoed by a German submarine near the coast of Ireland and 114 American men, women, and children went down to death on the sinking vessel.

To this deed President Wilson objected vehemently and declared that the government of the United States would not "omit any word or act necessary to the performance of its sacred duty of maintaining the rights of the United States and its citizens and of safeguarding their free exercise and enjoyment." The German government replied evasively. In two additional notes to it, President Wilson repeated his objections and warnings. At length in September 1915 the German government replied: "Liners will not be sunk by our submarines without warning and without safety of the lives of non-combatants, provided the liners do not try to escape or offer resistance." It looked as if President Wilson had won a great diplomatic victory.

Although war agitations continued to fan excitement in the United States, as the presidential campaign of 1916 drew near, the majority of the people still seemed in a mood to keep out of the European conflict. At least such appeared to be the judgment of political leaders. With the Progressive party now dying, the Republicans, counting on their recovered unity for success at the polls, nominated Charles E. Hughes as their candidate and in their platform declared that they would maintain American rights "at home and abroad." At the same time they announced: "We desire peace, the peace of justice and right, and believe in maintaining a straight and honest neutrality between the belligerents in the great war in Europe." Renominating President Wilson unanimously, the Democrats praised "the splendid diplomatic victories of our great President, who has preserved the vital interests of our government and its citizens and kept us out of war." The campaign was boisterous and the election was close. At first it was reported that Hughes had carried the country but belated returns from California shifted the balance and gave the presidency to Wilson for a second term by an electoral vote of 277 to 254.

Hoping, perhaps, that he might be helpful in bringing the war to an end, President Wilson, soon after his triumph at the polls, addressed "peace" notes to the belligerents in Europe. His appeal for a peace conference was fruitless. Growing firmer in his resolve to intervene in the diplomacy of the war, he declared to the Senate, in January 1917, that the United States ought to take part in the establishment of peace on certain principles: "peace without victory"; the right of nations to have liberty and self-government; independence of Poland; freedom of the seas; reduction of armaments; and the abandonment of entangling alliances. A few days later the German government announced that it would renew its unlimited submarine warfare. Then without reviving the verbal argument with Berlin, President Wilson dismissed the German ambassador in Washington, Count von Bernstorff, and severed relations with his government.

Within two months six American ships were torpedoed and sunk. By April it was plain that this time Germany would not be stayed or turned in pursuing her peculiar methods of warfare. On April 2, 1917, President Wilson called upon Congress to "declare the present course of Germany to be in fact nothing less than war against the government of the United States." Four days later the war resolution was passed by Congress with a few dissenting votes—fifty in the House of Representatives and six in the Senate.

Having adopted the war resolution, Congress began to frame and pass measures for winning the war, which slashed deeply into the ways of American life. It quickly decided that a volunteer army would not be sufficient for the task ahead or indeed founded on correct principles, and that a great armed force must be raised by a draft of able-bodied males. At first it fixed the age limits at twenty-one to thirty-one inclusive and later at eighteen to forty-five inclusive. To support the armed forces, Congress provided for the floating of loans running into the billions. It increased taxes in every direction, devised new taxes, and raised the rates of income taxes to the incredible figure of sixty-three per cent in the highest brackets—a figure that must have made the eyes of radicals and conservatives surviving from 1896 start from their sockets. Heavier taxes were laid on inheritances. A high excess profits tax was imposed on corporations and partnerships.

Upon the President, Congress conferred broad power to control, regulate, and commandeer natural resources, industries, labor, the sale and distribution of food supplies—in fact to regiment men and women, all callings and occupations, and all activities, in the interest of winning the war. At the same time freedom of press and speech was put under the government ban by Espionage and Sedition Acts, the most severe yet passed in the history of the country. Never before had life and property in the United States been subjected to restrictions so numerous, so onerous, and so deep-thrusting.

A disciplined master of the English language, skilled in the art of clothing noble sentiments in lofty and telling phrases, President Wilson employed his talents in framing war aims and delivering addresses on the subject to Congress, the American people, and the world. In his earlier diplomatic notes to Great Britain and Germany he had dwelt upon American rights of commerce and travel. In his war message of April 2, 1917, he sought to lift the war above such practical considerations. "The World," he said, "must be made safe for democracy. Its peace must be planted upon the tested foundations of political liberty. We have no selfish ends to serve. We desire no conquest, no dominion. We seek no indemnities for ourselves, no material compensation for the sacrifices we shall freely make. We are but one of the champions of the rights of mankind."

Later the President expounded the "war for democracy" as also a "war to end war," to establish permanent peace throughout the world, to make certain territorial changes in the interest of oppressed nationalities, and to force the adoption of new measures for the conduct of international relations. His specific objectives he summarized in fourteen points in a message to Congress on January 8, 1918. Chief among his points of political significance were these: open treaties of peace, openly arrived at, to supplant secret treaties, intrigues, and alliances; freedom of navigation on the seas; the removal of trade barriers among nations, "so far as possible"; reduction of armaments; more liberty for the nationalities in Austria-Hungary; and an association of nations to afford guarantees of rights and peace for all nations, large and small.

Respecting territorial matters, President Wilson favored the re-

CHIEF THEATER OF AMERICAN ACTION IN THE WORLD WAR

storation of Belgium, which Germany had invaded and overrun during the war; righting the wrong done to France in Alsace-

Lorraine; changes in Italian frontiers for transferring Italians to the homeland; restoration of Serbia and Rumania; alterations in the Turkish Empire; the independence of Poland; and fair treatment for Russia, then in the throes of revolution. What about subject peoples of European empires? Colonial claims, President Wilson maintained, should be adjusted in the interest of the subject peoples.

In the prosecution of the war—widened in December 1917 to include Austria-Hungary—detachments of American naval forces were sent to European waters to co-operate in the hunt for German submarines and to convoy merchant ships carrying supplies. In June 1917 the vanguard of the army, the American Expeditionary Force, commanded by General John J. Pershing, reached France. Before the end of the war over 2,000,000 American soldiers were sent to France; while nearly 2,000,000 more were in training at home for service abroad if needed. By October 1917, American soldiers were in European trenches. From that time forward they took part in increasing numbers in the great battles which finally subdued Germany and Austria-Hungary.

When the armistice came on November 11, 1918, more than 75,000 American soldiers and sailors had sacrificed their lives in the struggle. More than 200,000 had been wounded or were missing or were in German prison camps. In the meantime the United States had furnished to the Allies enormous financial credits and great quantities of supplies for civil and military uses.

In January 1919 agents of the Allied and Associated Powers met at Paris to draw up the treaties of the war settlement. President Wilson was there in person, accompanied by a peace commission which he had chosen himself. For months the delegates at the Paris conference labored and disputed over the terms to be imposed on the vanquished. Early in May the treaty with Germany was finished and, on June 28, German delegates, with bitterness of protest against its terms, signed it at Versailles. Afterward treaties were completed with Austria, Hungary, Bulgaria, and Turkey. In all these proceedings, Russia, still in the toils of the revolution that began in 1917, took no part.

By the various treaties the map of Europe and a part of Asia was refashioned. Alsace-Lorraine was handed over to France. Other parts of Germany were joined to neighboring countries. Poland won independence. Russia was reduced in size by the creation of small states on her western borders. Czechoslovakia and Yugoslavia were brought into existence. The German colonies in Africa were transferred to Great Britain and France, to be held as mandates under the League of Nations. The province of Shantung, which Germany had seized in China, was given to Japan for temporary administration. The German navy was surrendered and the German military power diminished to a mere shadow of its former strength.

In several respects the terms imposed on defeated Germany did not conform to the war aims which President Wilson had so eloquently proclaimed to the world. But compared with the terms which Germany had imposed on conquered Russia at Brest Litovsk the preceding year, the provisions of the Versailles Treaty were mild. Indeed if it had not been for President Wilson's moderating influence, they would have been harsher, and the government of France would have taken immediate steps to occupy and hold Germany down by military force for an indefinite period. President Wilson himself thought that the Versailles Treaty had many faults but he expressed the hope that its injustices would be corrected in peaceful councils of the Powers under the association of nations for which a section of the treaty provided, largely on his insistence.

According to the provisions of this section, known as the Covenant, a League of Nations was to be established. Within the League were to be included the Allied and Associated Powers, countries that had been neutral in the war, and in time the countries defeated in the war. The League was to be governed by an assembly consisting of one delegate from each country and a council composed of representatives from the great Powers, to be elected by the assembly.

The nations in the League were bound by the Covenant to keep the peace themselves and to join in protecting one another against external aggression. They were to submit their disputes to the council for arbitration and inquiry. If a member violated its pledge to follow peaceful methods, measures to coerce it might be taken by the League. Provisions were to be made for disarmament. Thus if the United States joined the League it would be under obligations to observe the rules of the Covenant and to take part regularly and continuously in the adjustment of controversies arising among the nations of the earth. Only by becoming a member of the League and sharing its responsibilities, President Wilson averred, could a lasting peace be achieved for the United States and all other countries.

In the summer of 1919 the Versailles Treaty, including the Covenant of the League of Nations, was laid before the Senate and people of the United States for discussion and action. Hitherto many plans for permanent world peace had been proposed and debated in the United States. Now large and loose theories were reduced to a very definite scheme for a League of Nations which, its sponsors claimed, would guarantee permanent peace. Instead of many nebulous projects, the people now had before them a blueprint for a world association and parliament.

By the very nature of politics, the debate over the League became entangled with debates over foreign and domestic affairs in general and particular. The Covenant of the League was tied into the treaty, which prescribed severe terms for the Germans. Americans of German origin made all they could of that fact. Americans of Irish origin disliked the provision giving Australia, Canada, New Zealand, and South Africa, as well as Great Britain and Ireland, each a delegate in the League Assembly, thus strengthening British power in the League. Other critics assailed the transfer of Shantung to Japan instead of to China, its former owner. The war had been unpopular in many sections of the United States among Americans of old and new stocks and, now that freedom of discussion was partially restored, opponents of the war could voice their dissatisfaction with the treaty which came out of the war.

A large number of liberals and radicals, who might have favored the idea of a league of nations in the abstract, were loath to do so on account of revelations respecting some sordid origins of the war that made them question the possible efficacy of the proposed League and its setup. In January 1919, for instance, a New York newspaper published a number of secret treaties by which Russia, Great Britain, France, and Italy, either before or during the war, had agreed to divide the spoils at the end of the conflict. These startling documents disclosed deep-seated imperialistic ambitions as among the real war aims of the Entente Allies. Moreover, while peace negotiations were pending, American troops, without a declaration of war by Congress, were waging war on Russia, a former associate of the United States, at Archangel and in Siberia —solely under orders of President Wilson.

Into the confused situation was injected the question: Who is now to govern the United States—League of Nations or no League? Dissatisfaction with the Democratic party, for various reasons, was intensifying. In the congressional campaign of 1918, while the war was still raging, President Wilson appealed to the voters to elect a Democratic Congress for the support of his policies. On November 5, 1918, the people had their first opportunity since the outbreak of the war to pass judgment on the Democratic administration, and their verdict was emphatic against it. The Republicans won a majority in both houses of Congress. This outcome, Theodore Roosevelt declared, was tantamount to a national repudiation of President Wilson's leadership and doctrines. No doubt some Republican enmity for the Democratic party and its President was transferred to the League of Nations, just as some Democratic enmity was enlisted in its behalf.

Reflecting the popular divisions of opinion, the Senate was in turbulence. At one extreme in positions was a large group of senators prepared to ratify the treaty as drafted and to approve the League of Nations as incorporated in the treaty. At the other extreme was a small number of irreconcilables, among whom Senator Borah was prominent, determined to keep the United States out of further European entanglements by defeating American participation in the League. Between the extremes stood Republican and Democratic senators ready to vote for the League if some modifications or reservations were made in its plan. Caught between opposing tempers, President Wilson refused to make any significant compromises as the debate went on for weeks and months. At length on March 19, 1920, both the treaty and the League definitely failed, by eight votes, to receive the two-thirds majority of senatorial votes required by the Constitution for adoption.

In the national election of that autumn a "solemn referendum" was taken on the League of Nations. Nominating James Cox, of Ohio, for President and Franklin D. Roosevelt for Vice-President, the Democrats championed the League before the country. Choosing as their standard-bearer Warren G. Harding, of Ohio, and Calvin Coolidge as candidate for Vice-President, the Republicans assailed the Democratic administration from top to bottom. Harding condemned the proposed League but vaguely approved an indefinite kind of international association in the interest of peace. Some of his supporters endorsed the League outright and asserted that the election of Harding would mean participation in it. Other supporters, with equal assurance, told the voters that a Republican triumph would keep the United States out of the League and all such foreign entanglements.

Whatever the election returns of 1920 actually did imply, as a verdict for or against the League, there was no question about the party outcome: the Democrats were blown from power in a tornado of ballots. Harding carried every Northern state and even Tennessee in the South. His popular vote was 16,150,000 as against 9,140,000 cast for Cox. Nearly 1,000,000 votes, the heaviest Socialist vote ever polled, were cast for the Socialist candidate, Eugene V. Debs, then in prison for having denounced the war as an imperialist and capitalist conflict. So the repudiation of President Wilson's policies which had been foreshadowed in the congressional elections of 1918 seemed to be confirmed and the Republicans came back to power—for what proved to be a twelve-year period.

☆

Irrespective of the New Freedom's merits as a political slogan and as exemplified between March 4, 1913, and August 1, 1914, the accomplishments of Wilson's administration had not closed the long struggle over domestic policies, including those affecting the distribution of wealth in the United States. Nor had it brought about a high degree of economic felicity by the summer of 1914. Business had in reality entered a slump during the preceding winter.

An expert in labor conditions, John B. Andrews, reported: "From the point of view of the wage earner seeking work, the year 1914 was the worst since the year following the financial panic of 1907." According to an authority on industrial tendencies, they too were moving downward, "in most instances reaching such an alarming state as to place the year on a par with the severe depression of 1907–08." If agriculture was in a better state than business, farmers were far from satisfied with the prices of their produce in the dull markets.

And as the Democrats, in their customary style, had promised prosperity through "lowering trade barriers," so the Republicans in their customary style laid the slump to the reduction of the protective tariff by the Democrats. Whatever the reason for it, an implacable discontent with the New Freedom was abroad in the land—a revulsion which materially reduced the Democratic majority in the House of Representatives in the congressional elections of 1914 and destroyed it in the congressional elections of 1916 when Wilson was re-elected President.

About this time the economic slump disappeared temporarily. The war in Europe had scarcely started in the summer of 1914 when Great Britain and France began to buy enormous quantities of farm produce, manufactures, and semifinished raw materials in the United States. From month to month their purchases increased in volume, as they poured their own money into this country and began to borrow huge sums from American banks and investors. By the end of 1916 most branches of manufacturing and agriculture were booming; unemployment had almost disappeared; wages were higher; businessmen and farmers were gathering in large profits.

Although this spurt of prosperity before the United States entered the war was largely due to the purchases made by the Entente Allies, Wilson's partisans attributed it in some measure to the New Freedom. But leading Democrats, including the President himself, knew that it was mainly artificial and that the defeat of the Allies or the ending of the war would bring in its train an economic crash in the United States. In fact, to some members of the administration this was an argument for enlarging the borrowing facilities of the Allies and, finally, for entering the war directly. At all events, after the United States did enter the war, the business and agricultural boom grew to huge dimensions.

Yet even during the war and economic boom the domestic struggle over matters of capital and labor, over conservation of resources, over problems of taxation, and all the other issues relative to American living standards continued among the people and on the floors of Congress. Indeed, in some respects, the war magnified the problems and sharpened the issues.

Opposition to the war, such as it was, and to various measures adopted in carrying on the war, prevailed largely among the farmers and industrial workers who had fostered populistic or socialistic movements during preceding years. The arrest, prosecution, and imprisonment of war dissenters and labor agitators, notably Debs, revealed that the war for liberty and democracy abroad could be accompanied by stern measures of repression at home, under the very administration of President Wilson, world spokesman for those exalted war aims.

The social order was disturbed by strikes, numerous and widespread. Progressive and radical Democrats and Republicans in Congress tried to "make the rich pay for the war," to impose heavy taxes on profits, and to "restore the government to the plain people." During the war they also developed postwar plans for government ownership of the railways and for other features of "social reconstruction" in the United States.

It was generally understood that the domestic struggle would go on after the war and that provisions would have to be made for dealing with the economic crisis bound to follow the peace. But President Wilson proposed remedies couched primarily in international terms. The United States, he said, would have to join the League of Nations and promote world trade in order to find market outlets for the enlarged productive capacity of American industry and agriculture. Americans must do this, he insisted, "or you have ruined the United States." Even the settlement of controversies between capital and labor within America, he contended, cannot be effected unless we have "frank discussion" and "friendly discussion" and "those are the very things that are offered to us among the nations of the world by the Covenant of the League of Nations."

Years before, Republican leaders had promised manufacturers and farmers ever-expanding markets and prosperity, if they would support imperialism. Now President Wilson proposed to resolve pressing domestic difficulties in industry and agriculture by having the United States join the League of Nations and by promoting the reduction of protective tariffs, by opening American ports more freely to commodities from foreign lands.

By their actions, however, a large majority of the American people—Democrats as well as Republicans, Progressives, and Socialists—took issue with President Wilson on this point. They eventually made it evident that, in their opinion, joining the League of Nations or trying to drum up more foreign trade would not settle any of the major domestic disputes respecting national economy, poverty, or labor relations; or, for that matter, advance the brotherhood of mankind very far. Indeed in February 1917, while the entrance of the United States into the "war for democracy" was imminent, Congress passed, over President Wilson's veto, an act restricting immigration, and put it into effect May 1, 1917. Again, under pressure from President Wilson himself, Congress passed, in 1918, the Webb Act, which eased up the Sherman Anti-Trust law and permitted American businessmen to form combinations, loose cartels, in the export trade, for the purpose of combatting foreign concerns more vigorously in the international competition for world markets. As a matter of fact the conviction was generally held that, whatever might be done about the League of Nations, the Americans would still have immense tasks to perform at home and that the struggle among domestic interests was not likely to be stopped or materially modified by even the most fortunate posture of international affairs.

The period of Republican rule from 1921–33, commonly described as the age of "normalcy," was marked by a foreign policy that practically ignored the League of Nations, though "observers" were sent to its headquarters at Geneva from time to time. Imperialist activities conceived as in the interest of trade were pushed everywhere. Former associates in the war were urged to pay the war debts they owed to the United States. The tariffs on imported manufactures were twice raised. Peace was made with Germany, reserving to the United States all the rights against that nation, established by the Treaty of Versailles, which the Senate had rejected.

American investors were encouraged to lend billions of dollars to Germany, thereby helping to restore her economic power and enabling her to make payments on the reparations to the victors in the war, especially on the heavy damages levied by Great Britain and France. Wilson's policy of refusing to recognize revolutionary Russia, on the ground that he did not approve its government, was continued. In this way Russia was treated as a pariah among nations; while the State Department encouraged American capitalists to make money out of Russian trade if they could. The floating of loans to foreign countries and capitalists was promoted; the export trade of the United States was pushed by federal agents; imperialist policy was revived in the Philippines; and efforts were made to keep ajar the so-called Open Door in China for American business enterprise.

Nevertheless under Republican auspices regard was paid to ideals of peace prevalent in the United States. At an arms-reduction conference held in Washington in 1921–22, Great Britain, Japan, and the United States agreed to stop their naval race for a specified time and limit the size of their battleship fleets. In 1928 the United States joined France in promoting the Kellogg-Briand Pact, an arrangement by which all the great nations of the earth bound themselves to outlaw war as an instrument of national policy and to settle their disputes henceforth by peaceful methods. Ardent advocates of internationalism hailed this act as putting an end to war and guaranteeing world order.

The age of normalcy also became in many ways an age of

disillusionment in respect of foreign affairs. As the strife among the governments of Europe and Asia for world power, economic privileges, and other advantages went forward within the League of Nations and outside its councils, indifference to its fate widened in the United States. For this spectacle Americans who had opposed the entry of the United States into the League had only derision; and idealists who had sought to carry America into the League got cold comfort from it. The treatment accorded to revolutionary Russia by European governments contributed little to the comity of nations. Imperialist rivalries flourished as before— in Africa, Asia, and the islands of the seas.

At the same time secret agreements, made long before 1914, between Russia, France, and Great Britain, were unearthed by historians working in the archives of Russia, Germany, and Austria thrown open to researchers by revolutions in all those countries. On the basis of clear documentary evidence scholars dissected the myth, propagated by those Powers, that Germany was wholly responsible for inaugurating the war; that on Germany must be placed all the war guilt; that the governments of Great Britain, France, and Russia united by the secret agreements were administered by innocent civilians suddenly and unexpectedly attacked by a bloodthirsty villain.

By reading copies of these diplomatic documents, scholarly works in European history founded on them or the publicity given to the findings, literate Americans in large numbers learned something of the innumerable lies, deceptions, and frauds perpetrated by the governments of Czarist Russia, Great Britain, and France, as well as of the Central Powers, at the expense of their own peoples and other nations. The gleaming mirage that pictured the World War as purely or even mainly a war for democracy and civilization dissolved beyond recognition. Countless Americans who in 1914–18 had yearned for a "brave new world" at the conclusion of the war were disheartened by the proofs of sinister purposes running against their dreams.

Although the Republicans could claim, with some justification in the election returns of 1920, that the country had turned its back on President Wilson's internationalism, they were not able, in domestic affairs, to stamp out the spirit of progressive or radical insurgency, old in American tradition and yet ever new in its application to changing conditions. In fact in 1924 they encountered a progressive revolt. Progressive Republicans and Democrats, disgusted with both the old parties, put into the field a third ticket, headed by Senator Robert M. La Follette, of Wisconsin, and Senator Burton K. Wheeler, of Montana. But the regular Democrats nominated for President John W. Davis, nominally of West Virginia, in reality a New York lawyer for the firm of J. P. Morgan and Company in Wall Street. In the election the Republican candidate, Calvin Coolidge, who had succeeded to the presidency on the death of Harding in 1923, received more than half the total vote cast. Yet the 4,800,000 votes polled by the Progressives indicated that the country was far from converted to Republican "normalcy."

Nor in truth did the election of 1928, in which the Republicans received a longer lease on power, indicate an exact return to any previous state of affairs. The Republican candidate, Herbert C. Hoover, who had been Secretary of Commerce since 1921, was not a mere replica of a McKinley, a Taft, or a Harding. In that office he had convinced many businessmen that he was a financial wizard. He had promoted the export of manufactures by the lavish use of public funds. He had encouraged American investors to "prime the pump" abroad for American industries by lending billions to foreign governments and corporations, thus enabling foreigners to "buy" American goods. Though Hoover praised "rugged individualism" and was commended as a "great business leader," he was widely known also as a philanthropist and a man of avowed social sympathies. He had headed American relief in Belgium during the World War and later disbursed American money abroad by the millions in relieving famine-stricken regions.

Never before in their history had the Republicans nominated for the presidency a man who had spoken with such anxiety about the depressing aspects of American society against which the spirit of progressive insurgency had been continuously directed. Nor had any Republican candidate advocated so repeatedly the removal of these afflictions by private co-operation and governmental action.

In 1923, for example, Hoover had urged insurance companies to attack the problem of unemployment by adding that evil to the list of casualties against which they provided underwriting: "There is one field of insurance not yet covered. You have covered the great range of accidents and disaster, but one great disaster that comes to our workfolk has yet been unguarded. . . . It is less than eighteen months ago when we had five millions of unemployed men in our streets, of men who wished to work but for whom no work could be found. There is nothing that leads to such despair and such decay of self-respect as the man who wants a job and wants to work, the support of whose family is in jeopardy."

Hoover had also opposed child labor and endorsed a constitutional amendment authorizing Congress to abolish it. He had commended and aided the work of associations for the improvement of housing conditions, public health, the care of children, and other substandard features of American society.

Gross inequalities in the distribution of wealth, long the subject of populistic, progressive, and socialistic criticism, Hoover had frankly faced, to the alarm of conservatives; and he proposed to attack them by the use of the inheritance tax. The inheritance tax, he declared in 1919, "does redistribute overswollen fortunes. It does make for equality of opportunity by freeing from the dead hand control of our tools of production. It reduces extravagance in the next generation and sends them to constructive service." To Republicans who had assailed the income tax of 1894 as communistic that must have sounded like treason to the Grand Old Party; and to scholastic economists, a foolish flouting of "natural law."

Nor did the Democrats in 1928 nominate a Cleveland Democrat. They selected a liberal, of progressive social sympathies, Alfred E. Smith, of New York. While legislator and governor in that state, Smith had consistently promoted social legislation in line with progressive aspirations. He had defended freedom of speech amid the hysteria of the World War and with a proclamation of liberty had pardoned a communist imprisoned on account of his opinions. With Smith's social and political doctrines, liberals and progressives were generally in agreement. But he was handicapped by two disqualifications for a popular appeal at the time: he was a Roman Catholic in a country loyal to its Protestant heritage; and he had consistently opposed prohibition since the adoption of the Eighteenth Amendment in 1919, in defiance of the powerful anti-saloon organizations behind it. If the votes cast in 1928 proclaimed another extension of Republican power, they did not in any case mean that the processes of American history were reaching a standstill.

In spite of their three successive victories in presidential elections and many pledges of a return to the "good old days" of free enterprise—no government interference with business—Republicans did not wipe out the measures of reform that had been accumulated since 1900. They did not reverse history and go back to the policies and legislation of the McKinley regime. The efforts which some of them exerted to effect such a reaction were defeated in Congress even when they had indisputable majorities in both houses. Retreats toward the age of McKinley by the wholesale repeal of laws, if desired by Republican die-hards, did not take place.

On the contrary, reformist measures, once condemned by conservatives of every type, were retained on the statute books, if occasionally with changes; and new laws conceived in the reform spirit were added. Moreover, the struggle to level down the special privileges of the plutocracy and raise the living standards of the masses went on within both great political parties, while the agitations of minor parties on the left wing gave the public no rest. The nature of constructive persistence even in the face of "normalcy" was illustrated in respect of every issue still before the nation—issues which had been before it for more than fifty years.

Hopes of abolishing or reducing to nominal rates the federal taxes on income and inheritances, entertained in some quarters, came to naught after the return of the Republicans to power in 1921. Twenty years previously nearly all the revenues of the federal government were derived from indirect taxes—customs duties and excises on consumption. At that time conservatives had decried income and inheritance taxes as socialistic or communistic. And advocates of such taxes had admitted publicly that they were framed to shift a part of the burden of taxation from the poor to the rich; while intransigents among them had declared that these taxes were steps toward the destruction of the plutocracy and greater equality in the distribution of national income.

On this question President Coolidge took a traditional position: "I do not believe that the government should seek social legislation in the guise of taxation. If we are to adopt socialism it should be presented to the people of this country as socialism and not under the guise of a law to collect revenue."

Yet of the $4,100,000,000, collected by the federal government in revenues in the fiscal year ended June 30, 1927, more than half came from income taxes on individuals and corporations. And President Coolidge's Secretary of Commerce, Herbert Hoover, publicly expressed the belief that "the present inheritance, income, and excess-profits tax tend to a better distribution of wealth." No clearer proofs could have been adduced to show that normalcy, in its effort to retreat, did not in fact go all the way back to the beginning of the twentieth century. Indeed, it advanced beyond the timid income-tax measure of 1913, enacted during the New Freedom.

Another phase of the domestic struggle to regulate national wealth in the public interest had been the contest over the conservation and use of national resources. As the significance of the electrical industry for general welfare dawned in national consciousness, a sharp contest opened over the way in which water power on the national domain and along navigable rivers should be put to use. The old style had been to turn such sites over to private concerns for perpetual ownership and allow private companies to produce and sell power without federal interference.

This policy outstanding progressives had attacked early in the century. They insisted that all water power should be publicly owned, that public power plants should be built, and that electricity should be distributed by public lines and sold at the lowest possible rates. Modifications of these propositions in the form of compromises, such as short-term leases of sites to companies, combined with strict regulation of rates and services, were also submitted to the country.

Before the World War had come to an end, the question of "federal power" was brought to the front in Congress. In 1920 a comprehensive federal water power act was passed and signed. The measure provided for the establishment of a water power commission and made a beginning at strict control over private utilities using federal power sites.

Not long afterward a project for building a great power plant in the Boulder Canyon of the Colorado River came up for review. Again a compromise was reached: ownership of the power site was retained in the hands of the government. The Secretary of the Interior was authorized to construct and operate a dam and other works on the site, and to allot the water for irrigation, domestic purposes, and the generation of electrical energy. The electrical power so produced he was permitted to sell, at rates sufficient to cover the cost, to states, municipalities, and private corporations for distribution. In selling this power, however, he was compelled to give priority to states and municipalities. In the end only a small portion of it went to private companies. Consequently Congress, under Republican leadership, moved nearer to the production and sale of power by means of public agencies, without the intervention of private enterprise.

When, early in Coolidge's administration, rumors circulated to the effect that during the administration of his predecessor, President Harding, great oil reserves had been corruptly turned over to private concerns, the Senate ordered an investigation. Scandals were uncovered, and prosecutions were begun against offenders. Day by day revelations of bribery and fraud broke into the front pages of the newspapers, giving the people lurid pictures of the way in which unscrupulous men had got hold of and exploited the natural resources of the nation. Private promoters, the testimony revealed, had contributed money to Republican campaign funds and to politicians, in return for leases to tremendous oil reserves from which to enrich themselves.

Under stinging rebukes from members of Congress, the Coolidge administration started lawsuits in the courts against parties charged with fraud, and after the cases were heard the oil lands surreptitiously obtained were restored to the United States Government. No longer was it possible, as it had been fifty years earlier, for private persons or corporations to enter into secret connivance with government officials and gain titles to huge sections of the public domain without risk of exposure or retribution. The public resolve to keep all that remained of the national heritage of resources had been effectively demonstrated.

Another dispute over the disposal of natural resources arose in connection with a great power plant which the government had begun to build at Muscle Shoals, in the Tennessee Valley, for the production of chemicals to be used in munitions during the World War. When peace came, Republicans and Democrats who clung to nineteenth-century traditions of free enterprise in such matters demanded that the plant be sold or leased to a private concern at a low or even nominal figure. With this view Harding, Coolidge, and Hoover agreed in principle if not as to details.

But progressives in Congress, led by Senator George W. Norris, of Nebraska, had other plans—plans for socialization—and fought for them tenaciously. After a seven-year battle they pushed through Congress a resolution providing for government ownership and operation of the Muscle Shoals plant, for the construction of new plants, and for priority to states and municipalities in the sale of power.

President Coolidge killed it with a pocket veto. Again, and still under the leadership of Senator Norris, Congress passed a similar bill in 1931. President Hoover vetoed it, saying that it would help to destroy the "initiative and enterprise" of the American people. Though defeated temporarily in their efforts, congressional advocates of "public power" were able to prevent the adoption of recommendations from Coolidge and Hoover for otherwise disposing of Muscle Shoals, and to keep the plant in the hands of the government.

While conservatives of both parties labored unsuccessfully to turn the power resources of the Tennessee Valley over to private enterprise on easy terms, in the postwar period, few among them proposed repeal of the laws enacted in aid of agriculture during President Wilson's administration. If they had desired to do this, the plight of agriculture would scarcely have permitted the undertaking. After 1921, with the disappearance of the war demand for food products, agriculture started on a course of steep and ruinous decline. The prices of farm produce fell swiftly. Farmers by the tens of thousands went into bankruptcy. Farm mortgages were foreclosed and freehold farmers driven into tenancy or off the land. To make things worse, under the Republican tariff law of 1921 the prices of manufactured commodities which farmers had to buy remained fixed at high levels or in many cases rose still higher. Once more the country resounded with agrarian laments. Even politicians well entrenched in urban centers could hardly fail to note the discontent.

In these circumstances Republicans in control of Congress added to, instead of subtracting from, the Wilson program of agricultural legislation. They kept in force the Farm Loan Act of 1916 extending long-term credits to farmers at low rates of interest and supplemented it by provisions for short-term credits at low rates of interest. The Warehouse Act of 1916, designed to protect farmers against deceptive and fraudulent transactions in the storage of their products, was supplemented by the Packers and Stockyards Act, which gave farmers a similar protection in the shipment and sale of livestock. In 1922 grain growers were safeguarded by legislation against speculators in grains, as cotton growers had been by an act of 1916 against speculators in that commodity. Producers of perishable fruits and vegetables, who had long suffered from cheating and false reports at the hands of middlemen, were afforded more adequate defense by the Perishable Commodities Act of 1930. At the same time federal agencies were established to push the sale of agricultural products abroad in the manner employed to expand the foreign markets for manufactures. Invincibly, government functions were expanding.

But none of these measures did more than touch the fringes of the distress in agriculture. Surpluses of crops continued to pile up. The downward tendency of prices remained unchecked. Ruin spread more widely in farming regions. Farmers were suffering from the kind of calamity that was soon to overtake the middle classes and industrial workers of the cities; and right in the middle of "Republican prosperity" they gave the signal for a new agrarian rebellion. They demanded bigger markets and higher prices for their produce. One of their leaders vented their sentiments in saying: "If we cannot have prosperity too, we will kick the legs out from under the table and all Americans will have to sit on the ground." How to get the markets and higher prices? That was the question.

So deep was the unrest among farmers that Congress was moved to attempt a cure in 1927 by passing a bill to aid in handling the agricultural surpluses. The bill provided for the sale abroad of certain commodities at low prices and for making up the loss by an equalization fee or tax laid on producers in proportion to their sales. This would, its sponsors claimed, dispose of surplus output and raise prices. But whatever the merits of the bill, Coolidge interposed with a veto. The next year Congress passed a similar bill. Again Coolidge applied the veto.

The defeated farm bills represented a positive effort to interfere with the "natural" course of farm production and prices. As such they were generally deemed "unsound" by urban economists. Herbert Hoover was known to be against them. But in the heat of the campaign in 1928 both he and the Democratic candidate, Alfred E. Smith, promised to "do something" about the farm problem.

After his inauguration in 1929, President Hoover proposed and Congress enacted, with modifications, an agricultural marketing bill to control the disposition of various agricultural products. The act was expected to promote the organization of producers on the land into associations and corporations, to discourage overproduction, to foster orderly marketing, and to eliminate "undue" fluctuations and depressions in prices. To administer the law the Farm Board was created and a fund of $500,000,000 put at its command to be used in interfering with the "natural" course of production and prices in agriculture. This experiment, dubious in character, had just been started when the panic of 1929 struck even the cities and knocked "the legs out from under the table" in a wholesale fashion which even farmers had not contemplated in their resentment over their own economic distress.

In respect of labor legislation and social improvement, historic subjects of strife in the United States between and within political parties, the so-called age of reaction and disillusionment was in many respects an age of progress, not of retreat.

The provisions of the Clayton Antitrust Act of 1914 passed by a Democratic Congress, called by Samuel Gompers the "Magna Charta of Labor," had declared that labor was not a commodity and that the activities of organized labor were not to be suppressed under arbitrary injunctions issued by the federal courts. These two provisions, often violated or ignored in fact, were not struck from the statute books by Republicans. They were strengthened instead by a stringent anti-injunction law underwriting the principles of collective bargaining, passed in 1932. The new bill was sponsored by two progressive Republicans, George W. Norris in the Senate and Fiorello H. La Guardia in the House of Representatives, supported by many regular Republicans, championed by Democrats who then had a majority in the lower house, and signed by President Hoover. At no time in the history of the labor movement had its leaders been more powerful in political councils; the Anti-Injunction Act was testimony to the fact.

The La Follette Seamen's Act of 1915 for improving the conditions of sailors on American merchant vessels and assuring them new "human rights" remained on the statute books as another evidence that the influence of organized labor in social legislation was not declining under normalcy. In 1927, Congress gave to longshoremen and harbor workers the benefit of compensation for injuries—a privilege earlier granted to workers on interstate railways. The Railway Labor Mediation Act of 1926 was also in the line of progressive legislation, not a reversal in any respect. If few labor candidates were elected to Congress and setbacks frequently occurred in labor disputes, organized labor was growing in political force and winning sympathy under presidents often dismissed as "reactionary" by radicals.

What was known as the "social movement" was also gaining momentum. A sign of its meliorist advance was the adoption by Congress in 1924, with the approval of President Coolidge, of a resolution amending the Constitution so that federal authorities could regulate or abolish child labor throughout the United States. The amendment was not ratified by enough states to make it law, but some of its aims were later realized in other ways. In the states, almost unobserved by those who kept their eyes only on "national" affairs, laws were being multiplied in the interests of public health, housing, care of dependents, and protection against the hazards of poverty and other misfortunes. By 1930 three fourths of the states had provided pensions for widows and deserted wives with dependent children. By the end of 1931 at least nine states had general old-age pension laws—a main socialist proposal—and the propaganda for national pension legislation was rising throughout the country. In short neither war nor reaction had stifled the American resolve to subdue the evils of poverty in the United States.

CHAPTER XXVII

Economic Crash and the New Deal Uprising

In the autumn of 1929, just as the country seemed safe and sound on the "high plateau of permanent prosperity," except for farmers, the business boom attributed to Republican statecraft burst with a resounding crash. The prime stocks of the leading corporations fell nearly forty points on the average in a single day, October 29, when more than 16,000,000 shares were dumped on the market at the New York Stock Exchange. This panic was followed by the explosion of banks, railway companies, and private concerns, by increasing woes among farmers already in straits, by the closing of factories, shops, and offices, and by a steep decline in the opportunities of employment for artists, writers, musicians, architects, engineers, playwrights, and teachers—indeed the whole white-collar class—from New York to California. In the opening months of 1933, it was estimated, 12,000,000 men and women were out of work. Ruin and hunger, if not starvation, haunted not only the shacks of tenants and sharecroppers on the land, not only the back streets inhabited by industrial and professional classes, but also the grand avenues of great cities.

For a moment leaders in business and politics thought that this was "just another panic." President Hoover said: "We have passed through no less than fifteen major depressions in the last century. . . . We have come out of each . . . into a period of prosperity greater than ever before. We shall do so this time." But as the depression dragged through tedious months and into years, belief in "prosperity just around the corner" turned into doubt or despair. As this revulsion of feeling intensified, trust in the "natural" and "normal" processes of "recovery" declined, and leaders in the economic, intellectual, and moral life of the nation vehemently declared their unwillingness to endure the crisis with pious resignation as a visitation of God or of natural forces beyond human control. Long years of research, debate, agitation, and legislative gains in respect of social improvement had prepared multitudes of Americans for a different attitude toward poverty, unemployment, and misery in "God's own country."

Outstanding personalities in business and professional circles such as Owen D. Young and Gerard Swope of the General Electric Company, leaders in the United States Chamber of Commerce, in the American Federation of Labor, in the Federal Council of the Churches of Christ in America, and in associations for civic advancement joined in demanding concerted action against the depression. They called for deliberate planning and collective measures to create economic well-being and prevent the return of such a national misfortune. It was openly asserted in high places that, if capitalists could not so conduct industrial enterprise as to avoid periodical depressions of the kind and maintain a steady level of employment, the government of the United States would have to assume the responsibility.

In previous panics presidents had said or acted as if they believed that neither they nor Congress had any constitutional power to meddle with business activities and relieve the distresses of the millions unemployed. But President Hoover accepted no such defeatist philosophy while this terrible depression harrowed the nation with bankruptcies, mortgage foreclosures, poverty, hunger, and degradation. He immediately called upon Congress to make provision for a large-scale construction of public works to put labor and capital in action again; and he urged the governors of states to press for similar remedial measures within their respective jurisdictions.

As the depression wore on, Hoover acted more energetically and creatively. He recommended, and Congress adopted, two proposals for interfering in the "natural course" of business enterprise —from calamity to calamity. The first was the establishment of the Reconstruction Finance Corporation, which placed federal credit at the disposal of banks, insurance companies, railways, and other concerns in financial difficulties. The second was the formation of the Home Owners' Loan Corporation to aid people in peril of losing their homes under foreclosures of mortgages. He also approved legislation extending federal credit to states and municipalities struggling with unemployment and poverty. The popular criticisms launched against President Hoover were not to the effect that he had done nothing, but that he had not done enough or the right things on a scale commensurate with the magnitude of the national catastrophe.

President Hoover was desperately engaged in wrestling with the depression when the time for taking a national referendum on Republican statesmanship—the presidential election of 1932—arrived, as prescribed by the Constitution of the United States. Though the Democrats had won a majority in the House of Representatives in the congressional election of 1930, they had proposed no constructive measures to overcome the depression. Millions of Americans were still unemployed; poverty had become aggravated to menacing proportions; agriculture and industry were in a bad plight. The whole society of the United States was in a state of anxiety and confusion. But Democratic tactics in the House of Representatives were principally confined to obstructing and harassing President Hoover in such undertakings as he ventured to sponsor in trying to cope with the economic disaster.

As far as appearances indicated, the Democratic party, historically committed to the creed of "the less government the better," was even more disinclined than the Republicans to make a frontal drive against the depression by resorting to governmental action. Under Wilson's leadership they had, it is true, interfered with "free enterprise" in significant respects, but they had officially admitted no change in their individualistic creed. Nor in their platform of 1932 did they give any hint that they intended to reverse fundamentally their long role of opposition to federal interference in the "natural course" of national economy.

Neither in their choice of a presidential candidate nor in their campaign did the Democrats give the slightest indication that they intended to embark on a program of wholesale government interference with the processes of industry, agriculture, and labor organization. The man whom they selected to head their ticket, Franklin D. Roosevelt, governor of New York, represented by his sponsors as "progressive," had not in the course of his political career espoused any public policies which could be deemed radical by any stretch of the imagination. In their campaign literature the Democratic managers pictured Mr. Roosevelt as a man who could "perfectly understand the viewpoint of the dirt farmer and the city laborer, the man in the street and the one in high places, . . . quietly, impartially, firmly uphold the rights of each and achieve a fair deal for all."

Whether from sheer unrest or a belief that the Democrats could and would restore prosperity, the voters at the election broke Republican control over the executive and legislative branches of the federal government. They cast 22,800,000 ballots for Roosevelt as against 15,700,000 for President Hoover, the Republican candidate, running to succeed himself. Furthermore they returned huge Democratic majorities to the Senate and the House of Representatives.

What were the Democrats to do with their victory? Some, of course, expected to settle back and enjoy the spoils of office. Others relied on the revered economic philosophy that prosperity would revive in America if enough foreign outlets could some way be found for the products of American factories and farms. Indeed this historic dogma had been reiterated in their platform and in speeches during the campaign. Although their candidate, Mr. Roosevelt, had lent countenance to it, he had endorsed an agrarian program of government intervention for farm relief and promised to adopt several measures of relief for unemployment and poverty.

If the backers of Franklin D. Roosevelt expected a period of Democratic "normalcy," they were disappointed. Between November 1932 and his inauguration in March 1933 another financial panic had hit the country with the force of a cyclone. In every direction banks crashed and closed their doors. On the day of his installation hundreds were in bankruptcy, and practically all the others were shut up under precautionary measures taken by state governments. On March 4, 1933, therefore, circumstances looked black for the enjoyment of political jobs and power in the old style.

As the Democratic organization in Congress had no plans whatever for dealing with the financial disaster, the burden of leadership became President Roosevelt's and he took it upon his own shoulders. Under his direction a multitude of measures known collectively as the New Deal, devised to meet the depression, were quickly adopted and put into effect. These measures were based on the belief that the main business of getting the country out of the depression belonged to the people and the government of the United States, and could not be disposed of by trying to get foreign markets in bankrupt Europe or Asia.

Among Roosevelt's associates in the new Cabinet only one, Cordell Hull, Secretary of State, stuck to the idea of lowering trade barriers as the principal or sufficient mode of escape from the crisis. He admitted that the people at home could do something to help themselves; but putting American economy on a high level of production and prosperity by domestic actions he belittled as an effort to lift oneself by one's bootstraps; so he began to search for new or bigger foreign markets for American goods. While heading the American delegation to the World Economic Conference at London in the spring of 1933, Secretary Hull sought to reach some working agreements with representatives of various foreign governments, also in economic grief, that would enlarge the volume of American exports and imports. He was laboring at this task, though not making much advance, when President Roosevelt practically put an end to the conference by an abrupt message, and turned to the promotion of a domestic program for tackling the depression at home.

Apart from the repeal of the Prohibition Amendment in 1933, the principal domestic measures of the New Deal, adopted during and after 1933, may be summarized in a small compass under six heads: (1) control over banking and currency; (2) federal credit to property owners and corporations in financial difficulties; (3) relief to farmers; (4) regulation and stimulation of business enterprise; (5) systematizing rights of collective bargaining for organized labor; and (6) social security for selected groups of people against the hazards of dependency, unemployment, poverty, and old age. Taken collectively, they represented an effort to establish in the United States a stable economy in place of alternating booms and panics and to protect the people against numerous misfortunes of specific kinds. In the struggle to create the institutions of the New Deal many lines of older social meliorism were brought to a focus.

With the banks shut and the circulation of money palsied on March 4, 1933, the first task undertaken by President Roosevelt was that of opening the banks and managing the currency. Though urged by some of his supporters to nationalize at once all banks of issue and vest in the federal government the sole power of issuing currency, the President chose a less extreme course—one more in accord with the interests of private banking, and yet extending the scope and nature of regulation. All banks were put under closer federal supervision; credit was extended to banks which, it was thought, could be put into sound condition; and banks beyond redemption were liquidated. The gold standard was abandoned. Gold and silver coins and bullion were called in, ordered to be deposited with the government; and the right of citizens to demand gold and silver coins in exchange for paper money was abolished. For a currency based on gold was substituted a currency issued and managed under the authorities of the United States. Thus the power of private banks possessing stores of gold and silver to dominate the issue of currency by the United States was abrogated.

To afford relief to individuals and concerns in peril of bankruptcy or of losing their homes or farms, the policy of granting federal credit and aid was extended and made more effective. The farm loan banks were reorganized and supplemented by other credit institutions. The amount of security farmers were required to give for loans was reduced, and to those who could provide such security money was lent at lower rates of interest, on long terms, with easy methods of repayment in installments. Through new special agencies similar arrangements were made to lend money to people in towns who were in debt, had mortgages on their homes, and were in danger of losing their property. The Reconstruction Finance Corporation, established under President Hoover's administration, was revised; and billions of dollars were lent to banks, railways, insurance companies, industries, and other enterprises whose earnings temporarily fell short of their needs. By these measures the United States Government became the biggest money borrower and lender in the country and assumed heavy responsibilities for the fortunes of property owners in distress.

Rejecting the idea that all the huge surpluses of wheat, corn, cotton, meat, and other prime farm products could be sold abroad, or even "dumped" on foreign countries by any method, sponsors of farm relief adopted another course. By the Agricultural Adjustment Act of 1933 and later amendments, Congress provided for the curtailment of farm production by direct action. Instead of providing for the expansion of the home market, it adopted plans for organizing farmers who raised the leading agricultural staples, for reducing the amount which they produced, and for compensating them for that reduction by subsidies of money proportioned to their respective acreages withdrawn from production. With these measures were coupled other acts designed to restrict farm production, including livestock, to existing markets, stabilize supply in relation to demand, and create what was called by the Secretary of Agriculture, Henry A. Wallace, an "ever-normal granary."

Yet the dream of selling more agricultural produce abroad was not wholly given up. Under a law passed by Congress in 1934, on the insistence of Secretary Hull, the President and Secretary of State were authorized, for a period of three years, later extended, to make reciprocal trade agreements with other countries, free from the necessity of submitting their treaties to the Senate for ratification. In these agreements they could lower, within limits, the tariff rates on manufactures and other commodities in return for pledges on the part of foreign governments to reduce their rates on American imports. By this means, it was argued, outlets for a large amount of cotton, corn, meat, and other farm produce could be found in foreign markets.

But American manufacturing interests were also suffering from surpluses which could not be sold; millions of people, more than ten million at the highest point of unemployment, were out of work. Who was to buy the mountains of manufactured goods piled up in warehouses?

An attack on this problem was made under the National Industrial Recovery Act of 1933. The act authorized the expenditure of billions of dollars for the construction of public works with a view to stimulating building activities and creating purchasing power for the workers. Under it also an immense effort was made to organize business enterprises in the United States for a drive to increase employment, production, and sales in the home market. Enterprises were grouped together according to their nature. Their representatives were given power to adjust supply to demand, to fix prices within limits, and otherwise regulate their operations. For the purpose of preventing excesses in stock-market speculation and in the financing of great supercorporations, the Securities and Exchange Commission was established and given autocratic authority over all such transactions.

In the New Deal program special favors were afforded to organized labor which warmly supported President Roosevelt in elections. The National Industrial Recovery Act made provisions for collective bargaining between employers and employees, but the Supreme Court in 1935 declared unconstitutional nearly all of that act. Then Congress passed the National Labor Relations Act, making collective bargaining generally mandatory on employers and employees. Industrial and other workers were authorized to form or join unions of their own choosing and to elect representatives empowered to bargain for them in matters of hours, wages, and working conditions. To enforce the act the National Labor Relations Board was created. By other legislation Congress tightened the hold of organized labor on the processes of industrial bargaining.

Although a split occurred in the ranks of the American Federation of Labor under William Green and another organization, the Congress of Industrial Organizations, was formed, at first under the leadership of John L. Lewis, head of the United Mine Workers, both national federations flourished. The Congress of Industrial Organizations was highly successful in organizing industrial and white-collar workers, especially outside the old-line crafts. Both branches of national organized labor, with support from the National Labor Relations Board, increased rapidly in membership.

Taking into account millions of workers largely unorganized, Congress added the Wages and Hours Act to the labor program. Under this statute steps were taken to fix standard hours and wages in numerous industries and enterprises—particularly those in which the hours were long and the wages low.

By a series of measures the Roosevelt administration attacked more directly the problems of unemployment, poverty, and misery. Billions of dollars were appropriated for immediate relief to the hungry and homeless, to be spent directly through federal agencies and in co-operation with state and local governments. Later, jobs were provided for millions of the unemployed, including large numbers of the white-collar classes, on numerous projects set up under the Works Progress Administration and other federal agencies.

Various forms of social security were instituted under the Social Security Act of 1935; for example, insurance against unemployment to a limited extent and, for certain classes of workers, insurance against dependence in old age, and grants in aid of persons suffering from poverty, blindness, and other afflictions. Federal grants of money were made to states with a view to encouraging the establishment of a complete scheme of old-age pensions in every state in the Union. Briefly stated, a "floor" of minimum security was placed under millions of people. At the same time new projects for including all persons exempted from such benefits were proposed and brought under debate by sponsors of the New Deal.

Despite criticisms brought against it, frequently outrageous, and its many undoubted shortcomings and extravagances, the New Deal did so much for discouraged and desperate people that it won great popular support. In the circumstances relatively few persons with political aspirations proposed to abolish it completely and entrust the welfare of the people entirely to competitive enterprise.

While indulging in many denunciations of the New Deal in general, the Republicans, in their platform of 1936, endorsed the chief relief principles of the New Deal and pledged themselves to apply those principles more efficiently and at less cost. The Republican candidate, Alfred M. Landon, who had been associated with progressive politics in the West, stood by the planks of the Republican platform during the campaign of that year and in one respect he outbid the New Deal—by offering larger aids to agriculture.

Nevertheless, the Democrats won the election. Renominated by acclamation, President Roosevelt promised to uphold and expand the Democratic program. Reviewing with praise the New Deal activities since 1933 and declaring that he had just begun his fight in the interest of general welfare, he so captivated the public that he received 27,500,000 votes as against 16,700,000 cast for Landon. Whatever their deficiencies, New Deal endeavors to overcome the depression and relieve misery, mainly by domestic measures, seemed to be anchored in the affections of an enormous majority of the voters, so many of whom had personal reasons for being grateful.

Yet in fact the depression was by no means mastered when President Roosevelt took the oath of office for a second term on January 20, 1937—the date as fixed by the Twentieth Amendment, which moved closer to the election the installation of the President, senators, and representatives. At least 6,000,000 Americans were still unemployed. Business was still far below the peak of 1928. And in the year 1937, notwithstanding domestic pump-priming, another crisis struck the stock market, and prices of stocks went down even more rapidly than in the crash of 1929.

Financial analysts for the *American Year Book* of 1937 reported: "A new depression overtook the country in September. Unemployment increased with almost unprecedented swiftness. Relief rolls expanded. . . . The number of commercial failures was increasing. . . . New financing continued during 1937 in a state of comparative stagnation. . . . The decline in [stock] prices during September, October, and November was not only drastic. In fact there are few instances on record where a larger percentage decline has occurred in so short a period of time." Meanwhile the national debt mounted and yet no end of borrowing was in sight. On the contrary New Deal "experts" were now advocating the adoption of borrowing and spending as a permanent fiscal policy for fostering and directing industrial and agricultural production.

During the early stages of the concentration on domestic problems and on measures designed to lift the nation out of the depression, the mood of the country seemed to become more and more concerned with the character of society in the United States, with its grave difficulties, its extraordinary opportunities, its values and potentialities. To this mood the term "isolationism" was often applied. The term was new. It had been coined as a term of reproach for opponents of President Wilson's type of internationalism. Now it was often employed against New Dealers by Americans who believed that general prosperity could only be recovered by lowering trade barriers and entering into some form of collective security with the other nations of the earth. Although President Roosevelt proposed that the United States join the World Court, created under the League of Nations, the Senate rejected the recommendation and he declined to press the issue.

The spirit of disgust with war and Europe was intensified by reports from an investigation of the munitions traffic, pursued by a special committee of the Senate, which unfolded a seamy story of international intrigues, sinuous diplomacy, and profiteering devoid of patriotism, running through the years of the "war for democracy" and the planning for "permanent world peace." Sworn testimony, covering hundreds of pages in the volumes issued by the Senate committee, demonstrated that many men who had applauded Wilson's idealism had in fact made huge sums of money out of the war. Widely publicized, the Senate committee's revelations deepened the dillusionment over the nature and results of that "great crusade." Even President Roosevelt was accused of isolationism and in his reply he lent verisimilitude to the criticism by saying: "We are not isolationists except in so far as we seek to isolate ourselves completely from war."

Out of the uproar over the munitions inquiry and the refusal of Great Britain, France, Italy, and other associates in the World War to pay the debts they owed to the government of the United States came two acts of Congress designed to keep the country out of the next European war, already visible on the horizon. The first was the Johnson Act of 1934, forbidding the flotation of any more loans in the United States for foreign governments that had in effect repudiated the aforesaid debts. The second act was the Neutrality Resolution of 1935. It prohibited the sale of "arms, munitions, and implements of war" to foreign belligerents in time of war and provided that Americans who insisted on traveling aboard the ships of belligerents in wartime must do so at their own risk.

The two acts, in the intentions of the authors, were to prevent a repetition of events which had facilitated the involvement of the United States in the recent European war. When the Neutrality Resolution expired in 1936 it was renewed and made more stringent. Supported by overwhelming majorities in the Democratic Congress, neutrality legislation appeared to represent a reasoned desire on the part of the American people to avoid being entangled in another European war.

By words and actions President Roosevelt indicated that he was in full accord with this desire to keep out of Europe's next war, should another one break. In 1933 he virtually closed the World Economic Conference in London, where the representatives of great Powers had assembled to consider ways and means of overcoming the terrible economic depression through agreements on international trade and currencies. He refused to bring special pressure on the Senate to secure the approval of American participation in the World Court project. He adopted a "good neighbor" policy in Latin America, substituting conferences and cordiality for the straight imperialist coercions of former years.

He induced Congress to free Cuba from the protectorate imposed upon her by the so-called Platt Amendment of 1901. He signed with commendation an act of the Democratic Congress under which the imperialist experiment in the Philippine Islands was to be liquidated by granting them independence, to become effective in 1946.

In his campaign for re-election in 1936, President Roosevelt encouraged the people to fortify their resolve against taking part in another foreign war. He said in his address at Chautauqua, for example: "The Congress of the United States has given me certain authority to provide safeguards of American neutrality in case of war. . . . We can keep out of war if those who watch and decide have a sufficiently detailed understanding of international affairs to make certain that the small decisions of each day do not lead toward war and if, at the same time, they possess the courage to say 'no' to those who selfishly or unwisely would let us go to war."

CHAPTER XXVIII

Global War and Home Front

WHILE Americans were entrapped in the wreckage of the depression, casting about fitfully for methods of full "recovery," and in a mood of revulsion against participation in any more foreign wars, the economy of Europe was falling into chaos and the democracy for which the world was to have been made safe, according to President Wilson's formula, began to collapse in those parts of Europe where it had existed. The depressed state of the Old World now damped plans for maintaining or starting booms in the United States by lending American money to foreigners so that they could buy the "surpluses" of American goods. As a matter of fact, all over central and eastern Europe the march of events for years had been away from the solution of any nation's domestic problems by the mere promotion of freer trade. The march had been in the direction of dictatorships, controlled economy, and revived imperialism.

From its establishment in 1917 by revolution, under V. I. Lenin's strategy, the government of Soviet Russia was frankly an unlimited dictatorship, described as communist and headed by men who, without equivocation, avowed their contempt for democracy, constitutional government, and civil liberties. In 1922 parliamentary government was overthrown in Italy by Fascist bands under the leadership of Benito Mussolini who derided democracy and civil liberty as "stinking corpses," but who went beyond the Russian revolutionists by glorifying war and brute force as good in themselves. One after another smaller states—Yugoslavia, Greece, Spain, and Poland—repudiated popular government in favor of strong-arm government.

Germany's experiment with a republic and a democracy under a constitution adopted at Weimar in 1919 was brief. In 1933, Adolf Hitler, commanding a private army of banditti, called National Socialists, achieved political supremacy in Germany, destroyed the republic, suppressed civil liberty, and started a more than savage persecution of Jews, Social Democrats, Communists, and Liberals. Years before 1933, Hitler had announced his ambitions and intentions in his book *Mein Kampf* (*My Battle*). As there exhibited they embraced a merciless battle at home against all his opponents and a war, east or west or in both directions, against the neighbors of Germany.

To gain time for his operations, however, Hitler spoke publicly of peaceful intentions. In fact he immediately began to rearm Germany and train soldiers for a career of conquest. Many European and American writers warned mankind that Hitler and Mussolini were planning assaults far and wide, but conservative heads of governments in Great Britain, France, and elsewhere—the neighbors against whom they had warlike designs—refused to heed the warnings. Rejoicing in the fascist suppression of communists in Italy and hoping later to turn the full force of Nazi Germany against Russia and communism, they gave comfort and aid to Mussolini and Hitler, even after these dictators became allies in a Rome-Berlin Axis and were joined by Japanese warlords; even after these three aggressors began open wars on their neighbors.

Although popular sympathies in the United States during the years of fascist aggression in Europe and Asia were undoubtedly on the side of the victims of Italy, Germany, and Japan, the American resolve to stay out of the next war, as expressed in the successive neutrality acts, seemed to remain unshaken. But after his second overwhelming triumph at the polls in 1936, President Roosevelt turned upon what his critics called his "isolationism." In an address at Chicago in October 1937, to the amazement of the country, he indicated a change in his position. He denounced, without naming them, Germany, Italy, and Japan, for bringing on "the present reign of terror and international lawlessness." He denied that the United States could keep out of war if it came: "Let no one imagine that America will escape, that it may expect mercy, that this Western Hemisphere will not be attacked." Then he declared that the peace-loving nations must make concerted efforts to restrain the three dangerous Powers—and to lower trade barriers.

When popular protests greeted his Chicago speech and President Roosevelt was asked to amplify his argument, he lapsed into silence. But early the following year, 1938, he called upon Congress for an extra appropriation for the Navy and expressed his opinion that dangers of war were drawing closer to the United States. Meanwhile he supported the government of Britain in its professed "non-intervention" policy in Spain where, aided by the armed might of Hitler and Mussolini, fascist rebels were demolishing the Spanish Republic, to whose assistance Russia alone had come, and by so doing he aided, if unwittingly, in the triumph of fascism there.

After Germany launched a war on Poland in the autumn of 1939 and Great Britain and France retaliated by declaring war on Germany, President Roosevelt called upon Congress to repeal the embargo provision of the neutrality legislation or modify it in such fashion as to permit Americans to sell munitions to the British and French governments. In his message to Congress, however, he assured Congress that the repeal which he demanded was in the interest of American abstention from the war—in the interest of "American neutrality, American security, and above all, American peace." Apparently accepting the President's explanation, Congress made changes in the Neutrality Act in the direction which he indicated; but tightened it in other respects. In vain opponents of repeal or alteration insisted that the changes were steps toward entry into another war along the very road Woodrow Wilson had traveled from 1915 to 1917.

On September 3, 1940, President Roosevelt informed Congress that he had, by executive act, acquired lease rights to naval and air bases in Newfoundland, in the British West Indies, and in British Guiana; and that in exchange for certain of these bases he had given Great Britain fifty of our "over-age destroyers."

Objectors charged that, besides being an arbitrary action which the President had no lawful right to take, it was a plain act of war as defined by international law—the transfer of war vessels by a presumptive neutral to a government at war with another power. But the President simply replied that his Attorney General, Robert H. Jackson, had pronounced the destroyer deal lawful. To members of his party in Congress inclined to interpret it as a war measure he gave some reassurance by declaring: "This is not inconsistent in any sense with our status of peace."

☆

It was amid the thrumming of war alarms that the presidential campaign of 1940 opened. Brushing aside the third-term tradition established by Jefferson, the Democrats nominated President Roosevelt for a third term; and on his insistence chose Henry A. Wallace, a member of his Cabinet, for Vice-President. Passing over party regulars, the Republicans selected as their candidate for the presidency Wendell Willkie, a former Democrat, utility lawyer, and public relations agent, who had long opposed President Roosevelt's domestic policies.

Whatever party managers had in view, peace was an issue uppermost in the minds of the people. On this issue both candidates seemed to be reassuring. "The American people," declared Wendell Willkie, "do not want war. . . . They are determined to keep America at peace. In that determination I stand with them. I am for keeping out of war." To Willkie's challenge President Roosevelt responded in the closing days of the campaign. France had fallen. Mussolini had stabbed her in the back. But speaking at Boston at that hour of European stress and strain, on October 30, 1940, Roosevelt gave a solemn pledge to his country: "And while I am talking to you mothers and fathers, I give you one more assurance. I have said this before, but I shall say it again and again and again. Your boys are not going to be sent into any foreign wars. They are going into training to form a force so strong that, by its very existence, it will keep the threat of war away from our shores. The purpose of our own defense is defense."

Franklin D. Roosevelt was granted a third term by a vote of 27,000,000 in round numbers against the 22,000,000 polled by Willkie. In his annual message of January 6, 1941, to Congress, he announced his intention to have the United States send to the nations at war with Hitler and Mussolini "in ever-increasing numbers, ships, planes, tanks, guns." This action, he realized, might lead to war and yet he said: "Such aid is not an act of war, even if a dictator should unilaterally proclaim it so to be."

Then he had drawn up and introduced into Congress, in January, a measure "to promote the defense of the United States," known as the Lend-Lease bill. After extensive hearings and a long debate, this bill, modified by amendments, became a law on March 11, 1941. The Lend-Lease Act authorized the President to sell, transfer, exchange, lend, lease, or otherwise dispose of ships, aircraft, implements of war, and other commodities to the "government of any country whose defense the President deems vital to the defense of the United States." In effect, it empowered the

President to sell or give, to any and all governments actually or nominally at war with the Axis Powers, war implements and supplies in immense quantities.

Under international law as hitherto recognized, this law was an act of war. Opponents of the bill so characterized the gift of military supplies to China in her conflict with Japan and similar aid to Great Britain and her Allies in their war on Germany and Italy. But it was entitled a bill to promote the defense of the United States; and its sponsors in Congress assured the country that it was intended to keep the country out of war.

On July 7, 1941, about two weeks after Hitler's armies invaded Russia, President Roosevelt notified Congress that the armed forces of the United States had occupied Iceland, jointly with British forces for the time being; and that he had ordered the American Navy to defend the sea lanes between the United States and that island.

In August the President and the British Premier, Winston Churchill, met "somewhere in the Atlantic," and agreed upon measures to be taken in providing for the safety of their respective countries against Germany and the governments associated with her. They also drew up at their conference a declaration of principles, soon called the Atlantic Charter, for the conduct of affairs, not only during the war but also after the destruction of Nazi tyranny.

On October 27, 1941, President Roosevelt informed the country that Germany had started war on the United States. "Hitler," said the President, "has attacked shipping in areas close to the Americas. . . . Many American-owned ships have been sunk on the high seas. One American destroyer was attacked on September 4. Another destroyer was attacked and hit on October 17. Eleven brave and loyal men of our Navy were killed by the Nazis. We have wished to avoid shooting. But shooting has started. . . . America has been attacked."

Although the attention of the American people was now directed especially to the war in Europe, trouble was brewing in another foreign quarter. The government of Japan, taken over by ruthless militarists, had for years been seizing territory in China and waging war on that country. Under the slogan of "Asia for the Asiatics," Japanese imperialists nourished projects for conquering and ruling immense areas of the mainland and islands in the Far East. This region they called Japan's "sphere of influence."

Japan's aggression, of course, ran counter to American foreign policy in the Orient and to the letter and spirit of treaties signed by the Japanese government and other Powers, including the United States. In upholding that policy President Roosevelt took the position that Japan was violating treaties and international law, destroying the independence of China, and transgressing American rights in the Orient.

In response to such complaints the Japanese government, by this time allied with Germany and Italy as the third party to the Axis, offered some concessions, but in the main adhered to its own imperialistic line. It insisted that the United States was violating Japan's rights as a belligerent by giving financial aid to the government of China and by sending munitions to that government at Chungking, by way of the Burma Road. For months, as indeed for years in the past, the State Department at Washington refused to surrender any part of its Far Eastern policy. Diplomatic exchanges between the governments of the United States and Japan continued without softening the asperity of their differences.

Eager to avoid the awful perils of a two-front war, Great Britain tried conciliation with Japan. For a long time the two countries had been formal allies united by treaty. Though, on the insistence of the United States, their alliance had been severed in 1922, they had managed to keep on workable terms. Yielding to protests from the Japanese government, Great Britain in 1940 closed the Burma Road to shipments of munitions and supplies bound for Chungking, still in the hope of warding off a war with Japan.

But the British closure of the Burma Road brought objections from the United States. When he heard rumors of the proposal Secretary of State Cordell Hull declared that the United States had a "legitimate interest in the keeping open of the arteries of commerce in every part of the world," and that shutting the road would "constitute unwarranted interposition of obstacles to world trade." When her agreement with Japan expired at the end of six months, Britain complied with American desires and opened the road again to the transport of munitions to Chungking.

By November 1941 the tension between the government of the United States and the government of Japan approached a climax, as Japanese armed forces moving southward into French Indo-China increased in number. Late in that month, according to the statement of Wilfred Fleisher, long a resident in Tokyo and a careful student of Japanese affairs, in his *Our Enemy Japan,* a kind of truce with Japan was reached in Washington, with the approval of the British and Australians and reluctantly of the Dutch. But Hu Shih, the Chinese ambassador, protested to President Roosevelt against the proposed truce; and the plan for avoiding an immediate conflict with Japan was dropped. Subsequent efforts to reach an agreement failed.

As early as January 27, 1941, the American ambassador to Tokyo, Joseph Grew, had reported to the State Department that Japanese military forces were planning a surprise attack on Pearl Harbor in case of trouble with the United States. On November 25 and November 28, 1941, Secretary Hull told "high officials" of the United States Government that relations with Japan were critical and that Japan might launch sudden attacks at various points. While negotiations were still going on with Japan, on December 7, a surprise attack did occur. By bombing planes and submarines Japanese forces, without warning, fell upon Pearl Harbor in the Hawaiian Islands and decimated American naval, land, and air forces in that American outpost.

One of two things had happened. Either President Roosevelt, as Commander in Chief, or Frank Knox, Secretary of the Navy, or Henry L. Stimson, Secretary of War, had not duly and sternly put the American officers in charge at Pearl Harbor on their guard for defense; or those officers had been inexcusably negligent in the performance of duty. Wherever the responsibility lay, the United States had been assaulted by Japan and was severely crippled for quick counterblows by the disaster at Pearl Harbor. At the same time the Japanese had attacked American and British imperial outposts in the Far East.

On December 8, 1941, the day after the attack on Pearl Harbor, the United States declared war on Japan, and so did Great Britain. Three days later Germany and Italy proclaimed war on the United States and agreed with Japan, their Axis colleague, not to make a separate peace. In a little while nearly all the world was engulfed in war. The conflict of 1914–18 had been comparatively limited—mainly to Europe and the Atlantic Ocean. Now all the continents and seas became scenes of armed combats. Only minor Powers, such as Switzerland, Sweden, Turkey, and Argentina, remained outside the circle of fighting or belligerency.

At first the combat activities of the United States, apart from the war on submarines in the Atlantic, were confined to the Pacific

THE THEATERS OF AMERICAN
The black and shaded areas show the

ACTION IN THE GLOBAL WAR
extreme limits of Axis conquests.

area. Handicapped by the destruction of American resources at Pearl Harbor, the United States was powerless to check the southward sweep of Japan's ships, planes, and armies for many months. Manila soon succumbed under Japanese assaults. British and Dutch forces quickly yielded to the invaders—at Hong Kong and Singapore and in the Dutch East Indies. After displaying extraordinary courage in defense, Americans had to give up all the Philippines.

Before the end of 1942, Japanese forces had spread out in a great arc covering all the islands southward and were close to the shores of Australia. There Americans and Australians stopped the advancing horde and opened an offensive war for recovering ground and wearing down Japanese strength. While Australia was being saved and the Japanese tide turned slowly backward, British and American troops landed in the French colonies of North Africa, in November 1942, and established a front there against Italians and Germans. After some initial setbacks, they began a conquering advance.

Before a year passed they had crushed the Italians and Germans in Africa, invaded and occupied Sicily, brought about the overthrow of Mussolini and his Fascist government, invaded the Italian mainland, forced the Italian government out of the war, and were driving the Germans slowly but steadily northward by incessant hammering and bombing. Meanwhile American air forces, in co-operation with the British, intensified the systematic destruction of German industrial cities, as Russian armies drove the Germans backward to the Dnieper River and beyond.

Hard fighting remained ahead in the opening weeks of 1944 but the powerful and terrifying Axis had been disrupted. The Italian people, formerly an Axis partner, was struggling on its own soil for survival. Hitler was on the defensive, retreating before the Russian onslaughts and weakening under the relentless blows of Allied forces. The Japanese, without prospect of aid from any quarter, were losing one island stronghold after another under American and Australian attacks by air, land, and sea. At this point the political complications of the Global War began to unfold in their fullness, even for American novices.

In respect of its regimenting and disruptive effects in American society, the Global War was so revolutionary that it made the World War look like an episode. Every branch of economy—agriculture, industry, and labor—all the relations of men, women, and children, every phase of education, every medium of expression and communication, all processes of government, all aspects of civil and military government, were affected by the impacts of the total war and presented far-reaching reactions. Many of the reactions—perhaps all of them—were of incalculable significance for destiny and opportunity in the United States.

Under Selective Service Acts of 1940, 1941, and 1942, provisions were made for armed forces numbering two or three times the 4,000,000 men raised for the war of 1917–18. Before the close of 1943 approximately 8,700,000 men had been enlisted—withdrawn from farms, industries, shops, mines, offices, college halls, and from all the professions—deranging the course of economy and social practices. Doctors were taken from medical practice, often leaving hospitals and whole communities without adequate medical services. Teachers by the thousands went to war or left their school-rooms to engage in war production; and all over the land, in town and country, no substitutes could be found to carry on the work of primary and secondary education as before. Small business enterprises not "essential" to war production were denuded of manpower and, hard pressed, were often shut up or driven into bankruptcy.

To release more men for the fighting fronts and to aid in the military and naval administration, tens of thousands of women were recruited as volunteers from homes, schools, colleges, and business positions, organized in auxiliary corps, put into uniforms, given disciplinary instruction and war indoctrination such as the armed forces were receiving, granted military ranking and titles, with economic benefits akin to those accorded to men in the services. Thousands were sent overseas to the battle fronts to render various services under military orders. Women nurses and doctors were also drawn into the tasks associated with war.

To supply war materials in greater quantities and varieties than ever before nearly every manufacturing plant adaptable to war production was wholly or in part shifted from the manufacture of civilian goods to the manufacture of war goods; and billions of dollars were pumped into the construction of gigantic new plants, to make the United States the "arsenal of the democracies," as President Roosevelt phrased it. Millions of men were transferred from all kinds of occupations to war industries or other work deemed essential to war efforts; and finally all men, within broad age limits, were warned that unless they were in essential work they were liable to be inducted into the armed forces.

Millions of women were also recruited, voluntarily, from civilian employments for war production industries to release more men for the armed forces. Among them were throngs of women who had never been gainfully employed. As the war proceeded, demanding constantly more womanpower, greater and greater calls were made upon women still outside war work.

This disruption of civilian economy, this transformation of old manufacturing plants into war plants and the construction of new plants often in districts purely rural, induced an enormous migration of men and women, boys and girls, singly and in families, from one end of the country to the other. Old towns and cities thus became terribly congested while, in the new centers of war production, the provision of adequate facilities for housing and sanitation lagged far behind the industrial expansion. Despite efforts of the governments, federal and local, to contend with the situation, menaces to health, education, welfare, and every other human value reached frightening proportions.

In these circumstances, especially with so many mothers employed for long hours, by day or by night, outside the home, family life was not only shattered but hordes of young children were turned into the streets to fend for themselves. Older children left school in droves to work in factories for fabulous wages and, refusing to return to schools, took their lives into their own keeping. With children unguided by teachers or parents, juvenile delinquency and crimes increased to an extent that threatened the moral basis of American society. In August 1943, J. Edgar Hoover, head of the federal police force, exclaimed: "The tragedy revealed by our latest survey is found in the fact that the arrests of boys and girls seventeen years of age increased 17.7% [last year]. In reviewing the further trends for the past six months we find an 89% increase in the arrests of girls for offenses against common decency."

While various women's organizations were rejoicing in the equalities of opportunity, honors, and monetary rewards offered to women by the war and were pushing the recruiting of women for war work of all kinds, individual women, and to some extent organized women, began to appreciate the social peril of juvenile delinquency and also the problems of caring for the babies of mothers engaged in war work. Amid the pressures for complete concentration on war, therefore, women interested in social welfare urged that responsibility for looking after the children be mainly assumed by governments, federal, state, and local.

There was no doubt that families were undergoing disintegration; for men were being drafted for war, women drawn into the auxiliary armed forces, war production, and civilian defense, children of school age crowding into war industries, adolescents left to roam the streets for excitement, and the energies of parents distracted from the care of homes and children. The fact was indisputable and its social import was recognized by leaders in public affairs. It was discussed in newspapers, in meetings of organizations concerned with public welfare, in journals devoted to surveys of social and economic conditions, and in popular magazines. It was emphasized during debates in Congress over a proposal to defer pre-Pearl Harbor fathers.

Yet no generally accepted and workable plans were devised for successfully countering disruptive effects of war activities and war regimentation on the homes and family life of the nation. New houses for war workers were built under the national housing authorities; nurseries were installed in factories; and more nurseries were established in urban and rural communities. But none of these undertakings was on a scale commensurate with the problem. And indeed they were at best inadequate substitutes for the provisions of orderly home living.

The war necessities, demanding men and women by the millions for the armed forces and war production, also broke into education, that adjunct of family life in the care and rearing of the young generations. Every branch of it, from the primary schools to colleges and universities, was deeply affected by the same intrusive tendencies. Old programs of instruction designed to prepare youth for civilian life and employment were either thrown away or recast in the interest of preparation for combat service or activities connected with it. The war sciences crowded aside the old liberal arts and civilian sciences, with their emphasis on humane letters and living.

As one leader in this educational upheaval put it: "What is probably the greatest mass-educational system the world has ever known is quietly teaching thousands of American men the science and skills of modern technical warfare." Not only that. A regimentation of education and educational thought in this direction gathered momentum from Maine to California, under the auspices of the military arm of the government. So serious was civilian alarm over this tendency, savoring of militarism, that one of the great foundations made a grant of money to a learned association for the purpose of examining anew the nature and utility of "liberal education" at every level of the American school system.

Authority over life and property far greater in its extent than that conferred upon President Wilson in the World War was granted to President Roosevelt—power almost without limit over industry, agriculture, wages, prices, use of plant facilities, the erection of new plants, and rationing of supplies for civilians. The enforcement of social legislation providing for safety in industries, for sanitary standards of housing, and for safeguarding the health and welfare of the people was relaxed or openly disregarded amid the rush of war mobilization. Industrial plants were commandeered entirely or compelled to divert a percentage of their production to war purposes. Men and women in numerous vital industries were "frozen" in their jobs—compelled to remain where they were employed instead of being free to seek and accept more attractive positions. New plants of staggering dimensions were built from coast to coast, often at the expense of the government. Through public financing of industries, the rationing of commodities, the fixing of prices, and the multiplication of federal officials to administer the new laws, the tentacles of the government reached wider and wider, and deeper and deeper, into the life, liberty, and property of the people as well as into old practices known as "free enterprise."

Strenuous efforts were made to hold down wages and strikes; and in 1943, by the Smith-Connally Act, Congress imposed heavy penalties on labor leaders who fomented strikes, and forbade organized labor to contribute money to the campaign funds of political parties. In many respects, of course, trade unions had gained advantages out of war industries; more millions were employed; and under the policies of the New Deal many of these millions were, in effect, compelled to join unions and pay dues in order to get war production jobs. On the whole, labor loyally cooperated in war activities, the Communists giving enthusiastic support, as the extraordinary output of munitions, armaments, and other goods demonstrated.

There had been "rackets" in the labor world, corrupt and disgraceful rackets, but responsible labor leaders deprecated these blots on the labor movement and sought to maintain equable relations with industry and the government. Finding themselves caught in the pinch of rising prices and government control, however, they began to draw together more closely in efforts to deal with their new situation. John L. Lewis, of the United Mine Workers, having left the Congress of Industrial Organizations, offered to take his organization back into the American Federation of Labor. Moves were made to consolidate the Federation and the Congress, with a combined membership of more than 10,000,000, or at least to effect working agreements on a common program for meeting the strains of war regimentation on trade-union policies and standards.

In the domain of opinion, as well as in other phases of national life, government controls expanded. The press, the radio, and the moving picture were put under the scrutiny or censorship of official agencies. Government films were produced and film industries were largely diverted to meet the purposes and demands of war propaganda. The Espionage Act of 1917 was kept alive and applied by the courts. And to this measure for the control of opinion and expression was added what was in effect a new sedition act—Title I of the Alien Registration Act of 1940—which introduced into American law, for the first time, a principle of the European state-police system: namely, that anyone may be arrested and punished, not for what he says or does, but because he is a member of an association whose avowed purposes are revolutionary. Universities, colleges, and schools all over the country were turned into institutions for military training, and their programs and methods of education were subjected to the approval, supervision, or direct dominance of military authorities.

In financial terms the war outstripped all human experience. On June 30, 1914, the net debt of the United States stood at $1,000,000,000 in round numbers. In 1930 the Treasury Department estimated that the cost of the first World War up to that time was in excess of $37,000,000,000; and it was reckoned that, counting pensions to soldiers and additional charges, its total cost would run to $100,000,000,000. These figures were staggering for Americans who had once boasted that their nation was not like the debt-burdened nations of the Old World. But before a year of the Global War had passed, Congress authorized an expenditure amounting to $240,000,000,000.

While the debt mounted, taxes grew in weight. Under the income-tax law of 1942 every single person with more than $600 a year and every married couple with more than $1200 a year, subject to certain deductions, had to pay an income tax rising steeply with the amount of the income. Tens of millions of Americans who had never paid a direct tax for the support of the federal government were compelled to make out returns and pay. In addition they were subjected to stamp taxes and other forms of indirect taxation, profuse in variety. Taxes on the earnings and excess profits of corporations reached heights that approached confiscation in the upper levels.

Under the impulse of war imperatives the industrial facilities of the United States for productive purposes were expanded with astounding swiftness. In 1939 the manufacturing plants of the country represented an investment of about $50,000,000,000—the accumulation of all the previous years. Within three years new plants, involving an additional investment of $22,000,000,000, were either built or under construction, many of them wholly or partly owned by the federal government. In terms of annual output in dollar values the production of wealth, which had fallen below $50,000,000,000 in the midst of the great depression following the panic of 1929, was lifted by 1943 to the neighborhood of $150,000,-000,000, revealing in this astronomic figure the titanic productive powers of capitalists, managers, and workers, equipped with the agencies of modern science and technology.

By seeming necessity the expansion of heavy industries for the production of steel, guns, ships, tanks, trucks, planes, and other implements of war expedited the long-time trend toward the concentration of capitalist activities and interests. For more than a hundred years, especially since the enactment of the Sherman Anti-Trust Act of 1890, farmers, owners of small industries, shopkeepers, and other heads of little economic units had inveighed against this tendency. Statesmen had called for a reversal of the process. Agitators had stirred up excitement about it. Political revolts had been raised against it. But nothing had forced a return to the system of village smithies, corner stores, horses, and buggies. Concentration had been accelerated by the World War under the leadership of President Wilson who, in his campaigns, had denounced the "masters of big business" and promised to emancipate the people from their dominion.

Now the Global War, fought in support of foreign policies world-wide in purpose and range, made heavy and unprecedented demands upon mass production industries directed by masters of big business. To get quickly and in fabulous amounts the quantities and kinds of implements absolutely needed for such a war, it was necessary for the government to turn immediately to industries already monstrous in size and force their immediate conversion from peacetime production into war production. As the demand for war goods rose higher and higher and plants covering ten, twenty, eighty, or more acres of ground had to be built, it was to the experienced managers of gigantic industries that the government had to resort for swift and efficient construction of new buildings.

Special efforts were made to favor little business concerns, but by the close of 1943 seventy per cent of the war business had gone to the hundred biggest business establishments. The building of at least one hundred plant extensions was assigned to the General Motors Company alone. In response to this stimulus great business leaders sprang to their duties and, with the co-operation of labor, turned out war goods in quantities that astounded the world. Ardent sponsors of the war execrated the tendency to concentration. Vice-President Wallace lashed out at the "monopolists" in wrathful language. New Deal members of Congress spread denunciation over pages of the *Congressional Record*, while on the insistence of the War and Navy departments the prosecution of trusts and combinations was relaxed by the Department of Justice. Businessmen claimed that they could not keep their industries going at full tempo and also spend days and weeks in courtrooms defending themselves against civil and criminal charges as monopolists. So the process of centralization went on under the "economic royalists" anathematized by President Roosevelt and the New Dealers. In these circumstances was raised anew, and in a novel form, Henry Adams' question of 1895: Are we in the midst of the last great centralization, with its overtones and undertones, with all its implications as a pattern of culture enclosing politics, education, ethics, and esthetics?

Permeating all the discussions about the immediate problems thrust upward by war mobilization, regimentation, and the disruption of family and national life were debates over two fundamental questions looking to the future. First: What kind of international settlement is to be made or can be made at the close of the armed combat? Second: What will American society look like when the war comes to an end, and what is to be done, or can be done, about the new problems and tasks arising on every hand?

As to the first of these questions, Americans were practically unanimous on the proposition that a peace more enduring than the truce patched up at Paris in 1919 must be made, if possible, if within the grasp of American statesmen and the people of the United States. But how was this end to be gained? There was the rub.

To the public were offered from various sources innumerable

plans for a pacific postwar world. The range was wide. It embraced a revived League of Nations, new types of world federations, the establishment of a world police force to hold down aggressors, the education of all nations in American principles of democracy, and economic schemes for bringing peace, prosperity, and fraternity to everybody, everywhere. Perhaps simplest of all, on its face, was a project for an open alliance between the United States, Great Britain, Russia, and China, committed to the maintenance of peace and the suppression by force of any and all nations attempting to defy their authority by arms. Yet none of these plans received an official blessing from President Roosevelt.

In the course of the World War, President Wilson had set forth his war aims in the form of definite points as a foreign policy for the United States—largely vain in respect of peace, as events proved. Before and during the Global War, President Roosevelt merely expounded his views on war aims as American foreign policy in the most general language.

In his annual message to Congress in January 1941, Roosevelt said: "In future days, which we seek to make secure, we look forward to a world founded upon four essential human freedoms.

"The first is freedom of speech and expression—everywhere in the world.

"The second is freedom of every person to worship God in his own way—everywhere in the world.

"The third is freedom from want—which, translated into world terms, means economic understandings which will secure to every nation a healthy peacetime life for its inhabitants—everywhere in the world.

"The fourth is freedom from fear—which, translated into world terms, means a world-wide reduction of armaments to such a point and in such a thorough fashion that no nation will be in a position to commit an act of physical aggression against any neighbor— anywhere in the world."

In the Atlantic Charter of August 1941 President Roosevelt and Premier Churchill announced principles of policy on which they agreed: "Their countries seek no aggrandizement, territorial or other; . . . they desire to see no territorial changes that do not accord with the freely expressed wishes of the peoples concerned; . . . they respect the right of all peoples to choose the form of government under which they will live." To these principles they added hopes for other changes, such as freer trade, co-operation among nations in the economic field; a peace which will "afford assurance that all the men in all the lands may live out their lives in freedom from fear and want"; freedom of the seas; the abandonment of force in the world; and general disarmament, "pending the establishment of a wider and permanent system of general security."

An indefinite kind of agreement on war aims and purposes was reached among countries at war with two or more Axis Powers, on January 2, 1942, when the agents of twenty-six governments signed at Washington a joint declaration and formed a loose organization known as the United Nations. Some of the official signers represented only governments in exile from countries overrun by Hitler, but they all "subscribed" to the principles of the Atlantic Charter and pledged their countries to employ all their military and economic resources in waging war on those Axis Powers with which they were then actually at war, to co-operate in waging the war, and to make no separate peace.

The signers of the United Nations Declaration were the President of the United States, the Prime Minister of Great Britain, the Soviet ambassador, the Chinese foreign minister, and officials from Australia, Belgium, Canada, Costa Rica, Cuba, Czechoslovakia, the Dominican Republic, El Salvador, Greece, Guatemala, Haiti, Honduras, India, Luxembourg, the Netherlands, New Zealand, Nicaragua, Norway, Panama, Poland, South Africa, and Yugoslavia. Later other governments joined the United Nations. Although this was not an alliance binding the United States by treaty, President Roosevelt expressed the hope that the union so formed would co-operate not only during the war but also in making the settlement at the end of the war.

Many complications lay in the way of reducing the broad principles of the Atlantic Charter to specific plans of action likely to guarantee their realization, especially in view of the fact that no one could foresee the exact state of things at the end of the war. Many Americans believed and publicly declared during the war that the idea of giving everybody, everywhere in the world, freedom of speech and expression, freedom of religious worship, freedom from want, and freedom from fear was a chimera; that these are freedoms which cannot be given gratuitously or imposed by force. The number of Americans who thought that some kind of alliance or world association should be formed to keep the peace was very large, according to every indication. But no simple or intricate plan that was set forth commanded wholesale approval.

In the discussion of plans for reordering the world, even Americans who had been champions of the League of Nations or some other form of permanent world organization, and who still were fervently international in their outlook, displayed strong diversities of opinion over specific proposals for achieving a world order. The plight of world affairs was in fact far more confused by 1943 than it had been at the conclusion of the World War. Russia signed the United Nations Declaration but its head, Joseph Stalin, let the other nations know that his government did not intend to restore to independence and self-government certain small countries on the western borders of the Soviet Republic. British authorities officially announced that the British Empire was not to be liquidated and that outside interference with the government of its dominions and dependencies would not be tolerated. As France was prostrate before Hitler's armies of occupation, there was only a self-constituted committee of Frenchmen to speak for her interests, but it cast about for allies and claimed a place for France in the postwar world. At a London conference attended by representatives of governments in exile, in September 1943, protest was made against the rumor that their affairs were to be controlled by any Anglo-American system of power, with or without the aid of Russia. Above all, it was recognized that Russia, owing to her tremendous victories over German forces and the terrifying strength of her armies, might well be the most powerful nation in the determination of the final settlement, and might oppose Pan-Slavism to Pan-Latinism, Pan-Arabianism, and Pan-Anglo-Saxonism, notwithstanding the declaration at Moscow signed by representatives of Russia, Great Britain, the United States, and China and announced on November 1, 1943.

That the debates over foreign and domestic problems would continue to be tempestuous and more and more penetrating was foreshadowed by the outcome of the congressional elections of 1942, nearly a year after the outbreak of the war. In the campaign, supporters of the Roosevelt administration demanded a wholesale repudiation of citizens who had formerly opposed getting into the war. Of the total vote cast at the polls, Republicans received 50.6%; the Democrats 47.4; and independents 2%. A large proportion of the candidates who had been against intervention prior to Pearl Harbor were successful at the polls. Although the Democrats managed to hold a majority in the House of Representatives and in the Senate, their sway was materially weakened in both houses. About 80% of the members in the House of Representatives who had voted against the Lend-Lease bill in 1941 were returned to their seats—a percentage larger than that of the members who had voted for it.

All members of the new Congress were fully committed to the vigorous prosecution of the war, but many of them soon began to show a virulent opposition to President Roosevelt's policies and administration. Again and again, in both chambers, combinations of Republicans and Democrats overrode his plans, proposals, and desires. They abolished his National Resources Planning Board, the domestic branch of the Office of War Information, and the National Youth Administration. They investigated and criticized the Lend-Lease Administration and demanded to know how the $60,000,000,000 appropriated to aid other nations enlisted in the war on the Axis Powers was being distributed and spent. They attacked in long debates the President's aides and advisers, demanded a reduction in the enormous bureaucracy of more than 3,000,000 federal civilian employees, and in some instances attempted to oust officials by cutting off their salaries.

Only on two fundamentals was there anything like universal agreement in Congress. The first was that the war must be supported by appropriations of money so large that they appalled the senators and representatives as they voted them. The second was that efforts to establish an enduring peace must be made. Evidences of the former appeared in the war appropriations by Congress equaling in amount more than the appropriations of all the Allied governments combined. Evidences of the latter were made manifest in two resolutions on the peace settlement—one by the House of Representatives and the other by the Senate.

The House of Representatives resolution, bearing the name of its author, J. W. Fulbright, of Arkansas, came up for final debate in September 1943 and was passed by an overwhelming majority. It read: "Resolved by the House of Representatives [the Senate concurring], That the Congress hereby expresses itself as favoring the creation of appropriate international machinery with power adequate to establish and to maintain a just and lasting peace, among the nations of the world, and as favoring participation by the United States therein through its constitutional processes."

The Senate, however, refused to concur with the House on the Fulbright resolution. For this proposal it substituted one of its own, cast in more circumspect terms. The Senate resolution, bearing the name of Tom Connally, chairman of the Foreign Relations Committee, gave a pledge that the United States would co-operate with its comrades in arms in securing a "just and honorable peace" and that the United States, "acting through its constitutional processes," would join with "free and sovereign nations" in the establishment and maintenance of international authority with power to prevent aggression and preserve the peace of the world.

While the Connally resolution was being debated in the Senate, with much deference to the constitutional right of that body to pass upon treaties negotiated by the Chief Executive, the proceedings were made somewhat academic by the announcement, on November 1, that President Roosevelt, on his own motion, had committed the United States to "united action" with Russia, Great Britain, and China to be "continued [after the war] for the organization and maintenance of peace and security." These four Powers pledged themselves to "consult with one another and as occasion requires with other members of the United Nations with a view to joint action on behalf of the community of nations." They also bound themselves not to employ their military forces, after the war, within the territories of other states "except for purposes envisaged in this declaration and after joint consultation." As the declaration, agreed to in Moscow, was not given the form of a treaty, the President did not submit it to the Senate for ratification before proclaiming it.

After the Moscow declaration was made public the Senate modified and adopted by an overwhelming majority the Connally resolution. It incorporated in the original proposal a section from that declaration and added a proviso that any commitment to a world organization must be made in the form of a treaty duly approved by the Senate, two thirds of the Senators concurring.

Other efforts to draw the great Powers together were made at two conferences held late in November 1943. At the first, in Cairo, President Roosevelt, Premier Churchill, and Generalissimo Chiang Kai-shek confirmed their unity and agreed that Japan was to be stripped of all the territories won by aggression against her neighbors. At the second conference, at Teheran in Iran, President Roosevelt, Premier Churchill, and Premier Stalin pledged themselves to solidarity in war and expressed a determination that the United States, Great Britain, and Russia would work together in the peace to follow victory. They also referred generally to the co-operation of all nations dedicated to liberty but refrained from giving any details as to a world organization at the end of the war.

☆

Formulating verbal declarations as to what the United States might or should do in conducting foreign relations after the war was easy in comparison with answering fundamental questions looking to the future on the home front after the war. These involved the demobilization of the armed forces unless used for world policing or another war, dismantling the regimenting machinery of the war administration, the provision of employment for the millions to be released from war activities—indeed all the issues of civilization in the United States. And by the people and their representatives in Congress home-front problems received a consideration more extensive, more searching, and more anxious than ever before displayed in the history of the Republic, even during the Revolution and the Civil War. Everybody presumably knew that the war boom, like the New Deal spending before it, had not permanently solved the problem of depressions and poverty, and that no kind of peace settlement with other nations would materially relieve the high tensions in domestic affairs.

In connection with the war and foreign policy, it is true, many advocates of internationalism revived and brought to the center of discussion the theory that only by joining other nations in promoting foreign trade and lowering or abolishing trade barriers could the United States find outlets for the surpluses of goods and enjoy steady prosperity. But this theory was not universally accepted. Moreover there was little assurance that all or even most, if any, of the nations associated with the United States in the war were willing to co-operate in such an undertaking. Along the shadowy shorelines of the foreign trade dominion other Americans also rekindled the false lights of imperialism.

Judging by debates in Congress, composed of a new House elected by the voters in 1942 and a Senate one third of which was renewed at the same election, another view was the most widely held. According to this outlook, whatever happened after the war in the way of international arrangements, the domestic problems of the United States would be greater, not smaller; more difficult, not less difficult, at the close of the global conflict. Equally prominent in the debates of Congress and popular discussions was the voicing of another conviction: the main burden of coping with these problems will fall upon the American people; it will be inescapable; and in discharging this responsibility Americans will be compelled to resort mainly to actions on the home front. In any event it was generally realized in Congress that, whatever the outcome of the Global War, the old conflicts of interests over problems of social welfare would continue; and that the social and economic conditions of the country, even in the midst of the war spending boom, were such as to evoke anxiety for the future.

As if forcibly to remind the nation of these conditions, Arthur J. Altmeyer, chairman of the Social Security Board, statistically and summarily described them in an address on March 13, 1943— an address reprinted in the *Congressional Record* of March 17 at the request of Senator Robert F. Wagner, a loyal supporter of the New Deal and President Roosevelt's foreign policies. A single paragraph in Mr. Altmeyer's address was an index to problems that would confront the nation, no matter what world settlement was made at the peace table: "I need only remind you that at one time, not so long ago, there were 28,000,000 people who were dependent upon their Government for the necessities of life. Not so very long ago, there were 12,000,000 workers unemployed through no fault of their own. Even today there are over 5,000,000 people who are still dependent upon their Government to supply them with the necessities of life and there are still approximately 1,500,000 workers unemployed through no fault of their own. On this very day, we know that there are 7,000,000 people who are unable to work because of sickness or physical disability of some sort and that 3,500,000 of these are permanently totally disabled. We know that 45% of the persons examined under the Selective Training and Service Act have physical defects which caused their rejection for general military service and which must affect their earning capacity in private life. Whether or not we establish a social security system, as a civilized and progressive Nation, we shall still have these problems and their economic consequences to solve and we will undertake to solve them."

Confirmation of the view that through the coming years the domestic conflict would persist, indeed increase rather than diminish in intensity, came from other official sources. The release of news by men in President Roosevelt's official family to the effect that he would be nominated and elected for a fourth term in order to carry forward his work at home and abroad indicated that the making of the peace would not bring to a close the struggle on the home front.

In a speech at Detroit on July 25, Vice-President Henry A. Wallace attacked President Roosevelt's opponents, whom he classified as "isolationists," "reactionaries," and "American Fascists." Having called the tune in this language, Wallace, while expressing his belief in "our democratic capitalistic system," proceeded to outline a sweeping program for world peace, the enlightenment of all peoples, "full production and full employment," and the establishment of world prosperity which, if attempted, would put a greater strain on historic capitalism in America than any important representative of the New Deal had ever yet proposed. To this address Alfred M. Landon shortly afterward replied by presenting his version of Republican policies and asserting that Vice-President Wallace had declared a "civil war."

No colorful vision of a warless and forever joyful world, such as that with which President Wilson had inflamed the imaginations of the people in his time, obscured for a moment the clashes of opinion in the grand coalition of United Nations or the persistent diversities of the "one world." Something superexcellent, beyond the defeat of the Axis Powers, might, it was conceded, arise from the Global War; but the contours of that superexcellence were not so plainly obtrusive on any horizon as to resolve all doubt.

While in war production, in family sacrifices, in blood and treasure, Americans bowed their backs to duty and necessity, they were poignantly aware of the overhanging portents—of conflicts already converging on the home front, of approaching tasks on this continent greater than the Republic had yet endured in its long history. And in their minds shadowy plans for a world order and for enforcing the four freedoms throughout the world in the "century of the common man" sank in the scale of weight as compared with concerns crucial to life in America and to the survival of constitutional government.

How far in the scale? History would give an indisputable answer, sometime. But a poll of the people in the forty-eight states reported by the American Institute of Public Opinion on October 2, 1943, furnished clues to the answer. Citizens from Maine to California were asked by the poll takers what they thought would be the "greatest problem facing this country" from 1944–48. Fifty-eight per cent of them named "jobs or the economic readjustment of the country as the most vital long-range issue ahead for the next few years." And only thirteen per cent named as the most vital issue the "problem of drawing up a lasting peace."

Could Americans really effect this readjustment—this wise and efficient ordering of their national life? Could full employment be provided for all the millions who had to have it for their very livelihood? The New Deal had failed to solve the problem of unemployment between 1933 and 1939, that is, before the war boom started; for there were still five or six million men and women without steady employment in 1938. And there was nothing in experience to indicate that the New Deal could solve the still greater problem of unemployment looming on the horizon of the coming peace. Nor did the fact that the most devastating panic in the nation's history had occurred under Republican auspices indicate that a return to the days of freer, if not free, enterprise, still yearned for in nostalgic circles, offered any better prospects, even if it was feasible.

It was here that two theories alien to the democratic processes of constitutional government entered into the discussion of destiny and opportunity ahead in the United States. One was communism in its new form of Russian despotic statism; the other, fascism; both were in a large measure outcomes of the frustrations and revolutions that followed the World War of 1914–18. Communism was supported in the United States by a political organization, the Communist party—which grew out of the labor unrest in America following the Russian Revolution of 1917. Though its membership was small, it was active in propaganda and tortuous in operations, on the Moscow line, in and through labor unions and old party machines, even to the point of considering its own ostensible dissolution in 1944. Fascism was represented by no openly organized party but believers in it carried on propaganda, aboveground and underground, and had their key members in places of influence.

Although true-blue defenders of communism and fascism differed in their professed objectives relative to human welfare, the systems were alike in two essential respects: in the suppression of civil liberties, representative government, and intellectual freedom; and in the regimentation of the people under a despotic leader untrammeled by popular elections, legislative bodies, and a free press. This was generally recognized in the United States. But it was said for both creeds that, in times of great social dislocations, depression, and unemployment, communist and fascist dictators had established order, given work to the idle, and organized industrial production, if mainly for war purposes; and that some such methods might be attempted or actually employed in the United States in case the postwar depression was far more calamitous than the breakdown of 1929–38.

That such a turn in American affairs would be disastrous to civil liberties and the democratic process of constitutional government was admitted by all citizens loyal to the American heritage. The very thought of it inspired leaders in business, industry, organized labor, and organized agriculture to great and concerted efforts in studying postwar problems and in planning measures for grappling with them by associational and co-operative undertakings, private and public, designed to maintain full production, furnish adequate employment, raise the standards of life throughout the nation, and sustain the American spirit.

Brief Reading List

GENERAL

BEARD, CHARLES A., and MARY R., *The Rise of American Civilization:* Vol. I, *The Agricultural Age;* Vol. II, *The Industrial Era;* Vol. III, *America in Midpassage* (1929–38); Vol. IV, *The American Spirit: A Study of the Idea of Civilization in the United States.*

BEARD, CHARLES A. (editor), *A Century of Progress—1833–1933;* (a symposium by specialists on invention, industry, transportation, agriculture, labor, banking, government and law, social progress, the position of women, natural science, medicine, education, the arts, and literature).

COLONIAL FOUNDATIONS AND POPULATION

NETTELS, CURTIS P., *The Roots of American Civilization* (the colonial age in general).

BRIDENBAUGH, CARL, *Cities in the Wilderness* (rise and growth of the leading colonial towns).

WERTENBAKER, T. J., *The Old South* (study of Southern culture and civilization).

CLARKE, M. P., *Parliamentary Privileges in the American Colonies* (establishing the rights of self-government).

HANSEN, M. L., *The Immigrant in American History.*

DU BOIS, W. E. B., *Black Folk: Then and Now* (the struggle of Negroes to win a place in American society).

GARIS, R. L., *Immigration Restriction* (historical).

ESSENTIALLY POLITICAL

SCHLESINGER, A. M., and HOCKETT, H. C., *Political and Social History of the United States* (Vols. I, II).

MORISON, S., and COMMAGER, H. S., *Growth of the American Republic* (Vols. I, II).

ECONOMIC

FAULKNER, H. U., *Economic History of the United States.*
BINING, A. C., *The Rise of American Economic Life.*
HACKER, L., *The Triumph of American Capitalism* (historical).

INVENTIONS

KAEMPFFERT, W., *A Popular History of American Invention* (Vols. I, II)

AMERICAN POLITICAL THEORIES

MERRIAM, C. E., *A History of American Political Theories* (to about 1900).
LEWIS, E. R., *A History of American Political Thought* (from the Civil War
to the World War).
COKER, F. W., *Democracy, Liberty, and Property* (extracts from great
writings on American political and social ideals from colonial times to
1941).
SMITH, B., *The Democratic Spirit* (extracts from great writings on the spirit
of political, social, and economic reforms).

LITERATURE IN RELATION TO AMERICAN
SOCIAL AND ECONOMIC LIFE

CURTI, M., *The Growth of American Thought* (general, with comprehensive bibliographies).
PARRINGTON, V. L., *Main Currents in American Thought* (Vols. I–III, from
colonial times to about 1930).
KAZIN, A., *On Native Grounds* (from about 1875 to 1942).

Appendix

SIGNERS OF THE DECLARATION OF INDEPENDENCE

Arranged by states, not in the order in which they appeared in the original copy of the document.

JOHN HANCOCK.

NEW HAMPSHIRE
Josiah Bartlett
Wm. Whipple
Matthew Thornton

MASSACHUSETTS
Saml. Adams
John Adams
Robt. Treat Paine
Elbridge Gerry

RHODE ISLAND
Step. Hopkins
William Ellery

CONNECTICUT
Roger Sherman
Sam'el Huntington
Wm. Williams
Oliver Wolcott

NEW YORK
Wm. Floyd
Phil. Livingston

Frans. Lewis
Lewis Morris

NEW JERSEY
Richd. Stockton
Jno. Witherspoon
Fras. Hopkinson
John Hart
Abra. Clark

PENNSYLVANIA
Robt. Morris
Benjamin Rush
Benja. Franklin
John Morton
Geo. Clymer
Jas. Smith
Geo. Taylor
James Wilson
Geo. Ross

DELAWARE
Cæsar Rodney
Geo. Read
Tho. M'Kean

MARYLAND

Samuel Chase
Wm. Paca
Thos. Stone
Charles Carroll of Carrollton

VIRGINIA

George Wythe
Richard Henry Lee
Th. Jefferson
Benja. Harrison
Thos. Nelson, jr.
Francis Lightfoot Lee
Carter Braxton

NORTH CAROLINA

Wm. Hooper
Joseph Hewes
John Penn

SOUTH CAROLINA

Edward Rutledge
Thos. Heyward, Junr.
Thomas Lynch, Junr.
Arthur Middleton

GEORGIA

Button Gwinnett
Lyman Hall
Geo. Walton

SIGNERS OF THE CONSTITUTION OF THE UNITED STATES

GO: WASHINGTON—
Presidt. and Deputy from Virginia

NEW HAMPSHIRE

John Langdon
Nicholas Gilman

MASSACHUSETTS

Nathaniel Gorham
Rufus King

CONNECTICUT

Wm. Saml. Johnson
Roger Sherman

NEW YORK

Alexander Hamilton

NEW JERSEY

Wil: Livingston
David Brearley
Wm. Paterson
Jona: Dayton

PENNSYLVANIA

B. Franklin
Thomas Mifflin
Robt. Morris
Geo. Clymer
Thos. Fitzsimons
Jared Ingersoll
James Wilson
Gouv Morris

DELAWARE

Geo: Read
Gunning Bedford Jun
John Dickinson
Richard Bassett
Jaco: Broom

MARYLAND

James McHenry
Dan of St. Thos Jenifer
Danl. Carroll

VIRGINIA

John Blair—
James Madison Jr.

NORTH CAROLINA

Wm. Blount
Richd. Dobbs Spaight
Hu Williamson

SOUTH CAROLINA

J. Rutledge
Charles Cotesworth Pinckney
Charles Pinckney
Pierce Butler

GEORGIA

William Few
Abr Baldwin

Attest   WILLIAM JACKSON Secretary.

PRESIDENTS AND VICE-PRESIDENTS

President	Born in	Party
1. George Washington	Virginia, 1732	No party
2. John Adams	Massachusetts, 1735 ...	Federalists ....
3. Thomas Jefferson	Virginia, 1743	Republicans ......
4. James Madison	Virginia, 1751	Republicans ......
5. James Monroe	Virginia, 1758	Republicans ......
6. John Quincy Adams	Massachusetts, 1767 ..	Republicans ......
7. Andrew Jackson	North Carolina, 1767 .	Republicans ......
8. Martin Van Buren	New York, 1782	Republicans ......
9. William Henry Harrison .	Virginia, 1773	Whigs ....
10. John Tyler	Virginia, 1790	Whigs ....
11. James K. Polk	North Carolina, 1795 .	Democrats ....
12. Zachary Taylor	Virginia, 1784	Whigs ....
13. Millard Fillmore	New York, 1800	Whigs ....
14. Franklin Pierce	New Hampshire, 1804	Democrats ....
15. James Buchanan	Pennsylvania, 1791 ...	Democrats ....
16. Abraham Lincoln	Kentucky, 1809	Republicans ......
17. Andrew Johnson	North Carolina, 1808 .	Republicans ......
18. Ulysses S. Grant	Ohio, 1822	Republicans ......
19. Rutherford B. Hayes	Ohio, 1822	Republicans ......
20. James A. Garfield	Ohio, 1831	Republicans ......
21. Chester A. Arthur	Vermont, 1830	Republicans ......
22. Grover Cleveland	New Jersey, 1837	Democrats ....
23. Benjamin Harrison	Ohio, 1833	Republicans ......
24. Grover Cleveland		Democrats ....
25. William McKinley	Ohio, 1843	Republicans ......
26. Theodore Roosevelt	New York, 1858	Republicans ......
27. William H. Taft	Ohio, 1857	Republicans ......
28. Woodrow Wilson	Virginia, 1856	Democrats ....
29. Warren G. Harding	Ohio, 1865	Republicans ......
30. Calvin Coolidge	Vermont, 1872	Republicans ......
31. Herbert Hoover	Iowa, 1874	Republicans ......
32. Franklin D. Roosevelt	New York, 1882	Democrats ....

OF THE UNITED STATES

Elected from	Years of Service	Died	Vice-President
1. Virginia	1789–1797	1799	John Adams
2. Massachusetts ...	1797–1801	1826	Thomas Jefferson
3. Virginia	1801–1809	1826	{ Aaron Burr, 1st term { George Clinton, 2nd term
4. Virginia	1809–1817	1836	{ George Clinton, 1st term { Elbridge Gerry, 2nd term
5. Virginia	1817–1825	1831	Daniel D. Tompkins
6. Massachusetts ...	1825–1829	1848	John C. Calhoun
7. Tennessee	1829–1837	1845	{ John C. Calhoun, 1st term { Martin Van Buren, 2nd term
8. New York	1837–1841	1862	Richard M. Johnson
9. Ohio	1841 (one month)	1841	John Tyler
10. Virginia	1841–1845	1862	
11. Tennessee	1845–1849	1849	George M. Dallas
12. Louisiana	1849–1850	1850	Millard Fillmore
13. New York	1850–1853	1874	
14. New Hampshire .	1853–1857	1869	William R. King
15. Pennsylvania	1857–1861	1868	John C. Breckenridge
16. Illinois	1861–1865	1865	{ Hannibal Hamlin, 1st term { Andrew Johnson, 2nd term
17. Tennessee	1865–1869	1875	
18. Illinois	1869–1877	1885	{ Schuyler Colfax, 1st term { Henry Wilson, 2nd term
19. Ohio	1877–1881	1893	William A. Wheeler
20. Ohio	1881 (6mos.)	1881	Chester A. Arthur
21. New York	1881–1885	1886	
22. New York	1885–1889	1908	Thomas A. Hendricks
23. Indiana	1889–1893	1901	Levi P. Morton
24. New York	1893–1897		Adlai E. Stevenson
25. Ohio	1897–1901	1901	{ Garret A. Hobart, 1st term { Theodore Roosevelt, 2nd term
26. New York	1901–1909	1919	Charles W. Fairbanks, 2nd term
27. Ohio	1909–1913	1930	James S. Sherman
28. New Jersey	1913–1921	1924	Thomas R. Marshall
29. Ohio	1921–1923	1923 .	Calvin Coolidge
30. Massachusetts ...	1925–1929	1933	Charles G. Dawes
31. California	1929–1933		Charles Curtis
32. New York	1933–		{ John N. Garner, 1st, 2nd term { H. A. Wallace, 3rd term

TERRITORIAL GROWTH OF THE UNITED STATES, 1783–1912

Territorial Division	Year Acquired	Area added. Square miles	Purchase price	Ceded by
Louisiana Purchase	1803	827,987	$15,000,000	France
Florida	1819	72,101	6,489,768[1]	Spain
Texas	1845	389,166	Annexed	....
Oregon Territory	1846	286,541	.........[2]	Great Britain
Mexican Cession	1848	529,189	18,250,000[3]	Mexico
Purchase from Texas	1850	......[4]	10,000,000	Texas
Gadsden Purchase	1853	29,671	10,000,000	Mexico
Alaska	1867	590,884	7,200,000	Russia
Hawaii	1898	6,449	Annexed	....
Porto Rico	1899	3,435	....	Spain
Guam	1899	210	....	Spain
Philippines	1899	115,026	20,000,000	Spain
Tutuila Group, Samoa	1899	77	....	(rights settled)
Panama Canal Zone (lease)	1904	436	10,000,000	Panama
Total		2,851,172	$96,939,768	

[1]Interest payments included.
[2]Date of settlement with Great Britain.
[3]Includes payments to American citizens for claims against Mexico.
[4]123,784 square miles which had become a part of the United States territory with the annexation of Texas in 1846.

Index